THE YI RIVER COMMENTARY
ON THE *BOOK OF CHANGES*

伊川易傳

WORLD THOUGHT IN TRANSLATION

A joint project of Yale University Press and the MacMillan Center for
International and Area Studies at Yale University, World Thought in
Translation makes important works of classical and contemporary political,
philosophical, legal, and social thought from outside the Western tradition
available to English-speaking scholars, students, and general readers. The
translations are annotated and accompanied by critical introductions that
orient readers to the background in which these texts were written, their
initial reception, and their enduring influence within and beyond their own
cultures. World Thought in Translation contributes to the study of religious
and secular intellectual traditions across cultures and civilizations.

Series editors

Stephen Angle
Andrew March
Ian Shapiro

THE YI RIVER COMMENTARY ON THE *BOOK OF CHANGES*

伊川易傳

Cheng Yi

Edited and Translated by L. Michael Harrington

Introduction by L. Michael Harrington and Robin R. Wang

Yale

UNIVERSITY

PRESS

New Haven and London

孔子与山东文化强省战略协同创新中心规划成果

Produced with the Assistance of the Confucius and Shandong Cultural Center for Strategic Innovation and Cooperation.

Yale University Press books may be purchased in quantity for educational, business, or promotional use. For information, please e-mail sales.press@yale.edu (U.S. office) or sales@yaleup.co.uk (U.K. office).

Set in Postscript Electra and Trajan type by Newgen.
Printed in the United States of America.

Library of Congress Control Number: 2018964796
ISBN 978-0-300-21807-7 (hardcover : alk. paper)

A catalogue record for this book is available from the British Library.

This paper meets the requirements of ANSI/NISO z39.48-1992 (Permanence of Paper).

10 9 8 7 6 5 4 3 2 1

CONTENTS

ACKNOWLEDGMENTS

I would like to thank Stephen C. Angle for recommending the publication of this translation in Yale University Press's World Thought in Translation series and for actively supporting it throughout the editorial process.

The translation and introduction were produced with the assistance of the Confucius and Shandong Cultural Center for Strategic Innovation and Cooperation (孔子与山东文化强省战略协同创新中心). Robin R. Wang and I would like to thank the Center for its generous financial support.

Additional support was provided by Duquesne University. I would especially like to thank James Swindal, dean of the McAnulty College of Liberal Arts, who encouraged this project both as dean and as chair of the Philosophy Department. Students in my Confucianism courses at Duquesne in the Fall 2010, Spring 2013, and Spring 2016 terms—especially Boram Jeong and Dong Minglai—also deserve a round of thanks for the time they spent helping me to clarify the translation and my approach to Song dynasty philosophy.

TRANSLATOR'S NOTE

The present translation follows the text of the *Yi River Commentary* as it is found in the 1865 printing of the *Er Cheng quanshu* 二程全書 (n.p.). I have checked this text against the more contemporary version, edited by Wang Xiaoyu 王孝魚 in the *Er Cheng ji* 二程集 (Beijing 北京: Zhonghua shuju 中華書局, 1981), and have noted cases in which the versions differ significantly in meaning. I have also noted cases in which both versions appear defective. Ts'ai Yung-ch'un provides a list of previous editions of the Chinese text in his doctoral dissertation from Columbia University, "The Philosophy of Ch'eng I: A Selection of Texts from the Complete Works, Edited and Translated with Introduction and Notes" (1950), 281–283. He also translates numerous short passages from the *Yi River Commentary* throughout the text of his dissertation.

Several other previously published works contain English translations of passages from the *Yi River Commentary*. The Song 宋 dynasty Confucians Zhu Xi 朱熹 and Lu Zuqian 呂祖謙 (1137–1181) included more than one hundred passages from the commentary in their anthology of Confucian texts, the *Jinsilu* 近思錄, translated by Wing-tsit Chan as *Reflections on Things at Hand* (New York: Columbia University Press, 1967). An appendix on pages 309–322 correlates quotations in the anthology with their original position in Cheng Yi's commentary. Chan's translation of Cheng Yi's "Preface to the Commentary on the *Book of Changes*" appears on pages 107–110. Kidder Smith translates small portions of the commentary on Hexagrams 1–4 and all the commentary on Hexagram 24 in his doctoral dissertation from the University of California, Berkeley, "Cheng Yi's (1033–1107) Commentary on the 'Yijing'" (1979), 50–64. He also translates Cheng Yi's preface, with comprehensive analysis and notes, on pages 105–108. Still another translation of the preface appears in Iulian K.

Shchutskii, *Researches on the I Ching,* trans. William L. MacDonald and Tsu-yoshi Hasegawa, with Hellmut Wilhelm (Princeton, NJ: Princeton University Press, 1979), 72–73. It is also worth mentioning Richard John Lynn's *The Classic of Changes* (New York: Columbia University Press, 1994). Although this is a translation of Wang Bi's commentary, Lynn nevertheless keeps a constant eye on Cheng Yi's commentary in the notes that conclude his translation of each hexagram.

The only complete translation of the *Yi River Commentary* into a modern Western language is Paul-Louis-Félix Philastre, *Le Yi king: Ou livre des changements de la dynastie des Tscheou* (Paris: E. Leroux, 1885–1893). Thomas Cleary's *The Tao of Organization* (Boston: Shambhala, 1995) purports to be a translation of the *Yi River Commentary* into English, but it silently omits nearly all the historical references and quotations of classical texts, as well the portions of the commentary that address the *Judgment* and *Symbol,* resulting in a severe abridgment that contains less than half of the original text.

The translation of a commentary on the *Book of Changes* demands a new translation of the *Book* itself. Some of the characters in the original text may be given different meanings, and some portions of the original text may be given different sentence structures, depending on the interpretive decisions of the commentator. For instance, Cary Baynes translates the beginning of the second line statement in Hexagram 42 as "someone does indeed increase him. Ten pairs of tortoises cannot oppose it."[1] Cheng Yi's commentary, however, requires that the *peng* 朋 character be translated as "friends" and not "pairs," and that the number ten modify "friends" instead of "tortoises." For his commentary to make sense to the reader, the original text of this passage must be translated as "sometimes ten friends add to it. None of the turtles is capable of drawing back." Because the commentary requires a text tailored to its interpretation, I have provided a new translation of the *Book of Changes* itself together with its ancient commentaries, as they are found in the *Zhouyi zhengyi* edition, compiled in the Tang dynasty. All text in boldface belongs to this edition, and the rest is Cheng Yi's commentary. Where Cheng Yi quotes another text in the course of his commentary, I have translated the quotation myself, though I provide references to existing English translations in my notes. I have allowed considerable ambiguity to remain in my translation of the original text. For instance, I have allowed *gang* 剛 to remain ambiguous when it appears in the early commentary known as the *Judgment,* as it generally refers not only to a *yang* line or group of *yang* lines but to any number of things that have a *yang* capacity or function. I translate it simply as "firmness." In Cheng Yi's commentary, however, I translate *gang* as "firm line" if it is clear that he is referring only to a line.

I have striven above all for consistency, especially when translating techni-
cal terms. In some cases, I have allowed the meaning to be ambiguous or the
reading of a passage to be awkward to preserve consistency of translation. For instance, I translate *wen* 文 as "pattern" even in some cases where "culture" would
provide a smoother reading, as when the sage-king Shun promulgates "pattern
and virtue" among the Miao tribe. The text would be less awkward if it said
that Shun promulgates "culture and virtue," but that translation would lose the
reference to the pattern that Cheng Yi discusses throughout his commentary.

To ensure that the presence of a character is apparent on each occasion of
its use, I split apart many two-character combinations that would ordinarily be
translated by a single English word. For instance, I translate *wenming* as "pattern and enlightenment," rather than the more common "civilization." Cheng
Yi often uses the *wenming* combination when interpreting passages that refer to
light, and the translation of "civilization" would not allow the reader to see why
Cheng Yi finds *wenming* to be especially appropriate in such contexts. Because
the components of many two-character combinations are not different in meaning, the reader should expect to encounter a significant amount of pleonasm.
For instance, the phrase "hardship or obstacle" (*jianxian* 艱險) could easily
be translated by a single English word. I translate the two characters separately
to ensure that each character announces its presence in the English translation wherever it occurs. When a single character has two obviously different
meanings, and there is no English word that encompasses them both, I have
not hesitated to translate the character with two different words. For instance,
I translate the title of the *Wenyan* 文言 commentary as *Remarks on the Text*
rather than *Remarks on the Pattern*. Variant translations of important characters
are included in the glossary at the end of the book.

There is no good way to translate the titles of the sixty-four hexagrams. Most
of the titles are single characters, some of which occur only rarely in classical
Chinese, and whose meaning later commentators derived from earlier commentaries. I do not follow James Legge's practice of leaving the titles in Chinese, as some of them are words used in everyday speech. There is no reason
to mystify the reader of Hexagram 17 with a title like "Sui," when in fact the
Chinese character is mundane and easily translated as "follow" (*sui* 隨). I also
do not follow the practice observed by some translators of expanding on the
meaning of the Chinese character when translating it. The title of Hexagram
1 is certainly associated with "pure *yang*," as Richard John Lynn translates it,
and with "heaven," as John Minford translates it.[2] But if you translate *qian* 乾
as "pure *yang*," how will you translate *yang*? If you translate it as "heaven," how
will you translate *tian* 天? To explain the title while translating it risks blurring

the meaning of Chinese characters that Cheng Yi, at least, is concerned with keeping distinct. I have elected instead to translate hexagram titles with short English words, preferably those that can serve as both nouns and verbs. These words are ambiguous enough not to explain the hexagram much more than the original Chinese title does, and they do not suggest an obvious Chinese character in the mind of the reader, unless the title character is itself already in common use (as in the case of the "Follow" or *sui* hexagram).

INTRODUCTION

L. Michael Harrington and Robin R. Wang

Little can be said with certainty about the classical Chinese text known as the *Book of Changes* (*I-Ching, Yijing* 易經), save that a version of it was used as a divination text during the Zhou 周 dynasty, and that it somehow reflects the divination practices of the preceding Shang 商 dynasty. Over the roughly three thousand years since its composition or compilation, its many commentators have reached dramatically different conclusions about its purpose, the syntax of individual passages within it, and the meaning of individual characters. The text cannot speak coherently in its original language, let alone in a translation, until its characters, statements, and overall purpose are given some definition by a commentator. At the same time, few contemporary readers in any language are familiar with the different commentary traditions, leading Richard J. Smith to begin his history of the *Book of Changes* by saying that there is "probably no work circulating in the modern world that is at once as instantly recognized and as stupendously misunderstood."[1] This inattention to history is largely the result of what has come to be known as the "book of wisdom" approach to the text, which treats its meaning as timeless and without context. A meaning that is not specific to any one time period can claim to be equally relevant for every generation of readers.

One response to the problem of turning the *Book of Changes* into a book of wisdom is to fall back on an explicitly historical approach. English-language scholarship on the Confucian commentary tradition, for instance, now generally restricts itself to placing each commentary in its historical context. The authors of *Sung Dynasty Uses of the I Ching* say that, "rather than arguing that it transcends human culture or contains a timeless wisdom, we have examined its specific use by specific people."[2] Tze-ki Hon identifies his goal as "to demonstrate how the *Yijing* commentaries can be an important source of information on the momentous political and social changes of eleventh-century China," eschewing the "book of wisdom" approach, which "ignores the history of the text."[3] Richard John Lynn expects that his notes comparing Wang Bi 王弼 (226–249), Cheng Yi 程頤 (1033–1107), and Zhu Xi 朱熹 (1130–1200) will help "emancipate the *Changes* from the notion that it can only be understood and appreciated as a timeless book of wisdom," and that his approach to Wang's commentary will treat it as "the historical product of a certain time and place."[4] Nonetheless, some of these same authors acknowledge the enduring value of the *Book of Changes*. Hon, for instance, says that "the *Yijing* speaks to everyone who is in the midst of change,"[5] and Lynn notes that "there is a core of insights here concerning the structure of human relationships and individual behavior that can, I believe, speak to this and any other age."[6]

It is possible to allow the *Book of Changes* to speak in the same voice to many ages, without ignoring the fact that its meaning has changed over time, by looking at it from the perspective of a single commentary. The commentary does not stand outside history. Instead, it articulates a conceptual position from a standpoint within a developing historical tradition. It presents the *Book of Changes* as it was seen by a tradition at a certain phase in its development, but the concepts it presents may be analyzed and employed by readers of many different time periods. There is no more valuable commentary for the contemporary reader to study for these purposes than the one authored by the Song 宋 dynasty Confucian and philosopher Cheng Yi, who took the sobriquet "Yi River" after the river that flows through his hometown of Luoyang 洛陽. A lecturer on the Confucian classics deeply involved in the political factionalism of the Northern Song dynasty, Cheng Yi composed or at least completed his commentary on the *Book of Changes* during the first of two periods of exile he suffered toward the end of his life. One of several titles used to identify this commentary was *The Yi River Commentary on the Book of Changes* (*Yichuan yizhuan* 伊川易傳).[7] Although this title was presumably intended to reflect only Cheng Yi's sobriquet, it highlights his stated purpose in composing the commentary: to help the reader "track the flow" of the original text.[8] His commentary has a special significance for the modern reader because most English translations and Chinese editions are based on it and on the work of his later popularizer and critic Zhu Xi.[9] To study Cheng Yi's interpretation is to be able to see the historical source of the contemporary understanding of the *Book of Changes* as it appears in, for instance, the pioneering translations and commentaries made by James Legge and Richard Wilhelm.[10] A second reason to pay special attention to the *Yi River Commentary* is that it has exceptional pedagogical and philosophical value. Its pedagogical value arises from the fact that, un-like many commentators, Cheng Yi provides full paragraphs of interpretation, rather than half-sentences or sentences, to explain each hexagram. Its value for the philosopher arises from the fact that Cheng Yi understands each hexagram, and each passage from the text, as contributing to the articulation of a coher-ent conceptual structure: the principle that governs the interaction between different capacities and functions in any state of affairs. This structure can be articulated independently of the *Book of Changes*, but Cheng Yi takes the book to be a necessary introduction to it.[11]

What is the text, or rather texts, that Cheng Yi adopts as the subject of his commentary? There is first a set of sixty-four figures (*gua* 卦), each composed of six lines (*yao* 爻) stacked one on top of the other.[12] Each line may be either bro-ken or solid. Each figure is given a name, and the text also contains short com-ments on each name and on each line of the figure. The figure itself is known as a hexagram, the comments on the name are called the "judgment" (*tuan* 彖), and the comments on each line are the "line statements" (*yaoci* 爻辭). In addition, two early commentaries known as the *Symbol* (*Xiang* 象) and the *Judgment* have been cut apart and folded into the text of the edition used by Cheng Yi. A third commentary known as the *Remarks on the Text* (*Wenyan* 文言) has been folded into the text of the first two hexagrams. For the remaining sixty-two hexagrams, Cheng Yi begins by quoting the relevant section from a fourth early commentary, the *Sequence of the Hexagrams* (*Xugua* 序卦). These early commentaries already make dramatic changes to the meaning of the original text. Cheng Yi also benefits from a number of later commentators, in particular Wang Bi and Kong Yingda 孔穎達 (574–648), whose commentaries formed the basis of the official commentary on the *Book of Changes* (*Zhouyi zhengyi* 周易正義) commissioned by the Tang 唐 dynasty emperor Li Shimin 李世民 (598–649). Last of all, Cheng Yi relies occasionally on the approach of his own teacher at the Imperial Academy, Hu Yuan 胡瑗 (993–1059), whose work has been described as resembling "outline notes for an early draft" of Cheng Yi's commentary.[13] All these commentators belong to a specific tradition of commentary on the *Book of Changes*, which became known as the tradition of meanings (*yi* 義) and principles (*li* 理).[14]

The following section of this introduction will summarize the approach used by the tradition of meanings and principles, but it will first identify Cheng Yi's attitude toward the tradition of using the *Book of Changes* as a divination text, and the tradition of regarding the symbols (*xiang* 象) and numbers (*shu* 數) that appear in the text as the key to determining its meaning. Once Cheng Yi's own approach has been identified, the remaining sections of the introduction examine his approach in two contexts: the seasonal changes of the cosmos and the political changes of the human world. In both these contexts, Cheng Yi's understanding of the term "change" (*yi* 易) should be kept in mind. Although other commentators identify several meanings for this term, Cheng Yi says only that it "refers to alteration and the avoidance of depletion."[15] In other words, it refers both to the change going on outside interpreters ("alteration") and to the change that the interpreters themselves make in response to the external changes they observe ("avoidance of depletion"). The purpose of the book is practical: it teaches readers to identify the propensity for change in the world around them so that they may themselves change effectively. Effective change requires knowing what is possible in the present moment, and so Cheng Yi says that the great rule for studying the *Book of Changes* is simply "to recognize the moment and understand its propensities."[16]

TRADITIONS OF INTERPRETING THE *BOOK OF CHANGES*

The *Book of Changes* easily lends itself to use as a divination text. Many of the hexagram judgments and line statements contain explicit prognostications (*zhan* 占), such as "good fortune" or "misfortune." The hexagrams provide an index to these prognostications that can then be manipulated by the diviner. Charged with deciding whether a particular course of action is viable, the diviner has only to use a method like flipping a coin or casting yarrow stalks to identify first a particular hexagram, and then a particular line in the hexagram, to arrive at a prediction.[17] Such an approach to the *Book of Changes* is able to sidestep many of the problems with interpreting it. It is not essential to know the different possible meanings of a hexagram, so long as one is able to arrive at the prediction of good fortune or misfortune. The diviner may learn nothing about the structure of reality from the book, gaining only the knowledge of what will happen without understanding why it will happen.

Cheng Yi does not deny the effectiveness of the divinatory approach to the *Book of Changes*.[18] He nonetheless never recommends it, and Zhu Xi attributes to him the claim that the *Book of Changes* is not in fact a divination text.[19] It is certainly true that Cheng Yi never uses divinatory language in his commentary unless the text itself has brought it up. In these contexts, he often argues that the text downplays the significance of divination. For instance, one passage in the text can be read as saying that "none of the turtles is capable of drawing back." Cheng Yi interprets this to mean that even divination cannot be used to oppose the will of the people.[20] In another passage, a line statement says that "there is not yet divination." Cheng Yi interprets this to mean that great people do not have to wait for divination to carry out their reform. They know what will work even without receiving the support of a prognostication.[21] In one case, Cheng Yi argues that the text does not literally mean divination when it uses divinatory language. The word "augury," he says, "does not signify the use of yarrow stalks or tortoise shells."[22]

A second approach to the *Book of Changes*, known as the "tradition of symbols and numbers," goes beyond merely using it as a tool for divination. In this tradition, the trigram symbols act as the basic units of meaning, from which the reader may then derive the meaning of the hexagrams. Any three lines in a hexagram, usually the top three and the bottom three, may be treated as a figure independent of the rest. The meaning of these trigrams is sometimes initially deduced from their shape. For instance, the *gen* trigram—consisting of one solid line above two broken lines—is the symbol of the mountain because the three lines of the trigram taken together look like a mountain. It also symbolizes the action of stopping because mountains put a stop to travel. Each trigram can be understood in a similar way, as symbolizing an elemental or topographical feature as well as an action.[23] When assembled into the hexagrams, the trigrams are able to generate additional symbols through their combination. For instance, when the mountain trigram is set above the fire trigram in Hexagram 22, it can symbolize the action of illumination, as the fire illuminates what grows on the mountain. One may go further and say that the eight trigram symbols were not chosen at random but are the eight building blocks of the cosmos. There could not be more or less than eight, just as there could not be more or less than sixty-four hexagrams. One is then led to ask what meaning is conveyed by the number eight, or the number sixty-four. This is the esoteric side of the symbols and numbers tradition, as it requires acceptance that there is an exact correlation between the text of the *Book of Changes* and the structure of reality.

Cheng Yi does not accept this exact correlation, saying only that the sixty-four hexagrams are "sufficient" to account for all the principles of the world.[24] He does not attribute any special significance to the number of hexagrams or to the number of trigrams. In general, he avoids the esoteric side of the symbols and numbers tradition, and he uses neither charts nor numerology to explain the meaning of the *Book of Changes*.[25] He makes frequent use of the trigram symbols, but they serve him in the same way as the names of the hexagrams. That is, they specify one of the contexts in which the hexagram may be understood. For instance, Hexagram 26 consists of the mountain trigram above the heaven trigram. The mountain trigram symbolizes the action of stopping, and so it helps to specify that the hexagram refers to lines in the upper trigram herding or stopping the lines in the lower trigram. The trigram symbols are often little more than a mnemonic device, assisting the reader in remembering which hexagram name goes with which configuration of lines.

Cheng Yi's preferred approach to the *Book of Changes* belongs to a third tradition, known as the "tradition of meanings and principles." In this tradition, it is not the exact correlation between the text and reality that must be accepted, but certain principles that lie outside the text and can be verified independently of it. These principles are not the immediate objects of our sense experience, but they can be inferred from what we see happening in the cosmos and in human affairs.[26] The two most basic components of these principles identified by Cheng Yi are *yin* 陰 and *yang* 陽. The reader who relies on the common understanding of *yin* and *yang* as two different kinds of things, or as qualities that are permanently attached to certain things, will quickly go astray when reading the *Yi River Commentary*. For Cheng Yi, *yin* and *yang* most often refer to capacities or functions possessed for a period of time by persons or things and identifiable only in a specific context. A single person may be *yin* at one time and *yang* at another, or both *yin* and *yang* at the same time but in different contexts. Women, for instance, are identified by Cheng Yi as *yin* in certain passages but as *yang* in others.[27] Noble people, too, are *yang* in some passages and *yin* in others.[28] The principles that govern the meaning of the *Book of Changes* articulate a dynamic relationship between *yin* and *yang* in these different contexts. The principle that "firmness and softness correspond to each other," for instance, indicates only that *yin* and *yang* tend to interact when there is nothing to obstruct them, not that they will always interact or that their interaction will always take the same shape.[29]

The enduring relevance of this approach depends on the degree to which its principles are not simply reflections of eleventh-century China. The most basic of them may be understood as saying that actions are not dependent solely on an agent. They are always coactions, dependent on someone who initiates and someone who carries out or yields to the action. The word *yang* designates the person or thing that initiates the action, while the word *yin* designates the person or thing that yields to it or carries it out. If there is no correspondence between something with a *yang* capacity and something with a *yin* capacity, no action will occur.[30] A second principle is that the action will be more or less effective depending on the relative positions of the one who initiates it and the one who yields to it or carries it out. The rider of a horse is better at initiating the action of traveling when seated above the horse while holding the reins. The horse in turn is better at carrying out the action of traveling when it is below the rider with its feet on the ground.[31] In this case, the position above is the *yang* position, and the position below is the *yin* position. Nonetheless, people with *yin* capacities in *yin* positions may still perform certain *yang* functions, just as the horse initiates its own movement in response to the rider. People with *yang* capacities in *yang* positions may also perform certain *yin* functions, just as the rider adjusts to follow the movement of the horse, even though that movement was originally initiated by the rider.

Each hexagram is a variation on four basic combinations of *yin* and *yang* capacities and positions. A trigram composed of three solid lines represents the *yang* capacity, and a trigram composed of three broken lines represents the *yin* capacity. The upper position in the hexagram represents the *yang* position, and the lower position represents the *yin* position. The four basic combinations that result are *yang* above *yang*, *yang* above *yin*, *yin* above *yang*, or *yin* above *yin*. The remaining sixty hexagrams are formed by modifying a single line in one or both of the trigrams already configured in one of these four basic relationships. In positing this method of hexagram construction, Cheng Yi differs from many other commentators, who swap one or more lines within an existing hexagram to construct a new one. For instance, where other commentators say that Hexagram 41 is constructed by exchanging the *yang* line in the third position for the *yin* line in the top position, Cheng Yi sees it as a variation on the *yin* above *yang* relationship and constructs it by altering the top lines in each of its two constituent trigrams.[32]

To use Cheng Yi's commentary in evaluating action is to highlight not what a thing is but what it is capable of doing in its present context. Different people and things may exercise the functions of *yin* and *yang*, and the hexagrams do not dictate anything about differences that are not relevant to these functions. The hexagrams also focus the reader's attention on configurations of capacities and functions rather than single causes. When one nation declares war on another, for instance, we are not directed to look for a single cause but positioned to see the overall structure of government in the nation with all its various capacities

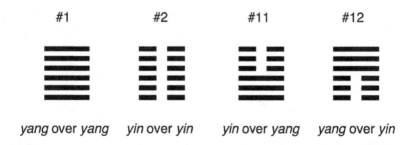

The four basic trigram relationships

and functions working together to produce the declaration as its result. It is like the work of the doctor in traditional Chinese medicine. Rather than identifying a single cause of a disease, the doctor looks at the overall structure of the human body to identify imbalances between its various functions, the disease being the result of this imbalance.[33] Cheng Yi rarely discusses the human body as a model for government—he prefers to examine the body of the cosmos (*tiandi* 天地). The progression of the seasons in the cosmos provides him with a standard for the less predictable patterns of human action.

THE *BOOK OF CHANGES* AND THE COSMOS

Daily temperatures are unpredictable, but seasonal temperatures are predictable. They follow the tilting of the sun in its path across the sky. When the path of the sun is at its furthest from being directly overhead, we have the greatest cause of cold. After this moment—that is, after the winter solstice—the path of the sun will become a cause of increasing heat. Together with the increasing cold of autumn comes the solidifying of water in the form of frost, ice, and snow, as well as an entry of living things into their phase of storing up rather than expending energy. Together with the increasing warmth of spring comes the rarefaction of water in the form of steam, together with the initiation of new activity on the part of living things. In the cosmos, then, the *yin* function is associated not only with receiving but also with cooling and solidifying, while the *yang* function is associated not only with initiating but also with heating and rarefying.

The *yin* and *yang* capacities in the cosmos are understood by Cheng Yi, following the Chinese cosmological tradition, as constituted by *qi* 氣. In his commentary, Cheng Yi regards *qi* broadly as the capacity of anything that can take on a *yin* or *yang* function. When the cosmic *qi* becomes warm, as a result of a particular configuration of the cosmos, it takes up a *yang* function. When it becomes cold, again as the result of the changed configuration of the cosmos, it takes up a *yin* function. The proportion of the cosmic *qi* with a *yang* function slowly accumulates from the winter solstice to the summer solstice, while the proportion of *qi* with a *yin* function slowly accumulates for the rest of the year.

This process can be depicted with twelve hexagrams in the *Book of Changes*, known as the sovereign hexagrams (*bigua* 辟卦) or ruling hexagrams (*jungua* 君卦). Their application to the calendar is attributed to the Han 漢 dynasty astronomer Jing Fang 京房 (77–37 BCE).[34] The lunar month that overlaps with the winter solstice is always identified as the eleventh month. The calendrical series based on the sovereign hexagrams identifies this month with Hexagram

24, when one *yang* line appears at the bottom of the hexagram to indicate the first appearance of the rarefying, heating, and initiating function in the cosmos. The succeeding lunar months are identified with the hexagrams that show the accumulation of *yang* step by step, until Hexagram 1 is reached in the fourth lunar month. The fifth lunar month is identified with the first appearance of the solidifying, cooling, and storing function in the cosmos, represented by Hexagram 44. The remaining lunar months are identified with the hexagrams that show the step-by-step accumulation of *yin*, until Hexagram 2 is reached in the tenth lunar month.

Cheng Yi accepts the sovereign hexagram series with one important modification. The series associates the tenth month with Hexagram 2 and the fourth month with Hexagram 1. Taken literally, Hexagram 1 describes a state where there is no *yin* capacity at all, while Hexagram 2 describes a state where there is no *yang* capacity. This can never happen in the cosmos, as it would imply the suspension of all activity. There can be no action at all without both the *yin* and the *yang* capacity. Cheng Yi notes that the calendrical tradition refers to the tenth month as "the month of *yang*" to make sure no one thinks that *yang* has entirely vanished during this month.[35] The sovereign hexagrams, then, do not indicate precisely the proportion between *yin* and *yang* in the cosmos but simply represent in a rough manner their accumulation and depletion over the course of the year.

Accumulation in quantity looks no different from an ascent into the heavens in the ordering of the sovereign hexagrams. The *yin* lines do not accumulate anywhere in a hexagram but are added to the lines already at the bottom of the

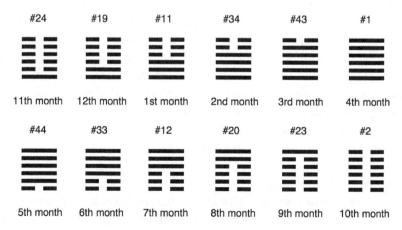

The sovereign hexagrams and their lunar months

hexagram. It is difficult, then, to take the sovereign hexagrams as representing the progression of the seasons according to traditional Chinese cosmology, which describes *yang* as descending at the same time as *yin* ascends, and vice versa. The sovereign hexagrams never depict either *yin* or *yang* as descending. The depletion of *yin* and *yang* occurs at the top of the hexagram rather than at the bottom, suggesting that they are depleted not by descending into the earth but by completing their ascent into the heavens. It may be that Cheng Yi does not consider this to be a problem. He certainly never considers it worthy of discussion. Because he does not regard *yin* and *yang* as indestructible substances, always equal in amount within the cosmos, he may not expect the depleted *yin qi* to descend from heaven to earth at all. Cheng Yi holds the general position that *yin* and *yang* capacities in *qi* are freshly generated each time they appear and are not simply the relocation of the previously existing *qi* that was endowed with such capacities.[36] The last of this year's *yin* capacity may vanish away completely in the heavens before the first of next year's *yin* capacity is newly produced within the earth. In other words, the *yin* of next year's winter is not the *yin* of this year's winter. It is also the case that the top and the bottom of the hexagrams do not refer to a literal top and bottom, even when referring to the cosmos. They refer only to positions from which a particular kind of action can best be undertaken. The top position of the hexagram does not have to represent the literal peak of heaven but wherever it is that *qi* with a *yin* or *yang* function is reduced to insignificance. In any case, Cheng Yi is happy to use both ways of speaking: to talk about the *yin* and *yang qi* as exhausted at the top of the hexagram, and as having descended to the bottom.

The ascent of the cosmic *qi* always occurs by accumulation, but the *yin* and *yang* capacities do not respond to ascent in the same way. Cheng Yi identifies rising as in the nature of *yang* and descending as in the nature of *yin*. When *yang* rises, then, it is fulfilling its nature, while the ascent of *yin* goes against its nature. During the spring months, the warming *yang qi* is able to initiate the activity of living things as it fulfills its nature in rising to interact with the *yin qi* above it. During the autumn months, the cooling *yin qi* is not able to yield to the *yang qi* because it is going against its own nature by ascending, and so there is no interaction between the two.

Other hexagrams can provide additional information about the seasonal progression, based on their likeness to the sovereign hexagrams. For instance, Hexagram 3 differs from Hexagram 24 only by having a *yang* line in the fifth position rather than a *yin* line. Cheng Yi interprets them both as referring to the beginning of *yang* in the cosmos. This is the first sign in his commentary that the sixty-four hexagrams do not represent sixty-four different situations, but a few situations repeated with a different emphasis. Hexagram 3 focuses on the difficulty that *yang* will have in accumulating while it is still small; Hexagram 24 focuses on the simple fact that *yang* has returned.

Although the sovereign hexagrams may be studied for what they reveal about the cosmos, Cheng Yi treats them primarily as a standard against which the more complicated activities of the human world can be measured.

THE *BOOK OF CHANGES* AND THE STATE

The use of the *Book of Changes* in politics requires a reader with a cultivated awareness of "kinds" (*lei* 類). The *lei* of two or more things is what they share, however different they may be in other respects. To be aware of the *lei* of something is to possess knowledge of it—in fact, the *lei* character in classical Chinese is sometimes used as a verb meaning "to know" something.[37] In Cheng Yi's commentary, the awareness of *lei* is especially important for noble people (*junzi* 君子), who hope to bring order to the human world. According to the commentary known as the *Symbol*, "Noble people use kinds and classes to distinguish things."[38] Cheng Yi comments, "They have never lost the method of putting things in their places." There are three respects in which the awareness of *lei* is important for noble people. First, they must be able to see the resemblance in kind between the cosmos and the state. Second, they must be able to join different things with the same kind of capacity (either *yin* or *yang*). Third, they must be able to see the resemblance in kind between the various hexagram positions and the various titles held by state officials.

A relevant similarity in kind between the cosmos and the state is the importance of accumulation. Just as the *yang* capacity in the cosmos only becomes effective when there is enough *qi* that has this capacity, so also a few people in the state are not effective by themselves. If they hope to have an influence on the activity of the state, they will have to recognize others of the same kind so as to join with them. The student with an awareness of *lei* will recognize that this forming of factions has the same basic structure as the seasonal growth of warmth or coolness in the cosmos. Tze-ki Hon takes Cheng Yi's recognition of the inescapable reality of factions to be one of the most distinctive features of his commentary.[39] It is certainly true that Cheng Yi emphasizes the fact that lines are only effective in blocks.

Or are they? In addition to the structure of *yang* driving out *yin*, and *yin* driving out *yang*, which replicate in the state the progression of seasons in the cosmos, there is also the possibility of correspondence and interaction between *yin* and *yang*. In the cosmos, this correspondence in the spring produces the rain that nourishes the earth and brings forth new life. In the state, correspondence is also to be valued, but here the possibilities for correspondence are more complex than those in the cosmos. In the state, one may occupy a position without having reached it through the process of accumulation. For instance, a solid line — that is, a line with a *yang* capacity — may occupy the fifth position of a hexagram. Hexagram lines are traditionally numbered from bottom to top, so the fifth position is the second highest position. A *yang* line may occupy this position even when all the other positions in the hexagram are occupied by broken lines — that is, lines with a *yin* capacity — as occurs in Hexagram 8. The *yang* line in this hexagram occupies its high position without being supported by an accumulation of *yang* lines in the positions below it. All the lines below it are *yin*, but it may still be effective by corresponding with them and with the *yin* line in the highest position above it. The meaning of the hexagram, according to Cheng Yi, is not the inefficacy of the *yang* line, but the close relationship it may develop with the *yin* lines by corresponding with them.

Only someone with a cultivated awareness of *lei* will be able to apply such a hexagram to an actual state. It requires seeing what position in the actual state corresponds to the fifth position in the hexagram. The fifth position is traditionally conceived as *yang*, being the central and therefore the most representative position of the upper trigram. It is the position from which someone can most effectively make decisions that will be carried out. In the China of Cheng Yi's time, this is the position of the emperor. The second position is traditionally conceived as *yin*, being the central and therefore the most representative position of the lower trigram. It is the position with the resources for effectively yielding to or carrying out decisions. Cheng Yi identifies this as the position of the government minister. When a *yang* line is put in the fifth position, it indicates that the person occupying this position knows how to bring about a desired action. Were a *yin* line in this position, it would refer to someone who does not know how to bring about the desired action but must delegate the decision-making process to another party. The *yin* line, in other words, is capable only of doing what someone else decides for it. Cheng Yi assists the reader of various hexagrams in cultivating an awareness of *lei* — in this case, of knowing how to match up hexagram lines and positions with actual people and their positions — by giving historical examples of people who were *yang* in *yang* positions (the sage-king Shun 舜), *yin* in *yang* positions (King Cheng 成王), and *yang* in *yin* positions (the Duke of Zhou 周公).[40]

The third and fourth positions account for government functions that lie somewhere between the straightforwardly *yang* and *yin* functions of the ruler and minister. Because the third is above the second line, it is *yang*, but it is also

top position . . . . without title

yang fifth position . . . . ruler (*jun* 君)

yin fourth position . . . . great minister (*dachen* 大臣)

yang third position . . . . . . .various marquises (*zhuhou* 諸侯)

yin second position . . . . . . minister (*chen* 臣)

initial position . . . . .without title

The positions and their titles

below the fifth, and so it is not unqualifiedly *yang*. It is the position of those who hold executive positions in government but are subject to a higher authority. Cheng Yi mentions once that this is the position of the "various marquises," the rulers of the various states within the Zhou dynasty, who were all at least nominally subject to the emperor.[41] The fourth position is below the fifth, and so it is *yin*, but it is not unqualifiedly *yin*, because it is also above the second position. It is the position of those who serve the decisions of the executive but are closer to the decision-making process than the average minister. Cheng Yi refers to it as the position of the great minister. The hexagram structure, then, can represent four hierarchically arranged positions in government: the ruler, great minister, various marquises, and lower ministers. Readers with an awareness of *lei* will know that the interpretation of the hexagrams does not require that each of these four positions be identified with a different person or group within the state. Because lines act in blocks, a hexagram with only two *yang* lines, one in the fourth position and one in the fifth, need not differ from a hexagram with only one *yang* line in the fifth position. The capacity of the great minister may be absorbed into that of the ruler in the first case, in which the two *yang* lines act in a block together, but it may be absorbed into that of the lower trigram in the latter case, in which it acts in a block with the other *yin* lines below it. Both hexagrams can then represent the correspondence between the ruler and the ministers, which is how Cheng Yi interprets them.

The bottom and top lines in the hexagram refer to people without positions in government. These include people capable of participating in government but who currently lack the opportunity, such as the noble people, as well as the large class of people who will never participate in government, sometimes summed up by Cheng Yi with the phrase "farmers, artisans, merchants, and traders."[42] Wang Bi claims that the bottom and top positions in the hexagram are neither *yin* nor *yang*, on the basis that they refer to times rather than government functions.[43] The initial position belongs to those who do not yet participate in government at the moment described by the hexagram, and the top line refers to people who are on their way out of the moment described by the hexagram. While Cheng Yi agrees with Wang Bi that these positions are primarily temporal, he takes an unusual step toward the symbols and numbers tradition by claiming that, since odd numbers are *yang* and even numbers are *yin*, the first position must be *yang* and the sixth must be *yin* for no other reason than that one is an odd numbered position and the other is even numbered.[44] When considering the meaning of these positions, however, Cheng Yi often reverses their function, identifying the initial position as *yin* and the sixth position as *yang*.[45] A *yin* function may be carried out most effectively when it is below *yang*, after all, and the initial position is below all the rest. The sixth position, because it is above all the rest, functions as a *yang* position. These positions refer to the largest percentage of the population by far, a massive group of people who are presumably not homogeneous in their capacities. Factions within this large group, however, cannot be represented by the hexagrams. In fact, the hexagrams cannot represent the difference between any groups with purportedly equal decision-making power, such as two sovereign nations. Relations between equals are always subsumed under relations between unequals. For instance, the people of two cities are significant not in their relation to each other but in relation to the emperor who stands above them.

The reader must negotiate a sizable gap when moving from these methods of interpretation to the actual text of the *Book of Changes* with Cheng Yi's commentary. The hexagram titles, judgments, and line statements of the *Book of Changes* do not clearly reflect any method of mapping the configurations of the seasons and government onto hexagrams. Hexagram 7, for instance, has only one *yang* line, in the second position. A reader using the method described earlier could interpret it as depicting a state in which the only person capable of making effective decisions is a minister. The title of the hexagram, however, is "Troop" (*shi* 師), and its meaning is entirely concerned with military affairs. The five *yin* lines refer to the army, and the *yang* line refers to its commander. As Cheng Yi frequently admonishes the reader, the title of a hexagram, as well as its judgment and line statements, address only the most important of the contexts in which the hexagram is relevant. Because a military expedition is the only case in which a subordinate is given absolute authority, this is the case addressed by the *Book of Changes* in Hexagram 7. The reader is left to infer the meaning of the hexagram in other contexts. Individual lines may also change their meanings as the text draws the reader's attention to specific challenges presented by the hexagram configuration. This specificity explains why Cheng Yi criticizes contemporary readers for trying to understand the "meanings and principles" before they actually look at the text of the *Book of Changes* itself.[46] Or, as he puts it in his preface to the commentary, "it never happens that one can develop the intention without acquiring anything from the statement."[47] That is, the intention of the *Book of Changes* may be understood only by working through the often wearying details of the titles, judgments, and line statements. Even for the philosopher, the *Yi River Commentary* must first and foremost be understood not as a guide to principles, but to the details of their expression in each hexagram. Any summary or introduction—Cheng Yi explicitly mentions the *Appended Statements* (*Xici* 繫辭) in this regard—should be set aside until the reader has become familiar with the "altering and moving without constancy" of the text itself.[48]

THE YI RIVER COMMENTARY
ON THE *BOOK OF CHANGES*

伊川易傳

PREFACE TO THE COMMENTARY
ON THE *BOOK OF CHANGES*

The *yi* character of the title refers to alteration—that is, to following the moment and altering or changing so that one may attend to the way. As "a book that is broad, great, total, and perfect," it "brings about submission to the principle of nature and the mandate" by developing the causes of darkness and light, exhausting the inclinations of affairs and things, and showing the way of things "both at their opening and when matters are brought to completion."[1] The worry and distress of the sages about later generations may be said to be extreme. Although we have come so far from antiquity, the classic that was left to us still persists. Earlier intellectuals nonetheless lost sight of its intentions by commenting only on the words, while later students recite the words but forget their savor. From the Qin dynasty onward, in fact, no one even comments on them. Born a thousand years later, I mourn this burying and obscuring of the text. This commentary was produced so that later generations may be enabled to track its flow and seek its source.

"The *Book of Changes* possesses the way of the sages in four respects: when they speak, they value its statements; when they move, they value its alterations; when they control tools, they value its shapes; when they use divination and augury, they value its prognostications."[2] The principle of good and bad fortune, of disappearance and growth, as well as the way "to advance and retreat, to persist and vanish"—these are perfected in the hexagram statements.[3] Those who unfold the statements and assess the hexagrams will be able to recognize their alterations. The symbol and the prognostication lie at their center. "When noble people occupy positions, they gaze on the symbol and explore the hexagram statement. When they move, they gaze on its alteration and explore its prognostication."[4] One may sometimes acquire something from a hexagram statement without attaining its intention, but it never happens that one can develop the intention without acquiring anything from the statement.

Principles are extremely minimal, while symbols are extremely manifest. Substance and function, however, have a single source, and so there is no space between what is clear and what is minimal. If one "gazes on their convergence and communication when putting legislation and ritual into action," there is nothing these statements will not bring to perfection.[5] This is why good students, in seeking the words, will necessarily begin with what is nearest to them. Those who change, departing from what is nearest to them, will not recognize the words. My commentary refers to the statements, but the acquisition of the intentions from the statements lies with the reader.

This preface was composed in the second year after the inauguration of the Yuanfu era of the Song dynasty, in the first month of the year referred to by the seventh heavenly stem and ninth earthly branch, by Cheng Yi, also known as Zhengshu, of Henan province.[6]

Part One

1. LEAD (QIAN 乾)

Lead: there are primacy, progress, profit, and purity.[1] In early antiquity, the sage began by drawing the eight trigrams, and so perfected the way of the three powers.[2] He put one of them on top of the other in order to exhaust the alterations of the world. This is why, when six lines have been drawn, the hexagram is complete. A Lead trigram on top of a Lead trigram constitutes the Lead hexagram, and the Lead hexagram refers to heaven. The name "heaven" refers to the form and substance of heaven, while the name "leader" refers to the nature and inclination of heaven. To lead is to be vigorous, and those who are vigorous without rest are called "leaders." As for heaven, if one speaks of it without qualification, it is the way. This is the heaven that "does not draw back from them."[3] If one speaks of its divisions, then, concerning its form and substance, it is called "heaven"; concerning its mastery and dominion, it is called "lord"; concerning its task and function, it is called "ghosts and spirits"; concerning its mysterious function, it is called "spirit"; concerning its nature and inclination, it is called "leader." The Lead hexagram refers to the beginning of the ten thousand things, and this is why it also refers to heaven, the *yang qi*, the father, and the ruler. Primacy, progress, profit, and purity are called the "four virtues." Primacy is the beginning of the ten thousand things; progress is the growth of the ten thousand things; profit is the success of the ten thousand things; purity is the completion of the ten thousand things. Only the Lead and Yield hexagrams have these four virtues.[4] In the other hexagrams, they are altered to follow the state of affairs in the hexagram. This is why primacy without qualification refers to the good and the great, profit is the master of straightforwardness and certainty, and the substances of progress and purity are also each in accord with a particular state of affairs. The meaning of these four virtues is broad and great.

The initial "nine" line: a hidden dragon should not be employed. The bottom line is referred to as the "initial" line. The number nine is the most abundant of the *yang* numbers, and this is why it is used to name the *yang* lines.[5] A principle has no form, and this is why a symbol is borrowed to clarify its meaning. The Lead hexagram has the dragon as its symbol. When considered as a thing, the dragon is a spirit whose alterations cannot be gauged. This is why it is used to symbolize the way of the Lead hexagram, which brings about alteration and transformation. As the *yang qi* either disappears or comes to rest, the sages either advance or retreat.[6] The initial "nine" line is at the bottom of the first hexagram and refers to the beginning or the impetus of things, when the *yang qi* is starting to sprout. The sages are ensconced in this minimal position, as though in the dragon's hiddenness and concealment. Because they should not yet be employed, it is proper that they be nourished in obscurity as they await their moment.

The second "nine" line: a dragon is seen in the field. There is profit in seeing great people. A field is something above the earth. The dragon goes out and is seen above the earth, and its virtue is already manifest. Concerning the sage, one may remark that this is the moment when Shun plows the field and fishes.[7] There is profit in seeing rulers of great virtue, so as to put their way into action; there is profit for rulers in seeing ministers of great virtue, so that they may share in bringing their task to completion; there is profit for the world in seeing people of great virtue, so as to receive their grace. The ruler of great virtue is the fifth "nine" line. The trigram substances of the Lead and Yield hexagrams are both uniform.[8] Because they are not divided into firm and soft lines, their virtue is the same and they correspond to each other.

The third "nine" line: noble people lead, and lead again, all day long. At dusk, if they are careful, there is danger but no blame. Although the third line is in the position of humanity, it is also at the top of the lower trigram substance.[9] It has not yet cast off those below, and it refers to those who are respected for their clarity. This is the moment when the mysterious virtue of Shun rises and is heard of.[10] If all day and into the dusk it does not relax but is alarmed and careful, then, although it is placed on a perilous terrain, there will be no blame. It also refers to people who are below but who already manifest the virtues of a ruler. The world will soon wed itself to them, and their peril and trouble should be recognized. Although the line statement is speaking about the affairs of a sage, if it did not also provide a warning, how could it be considered as having something to teach? This is the reason the *Book of Changes* was produced.

The fourth "nine" line: sometimes it leaps in the abyss. There is no blame. The abyss is where the dragon is content. "Sometimes" is a word that indicates doubt and signifies that something does not have to occur. Its leaping or not leaping depend only on whether it has reached the moment for achieving contentment. The movement of sages is never other than at their moment. This is the moment when Shun undergoes the test.[11]

The fifth "nine" line: a dragon flies in the heavens. There is profit in seeing great people. The position of advancement is the position of heaven. Because the sage has acquired the position of heaven, there is profit in seeing people who are below but of great virtue, so that together they may share in bringing the affairs of the world to completion. There is certainly also profit for the world in seeing a ruler of grand and great virtue.

The top "nine" line: the dragon is proud. There are regrets. The fifth "nine" line is positioned at the limit of centrality and straightforwardness. When the limit of the moment has been acquired, those who exceed it are proud. The top "nine" line has reached the point of pride or the limit, and this is why there are regrets. When there is excess, there will also be regrets. Only sages know when to advance and when to retreat, when to persist and when to vanish. Because they are not excessive, they do not reach the point of regret.

The employment of the "nine" lines: a group of dragons is seen. They have no heads. There is good fortune.[12] To employ the "nine" lines is to place oneself on the way of leadership and firmness, to use *yang qi* in occupying the Lead trigram substances, and so to be uniform in one's firmness. When firmness and softness sustain each other, there is centrality, but when one uses firmness uniformly, there is an excess of firmness. The statement "a group of dragons is seen" signifies that one gazes on the meaning of the various *yang* lines. If "they have no heads," then "there is good fortune." To consider firmness as what comes first in the world is the way of misfortune.

The *Judgment* says:[13] "How great is the primacy of the Lead hexagram! The ten thousand things owe it their beginning, because it unites heaven. The action of clouds brings the influence of rain, and the sundry things flow into their forms. Those who are greatly enlightened about the end and the beginning complete the moments of the six positions, ride the moments with the six dragons, and drive the heavens. The way of the Lead hexagram is alteration and transformation. Each makes its nature and mandate straightforward, and each preserves its alignment and great harmony, so that there are profit and

purity. It goes out ahead of the numberless things, and the ten thousand states are all serene." The words below the hexagram constitute the judgment. Fuzi attends to and explains it, and his explanation is called the *Judgment*.[14] The judgment speaks about the meaning of the hexagram as a whole. This is why, when knowledgeable people gaze on the words of each judgment, their understanding has exceeded the halfway point. "How great is the primacy of the Lead hexagram!": the *Judgment* applauds the primacy of the Lead hexagram, which begins the way of the ten thousand things, for its greatness. Primacy is to these four virtues what humaneness is to the five constant virtues.[15] If one speaks of it as a part of virtue, then it is just one state of affairs, but if one speaks of it without qualification, then it contains all four virtues. "The ten thousand things owe it their beginning, because it unites heaven": it is speaking about primacy. The uniting brought about by the primacy of the Lead hexagram refers to the way of heaven. The way of heaven is the beginning of the ten thousand things, and so things owe their beginning to heaven. "The action of clouds brings the influence of rain, and the sundry things flow into their forms": it is speaking about progress. The way of heaven is to act by revolving, and so it gives birth to and cultivates the ten thousand things. Those who are greatly enlightened about the way of heaven in its end and beginning will see that the six positions of the hexagram are each completed by reference to a moment. The initial and final lines of the hexagram are the way of heaven at its beginning and end. Riding the moments of these six lines is the revolution of heaven. To "drive the heavens" signifies undertaking the revolution of heaven. "The way of the Lead hexagram is alteration and transformation": it gives birth to and cultivates the ten thousand things. Colossal or tiny, aloft or below, each in its kind "makes its nature and mandate straightforward." What heaven grants is the mandate, and what a thing receives is its nature. "Each preserves its alignment and great harmony, so that there are profit and purity": the word "preserve" signifies constancy and persistence, and the word "alignment" signifies constancy and harmony. Each preserves its alignment and great harmony, and as a result, there is profit as well as purity. The way of heaven and earth, which is constant, continuous, and unceasing, is to preserve alignment and great harmony. Heaven is the progenitor of the ten thousand things, while the king is the ancestor of the ten thousand kingdoms. The way of the Lead hexagram "goes out ahead of the numberless things," and the ten thousand sorts of things make progress. The way of rulers is to be in the respected and watchful position of heaven, and everyone between the four seas attends to them. When the king gives substance to the way of heaven, "the ten thousand states are all serene."

The *Symbol* says:[16] "Heaven acts with vigor. Noble people use it to strengthen themselves without resting." The *Symbol* passage below the hexagram interprets the symbol of that particular hexagram, while the *Symbol* passage below a line interprets the symbol of that particular line. The symbol chosen for each of the various hexagrams may be considered its law. The way of the Lead hexagram has the extremely great symbols of overturning and cultivating. No one who is not a sage can give them substance, but the *Symbol* desires that all people be able to choose it as their law, and this is why it chooses to say that "heaven acts with vigor," and that is all. Extreme vigor is certainly sufficient for anyone to see the way of heaven. "Noble people use it to strengthen themselves without resting": they take the vigor of heavenly action as their law. "**'A hidden dragon should not be employed': *yang* is at the bottom.**" The *yang qi* is at the bottom, and noble people are placed in minimal positions. They should not yet be employed. "**'A dragon is seen in the field': the influence of its virtue is universal.**" It is seen above the earth, and the transformation of its virtue is extended to things. Its influence is already universal. "**'Lead, and lead again, all day long': they revert or return to the way.**" Whether they advance or retreat, whether in motion or at rest, they must use the way. "**'Sometimes it leaps in the abyss': in its advance, there is no blame.**" If it advances when it calculates that it should, when the moment is suitable, then "there is no blame." "**'A dragon flies in the heavens': great people create.**" The deeds of great people are the affairs of sages. "**'The dragon is proud. There are regrets': what is full should not continue.**" If it is full, then it will alter, and so "there are regrets." "**'The employment of the "nine" lines': the virtue of heaven should not be considered the head.**" The employment of the "nine" lines is the virtue of heaven. The virtue of heaven is *yang* and firm. If it turns to the employment of its firmness, and prefers to be first, then it will become excessive.

The *Remarks on the Text* says:[17] "**Primacy is the oldest of goods; progress is the convergence of excellences; profit is the harmonization of duties; purity is the management of affairs.**" The other hexagrams have the *Judgment* and the *Symbol*, and that is all. Only for the Lead and Yield hexagrams was the *Remarks on the Text* provided, which reveals and sheds light on their meaning. It unfolds the way of the Lead hexagram and its influence on human affairs. Primacy, progress, profit, and purity are the four virtues of the Lead hexagram. Concerning people, primacy is at the head of the crowd of goods, progress is the convergence of excellences and beauties, profit is harmonization and alignment with duties, and purity is employed in the management of affairs. "**When noble people give substance to humaneness, it is sufficient to make them elders.**"

They give substance to the law through the humaneness of the Lead hexagram, which is the way of rulers and elders, and "is sufficient to make them elders." To "give substance to humaneness" is to give substance to primacy. Those who draw close to something and make it effective may be said to give it substance. **"When they bring excellence to their convergence, it is sufficient to align with ritual."**[18] They acquire excellence in their mutual convergence, which is to align with ritual. If they were not aligned with ritual, they would be without principle. How could they then acquire excellence? Being without principle, how could they make progress? **"When they bring profit to things, it is sufficient to harmonize with duty."** They harmonize with duty, which is to be capable of bringing profit to things. If they had not acquired what is fitting, how could they bring profit to things? **"When they are pure and certain, it is sufficient to manage affairs."** Because they are pure and certain,[19] they can manage affairs. **"Noble people put these four virtues into action, and this is why the judgment says: 'Lead: there are primacy, progress, profit, and purity.'"** They put these four virtues into action, which is to align with the Lead hexagram. **"The initial 'nine' line statement says: 'A hidden dragon should not be employed.' What is signified by this? Confucius says: 'The dragon is virtuous but concealed. It does not change with the times, it is not completed by fame, it flees the times without despair, and when it is not seen, it does not despair. It does what brings it pleasure, and it draws back from what worries it. Steadfast, and unable to be uprooted—such is the hidden dragon.'"** From this point on, the *Remarks* is speaking about the employment of the Lead hexagram, or the way to employ the "nine" lines. The initial "nine" line is the minimum of *yang*. The dragon's virtue is hidden and concealed, which refers to sages and worthies "ensconced among the rustics."[20] They guard their way and do not alter themselves to follow the times. Their actions are obscure, and they do not seek to be known in the moment. They believe and take pleasure in themselves. If they see something they should do, then they move, but if they know something to be difficult, they evade it. They keep such a solid guard that no one will strive with them—this is the virtue of the hidden dragon. **"The second 'nine' line statement says: 'A dragon is seen in the field. There is profit in seeing great people.' What is signified by this? Confucius says: 'The dragon is virtuous— that is, straightforward and central. It is to be believed in its everyday speech, and it is prudent in its everyday acts. It safeguards against crookedness and persists in its sincerity. It does good for the times without attacking them. Its virtue is liberal and transformative. The *Book of Changes* says: 'A dragon is seen in the field. There is profit in seeing great people.' This is the virtue of the ruler.'"** The *Remarks* is referring to those who use the virtue of the dragon to place themselves with straightforwardness and centrality. The meaning of the straightforwardness and centrality acquired here is straightforwardness and centrality within a hexagram. To be believed every day and to be prudent every day—their creations must come one after the other like this. If they have already placed themselves on a terrain without excess, they have only to safeguard against crookedness. If they have already safeguarded against crookedness, they have only to persist in their sincerity. "It does good for the times without attacking them": it does not itself possess this good. "Its virtue is liberal and transformative": it makes itself straightforward so that things will be straightforward. All of these are affairs of great people. Although this is not the position of the ruler, these are the virtues of a ruler. **"The third 'nine' line statement says: 'Noble people lead, and lead again, all day long. At dusk, if they are careful, there is danger but no blame.' What is signified by this? Confucius says: 'Noble people advance their virtues and correct their vocation. They are loyal and believable, and so they advance their virtues. They correct their statements and set up their sincerity, and so they occupy their vocation. When they know what point to reach, they reach it and can agree with what is incipient. When they know the end, they come to the end and can agree with and persist in their duty. This is why they occupy positions above without arrogance and positions below without worry. This is why they lead, and lead again, careful to be in accord with the moment. Although they are in peril, there is no blame.'"** The third line occupies the top position in the lower trigram, but the virtue of the ruler is already manifest in it. What is it to do? It has only to advance its virtue and correct its vocation, and that is all. It accumulates loyalty and believability on the inside, and so it advances its virtue. It makes its words selective and its tendencies devoted, and so it occupies the position of its vocation. "When they know what point to reach, they reach it": they bring about knowledge. They seek to know what point to reach, and afterward they reach it. It is the knowledge that comes first, and this is why they "can agree with what is incipient." This is signified in the following passage: "To begin sorting according to principle is an affair of knowledge."[21] "When they know the end, they come to the end": they act by force. If they already know where the end is, they will advance by force and come to the end. Keeping guard comes afterward, and this is why they "can agree with and persist in their duty." This is signified in the following passage: "To bring to an end the sorting according to principle is an affair of sagehood." These are the beginning and the end of learning. Such is the learning of noble people, and this is why they know how to place themselves on the way of those above and below without arrogance or worry. They do not relax, and they recognize their trouble. Although they are on a perilous terrain, "there is no blame." "The fourth "nine" line statement says: 'Sometimes it leaps in the abyss. There is no blame.' What is signified by this? Confucius says: 'It is not constantly above or below, but this does not make it crooked. Its advances and retreats do not last, but it does not cast off its group. Noble people advance their virtues and correct their vocation, wanting to extend themselves to the moment. This is why there is no blame.'" Sometimes it leaps, and sometimes it remains in place: "It is not constantly above or below." Sometimes it advances, and sometimes it retreats. Whether it departs or arrives, it attends to what is fitting, and so "this does not make it crooked" or bent, and "it does not cast off its group" or kind. It advances its virtues and corrects its vocation, "wanting to extend" itself "to the moment." There is a moment to act, and a moment to stop, and they cannot be lasting. This is why the line statement says "sometimes." The deep abyss is where the dragon is content. The phrase "in the abyss" signifies that it leaps to arrive at a place of contentment. The abyss is deep, and so it says that "it leaps," but the meaning chosen is that it advances to arrive at a place of contentment. The word "sometimes" indicates that it is doubtful. It follows the moment, but it is not yet necessarily capable of anything. Noble people submit to the moment just as shadows follow forms. If they could cast it off, they would not be on the way. "The fifth 'nine' line statement says: 'A dragon flies in the heavens. There is profit in seeing great people.' What is signified by this? Confucius says: 'The same sounds correspond to each other, and the same kinds of *qi* seek each other. Water flows toward what is damp, while fire arrives at what is dry. Clouds attend to the dragon, while the wind attends to the tiger. Sages go to work, and the ten thousand things behold them. What is rooted in heaven relates to those above, while what is rooted in earth relates to those below, so that each thing attends to its own kind.'" People and sages agree in kind. The fifth line uses the virtue of the dragon to rise into the position of respect. If humankind in general cannot do otherwise than admire or wed itself to it, what will the case be like for those who have its same virtue? Those above correspond to those below, while those below attend to those above: "The same sounds correspond to each other, and the same kinds of *qi* seek each other." "Water flows toward what is damp, while fire arrives at what is dry": one attends to the dragon and the other to the tiger, but they both use a certain kind of *qi*. This is why "sages go to work, and the ten thousand things behold them." When those above have already seen those below, those below also see those above. The word "things" here refers to people. An ancient saying holds that people are things, and "people" is a name for things that discourse.[22] In the *Book of Changes*, the statement "there is profit in seeing great people" is always the same, but there are differences in its meaning. In the Fight hexagram, for instance, "there is profit in seeing great people" signifies that it is fitting to see people of great virtue, centrality, and straightforwardness, so that "its distinctions are enlightened."[23] The statement is made before the great people are seen. In the second and fifth lines of the Lead hexagram, however, the sages have already gone out. Those above and below see each other, and they share in bringing their affairs to completion. What is profitable is to see great people, but the statement is made after they have been seen. "What is rooted in heaven" is, for example, the sun, moon, stars, and planets. "What is rooted in earth" is, for example, insects, beasts, grasses, and trees. *Yin* and *yang* each attend to their own kind, and the case is not otherwise for people or things. "**The top 'nine' line statement says: 'The dragon is proud. There are regrets.' What is signified by this? Confucius says: 'It is esteemed but has no position. It is lofty, but the people are not with it. Worthy people occupy positions below and give no assistance. As a result, if it moves, there are regrets.'**" This "nine" line occupies the top position, and the position of respect is not proper for it. As a result, "the people are not with it," there is "no assistance," and "if it moves, there are regrets." "'**A hidden dragon should not be employed': it is at the bottom.**" Here and afterward the *Remarks* is speaking about the moments of the Lead hexagram. It "should not be employed": because it is at the bottom, it should not yet be employed. "'**A dragon is seen in the field': it is the moment for abiding.**"[24] It follows the moment, and so it stops. "'**Lead, and lead again, all day long': they put their affairs into action.**" They advance their virtue and correct their vocation. "'**Sometimes it leaps in the abyss': it puts itself to the test.**" It follows the moment, and so it employs itself. "'**A dragon flies in the heavens': those above set things in order.**" To acquire a position and act is how those above set things in order. "'**The dragon is proud. There are regrets': its depletion brings disaster.**" It is depleted and at its limit, and so the disaster is extreme. "'**Lead: there are primacy' and 'the employment of the 'nine' lines': the world is set in order.**" The way of "the employment of the 'nine' lines" is the same whether it concerns heaven or the sages. If they are able to employ them, then "the world is set in order." "'**A hidden dragon should not be employed': the *yang qi* is hidden and stored away.**" Here and afterward the *Remarks* is speaking about the meaning of the Lead hexagram. At the moment when *yang* is minimal, hidden, and stored away, it is also proper for noble people to be obscure and stored away. They should not yet be employed. "'**A dragon is seen in the field': it brings pattern and enlightenment to the world.**" When the virtue of the dragon is seen above the earth, the world sees the transformation of its pattern and enlightenment.[25] "'**Lead, and lead again, all day long': they act in accordance with the moment.**" They follow the moment and advance. "'Sometimes it leaps in the abyss': the way of the Lead hexagram is reform." It casts off its position below and rises to a position above. Those above and below are reformed. "'A dragon flies in the heavens': its position has the virtue of heaven." Its straightforward position is above. Its proper "position has the virtue of heaven." "'The dragon is proud. There are regrets': it is limited in accordance with the moment." Because the moment is already at its limit, its place in the moment is also at its limit. "'Lead: there are primacy' and 'the employment of the 'nine' lines': it sees the regulation of heaven." The way of "the employment of the 'nine' lines" is "the regulation of heaven." The law or regulation of heaven signifies the way of heaven. Someone asks: do the six lines of the Lead hexagram all refer to the affairs of sages? Response: only the sage will exhaust the way of the Lead hexagram. If one acquires or loses it, one will persist in either good or bad fortune. How could this be specific to the Lead hexagram? The various hexagrams are all like this. "'Lead: there are primacy': it begins and makes progress." The *Remarks* goes back over it again, delineating it in speech so as to exhaust its meaning. What has already begun must make progress. If there were no progress, it would be at rest. "'Profit and purity': these are nature and inclination." They are the "nature and inclination" of the Lead hexagram. If what has already begun and made progress does not also have "profit and purity," how could it not be at rest? "The Lead hexagram—that is, the beginning—can make use of beauty and profit to profit the world. There is no saying where the profit is. How great it is!" The way of the Lead hexagram—that is, the beginning—can make the numberless kinds be born and come to completion. The world is given "beauty and profit," and "there is no saying where the profit is." In fact, there is no place without profit, but no one can point to or name it. This is why the *Remarks* applauds the greatness of this profit, saying, "How great it is!" "How great it is, this Lead hexagram! Firmness, vigor, centrality, straightforwardness, uniformity, and spotlessness are its essence! The six line statements reveal and proclaim the innate development of its inclinations. They 'ride the moments with the six dragons, and drive the heavens.' 'The action of clouds brings the influence of rain.' The world is at peace." "How great it is" applauds the way of the Lead hexagram for its greatness. "Firmness, vigor, centrality, straightforwardness, uniformity, spotlessness"—the way of the Lead hexagram is formed and embraced by these six attributes. The word "essence" signifies the essence or limit of the six attributes. "The six line statements reveal and proclaim the innate development"—that is, they exhaust the meaning—"of its inclinations." When they ride the moments of the six line statements so as to undertake the revolution of the heavens, then the task and function of heaven is made manifest. This is why one sees that "the action of clouds brings the influence of rain," which refers to *yin* and *yang* acting liberally and smoothly, the way of harmony and peace in the world. **"Noble people use complete virtue in their action, an action that can be seen daily. To say that it is hidden indicates that it is concealed and not yet seen. Their action is not yet complete, and so noble people are not employed."** Concerning the completion of virtue, those of its affairs that can be seen are actions. When virtue is complete, it can afterward be influential in some function. At its initiation or starting point, it is still "hidden" and "concealed," and "not yet seen," and so its action is "not yet complete." What is not yet complete is not yet manifest, "and so noble people are not employed." **"Noble people gather things by learning about them; they distinguish things by asking about them; they occupy positions by their tolerance; they put things into action by their humaneness. The *Book of Changes* says: 'A dragon is seen in the field. There is profit in seeing great people.' This is the virtue of the ruler."** Sages are in positions below. Although it is already clear who they are, they have not yet acquired positions. They advance their virtue and correct their vocation, and that is all. They advance their virtue by learning, gathering, asking, and distinguishing; they correct their vocation by being tolerant in their positions and by acting with humaneness. The "virtue of the ruler" is already manifest in them, "there is profit in seeing great people," and they advance to put it into action. Those who advance to occupy positions are like Shun and Yu.[26] Those who advance to put the way into action are like Yi and Fu.[27] **"The third 'nine' line: it redoubles its firmness and is not at the center. It is above but not in the heavens; it is below but not in the fields. This is why it leads, and leads again, in accord with the moment and with care. Although there is peril, there is no blame."** The redoubling of firmness in the third line refers to an abundance of firmness. It has exceeded the center by occupying the top position in the lower trigram. It is at the top, but it has not yet reached the heavens, and it has already cast off the fields below it. This is a terrain of peril and trouble, but it accords with the moment and submits to its place. "It leads, and leads again," using alarm and care to defend against the peril. This is why, "although there is peril," it does not reach the point of blame. Noble people submit to the moment with alarm and care, and so they can be free. **"The fourth 'nine' line: it redoubles its firmness and is not at the center. It is above, but not in the heavens; it is below, but not in the fields; it is at the center, but not among people. This is why it happens only 'sometimes.' To happen only 'sometimes' indicates that it is doubtful, and this is why there is no blame."** The fourth line "is not in the heavens" and "not in the fields," and it has gone out above the people to a perilous terrain. The word "doubtful" indicates that it

is not yet resolved, and its place cannot be considered necessary for it. Sometimes it advances and sometimes it retreats, but only to a place where it will be
contented, and so "there is no blame." **"As for great people, they align their
virtue with heaven and earth, they align their light with the sun and moon,
they align their sequence with the four seasons, and they align their good or
bad fortune with ghosts and spirits. They come before heaven, and heaven
does not draw back from them; they come after heaven, and honor the moments of heaven. If heaven does not draw back from them, what will the case
be like for other people? What will the case be like for ghosts and spirits?"**
When great people align with "heaven and earth," "sun and moon," "the four
seasons," and "ghosts and spirits," they are aligning with the way. Heaven and
earth are the way, and ghosts and spirits are the traces of creation and transformation. When sages come before heaven, heaven does the same things that
they do; when they come after heaven, they are capable of submitting to
heaven—that is, they align with the way, and that is all. Because they align with
the way, how could people or ghosts and spirits draw back from them? **"To say
that it is 'proud' indicates that it knows how to advance without knowing how
to retreat, it knows how to persist without knowing how to vanish, it knows
how to acquire without knowing how to be deprived. Only sages know how to
advance and retreat, to persist and vanish, without losing their straightforwardness—only sages know this!"** The word "pride" refers to an extremity and
limit. Those who reach the point of pride do not know the principle of advancing and retreating, persisting and vanishing, or acquisition and deprivation. If
they were sages, they would know it and place themselves accordingly. They
would never lose their straightforwardness, and this is why they would not reach
the point of pride.

2. YIELD (*KUN* 坤)

Yield: there are primacy, progress, profit, and the purity of the mare. The Yield hexagram is the opposite of the Lead hexagram. The four virtues are the same, but the substance of the purity is different. The Lead hexagram has firmness and certainty as its purity, while in the Yield hexagram it is softness and submission that are pure. The mare is soft and submissive, and so brings vigor to its action. This is why the judgment chooses the mare as its symbol and says: "The purity of the mare." **Noble people have a long journey.** The actions of noble people are soft and submissive, and so they have both profit and purity. They align with the virtues of the Yield hexagram. **At first, there is confusion, but later acquisition and the mastery of profit.** *Yin* is what attends to *yang*. It waits for it to sing the melody, and then it harmonizes. If *yin* precedes *yang*, then it will be confused and in error. If it occupies a later position, then it will acquire something constant. "The mastery of profit": when there is profit for the ten thousand things, its mastery lies in yielding. Their birth and completion are both the task of the earth. The way of the minister is also like this: the ruler decrees and the minister acts. To labor over affairs is the mission of the minister. **The southwest acquires friends, while the northeast is deprived of friends. Contentment brings purity and good fortune.** The southwest is a *yin* region, while the northeast is a *yang* region.[1] *Yin* must attend to *yang*, and so be cast off from and deprived of its friends and kindred. Then it will be able to complete the task of transformation and cultivation, and will possess the good fortune of contentment and purity. When it acquires something constant, it will be contented. When it is contented with its constancy, it will be pure, and so it will have good fortune.

The *Judgment* says: "How extreme is the primacy of the Yield hexagram! **The ten thousand things owe it their birth, because it submits to and serves heaven. The benefit of the Yield hexagram is that it bears things, and the alignment of its virtue is without boundaries.**" The way to which things owe their birth may be described as "great," but the Lead hexagram has already been called "great," and this is why the Yield hexagram is called "extreme." The meaning of "extreme" falls a little short of the abundance indicated by the word "great." Whenever the sage distinguishes the respected from the humble, he is prudent and severe like this. The ten thousand things owe their beginning to the Lead hexagram, but they owe their birth to the Yield hexagram—these are the ways of the father and mother. To submit to and serve the influence of heaven so as to bring its task to completion is the benefit and virtue of the Yield hexagram. It constrains and bears the ten thousand things, and aligns with the boundlessness of the Lead hexagram. "**There are enclosure, immensity, brightness, and greatness. The sundry things are stirred to make progress. The mare is an earthly kind of thing, whose action on the earth is without boundaries. There are softness, submission, profit, and purity. Noble people have such action.**" The way of the Yield hexagram is given form and embraced by these four words: "enclosure," "immensity," "brightness," and "greatness." In the case of the Lead hexagram, the words are "firmness," "vigor," "centrality," "straightforwardness," "uniformity," and "spotlessness." "Enclosure" refers to its containing and embracing; "immensity" refers to its tolerance and generosity; "brightness" refers to its illumination and enlightenment; "greatness" refers to its liberality and benefit. Because it has these four, it can complete the task of serving heaven. "The sundry things are stirred" to acquire progress and success. The judgment chooses the mare as a symbol because it is soft and submissive as well as vigorous and active, and it is an earthly kind of thing. "Whose action on the earth is without boundaries": this signifies its vigor. If the Lead hexagram has vigor, while the Yield hexagram is submissive, then why is there also vigor in the Yield hexagram? Response: if it had no vigor, how could it be a match for the Lead hexagram? There could be no action in the Lead hexagram if the Yield hexagram were stopped. Its movement is also firm, but not so as to harm its softness. "There are softness, submission, profit, and purity": these are the virtues of the Yield hexagram and are how noble people act. The way of noble people is to align with the virtues of the Yield hexagram. "'**At first, there is confusion,' and the loss of the way. Later, there is submission, and the acquisition of constancy. 'The southwest acquires friends,' which is to act together with one's kindred. 'The northeast is deprived of friends,' which is to have delight in the end. The good fortune of contentment and purity lies in corresponding** to the earth without boundaries." The function of the Lead hexagram is what the *yang qi* does; the function of the Yield hexagram is what the *yin qi* does. When above form, they are said to be the way of heaven and earth; when below form, they are said to be the task of *yin* and *yang*. From the words "at first, there is confusion, but later acquisition," and so on, the judgment is remarking on the way of *yin*. If it goes first and sings the melody, then it is confused and has lost the way of *yin*. If it goes later and harmonizes, then it is submissive and has acquired its constant principle. The southwest is a *yin* region. Those who attend to their kindred will acquire friends. The northeast is a *yang* region. Those who cast off their kindred will be deprived of friends. If *yin* casts off its kindred and attends to *yang*, then it will be able to complete the task of giving birth to things, and in the end it will have good fortune and delight. "To act together with one's kindred" is its root, while to attend to *yang* is its function. The substance of *yin* is soft but restless. This is why, if it attends to *yang*, it can be contented and pure, and there will be good fortune. It will correspond to the way of the earth without boundaries. If *yin* is neither contented nor pure, how will it be able to correspond to the way of the earth? The *Judgment* says "without boundaries" three times, but it is not saying the same thing in each case. "The alignment of its virtue is without boundaries" indicates that heaven does not cease; "corresponding to the earth without boundaries" indicates that the earth is not depleted; "action on the earth is without boundaries" indicates that the mare is vigorous in its action.

The *Symbol* says: "The propensity of the earth is to yield. Noble people use it to bring benefits with their virtue and to bear things." Because the way of the Yield hexagram is as great as the way of the Lead hexagram, how could anyone other than a sage give it substance? The earth is beneficial, and its propensity is to submit or to collapse. This is why the *Symbol* chooses the symbols of submission and benefit, and says that "the propensity of the earth is to yield." When noble people gaze on the symbol of yielding and benefit, they use it to bring deep benefits with their virtue and to embrace and bear the numberless things.

The initial "six" line: it walks in the frost. The solid ice is reached. The *yin* lines are called "six" because this number refers to an abundance of *yin*. In the number eight,[2] *yang* is already born and there is no uniform abundance. *Yin* begins and is born at the bottom, but it is extremely minimal. When the sage sees that *yin* is begun and born, and is about to grow, he gives a warning about it. When "*yin* begins to crystallize," it will become frost. It is proper for those who walk in the frost to recognize that *yin* is becoming abundant step by step and "will reach the point of solid ice." Likewise, although small people are extremely minimal in their beginning, they should not be made to grow. If they grow, they will reach the point of abundance. **The *Symbol* says: "'It walks in the frost. The solid ice is reached': *yin* begins to crystallize. As it steadily brings about its way, it will reach the point of solid ice."** When *yin* begins to crystallize and become frost, as it becomes abundant step by step, "it will reach the point of solid ice." Although small people are minimal, as they grow, they will step by step reach the point of abundance, and this is why the *Symbol* gives a warning about them in the initial line. The word "steadily" signifies "with practice." With practice, they will reach the point of abundance. One becomes practiced by tracing and retracing something.

The second "six" line: there are straightness, squareness, and greatness. Even without practice, nothing is without profit. The second line is in a *yin* position in the lower trigram, and this is why it is the master of the Yield hexagram. The line statement is speaking about the way of the Yield hexagram as a whole. It is central, straightforward, and in a position below, which is the way of the earth. "Straightness, squareness, and greatness"—its virtue and function are formed and embraced by these three attributes, which exhaust the way of the earth. Because it is straight, square, and great, it can go without practice, and yet "nothing is without profit." The phrase "without practice" signifies that it is spontaneous. Since the line statement refers to the way of the Yield hexagram, when action is taken, it is the action of no one. If it were referring to sages, they would attend to and embrace the way of centrality. "Straightness, squareness, and greatness" are signified by Mencius when he says: "It is extremely great and extremely firm, because it is straight."[3] Since the line statement refers to the substance of the Yield hexagram, it changes the word "firm" to "squareness," just as the *Judgment* attaches the phrase "of the mare" to "purity." Since Mencius is speaking about *qi*, he puts "great" first, as greatness is the substance of *qi*. In the case of the Yield hexagram, it is "straightness" and "squareness" that come first, since it is great only because it is straight and square. Straightness, squareness, and greatness are sufficient to exhaust the way of the earth. This is what people ought to understand. The substances of the Lead and Yield hexagrams are uniform, so that all their positions correspond to one another. The second line is the master of the Yield hexagram, and so its correspondence with the fifth is not chosen for comment, and the fifth is not used for the way of the ruler. If this were the Lead hexagram, the second and fifth lines would correspond to each other. **The *Symbol* says: "There is movement in the second 'six' line: it is straight and square. 'Even without practice, nothing is without profit': the way of the earth is bright."** Its movement is in the service of heaven:

"It is straight and square." If it is straight and square, then it is also great. The meaning of the words "straightness" and "squareness" is that its greatness will not be depleted. The way of the earth is bright and clear, and its task is to be submissive and bring things to completion. How could practice come first and profit afterward?

The third "six" line: if its arrangement is enclosed, it can be pure. Sometimes it attends to the affairs of the king. By not completing them, it brings them to their end. The third line occupies the top position in the lower trigram and refers to those who have acquired positions. Concerning the way of ministers, it is proper for them to enclose and obscure their arrangement and beauty. If something good happens, they wed it to the ruler, and so they can be constant and acquire straightforwardness. Those above will not have hearts that are jealous and bad, and those below will acquire the way of softness and submissiveness. "It can be pure" signifies that they can be pure and certain in keeping guard, and also that they can be constant and continuous, without regret or blame. Sometimes they attend to the affairs of those above, but they do not dare to undertake the completion of such tasks. They simply honor their affairs by keeping guard over their end. To keep guard over one's mission so as to bring the affair to its end is the way of ministers. **The *Symbol* says: "'If its arrangement is enclosed, it can be pure': it reveals it according to the moment."** Fuzi, troubled that people might guard the words of the text without attaining their meaning, attends to it further and sheds light on it.[4] He says that, concerning the way of ministers placed below, it is not proper for them to possess the good that they accomplish. They must enclose and obscure their beauty, and then they will be straightforward and can be constant. Nonetheless, their duty—what it is proper for them to do—is revealed according to the moment, even though they do not possess what they accomplish. Not to lose what is fitting is to make use of the moment. If they do not enclose or store it away, they will not bring it to its end. If they enclose it but do not bring it to its end, they will not exhaust their loyalty. **"'Sometimes it attends to the affairs of the king': its knowledge is bright and great."** The *Symbol*, having brought up and interpreted the meaning of the sentence's former part, now extends itself to the latter part of the text. There are similar cases in other hexagrams. "Sometimes it attends to the affairs of the king" without being able to bring them to completion or possess their end, and this is the brightness and greatness of its knowledge. It is only because "its knowledge is bright and great" that it can enclose and obscure it. When shallow and dim people possess something good, they fear only that other people might not know it. How could they enclose their arrangement?

The fourth "six" line: it ties the sack. There is no blame and no praise. The fourth line occupies a position near the fifth, but this does not mean that they acquire each other. This is the moment when those above and below are locked away and separated. It places itself straightforwardly but on a perilous and doubtful terrain. If it obscures and stores away its knowledge, as though tying or knotting the mouth of a sack, exposing nothing, then it can be without blame. If this does not happen, it will be harmed. If it has already obscured and stored away its knowledge, then there will also be no praise for it. **The *Symbol* says: "'It ties the sack. There is no blame': if it is cautious, it will not be harmed."** If it can be cautious like this, then "it will not be harmed."

The fifth "six" line: a yellow skirt brings primacy and good fortune. Although the Yield hexagram refers to the way of ministers, the fifth position is really that of the ruler, and this is why the line statement gives a warning, saying that "a yellow skirt brings primacy and good fortune." Yellow is the color of centrality, and a skirt is clothing for one's lower part. Those who guard their centrality — which signifies that they guard their own role — and occupy positions below will have primacy and good fortune. The word "primacy" refers to greatness and goodness. The *Symbol* only says of this line that if it guards its centrality and occupies a position below, it will have primacy and good fortune. It does not exhaustively reveal its meaning. If the yellow skirt has already brought primacy and good fortune, then it should be recognized that occupying the position of respect will bring great misfortune to the world. Since the people of later ages have not attained this, its meaning has become obscure, and one cannot do otherwise than distinguish it. The fifth is the position of respect. In the other hexagrams, when a "six" line occupies the fifth position, it refers sometimes to softness and submission, sometimes to pattern and enlightenment, and sometimes to dimness and weakness. In the Yield hexagram, it refers to occupying the position of respect. *Yin* refers to the way of ministers and the way of women. Yi and Mang are examples of ministers who occupied the position of respect, and one can speak of similar cases.[5] Nu Wa and Wu are examples of women who occupied the position of respect, but these were alterations that are not constant, and one can speak of no other cases.[6] This is why the line statement gives a warning about the yellow skirt, but its remarks are not exhaustive. Someone wonders: in the Hide hexagram, there are exhaustive remarks on the affairs of Tang, Wu, and similar cases.[7] Why is it only in this case that it does not remark on them? Response: neglect and flourishing belong to the constant principle, but using *yin* to occupy the position of respect is an alteration that is not constant. **The *Symbol* says: "'A yellow skirt brings primacy and good fortune': the pattern is**

at the center." The pattern of yellow—that is, centrality—is at the center and does not exceed it. What accumulates on the inside is extremely beautiful, and it occupies a position below. This is why it "brings primacy and good fortune."

The top "six" line: dragons clash in the wilderness. Their blood is black and yellow. *Yin* is what attends to *yang*, but, at the limit of its abundance, it resists and contends with it. When a "six" line is already at the limit and still advances ceaselessly, there will necessarily be a clash. This is why the line statement says that they "clash in the wilderness." The word "wilderness" signifies an advance that reaches the outside. If they are already enemies, they must both be injured, and this is why "their blood is black and yellow." **The *Symbol* says: "'Dragons clash in the wilderness': their way is depleted."** When the abundance of *yin* reaches the point of its depletion and limit, there must be contention and injury.

The employment of the "six" lines: there are profit and endless purity. The employment of the "six" lines in the Yield hexagram is like the employment of the "nine" lines in the Lead hexagram—it is the way of employing *yin*. The way of *yin* is soft and is constant only with difficulty. This is why, concerning the way of employing the "six" lines, there is profit in constancy and in endless purity and certainty. **The *Symbol* says: "'The employment of the 'six' lines' brings 'endless purity': it is great at the end."** When the purity and certainty of *yin* have become insufficient, it will not be capable of the "endless end."[8] This is why, on the way of employing the "six" lines, there is profit in abundance and greatness at the end. If it can be great at the end, there will be endless purity.

The *Remarks on the Text* says: "The Yield hexagram is extremely soft, but its movement is firm. It is extremely tranquil, but its virtue is square. When it comes afterward, 'there are acquisition and the mastery,' and it possesses constancy. It encloses the ten thousand things and its transformation is bright. How submissive is the way of the Yield hexagram! It serves heaven and acts in accordance with the moment." The way of the Yield hexagram "is extremely soft," but if it is in movement, it will be firm. The substance of the Yield hexagram "is extremely tranquil," but if it is virtuous, it will be square. Its movement is firm, and this is why it corresponds to the Lead hexagram without drawing back. Its virtue is square, and this is why it gives birth to things while possessing constancy. The way of *yin* is not to sing the melody but to harmonize, and this is why to occupy a position that comes afterward is to acquire something. "The mastery of profit" and the completion of the ten thousand things are the constant tasks of the Yield hexagram. It encloses and embraces the ten thousand kinds, and so its task and transformation are bright and great. After the word "mastery," the *Remarks* omits the phrase "of profit."⁹ "How submissive is the way of the Yield hexagram! It serves heaven and acts in accordance with the moment": it serves the influence of heaven and acts without drawing back from the moment, and so the *Remarks* applauds the way of the Yield hexagram for its submissiveness. **"The family that accumulates what is good must have a surplus of delight; the family that accumulates what is not good must have a surplus of calamity. If the minister murders the ruler, if the son murders the father, these are not the work of a morning and an evening. What causes them arrives step by step, from a distinction that was not made early enough. The *Book of Changes* says: 'It walks in the frost. The solid ice is reached.' It is, in fact, speaking of submissiveness."** The cause that brings the affairs of the world to completion is nothing other than accumulation. If what a family accumulates is good, then blessings and delight will be extended to its children and grandchildren. If what it accumulates is not good, then disasters and calamities will flow into its later generations. The greatest of these, when they reach the point of the afflictions of murder and rebellion, are all reached because of accumulation and aggregation. They cannot be completed in a morning and an evening. The enlightened recognize that they can hardly do other than grow and that the accumulation of the small will complete something great. They distinguish it early, without submitting to its growth, and this is why the badness of the world has no cause of completion—because they recognize the warning of the line statement: "It walks in the frost." The frost that reaches the point of becoming ice, and a small badness that reaches the point of becoming great, both indicate submission to the growth of an affair and its propensities. **"Straight is their straightforwardness and square is their duty. Noble people use reverence to straighten the inside, and duty to square the outside. When reverence and duty are set up, virtue is not solitary. If 'there are straightness, squareness, and greatness,' then 'even without practice, nothing is without profit,' and there is no doubt about what is to be done."** "Straight" is a word for their straightforwardness, and "square" is a word for their duty. Noble people become masters of reverence so as to straighten what is inside them; they become guardians of duty so as to square what is outside them. When reverence is set up, they are straightened on the inside; when duty is given form, they are squared on the outside. Duty is given form on the outside, but it is not itself outside. When reverence and duty are set up, their virtue will be abundant. They do not expect to be great, but they are great: "Virtue is not solitary." There is nothing they employ that they do not themselves encompass, and there is nothing they influence that is not profitable. What doubt could there be? **"Although *yin* possesses beauty, it encloses it so as to attend to the affairs of the king. It does not dare** bring them to completion. Such is the way of the earth, the way of the wife, and the way of the minister. The way of the earth does not bring anything to completion, and so its alternation brings things to their end." The way of those below is not to occupy a position of accomplishment but to enclose and obscure their arrangement and beauty "so as to attend to the affairs of the king." They alternate with those above to bring these affairs to their end, but they do not dare to take possession of their completed task. They are like the way of the earth, which alternates with heaven in bringing things to their end, but heaven is the master of the completed task. The way of the wife is also like this. "**Heaven and earth alter and transform, and plants and trees are bountiful. If heaven and earth are locked away, worthy people conceal themselves. The *Book of Changes* says: 'It ties the sack. There is no blame, and no praise.' It is, in fact, speaking of prudence.**" The fourth line occupies a position in the upper trigram, near the ruler, but this does not mean that they have acquired each other. This is why it symbolizes separating and severing. When heaven and earth interact and affect each other, they alter and transform the ten thousand things, and plants and trees become bountiful and abundant. When ruler and minister are on each other's border, the way makes progress. When heaven and earth are locked away and separated, there will be no success for the ten thousand things. When the ways of ruler and minister are severed, worthy people conceal themselves and flee. In the moment of locking away and separating, the fourth line "ties the sack" to obscure and store itself away. Although there will now be no decree of praise, it can also acquire no blame. The line statement is saying that it is proper to be prudent and to guard oneself. "**Noble people are yellow at their center and develop their principle. They make their position straightforward, and occupy their own substance. Beauty is at their center and goes smoothly through their four limbs. What is revealed in their affairs and vocation is the extremity of beauty.**" They "are yellow at their center" when pattern occupies their center. As for noble people, pattern is at their center and they attain their principle. They occupy straightforward positions, and they do not lose sight of the fact that their substance is below. The fifth is the position of respect, but in the case of the *Yield* hexagram the *Remarks* chooses to refer only to the meaning of centrality and straightforwardness. Beauty accumulates "at their center" and develops smoothly "through their four limbs." "What is revealed" and seen "in their affairs and vocation" is the extreme abundance of virtue and beauty. "**Since *yin* is doubtful about *yang*, they must clash, because it resents the lack of *yang*. This is why it says 'dragon.' It is not as though it has cast off its own kind, and this is why it says 'blood.' As for the black and yellow, they are the mixture of heaven and earth. Heaven is black and the earth is** yellow." Since *yang* is great and *yin* is small, *yin* must attend to *yang*. When *yin* has reached the limit of abundance, it is commensurate with *yang*, which is to be "doubtful about *yang*." Since they do not attend to each other, they must clash. Although the hexagram is uniformly *yin*, there is fear and doubt because there is no *yang*. "This is why it says 'dragon,'" to show that *yin* will clash with *yang*. "In the wilderness" indicates that it advances ceaselessly and reaches the outside. When something has reached the limit of abundance and advances ceaselessly, there will be a clash. Although it has reached the limit of abundance, none of the lines has cast off the *yin* kind. They will contend with *yang*, and their injury should be recognized: "This is why it says 'blood.'" *Yin* is already at the limit of abundance, and reaches the point of contention with *yang*. *Yang* cannot be uninjured, and this is why the blood is black and yellow. Black and yellow are the colors of heaven and earth, and here they signify that both are injured.

3. BLOCK (*ZHUN* 屯)

The *Sequence of the Hexagrams* says: "After heaven and earth exist, the ten thousand things are born. What fills the space between heaven and earth is nothing but the ten thousand things, and this is why the Block hexagram is next. To block is to fill."[1] There is a blockage at the beginning and the birth of things. At the beginning and the birth of the ten thousand things, there is an impenetrable knot that permits no development, and this is why they fill and choke the space between heaven and earth. When they reach the point of a smooth development and a lush abundance, then the idea of choking will vanish. Heaven and earth give birth to the ten thousand things, and the Block hexagram refers to the beginning and the birth of things. This is why it comes immediately after the Lead and Yield hexagrams. Concerning the two trigram symbols, one may remark that they are clouds and thunder coming together, which symbolizes the beginning of the interaction between *yin* and *yang*. Concerning the two trigram substances, one may remark that the interaction begins at the bottom of the Shake trigram, while it begins at the center of the Pit trigram. *Yin* and *yang* interact with each other, which brings the clouds and thunder to completion. When *yin* and *yang* begin to interact, the clouds and thunder correspond to each other, but they do not yet bring the lake to completion. This is why they are the symbols of the Block hexagram. If they had already brought the lake to completion, then they would be the symbols of the Loose hexagram. Further, movement toward the center of an obstacle is also the meaning of the Block hexagram. If *yin* and *yang* did not interact at all, this would be the Clog hexagram. Because their interaction has begun, but it does not yet go smoothly, it is the Block hexagram. At the moment, the world is blocked by difficulties. It is not yet the moment of progress and freedom.

Block: there are primacy, progress, profit, and purity. It should not be employed. There is a long journey but profit in establishing the marquises.[2] The Block hexagram has a way of great progress. For those placed here, profit lies in purity and certainty. Without purity and certainty, how will they be able to cross through the blockage? At the start of the moment of blockage, they cannot yet have any journey to make. As for the blockage of the world, how could force alone be able to cross through it? One must be broadly supplied with assistance and help, and this is why there is "profit in establishing the marquises."

The *Judgment* says: "Block: firmness and softness begin to interact, but birth is difficult. There is movement at the center of the obstacle." Concerning the two symbols—cloud and thunder—one may remark that "firmness and softness begin to interact." Concerning the two substances—the Pit and Shake trigrams—one may remark that "there is movement at the center of the obstacle." When "firmness and softness begin to interact" but are not yet able to develop freely, there will be hardship and blockage. This is why the *Judgment* says that "birth is difficult." "There is movement at the center of the obstacle" also has the meaning of hardship and blockage. **"There are great progress and purity. The movement of thunder and rain is satisfying and full."** "There are great progress and purity" signifies that "the movement of thunder and rain is satisfying and full." When *yin* and *yang* begin to interact, there will be hardship and blockage because they are not yet able to develop freely. When they extend their harmony and cooperation, they will bring the thunder and rain to a completion that satisfies and fills the space between heaven and earth, and the birth of things will be successful. This is the way of great progress in the Block hexagram. And so they are capable of great progress only because of their grand purity. If they did not possess purity and certainty, how could they go out from the blockage? When people are placed in the Block hexagram, they have a way to bring about great progress, and it, too, lies in grand purity and certainty. **"Heaven's creativity is crude and hazy. It is fitting to establish the marquises and not to be serene."** Earlier the text was speaking about the meaning of heaven and earth giving birth to things. Here it is speaking about the affairs of the seasons. "Heaven's creativity" signifies the revolution of the seasons. The *cao* character of "crude" refers to a disorder without coherence or sequence, and the *mei* character of "hazy" refers to a gloom without any light. It is fitting that those faced with the revolution of the seasons establish or set up some kind of assistance and help. Then they will be able to cross through the blockage. Even if they assist themselves by establishing the marquises, it is still proper for them to be worried, diligent, alarmed, and trembling, without retiring to a place of serenity—this is the deep warning of the sage.

The *Symbol* says: "There are clouds and thunder: Block. Noble people use the warp and the weft." The *Symbol* says not that the Pit trigram refers to rain but that it refers to "clouds." Clouds are constituted by rain that is not yet complete. The rain cannot yet be brought to completion, and so there is a blockage. Noble people gaze on the symbol of the Block hexagram and use the warp and the weft on the affairs of the world, so as to cross through the blockage and difficulty. The warp and the woof, together with the thread used in weaving—these signify the act of organization.

The initial "nine" line: the boulder is massive. There is profit in occupying a position of purity, and profit in establishing the marquises. The initial line makes use of *yang* to occupy a position in the lower trigram, it has the powers of firmness and enlightenment, it faces a time of blockage and difficulty, and it occupies a position below. It is not yet able to make the journey readily and cross through the blockage, and this is why "the boulder is massive." It faces the blockage from the initial position. If the boulder were not massive and it advanced hastily, then it would confront the difficulty. This is why it is fitting that it occupy a straightforward position and make its tendencies certain. In general, when people are placed in a blockage or difficulty, they can seldom guard their straightforwardness. If they do not guard their purity and certainty, they will lose sight of their duty. How could they cross through the blockage of the moment? When people occupy positions in a time of blockage and face the blockage from below, what is fitting is that they have help. This is the way to occupy a position in the Block hexagram and to cross through the blockage, and this is why the line statement chooses the establishment of the marquises as its meaning. It signifies the seeking out of assistance and help. **The *Symbol* says: "Although 'the boulder is massive,' it tends to act on its straightforwardness."** When worthy people are in positions below, it is not yet the moment for profit. Although "the boulder is massive," and they cannot yet succeed in making the journey and crossing through the blockage of the moment, they nonetheless have the tendency and the function of crossing through the blockage. That is, they tend to put their straightforwardness into action. **"The esteemed descend to the impoverished: they are great at acquiring the people."** This "nine" line faces the moment of blockage and difficulty, it makes use of *yang*, and it arrives to occupy a position below the *yin* lines. It symbolizes "the esteemed" descending "to the impoverished." When facing the moment of the Block hexagram, *yin* softness cannot make itself persist. The crowd weds itself and attends to even a single line with the power of *yang* firmness. If it can also place itself in a humble position below, it will be "great at acquiring the people." Someone wonders: how could those who face the bottom of the Block hexagram possess anything estimable? As for those who use the powers of firmness and enlightenment to descend to *yin* softness, who use a power capable of crossing through the blockage to descend to those who are incapable of it—this is the esteemed descending to the impoverished. In the case of *yang* doing this for *yin*, how could it not be esteemed?

The second "six" line: it is like someone blocked, like someone thwarted. It rides a horse like someone in formation. If there are no bandits, there will be a marriage. The young woman of purity is not betrothed, but after ten years she will be betrothed. The second line uses *yin* softness to occupy a position in the time of blockage. Although it straightforwardly corresponds to a higher line, it is pressed against the initial firm line, and this is why there is blockage and difficulty. The word "thwarted" indicates that it backs up, and "like" is just a part of speech.[3] "It rides a horse" indicates that it wants to act. It wants to attend to its straightforwardly corresponding line, but it returns "like someone in formation" and cannot advance. The word "formation" refers to something divided up and sectioned out. It dismounts from the horse so as to constitute the formation and is in a different place from its horse. When the second line faces the time of blockage, although it cannot make the crossing, it occupies the center and has acquired straightforwardness. It has a corresponding line above it, and so it has not lost sight of its duty, but it is nonetheless pressed against and near to the initial line. *Yin* is what *yang* seeks out, and softness is what firmness usurps. When softness faces the moment of the Block hexagram, it will certainly have difficulty in crossing though it. Further, it is oppressed by a line that is *yang* and firm, and this is why there will be difficulty. Provided that it is not oppressed by the difficulty of the bandits, it will make the journey to seek out a marriage. The word "marriage" refers to straightforward correspondence, and "bandits" refers to an extreme lack of principle. The second line guards its centrality and straightforwardness, and it does not recklessly align with the initial line, so it "is not betrothed." If its purity and certainty do not change for a period of ten years, then at the limit of the Block hexagram it will necessarily develop, will obtain its straightforwardly corresponding line, "will be betrothed," and will bear children. If a young woman of *yin* softness, who can guard and rein her tendencies, must eventually obtain her development, what will the case be like for noble people, who guard the way without backing up? The initial line refers to people of worth, enlightenment, firmness, and straightforwardness but also to bandits who invade and oppress people. How can this be? Response: here its meaning is drawn from the second line, which uses softness to draw near to firmness, without accounting for the virtues of the initial line in any respect. This is how the *Book of Changes* chooses meanings for hexagram lines. **The Symbol says: "The difficulty of the second "six" line: it rides firmness. 'After ten years she will be betrothed': it reverts to what is constant."** The second "six" line occupies the moment of the Block hexagram, "it rides firmness," and it is pressed by a line that is *yang* and firm—this is its distress and difficulty. If it reaches a period of ten years, then the difficulty must eventually develop. At that time, "it reverts to what is constant," which indicates that it aligns with its straightforwardly corresponding line. The number ten is chosen because it is the end of the number series.

The third "six" line: one who approaches deer without the forester merely enters the center of the forest. Noble people see in its incipience that nothing is better than abandoning it. If they make the journey, there will be dismay. The third "six" line uses *yin* softness to occupy a firm position. When a soft line is already incapable of being contented with the blockage, and it occupies a firm position without centrality or straightforwardness, its movement will be faulty. Although it is greedy for what it seeks, it is not sufficient to make the crossing, and it does not have the support of a corresponding line. How could it be content? It is like "one who approaches deer without the forester." Those who enter the mountain forest must have the forester to direct them. If no one directs them, they will only become snared and enter the bushy center of the forest. Noble people see the state of affairs when it is incipient and minimal, that "nothing is better than abandoning it," and that they should not pursue it. "If they make the journey," they will ineptly be choosing depletion and dismay, and that is all. **The Symbol says: "'One who approaches deer without the forester': it attends to the game. Noble people abandon it: 'if they make the journey, there will be dismay' and depletion."** Those who move faultily toward an illicit state of affairs are attending to their desires. To be "without the forester" and still to approach the deer is to be greedy for game. When facing the moment of the Block hexagram, those who move when they should not move are like those without the forester who still approach the deer. They have the heart of attending to the game. If they were noble people, they would see the affair in its incipience, and then they would abandon and not attend to it. "If they make the journey," there should be dismay, and they will be trapped and depleted.

The fourth "six" line: it rides a horse like someone in formation, and seeks a marriage. If it makes the journey, there will be good fortune. Nothing is without profit. The fourth "six" line uses softness and submission to occupy a position near the ruler and acquires those above. Its power is insufficient to cross through the blockage. This is why it wants to advance but returns to a stop: "It rides a horse like someone in formation." It is not sufficient to cross through the blockage of the moment by itself, but if it can seek out worthy people to assist it, then it should make the crossing. The worthy people of *yang* firmness referred to by the initial line, to which it straightforwardly corresponds, are the ones to be married. If it "seeks a marriage" with this line that is *yang* and firm, and together they make the journey to give their shared assistance to a ruler of *yang* firmness, centrality, and straightforwardness, then they will cross through the blockage of the moment, there will be good fortune, and nothing will be without profit. As for those occupying the positions of duke and dignitary, their powers may not be sufficient to cross through the blockage of the moment by themselves, but if they can seek out worthy people below them, if they can employ and relate to them, then how could they not make the crossing? **The Symbol says: "It 'seeks' and 'makes the journey': there is enlightenment."** To recognize one's own insufficiency, to seek the assistance of worthy people and afterward to make the journey—this may be called "enlightenment." To occupy the terrain for acquiring things and bringing them about without having the capacity for it, and yet still seeking success by oneself, is the extremity of dimness.

The fifth "nine" line: its richness is blocked. A small purity brings good fortune, while a great purity brings misfortune. The fifth line occupies the position of respect, it acquires straightforwardness, and it faces the moment of the Block hexagram. If it had worthy people of firmness and enlightenment to assist it, then it would be able to cross through the blockage. It has no ministers, and this is why "its richness is blocked." Even in a time of blockage and difficulty, nothing takes away from the respect of the rulers, at least concerning their fame and position. It is only that there are some places where their influence cannot act and some places where their virtue and grace do not descend—such is the case when "its richness is blocked," which is the blockage faced by rulers. When there are places where their richness or grace does not descend, it is because authority and aptitude are no longer in them. If authority and aptitude have departed from them, and they want to straighten themselves out abruptly, they are seeking the way of misfortune. This was the case for the affairs of Duke Zhao of Lu and the Duke of Gaogui Village.[4] This is why, if there is "a small purity," it will bring "good fortune." The phrase "small purity" refers to straightening oneself out step by step, as did Pan Geng and Xuan of the Zhou dynasty.[5] They corrected their virtue and employed worthy people, returning to the government of the first kings, so that the various marquises returned to their courts. In fact, they steadily brought about their way, using no violence in their action.[6] Further, theirs was not the idleness of inaction, as it was for Xi and Zhao of the Tang dynasty.[7] If there were inaction, then the blockage would be constant, and they would reach the point of vanishing. **The *Symbol* says: "'Its richness is blocked': its influence is not yet bright."** Its richness and grace do not yet extend to those below, and so the influence of its virtue cannot yet be bright and great. Such is the blockage of the ruler.

The top "six" line: it rides a horse like someone in formation. It weeps blood like streams. This "six" line uses *yin* softness to occupy the end of the Block hexagram, it is at the limit of the obstacle, and it has no corresponding line to support it. If it occupies this position, it will not be content, but if it moves, it will have nowhere to go. "It rides a horse," that is, it wants to make the journey, but it is "like someone in formation"—that is, it does not advance. It is at the extremity of depletion and peril, and reaches the point at which it "weeps blood like streams," which is the limit of the Block hexagram. Since the Block hexagram has reached its limit, if it had the help of a line that was *yang* and firm, it would be able to cross through it. **The *Symbol* says: "'It weeps blood like streams': how could it grow?"** The blockage and difficulty are at their limit and depletion, but it does not know what to do. This is why it reaches the point at which "it weeps blood." Since it is so thoroughly upset, how could it grow or be continuous? As for the hexagrams, they refer to states of affairs, while the lines refer to the moments of these states of affairs. They are divided into three, and then doubled, which is sufficient to contain and tie up the crowd of principles, to draw out and expand them, to penetrate their kinds and how they grow, and to sum up the possible states of affairs in the world.

4. BLIND (*MENG* 蒙)

The *Sequence of the Hexagrams* says: "To block is to fill. The Block hexagram refers to the beginning and the birth of things. When things are born, they are necessarily blind, and this is why the Blind hexagram is next. The Blind hexagram refers both to blindness and to the youth of things." The Block hexagram refers to the beginning and the birth of things. At the beginning and the birth of things, when they are young and small, revelation has not yet been brought to their blindness and haziness. And so the Blind hexagram succeeds the Block hexagram. As for the trigrams, the Calm trigram is above and the Pit trigram below. The Calm trigram refers to the mountain and to stopping, while the Pit trigram refers to water and to the obstacle: below the mountain, there is an obstacle. To encounter the obstacle and be stopped, not knowing where to go, is the symbol of blindness. Water is a thing that must travel, but when it begins to go out, it does not yet have anywhere to go. This is why it refers to blindness. When it extends its advance, then it will have the meaning of progress.

Blind: there is progress. It is not that I seek the blind child, but that the blind child seeks me. The initial augury gives an answer. A second or third shows disdain for it. If it is disdained, then it will give no answer. There are profit and purity. The meaning of the word "progress" is the principle that blindness becomes openness and revelation. The powers of the trigrams bring about the way of progress at "the center of the moment." The fifth "six" line is the master of the Blind hexagram, while the second "nine" line refers to those who bring revelation to blindness. The word "I" signifies the second line. The second line is not the master of the Blind hexagram, but when the fifth line has already submitted to and lowered itself before the second, then the second brings revelation to the blindness. This is why the judgment remarks that the second line is the master.

"It is not that I seek the blind child, but that the blind child seeks me": the fifth line occupies the position of respect, but it possesses the virtues of softness and submission. When it is faced with the blindness of childhood, it corresponds straightforwardly to the second line. Further, they both possess the same virtue of centrality. It can employ the way of the second line to bring revelation to its blindness. The second line uses the virtues of firmness and centrality while in a position below. It refers to those who are believed in and welcomed by the rulers. It is proper that they guard themselves with the way and wait for rulers of extreme sincerity to seek them out. After the rulers correspond to them, they will be able to employ their way: "It is not that I seek anything from the blind child, but that the blind child arrives at seeking something from me." The word "augury" indicates the use of prognostication to resolve something. "The initial augury gives an answer": this signifies that, if someone of extreme sincerity and unity of intention comes to seek it out, then it will give an answer. If there is a second or third augury, then it will become disdainful and lethargic, and this is why "it will give no answer." Concerning the way of bringing revelation to blindness, the profit lies in purity and straightforwardness. Further, although the second line is firm and central, it nonetheless occupies a *yin* position. This is why it is fitting that the judgment give a warning.

The *Judgment* says: "Blind: below the mountain is an obstacle. When there is an obstacle, and it brings things to a stop, this is blindness. 'Blind: there is progress': progress is used to act at the center of the moment. 'It is not that I seek the blind child, but that the blind child seeks me': our tendencies correspond." "Below the mountain is an obstacle": when there is an obstacle inside, no one can be placed there, while those who are stopped outside cannot advance. They do not yet know what to do, and this is why the symbol has the meaning of darkness and blindness. "'Blind: there is progress': progress is used to act at the center of the moment": there can be progress in the Blind hexagram when one uses the way of progress in taking action. The way of progress signifies "the center of the moment." The word "moment" signifies the acquisition of correspondence with the ruler. The word "center" signifies the acquisition of the center as one's place. When one has acquired centrality, the moment has arrived. "'It is not that I seek the blind child, but that the blind child seeks me': our tendencies correspond": the second line possesses the worthiness of firmness and enlightenment, but it is placed below. The fifth line is "the blind child," but it occupies a position above. It is not the case that the second seeks the fifth. In fact, the tendencies of the fifth correspond with those of the second. When worthy people are below, how could they advance themselves to seek the rulers? Were they to seek the rulers by themselves, they could not possibly make the principle of their employment believable. And so, the people of antiquity had to wait for their rulers to bring about reverence and to exhaust ritual, and afterward they would make the journey. It was not that they desired respect and greatness for themselves. In fact, "they only respected virtue and took pleasure in the way. If they were not like this, they would not have been sufficient for the things they did."[1] "'The initial augury gives an answer': it uses firmness and centrality. 'A second or third shows disdain for it. If it is disdained, then it will give no answer': disdain is blindness." "The initial augury" signifies that people have come with sincerity and unity to seek the resolution of their blindness. In such a case, it is proper to use the way of "firmness and centrality," which will give an answer—that is, which will bring openness and revelation to it. "A second or third" indicates that they are bothersome and disjointed. The intentions of those who have come to augur are bothersome and disjointed. If they cannot be sincere and unified, then they will be disdainful and lethargic, and it will not be proper to give an answer. If an answer were given, they could not possibly believe what they had received. There would be nothing but bother and disdain, and this is why the *Judgment* says: "Disdain is blindness." Both those who seek and those who give the answer are either bothersome or disdained. "To nourish the straightforwardness of the blind is the task of the sage." The hexagram judgment says: "There are profit and purity." The *Judgment* returns to this point and expands its meaning. It sheds light on the fact that the judgment does not stop at giving a warning to the second line but is really about the way of bringing nourishment to the blind. Those who have not yet been brought to revelation are said to be blind. To take the blind—those who have not yet been brought to revelation—and make them uniform and unified, and nourish their straightforwardness, is to produce the accomplishment of a sage. If those who bring revelation "enact prohibitions afterward, they will be flouted and defied, and they will find it difficult to be victorious."[2] To nourish the straightforwardness of the blind is the best that learning can do. Of the Blind hexagram's six lines, the two *yang* lines are those that bring order to the blind, while the four *yin* lines are all placed in blindness.

The *Symbol* says: "Below the mountain, a spring goes out: Blind. Noble people use it to give purpose to action and to cultivate virtue." "Below the mountain, a spring goes out": it goes out and encounters an obstacle. It does not yet have anywhere to go, and this symbolizes the Blind hexagram. When people are in the blindness of youth, they do not yet know what is suitable. Noble people gaze on the symbol of the Blind hexagram, and "use it to give purpose to action and to cultivate virtue." When they gaze on how it goes out and cannot yet develop or act, they give purpose and resolution to how it will act. When they gaze on how it begins to go out and does not yet have any direction, they nourish and cultivate its enlightenment and virtue.

The initial "six" line: it brings revelation to blindness. There is profit in the employment of punishment on people, in the employment of shackles and manacles to persuade them. Making a journey will bring dismay. The initial line uses the dimness of *yin* to occupy the bottom position and refers to the blindness of the people below. The line statement speaks of the way to bring them revelation. In bringing revelation to the blindness of the people below, it is proper to shed light on the punishments and prohibitions. When these are shown to them, it will make them know how to tremble. Afterward, one may attend to them with teaching and direction. Since antiquity, sage-kings have brought order by providing the punishments and penalties that make the crowd equable. They shed light on the teachings and transformations that make its customs good. When the punishments and penalties have been set up, there can afterward be the action of teaching and transformation. Although sages value virtue and do not value punishment, they have never yet tasted partiality to one and neglect of the other. This is why, at the beginning of their government, the setting up of the laws occupies the first place. In the initial moment of bringing order to the blind, one exercises authority by means of punishment "to persuade them" to drive out the "shackles and manacles" of darkness and blindness. The phrase "shackles and manacles" signifies what chains and bolts them down. If they do not drive out the shackles and manacles of darkness and blindness, nothing can make the teaching of the good to enter them. When the punishments and prohibitions have been administered, even if their hearts cannot yet be exemplary, it is still proper for them to tremble and attend to authority without daring to indulge the desires of their darkness and blindness. Afterward, they will become able step by step to recognize the way of the good and to reform the wrongness of their hearts. Then they will be able to "convert their manners and change their customs."[3] If punishments were employed without qualification to bring order, no revelation could ever be brought to the blind, despite their trembling. If they avoided the punishment but had no sense of shame, they could neither acquire nor complete their order and transformation.[4] This is why, if it makes the journey, there should be dismay. **The *Symbol* says: "'There is profit in the employment of punishment on people': it makes the law straightforward."** When beginning to bring order to the blind, one sets up defenses and perimeters, and sheds light on the punishments and penalties—that is, one "makes the law straightforward." When this is brought about, they will step by step reach the point of transformation. Someone wonders: in the initial moment of bringing revelation to the blind, how is this hasty employment of punishment not a case of "putting to death without teaching"?[5] The question does not recognize that teaching can result only when laws, controls, and punishments have been set up. In fact, when later generations discuss punishment, they do not recognize that teaching and transformation are at its center.

The second "nine" line: to include the blind brings good fortune. To accept a woman brings good fortune. The son conquers the family. The word "include" refers to enclosing or embracing. The second line occupies a position in a time of blindness, it possesses the powers of firmness and enlightenment, and it corresponds to the ruler referred to by the fifth "six" line. The virtue of centrality is the same in both of them, and they refer to those who face command over this moment. They must broaden what they enclose or embrace, and feel sorrow and sympathy for those in darkness and stupidity, and then they will be able to bring revelation to the blindness of the world and complete the task of bringing order to the blind. When their way is broad and their influence is liberal like this, there will be "good fortune." The hexagram has only two *yang* lines, and the firmness of the top "nine" line is excessive. Only the second "nine" line has the virtues of firmness and centrality. It corresponds to the fifth line and refers to those who alone are enlightened and who are employed in the moment. Were they to rely on their enlightenment and give themselves unqualified command, their virtues would not be immense.[6] This is why it is proper "to accept" what is good even from the softness and dullness of "a woman," so that one's enlightenment may broaden. The statement also uses the word "woman" because many of the various lines are *yin*. No one in the world will extend themselves to the sagehood of Yao and Shun without daily asking of the people below them, choosing what is good in everyone.[7] If the second line can "include" and "accept," it will conquer and cross through the affairs of the ruler, just like the son who can set the family in order. The fifth line is soft and *yin*, and this is why the task of bringing revelation to the blind belongs entirely to the second. To describe it in terms of a family: the father is the fifth line and the son is the second. The second line can master the task of the Blind hexagram just as "the son conquers" or brings order to "the family." **The *Symbol* says: "'The son conquers the family': firmness and softness respond to each other."** The son who conquers or brings order to the family receives unqualified command from a father who believes in him. The second line can master the task of the

Blind hexagram because it receives unqualified command from a fifth line that believes in it. The inclinations of the second and fifth lines, of firmness and softness, respond to each other. This is why they acquire the way of acting with firmness and centrality, and complete the task of bringing revelation to the blind. If the inclinations of the higher and lower lines did not respond to each other, even if the second line were firm and central, how could it officiate in this affair?

The third "six" line: it should not employ or choose the woman. She sees the gold of her husband, but does not possess him. There is no long-term profit. The third line uses *yin* softness to place itself in blindness and dullness, without centrality or straightforwardness, and refers to the faulty movement of a woman. It corresponds straightforwardly to the top line, but it cannot go far to attend to it. Nearby it sees the second "nine" line, to which the group of blind lines has wedded itself, and which has acquired the abundance of the moment. This is why the third line abandons its straightforwardly corresponding line and attends to the second, like a woman who "sees the gold of her husband." It is proper that a woman attend to a man because of straightforwardness and ritual. If she enjoys and attends to him because she has seen all his gold, she will not be able to preserve her possession of his body. There is no journey she can make that will be profitable. **The *Symbol* says: "'It should not employ or choose the woman': her action is not submissive."** When a woman is like this, "her action" is crooked, crass, and "not submissive." She should not be chosen.

The fourth "six" line: to be trapped in blindness brings dismay. The fourth line uses *yin* softness and is blind and dull. Firmness and enlightenment do not relate to or support it, it has no means of bringing revelation to its own blindness, and it refers to those who are trapped in darkness and blindness. Its dismay should be extreme. The word "dismay" refers to insufficiency and signifies that there may be too little of something. **The *Symbol* says: "The 'dismay' of being 'trapped in blindness': it alone is far from reality."** In the moment of the Blind hexagram, it is *yang* firmness that brings revelation to the blind. The fourth line is *yin* and soft, and is the farthest from the firm lines. It refers to people of stupidity and blindness who are not close to or near worthy people and who have no means of acquiring enlightenment. This is why they are "trapped in blindness." They should be disappointed and dismayed, as they alone are far from people of worth and enlightenment. Their inability to relate to worthy people is what brings about the trap—their dismay should be extreme. The word "reality" here signifies *yang* firmness.

The fifth "six" line: the child is blind. There is good fortune. The fifth line uses softness and submission to occupy the position of the ruler. It corresponds to the second line below it, and it uses its virtues of softness and centrality in delegating command to the powers of firmness and enlightenment, which is sufficient to bring order to the blindness of the world. This is why "there is good fortune." The word "child" is chosen because it has not yet been brought to revelation, and it is supplied by other people. It refers to rulers who, if they can delegate command with extreme sincerity to worthy people and so bring their task to completion—how is this different from going out and doing it themselves? **The *Symbol* says: "There is good fortune when 'the child is blind': there are submission and lowliness."** To abandon oneself and attend to other people is "submission" or attentiveness. To diminish one's tendencies and seek something from those below is humility or "lowliness." Those who can be like this will gladden the world.

The top "nine" line: it strikes the blind. There is no profit for the bandit, but profit in resisting bandits. This "nine" line occupies the end position of the Blind hexagram, which is to face the moment when the blindness reaches its limit. When the stupidity and blindness of people have reached their limit, as when the Miao people would not be administered, but became bandits and disorderly, it is proper to strike and attack them.[8] Nonetheless, this "nine" line occupies the top position. Its firmness is at the limit and not the center, and this is why the line statement warns that "there is no profit for the bandit." To set the blindness of people in order is to resist bandits, while to indulge in firmness and violence is to be a bandit. When Shun took the field against the Miao people, and the Duke of Zhou put the three deputies to death, they were resisting bandits.[9] When the Qin emperor Huang and the Han emperor Wu depleted their soldiers through putting to death and attacking, they were bandits.[10] **The *Symbol* says: "There is 'profit in' employing resistance against 'bandits': those above and below are submissive."** "There is 'profit in' employing resistance against 'bandits'": those above and below both acquire submissiveness. When those above are not excessively violent, and those below strike or drive out their blindness—this is the meaning of "resisting bandits."

5. NEED (*XU* 需)

The *Sequence of the Hexagrams* says: "The Blind hexagram refers both to blindness and to the youth of things. When things are young, they should not be without nourishment, and this is why the Need hexagram is next. The Need hexagram refers to the way of eating and drinking." As for the youth and immaturity of things, they must wait to be nourished so that they can be brought to completion. What is needed for the nourishment of things is eating and drinking, and this is why the *Sequence* says: "The Need hexagram refers to the way of eating and drinking." "The cloud ascends to heaven," which is the symbol of soaking something with steam. Eating and drinking are what soak into things and add to them. This is why the Need hexagram refers to the way of eating and drinking, and why it succeeds the Blind hexagram. The great idea in this hexagram is its meaning of requirement and waiting, and the *Sequence* chooses as its example the greatest of requirements. The nature of leading or vigor is such that it must advance, but the Lead trigram is placed below a pit or obstacle. The obstacle constitutes a hindrance, and this is why it waits for what it requires and advances only afterward.

Need: it is trustworthy. There are brightness and progress. Purity brings good fortune. There is profit in traversing a great stream. Those in need must wait for what they require. Concerning the two trigram substances, one may remark that the Lead trigram has a firmness and vigor that advance upward, but it encounters an obstacle and is not yet able to advance. This is why the trigrams mean to need and to wait. Concerning the powers of the hexagram, one may remark that the fifth line occupies the position of the ruler and is the master of the Need hexagram. It has the virtues of firmness, vigor, centrality, and straightforwardness. It is sincere and believable—that is, its center is replete and full,

59

and to have a full center is to be trustworthy. Since it is trustworthy, its light will be bright, and it will be capable of progress and development. It will acquire purity and straightforwardness, and there will be good fortune. Since its need is like this, how could it be unable to make the crossing? Although there is an obstacle, it is not difficult, and this is why "there is profit in traversing a great stream." In general, "purity brings good fortune" indicates either that there is already straightforwardness and good fortune, or that if one acquires straightforwardness there will be good fortune. It is proper to make this distinction.

The *Judgment* says: "To need is to require. The obstacle is ahead. Those who are firm and vigorous will not be snared, which means that they will not be trapped and depleted." The meaning of the Need hexagram is requirement. When "the obstacle is ahead," no one should advance hastily, and this is why one waits for what is needed, and then acts. Those who possess the firmness and vigor of the Lead trigram will be able to wait for what they need, and will not move lightly. This is why they are not snared by the obstacle, which means that they will not reach the point of being "trapped and depleted." As for people of firmness and vigor, their motion is necessarily restless. To be capable of waiting for what they need and then moving is the best they can do to place themselves. This is why Fuzi applauds them, saying: "Which means that they will not be trapped and depleted."[1] **"'Need: it is trustworthy. There are brightness and progress. Purity brings good fortune': its position is the position of heaven, because of its straightforwardness and centrality."** The fifth line occupies the center of its trigram with firmness and fullness, which are the symbols of trustworthiness. It will acquire what it needs, and this, too, means that "it is trustworthy." It has the firmness of the Lead trigram as well as extreme sincerity, and this is why it has the virtues of brightness and enlightenment, and is capable of progress and development. It has acquired purity and straightforwardness, and so there will be good fortune. This can happen because it occupies the position of heaven and has acquired straightforwardness and centrality. It occupies "the position of heaven," which designates the fifth position. "Because of its straightforwardness and centrality": the *Judgment* is also remarking on the second line, and this is why it says "straightforwardness and centrality." **"'There is profit in traversing a great stream': a journey will accomplish something."** It is already trustworthy, pure, and straightforward. Even when traversing obstacles and hindrances, if it makes the journey, it will accomplish something. This is the best that the way of the Need hexagram can do. Since it has the firmness of the Lead trigram and is capable of what it needs, how could it be without profit?

The *Symbol* says: "The cloud ascends to heaven: Need. Noble people use eating and drinking, finding repose and pleasure." The *qi* of the cloud steams and ascends or rises to heaven. One must wait for the *yin* and *yang qi* to become harmonious and orderly, and afterward the rain will be brought to completion. When the cloud begins to ascend to heaven, the rain is not yet complete, and this is why it has the meaning of waiting for what one requires. The *yin* and *yang qi* are interacting and affecting each other, but they have not yet brought the rain or the lake to completion. They are like noble people who herd their powers and virtues but who do not yet employ their influence. Noble people gaze on the symbol of the cloud ascending to heaven, which is in need of something to become rain, and they cherish their way and virtue. They are content to wait for the moment, "eating and drinking" to nourish their substance or *qi*, and "finding repose and pleasure" to harmonize the tendencies of their hearts. This is called "occupying a position of ease while awaiting the mandate."[2]

The initial "nine" line: it is in need in the outlands. There is profit in employing what lasts, and no blame. Those in need have encountered an obstacle. This is why they are first in need, and advance afterward. The initial line is the farthest from the obstacle, and this is why "it is in need in the outlands." The word "outlands" refers to a vast and faraway terrain. When placed somewhere vast and far away, there is profit in being contented and in guarding one's constancy. In such a case, there will be "no blame." Those who cannot be contented and constant will move restlessly and confront the difficulty. How could they be in need in a faraway place? How could they be without excess? The *Symbol* says: "'It is in need in the outlands': it does not act to confront the difficulty. 'There is profit in employing what lasts, and no blame': it has not yet lost its constancy." Those placed in a vast and faraway place do not act to confront and brave the obstacle and difficulty. Considered as a thing, *yang* is something that advances upward with firmness and vigor. The initial line can be in need and wait on a vast and faraway terrain, without advancing to confront the obstacle and difficulty. If it returns to a fitting place of contentment and does not lose its constancy, then it should have "no blame." Even they do not advance, those with the tendency to move will not be able to be contented with their constancy. Noble people in the moment of the Need hexagram are contented and tranquil, and keep guard over themselves. Although their tendencies have requirements, they are as idle as if they could remain here until the end of their lives. This is to be able to employ what is constant.

The second "nine" line: it is in need in the sand. There are small remarks but good fortune in the end. The Pit trigram refers to water, and near water there is sand. The second line is nearing the obstacle step by step, and this is why "it is in need in the sand." As it nears the obstacle and difficulty step by step, although it has not yet reached the point of distress and harm, there are already "small remarks." In general, the greatness or smallness of the distress or difficulty is peculiar to each line statement. When it is small, it only reaches the point that there are remarks, since the injuries caused by spoken words are extremely small. The second line uses the power of *yang* firmness, occupies a soft position, guards its centrality, and places itself with tolerance and generosity—this is the best that the Need hexagram can do. Although it is going nearer to the obstacle step by step, it has not yet reached the obstacle, and this is why "there are small remarks," and it is injured by spoken words. The harm is not great, and in the end it will acquire good fortune. **The *Symbol* says: "'It is in need in the sand': the center overflows. Although 'there are small remarks,' there is good fortune in the end."** The word "overflows" refers to the span of its tolerance. Although the second line is near the obstacle, it uses tolerance and generosity to occupy the center. This is why, although small remarks or spoken words are extended to it, it will acquire good fortune in the end, which is to place oneself well.

The third "nine" line: it is in need in the mud and brings about extreme banditry. The word "mud" refers to something at the water's edge. When it advances to the edge of the obstacle, it is proper that it bring about the extremity of bandits or difficulties. The third line is firm and without centrality, it occupies the top of the vigor trigram substance, and it symbolizes advancement and movement. This is why it brings about the bandits. If it is not "reverent and cautious," it will also bring about deprivation and defeat. **The *Symbol* says: "'It is in need in the mud': there is disaster outside it. I myself bring about the bandits. If it is reverent and cautious, it will not be defeated."** The third line is pressed against the obstacle and difficulty in the upper trigram substance, and this is why the *Symbol* says: "There is disaster outside it." "Disaster" is a general term for distress and difficulty. One of its roles is to be a word for a mistake. The third line brings about bandits because it advances by itself and besets the obstacle. This is why it says "I myself," because by itself it brings about the bandits. If it can be "reverent and cautious," if it calculates what is fitting before it advances, then there will be no deprivation or defeat. In the moment of the Need hexagram, one first has requirements and afterward advances. Its meaning is that one moves in accordance with the characteristics of the moment. Its warning is not that no one should advance, but that one should straightaway be made reverent and cautious, so as not to lose sight of what is fitting.

The fourth "six" line: it is in need in blood and goes out from its cave. The fourth line uses a disposition of *yin* softness, is placed in the obstacle trigram, faces the advance of the three *yang* lines below it, and refers to those who are injured by the obstacle and difficulty. This is why the line statement says that it "is in need in blood." Since they have been injured by the obstacle and difficulty, they cannot be contented with their place and must lose the position they occupy. This is why it says that it "goes out from its cave." The word "cave" refers to a place where things are contented. They submit by attending to the moment and do not struggle with the obstacle and difficulty, and so they will not reach the point of misfortune. Those who make use of softness to occupy *yin* positions are unable to struggle. Were a *yang* line to occupy this position, there would necessarily be misfortune. In fact, being without the virtues of centrality and straightforwardness, and using firmness alone to struggle with the obstacle—these are quite sufficient to bring about misfortune. **The *Symbol* says: "'It is in need in blood': it submits by listening."** The fourth line uses *yin* softness to occupy the center of the obstacle and difficulty. It cannot place itself with certainty, and this is why it retreats and "goes out from its cave." In fact, *yin* softness cannot struggle with the moment. If it cannot remain in place, it will retreat. This is a case of submitting or attending by listening to the moment, and so it does not reach the point of misfortune.

The fifth "nine" line: it is in need in food and wine. Purity brings good fortune. The fifth line uses *yang* firmness to occupy the center, it acquires a straightforward position in the position of heaven and it is capable of exhausting its way. Since this is how it is in need, what could it need that it does not obtain? This is why it reposes and is content with "food and wine" while awaiting it. It must acquire what it requires. To have acquired purity and straightforwardness, and to be successful at getting what one needs—this may be called "good fortune." **The *Symbol* says: "'Food and wine. Purity brings good fortune': it uses centrality and straightforwardness."** "It is in need in food and wine": there are purity and good fortune because the fifth line acquires centrality and straightforwardness, and exhausts its way.

The top "six" line: it enters its cave. There are three men, guests, who arrive, though not quickly. If it is reverent, there will be good fortune in the end. In the Need hexagram, there is an obstacle ahead. There is the moment of need, and afterward one advances. The top "six" line occupies the end position of the obstacle trigram. If it is at the end, there will be alteration. It is at the limit of the Need hexagram, it has continued a long time, and now it makes its acquisition. *Yin* stops in the sixth position, and so this line is contented in its place. This is why "it enters its cave." The word "cave" refers to a place of contentment. If it has stopped where it is contented, those behind it will necessarily reach it. The phrase "three men, guests" signifies the three *yang* lines of the lower trigram. The three *yang* lines of the Lead trigram are not things that belong below. They refer to those who advance in the moment of the Need hexagram. The Need hexagram has reached its limit, and this is why they all advance upward. The phrase "though not quickly" indicates that they are not rushed, but arrive on their own. The top "six" line is in the Need hexagram and has acquired a place of contentment. When the group of firm lines arrives, if it does not raise up a heart of jealousy and illness, of wrathfulness and struggle, if it waits on them with extreme sincerity and exhaustive reverence, then although the firm lines are extremely violent, what principle would make them invaders and usurpers? This is why "there is good fortune in the end." Someone wonders: can a *yin* line occupying a position atop three *yang* lines acquire contentment? Response: the three *yang* lines belong to the substance of the Lead trigram, and they tend to advance upward. Since this is a "six" line in a *yin* position, they cannot stop here and remain straightforward. This is why their intention is not to contend and strive. If it is reverential toward them, there will be good fortune. **The Symbol says: "'Guests, who arrive, though not quickly. If it is reverent, there is good fortune in the end': although its position is not proper for it, it does not yet have a great loss."** "Its position is not proper for it" because it makes use of *yin* and it is at the top. When a "six" line occupies a *yin* position, it is considered contented. The *Symbol*, in turn, exhausts the meaning of this, shedding light on the fact that it is fitting for *yin* to be below, yet here it occupies the top: "Its position is not proper for it." Nonetheless, if it can be reverent and cautious when placing itself, the *yang* lines will not be able to usurp it, and it will acquire good fortune in the end. Although its position is not proper for it, it has not yet reached the point of "great loss."

6. FIGHT (*SONG* 訟)

The *Sequence of the Hexagrams* says: "If there are eating and drinking, then fights must break out, and this is why the Fight hexagram is next." What people need is to eat and drink. Since they have this requirement, it causes contention and fighting to arise, and so the Fight hexagram succeeds the Need hexagram. As for the trigrams, the Lead trigram is above and the Pit trigram below. Concerning the two trigram symbols, one may remark that the action of the heavenly *yang* is to ascend, while the nature of water is to descend. Their actions draw back from each other, and so they bring a fight to completion. Concerning the two trigram substances, one may remark that "there is firmness above, and an obstacle below." When firmness and an obstacle respond to each other, how could there not be a fight? Further, when people have obstacles and hindrances on the inside but are firm and strong on the outside, they get into fights.

Fight: it is trustworthy. The obstructions make it careful. Centrality brings good fortune, but there is misfortune in the end. Concerning the way of fighting, one must be trustworthy and full. To have no fullness at one's center is to have deceit and faults, which is the way of misfortune. The trigram centers are full, which is the symbol of being trustworthy. A fight is when people contend and make distinctions, and wait for someone else to resolve them. Although "it is trustworthy," it must also be obstructed and choked, and does not yet develop. If there were no obstructions, then it would already be enlightened, and there would be no fight. As long as the state of affairs has not yet been distinguished, neither good nor bad fortune is the necessary result. This is why it is trembling and careful. "Centrality brings good fortune": if it acquires centrality, then there will be good fortune. "There is misfortune in the end": when the affair reaches its end or limit, there will be misfortune. **There is profit in seeing**

great people, but no profit in traversing a great stream. Those who fight seek
to distinguish the twisted and the straight, and this is why "there is profit in seeing great people." If the people are great, they will be able to use their firmness,
enlightenment, centrality, and straightforwardness to resolve the fight. A fight
is not an affair of harmony and peace, and so it is proper to select a terrain of
contentment and to place oneself there. One should not be snared by perils and
obstacles, and this is why "there is no profit in traversing a great stream."

**The *Judgment* says: "Fight: there is firmness above, and an obstacle below.
There is an obstacle, but it is vigorous: Fight."** As for the trigrams of the Fight
hexagram, the firm trigram is above and the obstacle below—there is an obstacle but also vigor. Further, the hexagram is constituted by an obstacle and vigor
responding to each other. The inner trigram refers to the obstacle, the outer
trigram refers to vigor, and together they constitute the Fight hexagram. Were
there vigor but no obstacle, it would not give birth to a fight. Were there an obstacle but no vigor, there could also be no fight. In this case, there are both an
obstacle and vigor, and as a result, there is a fight. **"'Fight: it is trustworthy. The
obstructions make it careful. Centrality brings good fortune': firmness arrives
and acquires centrality."** The way of the Fight hexagram is certainly like this,
but the *Judgment* is also speaking about the powers of the hexagram. Since the
second "nine" line has arrived from the firmness of the outer trigram to bring
the fight to completion, the second line is the master of the Fight hexagram. It
uses its firmness to place itself at the center, and it possesses the symbol of the
full center. This is why "it is trustworthy." Since it is placed in a moment of the
Fight hexagram, although it is trustworthy and believable, it must also be hindered, obstructed, and choked with hardships, and so it will have to be careful
and troubled. If there were no obstructions, the fight could not be brought to
completion. Further, it occupies the position at the center of the obstacle and
snare, which also means that it is obstructed and choked, careful and troubled.
The second line makes use of *yang* firmness, it arrives from the outer trigram,
and it has acquired centrality. This means that it arrives at the fight with firmness but without excess. As a result, there will be good fortune. The meaning
of some hexagrams is chosen mostly because of the causes that complete the
hexagram, and this is one of those cases. When the meaning of the hexagram is
not chosen because of the causes that complete it, then the *Judgment* will not
say much about the lines that have been altered. In the hexagram judgment,
the second line is good, but in the line statement, the center line does not seem
to be good. In fact, the hexagram judgment chooses to remark that it is good
only concerning being trustworthy and acquiring centrality, while the line state-

ment considers its meaning to be someone coming from below to fight against someone above—they have not chosen to speak about the same thing. "**There is misfortune in the end': the fight should not be brought to completion.**" The fight is not a good state of affairs, but it cannot be put in the past. How could anyone bring this affair to its end and limit? Should someone intend to bring the affair to its limit, "there is misfortune." This is why the *Judgment* says that it "should not be brought to completion." The word "completion" signifies the depletion and exhaustion of the state of affairs. "**There is profit in seeing great people': they value centrality and straightforwardness.**" Those who fight seek to distinguish what is right and what is wrong. When making distinctions, it is proper to be central and straightforward, and this is why "there is profit in seeing great people." What they value are centrality and straightforwardness. If those who hear them are not such people, those who fight will sometimes not acquire centrality or straightforwardness. The fifth "nine" line refers to great people of centrality and straightforwardness. "**No profit in traversing a great stream': it enters the abyss.**" Those in a fight with people should place themselves on a contented and level terrain. Were they to tread through perils and obstacles, they would ensnare themselves, which is to enter a deep abyss. The center of the trigram is the symbol of centrality and straightforwardness, but also of the obstacle and snare.

The *Symbol* says: "**The actions of heaven and water draw back: Fight. Noble people use it to produce a state of affairs, with skill at its beginning.**" Heaven ascends and water descends—their actions draw back from each other. The two trigram substances draw back from and repulse each other, which is the cause of a fight. Were the upper and lower trigrams submissive to each other, what could cause them to muster for a fight? Noble people gaze on the symbol and know that human inclinations have a way of bringing about contention and fights. This is why, in producing a state of affairs, they must generally use "skill at its beginning." If they sever the starting point of the fight at the beginning of the state of affairs, then the fight will have no reason to be born. The meaning of the phrase "skill at its beginning" is broad. Some kinds of it are, for instance, caution in one's interactions and ties, and enlightenment in one's sanctions and contracts.

The **initial "six" line: the affair is not endless. There are small remarks but good fortune in the end.** This "six" line uses softness and weakness to occupy the bottom of the hexagram and refers to those who cannot bring their fight to its end and limit. This is why the line statement gives a warning about the power of the Fight hexagram's initial line, because it is a "six." It says that if "the affair is not" lengthy or "endless," then it will acquire "good fortune in the end," even though "there are small remarks." In fact, a fight is not an affair that should be lengthy. Good fortune will be difficult for those who use the power of *yin* softness to fight from the bottom. It is supported by a corresponding line above it and can keep the affair from becoming endless. This is why, although there are small remarks, it will acquire good fortune in the end. When there are remarks, this is the smallest of disasters. To keep the affair from becoming endless and from reaching the point of misfortune is the good fortune of the Fight hexagram. **The *Symbol* says: "'The affair is not endless': the fight should not be lengthy."** This "six" line makes use of softness and weakness at the bottom of the Fight hexagram, which certainly means that it should not be lengthy or endless. If the fight becomes endless, it will not be victorious, and afflictions and difficulties will be extended to it. Further, the *Symbol* specifically warns the initial line of the Fight hexagram that a fight is not an affair that should be lengthy. **"Although there are small remarks, its distinctions are enlightened."** It is soft and weak, it occupies the bottom position, and its powers are not capable of a fight. Although it keeps the affair from becoming endless, there will necessarily be a small disaster because it is in a fight. This is why "there are small remarks." Since it keeps the affair from becoming endless, and it corresponds straightforwardly to the *yang* and firm line above it, the principle by which it makes distinctions is enlightened. This is why it acquires good fortune in the end. If such were not the case, how could it avoid the opposite? The meaning of the Fight hexagram is that those in the same positions correspond to each other and agree with each other. This is why the initial and fourth lines obtain enlightened distinctions. If their positions were the same and they did not acquire each other, they would fight each other. This is why the second and fifth lines oppose each other as enemies.

The second "nine" line: it is not capable of a fight. It recoils and escapes to the people of its district, three hundred households. There are no mistakes. The second and fifth lines are on terrains that correspond to each other. Since they are both firm and do not agree with each other, they fight each other. The second "nine" line arrives from the outer trigram, it uses firmness to place itself in the obstacle trigram, it is the master of the Fight hexagram, and it is the enemy of the fifth. Since the fifth line uses centrality and straightforwardness to place itself in the position of the ruler, how could it be an enemy? This is to be in a fight of which duty is not capable. If it could recognize that its duty will not permit this, it would retreat and recoil, escaping and evading the fight. In a restricted place with few people, it will acquire neither excess nor mistakes. It will necessarily escape, evading its enemy's terrain. The phrase "three hundred households" refers to the extreme smallness of the district. Were it in a strong and great place, it would be like someone struggling. How could it be without mistakes? The word "mistake" refers to an excess, as when one's place is not proper, and is different from recognizing that a deed is bad and doing it anyway. **The *Symbol* says: "'It is not capable of a fight. It recoils and escapes': it absconds."** Its duty has made it no enemies, and this is why it cannot fight. "'It recoils and escapes': it absconds"—that is, it evades it and departs from such a place. **"From below, it fights with those above: it reaches distress as though plucking it."** "From below, it fights with those above": it fractures its duty and contracts its propensity. It reaches the point of affliction and distress as though it chose them by picking or plucking them. The *Symbol* is saying that this is easy to do.

The third "six" line: it eats of its former virtue. There is purity. Danger brings good fortune in the end. Although the third line occupies a firm position and corresponds to the top line, its root or disposition is *yin* and soft, it places itself in the obstacle trigram, it is securely between two *yang* lines, and it refers to imperiled and troubled people who do not fight. The wage one receives is proportioned to one's virtue. "It eats of its former virtue": this signifies that it has placed itself in a simple role. The word "purity" signifies that it guards itself with solidity and certainty. "Danger brings good fortune in the end": this signifies that, although it has placed itself on a perilous terrain, if it can recognize its peril and trouble, it will necessarily obtain good fortune in the end. If it guards its simple role without seeking anything, it will not fight. Its placement is perilous because it is in the obstacle trigram, because the lines it rides and serves are both firm, and because it occupies a position in the moment of the Fight hexagram. **Sometimes it attends to the affairs of the king, but it does not bring them to completion.** What is soft attends to what is firm; what is below attends to what is above. The third line does not fight, but it attends to the top "nine" line, which does. This is why the line statement says: "Sometimes it attends to the affairs of the king, but it does not bring them to completion." This signifies that it attends to the top line, but that it does not bring anything to completion. The Fight hexagram refers to an affair of firmness and vigor, and this is why the initial line does not make it endless, and the third attends to the top line. Both of them are incapable of a fight. These two lines, being *yin* and soft, do not bring it to an end, and so they acquire good fortune. The fourth line is also incapable of fighting and adapts itself to acquire good fortune. In the Fight hexagram, it is good to be able to stop. **The *Symbol* says: "'It eats of its former virtue': attending to**

those above brings good fortune." Since it guards its simple role, it attends to what is done by those above but is not itself the cause of it. This is why "it does not bring them to completion" and acquires good fortune in the end.

The fourth "nine" line: it is not capable of a fight, but returns to approach the mandate. It adapts itself to contentment and purity. There is good fortune. The fourth line uses *yang* firmness to occupy the vigor trigram substance, it does not acquire centrality or straightforwardness, and it refers to those who are fighters at their root. It serves the fifth, walks on the third, and corresponds to the initial line. Its duty is not capable of fighting the fifth line or the ruler; the third line occupies a position in the lower hexagram, is soft, and will not agree to fight with it; the initial line straightforwardly corresponds to it, is submissive and attentive, and will not agree to fight with it. Although the fourth line, being firm and vigorous, wants to fight, no one will agree to oppose it as an enemy. There is nothing causing it to muster for a fight, and this is why "it is not capable of a fight." Further, it occupies a soft position and corresponds to a soft line, which also means that it is able to stop. Since its duty is not capable of a fight, if it can conquer its heart of firm wrath and desire for fighting, if it can return and approach the mandate, reform its heart, pacify its *qi*, alter and become content and pure, then there will be good fortune. The word "mandate" here refers to the straightforward principle. To lose the straightforward principle is to face the mandate, and this is why to approach the mandate is considered a return. To face something is not to be submissive. The *Book of History* says that "he faces the mandate and ravages those of his class,"[1] and Mencius says that "they face the mandate and tyrannize the people."[2] If firmness and vigor are without centrality and straightforwardness, they will move restlessly. This is why it is not content. Its place is neither central nor straightforward, and this is why it is not pure. Being neither content nor pure, it prefers to fight. If its duty is not capable of a fight, and it does not fight, but reverts to and approaches the straightforward principle, if it alters what is neither contented nor pure so that it becomes contented and pure, then there will be good fortune. **The *Symbol* says: "'It returns to approach the mandate. It adapts itself to contentment and purity': it loses nothing."** If it can be like this, then it will lose nothing, and so there will be good fortune.

The fifth "nine" line: in the fight, there is primary good fortune. It uses centrality and straightforwardness to occupy the position of respect and refers to those who set fights in order. Those who set fights in order acquire centrality and straightforwardness, and so there is primary good fortune. The phrase "primary good fortune" refers to great good fortune that exhausts what is good.

Sometimes good fortune is great without exhausting what is good. **The *Symbol* says: "'In the fight, there is primary good fortune': it is central and straightforward."** What influence could the way of centrality and straightforwardness possess if there were no primary good fortune?

The top "nine" line: sometimes a sash and belt are bestowed on it. At the end of the day they are stripped off three times. This "nine" line uses *yang* to occupy the top position, it is at the limit of firmness and vigor, it is placed at the end of the Fight hexagram, and it refers to those who bring fights to their limit. When people indulge their firmness and strength, bringing the fight to its depletion and limit, it is certainly by principle that they choose to be afflicted and are deprived of their bodies. Provided that they are sometimes made to fight well and be victorious, ceaselessly bringing the fight to its limit and depletion, and reaching the point at which they receive the rewards of clothing and the mandate—this is still to obtain something by hostility and contention with other people. How could they contentedly preserve it? This is why, at the end of a single day, it is stripped off or seized three times. **The *Symbol* says: "Because of the fight, it receives clothing: it is still not sufficiently reverent."** It brings the affair of the fight to its depletion and limit. Provided that it is made to receive the favor of clothing and the mandate—if "it is still not sufficiently reverent" and may become impoverished and bad, what will the case be like when affliction and distress follow it?

7. TROOP (*SHI* 師)

The *Sequence of the Hexagrams* says: "If a fight breaks out, a crowd must arise. This is why the Troop hexagram is next." The troop is mustered because there is contention, and so the Troop hexagram succeeds the Fight hexagram. As for the trigrams, the Yield trigram is above and the Pit trigram below. Concerning the two trigram substances, one may remark that "at the center of the earth, there is water," which symbolizes the gathering of a crowd. Concerning the meaning of the two trigrams, one may remark that the inner trigram refers to the obstacle and the outer trigram to submission. To act with submission while placed on a way of obstacles is the meaning of the Troop hexagram. Concerning the lines, one may remark that a single *yang* line is master over a crowd of *yin* lines, which symbolizes uniting the crowd. In the Close hexagram, too, a single *yang* line is master over a crowd of *yin* lines, but it is positioned above and symbolizes the ruler. In the Troop hexagram, a single *yang* line is master over a crowd of *yin* lines, but it is positioned below and symbolizes the general or commander.

Troop: there is purity. Stern people bring good fortune and no blame. The way of the troop makes use of straightforwardness as its root. If the troop is mustered and the crowd is moved to poison the world, but they do not make use of straightforwardness, then the people will not be attentive and will become a strong barrier. This is why purity is considered the master of the troop. Although his movement may be straightforward, the troop commander must be a stern person if there are to be "good fortune and no blame." In fact, there are sometimes good fortune and blame together, and sometimes no blame and no good fortune. When there are good fortune and no blame, this is the exhaustion of the good. The phrase "stern people" is a name for people who are respected and severe. The troop commander rallies the crowd. If he is not someone that the crowd respects, believes in, trembles at, and obeys, how will he be able to make the human heart attend to him? This is why, when Sima Rangju was promoted from a minimal and impoverished position to supervise the crowd, but the crowd did not yet obey him in its heart, he requested that Zhuang Jia be named general.[1] What the judgment calls "stern people" must not simply be those who occupy venerable and esteemed positions. They are the ones trembled at and obeyed by the crowd because of their power, skill, virtue, and vocation. For instance, when Rangju had put Zhuang Jia to death, then the crowd trembled at and obeyed him in its heart, and he was a stern person. A further instance is the marquis of Huaiyin, who arose from a minimal and impoverished position and succeeded in becoming a great general.[2] In fact, he possessed the skill to make people respect and tremble at him.

The *Judgment* says: "The troop is the crowd, and purity is straightforwardness. Those who can make straightforward use of the crowd should become kings." Someone able to make every person in the crowd straightforward should become the king of the world. When the crowd has become obedient and attentive in its heart and is wedded to straightforwardness—this is where the way of the king stops. "It is firm and central, but there is also correspondence. There are obstacles to action, but it is submissive." The *Judgment* is speaking about the second line, which makes use of firmness and places itself at the center. That is, it is firm and has acquired the way of centrality. The fifth "six" or ruling line corresponds to it straightforwardly, indicating that the fifth believes in it and gives it unqualified command. Although this is the way of "obstacles to action," if "it is submissive" in its movement it may be called a soldier of duty or the king's commander.[3] The upper trigram refers to submissiveness and the lower trigram to the obstacle: "There are obstacles to action, but it is submissive." "By this means it poisons the world and the people attend to it. There is good fortune, and further, what blame could there be?" The troop is never mustered for a march without doing injury to resources and harm to people, and so "it poisons" or harms "the world." Nonetheless, the people attend to it in their hearts because it is moved by duty. In antiquity, "it took the field in the east and the west hated it" because the people attended to it in their hearts.[4] This is why, in such a case, there will be good fortune and no blame. The phrase "good fortune" signifies that it will necessarily be capable of it. "No blame" signifies that it has aligned itself with duty. "And further, what blame could there be?": the meaning of this is certainly that there is no blame.

The *Symbol* says: "At the center of the earth, there is water: Troop. Noble
people use it to embrace the people and herd the crowd." "At the center of
the earth, there is water": water gathers at the center of the earth and symbolizes the gathering of the crowd. This is why it is the symbol of the Troop hexagram. Noble people gaze on this symbol—"at the center of the earth, there is
water"—and they use it to embrace and preserve the people, and to herd and
gather the crowd.

The initial "six" line: the troop uses signals to depart. If these are lacking,
there will be advantage and misfortune. The initial line is the beginning of the
Troop hexagram, and this is why the line statement remarks on the meaning
of the troop's departure and the way of putting troops into action. It is speaking about the mustering of troops in a kingdom or state. If this aligns with duty
and principle, then it "uses signals" or laws, a phrase signifying that the troop
moves only to prohibit disorder and put violence to death. If its movement is
not in accordance with duty, then it will be on the way to misfortune even if
it is good. To be good here signifies to conquer and be victorious, while "misfortune" signifies calamity for the people and harm for one's duty. When one
speaks of putting troops into action, the word "signals" signifies calling out the
decrees that rein and control them. The way of putting troops into action is
rooted in the calling out of decrees that rein and control so that one may unite
and control the crowd. If signals are not used, there will be misfortune, even
if the troop is good. It will still be on the way to misfortune, even if it is made
victorious and triumphant. When the control of the troop has no law, by some
felicity it may avoid defeat and even be victorious. The moment has this as a
possibility, and so the sage gives a warning about it. The *Symbol* says: "'The
troop uses signals to depart': the loss of these signals brings misfortune." It is
proper that "the troop uses signals to depart." If it loses these signals, there will
be "misfortune." Although by some felicity it may be victorious, it will also be
on the way to misfortune.

The second "nine" line: at the center of the troop, there are good fortune
and no blame. The king bestows the mandate three times. The second "nine"
line is the only *yang* line in the Troop hexagram, and the crowd of *yin* lines is
wedded to it. The fifth line occupies the position of the ruler, and corresponds
straightforwardly to the second. The second is the master of the Troop hexagram and refers to someone with unqualified control over a state of affairs. To
occupy a position below and have unqualified control over a state of affairs
should happen only in the case of a troop. Since antiquity, when the mandate
is given to the generals, they acquire unqualified control over affairs outside the

frontier. They gain unqualified control over the troop by acquiring the way of centrality, and this is why "there are good fortune and no blame." In fact, if they rely on the fact that their control is unqualified, they will lose the way of those below. If it were not unqualified, they would not possess the principle of completing their task. This is why the acquisition of centrality brings good fortune. In general, when the authority and harmony in the way of the troop are both extreme, there will be good fortune. When they have placed themselves so as to exhaust the good, they will be able to complete their task and bring contentment to the world. This is why the king reaches the point of "bestowing" favors and "the mandate three times." In general, when a state of affairs occurs three times, it has reached its limit. Since the fifth "six" line is in a position above and has delegated unqualified command to the second, it will now grant a number of benefits or favors. But if the rituals do not name them, its authority will have no weight and those below will not believe in it. There are other hexagrams in which the second "nine" line is given command by the fifth "six" line, but only in the Troop hexagram is it the unqualified master of its affairs. The crowd of *yin* lines is wedded to it, and this is why the meaning of this hexagram is extremely great. Those on the way of ministers should not dare to take unqualified control over their affairs. It is only when the affair is outside the frontier that control over it may be unqualified. Although the control may reside in it, nonetheless, the effect that can be brought about by the force of the troop is always agreed to by the ruler and proper for it to do. The intellectuals of the times have discussed how the Lu kingdom made libations to the Duke of Zhou using the rituals and music of the son of heaven.[5] If they consider only the Duke of Zhou's capacity as minister, and not what he accomplished with that capacity, then the rituals and music for a minister should have been employed, and not those that were actually employed. But in this, they do not recognize the way of the minister. As for those who occupy the position of the Duke of Zhou, they will manage the affairs of the Duke of Zhou. If they can do something because of their position, it is always proper for them to do it, and if they are like the Duke of Zhou, then they will exhaust their mission. Such is also the case for the way of the child. Only Mencius recognizes its meaning, and this is why he says: "One should manage the affairs of one's relatives as Zengzi did."[6] He does not taste a surplus of filial piety in Zengzi. In fact, if children are personally capable of doing something, it is always proper for them to do it. **The Symbol says: "'At the center of the troop, there is good fortune': it serves the favor of heaven. 'The king bestows the mandate three times': he cherishes the ten thousand kingdoms.'"** "At the center of the troop, there is good fortune," because it serves the favor and command of heaven. The word "heaven" here refers to the king.

If ministers were not given favor and command by their rulers, how could they acquire the unqualified aptitude for taking the field, or possess the good fortune of completing their task? The *Symbol* considers the second line to be the unqualified master of its affairs, and this is why it reveals this meaning, which is different from the view of the aforementioned intellectuals of the times. The king bestows his kindness and the mandate three times to solemnize their completed task, and so "he cherishes the ten thousand kingdoms."

The third "six" line: the troop sometimes has a carriage of officiants. There is misfortune. The third line occupies the top position in the lower trigram and refers to those who occupy positions that are proper for command. Not only are its powers *yin* and soft, so that it is neither central nor straightforward, but also, in the affairs of a troop on the march, it is proper that one person have unqualified command. Because those above believe in and delegate command to the second line, with its powers of firmness and centrality, it must possess the unqualified management of its affairs, and then it will complete its task. Were a crowd of people sometimes made the masters of them, this would be the way of misfortune. The phrase "carriage of officiants" refers to a crowd of masters and is, in fact, pointing to the third line.[7] The third line occupies the top position in the lower trigram, and this is why the line statement reveals this meaning. In the affairs of an army on the march, it will necessarily be overturned and defeated if one person does not have unqualified command. **The *Symbol* says: "'The troop sometimes has a carriage of officiants': it will not accomplish anything great."** If it delegates command to or invests it in two or three others, how could it complete its task? And how could it merely fail in its task? As a result, it will bring about misfortune.

The fourth "six" line: the troop camps on the left. There is no blame. The advance of the troop makes use of strength and courage. The fourth line uses softness to occupy a *yin* position and refers to those who cannot advance to conquer and triumph. It retreats, recognizing that it cannot advance, and this is why it "camps on the left." The phrase "camps on the left" refers to retreat and abandonment. To calculate what is fitting and advance or retreat—this is to do what is proper, and this is why "there is no blame." To see the possibility and advance or to recognize the difficulty and retreat—these are "what is constant" for the troop. The line statement chooses to mention only a case where retreat is fitting, and does not discuss whether its power is capable of this or not. To measure one's incapacity for victory, and to keep the troop intact by retreating, is far better than being overturned and defeated. If the troop retreated when it should have advanced, there would be blame. The *Book of Changes* reveals this meaning so that it may be shown to later generations—its humaneness is deep. **The *Symbol* says: "'The troop camps on the left. There is no blame': it does not yet lose what is constant."** The way of putting the troop into action is to accord with the moment and use a fitting influence, which is "what is constant" for it. This is why those who "camp on the left" will necessarily be without any loss. If they retreat and camp like the fourth line, they will acquire what is fitting, and as a result, there will be no blame.

The fifth "six" line: the field has game. There is profit in holding to one's remarks, and no blame. The oldest son commands the troop, and the younger sons are in the carriage of officiants. Purity brings misfortune. The fifth is the position of the ruler and is the master of mustering the troop. This is why the line statement speaks about the way of mustering troops and giving command to the general. The troops should only be mustered when "the Man and Yi tribes are harassing the Xia, and there are bandits and traitors, as well as vile and devious people,"[8] who give birth to harm for the people. Since their arrival should not be cherished, a statement is afterward issued putting them to death. It is like the case of game animals entering the center of a field, invading and harming its planting and harvest. Since it is dutiful and fitting to choose them for the hunt, they are chosen for the hunt, and those who move like this will acquire no blame. Were they to move lightly to poison the world, their blame would be great. The phrase "in holding to one's remarks" refers to issuing a statement, to shedding light on the crime and campaigning against it. Were they emperor Huang of the Qin dynasty or Wu of the Han dynasty, who depleted the mountains and forests so as to squeeze out the game animals, this would not be a case of "the field has game."[9] Concerning the way of giving command to generals and supervising the troops, it is proper that the oldest son command the troop. The second line is in a position below and is the master of the Troop hexagram—it is the "oldest son." Were the crowd of younger sons to be the masters, there would be misfortune, even if their actions were straightforward. The phrase "younger sons" generally refers to those who are not the oldest. Since antiquity, those who did not give unqualified command to their generals have brought about their overturning and defeat. Such was the case for Xun Linfu of the Jin state in the clash at Bi, and also for the defeat of Guo Ziyi at Xiangzhou during the Tang dynasty.[10] **The *Symbol* says: "'The oldest son commands the troop': he acts at the center. 'The younger sons are in the carriage of officiants': they are made into something improper."** The phrase "oldest son" signifies the second line, which uses the virtues of centrality and straightforwardness to align with those above. It receives command from them so that it may act. If it were in turn to make surplus people into a crowd of officiants over its affairs, their command would make them into "something improper," and their misfortune would be fitting.

The top "six" line: great rulers give possessors the mandate. They found the states and serve the families. Small people should not be employed. The top line is the end of the Troop hexagram and refers to the completion of its task. The "great rulers" use titles and mandates to reward the "possessors" of this accomplishment. "They found the states": this refers to installing them among the various marquises, and "serve the families" refers to making them dignitaries and great officials. The word "serve" indicates to "receive." Although small people may possess accomplishments, they should not be employed. This is why the line statement warns that they "should not be employed." When the troop is mustered for a march, there is more than one way to complete its task. It is not necessary that everyone be a noble person, and this is why it warns that small people who possess accomplishments should not be employed. They should be rewarded with gold, silk, and positions with wages, but they should not be made to possess the state or act as governors. If small people are easily brought to arrogance and fullness during moments of peace, what will the case be like when they have accomplished something? This is why Ying and Peng of the Han dynasty vanished away.[11] Such is the sage's deep apprehension and far-reaching warning. He speaks without qualification about the meaning of the end of the Troop hexagram, and chooses not to speak about the meaning of the line, because the former is so great. Were one to say something about the line, it would be that a "six" line uses softness to occupy the limit position in the submission trigram. Since the Troop hexagram is already at its end, and this line occupies a terrain without position, it refers to those who place themselves well and are without blame. **The *Symbol* says: "'Great rulers give possessors the mandate': in straightforward agreement with their accomplishment. 'Small people should not be employed': they will necessarily bring disorder to the kingdom."** Great rulers wield the blade of kindness and reward "in straightforward agreement" with the accomplishments of the army on the march. Although they are rewarding accomplishments at the end of the Troop hexagram, they should not give command or employment to small people, even those who possess accomplishments. Were they to be employed, they would "necessarily bring disorder to the kingdom." There are cases in antiquity of small people who relied on their accomplishments and brought disorder to their kingdoms.

8. CLOSE (*BI* 比)

The *Sequence of the Hexagrams* says: "If there is a crowd, it must draw close together. This is why the Close hexagram is next." To be close to something is to relate to it and assist it. Human beings are of such a kind that they must relate to and assist each other, and only afterward can they be contented. This is why, if there is already a crowd, "it must draw close together," and so the Close hexagram succeeds the Troop hexagram. As for the trigrams, the Pit trigram is above and the Yield trigram below. Concerning the two trigram substances, one may remark that water is above the earth. When things are next to each other, so close that there is nothing between them, it is still not like when water is above the earth. This is why these substances refer to the Close hexagram. Further, the crowd of lines is entirely *yin* except for the fifth, which makes use of *yang* firmness to occupy the position of the ruler. The crowd relates to and depends on it, and those above relate to those below. This is why these lines constitute the Close hexagram.

Close: there is good fortune. If the origin is augured, there will be primacy, endlessness, purity, and no blame. The Close hexagram refers to the way of good fortune. When people relate and draw close to each other, they themselves constitute the way of good fortune. This is why the *Mixed Hexagrams* says: "Closeness brings pleasure, while the troop brings worry."[1] When people relate and draw close to each other, they must possess the way. If they do not possess the way, then they will have regrets, and there will be blame. This is why they must unfold the origin and prognosticate the resolution, so that they will draw close when they should draw close. The word "augured" signifies that the resolution is prognosticated and its measure is foretold. It does not signify the use of yarrow stalks or tortoise shells. If those who draw close acquire primacy, endlessness, and purity, then there will be no blame. "Primacy" signifies

possessing the way of the ruler or elder; "endlessness" signifies being able to
be constant and continuous; "purity" signifies acquiring the way of straightforwardness. When those above draw close to those below, they must have all three
of these. When those below attend to those above, they must seek all three of
these, and then there will be no blame. **Those who are not serene start to arrive. Later, there will be misfortune for the grand.** People who cannot by themselves preserve their contentment and serenity begin to arrive. They are seeking
to relate and draw close to someone. If they can draw close to someone, then
they will be able to preserve their contentment. Since they are facing a moment
without serenity, it is certainly fitting that they do their best to seek closeness. If
they set themselves up alone, relying on themselves without quickly tending to
seek closeness, and it grew late, then there would be misfortune, however grand
they were. If there is misfortune even for the grand, what will the case be like
for those who are soft and weak? "Grand" is a name for those who set themselves up with firmness. The Zuo commentary says: "Zinan is grand."[2] It also
says: "This signifies that we are not grand."[3] In general, when things are born
between heaven and earth, they cannot persist by themselves, without relating
and drawing close to each other. Although their firmness and strength may be
extreme, they cannot set themselves up alone. The way of the Close hexagram
comes about because of two tendencies that seek each other. If the two tendencies did not seek each other, then this would be the Split hexagram. The rulers
cherish and foster those below them, while those below relate to and assist[4]
those above. It is always like this among blood relations, friends, and village
factions. This is why it is proper for those above and below to align their tendencies, so that they may attend to each other. Were they not to have the intention
of seeking each other out, then they would cast each other off, and there would
be misfortune. In the great majority of cases, when people's inclinations seek
each other out, they will align. But if they "constrain each other," they will split
apart.[5] To constrain each other is to wait on each other without anyone going
first. When people relate to each other, they will certainly possess the way, and
so their tendency or desire for closeness should not be slackened.

**The *Judgment* says: "'Close: there is good fortune': to be close is to assist.
Those below submit and attend to it."** "Close: there is good fortune": the Close
hexagram refers to the way of good fortune. When things relate and draw close
to each other, it is the way of good fortune. "To be close is to assist": the *Judgment* is explaining the meaning of the Close hexagram. Those who are close
relate to and assist each other. "Those below submit and attend to it": it is interpreting the reason this is the Close hexagram. The fifth line makes use of *yang*
to occupy the position of respect, while the group of lines below it submits and

attends to it, or relates to and assists it, and so they constitute the Close hexagram. "'**If the origin is augured, there will be primacy, endlessness, purity, and no blame': it uses firmness and centrality.**" Those who unfold the origin and augur its resolution are on the way of drawing close to each other. If they acquire "primacy, endlessness, and purity," there should afterward be no blame. The *Judgment* says "primacy, endlessness, and purity" as in the case of the fifth line. It uses *yang* firmness to occupy a central and straightforward position, which is to exhaust what is good about the way of the Close hexagram. To occupy the position of respect with *yang* firmness is the virtue of the ruler, or "primacy." Those who occupy central positions and acquire straightforwardness will be capable of endlessness and purity. The hexagram judgment remarks on the way of the Close hexagram at its root and inclusively, while the *Judgment* remarks on primacy, endlessness, and purity—which is the case of the fifth "nine" line using firmness to place itself in a central and straightforward position. "'**Those who are not serene start to arrive': those above and below correspond.**" When the lives of people cannot be preserved in contentment and serenity, they "start to arrive" and seek to depend on or become close to someone. The people cannot preserve themselves, and this is why they gird themselves with a ruler in their search for serenity. Rulers cannot set themselves up alone, and this is why they preserve the people in contentment. When "those who are not serene" arrive and draw close, those above and below will correspond to each other. Concerning the public acts of sages, one may remark that they certainly sought the closeness of the world with extreme sincerity, so as to make the people contented. Concerning the private acts of the later kings, one may remark that, if they do not seek the dependence of the people below them, they will be in extreme peril of vanishing. This is why the tendencies of those above and below must correspond to each other. Concerning the hexagram, one may remark that the group of *yin* lines above and below draws close to the fifth line, while the fifth line draws close to the crowd—"those above and below correspond." "'**Later, there will be misfortune for the grand': this is the way of depletion.**" The crowd must draw close together, and later it will be able to have success in its life. When the things between heaven and earth have not yet related or drawn close to each other, they cannot be successful. If their tendency to attend to each other is not swift but late, then they will not be able to draw close completely. Although they may be grand, they will also have misfortune. If they do not relate or draw close to anyone, they will bring about the misfortune of being trapped and contracted, which is "the way of depletion."

The *Symbol* says: "**On the earth, there is water: Close. The first kings used it to establish the ten thousand states and relate to the various marquises.**" As for the things that relate and draw close to each other, with nothing between them, none are like water on the earth, and so it is the symbol of the Close hexagram. The first kings gazed on the symbol of the Close hexagram, and "used it to establish the ten thousand states and relate to the various marquises." They established or set up the ten thousand states, and so they drew close to the people; they related to and fostered the various marquises, and so they drew close to the world.

The initial "six" line: it is trustworthy. It draws close with no blame. The initial "six" line is at the beginning of the Close hexagram. The way of drawing close to each other is rooted in being sincere and believable. If those whose center or heart is not believable relate to other people, what person would agree with them? This is why, at the beginning of the Close hexagram, one must be trustworthy and sincere, and then there will be "no blame." The word "trustworthy" refers to being believable at one's center. **It is trustworthy. It fills the pot. It arrives in the end and possesses another. There is good fortune.** Sincerity and believability replenish and fill it on the inside, as when something fills to satiety the center of a pot. The word "pot" refers to a vessel with a simple disposition. The line statement is remarking that, if the pot is full at its center, and no pattern or ornament is attached to it on the outside, then it will be able to arrive in the end at the good fortune of possessing another. The word "another" indicates that it is not here, but comes from the outside. If sincerity fills and replenishes it on the inside, and there is nothing in it that is not believable, how could it employ external ornamentation to seek closeness? When one's center is filled with sincerity and believability, it is proper that even the other people outside be affected by it and arrive or attend to it. Closeness is rooted in being trustworthy and believable. **The *Symbol* says: "In the initial 'six' line, 'it draws close': it 'possesses another. There is good fortune.'"** The *Symbol* is remarking on the initial "six" line of the Close hexagram, at the beginning of the way of drawing close. Those who can be trustworthy at the beginning will bring about the good fortune of possessing another in the end. If they were not sincere at the beginning, how could they acquire good fortune in the end? The misfortune of the top "six" line is that it is "without a head."[6]

The second "six" line: it draws close inside itself. Purity brings good fortune. The second and fifth lines correspond straightforwardly, they both acquire centrality and straightforwardness, and they refer to those who draw close using the way of centrality and straightforwardness. The second line is placed in the inner trigram. The phrase "inside itself" signifies "from itself." Even though the selection and employment of one's powers lies in those above, the dedication of one's body to the state must come from oneself. If the self advances by aligning with the way of the ruler it seeks to acquire, then it will acquire straightforwardness and there will be good fortune. When those above seek it out, its correspondence using the way of centrality and straightforwardness is "inside itself," so "it does not lose sight of itself." To do one's best to seek closeness is not the way that noble people give themselves weight, and so it will lose sight of itself. **The *Symbol* says: "'It draws close inside itself': it does not lose sight of itself."** If it guards itself with the way of centrality and straightforwardness, waiting to be sought by those above, then "it does not lose itself." The *Book of Changes* gives a profoundly severe warning. Although the second line is central and straightforward, its disposition is soft and it belongs to the submission trigram substance. This is why it gives a warning about the good fortune of purity and about losing sight of oneself. Since it is warned to guard itself while waiting to be sought by those above, if it does not, but goes on to make the crossing, will there afterward be misfortune? Response: when scholars make themselves correct, this is their way of seeking those above. To "diminish their tendencies and disgrace themselves" is not the way that they give themselves weight.[7] This is why, though the hearts of Yi Yin and the Marquis of War were ardent enough to save the world, they had to wait for the rituals to be performed before going out.[8]

The third "six" line: it draws close to outlaws. The third line is neither central nor straightforward, and it draws close to no one who is central and straightforward. The fourth line is *yin* and soft, and is not at the center, while the second persists in corresponding and drawing close to the initial line. Neither of them is central and straightforward—they are the "outlaws." When it draws close to outlaws, its loss should be recognized, and the line statement does not presume to remark on its regret and dismay. This is why it should be "injured." The second line is central and straightforward, but it may be called an outlaw. Its meaning is chosen following the moment and is not the same in each case. **The *Symbol* says: "'It draws close to outlaws': is it not also injured?"** When people draw close to each other, they seek contentment and good fortune. Since "'it draws close to outlaws,'" it will necessarily be about to acquire regret and dismay, and it should also be "injured." This is a deep warning that it will lose itself by drawing close.

The fourth "six" line: it draws close on the outside. There are purity and good fortune. The fourth and the initial line do not correspond to each other, but the fifth line draws close to it: "It draws close" to the fifth "on the outside." It will acquire purity and straightforwardness, and there will be good fortune. It is straightforward that rulers and ministers draw close to each other; it is fitting that they draw close to each other and agree with each other. The fifth line with its *yang* firmness, centrality, and straightforwardness, refers to worthy people. It occupies the position of respect and is above the fourth line. To draw close straightforwardly is to relate to worthy people and attend to those above. This is why there are "purity and good fortune." When a "six" line occupies the fourth position, this, too, gives the meaning of acquiring straightforwardness. Further, when people who are *yin*, soft, and without centrality can draw close to worthy people of firmness, enlightenment, centrality, and straightforwardness, they will acquire straightforwardness and good fortune. Further, those who draw close to worthy people and attend to those above must use the way of straightforwardness, and then there will be good fortune. These numerous analyses require each other so that they may begin to perfect their meaning. **The *Symbol* says: "'It draws close on the outside' to worthy people: it attends to those above."** "It draws close on the outside": this signifies that it attends to the fifth line. The fifth line refers to worthy people of firmness, enlightenment, centrality, and straightforwardness. Further, it occupies the position of the ruler, and the fourth line draws close to it. That is, it draws close to worthy people and attends to those above, and so there is good fortune.

The fifth "nine" line: it clarifies what draws close. The king employs three barriers and loses the game that is ahead. The people of the district do not reprove them. There is good fortune. The fifth line occupies the position of the ruler, it is placed with centrality and acquires straightforwardness, and it exhausts what is good about the way of the Close hexagram. As for the way of rulers who draw close to the world, it is proper that they clarify and shed light on the way of the Close hexagram, and that is all. For instance, they make their intentions sincere so as to wait on things, "they efface themselves so that they may extend themselves to other people,"[9] "they reveal a government whose influence is humane,"[10] and they make the world receive their favor and grace. This is the way that noble people relate and draw close to the world. In such a case, who in the world would not relate and draw close to those above? But if they are violent and of small humaneness, if they draw back from the way and crave praise while still wanting to seek out closeness with those below, then their way will shrink. How could they acquire closeness with the world? This is why the sage uses the straightforwardness of the fifth "nine" line to exhaust the way of closeness, and chooses the three barriers as his example. He says: "The king employs three barriers and loses the game that is ahead. The people of the district do not reprove them. There is good fortune." The first kings made use of the four seasonal hunts, and could not neglect them. This is why they unfolded the humaneness of their hearts with the ritual of the three barriers. As is said in the *Book of Rites*, "the son of heaven does not entirely surround it."[11] This is also the meaning of Cheng Tang's prayer about the nets.[12] When the son of heaven held hunts, he entirely surrounded three sides, but he left one path open ahead so that the game could depart. He was not so cruel as to exhaust things—there is humaneness in preferring them to live. He only chose those who did not "employ his mandate," who did not go out but entered again.[13] All the wild game that departed on the open path ahead avoided him, and this is why it says that he "loses the game that is ahead." The kings clarified and shed light on the way of the Close hexagram, and the world spontaneously arrived and drew close to them. They fostered those who arrived, but it was certainly not because of their congeniality that things sought to draw close to them. It is like the three barriers in the field: the game that departs passes through and is not trailed, while those that arrive are chosen. The greatness in the way of kings is that the people become radiant without recognizing what is happening. "The people of the district do not reprove them. There is good fortune": it is saying that it reaches the public and not the private, not discriminating between those adjacent and far away, between the relation and the stranger. The word "district" refers to those who occupy the district. What the *Book of Changes* means by "district" is always the same. It is where the king has his capital, at the center of the states held by the various marquises. The word "reprove" refers to confining or restricting. Those who wait on all things as though they were one are not confined or reproved by those who occupy the district. In a case like this, there will be good fortune. Sages use what is great and public rather than what is private when they set the world in order, as may be seen in how they clarify those who draw close. Not only is the way of rulers drawing close to the world like this—it is not otherwise in the great majority of cases where people draw close to each other. Concerning the ministers and rulers, one may remark that those who drain their loyalty and sincerity and bring about the full force of their power are clarifying the way of drawing close to one's rulers. Whether they are employed or not lies with the rulers, and that is all. They should not seek to draw them close by groveling, toadying, or a chance rendezvous. The case of friendship is also like this. One may correct oneself and wait on other people with sincere intentions, but whether they relate to one or not lies entirely in them, and that is all. One should not seek to draw them close by "clever words and a commanding countenance," by attending to them twistedly, or by aligning with them recklessly.[14] It is never otherwise for village factions, blood relations, or the crowd of people. This is the meaning of the three barriers and of losing the game that is ahead. **The *Symbol* says: "'It clarifies what draws close,' and 'there** is good fortune': the position is straightforward and central." "It clarifies what draws close," and so "there is good fortune": it uses the position that it occupies to acquire straightforwardness and centrality. To place oneself on a terrain of straightforwardness and centrality is to be on the way of straightforwardness and centrality. The Close hexagram considers impartiality to be good, and this is why the *Symbol* says that it is "straightforward and central." In general, when it says that the fifth line is straightforward and central, it has placed itself straight-forwardly and acquired centrality, as in the Close and Follow hexagrams.[15] When it says that the fifth line is central and straightforward, it has acquired both centrality and straightforwardness, as in the Fight and Need hexagrams.[16] **"It abandons those that rebel and chooses those that submit: it 'loses the game that is ahead.'"** According to the ritual of choosing those that do not employ its mandate, it abandons those that submit and chooses those that rebel. Everyone who submits to its mandate and departs will avoid it. The Close hexagram puts it in reverse order, saying that the rebellious are those who depart and the sub-missive are those who arrive. This is why "it loses the game" that departs ahead of it. It is saying that those who arrive are fostered and those who depart are not trailed. **"'The people of the district do not reprove them': those above act with centrality."** They are not reproved or confined so that they relate only to those nearby. Those above act toward those below with centrality—that is, impartial-ity—treating the nearby and far away as though they were one.

The top "six" line: it draws close without a head. There is misfortune. This "six" line occupies the top position, at the end of the Close hexagram. The word "head" signifies the beginning. Concerning the way of the Close hexagram, in general, when the beginning is good, the end will also be good. Sometimes the beginning does not make it to the end, and sometimes it does, but there has never been an end without a beginning. This is why, if "it draws close without a head" and reaches the end, "there is misfortune." The line statement says this concerning the end of the Close hexagram. The top "six" line is *yin* and soft, it is without centrality, it places itself at the limit of the obstacle trigram, and it will certainly not be capable of achieving its end. It often happens in the world that people break up at the end because they did not use the way when they began to draw close. **The *Symbol* says: "'It draws close without a head': its end is no-where."** Since "it draws close without a head," where will it end up? Even those who draw close with a head may still sometimes draw back from each other at the end. If they do not use the way at the beginning, how could their end be preserved in its turn? This is why the *Symbol* says that "its end is nowhere."

9. SMALL HERD (*XIAOXU* 小畜)

The *Sequence of the Hexagrams* says: "If things draw close together, they must have been herded, and this is why the Small Herd hexagram is next." When things draw close to and depend on each other, they constitute a gathering, and a gathering is a herd. Further, when they relate to and draw close to each other, their tendencies herd each other, and so the Small Herd hexagram succeeds the Close hexagram. To herd is to bring to a stop. If things are stopped, then they have been gathered. As for the trigrams, the Low trigram is above and the Lead trigram below. The Lead trigram is a thing that remains above, but here it occupies a position below the Low trigram. For herding and bringing firmness and vigor to a stop, there is nothing like lowliness and submission. It is lowliness that does the herding, and this is why it is the symbol of the Herd hexagram. Since lowliness is *yin*, and its substance is soft and submissive, it can only use lowliness, softness, and submission on firmness and vigor. It cannot bring them to a stop by force, and so its way of herding is small. Further, the fourth line is the only *yin* line, and it has acquired a position, being what the five *yang* lines all enjoy. To acquire a position by acquiring softness is the way of lowliness. It can herd the tendencies in the group of five *yang* lines, and as a result, it is the symbol of the Herd hexagram. The Small Herd hexagram signifies that the small is used to herd the great. Those that herd and gather are small, and the affair that they herd is small, and this is why the line is *yin*. The *Judgment* focuses on the fourth "six" line's herding of the various *yang* lines as the meaning of the complete hexagram and does not say anything about the two trigram substances. In fact, it has brought up what carries the most weight.

Small Herd: there is progress. Dense clouds but no rain come from our western outlands. A cloud is nothing but *yin* and *yang qi*. If the two kinds of *qi*

interact and harmonize, one of them will certainly herd the other and bring
the rain to completion. When *yang* sings the melody and *yin* harmonizes, the
one submits to the other, and this is why there is harmony. If *yin* were to go
before *yang* and sing the melody, it would not be submissive, and this is why
there would be no harmony. If there were no harmony, then the rain could
not be brought to completion. Although the clouds that have been herded and
gathered may be dense, if they do not bring the rain to completion, it is because
they come from the western outlands. The northeast is a *yang* region, while the
southwest is a *yin* region.[1] The melody is sung by *yin*, and this is why there is
no harmony, and the rain cannot be brought to completion. It always seems
to the human gaze that the *qi* of the mustered clouds comes from one of the
four faraway regions, and this is why the judgment calls them "outlands." It is
speaking about the fourth line when it says that they "come from our western
outlands." The *yang* lines are herded by the fourth line, which is the master of
the Herd hexagram.

The *Judgment* **says: "Small Herd: softness acquires a position, and those above
and below correspond to it. It is called Small Herd."** The *Judgment* is speaking
about the meaning of the complete hexagram. A *yin* line occupies the fourth
position, and further, it is placed in a position above, and so "softness acquires
a position." The five *yang* lines above and below all correspond to it and refer
to what is herded. The herding of five *yang* lines with a single *yin* line is something that can happen, but it cannot be a certainty. As a result, this is the Small
Herd hexagram. When the *Judgment* interprets the meaning of the complete
hexagram, and then attaches the phrase "it is called," it always repeats the name
of the hexagram. It is proper that the text have this propensity. When it merely
says the name of the hexagram—since the Hide hexagram is the only other one
to have the phrase "it is called"—the text still has this propensity.[2] **"There are
vigor and lowliness, firmness and centrality, and the tendency to act, which
is progress."** The *Judgment* is speaking about the powers of the trigrams. The
inner trigram is vigorous and the outer trigram lowly: "There are vigor and" the
capacity for "lowliness." The second and the fifth lines both occupy the center
of a trigram, and so there are "firmness and centrality." The nature of *yang* is to
advance upward, but the substance of the Lead trigram is at the bottom, and so
its tendency is toward action. When a firm line occupies the center of a trigram,
there is a firm line acquiring centrality, but also a center that is firm. It is saying
that the *yang* lines are herded by softness and lowliness, but that there can be
progress because of the firm centers. Concerning the meaning of the complete
hexagram, one may remark that *yin* is herding *yang*; concerning the powers of

the trigrams, one may remark that *yang* is firm and central. The powers of the trigrams are such that, although the herding is small, there can be progress. **"'Dense clouds but no rain': it is still on its journey. 'Come from our western outlands': their influence is not yet active."** The way of the Herd hexagram cannot complete anything great, as when dense clouds do not bring the rain to completion. When *yin* and *yang* interact and harmonize, their interaction is certain and they bring the rain to completion. If these two kinds of *qi* do not harmonize, *yang* "is still on its journey" upward, and this is why they do not bring the rain to completion. In fact, the *qi* "from our" *yin* region has gone first and sung the melody, and this is why there is no harmony and the rain cannot be brought to completion. Its accomplishment or "influence is not yet active." The impossibility of the Small Herd hexagram completing anything great is like the impossibility of clouds from the western outlands bringing the rain to completion.

The *Symbol* says: "The wind travels above the heavens: Small Herd. Noble people use it to make their pattern and virtue marvelous." The firmness and vigor of the Lead trigram are herded by the Low trigram. As for the nature of firmness and vigor, it is only softness and submission that can herd and stop them. Although they can herd and stop them, they nonetheless cannot control this firmness and vigor with certainty. The bonds of softness and submission can only exasperate them, and this is why these trigrams constitute the Small Herd hexagram. Noble people gaze on the meaning of the Small Herd hexagram, and "marvel at" or make beautiful "their pattern and virtue." Herding and gathering have the meaning of collecting into a herd. If what noble people collect into a herd is great, then they use the warp and the weft of the way and virtue on their vocation. If it is small, then they use the powers or talents of pattern and arrangement. Noble people gaze on the symbol of the Small Herd hexagram and use it to make their pattern and virtue marvelous or beautiful. The way or meaning of pattern and virtue here is small.

The initial "nine" line: to return is its own way. What blame could there be? There is good fortune. The initial "nine" line is *yang* and belongs to the Lead trigram substance. The *yang qi* is something that ascends, and further, it has the powers of firmness and vigor. It is sufficient to advance upward, returning with those lines above it that have the same tendencies. To advance and return to what is above is its way, and this is why the line statement says: "To return is its own way." When it has returned by its own way, how could it possess either excess or blame? There is no blame, and further, "there is good fortune." When various line statements say that "there is no blame," they are indicating that, when the case is like this, there is no blame. This is why it is said that "when there is no blame, one's goodness alleviates one's excess."[3] Although this statement makes the meaning of the line to be good at its root, it does not harm the additional meaning that, if it were not like this, there would be blame. The way of the initial "nine" line is the cause of its actions, and so it has neither excess nor blame. This is why it says: "What blame could there be?" This sheds extreme light on the fact that there is no blame. **The *Symbol* says: "'To return is its own way': it means there is good fortune."** Its powers are *yang* and firm, and its way is the cause of its return: "It means there is good fortune." The initial line corresponds straightforwardly to the fourth, which in the moment of the Herd hexagram indicates that the one herds the other.

The second "nine" line: it is guided in its return. There is good fortune. The second line uses *yang* to occupy the center of the lower trigram substance, and the fifth uses *yang* to occupy the center of the upper trigram substance. They both use *yang* firmness to occupy the center, they are herded by *yin*, and they want to return upward together. Although the fifth line is above the fourth, they are both herded by the same line. For all these reasons, their tendencies are the same. As for those with the same distress, they worry about each other. The second and fifth lines have the same tendencies, and this is why they guide and link up with each other in their return. If the two *yang* lines advance together, the *yin* line cannot be victorious over them, and they will return successfully. This is why the line statement says that "there is good fortune." Someone asks: if they return successfully, will they cast off what herds them? Response: in general, the line statements say that if something is the case, then something else can happen. If it were already happening, then the moment would already be altering. What value would there be in warning or reproving anyone? How could the fifth line, belonging to the Low trigram substance when the Low trigram herds the Lead trigram, still be guided by the second? Response: those who bring up the two trigram substances may remark that the Low trigram herds the Lead trigram. Concerning the hexagram as a whole, one may remark that a single *yin* line herds five *yang* lines. In the *Book of Changes*, the meaning is chosen following the moment—every case is like this. **The *Symbol* says: "At the center, 'it is guided in its return': it also does not lose itself."** The second line occupies the center and acquires straightforwardness. Whether it is firm or soft, whether it advances or retreats, it does not lose the way of centrality. When the *yang* lines return, their propensity will necessarily be strong. The second line places itself at the center, and this is why it does not reach the point of excessive firmness even though it makes a strong advance. If it were excessively firm, it would lose itself. The line statement stops at saying that "it is guided in its return" and gives good fortune as the meaning. The *Symbol* goes on to reveal and shed light on the beauty of being at the center.

The third "nine" line: the carriage throws its spokes. Husband and wife oppose their stares. The third is a *yang* line occupying a position without centrality, it is profoundly close to the fourth, and the inclination of the *yin* and *yang* lines is to seek each other. Further, they are intimately close and without centrality. The *yin* line herds and controls it, and this is why it cannot advance ahead, like a "carriage" that "throws" or drives out "its" wheels or "spokes." The line statement is saying that it cannot travel. "Husband and wife oppose their stares": *yin* is controlled by *yang*, but here it opposes and controls *yang*, like a husband and wife who oppose their stares. The phrase "oppose their stares" signifies that they look at each other with angry stares. She does not submit to her husband but opposes and controls him. It is never the case that the wife is confused by the favor of her husband, that she succeeds in opposing and controlling her husband, unless her husband has lost the way. Then his wife can control him, and this is why the third line refers to throwing spokes and opposing stares. **The *Symbol* says: "'Husband and wife oppose their stares': they cannot make their home straightforward."** "Husband and wife oppose their stares": this is, in fact, because "they cannot make their home" and family "straightforward." The third line does not use the way to place itself, and this is why the fourth controls it and prevents it from advancing. It is like a husband who cannot make his home and family straightforward, and this is why he brings about the opposed stares.

The fourth "six" line: it is trustworthy. Its blood departs and its care goes out. There is no blame. The fourth line is placed near the position of the ruler during the moment of the Herd hexagram and refers to those who herd their rulers. If it is trustworthy and sincere on the inside, then the tendencies of the fifth line will believe in it and attend to its herding. There is only one *yin* line in the hexagram, but it herds the crowd of *yang* lines. The tendencies of the various *yang* lines are bound to the fourth. Should the fourth want to herd them by force—a single soft line becoming the enemy of a crowd of firm lines—then it would necessarily see injury and harm. If it is nothing but exhaustively trustworthy and sincere in corresponding to them, then it will be able to affect them. This is why its injury and harm are far away, and its peril and trouble are avoided. In a case like this, it can be without blame, but if such is not the case, it will not avoid harm. This is the way of using softness to herd firmness. The rulers are authoritative and severe, and yet their desires can be herded and stopped by ministers who are minimal and paltry. In fact, the ministers affect them by being trustworthy and believable. **The *Symbol* says: "'It is trustworthy. Its care goes out': those above align their tendencies."** Since the fourth line is trustworthy, the fifth believes in it and gives it command. It aligns its tendencies with it, and so "its care goes out" and there is no blame. If its care goes out, it should be recognized that "its blood departs." The *Symbol* has brought up the lighter part of the line statement. Once the fifth has aligned its tendencies, the crowd of *yang* lines all attend to it.

The fifth "nine" line: it is trustworthy, as though it were entwined. It is wealthy by means of its neighbor. The Small Herd hexagram refers to the moment when the crowd of *yang* lines is herded by a single *yin* line. The fifth line uses centrality and straightforwardness to occupy the position of respect. Since it is trustworthy and believable, the lines of its kind all correspond to it. This is why the line statement says "as though it were entwined," signifying that they guide and link up with each other. The fifth line must support and coax them to make the crossing together—that is, "it is wealthy by means of its neighbor." The propensity of the fifth line to occupy the position of respect is like wealthy people who unfold their resources and force so as to share them with the neighbors who are close to them. Noble people are trapped by small people; straightforward people are imperiled by a group of crooked people. In such a case, those below must entwine themselves around and coax those above,[4] so that they make the same advance, while those above must support and draw up those below, so that they may merge their forces. Not only do they unfold their own force so that it extends to other people, but the completion of their own force owes something to the help of those below. **The *Symbol* says: "'It is trustworthy, as though it were entwined': it is not wealthy alone."** "It is trustworthy, as though it were entwined": in fact, its neighbors and those of its kind all guide it, entwining themselves around and attending to it. It has the same desires as the crowd, and so it does not possess its wealth alone. When noble people are placed in hardship and peril, they are nothing but extremely sincere. This is why they acquire the help of a forceful crowd, and they will be able to make the crossing with this crowd.

The top "nine" line: it has already rained. It is already in place. It values the loading up of virtue. The purity of the wife brings danger. This "nine" line is at the limit of the Low or submission trigram, it occupies the top position in the hexagram, it is placed at the end of the Herd hexagram, and it refers to those who attend to what herds them, and are stopped. The fourth line is what stops it. "It has already rained": there is harmony. "It is already in place": it is stopped. When *yin* herds *yang*, there can be no stopping if there is no harmony. When there are harmony and stopping, the way of the Herd hexagram is complete. The Great Herd hexagram refers to a herd that is great, and this is why the herd is scattered at its limit. The Small Herd hexagram refers to a herd that is small, and this is why the herd is completed at its limit. "It values the loading up of virtue": the fourth line employs the virtues of softness and lowliness. When they have accumulated to satiety, it reaches the point of completion. The herding of firmness by *yin* softness cannot be completed in a morning and an evening but is reached through accumulation and piling up. Should it not be warned about this? The phrase "loading up" refers to accumulating and satiating. The *Book of Poetry* says: "The sound of his wailing loaded up the streets."[5] "The purity of the wife brings danger": the word "wife" here signifies the *yin* line. When *yin* herds *yang*, when softness controls firmness, and when the wife guards this with purity and certainty, it is a way of peril and danger. How could everyone be contented when the wife controls her husband and the minister controls the ruler? **The moon is almost full. Noble people take the field. There is misfortune.** When the moon is full, it becomes the enemy of the sun. If it is "almost full," this is remarking that it is about to become an enemy in its abundance. Why does the line statement say that it is almost full, when *yin* is already capable of herding *yang*? Here it herds the *yang* tendencies with softness and lowliness, since it cannot control them with force. But if it does not cease, it is about to use its abundance against *yang*, and "there is misfortune." Since it is almost full, a warning may be given, saying that the wife is about to become an enemy. If noble people move, they will bring misfortune. The phrase "noble people" here signifies the *yang* lines and to "take the field" refers to movement. It is almost full or in the moment when it is about to be full. Were it already full, the *yang* lines would already have disappeared. What value could there be in a warning? **The *Symbol* says: "'It has already rained. It is already in place': virtue is accumulated and loaded up. 'Noble people take the field. There is misfortune': there is room for doubt."** "It has already rained. It is already in place": this says that the way of the Herd hexagram is accumulated to satiety and completed. Since *yin* is about to reach the limit of abundance, if noble people move, there will be misfortune. If *yin* is the enemy of *yang*, then it will necessarily make *yang* disappear. If small people resist noble people, they will necessarily harm the noble people. How could they not be doubtful and apprehensive? If they know how to be doubtful and apprehensive ahead of time, disquieted and troubled, and seek the means of controlling them, then they will not reach the point of misfortune.

10. WALK (*LÜ* 履)

The *Sequence of the Hexagrams* says: "After things have been herded, there will be a ritual. This is why the Walk hexagram is next." As for the gathering of things, it discriminates the great from the small, it ranks the lofty above those below, and it divides the beautiful from the bad. "After things have been herded, there will be a ritual" refers to this, and so the Walk hexagram succeeds the Herd hexagram. One's walk is one's ritual, and one's ritual is how one walks. As for the trigrams, heaven is above and the lake below. Heaven is above, while the lake is placed below, and this division of those above from those below gives meaning to respect and humility. It is the propriety of principle, the root of ritual, and the way of a constant walk. This is why it symbolizes the Walk hexagram. A walk can be a treading, but it can also be a padding. To walk on a thing is to tread on it, while to be walked on by a thing is to be a pad for it. Softness serves as a pad for firmness, and this is why these trigrams constitute the Walk hexagram. The *Judgment* does not say that firmness walks on softness but that "softness is a walk for firmness." It is a constant principle that firmness rides on softness and is not sufficient to constitute a way. This is why the *Book of Changes* remarks only that "softness rides on firmness" and does not remark that firmness rides on softness.[1] When it remarks that someone is to be a walk and a pad for firmness, this seems to mean submissiveness with humility and correspondence with enjoyment.

It walks on the tail of a tiger and is not bitten. There is progress. The Walk hexagram refers to the way that people walk. Since heaven is above, while the lake is placed below, softness is serving as a walk and a pad for firmness. Those above and below each do their duty. They are extremely submissive in their affairs and extremely proper in their principles. When people walk and act like this, although they may be walking on an extremely perilous terrain, there is nevertheless nothing that can harm them. This is why "it walks on the tail of a tiger" but does not seem to be bitten or gnawed on, and so it can make progress.

The *Judgment* says: "Walk: softness is a walk for firmness.[2] It enjoys and corresponds to the leader. As a result, 'it walks on the tail of a tiger and is not bitten. There is progress.'" The Joy trigram makes use of *yin* softness to be a walk and a pad for the *yang* firmness of the Lead trigram: "Softness walks on, or is a walk for, firmness." The Joy trigram refers to enjoyment, submissiveness, and correspondence to the firmness of the Lead trigram, and it serves as its walk and pad. That those below submit to those above, and that *yin* serve *yang*—this is the straightforward principle of the world. If what walks and is walked on are like this, there will be extreme submissiveness and extreme propriety. Although "it walks on the tail of a tiger," it will see neither injury nor harm. When its walk and action are like this, its progress should be recognized. "It is firm, central, and straightforward. It walks in the position of a lord without infirmity, which is to be bright and enlightened." The fifth "nine" line makes use of *yang* firmness, centrality, and straightforwardness. It has the walk of respect and the position of a lord. Were it to be without infirmity or defect, it would acquire what is best in the way of the Walk hexagram—that is, "to be bright and enlightened." The word "infirmity" signifies any blemish or defect, as is the case when "it walks resolutely." "Bright and enlightened" refers to abundant virtue and radiant brightness.

The *Symbol* says: "There are heaven above and the lake below: Walk. Noble people use it to distinguish what is above and below and to determine the tendencies of the people." Heaven is above, while the lake occupies a position below, in accordance with the straightforward principle of those above and below. It is proper that the walk of people be like this, and this is why such a symbol is chosen for the Walk hexagram. Noble people gaze on the symbol of the Walk hexagram, and they use it to distinguish and discriminate the division of those above from those below, so as to "determine the tendencies of the people." When they have shed light on the division of those above from those below, the tendencies of the people will be determinate. When the tendencies of people are determinate, one will be able to speak of setting them in order. If the tendencies of the people are not determinate, the world can be neither acquired nor set in order. As for the dukes, dignitaries, great officials, and others of ancient times, their positions were proportionate with their virtues. They occupied them until the end of their lives, and they all had their roles to play. When their positions were not yet proportionate with their virtues, their rulers brought them up and advanced them. Scholars made their learning correct, and when their learning had become extreme, their rulers sought them out. They never put themselves forward. Farmers, artisans, merchants, and traders set their affairs in motion, and their feasts stayed within their boundaries. This is why they all had determinate tendencies, and the hearts of the world could be one. In later times, everyone from the numberless scholars to the dukes and dignitaries daily tends toward respect and glory, while the farmers, artisans, merchants, and traders daily tend toward wealth and extravagance. The hearts of the countless millions interact wantonly for profit, and the world is confounded. In such a case, how could their hearts be one? It is difficult for their desires to be other than disorderly, and this is because those above and below do not have determinate tendencies. Noble people gaze on the symbol of the Walk hexagram, and they divide and "distinguish what is above and below." They make it so that each has its proper division by determining the hearts and tendencies of the people.

The initial "nine" line: it walks with simplicity. If it makes the journey, there is no blame. Those who walk do not place themselves, which means that they are traveling. The initial line is placed at the very bottom and refers to those who are simple and in positions below. It has the power of *yang* firmness and should be able to advance upward. "If it makes the journey" while contented with the simplicity of its humble position below, then "there is no blame." As for people who cannot content themselves with the simplicity of abject poverty, they will advance. They will move out of greed and restlessness, seeking to depart from their abject poverty, not because they want to do anything. When they have acquired their advance, they will necessarily overflow with arrogance. This is why there is blame in making a journey. If they are worthy people, then they will be content to walk with simplicity and to take pleasure in their place. If they advance, it is to do something. This is why, if they acquire their advance, they will have done nothing but what is good. They will have guarded the simplicity of their walk. **The *Symbol* says: "On its journey 'it walks with simplicity': it acts only on its aspirations."** To make a journey while being content to walk with simplicity, and not for reckless profit, is to act only on one's tendencies and aspirations. The word "only" here indicates "without qualification." As for those who have the heart for desiring esteem and the heart for the way of action, these will interact and clash at their center. How could they be content to walk with simplicity?

The second "nine" line: the way it walks is flat, and flat again. The purity of secluded people brings good fortune. The second "nine" line occupies a soft position, it is tolerant and generous, it acquires centrality, and it walks on what is "flat, and flat again," which is the way of peace and ease. Although it walks on a way that is flat and easy, it is still necessary that people of seclusion, tranquility, contentment, and idleness be placed here. Then it will be capable of purity and certainty, and there will be good fortune. The second "nine" line, being *yang*, tends to advance upward. This is why the line statement warns it to be a secluded person. **The *Symbol* says: "'The purity of secluded people brings good fortune': at their center, they do not disorder themselves."** The way of the Walk hexagram lies in contentment and tranquility. Since its center is idle and straightforward, its walk is contented and generous. If there were restless movement at its center, how could it be contented with its walk? This is why it must be a secluded person, and then it will be capable of solidity and certainty, and there will be good fortune. In fact, its center and heart will be contented and tranquil, and it will not disorder itself with the desire for profit.

The third "six" line: the nearsighted can look, and the lame can walk. People walk on the tail of a tiger and are bitten. There is misfortune. Warlike people do the deeds of great rulers. The third line uses *yin* to occupy a *yang* position. Its tendency or desire is for firmness, but its substance is *yin* and soft at its root. How could it be solid in its walk? This is why it is like the look of those who are sightless or nearsighted: their sight is not enlightened. It is like the walk of those who are lame or hobbled: they do not travel far. Since its power is not sufficient, and further, it is not placed at the center, its walk will not be straightforward. Its walk is like this because it uses softness to busy itself with firmness. In such a case, it walks on a perilous terrain. This is why the line statement says that "people walk on the tail of a tiger." Those who walk on a perilous terrain without a good walk will necessarily extend themselves to affliction and distress. This is why it says that they "are bitten. There is misfortune." "Warlike people do the deeds of great rulers": warlike and violent people who occupy positions above other people, who indulge their restlessness and rashness and nothing else, will not be able to walk submissively, or at least, they will not get very far. It is neither central nor straightforward, and its tendency is firm, which is why the group of *yang* lines agrees with it.[3] As a result, its firmness is restless, it treads on peril, and it will acquire misfortune. **The *Symbol* says: "'The nearsighted can look': but they are not sufficient for enlightenment. 'The lame can walk': but they are not sufficient for travel."** As for people of *yin* softness, if their powers are not sufficient, they cannot look with enlightenment, and they cannot travel far. In such a case, they will busy themselves with firmness. When their walk is like this, how could they avoid harm? **"The misfortune of those who 'are**

bitten': their position is not proper for them. 'Warlike people do the deeds of great rulers': their tendencies are firm." It uses softness to occupy the third position. Its walk is not straightforward, and so it brings about affliction and harm. It receives a bite, and there is misfortune. Warlike people are taken as the example because it is placed in a *yang* position. Its powers are weak, but its "tendencies are firm." Since its tendencies are firm, its movement is at fault. Its walk is not caused by the way, as in the case of a warlike person who does the deeds of a great ruler.

The fourth "nine" line: it walks on the tail of a tiger. It is startled, and startled again, but there is good fortune in the end. The fourth "nine" line is *yang* and firm, it belongs to the Lead trigram substance, and its firmness is victorious even though it occupies the fourth position. It is near the ruler but on a terrain of numerous troubles, which means that they do not acquire each other. The fifth line in turn is excessively firm and resolute, and this is why "it walks on the tail of a tiger." "It is startled, and startled again": it has a trembling and troubled appearance. If it can be trembling and troubled, it is proper that "there is good fortune in the end." In fact, although this "nine" line is firm, its tendencies are soft; although the fourth position is near the ruler, it does not place itself there. This is why, if it is able to be alarmed, cautious, trembling, and troubled, it will avoid the peril and obtain good fortune in the end. **The *Symbol* says: "'It is startled, and startled again, but there is good fortune in the end': it tends to travel."** If it can be "startled, and startled again," trembling and troubled, then it will acquire "good fortune in the end." Its tendency is to travel and not to place itself. If it departs from the peril, it will obtain good fortune. *Yang* firmness is capable of traveling, but it occupies a soft position, and so it uses submissiveness to place itself.

The fifth "nine" line: it walks resolutely. Purity brings danger. The word "resolutely" here refers to its firm resolution. The fifth line makes use of *yang* firmness and the substance of the Lead trigram to occupy the position of extreme respect. It refers to those who give command to their firm resolution and then act. In a case like this, even though they have acquired straightforwardness, there will still be peril and danger. The sages of antiquity who occupied positions of respect in the world had sufficient enlightenment to illuminate others, sufficient firmness to become resolute, and sufficient propensity to be without qualification. Nonetheless, they never tasted this without exhausting the discussions of the world. Even with people as minimal as grass and wood cutters, they still chose to have discussions.[4] It is because of this that they were sages. "It walks in the position of the lord, which is to be bright and enlightened" is said of them.[5] They could have given themselves command with firmness and enlightenment and acted resolutely, without being concerned. Although this would have made them straightforward, it would also have been a perilous way. How could they have kept guard with certainty? If, when those possessing the powers of firmness and enlightenment give themselves unqualified command, it constitutes a perilous way, what will the case be like for those whose firmness and enlightenment are not sufficient? When the *Book of Changes* says that "purity brings danger," its meaning is not the same in every case. This can be seen in the hexagram that follows.[6] **The *Symbol* says: "'It walks resolutely. Purity brings danger': its position is straightforward and proper for it."** The *Symbol* warns those who walk resolutely, because they are straightforward and the position of respect is proper for them. If they occupy the position of extreme respect, seize their propensity to be without qualification, give themselves command with firm resolution, and are neither trembling nor troubled—although this will make them straightforward, it will still be a perilous way.

The top "nine" line: it looks over its walk and assesses whether it is auspicious. Cycling through it brings primary good fortune. This top line is placed at the end of the Walk hexagram. From its position at the end, it looks over where it has walked and traveled to assess whether it was good or bad, an affliction or a blessing. There are goodness and good fortune in encompassing it. The phrase "cycling through" signifies that it is intact and perfect in encompassing and cycling through it, that there is nothing it does not reach. When people assess or look over the end of their walk, the best case is if they can encompass it, intact from beginning to end, without finding an infirmity. As a result, there is "primary good fortune." The good and bad fortune of people is bound to their walk. If it has more or less of the good or the bad, their good or bad fortune will be smaller or greater. **The *Symbol* says: "In the top line, there is 'primary good fortune': it has great delight."** This top line is at the end of the Walk hexagram. If people have a good walk, their good fortune will be extreme. If they encompass and cycle through it to the end without finding any inadequacy, they will be people with a great grasp of blessing and delight. What is esteemed in a person's travels is that they have an end.

11. FREE (*TAI* 泰)

The *Sequence of the Hexagrams* says: "Once people have walked in freedom, they will be contented. This is why the Free hexagram is next." When people go walking and acquire their place, they will be relaxed and free. If they are free, then they will be contented, and so the Free hexagram succeeds the Walk hexagram. As for the trigrams, the Yield or *yin* trigram is above and the Lead or *yang* trigram below. When the heavenly and earthly *qi*—that is, the *yin* and *yang qi*—interact with each other and harmonize, then the ten thousand things will be born and brought to completion. This is why the trigrams symbolize a free development.

Free: those who are small go on a journey, while those who are great arrive. There are good fortune and progress. "Those who are small" signifies the *yin* lines, while "those who are great" signifies the *yang* lines. To "go on a journey" is to make a journey to the outer trigram. To "arrive" is to arrive and occupy the inner trigram. The *yang qi* has fallen to the bottom, while the *yin qi* is above and interacts with it. When *yin* and *yang* harmonize smoothly, the ten thousand things are born and achieve success, which indicates that heaven and earth are free. Concerning human affairs, one may remark that "those who are great" are the rulers above, while "those who are small" are the ministers below. The rulers unfold their sincerity so that they may give command to those below, while the ministers exhaust their sincerity so that they may manage the affairs of the rulers. The tendencies of those above and below develop together, which indicates that the imperial court is free. *Yang* refers to noble people, while *yin* refers to small people. Noble people arrive, and so their place is inside; small people go on a journey, and so their place is outside. This is the case of noble people acquiring positions, while small people are at the bottom, which indicates that

the world is free. The way of the Free hexagram brings "good fortune and progress." The judgment says neither "primacy and good fortune" nor "primacy
and progress." The moments are either of corruption or of prosperity, and their
order is either small or great. Although this is the Free hexagram, how could
there be only one variety of it? When the judgment says "there are good fortune
and progress," it is able to contain them all.

**The *Judgment* says: "'Free: those who are small go on a journey, while those
who are great arrive. There are good fortune and progress.' As a result, heaven
and earth interact and the ten thousand things develop. Those above and
below interact, and their tendencies become the same."** "Those who are small
go on a journey, while those who are great arrive": the *yin* lines go on a journey and the *yang* lines arrive. "As a result," the *yin* and *yang qi* of "heaven and
earth interact" with each other, and the ten thousand things are successful and
develop freely. In the case of people, the inclinations of those above and below
interact and develop, and their tendencies, like their intentions, become the
same. **"*Yang* is inside and *yin* outside; vigor is inside and submission outside;
noble people are inside and small people outside. The way of noble people
grows, while the way of small people is disappearing."** *Yang* arrives to occupy
the inner trigram, while *yin* makes the journey to occupy the outer trigram.
That is, *yang* is advancing while *yin* is retreating. The Lead or vigor trigram is
on the inside while the Yield or submission trigram is on the outside: "Vigor is
inside and submission outside," which is the way of noble people. When noble
people are inside, while small people are outside, "the way of noble people
grows, while the way of small people is disappearing." And so these two trigrams
constitute the Free hexagram. Having already chosen to speak about the harmonious interaction of *yin* and *yang*, the *Judgment* now chooses to say that "the
way of noble people grows." When *yin* and *yang* interact harmoniously, the way
of noble people is growing.

**The *Symbol* says: "Heaven and earth interact: Free. The princes use it to make
the way of heaven and earth resourceful and complete, and to assist the fitness of heaven and earth, so as to do everything for the people."** When heaven
and earth interact, and *yin* and *yang* harmonize, the ten thousand things will
be lush and successful, and so they will be free. It is proper that rulers give substance to this symbol of the free development of heaven and earth, and "use it
to make the way of heaven and earth resourceful and complete, and to assist the
fitness of heaven and earth, so as to do everything for" the lives of the people.
The phrase "resourceful and complete" signifies that they give substance to the
way of free interaction between heaven and earth, which is the starting point of

an influence that is resourceful, controlling, and complete. "To assist the fitness of heaven and earth": when heaven and earth freely develop, the ten thousand things will be lush and successful. Rulers give substance to it through laws and controls, making the people employ the moments of heaven, cause the earth to be profitable, assist and help in the task of its transformation and cultivation, and bring the profit of its thickness and beauty to completion. For example, when the *qi* of spring reveals and gives birth to the ten thousand things, then the laws of sowing and planting are constituted. When the *qi* of autumn makes the ten thousand things complete and full, then the laws of bringing in and harvesting are constituted. This is "to assist the fitness of heaven and earth," so as to do everything to assist and help the people. The lives of the people necessarily depend on the laws and controls constituted by the rulers above them, which teach, administer, assist, and aid them. Then they will acquire success in their birth and nourishment. This is "to do everything" for them.

The initial "nine" line: it uproots the rushes by the rhizome. With things of this sort, it takes the field. There is good fortune. The initial line makes use of *yang* to occupy the bottom position and refers to those in positions below who have the powers of firmness and enlightenment. If this were the moment of the Clog hexagram, noble people would retreat and their place would be depleted. But in the moment of the Free hexagram, their tendency is to advance upward. The advance of noble people must be guided and supported by friends of their own kind, just like the roots of rushes. When one of them is uprooted, the rest are guided and linked up with it as well. The word "rhizome" refers to roots that guide and link up with each other, and this is why they constitute the symbol. The word "sort" refers to a kind. When worthy people advance with those of their own kind, their same tendencies put their way into action, and so "there is good fortune." The advance of noble people must be with those of their own kind. Not only is their tendency first to be with each other, but also they take pleasure in doing good together, and so each depends on the other when making the crossing. This is why noble people, like small people, have never yet been able to set themselves up alone without depending on help from friends of their own kind. Since antiquity, when noble people acquire positions, the worthies of the world have met them at the imperial court. With the same tendencies and allied forces, they bring the freedom of the world to its completion. When small people are in positions, dissimilar people advance with them. Afterward their faction is victorious, and the world enters the Clog hexagram. In fact, each attends to its own kind. **The *Symbol* says: "'It uproots the rushes. It takes the field. There is good fortune': it tends toward the outside."** If the moment of the Free hexagram is about to occur, the group of worthy people will all want to advance upward. The tendencies of the three *yang* lines have the same desire to advance, and this is why the symbols of "rushes by the rhizome" and "with things of this sort, it takes the field" are chosen. "It tends toward the outside": it advances upward.

The second "nine" line: it contains the barren. It is employed to wade the river. It does not overlook what is distant. Friends vanish. It acquires and values the action of the center. The second line uses *yang* firmness to acquire the center, and corresponds to the fifth line above, while the fifth line uses softness and submissiveness to acquire the center, and corresponds to the second line below. The ruler and ministers have the same virtue. Because of their powers of firmness and centrality, those above give them unqualified command. Although the second line occupies the position of the minister, it is the master of bringing order to the Free hexagram. This is signified by the passage from the *Judgment* that reads: "Those above and below interact, and their tendencies become the same." This is why, concerning the way of bringing order to the Free hexagram, the second line is said to be the master. "It contains the barren. It is employed to wade the river. It does not overlook what is distant. Friends vanish": these are the four ways to place oneself in the Free hexagram. When the inclinations of people are contented and indulged, the government becomes relaxed and slackened, the laws and measures become neglected and lax, and there will be no rein on the numberless affairs. The way of setting things in order must contain or enclose a measure of barrenness and dirt. In such a case, its influence will be tolerant and generous when delineating what has decayed the most. It will reform the state of affairs using principle, and people will be contented. Were it to have no measure of "enclosure" or "immensity," its heart would be wrathful and ill, and so its apprehension would be neither deep nor far-reaching, and its distress would be both violent and exasperating.[1] The depth of the decay would not yet be driven out, even as distress would already be born nearby. This is why "it contains the barren." "It is employed to wade the river": in a time of freedom and serenity, the inclinations of people become practiced in continuous contentment. They are content to guard what is ordinary, they sloppily retrace their steps, and they are scared of further alteration. They are without the courage to wade the river—that is, they cannot do anything in this moment. The phrase "wade the river" signifies that its firmness and purpose are sufficient to cross the depth and surpass the obstacle. Since antiquity, times of freedom and order must step by step reach the point of scarcity and decline. In fact, it is because they habitually practice contentment and leisure, which is to retrace their steps. When there are no rulers of firmness and decisiveness with endless and relentless assistants, they will not be capable of extraordinary specificity when they are aroused to reveal and reform the decay. This is why the line statement says: "It is employed to wade the river." Someone wonders: earlier it said that "it contains the barren," which is to contain or enclose an all-embracing tolerance, but here it says that "it is employed to wade the river," which is to be aroused and to reveal, to modify and to reform. These statements seem to be the reverse of each other. This is not to recognize that a measure of enclosure and embrace,[2] together with the employment of a firm and purposeful influence, belongs to the deeds of sages and worthies. "It does not overlook what is distant": in moments of freedom and serenity, if people's hearts become habituated to freedom, then they will be reckless, contented, and leisurely, and that is all. How could they turn to deep reflection and far-reaching apprehension, and extend it to what is distant and far away in their affairs? It is proper that those who bring order and freedom encompass and extend themselves to the numberless affairs. Although they may be distant and far away, they should not be overlooked. When an affair is still minimal and concealed, or when the powers of worthy people are still crass and rustic[3]—these are both cases of being distant and far away. In the moment of the Free hexagram, they will certainly be overlooked. "Friends vanish": since it is already the moment of the Free hexagram, people have become practiced in contentment, indulging their inclinations and losing the reins. Those who are about to restrict them and make them straightforward will not be capable of it unless they sever and drive out their private agreements with friends. This is why it says: "Friends vanish." Since antiquity, when those who set up laws and controls over affairs are guided by people's inclinations, they are often unable to act. As for prohibiting wastefulness and extravagance, this does harm to one's neighbors and relations, while setting a limit on the produce of the fields will interfere with the esteemed families. In cases of this kind, if those who must act are unable to decide in favor of the great public, this is to be guided by friends and those close to one. If those who bring order to the Free hexagram are incapable of making "friends vanish," it will be difficult for them to do it. Concerning the way of bringing order to the Free hexagram, those who possess these four ways will be able to align with the virtue of the second "nine" line, and this is why it says: "It acquires and values the action of the center." The meaning of what it says is that they can match up or align with the action of the central line. The word "values" here indicates that they match up with it.[4] **The *Symbol* says: "'It contains the barren. It acquires and values the action of the center': so that it may be bright and great."** The *Symbol* only brings up the statement that "it contains the barren," but it is developing and interpreting the meaning of all four statements. It is saying that those who are like this will be able to match or align with the virtues in the action of the central line. Their way will be bright, enlightened, clear, and great.

The third "nine" line: there is no plain without a sinkhole. There is no journey without a return. There is purity in hardship, and no blame. It is trustworthy, and without anxiety. Eating is a blessing. The third line occupies the center of the Free hexagram, at the top of the various *yang* lines, and refers to an abundance of freedom. The principle of things is like tracing a circle: those at the bottom will necessarily rise, while those that occupy the top will necessarily fall. When freedom has been continuous, it will necessarily become clogged up. This is why, in the abundance of freedom, when the *yang* lines are about to advance, the line statement gives a warning, saying that there is no constant contentment or plain without an obstacle or sinkhole—which signifies that there is no constant freedom. There is no journey that is constant, that does not come back—which signifies that it is proper for the *yin* lines to return. Since plains have sinkholes, and journeys have returns, things will become clogged. It is proper to recognize such necessity in the principle of heaven so that, at the moment when the Free hexagram starts, no one will dare to be contented and leisurely. If people are constantly reflective and apprehensive about their hardship and peril, if they make their influence straightforward and certain then, when such is the case, there should be no blame. When those placed on the way of the Free hexagram have been able to be pure in their hardship, they should be constant in the preservation of their freedom. If they do not labor with worry or anxiety, they will acquire what they seek and will not lose what they hope for. If they are trustworthy like this, then they will add to their possession of blessings and wages, or "eating." To have wages or "eating" signifies a blessing or jubilation. As for those who place themselves well in the Free hexagram, their blessings should grow. In fact, if their virtue and goodness accumulate daily, their blessings and wages will escalate daily. If their virtue overshoots their wages then, even if they possess abundance, it will never satiate them. Since antiquity, amplitude and abundance have never yet come about without the loss of the way, without perishing in defeat. **The *Symbol* says: "'There is no journey without a return': this is the border between heaven and earth."** "There is no journey without a return": the *Symbol* is speaking of the border on which heaven and earth interact. When *yang* has fallen to the bottom, it must return to the top, and when *yin* has risen to the top, it must return to the bottom. This is the constant principle of contraction and expansion, of going on a journey and arriving. It accounts for the way of heaven and earth interacting on their border and sheds light on the principle of inconstancy in the Clog and Free hexagrams, so as to give a warning.

The fourth "six" line: it flutters, and flutters again. Without wealth, it makes use of its neighbors. Without a warning, it is trustworthy. The place of the fourth "six" line exceeds the center of the Free hexagram. It is *yin* and it is in the upper trigram, so its tendency is to return to the lower trigram. The tendency of the two *yin* lines above it is also to rush to the bottom. "It flutters, and flutters again": this indicates the appearance of rapid flight. The fourth line "flutters, and flutters again" toward the bottom, just the same as its neighbors. The word "neighbor" refers to someone of one's own kind and signifies the fifth and top lines. When people are wealthy and those of their own kind attend to them, it is for the sake of profit. When they are not wealthy and others attend to them anyway, it is because their tendencies are the same. The three *yin* lines are all things that belong at the bottom. When they occupy positions above, they lose their reality, and all their tendency or desire is to travel downward. This is why, "without wealth," they attend to each other. They do not wait for a warning or for further information because they align with each other in the sincerity of their intentions. As for *yin* and *yang* in their rise and fall—that is, the Clog and Free hexagrams in the revolution of the moments—sometimes they interact and sometimes they are scattered. This is a constant principle. When the Free hexagram has exceeded its center, it is about to alter. Concerning the third line, the sage says that there is "purity in hardship" and "a blessing." In fact, the third line is about to reach the center and may preserve itself if it recognizes the sage's warning. The fourth line has already exceeded the center, and principle requires that it be altered. This is why he speaks without qualification about the way of beginning and ending, of reverting or returning. If it were the fifth line, the master of the Free hexagram, then he would remark on the meaning of its place in the Free hexagram. **The Symbol says: "'It flutters, and flutters again. Without wealth': they all lose their reality. 'Without a warning, it is trustworthy': it is the aspiration of their center and heart."** "It flutters, and flutters again": this refers to its rapid journey downward. It does not wait to become wealthy, yet its neighbors attend to it. The three *yin* lines are above, and this is why they have all lost their reality. At its root, *yin* is a thing that belongs below, but here it occupies a position above. This is to lose one's reality. They do not wait for information or warnings but agree with each other in the sincerity of their intentions. In fact, this is what they aspire to in their center and heart. What is proper or according to principle belongs to heaven, while what makes the crowd to be the same belongs to the moment.

The fifth "six" line: Di Yi gives the bride away at her wedding, bringing jubilation and primary good fortune. The *Grand Scribe's Records* refers to Tang as Tian Yi.[5] After him, there was Di Zuyi, who was also a worthy king. Much later, there was Di Yi. The "Numerous Officers" chapter of the *Book of History* says that "from Cheng Tang to Di Yi, there was no one without enlightenment and virtue, who was not anxious, and who did not make libations."[6] As for the one named Di Yi, it is not yet known who he was. If one uses the meaning of the line when gazing on this question, then Di Yi is the one who established rituals and laws to control royal ladies who take spouses below them. Since antiquity, although lordly women have often taken spouses below them, it was only after Di Yi that they were controlled by rituals and laws. They diminish their respect and esteem, so that they submit and attend to their husbands. The fifth "six" line uses *yin* softness to occupy the position of the ruler, and it corresponds to the second "nine" line below it, which refers to a worthy person of firmness and enlightenment. If the fifth line can delegate command to worthy ministers, and submit and attend to them, then it will be like the wedded bride of Di Yi. If it diminishes its respect so as to submit and attend to the *yang* line, this may be considered to be "jubilation" and "primary good fortune." "Primary good fortune" refers to great good fortune that exhausts what is good. It signifies that it has completed the task of bringing order to the Free hexagram. **The *Symbol* says: "'Bringing jubilation and primary good fortune': it is central and acts on its aspirations."** The reason it can obtain "jubilation" and blessings, as well as "primary good fortune," is that it aligns with the way of centrality and acts on its tendencies and aspirations. It possesses the virtue of centrality, and so it can give command to worthy people of firmness and centrality. Its tendency and aspiration are to listen and attend to them. If this were not what it desired, how could it attend to them?

The top "six" line: the rampart returns to the ditch. It should not employ the troops. Its own district receives information and the mandate. Purity brings dismay. When one digs a ditch, the earth is accumulated and piled up until it completes a rampart, just as the way of bringing order is accumulated and piled up until it completes the Free hexagram. When the Free hexagram is extended to its end, it is about to revert to the Clog hexagram, just as the slope of an earthen rampart crumbles and returns or reverts to the ditch. Since the top line is a "six" and constitutes the end of the Free hexagram, it refers to the placement of small people, whose actions will soon bring about the Clog hexagram. "It should not employ the troops": rulers are able to employ the crowd because those above and below have mutual inclinations, and their hearts are attentive. Here, when the Free hexagram is about to end, and they have lost the way of freedom, those above and below do not have mutual inclinations. The hearts of the people are cast off and scattered, and do not attend to those above. How could they be employed? If they were employed, there would be disorder. When the crowd should not be employed, it starts to give "information and the mandate" to its own nearby relations. Although they are made to acquire straightforwardness by receiving information and the mandate, they may also be disappointed and dismayed. The "district" is the position it occupies and signifies its nearby relations. In the great majority of cases, when giving information and the mandate, one must begin with those nearby. There are two general meanings of "purity brings misfortune" and "purity brings dismay": sometimes there will be misfortune or dismay if one guards one's purity and certainty like this, and sometimes there will be misfortune or dismay even if one acquires straightforwardness. In the present case, the line statement does not say that "purity brings misfortune," but only that "purity brings dismay." It is about to reach the Clog hexagram, and it starts to give information and the mandate, which may bring about disappointment and dismay. It is not that information and the mandate are the causes of the Clog hexagram. **The *Symbol* says: "'The rampart returns to the ditch': its mandate is disordered."** "The rampart returns to the ditch": although it gives the mandate, the disorder cannot be stopped.

12. CLOG (*PI* 否)

The *Sequence of the Hexagrams* says: "Those who are free will develop. Things cannot develop to the end, and this is why the Clog hexagram is next." As for the principle of things, it is to make a journey and then arrive. When things develop freely to their limit, they must become clogged, and so the Clog hexagram succeeds the Free hexagram. As for the trigrams, heaven is above and earth below. When heaven and earth interact with each other, and *yin* and *yang* harmonize smoothly, this is freedom. If heaven is placed above and the earth below, this is the separation and severance of heaven and earth. They do not interact with each other and develop, and so the trigrams constitute the Clog hexagram.

It is clogged by no one. When heaven and earth interact, the ten thousand things are born at their center. Afterward, the three powers are brought to perfection.[1] Humans are the most spiritual of them, and this is why they stand at the head of the ten thousand things. In general, everything born at the center of heaven and earth is on the way of humanity. When heaven and earth do not interact, they do not give birth to the ten thousand things, which is not the way of anyone. This is why the judgment says, "it is clogged by no one," signifying that this is the way of no one.[2] To grow and to disappear, to close and to open — these do not rest from causing each other. When the Free hexagram reaches its limit, it turns around. When the Clog hexagram reaches its limit, it collapses. If there is no principle by which things are constant and without alteration, how could the way of humanity be otherwise? If things have already become clogged up, then there will be freedom. **There is no profit in the purity of noble people. Those who are great go on a journey, while those who are small arrive.** As for the interaction and development of those above and below, as well as the harmonization and convergence of firmness and softness — this is the way of noble people. What has become clogged is the reverse of this, and this is why "there is no profit in the purity of noble people." The straightforward way of noble people is that they do not act when something is clogged or choked. "Those who are great go on a journey, while those who are small arrive": *yang* goes on a journey, while *yin* arrives. They symbolize the way of small people growing, and the way of noble people disappearing. This is why they constitute the Clog hexagram.

The *Judgment* says: "'It is clogged by no one. There is no profit in the purity of noble people. Those who are great go on a journey, while those who are small arrive.' As a result, heaven and earth do not interact, and the ten thousand things do not develop. Those above and below do not interact, and the world is without kingdoms. *Yin* is inside and *yang* outside; softness is inside and firmness outside; small people are inside and noble people outside. The way of small people grows, while the way of noble people is disappearing." When the heavenly *qi* and the earthly *qi* do not interact, the ten thousand things do not possess the principle of birth and completion. When the duties of those above and below do not interact, the world does not possess the way of kingdoms and states. The establishment of kingdoms and states is what constitutes order. When the influence of government sets the people in order, the people gird themselves with the rulers and attend to their mandate. Those above and below interact with each other, and so there is order and contentment. Currently, "those above and below do not interact," and so the world is without the way of kingdoms and states. *Yin* softness is inside, while *yang* firmness is outside. Noble people make the journey to occupy the outer position, while small people arrive to take up the inner position. "The way of small people grows" at the moment when "the way of noble people is disappearing."

The *Symbol* says: "Heaven and earth do not interact: Clog. Noble people use it to elude difficulty by being thrifty with their virtue. They should not glory in their wages." "Heaven and earth do not interact" with each other and develop. This is why these trigrams constitute the Clog hexagram. In the moment of the Clog or choke hexagram, the way of noble people disappears. It is proper that they gaze on the symbol of the Clog or choke hexagram, and be thrifty or take away from their virtue,[3] so as to evade or avoid affliction and difficulty. They should not glory in occupying positions with wages. The Clog hexagram refers to the moment when small people acquire the object of their tendencies. If noble people occupy a clear and glorious terrain, affliction and distress will necessarily be extended to them. This is why it is fitting that they be placed in obscurity, depleting and restricting themselves.

The initial "six" line: it uproots the rushes by the rhizome. With things of this sort, purity brings good fortune and progress. The Free and Clog hexagrams both choose rushes as symbols. Since the group of *yang* lines in the former and the group of *yin* lines in the latter are the same in being at the bottom, they symbolize things that are guided and linked up with one another. In the moment of the Free hexagram, taking the same field constitutes good fortune, and in the moment of the Clog hexagram, possessing the same purity constitutes progress. At the beginning, the inner trigram referred to small people and the outer trigram to noble people, and together they gave the meaning of the Clog hexagram. But now the initial "six" line, at the bottom of the Clog hexagram, constitutes the way of noble people. The *Book of Changes* follows the moment in choosing its meanings, altering and moving without constancy. In the moment of the Clog hexagram, those at the bottom are the noble people. The three *yin* lines of the Clog hexagram all have corresponding lines above them, but in a moment of clogging and separation they are separated and severed, and do not communicate with each other. This is why the meaning of the line statement is that there is no correspondence. If the initial "six" line can, with other things of its kind, rein itself in with purity and certainty, then it will place itself in the good fortune of the Clog hexagram, and will make progress on its way. Those who can advance while facing the Clog hexagram are small people. If they were noble people, they would expand their way and avoid affliction, and that is all. Whether noble people advance or retreat, they never taste anything different from those of their kind. The *Symbol* says: "'It uproots the rushes.' 'Purity brings good fortune': it tends toward the ruler.'" This line is a "six" that guards itself at the bottom of the hexagram; it sheds light on the way of noble people placed at the bottom.[4] The *Symbol*, in turn, unfolds and sheds light on it by taking it as the symbol of the noble person's heart.[5] When noble people keep guard and rein themselves with certainty while placed at the bottom, they do not take pleasure in not advancing or in their solitary goodness. But their way has started to become clogged, and they should not advance—this is why they are contented here. Their hearts certainly do not taste their absence from the world. They tend constantly toward making an acquisition of the ruler and advancing, so that they may make the crossing and render the world healthy. This is why the *Symbol* says: "It tends toward the ruler."

The second "six" line: it contains its service, which is the good fortune of small people. In the clogging of great people, there is progress. The disposition of the second "six" line is *yin* softness, but it occupies a position that is central and straightforward. Concerning the *yin* softness of small people, one may remark that, in the lower trigram where the clogging starts, they tend to contain and herd their service and submission to those above, so that they may seek to cross through it. Their clogging refers to profit for themselves, which is the good fortune of small people. When great people face the Clog hexagram, they place themselves according to the way. How could they be willing to bend themselves and contract the way? In their service and submission to those above, they simply keep guard over their clogging by themselves, and that is all. The clogging of the self is progress on the way. Someone asks: when those above and below do not interact, how can there be service? Response: when straightforwardness has become clogged, the heart of a small person who submits to those above is not entirely untasted. **The *Symbol* says: "'In the clogging of great people, there is progress': it does not bring disorder to the group."** When great people are in the moment of the Clog hexagram, they guard their straightforwardness and rein themselves in. They are not mixed up with or disordered by the group or kind of small people. Although there is the clogging of the self, there is also progress on the way, and this is why "in the clogging there is progress." If they did not use the way, and they themselves made progress, then the way would become clogged. The line statement does not say "noble people." It says "great people," because the way of those who can be like this is great.

The third "six" line: it contains a disappointment. The third line uses *yin* softness, is neither central nor straightforward and occupies a position in the Clog hexagram. Further, it is quite near to those above. It cannot guard the way or be contented with the mandate, and it brings these transgressions to their depletion — that is, it brings the inclination and condition of small people to its limit. Whatever they contain or herd, whatever they do with skill and apprehension, it will always reach the point of crookedness and transgression, and they should be disappointed and humiliated. **The *Symbol* says: "'It contains a disappointment': its position is not proper for it."** A line that is *yin* and soft occupies a position in the Clog hexagram, and is neither central nor straightforward — it should be disappointed, since its place "is not proper for it." It is not placed in the proper position, which indicates that it has not made use of the way.

The fourth "nine" line: when it has the mandate, there is no blame. Those of its rank are cast into jubilation. The fourth line uses *yang* firmness and the vigor trigram substance to occupy a position near the ruler. It refers to those who have enough power to cross through the clogging and who have acquired lofty positions. They are sufficient to assist those above in crossing through the clogging, but they are faced with the moment when the way of the ruler starts to become clogged, and they are placed on a terrain that presses them near to it. It would detest them and would choose to be jealous were they to occupy an accomplished position, and that is all. Should they be able to make a move, it must go out from the mandate of the ruler. If the blade of authority is wielded solely by those above, then there will be no blame, and they will put their tendencies into action. If they can make all their affairs go out from the mandate of the ruler, they will be able to cross through the moment of the Clog hexagram, and everyone of their rank or kind will depend on or be "cast into" blessing and "jubilation." To be cast into is to be connected to. When the way of noble people is put into action, they advance together with those of their own kind, so as to cross through the clogging of the world, and then "those of its rank are cast into jubilation." When small people advance, they, too, do the same as those of their own kind. **The *Symbol* says: "'When it has the mandate, there is no blame': it puts its tendencies into action."** "When it has the mandate" of the ruler, then "there is no blame." It can then cross through the Clog hexagram, which is to put "its tendencies into action."

The fifth "nine" line: to restrain a clog is good fortune for great people. It vanishes, and vanishes again. It is bound to a grove of mulberry trees. The fifth line uses the virtues of *yang* firmness, centrality, and straightforwardness to occupy the position of respect. This is why it can restrain or put to rest the clogging of the world, which "is good fortune for great people." Great people in their proper position can use their way to restrain or put to rest the clogging of the world, and slowly bring it to freedom. But they have not yet cast off the clog, and this is why the line statement gives the warning that "it vanishes." If the clog is already restrained or put to rest, and is step by step reverting to freedom, they should not readily become contented or indulgent. It is proper that they be deeply apprehensive, give far-reaching warnings, and constantly deliberate on the return of the clog. When it says that "it vanishes, and vanishes again. It is bound to a grove of mulberry trees," it signifies the way of being contented and certain, as though anchored or "bound to a grove of mulberry trees." Considered as a thing, the mulberry tree has roots that are deep and certain. The word "grove" signifies that they live in a thicket, and so their certainty is extreme. Such is the depth of the sage's warning. The Han dynasty's Wang Yun and the Tang dynasty's Li Deyu did not recognize this warning, and so they brought about affliction and defeat.[6] The *Appended Statements* says: "To be in peril is to be contented with one's position; to vanish is to preserve one's persistence. To be disordered is to possess order. This is why noble people are contented without forgetting their peril; they persist without forgetting that they will vanish; they are orderly without forgetting about disorder. By making themselves

contented, they are able to preserve the state."[7] **The *Symbol* says: "'Good fortune for great people': their position is straightforward and proper for them."**
They possess the virtues of great people, and they acquire a straightforward position of extreme respect. This is why they can restrain the clogging of the world,
so that there will be good fortune. Without this position, how could they do it,
even if they possessed the way? This is why the position of the sage is referred
to as "great and precious."[8]

**The top "nine" line: the clog collapses. First there is a clog, and afterward
happiness.** The top "nine" line refers to the end of the Clog hexagram. When
the principle of a thing is at its limit, it must reverse itself. This is why, when the
Free hexagram is at its limit, there will be the Clog hexagram, and when the
Clog hexagram is at its limit, there will be the Free hexagram. In the top "nine"
line, the Clog hexagram has reached its limit, and this is why the way of the
Clog hexagram "collapses," overturns, and alters. First, it is at its limit—this is
the Clog hexagram. Afterward, it collapses—this is happiness. When the Clog
hexagram collapses, the Free hexagram comes about. That is, there is "afterward
happiness." **The *Symbol* says: "When the clog comes to its end, it collapses:
how could it grow?"** "When the clog comes to its end," it must collapse. How
could there be a principle by which the clog could grow? When something is
at its limit, it must reverse itself—this is a constant principle. Nonetheless, to
make peril revert to contentment, to change disorder into order, one must first
have the power of *yang* firmness, and afterward one will be capable of it. This is
why the top "nine" line of the Clog hexagram can make the clog collapse, while
the top "six" line of the Block hexagram cannot alter the blockage.

13. SAME MEN (*TONGREN* 同人)

The *Sequence of the Hexagrams* says: "Things cannot be clogged up to the end, and this is why the Same Men hexagram is next." When heaven and earth do not interact, they constitute the Clog hexagram. When those above and below are the same as each other, they constitute the Same Men hexagram. The meanings of the Same Men and Clog hexagrams are the reverse of each other, and this is why the one succeeds the other. Further, in a time when the Clog hexagram is faced, there will necessarily be people of the same force who can cross through it, and so the Same Men hexagram succeeds the Clog hexagram. As for the trigrams, the Lead trigram is above and the Cast trigram below. Concerning the two trigram symbols, one may remark that heaven is above, and the nature of fire is to flame upward. It is the same as heaven, and this is why they constitute the Same Men hexagram. Concerning the two trigram substances, one may remark that the fifth line occupies a straightforward position and is the master of the Lead trigram. The second line is the master of the Cast trigram, and the two lines correspond to each other with centrality and straightforwardness. Those above and below are the same as each other, which is the meaning of the Same Men hexagram. Further, the hexagram has only one *yin* line, and the crowd of *yang* lines is the same in their desire for it, which is also the meaning of the Same Men hexagram. There are certainly other hexagrams that have only one *yin* line, but in the moment of the Same Men hexagram, the second and fifth lines correspond to each other, and heaven and fire are the same as each other. This is why its meaning is so great.

The same men are in the wilderness. There is progress, profit in traversing a great stream, and profit in the purity of noble people. The *ye* character of "wilderness" signifies what is vast, and the meaning chosen for it is far away and outside. As for the "same men," when they use the way of the world's great sameness, then sages and worthies will set their hearts on the great public. As for the sameness of ordinary people, when they use their private intentions to align with each other, they will set their inclinations on intimate closeness. This is why they must be "in the wilderness," which signifies that they do not use the private inclination of intimate nearness, but are in the outlands and wilderness, a vast and faraway terrain. Since they are not bound to anything private, they will reach the way of great and public sameness, where nothing is so far away that it is not the same—their progress should be recognized. If they are capable of great sameness with the world, this indicates that everyone in the world is the same as they are. When everyone in the world is the same as they are, how could they not cross through obstacles and hindrances? How could they not make progress through hardships and perils? This is why "there is profit in traversing a great stream, and profit in the purity of noble people." Earlier the judgment says that they are "in the wilderness," which signifies only that there is no intimate closeness. Here it says that it is fitting to use the straightforward way of noble people. The "purity of noble people" signifies the way by which the world reaches great and public sameness. This is why, although they may occupy a position a thousand miles away, or be born a thousand years later, so long as they are aligned, tallied up, and reined in, so long as they unfold things and put them into action, there will be no one in the crowd of a million people in the breadth between the four seas who will not be the same as them. But if they are small people, they will employ only their private intentions. As for what is wrong, so long as they are close to it, they will make themselves the same as it. As for what is right, so long as they detest it, they will make themselves different from it. This is why those who are the same as them constitute a groveling faction. In fact, their hearts are not straightforward. This is why, concerning the way of the Same Men hexagram, there is profit in the purity and straightforwardness of noble people.

The *Judgment* says: "Same Men: softness acquires its position. It acquires centrality and corresponds to the leader. It is called Same Men." The *Judgment* is speaking about the meaning of the complete hexagram. "Softness acquires its position" signifies that the second line is *yin* and occupies a *yin* position. It has acquired the position that is straightforward for it. The fifth line is central and straightforward, and the second line, with its centrality and straightforwardness, corresponds to it. It "acquires centrality and corresponds to the leader." The fifth line is firm, vigorous, central, and straightforward, while the second line uses softness, submissiveness, centrality, and straightforwardness in corresponding to it. Each has acquired what is straightforward for it, and their virtues are the same. This is why they constitute the Same Men hexagram. The fifth line is the master of the Lead trigram, and this is why it says the second line "corresponds to the leader." The *Symbol* chooses the trigram symbols of heaven and fire, but the *Judgment* concerns the second line exclusively. "**The Same Men hexagram says:**" These five words are a gloss on the text. "'**The same men are in the wilderness. There is progress, profit in traversing a great stream': the leader acts.**" Those who are extremely sincere and not private can tread on obstacles and difficulties, which is the action of a leader. To be "not private" is the virtue of heaven. "**Pattern and enlightenment make use of vigor. By being central and straightforward, they correspond. This is how noble people are straightforward.**" The *Judgment* uses the two trigrams to say something about the meaning of the hexagram. One possesses the virtues of pattern and enlightenment, while the firmness and vigor of the other use the way of centrality and straightforwardness in corresponding to it. This is the straightforward way of noble people. "**Only noble people can develop the tendencies of the world.**" The tendencies of the world have ten thousand peculiarities, but their principle is one. Noble people are enlightened by the principle, and this is why they can develop the tendencies of the world. Sages look at the hearts of the countless millions as one heart. They develop its principle and that is all. Because they possess pattern and enlightenment, they can elucidate the principle, and this is why they can shed light on the meaning of great sameness; because they possess firmness and vigor, they can conquer themselves, and this is why they can exhaust the way of great sameness. Afterward, they can align with centrality and straightforwardness when "the leader acts."

The *Symbol* says: "**Heaven agrees with fire: Same Men. Noble people use kinds and classes to distinguish things.**" The *Symbol* does not say "fire is below heaven," or "below heaven, there is fire," but "heaven agrees with fire." Heaven is above, and the nature of fire is to flame upward. In this respect, fire is the same as heaven, and this is why these trigrams constitute the meaning of the Same Men hexagram. Noble people gaze on the symbol of the Same Men hexagram, and they "use kinds and classes to distinguish things." That is, they use the kind and class of each to distinguish the sameness and difference between things, as between the factions of noble and small people, the principles of goodness and badness or of right and wrong, the casting off and alignment of things in their inclinations, and the difference and sameness in the principles of affairs. In general, noble people can distinguish and shed light on difference and sameness, and this is why they have never lost the method of putting things in their places.

The initial "nine" line: the same men are at the gate. There is no blame.
This "nine" line occupies the initial position of the Same Men hexagram, is
not bound to any corresponding line, and refers to being without partiality or
privacy. The phrase "same men" refers to what is public, and this is why they go
out by "the gate." The same men go out by the gate, which signifies that they
are outside. If they are outside, they do not have the partiality of privacy and
familiarity, but are public in their sameness and liberality. In a case like this,
there will be no excess or blame. **The *Symbol* says: "'The same men' go out
from 'the gate': further, who could be blamed?"** "The same men go out from
the gate" to the outside—that is, they are the same in their breadth, without partiality or privacy. This is sameness among people. To differentiate the beneficial
from the meager, or the relation from the stranger, is to cause or give birth to
excess and blame. But where there is no partiality or faction—who could be
blamed for this?

The second "six" line: the same men are in the sect. There is dismay. The
second and fifth lines correspond straightforwardly, and this is why the line
statement says that "the same men are in the sect." The *zong* character of "sect"
refers to a faction. To be the same as those to whom one is bound or corresponds is to be partial in agreeing with them. On the way of the Same Men
hexagram, this constitutes a shrunken privacy, and this is why there should be
dismay. If the second line were *yang*, it would have the virtues of firmness and
centrality. Their sameness would come about through the way of centrality,
and so it would not constitute privacy. **The *Symbol* says: "'The same men are
in the sect': it is the way of dismay."** Various hexagrams consider a central and
straightforward correspondence to be good, but in the Same Men hexagram
there should be dismay. This is why the ruler is not chosen as the meaning of
the fifth line. In fact, privacy and closeness are not the way of the ruler. Those
who are the same in private should be dismayed.

**The third "nine" line: it stashes its weapons in the bushes and rises above the
lofty hill. For three years, it is not mustered.** The third line uses *yang* to occupy
a firm position, does not acquire the center, and refers to people of firmness
and violence. In the moment of the Same Men hexagram, all tendencies become the same. The hexagram has only one *yin* line, and the tendencies of the
various *yang* lines all desire sameness with it. Further, the third line is close to
it. The second line uses the way of centrality and straightforwardness to correspond to the fifth, but the third uses firmness and strength to occupy a position
between the second and fifth. It wants to strive with the latter and be the same
as the former. Such a thing will not be made straight by principle or made vic-

torious by duty, and this is why it does not dare to reveal it clearly. "It stashes" or stores away its arms or "weapons" at the center of the forest or "bushes." It cherishes what is bad, what will not be made straight by inner purity, and this is why it is also trembling and troubled. In this moment, "it rises above the lofty hill" with concern and hope. When it has done this continuously for three years, it will not dare to be mustered at their end. This line statement sees deeply into the inclinations and condition of small people, but it does not say that there is misfortune. It has not dared to reveal itself, and this is why it does not reach the point of misfortune. **The *Symbol* says: "'It stashes its weapons in the bushes': it is the enemy of firmness. 'For three years, it is not mustered': how could it act?"** Its enemy is the fifth line. Since that line is both firm and straightforward, how could it strive with it? This is why it is trembling and scared, why it stashes and stores away. If it reaches the point of three years without being mustered, how could it act in the end?

The fourth "nine" line: it rides the battlement but does not conquer or assault it. There is good fortune. The fourth line is firm but neither central nor straightforward. Its tendency or desire is to be the same as the second line, and it is also hostile to the fifth. A "battlement" or embankment is used as a perimeter or separator. The fourth line is quite near the fifth, as though it were its separator or battlement. "It rides the battlement" and wants to "assault it," but it recognizes that this is not made straight by duty, and so it "does not conquer." Since it can recognize that this is not made straight by duty, and it does not make the assault, there will be good fortune. If it were to indulge in crooked desires, unable to revert to reflection on duty and principle, and at fault in its actions of assaulting and striving, then its misfortune would be great. The third line uses firmness to occupy a firm position, and this is why it pushes its strength to the end and cannot reverse itself. The fourth line uses firmness to occupy a soft position, and this is why it means to be trapped and capable of reversion. If it can reverse itself, there will be good fortune. Since it trembles before duty and is capable of modification, its good fortune is fitting. **The *Symbol* says: "'It rides the battlement': its duty is not to conquer. Its good fortune is to be trapped and to revert to the regulations."** "It rides the battlement but does not conquer or assault it" because "its duty is not to conquer." A crooked assault on straightforwardness will not be made victorious by duty. What causes it to acquire good fortune is that duty will not make it victorious, so that it is trapped and depleted, and it reverts to the laws and regulations. The crowd of *yang* lines wants to be the same as the second line, but only the third and fourth have the meaning of contention and strife. These two lines occupy positions between the second and the fifth. The initial and the final lines are far away, and this is why another meaning is chosen for them.

The fifth "nine" line: there are the same men. At first it calls out and wails, but afterward it laughs. Great troops conquer, and they encounter one another. The fifth "nine" line is the same as the second, but they are separated by two *yang* lines: the third and the fourth. The fifth is made straight by duty and made victorious by principle, and this is why it is not victorious over its indignation at this impediment, to the point that "it calls out and wails." Nonetheless, the crooked is not victorious over the straightforward. Although something separates these two lines, they must acquire alignment in the end, and this is why "afterward it laughs." "Great troops conquer, and they encounter one another": the fifth line corresponds straightforwardly to the second, while two unprincipled *yang* lines separate and strive with them. They must employ "great troops" to conquer and be victorious over them, and then they will be able to "encounter one another." The line statement speaks of "great troops," and says that they "conquer," to show the strength of the two *yang* lines. The fifth "nine" line occupies the position of the ruler, but the ruler is not chosen as the meaning of the "same men" here. In fact, the fifth line corresponds to the second with unqualified privacy and intimacy, and loses the virtues of centrality and straightforwardness. It is proper that the ruler possess great sameness with the world. To be alone and in private with one person is not the way of the ruler. Further, when they are separated at first, it calls out and wails, but after they have encountered each other it laughs—these are the inclinations of privacy and intimacy, and not the substance of great sameness. If the second line in the lower trigram is the same as those in its sect, and so "there is dismay," what will the case be like for rulers? The fifth line is not chosen as the way of the ruler, and this is why it says nothing about the way of the ruler. It only sheds light on two people with sameness of heart and means that there can be no separation between them. The *Appended Statements* says that "the way of noble people is sometimes to go out and sometimes to remain in place, sometimes to remain silent and sometimes to speak. When two people have sameness of heart, their sharpness can cut through metal."[1] When they are the same in their centrality and sincerity, they will be nothing other than the same whether they go out or remain in place, whether they speak or remain silent, and the world will not be able to come between them. The word "sameness" refers to unity. What is one cannot be divided, since the divisible is two. What is one can develop through metal and stone, or brave water and fire. There is no place it cannot enter, and this is why it says that "their sharpness can cut through metal." This principle is extremely minimal, and this is why the sage applauds it, saying that "the words of sameness of heart have a perfume like orchids."[2] He is saying that the savor of such words and intentions is deep and wide. **The *Symbol* says: "'At first' there are 'the same men': it is made straight by centrality. There are 'great troops,' and they 'encounter one another': it is saying that they conquer them."** "At first" it calls out and wails, because it is made straight by centrality, sincerity, and principle. This is why such a line is not at all victorious over its wrathfulness. Although its enemy is firm and strong, to the point that it employs great troops, it is nonetheless made straight by duty and made victorious by principle. In the end it will be able to conquer it, and this is why the *Symbol* says that they can "conquer them." The phrase "conquer them" signifies that they can be victorious, which shows the strength of the two *yang* lines.

The top "nine" line: the same men are in the outlands. There are no regrets. The word "outlands" refers to a terrain that is outside and far away. Those who seek sameness must relate to and agree with each other. The top "nine" line occupies the outside of the hexagram, has no corresponding line, and refers to those who are without agreement or sameness in the end. When there is sameness at the beginning, there is sometimes splitting apart and regret when it reaches the end. It is placed far away and has no line to agree with it. This is why, although there is no sameness, there are also "no regrets." Although its tendency to desire sameness is not successful, in the end it has nothing to regret. **The *Symbol* says: "'The same men are in the outlands': their tendencies do not yet acquire their object."** It occupies a position far away, and there is no sameness. This is why, in the end, it has nothing to regret. Nonetheless, it is on the way of the Same Men hexagram and its tendency to seek sameness has not acquired its object. Although it succeeds in having no regrets, it is not in a good place.

14. GREAT GRASP (*DAYOU* 大有)

The *Sequence of the Hexagrams* says: "If the same men are in agreement, other things will necessarily wed themselves to them. This is why the Great Grasp hexagram is next." When the same men are in agreement, other things wed themselves to them, and so the Great Grasp hexagram succeeds the Same Men hexagram. As for the trigrams, "fire is above heaven." Fire has a lofty place, and its light extends far away. In the crowd of the ten thousand things, none is unilluminated and unseen, which is the symbol of the Great Grasp hexagram. Further, a single soft line occupies the position of respect, while a crowd of *yang* lines corresponds to it. It occupies the position of respect and holds onto its softness: things wed themselves to it. Those above and below correspond to it, which is the meaning of the Great Grasp hexagram. The Great Grasp hexagram refers to the abundance of greatness and the thickness of what is grasped.

Great Grasp: there are primacy and progress. The powers of this hexagram are capable of primacy and progress. In general, when the judgment prefaces the virtues of the hexagram with the name of the hexagram, it indicates that they are the meaning of the hexagram. This is the case for judgments such as "Close: there is good fortune" and "Meek: there is progress." In some cases, because of the meaning of the hexagram, the judgment must give a particular warning. This is the case for judgments such as "Troop: there is purity. Powerful people bring good fortune," and "The same men are in the wilderness. There is progress." In other cases, the judgment's remarks concern the powers of the trigrams, as in the case of "Great Grasp: there are primacy and progress." Because of the firmness and vigor of the first trigram, and the pattern and enlightenment of the second, "there are correspondence to heaven and action according to the moment." This is why there can be "primacy and progress."

The *Judgment* says: "Great Grasp: softness acquires the position of respect and great centrality. Those above and below correspond to it. It is called Great Grasp." The *Judgment* is explaining why this is the Great Grasp hexagram. The fifth line is *yin* and occupies the position of the ruler: "Softness acquires the position of respect." By placing itself at the center, it acquires the way of "great centrality." It is venerated by the various *yang* lines: "Those above and below correspond to it." The crowd will certainly wed itself to those who occupy the position of respect while holding to softness. Further, it grasps the virtues of an empty center, pattern and enlightenment, and great centrality, and this is why those above and below have the same tendency to correspond to it. And so they constitute the Great Grasp hexagram. "**Its virtues are firmness and vigor, as well as pattern and enlightenment. There are correspondence to heaven and action according to the moment. As a result, 'there are primacy and progress.'**" As for the virtues of the trigrams, the inner trigram has firmness and vigor while the outer has pattern and enlightenment. The fifth "six" line, or ruler, corresponds to the second "nine" line in the Lead trigram. Because the nature of the fifth line is soft, submissive, and enlightened, it can correspond with submissiveness to the second line. The second line is the master of the Lead trigram, and so it corresponds to the leader. It corresponds with submissiveness when the leader acts, which is to submit to heaven and the moment. This is why the *Judgment* says: "There are correspondence to heaven and action according to the moment." Such are its virtues, and "as a result, 'there are primacy and progress.'" Wang Bi says: "If one does not develop greatly, how could one be the cause of the great grasp? If there is a great grasp, there must also have been 'primacy and progress.'"[1] He has not understood the meaning of the hexagram, or how the Cast and Lead trigrams complete the meaning of the Great Grasp hexagram. The meaning of the Great Grasp hexagram is not that it already possesses primacy and progress but that they are caused by the trigram powers, and this is why the hexagram acquires primacy and progress. Sometimes a great grasp may not be good or may be incapable of progress. Of the various hexagrams that possess primacy, progress, profit, and purity, the *Judgment* always explains that it is "great progress," although one may fear or wonder whether the case is the same for the Lead and Yield hexagrams.[2] If the hexagram does not contain both profit and purity, then the *Judgment* explains only that there are "primacy and progress." This exhausts the meaning of primacy, which here has the meaning of greatness and goodness. Only four hexagrams contain the phrase "primacy and progress": the Great Grasp, Blight, Rise, and Tripod hexagrams, though the *Judgment* of the Rise hexagram follows the other hexagrams poorly when it produces the phrase "great progress." Someone asks: how can the primacy of the other hexagrams not be the same as in the Lead hexagram? Response: the primacy of the Lead hexagram has the meaning of "beginning," the meaning of what "goes out ahead of the numberless things."[3] In the other hexagrams, it cannot have this meaning, but only goodness and greatness, and that is all. Someone asks: primacy may be great, but how can it be good? Response: those who are primary are first among things. How could what is first among things not be good? A state of affairs that comes to its completion will later be defeated. Defeat does not come first, and then completion. What is flourishing will later become scarce; what is scarce will certainly flourish later; what is acquired will later be lost. If it had not been acquired, how could it be lost? Whether it concerns goodness and badness, order and disorder, or right and wrong—in the affairs of the world, it is never otherwise: the good must come first. This is why the *Remarks on the Text* says: "Primacy is the growth of the good."

The *Symbol* says: "Fire is above heaven: Great Grasp. Noble people use it to curb the bad and disclose the good, submitting to heaven and its mandate of restraint." The fire is lofty and "above heaven." It makes the crowd or multitude of the ten thousand things be illuminated and seen, and this is why these trigrams constitute the Great Grasp hexagram. The Great Grasp hexagram has the meaning of being complicated and numberless. Noble people gaze on the symbol of the Great Grasp hexagram, and curb or sever the crowd of bad things, while disclosing or shedding light on the good kinds of thing, so as to honor and submit to heaven and its mandate of restraint and beauty. In the crowd or multitude of the ten thousand things, each is peculiarly good or bad. When noble people feast on the abundance of the Great Grasp hexagram, it is proper that they alternate with the art of heaven and bring order and nourishment to the numberless kinds of thing. The way of bringing order to the crowd is "to curb the bad and disclose the good," and that is all. They admonish the crowd about the bad and persuade it of the good, and so they submit to the mandate of heaven and bring contentment to the group of living things.

The initial "nine" line: if it does not interact with harm, it will be without blame. If there is hardship, there will be no blame. A "nine" line occupies the initial position of the Great Grasp hexagram. It has not yet reached the point of abundance, it is placed in a humble position, and it does not correspond to anything. It does not yet have the losses of arrogance and fullness, and this is why "it does not interact with harm." That is to say, it is not yet traversing harm. In the great majority of cases when wealth is grasped, it is rare that one does not also grasp harm. If someone with the worthiness of Zigong is unable to avoid it exhaustively, what will the case be like for those below him?[4] "It will be without blame. If there is hardship, there will be no blame": the line statement is saying that to grasp wealth is not at root to grasp blame, but people become blame-worthy because they grasp wealth. Were they able to feast on their wealth, and recognize that they are in a difficult place, then there would be no blame. But if they are placed so as to grasp wealth and cannot reflect on their hardship with alarm and trembling, then a heart of arrogance and extravagance will be born in them, and so there will be blame. **The *Symbol* says: "The initial 'nine' line of the Great Grasp hexagram: 'it does not interact with harm.'"** Those who are in the initial position of the Great Grasp hexagram, but who can think about their hardship and difficulty, will not cause a heart overflowing with arrogance to be born in themselves. And so, they will not interact with or traverse harm.

The second "nine" line: the great carriage is used to bear loads. There are a long journey and no blame. This "nine" line uses *yang* firmness to occupy the second position, and the ruler or fifth "six" line delegates command to it. Since it is firm and vigorous, its power will be victorious; since it occupies a soft position, it is meek and submissive; since it has acquired centrality, it is not excessive. With such power, it can be victorious in its command over the Great Grasp hexagram, just as the strong and mighty timbers of a great carriage can be victorious in bearing things of great weight. They are capable of taking command over traveling far with a great weight, and this is why "there are a long journey and no blame." The Great Grasp hexagram refers to a moment of thickness and abundance, when one's grasp has not yet reached its limit. This is why the power of the second line can be used for a journey with no blame. If it had reached the point at which abundance was at its limit, it would not be able to make the journey. **The *Symbol* says: "'The great carriage is used to bear loads': they accumulate at the center, but it is not defeated."** Loads of great weight accumulate at the center of a great and mighty carriage, but it is not taken away or defeated. It is like the strength of the timber or force in the second "nine" line, which can be victorious in its command over the Great Grasp hexagram.

The third "nine" line: the dukes employ progress toward the son of heaven. Small people are not capable of it. The third line occupies the top position in the lower trigram substance. It is in a position below, but it occupies a position above other people, and it symbolizes the various marquises who rule over people. The dukes and marquises ascend to serve the son of heaven, while the son of heaven occupies the position of respect in the world. To administer a piece of land is nothing other than to be the king's minister. How could those in positions below dare to have an unqualified grasp on what is theirs? In general, the wealth of the land and earth, and the crowd of people—they are all in the grasp of the king. This is a straightforward principle. This is why it is proper that the third line, which occupies the position of the various marquises in the moment of the Great Grasp hexagram, and so has wealth and abundance in its grasp, must "employ progress" and development toward the son of heaven. This signifies that it considers what it grasps as grasped by the son of heaven, which is the constant duty of ministers. Were small people to be placed here, they would have an unqualified grasp on their wealth, considering it private. They do not know the way dukes honor those above. This is why the line statement says: "Small people are not capable of it." **The *Symbol* says: "'The dukes employ progress toward the son of heaven': small people do harm."** It is proper that "the dukes employ progress toward the son of heaven." Were small people to be placed here, they would do harm. Since antiquity, when the various marquises have been able to guard the reins of the minister, being loyal and submissive, and honoring those above, they have given bountiful nourishment to the crowd and become a screen that soars around the king. They thicken and enhance their resources, waiting for the levies and grants of those above. Were small people to be placed here, they would not recognize the way for a minister to honor those above. They would consider what is theirs as private to themselves. When the people come in a crowd, when resources are thick, they will poach them for their own wealth and strength, adding to themselves without submissiveness. This is how "small people do harm" in the moment of the Great Grasp hexagram. Further, the Great Grasp hexagram refers to the harm of small people.

The fourth "nine" line: it is without profusion. There is no blame. The fourth "nine" line occupies the moment of the Great Grasp hexagram, it has already exceeded the center, and it refers to the abundance of the Great Grasp hexagram. Excess abundance is what causes misfortune and blame to be born. This is why the way to place itself is to be "without profusion," and then it will acquire no blame. The phrase "without profusion" signifies that it can be meek and take away from itself, without placing itself in great abundance, and this is why it will acquire no blame. The fourth line is near the lofty position of the ruler. Were it to place itself in great abundance, it would bring about misfortune and blame. The word "profusion" refers to an appearance of abundance and multiplicity. The "Bear Along Quickly" poem says: "The water of the Wen is rushing, and rushing again. A profusion, and a profusion again, of people travel it."[5] The condition here is that of an abundance and multiplicity of travelers. The "Great Enlightenment" ode says: "The team of four bays is profuse, and profuse again."[6] It is remarking on the abundance of King Wu's warhorses. **The *Symbol* says: "'It is without profusion. There is no blame': it sheds light and distinguishes with discernment."** This line refers to those who do not place themselves in abundance and who acquire no blame. In fact, they grasp the wisdom to shed light on and distinguish things. The word "discernment" refers to enlightened wisdom. Worthy and wise people shed light on and distinguish the principles of things. When facing abundance at its starting point, they know that their blame is about to become extreme. This is why they can take from and impede themselves, and do not dare reach the limit of satiety.

The fifth "six" line: it trusts its fellow, as though interacting, as though authoritative. There is good fortune. The fifth "six" line faces the moment of the Great Grasp hexagram, it occupies the position of the ruler, its center is empty, and it symbolizes being trusted and believed. If those who rule hold to softness and guard their centrality, if they are trustworthy and believable, and respond to those below, then those below will also be exhaustively believable and sincere in managing the affairs of those above. Those above and below will be trustworthy and believable in their interactions with each other. It uses softness to occupy the position of respect, it faces the moment of the Great Grasp hexagram, and people's hearts are contented and at ease. Were it to value softness and submission without qualification, then it would give birth to usurpation and lethargy. This is why it must be "as though authoritative," and then "there is good fortune." The phrase "as though authoritative" signifies that it grasps authority and severity. Since it uses softness and harmony to be trustworthy and believable in responding to those below, the crowd will tend to enjoy and attend to it. Further, by grasping authority and severity, it makes it tremble in its grasp. This is to place oneself well in the Grasp hexagram, and its good fortune should be recognized. **The *Symbol* says: "'It trusts its fellow, as though interacting': it is believable when revealing its tendencies. There is good fortune in being 'as though authoritative': it is at ease and not prepared."** The tendency of those below is to attend to those above. When those above are trustworthy and believable in responding to those below, those below will also be sincere and believable in managing the affairs of those above. This is why "it trusts its fellow, as though interacting." Because those above are trustworthy and believable when they reveal their trustworthy and believable tendency to those below, those below attend to those above like an echo corresponding to one's voice. That there is good fortune because it is "as though authoritative" signifies that, if it were not authoritative or severe, those below would be at ease and lethargic, being neither warned nor prepared. This signifies the way of those who are not modest, trembling, or prepared for those above. The word "prepared" here signifies that they are prepared for those above to seek out and reproach them.

The top "nine" line: heaven itself upholds it. There is good fortune. Nothing is without profit. The top "nine" line is at the end of the hexagram and occupies a terrain without position—that is, it is at the limit of the Great Grasp hexagram and does not occupy the position that it grasps. It is placed at the top of the Cast trigram, which is to be at the limit of enlightenment. It is only because of its extreme enlightenment that it does not occupy the position that it grasps, and it does not reach the point of excess or the limit. Since it grasps the limit but does not place itself there, it is without the disaster of fullness and satiety, and it is able to submit to principle. The top line walks on the trustworthy and believable fifth line, which means that it treads or walks on what is sincere and believable. The fifth grasps the virtues of pattern and enlightenment, and the top line can diminish its tendencies in order to correspond to it, which means that it values the worthy and venerates the good. To place oneself like this is extreme alignment with the way. It is proper that it feast on blessings and delights, and so "heaven itself upholds it." Its action is submissive to heaven, and it obtains the sustenance of heaven. This is why all its journeys bring good fortune, and "nothing is without profit." **The *Symbol* says: "In the top line of the Great Grasp hexagram, 'there is good fortune': heaven itself upholds it."** The top line of the Great Grasp hexagram grasps the limit, and it is proper that there be alteration, but it submits to heaven and aligns with the way in what it does. This is why heaven upholds and helps it, and so "there is good fortune." Noble people are satisfied without overflowing, and so heaven upholds them. The *Appended Statements* explicates this, saying that "heaven helps those who are submissive, and other people help those who are believable. It walks on a believable line, and it reflects on its submissiveness. Further, it values the worthy, and as a result, 'heaven itself upholds it. There is good fortune. Nothing is without profit.'"[7] "It walks on a believable line": this signifies that it walks on the fifth line. The fifth line has an empty center, which indicates that it is believable. "It reflects on its submissiveness": this signifies that it meekly retreats without occupying its position. "It values the worthy": this signifies that it tends to attend to the fifth line. In the time of the Great Grasp hexagram, those who are full and thick should not place themselves in positions of fullness—this is not what is fitting. Among the six lines, those at the center take pleasure in seizing the positions for which they have an aptitude. Only the initial and top lines do not place themselves in their positions, and this is why "there is no blame" for the initial "nine" line, and "nothing is without profit" for the top "nine" line. The top "nine" line is at the top, but it walks on a believable line and reflects on its submissiveness. This is why it acquires good fortune even though it is at the top. In fact, "heaven itself upholds it."

15. MEEK (QIAN 謙)

The *Sequence of the Hexagrams* says: "Those whose grasp is great should not become full, and this is why the Meek hexagram is next." Those whose grasp has become great should not reach the point of fullness and satiety. They must be meek and take something away from themselves. This is why, after the Great Grasp hexagram, the Meek hexagram is next. As for the trigrams, the Yield trigram is above and the Calm trigram below. "At the center of the earth, there is a mountain": the substance of the earth is humble and in a position below, while a mountain is a lofty and great thing. Because it occupies a position below the earth, it is the symbol of meekness. The use of venerable and lofty virtues while one is placed below something humble is the meaning of the Meek hexagram.

Meek: there is progress. Noble people achieve their end. The Meek hexagram possesses the way of progress. To possess virtue without occupying a position is what the word "meekness" signifies. When people place themselves with meekness and lowliness, how could they go on a journey without making progress? "Noble people achieve their end": the tendencies of noble people are persistently meek and lowly. They attain the principle, and this is why they take pleasure in heaven and do not struggle with it. They are replenished on the inside, and this is why they retreat and abdicate, and do not seek sympathy. They are content to walk in meekness, and to the end of their lives they do not change. People add to and respect those who humble themselves. When they obscure themselves, it only adds to the brightness and clarity of their virtue. This is what is signified by "noble people achieve their end." As for small people, when they have a desire, they must struggle to achieve it, and when they have a virtue, they must attack everyone with it. Although they may exhort themselves to be adoring and meek, they are incapable of acting with contentment and keeping guard with certainty. That is, they are incapable of achieving their end.

The *Judgment* says: "'Meek: there is progress.' The way of heaven sustains those below and is bright and enlightened. The way of earth is humble and acts on those above." The phrase "sustains" should instead be "borders."[1] The *Judgment* sheds light on the meaning of the Meek hexagram and its capacity for progress. The way of heaven uses its *qi* to border those below. This is why it can transform and cultivate the ten thousand things. Its way is "bright and enlightened." "Borders those below": this signifies that it interacts with those below. The way of earth uses a place of humility, and so its *qi* acts on those above—that is, it interacts with heaven. It is everywhere humble and diminished, and so there is progress. "The way of heaven makes the full inadequate but adds to the meek." Concerning the action of heaven, the *Judgment* remarks that it will make those who are full inadequate but that it will add to those who are meek. This is the case for the sun and moon, and for the *yin* and *yang qi*. "The way of earth alters the full and lets the meek flow." Concerning the propensity of the earth, the *Judgment* remarks that those who are full or satiated will collapse and be altered, and revert to what has snared them. There will be a flowing into and concentrating, an adding to and increasing, of those who at the bottom of humility. "Ghosts and spirits harm the full and bless the meek." The phrase "ghosts and spirits" signifies the traces of creation and transformation. They afflict and harm those who are full and satiated, while they bless and uphold those who are meek, who have had something taken away from them. In general, if there is excess, something will be taken away from it. If there is insufficiency, something will be added to it. This is always the case. "The way of humans detests the full and prefers the meek." It is human inclination to be made ill by and to detest those who are full and satiated, while preferring and agreeing with those who are meek and lowly. Meekness is the extremity of human virtue. This is why the sage delineates it in words, warning people against fullness and persuading them to be meek. "Meekness is respected and bright. It is humble and yet nothing may overshoot it. This is the end of noble people." To be meek is to be humble and lowly, but the way of meekness is respected and great, bright and clear. Although its place is humble and contracted, its virtue is so full and lofty that nothing further can be attached to its value—that is, "nothing may overshoot it." Noble people are extremely sincere in their meekness. It lasts and does not alter, and so they achieve their end. This is why it is "respected and bright."

The *Symbol* says: "At the center of the earth, there is a mountain: Meek. Noble people use it to accrue from the many and add to the few. They balance things with their level influence." The substance of the earth is at the bottom of humility. The mountain is lofty and great, yet it is at the center of the earth. Together they symbolize someone who is at the bottom of humility on the outside, but collects loftiness and greatness on the inside. This is why these trigrams constitute the Meek hexagram. The *Symbol* does not say "the mountain is at the center of the earth," but "at the center of the earth, there is a mountain." It is remarking that at its center, at the bottom of humility, it collects what is venerable and lofty. Were it to remark that what is venerable and lofty is collected at its center, at the bottom of humility, then the principle of the text would not be submissive. Such is always the case for the various symbols, as should be apparent to anyone who gazes on the text. "Noble people use it to accrue from the many and add to the few. They balance things with their level influence": noble people gaze on the symbol of the Meek hexagram. There is a mountain, and it is below the earth—that is, the lofty descends and the humble ascends. They see the meaning of impeding the lofty and bringing up those below, of taking from the excessive and adding to the insufficient. When they influence affairs, they accrue or choose from the many, and they increase or add to the few. They balance things that are many or few by evening out their influence and making it to become level.

The initial "six" line: it is meek, and meek again. Noble people are employed to traverse a great stream. There is good fortune. The initial "six" line uses softness and submission to place itself meekly. Further, it occupies the bottom position of a trigram, which is to place oneself at the very bottom of humility. It combines meekness with further meekness, and this is why the line statement says that "it is meek, and meek again." Those who can act like this are noble people. They place themselves in extreme meekness so that they may share themselves with the crowd. If they are without distress or harm even when they are "employed to traverse" the obstacle or difficulty, what will the case be like when they occupy positions of peace and ease? How could they be without good fortune? Since the initial line places itself meekly by using softness to occupy the bottom position, how could it not acquire excessive meekness? Response: it is ordinary for softness to occupy a position below. But here it seems to be extremely meek, and this is why "it is meek, and meek again." It does not yet seem to have lost anything. **The *Symbol* says: "'It is meek and meek again': it uses humility in going to the pasture."** "It is meek, and meek again": this refers to extreme meekness, and signifies that noble people use the way of meekness and humility to go to the pasture. To go to the pasture is to place oneself, as when the *Book of Poetry* says: "She went to the pasture and came back with wildings."[2]

The second "six" line: its meekness is eloquent. There are purity and good fortune. The second line uses softness and submission to occupy the center—that is, the virtue of meekness accumulates at the center. The virtue of meekness is replete and accumulated at the center, and this is why it is revealed on the outside. It is seen in the tone of one's voice and the shade of one's countenance, and this is why the line statement says that "its meekness is eloquent." To occupy the center and acquire straightforwardness is to possess the virtues of centrality and straightforwardness. This is why it says that "there are purity and good fortune." In general, when it speaks of purity and good fortune, it indicates either that there are purity and good fortune or that there will be good fortune if one acquires purity. The purity and good fortune of the second "six" line are what it possesses in itself. **The *Symbol* says: "'Its meekness is eloquent. There are purity and good fortune': it is acquired by the center or heart."** The second line possesses the virtue of meekness because extreme sincerity accumulates at its center. As a result, it is revealed in the tone of its voice. The center or heart acquires this by itself, without being exhorted to do it.

The third "nine" line: it labors in meekness. Noble people achieve their end. There is good fortune. The third line uses the virtue of *yang* firmness to occupy a position in the lower trigram substance. The crowd of *yin* lines venerates it, it acquires a position with its walk, and it is the top line in the lower trigram. It is given command by the ruler above and attended to by the crowd below, and it refers to those who labor at their task while wielding the virtue of meekness. This is why the line statement says that "it labors in meekness." There were people in antiquity, such as the Duke of Zhou, for whom this was proper. It was proper for him to take great command over the world, since he honored a master above him who was young and weak. He went "to the pasture" with meekness and modesty, shuddering, and shuddering again, as though he were trembling.[3] One could say that he was capable of meekness in his labor. Although noble people may be capable of laboring in meekness, they must still act on it and "achieve their end," and then there will be good fortune. As for taking pleasure in loftiness and being made happy by victories, these are the ordinary inclinations of people. It is certainly seldom that one can be meek in a moment of peace. What will be the case for those who can acquire respect only by laboring at their task? Even though they may be made to recognize that meekness is good, and may be exhorted to act on it, if they do not forget the heart that carries sympathy for itself, then they will not be able to make it constant and continuous. They will want to achieve their end, but will be unable to acquire it. Only noble people are content to walk with meekness and submission as their constant act. This is why it continues in them without alteration, and they may be said to achieve their end. Since they achieve their end, there will be good fortune. This third "nine" line uses firmness to occupy a straightforward position—that is, it can achieve its end. The virtue of this line is extremely abundant, and this is why the *Symbol* statement gives it special weight. **The *Symbol* says: "'It labors in meekness. Noble people': the ten thousand people obey."** The ten thousand people respect and obey the noble person who can labor in meekness. The *Appended Statements* says: "To labor without making it into a boast, to accomplish something without making it into a virtue—these are extremely beneficial. They describe those who accomplish something while descending below other people, whose virtue is said to be abundant and whose ritual is said to be modest. By bringing about modesty in their meekness, they persist in their positions."[4] To labor without seeking sympathy for oneself or boasting, to accomplish something without considering oneself to be virtuous—these are the extremes of virtue, immensity, and beneficence. They speak of laboring at one's task while making oneself meek by descending below other people. Their "virtue is said to be abundant" and their "ritual is said to be modest": concerning their virtue, one may remark that it is extremely abundant; concerning the ritual by which they place themselves, one may remark that it is extremely modest. This is what is signified by the word "meekness." As for their meekness, it signifies that they bring about modesty to persist in their positions. The word "persist" here refers to keeping guard. They bring about modesty and lowliness to keep guard over their positions. This is why they are lofty without peril and satisfied without overflowing. As a result, they can achieve their end and possess good fortune. As for the walking in meekness of noble people, it is their constant act and is not done to preserve their positions. When it says that they "persist in their positions," it is because they can bring about modesty and so persist in their positions. It is simply saying that the way of meekness is like this. If it were saying that they become good to possess titles and fame—how could noble people become good so as to be titled and famous? It would be saying that titles and fame are the reasons why they become good.[5]

The fourth "six" line: nothing is without profit. It gestures with meekness. The fourth line occupies a position in the upper trigram substance and is quite near to the position of the ruler. Further, the fifth "six" line or ruler places itself with meekness and softness, and the third "nine" line possesses great accomplishment and virtue. Those above give it command, and the crowd below venerates it. Since the fourth line occupies a position above, it is proper that it be modest and trembling when honoring its meek and virtuous ruler, and that it be humble and lowly when abdicating before the meek and laboring minister. In its movement, production, and influence, "nothing is without profit" when it "gestures with meekness." The word "gesture" refers to a shape that influences by cutting into sections, as when people gesture with their hands. Whether it moves or rests, advances or retreats, it must be meek in its influence. This is, in fact, because it occupies a terrain where there is a great deal of trouble, and because it is above a worthy minister. **The *Symbol* says: "'Nothing is without profit. It gestures with meekness': it does not draw back from the regulations."** In general, there are fitting places for people to be meek in their influence, and they should not exceed what is fitting. For example, the fifth "six" line sometimes employs "invasion and attack." Only the fourth line places itself on a terrain that is near the ruler and above a laboring minister. This is why, in general, in its movement and production, nothing is without profit when it is meek in its influence. In a case like this, it will afterward come to be at the center of the laws and regulations. This is why the *Symbol* says that "it does not draw back from the regulations," which signifies that it acquires what is fitting.

The fifth "six" line: it has no wealth but uses its neighbors. There is profit in employing invasion and attack. Nothing is without profit. The crowd weds itself to wealth. Only this resource is capable of gathering people. The fifth line has the respect of the ruler's position, but it holds to meekness and submission and responds to those below. The crowd weds itself to it, and this is why "it has no wealth but" is able to use "its neighbors." The word "neighbors" refers to those who are nearby. It has no wealth, but it acquires a relationship with other people. When the rulers wield meekness and submission, the hearts of the world wed themselves to them. Nonetheless, the way of the ruler should not value meekness and softness without qualification. They must necessarily make the crossing together with authority in war, and afterward they will be able to cherish the world and make it obedient. This is why "there is profit in employing" the actions of "invasion and attack." When authority and virtue are both manifest, they will afterward exhaust what is fitting concerning the way of the ruler, and nothing will be without profit. In fact, it is proper that the meekness and softness of the fifth line defend themselves against excess, and this is why the line statement reveals this meaning. **The *Symbol* says: "'There is profit in employing invasion and attack': it takes the field against the disobedient."** "It takes the field against" everyone who cannot be made obedient through pattern, virtue, meekness, and lowliness. If it does not employ authority in war against those who cannot be made obedient through pattern and virtue, how can it bring peace and order to the world? It will not be on the central way of the ruler but will be excessively meek.

The top "six" line: its meekness is eloquent. There is profit in employing the action of troops. It takes the field against the district of the states. This "six" line uses softness to place itself in a soft position at the limit of the submission trigram. Further, it is placed at the limit of the Meek hexagram and refers to the limit of meekness. It uses the limit of meekness, but it occupies a lofty position, and so its tendency toward meekness has not yet been successful. This is why it reaches the point of being revealed in the tone of its voice. Further, because softness has placed itself at the limit of meekness, this must be seen in its voice and countenance. This is why the line statement says that "its meekness is eloquent." Although it occupies a terrain without position and does not have command over the affairs of the world, it is still the case that the firmness and softness of a person's own actions must make the crossing together. The top line is at the limit of the Meek hexagram. If it reaches the point at which it becomes too extreme, then it will revert to excess meekness. This is why the profit lies in setting oneself in order with warlike firmness. The phrase "the district of the states" refers to one's own private possessions. "The action of troops" signifies the employment of warlike firmness. "It takes the field against the district of the states": this signifies that it sets its own private possessions in order. **The *Symbol* says: "'Its meekness is eloquent': its tendencies have not yet acquired their object. It should employ 'the action of troops': 'it takes the field against the district of the states.'"** It is at the limit of the Meek hexagram and occupies the top position, and so it has not yet acquired the meekness that it tends toward or desires. This is why it is not victorious over its ardency, and reaches the point of eloquence. Although its position is not proper for it, and its meekness is already excessive and at its limit, it is fitting that it set its private things in order with warlike firmness. This is why the line statement says that "there is profit in employing the action of troops. It takes the field against the district of the states."

16. CHEER (*YU* 豫)

The *Sequence of the Hexagrams* says: "Those whose grasp is great, yet who are capable of meekness, must be of good cheer. This is why the Cheer hexagram is next." It serves the meaning of the two preceding hexagrams, and so it succeeds them. Those whose grasp is already great, yet who are capable of meekness, will also have cheer and pleasure in their grasp. The word "cheer" means contentment, harmony, enjoyment, and pleasure. As for the trigrams, the Shake trigram is above and the Yield trigram below, which symbolizes submissiveness and movement. There is movement, but with harmony and submissiveness, and as a result there is cheer. The fourth "nine" line is the master of the movement. The groups of *yin* lines above and below share a correspondence to it. Further, the Yield trigram serves it submissively. As a result, when it moves, those above and below correspond to it submissively, and this is why these lines have the meaning of harmony and cheer. Concerning the two trigram symbols, one may remark that thunder goes out above the earth. At the beginning, *yang* is hidden and locked away at the center of the earth. As soon as it moves, it goes out from the earth, and it is aroused to reveal itself in sound. It develops smoothly with harmony and cheer. This is why these trigrams constitute the Cheer hexagram.

Cheer: there is profit in establishing the marquises and putting the troops into action. The Cheer hexagram refers to submission and movement. Given that it has this meaning, the profit in the Cheer hexagram lies in "establishing the marquises and putting the troops into action." As for "the establishment of the marquises, they are like a screen of trees," and so they share in bringing contentment to the world.[1] If the various marquises are harmonious and submissive, then the ten thousand people will possess enjoyment and obedience when mustered to become a troop of soldiers. If the heart of the crowd possesses harmony and enjoyment, then it will be submissive and attentive, and something will be accomplished. This is why, concerning the way of enjoyment and cheer, "there is profit in establishing the marquises and putting the troops into action." Further, the upper trigram refers to movement and the lower trigram to submissiveness, which symbolizes the various marquises attending to the king, and the crowd of troops submitting to his decree. To rule the ten thousand kingdoms, to gather a great crowd, to make it attend and obey—this would be impossible without harmony and enjoyment.

The *Judgment* says: "Cheer: firmness corresponds, and its tendency is to act. There is submission in its movement: Cheer." The phrase "firmness corresponds" signifies that the fourth line corresponds to the group of *yin* lines. The firm line has acquired a crowd of corresponding lines. "Its tendency is to act" signifies that *yang* has a tendency to ascend and act. When it moves, those above and below will attend to it submissively. That is, its tendency acquires their action. "There is submission in its movement: Cheer": the Shake trigram refers to movement and the Yield trigram to submission. Together they refer to movement and then submission to principle, or submission to principle and then movement, or further, to movement and then the submission of the crowd—and so these trigrams constitute the Cheer hexagram. "There is cheerful submission in its movement. This is why heaven and earth resemble it. Is this not the case in which to establish the marquises and put the troops into action?" If it makes use of cheerful submission and then moves, "heaven and earth resemble it" and will not draw back. In "the case in which to establish the marquises and put the troops into action," how could there not be submission? As for the way of heaven and earth, or the principle of the ten thousand things, it is nothing but extreme submission, and that is all. And so, when "great people" either "precede heaven" or "follow heaven," and it "does not draw back," this, too, is submission to principle, and that is all.[2] "Heaven and earth are submissive in their movement. This is why the sun and moon are not excessive, and the four seasons do not waver. If sages are submissive in their movement, then punishments and penalties will be clear and the people will obey." The *Judgment* now turns to delineate in words the way of submissive movement. The revolutions of heaven and earth "are submissive in their movement," and so the measure of the days and months neither exceeds its period nor strays. Likewise, the action of the four seasons neither violates its period nor wavers. "Sages are submissive in their movement," and this is why their traditions are straightforward and the people will be mustered to goodness. "Punishments and penalties will be clear" and uncomplicated, and the ten thousand people "will obey." "How great are the moment and the meaning of cheer!" Although the

Judgment has already spoken about the way of cheerful submission, the savor of its implications is an endless abyss. Even when one's words are exhausted, it still has a surplus of intentions. This is why it applauds it, saying: "How great are the moment and the meaning of cheer!" It wants people to polish and savor its principle, so that they become gladdened and softened, and soak themselves from swimming in it, so that they may understand it. "The moment and the meaning" signify the moment and the meaning of the Cheer hexagram. When the word "great" is employed together with "moment" and "meaning" in various hexagrams, it is always to applaud their greatness. Cheer is one of the eleven hexagrams that are like this: in the Cheer, Flee, Pair, and March hexagrams, the *Judgment* speaks of the moment and the meaning; in the Pit, Split, and Limp hexagrams, it speaks of the moment and the function; in the Feed, Great Excess, Loose, and Hide hexagrams, it speaks only of the moment. In each case, it refers to their greatness.

The *Symbol* says: "Thunder is aroused to go out from the earth: Cheer. The first kings produced music to venerate virtue. Its magnificence was offered to the lord on high, making him a match for their progenitors and old men." Thunder is the arousing and revealing of the *yang qi*, when *yin* and *yang* approach each other and bring their sound to completion. At the beginning, *yang* is hidden and locked away at the center of the earth. As soon as it moves, it "is aroused to go out from the earth" and to shake. At the beginning, it is locked away and impenetrable, but as soon as it is aroused to reveal itself, its development will be smooth, harmonious, and cheerful. This is why these trigrams constitute the Cheer hexagram. The Yield trigram refers to submissiveness and the Shake trigram to revelation. Harmony and submissiveness accumulate at the center and reveal themselves in sound — this is symbolized by music. When the first kings gazed on the symbol of thunder aroused to go out from the earth, and harmoniously and smoothly revealed in sound, they produced musical sounds to solemnize and venerate accomplishments and virtue. Their magnificent abundance reached the point of being "offered to the lord on high," which unfolded by "making him a match for their progenitors and old men." The word "magnificence" refers to abundance. The *Book of Rites* refers to a "magnificent oblation," where "magnificent" signifies "abundant."[3] An offering to the lord on high, "making him a match for their progenitors and old men," is the extreme of abundance.

The initial "six" line: cheer is eloquent. There is misfortune. The initial "six" line uses *yin* softness to occupy the bottom position. The fourth line is the master of the Cheer hexagram, and the initial line corresponds to it. That is, small people without centrality or straightforwardness are placed in the Cheer hexagram, and are favored by those above. Their tendencies or intentions are at the limit of satisfaction. They cannot be victorious over their cheer, reaching the point at which it is revealed in the sound of their voices. Those who are lightweight and shallow like this must reach the point of misfortune. The word "eloquent" refers to what is revealed in sound. **The *Symbol* says: "In the initial 'six' line, 'cheer is eloquent': when its tendencies are depleted, 'there is misfortune.'"** When it says "the initial 'six' line," it signifies that it uses *yin* softness to place itself in the bottom position. Its tendencies or intentions are depleted or at their limit, and it cannot be victorious over its cheer, reaching the point that it is "eloquent." It will necessarily become arrogant and indulgent, and will bring about misfortune.

The second "six" line: there is the security of stone, but not at the end of the day. Purity brings good fortune. Those who surrender themselves to the way of leisure and cheer will lose their straightforwardness. This is why few of the various lines in the Cheer hexagram have acquired straightforwardness—their powers are aligned with the moment.[4] Of all the lines, only the second "six" line places itself with centrality and straightforwardness. Further, it has no corresponding line, which symbolizes keeping guard over itself. Of those that face the moment of the Cheer hexagram, it alone can guard itself with centrality and straightforwardness. This may be called the wielding of its "special setup."[5] In such a case, its reining in of itself and its security are like the solidity of stone. "There is the security of stone": its security is like that of stone. As for the cheer and pleasure of people, their hearts enjoy them. This is why they linger, and linger again, and succeed in reaching the point at which they give themselves over to addiction and cannot put it in the past. The second line guards itself with centrality and straightforwardness, its security is like that of stone, and the rapidity of its departure is such that it does not await "the end of the day." This is why there are "purity" and straightforwardness, and also "good fortune." Those who are placed in the Cheer hexagram should not be content with its continuation. If it continues, they will drown in it. To be like the second line may be called "seeing the incipient and going to work."[6] Because the second line sees the incipient, Fuzi speaks about the limit of the way of recognizing the incipient, saying: "To recognize the incipient, is this not spiritual? Noble people do not flatter when interacting with those above and are not disdainful when interacting with those below. Is this not to recognize the incipient? The incipient is the minimum of movement and sees good fortune ahead of time. Noble people see the incipient and go to work without awaiting the end of the day. The *Book of Changes* says: 'There is the security of stone, but not at the end of the day. Purity brings good fortune.' As for those whose security is like stone, their decisions should be understood rather than employed at the end of the day. Noble people recognize both what is minimal and what is on display, both the soft and the firm—the hope of the ten thousand men!"[7] As for seeing affairs when they are incipient and minimal, is this not spiritual and mysterious? Noble people do not reach the point of flattery when interacting with those above and do not reach the point of disdain when interacting with those below. In fact, they recognize the incipient. If they did not recognize the incipient, it would reach the point of excess without being put in the past. They are modest and lowly when interacting with those above; this is why the excess here is flattery. They are harmonious and at ease when interacting with those below; this is why the excess here is disdain. Noble people see the incipient or minimal, and this is why it does not reach the point of excess. What is called the incipient is the minimal movement at the beginning. The impetus of good or bad fortune may be seen ahead of time, when it is not yet manifest. Fuzi only speaks of good fortune because, if it is seen ahead of time, how could it reach the point at which there is misfortune? Noble people are enlightened and wise, seeing affairs while they are incipient and minimal. This is why, if they can make their security like stone and guard themselves with solidity, they will be enlightened and without bewilderment. If they see movement while it is minimal, how could they await the end of the day? The word "decisions" refers to their discrimination. What is cut out and discriminated may be seen. What is minimal and what is on display are opposed to each other like the soft and the firm. If noble people see what is minimal, they will also recognize what is on display. If they see what is soft, they will also recognize what is firm. Those who recognize the incipient like this are admired by the crowd. This is why he applauds them, saying that they are "the hope of the ten thousand men!" **The *Symbol* says: "'But not at the end of the day. Purity brings good fortune': it is central and straightforward."** It is capable of purity and good fortune that are "not at the end of the day"—that is, it possesses the virtues of centrality and straightforwardness. Since "it is central and straightforward," it will guard itself with solidity, make early distinctions, and depart rapidly.[8] The *Symbol* speaks of the way in which the second "six" line places itself in the Cheer hexagram, and the intention of its teaching is deep.

The third "six" line: gaping at cheer brings regrets. Lingering brings regrets. The third "six" line is *yin* occupying a *yang* position and refers to people without centrality or straightforwardness. When they place themselves in the Cheer hexagram without centrality or straightforwardness, their every movement will bring regrets. The word "gaping" refers to looking upward. Although it regards with hope the fourth line above it, it will not be chosen by the fourth because it is neither central nor straightforward. This is why it has regrets. The fourth line is the master of the Cheer hexagram, and the third is quite near to it. If it lingers, and lingers again, without going ahead, it will see itself deserted and severed, and it will have regrets. In fact, those who place themselves without straightforwardness will have regrets and dismay whether they advance or retreat. What sort of action is proper for it? It should make itself straightforward, and that is all. Noble people place themselves on the way and control their hearts with ritual. Although they are placed in the moment of the Cheer hexagram, they will not lose their centrality and straightforwardness. This is why they are without regret. **The *Symbol* says: "'Gaping at cheer brings regrets': its position is not proper for it."** It does not place itself properly, and so it loses its centrality and straightforwardness. As a result, it will have regrets whether it advances or retreats.

The fourth "nine" line: it is the cause of cheer, it acquires greatness, and it is without doubt. Its friends team up, and it clasps them. The Cheer hexagram refers to cheer because of the fourth "nine" line. When it moves, the crowd of *yin* lines enjoys and submits to it as the master of the movement trigram, and this is the meaning of the Cheer hexagram. The fourth is the position of the great minister, and the ruler or fifth "six" line submits and attends to it. It uses *yang* firmness and is given command over the affairs of those above, which is the cause of cheer. This is why the line statement says that it is "the cause of cheer." The phrase "it acquires greatness" is saying that it acquires a great action with its tendencies, and this brings about the cheer of the world. "It is without doubt. Its friends team up, and it clasps them": the fourth line occupies the position of the great minister, it serves a soft and weak ruler, and it faces command over the world, which is a terrain of peril and doubt. It is proper that those above delegate command only to it, and there is no one of the same virtue among those below to help it. As a result, it is doubtful. It is proper that it do nothing but exhaust its extreme sincerity and be without doubt or apprehension. Then it is proper that friends of its own kind team up and gather. As for those who want to be believed by those above and below, they have only to be extremely sincere, and that is all. If they exhaust their extreme sincerity, how could they be distressed at having no help? The word "clasps" refers to a gathering. It is called "clasp" from the clasp that chooses and gathers some of the hair. Someone asks: since the hexagram has only one *yang* line, how could it acquire help from those of the same virtue? Response: there is a principle by which those who occupy positions above will necessarily acquire the help they seek, so long as they are extremely sincere. This is the case for the fifth "nine" line of the Pair hexagram, where the line statement says that "something falls from heaven." The fourth line uses *yang* firmness, is set near the position of the ruler, and is the unqualified master of the Cheer hexagram. It is fitting that the sage give a warning so that it does not do otherwise. The Cheer hexagram refers to the way of harmony and submissiveness. Because of its way of harmony and submissiveness, it will not lose what is straightforward for a minister. If the unqualified master of the Cheer hexagram is like this, it will take command over the affairs of the world and bring about the moment of cheer. This is why he warns it only to be extremely sincere and without doubt. **The *Symbol* says: "'It is the cause of cheer, it acquires greatness': it tends toward a great action."** It is itself the cause that brings the world to pleasure and cheer. This is why "it acquires greatness," which signifies that its tendencies acquire a great action.

The fifth "six" line: purity brings illness. What lasts will never die. The fifth "six" line uses *yin* softness to occupy the position of the ruler, it faces the moment of the Cheer hexagram, it sinks into and drowns in cheer, and it refers to those who cannot set themselves up. The aptitude that masters others, the gathering that weds others to itself—these belong only to the fourth line. The *yang* firmness of the fourth line acquires the crowd and cannot be controlled by soft and weak rulers who have given themselves over to bewilderment. Soft and weak rulers who cannot set themselves up will be controlled by ministers of unqualified aptitude. The word "purity" here refers to occupying and acquiring the position of the ruler, whose "illness" or bitterness lies in being controlled by those below. Since a "six" line occupies the position of respect, its position has not yet vanished, even though it has lost its aptitude. This is why the line statement says: "Purity brings illness. What lasts will never die." It is remarking that there is illness in purity, that this illness is constant and that it will never die. Such is the case of the rulers during the final ages of the Han and Wei dynasties.[9] There is no single way that brings rulers into peril and makes them vanish, but many consider it to be the Cheer hexagram. It does not remark that the fourth line has lost its straightforwardness but that the fifth line seems to be oppressed by its strength. At its root, the fourth line has not lost anything, and this is why it remarks that the meaning of the fourth line is the great minister with command over the affairs of the world. Of the fifth line, it remarks that it occupies the position of respect with softness and weakness, and that it is unable to set itself up, which means that authority and aptitude have departed from it. Each meaning is chosen in accordance with its particular line, and this is why they are not the same. If the fifth line does not lose the way of the ruler and yet the fourth is the master of the Cheer hexagram, it is because it has given command to someone who can bring a feast of contentment to the task. Such were the cases of Tai Jia and King Cheng.[10] In the Blind hexagram, too, a *yin* line occupies the position of respect while the second line, being *yang*, is the master of the Blind hexagram. There it brings good fortune, while here it brings illness, because the moments are not the same. It is fitting that the child, who is blind, owe something to another person. But to lose everything to another person by giving oneself over to cheer is the way to bring oneself into peril and to vanish. This is why, when they correspond to each other in the Blind hexagram, the one delegates command to the other, but when they press against each other in the Cheer hexagram, the one loses its aptitude to the other. Further, the hearts of those above and below are wedded without qualification to the fourth line. **The *Symbol* says: "In the fifth 'six' line, 'purity brings illness': it rides on firmness. 'What lasts will never die': centrality has not yet vanished."** If there is purity, there will be illness. It "rides on firmness" because a firm line presses against it. "What lasts will never die": the "centrality" of the position of respect "has not yet vanished."

The top "six" line: the gloom of cheer is completed. If it adapts, there will be no blame. The top "six" line is *yin* and soft, it does not possess the virtues of centrality and straightforwardness, and it uses *yin* to occupy the top position. As a result, it is not straightforward. It faces the moment when the Cheer hexagram is at its limit. If it is proper that even noble people occupying positions in such a moment be warned and troubled, what will the case be like for people of *yin* softness? When they give themselves over to indulgence in the Cheer hexagram, they become dark and confused, and do not know how to reverse themselves. They are now at the end of the Cheer hexagram, and this is why their darkness and gloom are already complete. If they could adapt and alter themselves, they would be able to be without blame. To be at the end of the Cheer hexagram means that there is alteration. When people lose themselves, if they can alter themselves, they are always able to be without blame. This is why, although "the gloom of cheer" is already "complete," it will still be good if it can alter itself. The sage reveals this meaning to persuade people to relocate to the good. This is why he does not go on to speak about the misfortune of gloom, but says without qualification that those who adapt are without blame. **The *Symbol* says: "In the top line, there is 'the gloom of cheer': how could it grow?"** The darkness and gloom of the Cheer hexagram has reached its end and limit, and blame for the disaster will now be extended to it. How could it grow in such a state? It is proper that it rapidly adapt.

17. FOLLOW (*SUI* 隨)

The *Sequence of the Hexagrams* says: "When there is cheer, people will neces-sarily follow it, and this is why the Follow hexagram is next." As for the way of enjoyment and cheer, it is what things follow, and so the Follow hexagram succeeds the Cheer hexagram. As for the trigrams, the Joy trigram is above and the Shake trigram below. The Joy trigram refers to enjoyment and the Shake trigram to movement. To enjoy and then move, to move and then enjoy—both of these are the meaning of the Follow hexagram. It is the case that women fol-low men, and here a young woman attends to a grown man—this is the mean-ing of the Follow hexagram. Further, the Shake trigram refers to thunder and the Joy trigram to the lake. Thunder shakes at the center of the lake, and the lake follows it and moves—this is the symbol of the Follow hexagram. Further, concerning the alteration of the trigrams, one may remark that the top line of the Lead trigram has arrived to occupy the bottom position of the Yield trigram, and the initial line of the Yield trigram makes the journey to occupy the top position of the Lead trigram. The *yang* line has arrived at the bottom of the *yin* lines. Since the *yang* line is below the *yin* lines, the *yin* lines must enjoy and follow it, which constitutes the meaning of the Follow hexagram. In general, when one has already chosen the meaning of the complete hexagram from its two trigram substances, then one goes on to choose the meaning of the lines, and then there is still the choice of the meaning of the hexagram's alteration. The case of choosing meanings for the Follow hexagram in particular is delin-eated perfectly.

Follow: there are primacy, progress, profit, and purity, and no blame. The way of the Follow hexagram can bring about great progress. The way of noble people is what the crowd follows, whether they themselves are followed by other people, or they watch over affairs and select what is to be followed—both are instances of following. When this following acquires the way, it can bring about great progress. In general, when rulers attend to the good, and the ministers below them honor their mandate, and learned people attend to their duty, watching over affairs and attending to their growth—all of these are instances of following. Concerning the way of the Follow hexagram, the profit lies in purity and straightforwardness. When the following acquires straightforwardness, it will afterward be capable of great progress, and there will be no blame. If it loses its straightforwardness, then there will be blame. How could it make progress?

The *Judgment* says: "Follow: firmness arrives at the bottom of softness. The one moves, and the other enjoys and follows. There are great progress and purity, and no blame. The world follows the moment." "Firmness arrives at the bottom of softness. The one moves, and the other enjoys": and so this is the Follow hexagram. The *Judgment* is saying that the top "nine" line of the Lead trigram has arrived to occupy the bottom position of the Yield trigram, while the initial "six" line of the Yield trigram makes the journey to occupy the top position of the Lead trigram. The top line makes use of *yang* firmness to arrive at the bottom of *yin* softness. As a result, the top has gone below the bottom, and the esteemed has gone below the impoverished. Those who can be like this are the ones that things enjoy and follow. Further, the lower trigram refers to movement and the upper trigram to enjoyment. If there is movement, there can be enjoyment, and so the one follows the other. When the case is like this, there can be "great progress" and the acquisition of "purity." If there can be great progress and the acquisition of purity, then there will be no blame. If there can be neither progress nor the acquisition of purity, this cannot be the way of the Follow hexagram. How could one make the world to follow? What the world follows is the moment, and this is why it says: "The world follows the moment." **"How great is the meaning of 'follow the moment'!"** The way of noble people is to move by following the moment, to attend to what is fitting, and to suit themselves to its alterations. Those who cannot bring about legislation and opportunity, or take the way of creation to its depths, or recognize the incipient with capacity and aptitude—they cannot be put into agreement with this way. This is why the *Judgment* applauds it, saying: "How great is the meaning of 'follow the moment'!" In general, it applauds things because it desires that people recognize the greatness of their meaning, explore them, and understand them. This applauding—"how great is the meaning of 'follow the moment'"—is not the same as in other hexagrams, such as the Cheer hexagram. In other hexagrams, the moment and the meaning are considered two states of affairs.

The *Symbol* says: "At the center of the lake, there is thunder: Follow. Noble people use it to welcome obscurity and enter into repose and rest." When thunder shakes at the center of the lake, the lake follows its shaking and moves, which symbolizes the Follow hexagram. Noble people gaze on the symbol and follow the moment in their movement. To follow what is fitting for the moment—such is the case for all the ten thousand affairs, but the *Symbol* chooses to speak only of the case that is nearest and that sheds the most light. "Noble people use it to welcome obscurity and enter into repose and rest": when noble people are in the daylight, they strengthen themselves without rest, but when they welcome darkness and obscurity, they enter and occupy a place inside, reposing and resting to make their bodies contented. The place they occupy follows the moment, and is suited to what is fitting for it. The *Book of Rites* says that "noble people in the daylight do not occupy a place inside, while at night they do not occupy a place outside."[1] This is the way to follow the moment.

The initial "nine" line: the governors possess something adaptable. Purity brings good fortune. Those who go out by the gate to interact will accomplish something. This "nine" line occupies the moment of the Follow hexagram, it belongs to the substance of the Shake trigram, it is the master of movement, and it refers to those who follow something. The word "governors" refers to masters and guardians. They have something to follow—that is, they are masters and guardians of something that is altering and changing. This is why the line statement says: "The governors possess something adaptable." "Purity brings good fortune": if what they follow acquires straightforwardness, there will be good fortune. If they possess something adaptable, and it does not acquire straightforwardness, then its movement will be excessive. "Those who go out by the gate to interact will accomplish something": what the human heart attends to is often what it relates to and loves. As for the inclinations of ordinary people, when they love something, they see it as right, and when they detest something, they see it as wrong. This is why they often attend to the words of their wives and children, even when they result in loss, but detest the words of those they dislike, even when they are good. Were they to follow what they relate to and love, they would be agreeing with their private inclinations. How could they align with the straightforward principle? This is why they "will accomplish something" if they "go out by the gate to interact." The phrase "go out by the gate" signifies that there is nothing private or intimate. Their interactions are not private, and this is why they follow what is proper and will accomplish something. **The *Symbol* says: "'The governors possess something adaptable': if what they attend to is straightforward, there will be good fortune."** When they possess something to follow and it has altered, what they attend to must acquire straightforwardness, and then "there will be good fortune." If what they attend to is not straightforward, there will be regret and dismay. "'**Those who go out by the gate to interact will accomplish something': they lose nothing.**" If they interact by going out by the gate, they are not guided by anything private, and their interactions will necessarily be straightforward. If they are straightforward, "they lose nothing" and "will accomplish something."

The second "six" line: it binds itself to the small child and loses the stern man. The second line corresponds to the fifth but is close to the initial line, and the earlier line follows this nearby soft line. It cannot keep guard with certainty, and this is why the line statement gives a warning about it, saying that if "it binds itself to the small child," then "it loses the stern man." The initial *yang* line, in the bottom position, is the "small child," while the straightforwardly corresponding fifth line, in a position above, is the "stern man." Should the tendencies of the second bind it to the initial line, it will lose its straightforward correspondence to the fifth "nine" line—that is, it "loses the stern man." To bind itself to the small child and lose the stern man is to abandon its straightforward correspondence and attend to what is not straightforward. Its blame will be great. The second line possesses the virtues of centrality and straightforwardness, and so it will not necessarily reach such a point, but it is in the moment of the Follow hexagram, and so it is proper to give a warning about it. **The *Symbol* says: "'It binds itself to the small child': they do not agree at the same time."** If people acquire straightforwardness in what they follow, they will be far from crooked. If they attend to what is wrong, they will lose what is right—there is no principle by which one may attend to both. Were the second to bind itself to the initial line, it would lose the fifth. It cannot agree with them at the same time. And so, the *Symbol* warns people to attend solely and without qualification to the straightforward and proper.

The third "six" line: it binds itself to the stern man and loses the small child. When it follows, it will seek and then acquire something. There is profit in occupying a position of purity. The phrase "stern man" refers to the fourth "nine" line, while the "small child" is the initial line. A *yang* line in a position above is the stern man, while a line occupying a position below is the small child. Although the third and the initial line belong to the same trigram substance, the third is quite near to the fourth, and this is why it "binds itself" to the fourth. In the great majority of cases, a line that is *yin* and soft cannot set itself up. It ordinarily relates and binds itself to something near it. Here it binds itself to the fourth line above it, and this is why it loses the initial line below it. By abandoning the initial line to attend to a higher line, it acquires what is fitting in the Follow hexagram. If it follows what is above it, then it is good. Just as those in darkness follow the light, when those who manage affairs attend to what is good, they are following what is above them. When they turn their backs on what is right and attend to what is wrong, or when they abandon the enlightened and pursue the dim, they follow what is below them. The fourth has no corresponding line—that is, it has no one who follows it. But it acquires the nearby third line as a follower, which will necessarily agree with it and relate to its goodness. This is why, when the third line follows the fourth, if it is searching for something, it will necessarily acquire it. When people follow those above, and those above agree with them, they will acquire what they seek. Further, they should in general acquire what they seek. Even though this is the case, they should certainly do no wrong to principle or bend the way in following those above, choosing love and enjoyment as the means of success in acquiring what they seek. In such a case, they would be small people, who become crooked flatterers in their rush toward profit. This is why the line statement says that "there is profit in occupying a position of purity." If they place themselves straightforwardly—and this is what is signified by seeking something that one will necessarily acquire—then they follow as noble people do, by making their affairs straightforward. **The *Symbol* says: "'It binds itself to the stern man': it tends to abandon those below."** Since it is already following those above, its tendency is now to abandon those below without attending to them. In the Follow hexagram, it is good to abandon those below and attend to those above or to abandon the humble and attend to the lofty.

The fourth "nine" line: when they follow, it obtains them. Purity brings misfortune. If it is trustworthy, it is on the way. If it uses enlightenment, how could there be blame? The fourth "nine" line uses the power of *yang* firmness and places itself in the limit position for a minister. If it is followed and "obtains them," although this is straightforward, there will be misfortune. The phrase "it obtains them" signifies that the hearts of the world follow it, and it acquires them. Concerning the way of the minister, it is proper to ensure that kindness and authority go out solely from those above, so that the hearts of the crowd will all follow the ruler. Were the human heart to attend to itself, it would be on a way of peril and doubt, and this is why there is misfortune. As for those who occupy this terrain, what can they do? They can only accumulate trustworthiness and sincerity at their center, move by aligning with the way, and place themselves with enlightenment and wisdom. In such a case, what blame could there be? Among the people of antiquity, there were some who put this into action, such as Yi Yin, the Duke of Zhou, and Kong Ming.[2] In all these cases, their virtue was extended to the people and the people followed them. They made the people to follow them, and so they completed the task of their ruler and brought contentment to their state. Extreme sincerity persisted at their center: "It is trustworthy." In their influence, there was nothing that was not centered on the way: "It is on the way." Only because of their enlightenment and wisdom were they able to be like this: "It uses enlightenment." What excess or blame could there be? As a result, those below believed in them and those above did not doubt them. This is a position at the limit, but it is not resented for pressing against those above. Its propensity is weighty, but it is not the excess of unqualified strength. Those who are not sages or great worthies will not be capable of it. Next after these examples is Guo Ziyi of the Tang dynasty, whose authority could shake and master others, and whose mastery was not to be doubted.[3] He, too, caused there to be sincerity and trustworthiness at his center, and placed himself without losing anything much. Without enlightenment and wisdom, could he have acted like this? **The *Symbol* says: "'When they follow, it obtains them': its meaning is misfortune. 'If it is trustworthy, it is on the way': enlightenment brings accomplishment."** It occupies a position near the ruler, and "it obtains them": its meaning is certainly misfortune. If it can be "trustworthy" and "on the way," then there will be no blame. This is, in fact, the accomplishment of enlightenment and wisdom.

The fifth "nine" line: it trusts in the excellent. There is good fortune. The fifth "nine" line occupies the position of respect, it has acquired straightforwardness, and its center is full. This is a case of being sincere at one's center while following what is good, and its good fortune should be recognized. The word "excellent" here refers to what is good. From the ruler on down to the numberless people, the good fortune of following the way lies only in following what is good, and that is all. This line corresponds to the straightforwardness and centrality of the second, which has the meaning of following what is good. **The *Symbol* says: "'It trusts in the excellent. There is good fortune': its position is straightforward and central."** It places itself in a straightforward and central position, and it causes the way of straightforwardness and centrality to come about. The trustworthiness and sincerity of what it follows refer to straightforwardness and centrality, and are signified by the word "excellent." Its good fortune should be recognized. The excellent line in which it trusts is the second "six" line. In the Follow hexagram, it is good to acquire centrality. What the Follow hexagram defends itself against is excess. In fact, when the heart follows what it enjoys, it does not recognize its own excess.

The top "six" line: it chains and binds itself. When it attends to it, it anchors itself. The king employs progress on the western mountain. The top "six" line uses softness and submissiveness to occupy the limit position in the Follow hexagram and refers to the limit case of following. The phrase "it chains and binds itself" signifies the limit case of following, which is to follow as though chained or constrained, as though yoked or bound up. "When it attends to it, it anchors itself": it further attends to it, and anchors or binds itself, which signifies that it follows with the certainty of someone knotted to it. "The king employs progress on the western mountain": the limit case of following is like this. In the past, King Tai employed this way, and made progress in his royal vocation on the western mountain. To evade the difficulty posed by the Di tribe, King Tai departed from the Bin region and arrived at Mount Qi. The people of Bin, both the old and the young, followed along by aiding and accompanying him "as though gathering at the market."[4] In fact, the hearts of the people followed as certainly as though they were knotted to him. He employed this way, and this is why he was able to make progress and become abundant in his royal vocation on the western mountain. The phrase "western mountain" refers to Mount Qi. In fact, the royal vocation of the Zhou was first mustered here. The top line occupies the limit position of the Follow hexagram, which certainly constitutes a great excess. Nonetheless, it is good both to make the people follow one and to follow the good with certainty, as in this case. When the line is applied to other cases, it refers to excess. **The *Symbol* says: "'It chains and binds itself': the top line depletes it."** To follow with the certainty of someone chained and bound, anchored and constrained, is to deplete and bring to its limit the way of the Follow hexagram.

18. BLIGHT (*GU* 蠱)

The *Sequence of the Hexagrams* says: "Those who follow people for happiness must have affairs to manage, and this is why the Blight hexagram is next." It receives its meaning from the two preceding hexagrams, and so it succeeds them. As for those who follow people for happiness and enjoyment, they must have affairs to manage. If they did not have affairs to manage, then why would they be happy? Why would they follow? And so the Blight hexagram succeeds the Follow hexagram. A blight is a state of affairs. It is not that the particular affair to be managed is a blight; the word "blight" simply indicates that there is such an affair. As for the trigrams, "below the mountain, there is wind." The wind is below the mountain. If it encounters the mountain and comes back, then things will be disordered, and this is the symbol of blight. The meaning of blight is decline and disorder. The character has two parts, one of which refers to insects and the other to a vase.[1] A vase in which there are insects has the meaning of blight and decline. The Zuo commentary says: "The wind falls below the mountain. The woman bewilders the man."[2] Since the grown woman descends below the young man, her inclinations are disordered. Since the wind encounters the mountain and comes back, all things are frustrated and disordered, which constitutes the symbol of having affairs to manage. This is why the *Sequence of the Hexagrams* says: "A blight is a state of affairs."[3] When there is already a blight and one sets it in order, this, too, is an affair to be managed. Concerning the hexagram symbol, one may remark that it refers to what brings the blight to completion. Concerning the powers of the trigrams, one may remark that they refer to what sets the blight in order.

Blight: there are primacy and progress. There is profit in traversing a great stream. If the blight has already occurred,[4] there is a principle by which it will return to order. Since antiquity, order has necessarily been the effect of disorder. If there is disorder, it will open the path to order—this is a spontaneous principle. For instance, if the powers of the trigrams are used to set the blight in order, they will be able to bring about primacy and progress. The greatness of the Blight hexagram lies in crossing through the hardships, difficulties, obstacles, and hindrances of the moment. This is why the judgment says: "There is profit in traversing a great stream." **Before the first stem there are three days. After the first stem there are three days.** The first stem is the head of a numerical series or the beginning of a state of affairs. For instance, the first and second stems are the first two in the series of heavenly stems.[5] Whether it refers to the first stem of a numerical series or to the first stem of a causal series, it is always called the "head" or the "impetus" of the state of affairs. Concerning the way of bringing order to blight, it is proper to be reflective and apprehensive about what comes before and after it by three days. In fact, to unfold the origin of what comes before and after is the way to achieve a continuous salvation from decay. "Before the first stem" signifies that it takes place before this—that people study how to bring it about. "After the first stem" signifies that it takes place after this—that they are apprehensive concerning what it is about to become. It goes on for one day, for two days, and reaches the point of three days. The judgment is remarking on how deep their apprehension is and how far they unfold what they apprehend. If they study how to bring it about, then they will also recognize the way of its salvation. If they are apprehensive concerning what it is about to become, then they will recognize the starting point of its perfection. If they are good at saving it, then they can bring reform to what had earlier decayed. If they are good at perfecting it, then they can bring continuity to what will later bring profit. The sage-kings of antiquity were like this, and so they renewed the world and handed it down to later times. Those who brought order to the blight of later times were not enlightened by the reproof of the sage expressed in "before the first stem" and "after the first stem." Their apprehension was shallow and only concerned affairs that were nearby. This is why their labor to save the times did not bring reform to their disorder. Even before their task was completed, its decay had already been born. The first stem is at the head of the state of affairs, while the seventh stem is at the head of a subsequent alteration.[6] When it concerns controlling or producing the various kinds of government and teaching, the text will use the phrase "first stem" to bring up their head. When it concerns the affair of revealing someone's calling or the influence of some decree, the text will use the phrase "seventh stem," since the seventh is a subsequent stem, and here there is a subsequent alteration.

The *Judgment* says: "Blight: firmness ascends and softness descends. There are lowliness and stopping: Blight." The *Judgment* is speaking about both the alteration of the hexagram and the meaning of the trigram substances. "Firmness ascends and softness descends": this signifies that the initial "nine" line of the Lead trigram ascends to become the top "nine" line of the hexagram, while the top "six" line of the Yield trigram descends to become the initial "six" line of the hexagram. *Yang* firmness is respected and positioned at the top, and now this line has made the journey to occupy the top position. *Yin* softness is humble and positioned at the bottom, and now this line has arrived to occupy the bottom position. Men, even when young, occupy positions above; women, even when grown, occupy positions below. When the respected and the humble acquire straightforwardness, when those above and below submit to principle—this is the way to set a blight in order. Because the firm line is now above, and the soft line below, the trigrams have altered to become the Calm and Low trigrams. The Calm trigram refers to stopping and the Low trigram to submissiveness. The lower trigram refers to lowliness and the upper trigram to stopping. Together they refer to stopping in lowliness and submissiveness. The way of lowliness and submissiveness is used to set the blight in order, and as a result, there are "primacy and progress." "'Blight: there are primacy and progress': the world is set in order." When one is on the way of setting blight in order—as in the case of the powers of the trigrams—then "there are primacy and progress" and "the world is set in order." As for those who bring order to disorder, if they can bring straightforwardness to the duties of the respected and the humble, those above and those below, then those below will be lowly and submissive, while those above will be able to stop, to be equable and contented in their determinations. When all states of affairs have stopped at submissiveness, how could their blight not be set in order? This way is great and good, and makes progress. In a case like this, the world will be set in order. "'There is profit in traversing a great stream': the journey is the affair to be managed." When the world faces the border of decline and disorder, it is fitting to traverse hardships and obstacles by making the journey and crossing through them: "The journey is the affair to be managed." "'Before the first stem there are three days. After the first stem there are three days': if it ends, then it will have a beginning. This is the action of heaven." As for what has a beginning, it must also have an end; if it has already ended, it must have a beginning—this is the way of heaven. Sages recognize the way of ending and beginning, and this is why they can be the origin and beginning. They study how to bring something about, they end it opportunely, and they perfect what it is about to become. "Before the first stem" and "after the first stem," they are apprehensive, and so they are able to set the blight in order and bring about "primacy and progress."

The *Symbol* says: "Below the mountain, there is wind: Blight. Noble people use it to dust off the people and cultivate their virtue." "Below the mountain, there is wind": if the wind encounters a mountain and comes back, it will scatter and disorder all things. This is why these trigrams constitute the symbol of having affairs to manage. Noble people gaze on the symbol of having affairs to manage and use it to "dust off" or make the crossing with "the people," and to nourish or "cultivate their virtue." In their own case, they nourish their virtue; concerning the world, they make the crossing with the people. Of all the affairs managed by noble people, none is greater than these two.

The initial "six" line: it manages the blight of the father. There is a son. The old man is without blame. There is danger, but good fortune in the end. Although the initial "six" line occupies the bottom position, it is the cause of the hexagram's completion and has the meaning of mastery. Since it is the master while occupying the lowest position in the inner trigram, it refers to the son who "manages the blight of the father." As for the way of the son who manages the blight of his father, if he can be ready to manage his affairs, this indicates that "there is a son," and the old man will acquire no blame. If such is not the case, then he will be a burden to his father. This is why he must be careful of the danger, and then he will acquire "good fortune in the end." As for those in humble places who officiate in the affairs of respected people, it is proper that they themselves be alarmed and trembling. The power of this "six" line is capable of lowliness and submissiveness, its substance is *yin* and soft, it is at the bottom, and it has no corresponding line, but it is nonetheless the master or manager. As a result, it does not have the meaning of being able to make the crossing. Concerning its incapacity to manage anything, one may remark that this is an extremely small part of the meaning. This is why the line statement speaks without qualification about the way of a son managing blight. He must be capable of making the crossing, and then he will not burden his father. If he is capable during the danger, there should be "good fortune in the end." Then the great law of the son who manages the blight will be seen perfectly. The *Symbol* says: "'It manages the blight of the father': he intends to serve the old man." As for the way of the son who "manages the blight of the father," his intention is to serve what is proper in the affairs of his father. This is why he extols and reveres his affairs, to situate his father on a terrain without blame. If he constantly cherishes care during the danger, he will acquire good fortune in the end. To exhaust sincerity in the affairs of one's father is the way of good fortune.

The second "nine" line: it manages the blight of the mother. There can be no purity. The second "nine" line is *yang* and firm, and the fifth "six" line corresponds to it—that is, it uses the power of *yang* firmness in a position below to manage the affairs of *yin* softness above it. This is why the meaning of a son managing the blight of his mother is chosen. Its meaning is near that of a minister using *yang* firmness to assist a ruler who is soft and weak. The second line belongs to the Low trigram substance and is placed in a soft position, both of which have submissiveness as their meaning. This is the way of managing the blight of one's mother. As for the relationship between mother and son, it is proper that he use softness and lowliness to assist and direct her, so that she is made to do her duty. If he is not submissive,[7] but brings about her defeat and blight, this is the crime of the son. How could there be no way for him to attend to and embrace a general sort of submissiveness? Concerning women, one may remark that their *yin* softness should be recognized. Were the son to expand himself using the way of *yang* firmness, hastily improving and brushing her off, then he would injure his own kindness and do great harm to her. So what is his means of entry? It lies in contracting himself and lowering his intentions, becoming lowly and submitting to a general sort of service. He makes his person to be straightforward and his affairs to be orderly, and that is all. This is why the line statement says that "there should be no purity," signifying that he should not be pure and certain, exhausting the way of firmness and straightness. In a case like this, he will bring about the way of centrality. Further, how could he be made to manage an extremely lofty affair? If the ruler is soft and weak, he may exhaust his sincerity and drain his loyalty only if he brings about the way of centrality. Further, how could he be made to do anything great? Even though a sage like the Duke of Zhou assisted King Cheng, and King Cheng was not extremely soft or weak, he could make him to be King Cheng, and that is all. He could keep guard and bring things to completion without losing sight of the way, but he certainly could not be made to manage the affairs of Xi, Huang, Yao, and Shun.[8] The second line belongs to the Low trigram substance and it acquires centrality—that is, it can be lowly and submissive, and it acquires the way of centrality. It aligns with the meaning of "there should be no purity," and it acquires the way to manage the blight of the mother. **The *Symbol* says: "'It manages the blight of the mother': it acquires the way of centrality."** The second line "acquires the way of centrality" and is not excessively firm. Such a person will be good at managing the affairs of its mother.

The third "nine" line: it manages the blight of the father. There are small regrets but no great blame. The third line uses the power of *yang* firmness, it occupies the top position in the lower trigram, and it refers to the master or manager: the son who manages the blight of his father. It uses *yang* to place itself in a firm position and it is without centrality—that is, it is excessively firm. Nonetheless, it belongs to the Low trigram substance and does nothing without submissiveness, even though it is excessively firm. Submissiveness is the root of managing the affairs of one's relations. Further, it occupies a position that is straightforward for it, and this is why there is no great excess. It uses the power of *yang* firmness and is capable of managing affairs. Although it is excessively firm and has very small regrets, there is no great excess or blame in the end. Nonetheless, there are small regrets, because it has already lost what is good in managing the affairs of one's relations. **The *Symbol* says: "'It manages the blight of the father': in the end there is no blame."** The power of the third line is used to manage "the blight of the father." Although "there are small regrets," in the end there is no great blame. In fact, it is able to manage affairs with firmness and decisiveness. It does not lose straightforwardness and possesses submissiveness, and so "in the end there is no blame."

The fourth "six" line: it is generous with the blight of the father. Making a journey brings the sight of dismay. The fourth line uses *yin* to occupy a *yin* position, its powers are softness and submissiveness, and it is placed so as to acquire straightforwardness. This is why it refers to those who are tolerant and generous when placing themselves over their fathers' affairs. As for the powers of softness and submissiveness, when placed straightforwardly they can only trace out what is ordinary and keep guard over themselves, and that is all. If they make the journey and manage excessive or extraordinary affairs, they will not be victorious but will have the "sight of dismay." When nothing corresponds to or helps something that is soft and *yin*, and yet it makes a journey, how could it make the crossing? **The *Symbol* says: "'It is generous with the blight of the father': its journey acquires nothing."** The power of the fourth line may be used to guard what is ordinary and to occupy a moment of tolerance and generosity. If it wants to make a journey, it "acquires nothing." If it attaches anything to its command, it will not be victorious.

The fifth "six" line: it manages the blight of the father. It employs the praiseworthy. The fifth line occupies the position of respect, it uses a disposition of *yin* softness, and it faces the management of the ruler's affairs. It corresponds to the second "nine" line below it—that is, it can delegate command to a minister of *yang* firmness. Although it can correspond to worthy people of *yang* firmness below it and can delegate command to them, its own reality is nonetheless *yin* and soft. This is why it is not capable of managing affairs that inspire, begin, open up, or institute anything. It should serve the vocation of its predecessors, and this is why "it manages the blight of the father." As for the affair of inspiring a vocation or bringing it to its end, no one without the powers of firmness and enlightenment will be capable of it. Although the rulers of succeeding times may be supplied only with softness and weakness, if they can delegate command to firm and worthy people, they should be able to keep a good succession going and acquire a praiseworthy reputation. Tai Jia and King Cheng both made use of their ministers and employed "the praiseworthy."[9] **The Symbol says: "'It manages the father. It employs the praiseworthy': it is served by the virtuous."** "It manages the blight of the father," and employs those who possess a praiseworthy reputation. It makes use of worthy people in positions below, who serve and assist it with their virtues of firmness and centrality.

The top "nine" line: it is not an affair of the king or the marquises. This affair is lofty and valuable. The top "nine" line occupies the end position in the Blight hexagram, it does not bind itself or correspond to the lines below it, and it is placed outside of affairs—that is, on a terrain where there are no affairs to manage. It uses the powers of firmness and enlightenment without a corresponding line to support it, it is placed on a terrain where there are no affairs to manage, and it refers to worthy or noble people who are not equal to the moment, who guard themselves in a lofty and unpolluted place, and who do not burden themselves with matters of the times. This is why the line statement says that "it is not an affair of the king or the marquises. This affair is lofty and valuable." People of antiquity who took such action include Yi Yin and Taigong Wang at the beginning, and the case of Zengzi and Zisi is also relevant.[10] They did not contract their way and succumb to the moment. When they could no longer provide their influence to the world, they made themselves better. In this respected and lofty, truehearted and valuable affair, they kept guard over their tendencies and reined themselves in, and that is all. There is also not a single way to what is lofty and valuable for scholars. Sometimes they cherish and chain themselves to the way and virtue, not being equal to the moment, and guard themselves in a lofty and unpolluted place; sometimes they recognize the way of stopping at what is sufficient, retreating and preserving themselves; sometimes they calculate their ability and take the measure of their role, contenting themselves without seeking recognition; sometimes they clarify, secure, and guard themselves, not managing the affairs of the world even a little, and do nothing but keep themselves unpolluted. Although their place may be peculiarly suited to acquisition or loss, to smallness or greatness, they always manage their own lofty and valuable affairs. When the *Symbol* says that "its tendencies should be taken as regulations," it signifies that its advance and retreat are aligned with the way. **The *Symbol* says: "'It is not an affair of the king or the marquises': its tendencies should be taken as regulations."** Those who place themselves outside of affairs, like the top "nine" line, are not burdened by matters of the times and do not minister to the affairs of the "king or the marquises." In fact, they use the way in their advance and retreat, and their employment and abandonment follow the moment. How could anyone but the worthy be capable of this? Those tendencies that persist in them should constitute laws and regulations.

19. WATCH (*LIN* 臨)

The *Sequence of the Hexagrams* says: "Those who have affairs to manage can afterward be great. This is why the Watch hexagram is next." "Those who keep watch are great," and "a blight is a state of affairs." If they have affairs to manage, then they can become great, and this is why the Watch hexagram is next. Han Kangbo says: "One's vocation may become great because one manages affairs at their birth."[1] The two *yang* lines start to grow and become abundant and great, and this is why they constitute the Watch hexagram. As for the trigrams, "on the lake, there is earth." The earth that is on the lake is the shore. The shore and the water border each other. The shore watches over the water from nearby, and this is why they constitute the Watch hexagram. Of the things of the world that are profoundly near and watch over each other, none is like earth and water. This is why the symbol "on the earth, there is water" constitutes the Close hexagram, while "on the lake, there is earth" constitutes the Watch hexagram. Those who keep watch are watching over the people, and watching over affairs. In general, they watch over all these things. As for the hexagram, the meaning chosen is that of someone above watching over those below and watching over the people.

Watch: there are primacy, progress, profit, and purity. The judgment is remarking on the powers of the trigrams. When the way of the Watch hexagram resembles the powers of its trigrams, then it will make great progress and be straightforward. **When the eighth month is reached, there will be misfortune.** The two *yang* lines start to grow at the bottom. This is the moment when the way of *yang* welcomes its abundance. The sage gives a warning about it in advance, saying that although *yang* has started to grow, "when the eighth month is reached" its way will disappear. That is, "there will be misfortune." In the great

majority of cases when the sage gives a warning, it is necessarily at the moment
when something is starting to become abundant. If something starts to become
abundant, but one is apprehensive about scarcity, then one should be able to
defend against its reaching the limit of satisfaction, and plan to make it endless
and continuous. If there were already scarcity, and then the sage gave his warning, he would not achieve anything by it. Since antiquity, the contentment and
order of the world have never been continuous without bringing about disorder.
In fact, no one can give a warning to those who possess abundance. When they
start to possess abundance, they do not recognize the warning. This is why
habitual contentment and wealth give birth to arrogance and extravagance. If
people take pleasure in relaxation and indulgence, then their doctrines and
precepts will go into decline. If they forget about affliction and disorder, then
they will sprout quarrels and strife. As a result, they will gradually become licentious without recognizing that they have reached the point of disorder.

The *Judgment* says: "Watch: firmness is gradual and grows. There are enjoyment and submission. Firmness is central and corresponds. There are great
progress and the use of straightforwardness, which is the way of heaven." The
word "gradual" signifies step by step. The two *yang* lines grow at the bottom
and advance step by step. The Joy trigram is below and the Yield trigram above,
indicating that there are harmonious "enjoyment and submission." A firm line
acquires the way of centrality and has a corresponding line to help it. As a result,
it is capable of "great progress" and the acquisition of straightforwardness, and
it aligns with the way of heaven. When those who are firm and straightforward
are also harmonious and submissive, they are on the way of heaven. The reason their task of transformation and cultivation never rests is that they are firm
and straightforward, harmonious and submissive, and that is all. When this is
the case, one may watch over people, affairs, or the world itself without being
deprived of great progress and the acquisition of straightforwardness. The Joy
trigram refers to enjoyment, an enjoyment that is harmonious. The *Judgment* of
the Solve hexagram says that there are "resolution and harmony."[2] "'When the
eighth month is reached, there will be misfortune': it disappears and does not
continue." In the Watch hexagram, two *yang* lines are born. It is the moment
when *yang* starts to become abundant step by step. This is why the sage gives a
warning, saying that although *yang* is starting to grow, nonetheless, "when the
eighth month is reached," it will disappear and "there will be misfortune." The
eight months signify the eight months during which *yang* is alive. *Yang* begins
and is born in the Turn hexagram. From the Turn hexagram to the Flee hexagram there are eight months altogether, referring to the period from December

to July.³ In the latter hexagram, two *yin* lines are growing and *yang* is disappearing, and this is why the *Judgment* says that "it disappears and does not continue." Concerning the *yin* and *yang qi*, one may remark that their disappearance and growth are like tracing a circle that cannot be changed. Concerning human affairs, one may remark that *yang* refers to noble people, while *yin* refers to small people. As for those who face the moment when the way of noble people is growing, the sage reproves them, making them recognize the principle that there is misfortune at its limit. If they deliberate on how to prepare for this, they will be constant, without reaching the limit of satiety, and there will be no misfortune.

The *Symbol* says: "On the lake, there is earth: Watch. Noble people use it to reflect and teach without becoming depleted. They embrace and preserve the people without boundaries." "On the lake, there is earth": the lake has a shore, which is the border of the water. Of all the things that watch over each other by containing and embracing each other, none are like water on the earth, and this is why "on the lake, there is earth" constitutes the symbol of the Watch hexagram. Noble people gaze on the symbol of relating to and watching over something, and they "reflect and teach without becoming depleted." When they relate to and watch over the people, their intention and reflection is to teach and direct them. They do this "without becoming depleted" because their extreme sincerity is tireless. When they gaze on the symbol of containing and embracing, they will have the heart to "embrace and preserve the people." They do this "without boundaries" because they are broad and great, without boundaries or perimeters. Containing and embracing include the idea of breadth and greatness, and this is why the symbol has the meaning of acting "without becoming depleted" and "without boundaries."

The initial "nine" line: it stirs it to watch. Purity brings good fortune. "To stir is to affect."⁴ In the moment when the *yang* lines are growing, they are affected and moved by the *yin* lines. The fourth line corresponds to the initial line, indicating that it affects it. When compared with other hexagrams, their correspondence to each other carries special weight. The fourth line is near the position of the ruler, while the initial line has acquired a straightforward position and is affected by and corresponds to the fourth. This is to use the way of straightforwardness, to believe in and delegate command to those in their proper positions, to act on one's tendencies, to obtain something from those above, and to put the way of straightforwardness into action. As a result, there will be good fortune. In other hexagrams, the initial and top line statements do not speak about acquiring a position or losing a position. In fact, the meaning of initiating or ending carries more weight in those hexagrams, while in the Watch hexagram it is the fact that the initial line has acquired a straightforward position that carries the most weight. In general, when it says that "purity brings good fortune," sometimes it indicates that there will be good fortune because there is already straightforwardness, sometimes that there will be good fortune if straightforwardness is acquired, and sometimes that there will be good fortune if one keeps guard over one's purity and certainty. Each line statement follows its own state of affairs.[5] **The *Symbol* says: "'It stirs it to watch. Purity brings good fortune': its tendency is to act straightforwardly."** The phrase "purity brings good fortune" signifies that the tendency of this "nine" line is to act straightforwardly. Because the "nine" line occupies a *yang* position, and because it corresponds straightforwardly to the fourth, its tendency is straightforward.

The second "nine" line: it stirs it to watch. There is good fortune. Nothing is without profit. The second line refers to *yang* starting to grow and become abundant step by step. It is affected and moved by the fifth "six" line, a ruler of centrality and submissiveness. They interact as though they were relations, and this is why it seems to believe in and delegate command to it, and it puts its tendencies into action. "There is good fortune" for what it watches over, and "nothing is without profit." It is already the case that there is good fortune; there is good fortune because it is like this. It is about to be the case that nothing is without profit; nothing is without profit in its influence and action. **The *Symbol* says: "'It stirs it to watch. There is good fortune. Nothing is without profit': it does not yet submit to the mandate."** The phrase "not yet" indicates that it is not hasty. In the *Mencius* someone asks: "Have you persuaded the state of Qi to attack the state of Yan?" Mencius responds: "Not yet."[6] He also says of Zhongzi: "The grain that he ate, was it that which was planted by Boyi? Or was it that which was planted by Robber Zhi? This is not yet possible to know."[7] In the *Grand Scribe's Records*, Hou Ying says: "People are certainly not yet easy to know."[8] When people of antiquity employed this phrase, their intention was always like that. Today, the great majority of people employ it as the opposite of the word "already." This is why their intention seems different, but in reality there is nothing peculiar about it. The second "nine" line is affected by and corresponds to the fifth so as to watch over those below. In fact, when it uses its growing virtue of firmness, and further, when it acquires centrality, then they affect each other in their extreme sincerity, not because it has submitted to the mandate of those above. As a result, "there is good fortune," and "nothing is without profit." The fifth line belongs to the submissiveness trigram substance, and the second belongs to the enjoyment trigram substance. Further, *yin* and *yang* lines correspond to each other, and this is why the *Symbol* specifically sheds light on the fact that enjoyment and submissiveness are not the causes here.

The third "six" line: it watches with sweetness. There is no long-term profit. Since it worries about it, there is no blame. The third line occupies the top position in the lower trigram and refers to those who watch over people. It is *yin* and soft, and belongs to the enjoyment trigram substance. Further, it is placed without centrality or straightforwardness and refers to those who watch over people using sweetness and enjoyment. To be above and use sweetness and enjoyment when watching over those below is an extreme loss of virtue, so that nothing can be profitable. The nature of the Joy trigram is already to indicate enjoyment, and further, this line rides above two *yang* lines. The *yang* lines are starting to grow and advance upward, and this is why it cannot be contented but adds to its sweetness. Since it recognizes its peril and trouble, and "worries about it," if it can be constrained by meekness, guard its straightforwardness, and place itself with extreme sincerity, then "there is no blame." If enjoyment causes it to become crooked, but it is able to worry about it and modify itself— how could it be blamed for this? **The *Symbol* says: "'It watches with sweetness': its position is not proper for it. 'Since it worries about it': the blame does not grow."** The line refers to people of *yin* softness, it is placed without centrality or straightforwardness, and it occupies the top position of the lower trigram. It also rides on two *yang* lines, which is not to be placed in its proper position. Since it can recognize this, and be troubled and worried about it, then it will necessarily be strongly exhorted to modify itself. This is why its excess and blame will not grow.

The fourth "six" line: its watch is extreme. There is no blame. The fourth line occupies the bottom position in the upper trigram, and is close to the lower trigram substance—this is to be quite watchful over those below, and is the extreme of watchfulness. On the way of the Watch hexagram, nearness is valued, and this is why its closeness is extreme. The fourth line occupies a straightforward position and descends to correspond with the *yang* firmness of the initial line. It is placed near the position of the ruler, it guards its straightforwardness, and it delegates command to the worthy. It relates to and watches over those below, and as a result, "there is no blame." It has placed itself properly. **The *Symbol* says: "'Its watch is extreme. There is no blame': its position is proper for it."** It occupies a position near the ruler, indicating that it has acquired command; it uses *yin* to place itself in the fourth position, indicating that it has acquired straightforwardness; it corresponds to the initial line, indicating that it descends to worthy people. And so "there is no blame," because in fact, "its position is proper for it."

The fifth "six" line: it knows how to watch. This is fitting for great rulers. There is good fortune. The fifth line uses softness at the center of the submission trigram substance, and it occupies the position of respect. It corresponds to the second line below it, which refers to a minister of firmness and centrality. This is to be able to delegate command to the second line, and not to labor over setting anything in order. It refers to those who know how to watch over those below. As for the body of a single person watching over the breadth of the world, if he trifles with trifles and delegates command to himself, how will he be able to encompass the ten thousand affairs? This is why he gives command to himself only concerning what he knows, and he gives what he does not know to someone suitable and sufficient for it. He can do nothing but choose the good people of the world and delegate command to the aware and enlightened people of the world. Then there will be nothing that he does not encompass. If he does not give command to himself concerning what he knows, then his knowledge will be great. The fifth line submits and corresponds to the second "nine" line, which refers to a worthy person of firmness and centrality. It delegates command to it so that it may watch over those below, which is to know how to watch over the world with enlightenment. This is what is "fitting for great rulers," and their good fortune should be recognized. **The *Symbol* says: "'This is fitting for great rulers': it signifies centrality in action."** The ways of rulers and ministers align. In fact, their two kinds of *qi* seek each other out. The fifth line possesses the virtue of centrality, and this is why it can delegate command to worthy people of firmness and centrality. It acquires what is fitting for great rulers, and it completes the task of knowing how to watch. In fact, this comes about because it puts the virtue of centrality into action. As for people of worth and power in relation to the ruler, if their ways were not the same, or their virtues did not align, how could they be employed?

The top "six" line: its watch is truehearted. There are good fortune and no blame. The top "six" line is at the limit of the Yield trigram, which refers to extreme submissiveness. It also occupies the end position of the Watch hexagram, which refers to a truehearted and beneficial watch. Although it does not correspond straightforwardly to the initial or second line, *yin* is nonetheless sought out by *yang* in the great majority of cases. Further, it is extremely submissive, which is why its tendency is to attend to the two *yang* lines. It is respected, but it corresponds to what is humble; it is lofty, but it attends to those below. It respects worthy people and it chooses what is good, which is extremely truehearted and beneficial. This is why the line statement says: "Its watch is truehearted," and so "there are good fortune and no blame." Since a line that is *yin* and soft is in a position above, and it cannot keep watch, it is fitting that there be blame. Since it is truehearted and beneficial by its submission to the firm lines, "there are good fortune and no blame." A "six" line occupies the end position of the Watch hexagram, but it does not choose to speak of the limit as its meaning. There is no excess or limit in the Watch hexagram, and this is why its stopping point has benefit as its meaning. The top is a terrain without a position, and so it stops at saying that it is at the top. **The *Symbol* says: "The good fortune of a truehearted watch: it tends toward what is inside."** "It tends toward what is inside": it corresponds to the initial and second lines. Its tendency is to submit to *yang* firmness, and to be truehearted and devoted. Its good fortune should be recognized.

20. GAZE (*GUAN* 觀)

The *Sequence of the Hexagrams* says: "Those who keep watch are great. After things become great, one can gaze on them, and this is why the Gaze hexagram is next." And so the Gaze hexagram succeeds the Watch hexagram. In general, any gazing or looking at things constitutes a gaze,[1] but to be gazed at by those below also constitutes a gaze.[2] For example, the phrase "gazing platform" contains the word "gaze" because something is gazed at by those below. When rulers gaze on the way of heaven above them and gaze on the customs of the people below them, these, too, constitute gazes. When they correct their virtue and put their government into action, they are regarded with admiration by the people, and so this, too, constitutes a gaze. "The wind travels above the earth": it pierces the ten thousand kinds entirely, which symbolizes an all-encompassing gaze. The two *yang* lines are above and the four *yin* lines are below. *Yang* firmness occupies the position of respect, and it is gazed on by the group of lines below it, which has the meaning of an admiring gaze. The various line statements choose only the meaning of a gazing or seeing that follows the moment.

Gaze: there is washing but no offering. It is trustworthy, as when it is grave. I have heard what the venerable Hu Yizhi says, that noble people who occupy positions above constitute the ceremonial exemplars for the world.[3] They ought to bring their solemnity and reverence to the limit, and then "those below will gaze on" and admire "them, and be transformed." This is why the world gazes on them. It is proper that its gaze be like the sacrifice in the ancestral temple, but at the beginning, at the moment of the washing. It should not be like the moment after the offering has been made. Then the people below will exhaust their extreme sincerity. With such graveness, they will regard them with admiration. The word "washing" signifies the beginning of the sacrifice and libation.

There is a washing of the hands and a pouring of dark wine on the earth. This is the moment when the spirit is sought. The word "offering" signifies the moment when the raw or cooked meats are set out. The washing is the beginning of the affair, when people's hearts exhaust the sincerity of their essence and achieve a severe sobriety. After the offering has been made, the rituals become numerous, complicated, and ornate. People's hearts become scattered, and the unity of their essence is not as it was at the beginning, at the moment of the washing. When those who occupy positions above make their exemplary ceremonies straightforward, then the people below will gaze on them. It is proper that they be solemn and severe as at the beginning,[4] at the initial washing of the hands, without letting the sincerity of their intentions become at all scattered, as it is after the offering has been made. Then the people of the world will not do otherwise than exhaust their trustworthiness and sincerity. "With such graveness, they will regard them with admiration": to be grave is to be admiring and hopeful.

The *Judgment* says: "The greatness that is gazed on is above. There are submission and lowliness, centrality and straightforwardness, in the gaze of the world." The fifth line occupies the position of respect. It uses the virtues of *yang* firmness, centrality, and straightforwardness—these are gazed on by those below. Its virtues are extremely great, and this is why the *Judgment* says that "the greatness that is gazed on is above." The Yield trigram is below and the Low trigram above, which refers to the capacity for "submission and lowliness." The fifth line occupies a position of "centrality and straightforwardness." It uses the virtues of lowliness and submission, centrality and straightforwardness, so as to be gazed on by the world. **"'Gaze: there is washing but no offering. It is trustworthy, as when it is grave': those below will gaze on it and be transformed."** The way of being gazed on is to be severe and reverent as at the beginning, at the moment of the washing. Then the people below it, in their extreme sincerity, will regard it with admiration and will attend to their own transformation. The phrase "no offering" signifies that the sincerity of their intention does not become at all scattered. **"It gazes on the spiritual way of heaven and the unwavering four seasons. Sages use the spiritual way when providing their teaching, and the world obeys."** The way of heaven is extremely spiritual, and this is why the *Judgment* says "spiritual way." Those who gaze on how the revolution of heaven and the four seasons neither strays nor wavers will see what is spiritual and mysterious. Sages see "the spiritual way of heaven," and they give substance to the spiritual way by "providing their teaching." This is why the world is never without obedience to them. As for the way of heaven, it is extremely spiritual, and this is why it neither strays nor wavers in the revolution of the four seasons or the transformation and cultivation of the ten thousand things. This extremely spiritual way cannot be spoken with a name. Sages merely sanction it in silence, give substance to its mysterious function, and provide it in their government and teaching. This is why the people of the world soak themselves from swimming in its virtue without recognizing its accomplishment. They drum and dance to its transformations without gauging its function. They spontaneously admire and gaze on it; they gird themselves with it and obey. This is why it says that sages "use the spiritual way when providing their teaching, and the world obeys."

The *Symbol* says: "The wind travels above the earth: Gaze. The first kings used it to inspect the regions, gaze on the people, and provide their teaching." "The wind travels above the earth": by encompassing and extending itself to the numberless things, it symbolizes a wide-ranging cause and an all-encompassing perception. This is why the first kings gave substance to it in the ritual of inspecting the regions, gazing on the customs of the people, and providing their government and teaching. The son of heaven makes the rounds and inspects the four regions, gazes on and looks into the customs of the people, and provides his government and teaching. For example, if there is wastefulness, he conjoins it with thrift. If there is thrift, he makes it manifest with a ritual. To inspect the regions is to gaze on the people, while to provide one's teaching is to be gazed on by the people.

The initial "six" line: the child gazes. Small people are without blame. Noble people are dismayed. This "six" line uses a disposition of *yin* softness to occupy a position far away from the *yang* lines. As a result, it refers to those who gaze on or see only what is shallow and nearby, just as in childhood or youth. This is why the line statement says: "The child gazes." Above it is a line that is *yang* and firm, central and straightforward, which refers to a sagely and worthy ruler. Those near it see the abundance of its way and virtue—what they gaze on is deep and far away. The initial line is far away from it—what it sees is unenlightened, just like the gaze of a blind child. The phrase "small people" refers to the people below. What they see is dark and shallow, and they cannot understand the way of noble people. This is their ordinary role, and it is not sufficient to make one call them excessive or blameworthy. If noble people are like this, they should be scorned and dismayed. The *Symbol* says: "'The initial 'six' line: the child gazes': this is the way of small people." What it gazes on is unenlightened, like the gaze of a child or youth. Such is the role of small people, and this is why the *Symbol* says: "This is the way of small people."

The second "six" line: the spy gazes. There is profit in a woman's purity. The second line corresponds to the fifth—that is, it gazes on the fifth. The fifth line refers to the way of *yang* firmness, centrality, and straightforwardness. It cannot be gazed on or seen by the second line, which is *yin*, dim, soft, and weak. This is why it is like nothing so much as the gaze of the peeping spy. Although the gaze of the peeping spy sees a little, it cannot be extremely enlightened. Since the second line has not been able to shed light on or see the way of *yang* firmness, centrality and straightforwardness, its profit is like the purity of a woman. Although she cannot see with extreme enlightenment, she can be submissive and attentive. This is the way of the woman and constitutes a woman's purity. Since the second line has not been able to shed light on or see the way of the fifth "nine" line, but can resemble the submissiveness and attentiveness of a woman, it will not lose its centrality and straightforwardness, which is where its profit lies. **The *Symbol* says: "The spy gazes on the woman's purity: it may still be uncouth."** Since noble people cannot gaze on or see the great way of *yang* firmness, centrality, and straightforwardness, they seem to be nothing but peeping spies. Although they can be submissive and attentive, which is just the same as a woman's purity, they may still be disappointing and uncouth.

The third "six" line: it gazes on its life, on its advances and retreats. Although the third line does not occupy its own position, it is placed at the limit of the submissiveness trigram, and it refers to those who can submit to the moment in their advances and retreats. Were it to occupy its proper position, it would not have the meaning of advancing and retreating. It gazes on "its life" or "the life that it lives": this signifies the movement, production, and influence that go out from oneself. It gazes on the life that it lives and follows what is fitting in its advances and retreats. And so, although it is not placed straightforwardly, it does not yet reach the point of losing sight of the way. It follows the moment in its advances and retreats, and it seeks to keep itself from losing sight of the way. This is why there are no regrets or blame—because it can be submissive. **The *Symbol* says: "'It gazes on its life, on its advances and retreats': it does not yet lose sight of the way."** Since it gazes on its own life, it advances and retreats by submitting to what is fitting. This is why it does not yet reach the point of losing sight of the way.

The fourth "six" line: it gazes on the brightness of the state. There is profit in employing the king's visitor. One can gaze on nothing with more light on it than what is nearby. The fifth line uses *yang* firmness, centrality, and straightforwardness to occupy the position of respect, and it refers to the sagely and worthy ruler. The fourth line, being quite near to it, gazes on or sees its way, and this is why the line statement says that "it gazes on the brightness of the state." It gazes on or sees the abundant virtue and bright radiance of the state. It is not pointing to the person of the ruler when it says "state." Were it speaking of the ruler—how could one stop at gazing on the actions of a single person? It is proper to gaze on the government and transformation of the world, and then the way and virtue of the ruler can be seen. Although the fourth line is *yin* and soft, and it occupies a straightforward position in the Low trigram substance, it is quite near to the fifth. It refers to those who can be submissive and attentive to what they gaze on or see. "There is profit in employing the king's visitor": when those above are enlightened sages, they will cherish and chain themselves to people of power and virtue. The latter will all aspire to advance to the imperial court, so as to assist and gird it while the world makes the crossing to health. The fourth line has gazed on or seen the virtue of the ruler and the order of the state, as well as their bright splendor and abundant beauty. It is fitting for it to visit the king's court so as to make the force of its wisdom effective, and to ascend and assist the ruler in influencing and gratifying the world. This is why it says: "There is profit in employing the king's visitor." In antiquity, when there were people of worth and virtue, the rulers held the ritual of visitation. This is why, when councilors with the rank of scholar advanced to the king's court, they were called "visitors." **The *Symbol* says: "'It gazes on the brightness of the state': it values a visit."** Noble people cherish and carry with them their power and vocation. Their tendency is to make the whole world better at the same time. Nonetheless, they also retain and cherish their guarding of themselves, which happens at moments when there is no enlightened ruler, when no one can employ their way, and when they cannot put this in the past. How could this be the tendency of noble people? This is why Mencius says: "To be set at the center of the world, to give the people between the four seas their determinations—noble people take pleasure in this."[5] To have gazed on or seen the abundant virtue and bright splendor of the state—this is what people of antiquity called "an extraordinary encounter." And so their tendency and aspiration is to climb and advance to the king's court so as to put their way into action. This is why the *Symbol* says: "'It gazes on the brightness of the state': it values a visit." The *shang* character of "values" here signifies their tendency to do something. Their tendency, intention, and aspiration is to make an adoring visit to the king's court.

The fifth "nine" line: it gazes on its life. Noble people are without blame. The fifth "nine" line occupies the position of the ruler. The order or disorder of the moment, and the beauty or badness of the customs, are bound to it and nothing else. "It gazes on its own life": should the customs of the world all be those of noble people, then their own government and transformation are good, which is to be without blame. Were the customs of the world not yet aligned with the way of noble people, then their own government and order would not yet be good, and they could not avoid blame. **The *Symbol* says: "'It gazes on its life': it gazes on the people."** The phrase "its life" refers to what goes out from oneself. If rulers want to gaze on whether their own influence is good or lacking, it is proper for them to gaze on the people. If the customs of the people are good, then their government and transformation are good. Wang Bi also says this: "They gaze on the people so as to examine their own way."[6]

The top "nine" line: it gazes on its life. Noble people are without blame. The top "nine" line places itself at the top using the virtue of *yang* firmness. Those below gaze on it, and it is not in its proper position. Such is the case for worthy or noble people who are not in positions but whose way and virtue are gazed on and admired by the world. "It gazes on its life": it gazes on the life that it lives. This signifies what goes out from oneself—that is, virtue, vocation, action, and duty. They are already what the world gazes on and admires, and this is why it gazes on the life that it lives. Were all this to be the life of a noble person, then there would be neither excess nor blame. If it is not yet the life of a noble person, how can it make people gaze on and admire it as a sympathetic model? In such a case, there will be blame. **The *Symbol* says: "'It gazes on its life': its tendencies are not yet at peace."** Although it is not in its proper position, people nonetheless gaze on its virtue and employ it in their ceremonies and laws.[7] This is why it is proper for it to be cautious and inspect itself, and to gaze on the life that it lives, so that it is constantly without the loss of a noble person's life. Then people will not lose what they hope for and will transform themselves. It should not, simply because it is not in a position, be content to surrender its intentions when it has no affairs to manage. This is why its tendencies or intentions have not yet acquired contentment, and this is why the *Symbol* says that "its tendencies are not yet at peace." The word "peace" here signifies contentment and serenity.

21. BITE DOWN (*SHIHE* 噬嗑)

The *Sequence of the Hexagrams* says: "After they gaze, something will align with them. This is why the Bite Down hexagram is next. To bite down is to align." Since they possess the ability to gaze, they will afterward come into alignment. And so the Bite Down hexagram succeeds the Gaze hexagram. To bite is to chew, and to bite down is to align. At the center of the mouth, there is something taking up space. After it is chewed, there will be alignment again. There are firm lines at the top and bottom of the hexagram, and soft lines at the center. There are firmness outside and emptiness at the center, which symbolize a person's jaws. But at the center of this empty center, there is still one firm line, which symbolizes having something between one's jaws. If there is something at the center of the mouth, it will separate the upper from the lower jaw, and one will be unable to bite down. It must be chewed, and then one will be able to bite down. This is why these lines constitute the Bite Down hexagram. Sages make use of this hexagram symbol to unfold the affairs of the world. Concerning the mouth, this symbol refers to something separating the jaws so that they are unable to align; concerning the world, it refers to strong dissension and insidious crookedness that make a space of separation between things, and this is why the affairs of the world are unable to align. It is proper to employ punishments and penalties. In small cases, one may be admonished or warned, while in great cases, one may be put to death or executed, so that the cause of separation is expelled or driven out. Afterward, the order of the world may be brought to completion. In the world in general, or in just a single state or a single family, or even in the ten thousand affairs, when there is no harmony or alignment, it is always because there is something between them. If there were nothing between them, then they would align. Even when heaven and earth give birth and bring the ten thousand things to completion, they must all align, and afterward they will be successful. In general, if things are not yet aligned, there is always something between them. For example, when ruler and minister, father and son, blood relations, or friends cast off or betray each other, or there is hatred and division between them, it is because an insidious crookedness has made a space between them. If it is expelled or driven out, then they will harmonize and align. This is why separation between things does great harm to the world. Sages gaze on the symbol of the Bite Down hexagram, and then they unfold the ten thousand affairs of the world. If they always drive out this separation between things and bring them into alignment, then nothing will be without harmony and order. The Bite Down hexagram refers to the great function of bringing order to the world. To drive out the spaces between things in the world, one must have command over punishments and penalties, and this is why the hexagram judgment chooses the employment of punishments as its meaning. As for the two trigram substances, light illuminates and authority shakes—together they symbolize the employment of punishments.

Bite Down: there is progress, and profit in the employment of trials. "Bite Down: there is progress": the hexagram itself has the meaning of progress. When the affairs of the world do not make progress, it is because there is something between them. If one bites down on it, then there will be progress and development. "Profit in the employment of trials": concerning the way of biting down on it, it is fitting to employ punishments and trials. How could the space between things in the world be driven out without punishments and trials? The judgment does not say that there is profit in the employment of punishments, but that there is "profit in the employment of trials." The upper trigram symbolizes a light that illuminates, and so there is profit in examinations and trials. A trial is held to study and examine someone's inclinations and falsehoods. Those who have identified the inclinations also recognize the way that brought about the space between things. Afterward, they will be able to provide a defense against it, together with the punishment of the person.

The *Judgment* says: "There is something at the center of the jaws. It is called Bite Down. If one bites down, there will be progress." "There is something at the center of the jaws": this is why it is the Bite Down hexagram. If there is something in the space between the jaws, it is harmful. If one bites down on it, the harm vanishes. Then there will be progress and development, and this is why the *Judgment* says: "If one bites down, there will be progress." **"Firmness is divided by softness. There are movement and enlightenment. Thunder and lightning are aligned and arranged."** The *Judgment* is remarking on the powers of the trigrams. The firm lines and soft lines have spaces between them: "Firmness is divided by softness." They are not mixed together, which symbolizes an enlightened argument. Enlightened argument is the root of examining and trying cases. "There are movement and enlightenment": the Shake trigram is below and the Cast trigram above. Together they refer to movement and enlightenment. "Thunder and lightning are aligned and arranged": thunder shakes and lightning dazzles. They require each other's cooperation in order to be seen, and so they are "aligned and arranged." Illumination cooperates with authority in its action—this is the way of employing trials. If one is capable of illumination, no inclination will remain concealed; if one possesses authority, no one will dare not to tremble. The *Judgment* earlier remarked on the two trigram symbols—"movement and enlightenment"—and this is why it now remarks on the idea of authority and enlightenment cooperating in their function. **"Softness acquires centrality and travels upward. Although its position is not proper for it, there is profit in the employment of trials."** The fifth "six" line uses softness to occupy a central position—this is the meaning of employing softness and acquiring centrality. The phrase "travels upward" signifies that it occupies the position of respect. "Although its position is not proper for it": this signifies that the use of softness to occupy the fifth position is not proper. "There is profit in the employment of trials": concerning the way of bringing order to trials, thorough firmness will result in injury because it is severe and violent, while excess softness will result in loss because it is tolerant and compliant. The fifth line is the master of employing trials. Since it uses softness to place itself in a firm position, and it acquires centrality, it will also acquire what is fitting for the employment of trials. If the use of softness to occupy a firm position indicates that "there is profit in the employment of trials," would the use of firmness to occupy a soft position be profitable or not? Response: firmness and softness are dispositions, while their employment is the position they occupy. It is not fitting to employ softness in bringing order to trials.

The *Symbol* says: "There are thunder and lightning: Bite Down. The first kings used it to shed light on the penalties and enforce their laws." The *Symbol* never situates anything backward, but one may wonder whether the text here is not inverted.[1] Thunder and lightning are things that require each other's cooperation in order to be seen, and this, too, is the symbol of the Bite Down hexagram. Lightning sheds light, and thunder has authority. The first kings gazed on the symbol of thunder and lightning when putting their enlightenment and authority into laws, and they used it to shed light on the punishments and penalties, and to give dominion to their laws and decrees. Laws shed light on the principles of affairs, and constitute a line of defense.

The initial "nine" line: it puts on the shackles that destroy the toes. There is no blame. This "nine" line occupies the initial position, it is placed at the very bottom, and it has no position. It symbolizes the people below, and it refers to people who receive punishments. When punishments are first employed, it is proper that a small crime receive a light punishment. The word "shackles" refers to wooden shackles. The excess is small, and this is why the shackles are put on the feet, so as to destroy or injure the toes. When people with small excesses are shackled and their toes destroyed, it is proper that they be admonished and troubled, so that they do not dare to advance in what is bad. This is why they acquire "no blame." The *Appended Statements* says: "When a small admonition gives a great reproof, this is a blessing for small people."[2] It is saying that they are admonished at its initial point, while it is small, and this is why they acquire no blame. The initial and top lines are both without positions and refer to people who receive punishments. The remaining four lines all refer to people who employ punishments. The initial line occupies the very bottom and has no position, and the top line is placed above the position of respect. Since it exceeds the position of respect, it, too, has no position. Wang Bi considers this position to be neither *yin* nor *yang*, but *yin* and *yang* are bound respectively to the even and odd numbers.[3] How could one embrace the idea of a position without them? Nonetheless, it is not said of the initial and top lines in the various hexagrams either that their positions are proper for them or that their positions are not proper for them. In fact, it is their meaning of initiation and ending that is great. The position of the initial "nine" line in the Watch hexagram is considered straightforward, while the *Symbol* says of the top "six" line in the Need hexagram that "its position is not proper for it," and the *Remarks on the Text* says that the top "nine" line of the Lead hexagram has "no position." But the *wei* character of "position" as referring to a title is not the position of *yin* and *yang*.[4] **The *Symbol* says: "'It puts on the shackles that destroy the toes': it will not travel."** If "it puts on the shackles that destroy" or injure "the toes," they will recognize the admonition and reproof, and will not dare to let what is bad in them grow. This is why the *Symbol* says that "it will not travel." As for the controls and punishments used by people of antiquity, if the crime was small, they put shackles on the toes. In fact, by choosing to prohibit or stop them from traveling, they kept them from advancing in their badness.

The second "six" line: it bites the skin and destroys the nose. There is no blame. The second is the position that corresponds to the fifth, and it refers to those who employ punishments. These four line statements all choose biting as their meaning. The second occupies the center and acquires straightforwardness—that is, its employment of punishments acquires centrality and straight-forwardness. When the employment of punishments acquires centrality and straightforwardness, then those who are criminal and bad will easily be made obedient. This is why the biting of the skin is chosen as its symbol. The flesh or skin of people is easily entered by biting and chewing. The word "destroys" refers to consuming. It enters so deeply that it consumes the nose. The second line uses the way of centrality and straightforwardness, and its punishments easily bring obedience. Nonetheless, it rides the firmness of the initial line—that is, it employs its punishments on firm and strong people. When firm and strong people are punished, they will necessarily require deep pain. This is why it reaches the point of destroying the nose, and then "there is no blame." The way of centrality and straightforwardness, which easily makes people obedient, and the severity of the punishment used to constrain firm and strong people,[5] are meanings that do not interfere with each other. **The *Symbol* says: "'It bites the skin and destroys the nose': it rides on firmness."** It is so deep that it "destroys the nose" because "it rides on firmness." To ride firmness here is to employ punishments on firm and strong people. It cannot be anything but deep and severe. If it is deep and severe, it will acquire what is fitting, and this, too, may be called "centrality."

The third "six" line: it bites the dried meat and encounters poison. There is some small dismay but no blame. The third line occupies the top position in the bottom trigram, and it refers to those who employ punishments. Since a "six" line occupies the third position, it is placed in a position that is not proper for it. Since it has placed itself without acquiring what is proper, and yet it punishes other people, they will not obey it. Instead, they will hate and abhor it, upending and confronting it. It will be like someone who bites and chews on something dry, solid, and tough, and who encounters the savor of something poisonous and bad. It is instead the mouth that is injured. If it employs punishments, but no one obeys it, it will instead bring about hatred and injury. That is, it should be scorned and dismayed. Nonetheless, the great opportunity for those who face the moment of the Bite Down hexagram is that they bite down on what has come between things. Although they have placed themselves in a position that is not proper for them, and they have such difficulty in bring-ing strong dissension into obedience that they reach the point of encountering poison, it is nonetheless not the employment of punishments that is not proper. This is why, although there should be dismay, it is small while they are biting down, and so there is "no blame." **The *Symbol* says: "'It encounters poison': its position is not proper for it."** The third "six" line uses *yin* to occupy a *yang* position, and so it places itself in a position that is not proper for it. Its place is not proper for it, and this is why it is difficult to bring those it punishes into obedience. Instead, they poison it.

The fourth "nine" line: it bites the dry meat on the bone and acquires a metal arrow. There is profit in hardship and purity, and also good fortune. The fourth "nine" line occupies the position near the ruler and refers to those who face command over the Bite Down hexagram. The fourth line has already exceeded the center, which indicates that the space between things is greater and the punishments to be employed are deeper. This is why the line statement says that "it bites the dry meat on the bone." The phrase "meat on the bone" refers to meat still joined to the bone. Dried meat together with the bone is extremely solid and difficult to bite. It bites something extremely solid and "acquires a metal arrow." Metal is chosen because it is firm, and the arrow is chosen because it is straight. The fourth nine line possesses the *yang* virtues of firmness and straightness, and so it acquires a way that is firm and straight. Although it employs a way that is firm and straight, there is profit in conquering the hardship of its affairs and in guarding itself with purity and certainty. Then there will be "good fortune." The fourth "nine" line is firm, but it belongs to the enlightenment trigram substance; it is *yang*, but it occupies a soft position. Since it is firm and enlightened, it will be injured by its own purposes, and this is why it is warned to recognize its difficulty. Since it occupies a soft position, it will not guard itself with certainty, and this is why it is warned about solidity and purity. Some people are firm without being pure, but people who have lost their firmness are generally never pure. The fourth is the best position in the Bite Down hexagram. **The *Symbol* says: "'There is profit in hardship and purity, and also good fortune': it is not yet bright."** In general, when something is said to be "not yet bright," its way is not yet bright and great. It is warned that "there is profit in hardship and purity." In fact, what is insufficient here is that it has not yet acquired centrality and straightforwardness.

The fifth "six" line: it bites the dry meat and acquires the yellow metal. There are purity and danger, but no blame. The fifth line is higher in the hexagram and it "bites the dry meat," which is easier than the "dry meat on the bone" of the fourth line. The fifth line occupies the position of respect, and it rides on the propensity of a higher line to punish those below—its propensity is at ease. It is almost at the limit of the hexagram, and so the space between things is extremely great and it is not easy to bite down. This is why it "bites the dry meat." It "acquires the yellow metal": yellow is the color of centrality, and metal is something firm. The fifth line occupies the center—that is, it acquires the way of centrality. It is placed in a firm position and is assisted by the firmness of the fourth line—this is to acquire the yellow metal. The fifth has no corresponding line, but the fourth occupies the position of the great minister—this is to acquire someone to help it. "There are purity and danger, but no blame": although the fifth "six" line is placed with centrality and firmness, it nonetheless really belongs to a soft trigram substance. This is why the line statement warns that it must be straightforward and certain, cherishing the peril and danger, and then it will acquire no blame. As for those who use softness to occupy the position of respect while facing the moment of the Bite Down hexagram, how could they do it without purity and certainty, or without cherishing their peril and trouble? **The *Symbol* says: "'There are purity and danger, but no blame': it acquires what is proper."** The reason it can be without blame is that what it does is to acquire "what is proper." The word "proper" here signifies occupying the center and employing firmness while being able to guard one's straightforwardness and apprehend the peril.

The top "nine" line: it shoulders a shackle that destroys the ears. There is misfortune. The top line exceeds the position of respect and has no position of its own. This is why it refers to those who receive punishments. It occupies the end position of the hexagram, where the space between things is great and the biting has reached its limit. The *Appended Statements* says that "the bad has accumulated and cannot be confined. The criminal is great and cannot be set loose."[6] This is why "it shoulders a shackle that destroys the ears," and its misfortune should be recognized. To shoulder is to carry, and signifies that the shackle is around its neck. **The *Symbol* says: "'It shoulders a shackle that destroys the ears': its awareness is not enlightened."** When people are deaf, dim, and unawakened, they accumulate what is criminal and bad until they reach their limit. As for the controls and laws made by people of antiquity, those whose crimes were great shouldered a shackle, which indicated that they had listened to no one and recognized nothing. Through accumulation, they had brought the bad in themselves to completion. This is why a shackle was used to destroy or injure their ears, to reprove them for their unenlightened awareness.

22. DRESS (*BI* 賁)

The *Sequence of the Hexagrams* says: "To bite down is to align. Things should not align recklessly, and that is all. This is why the Dress hexagram is next. To dress is to ornament." If things are aligned, then they will necessarily have a pattern, and pattern is ornament. If there is an alignment and gathering of people, then there will be authority and ceremonies, or an above and a below. If there is an alignment and gathering of things, then there will be succession and sequence, or rows and columns. If they are aligned, then they will necessarily have a pattern, and so the Dress hexagram succeeds the Bite Down hexagram. As for the trigrams, "below the mountain, there is a fire." The mountain is where grasses, trees, and a hundred kinds of thing are gathered. If there is fire below it, then what is above will be illuminated and seen. The grasses, trees, and sundry sorts will all receive a bright color, and so these trigrams symbolize the possession of dress and ornament. This is why they constitute the Dress hexagram.

Dress: there are progress and a small profit. It has a long journey. Once a thing is ornamented, it will afterward be capable of progress. This is why the *Book of Rites* says: "What has no root cannot set itself up; what has no pattern cannot act."[1] If a thing has reality and ornament is attached to it, then it will be able to make progress. The way of pattern and ornament can increase a thing's bright coloration, and this is why there can be "a small profit" in its advance.

The *Judgment* says: "'Dress: there is progress.' Softness arrives and gives its pattern to firmness, and this is why there is progress. A piece of firmness ascends and gives its pattern to softness, and this is why there is 'a small profit. It has a long journey.' There is a pattern of heaven. Coming to a stop in pat-

tern and enlightenment is the pattern of humanity." This hexagram symbolizes dress and ornament. Concerning the two substances of the upper and
lower trigrams, one may remark that firmness and softness interacting with each
other constitute a pattern or ornament. The lower trigram substance has the
Lead trigram as its root. When softness has arrived and given its pattern to the
central line, it then becomes the Cast trigram. The upper trigram substance has
the Yield trigram as its root. When firmness has made the journey and given its
pattern to the top line, it then becomes the Calm trigram. That is, "below the
mountain, there is fire," or a coming to a stop in pattern and enlightenment,
and this completes the Dress hexagram. In the affairs of the world, what has no
ornament cannot act, and this is why progress is possible in the Dress hexagram.
"Softness arrives and gives its pattern to firmness, and this is why there is progress": when softness has arrived and given its pattern to firmness, it completes
the symbol of pattern and enlightenment, and so the Dress hexagram is constituted by pattern and enlightenment. The way of the Dress hexagram can bring
about progress—it is really because of their ornamentation that things can
make progress. "A piece of firmness ascends and gives its pattern to softness, and
this is why there is 'a small profit. It has a long journey'": the central line, which
is a piece of the Lead trigram, makes the journey and gives its pattern to the top
line of the Calm trigram. Abundance is attached to affairs because of their ornamentation, and they can act because of their ornamentation. This is why
"there is 'a small profit. It has a long journey.'" As for the journey and the possibility of profit, they must be rooted in something. The way of dress and ornament is not capable of increasing a thing's reality, but it can attach pattern and
color to it. Affairs become clear and abundant because of their pattern. This is
why "there is a small profit. It has a long journey." The *heng* character of "progress" here refers to development, and "journey" refers to the advance that is attached to something. The alterations of the two trigrams share in completing
the meaning of the Dress hexagram. The *Judgment* says only that the upper and
lower trigrams by themselves are each the master of a single state of affairs. In
fact, the enlightenment of the Cast trigram is sufficient to bring about progress.
When it has received the pattern of softness, it is able to make a small advance.
"There is a pattern of heaven. Coming to a stop in pattern and enlightenment
is the pattern of humanity": this statement concerns the preceding text, which
says that when *yin* and *yang* or firmness and softness give their patterns to each
other, this is the pattern of heaven.[2] To come to a stop in pattern and enlightenment is the pattern of humanity. "Coming to a stop" signifies placing oneself in
pattern and enlightenment. Each disposition necessarily has its pattern, which
serves as the principle of its spontaneous activity. The principle necessarily has

an aim on which it waits, which serves as the root of birth and life. When there is "above," there will also be "below"; when there is "this," there will also be "that"; when there is a disposition, there will also be a pattern. Not one thing can be set up alone, and if there are two, then there will be a pattern. As for those who do not know the way, how could they understand this? The "pattern of heaven" is the principle of heaven, while the "pattern of humanity" is the way of humanity. **"One gazes on the pattern of heaven by examining the alteration of the seasons."** The "pattern of heaven" signifies the intersection and configuration of the sun, moon, planets, and stars, as well as the alternation and alteration of cold and heat, *yin* and *yang*. One gazes on their revolutions by examining the relocation and modification of the four seasons. **"One gazes on the pattern of humanity by transforming and completing the world."** The "pattern of humanity" is the coherence and sequence in the principle of humanity. "One gazes on the pattern of humanity" by teaching and transforming the world. When the rituals and customs of the world are complete, it is because sages have employed the way of the Dress hexagram. "Below the mountain, there is a fire": this is chosen as the symbol of the Dress hexagram. "Softness arrives and gives its pattern to firmness. Firmness ascends and gives its pattern to softness": this is chosen as the alteration of the trigrams. As for the hexagrams in general, sometimes the complete hexagram is determined by the meaning of its two trigram substances and their two symbols. For example, the *Judgment* of the Block hexagram says "there is movement at the center of the obstacle," and the *Symbol* says "there are clouds and thunder." The *Judgment* of the Fight hexagram says "there is firmness above, and an obstacle below," and the *Symbol* says "heaven and water draw back from each other." Sometimes a single line is chosen as the cause of the complete hexagram. For example, "when softness acquires a position, and those above and below correspond to it," it is called the Small Herd hexagram. Or take the case where "softness acquires the position of respect and great centrality. Those above and below correspond to it." This is called the Great Grasp hexagram. Sometimes only the two trigram substances are chosen as the cause, when they mean either disappearance or growth. For example, when "there is thunder at the center of the earth," it is the Turn hexagram, and when "the mountain is dependent on the earth," it is the Wear hexagram. Sometimes the two trigram symbols are chosen, but the interaction and alteration of two lines is chosen at the same time as the meaning of the hexagram. For example, the *Symbol* of the Add hexagram says "there are wind and thunder," but the *Judgment* says at the same time that "there is taking from those above and adding to those below." The *Symbol* of the Take hexagram says "below the mountain is a lake," but the *Judgment* says at the same time that "there is taking from those below and adding to those above." Sometimes, when the complete hexagram has already been determined by the two trigram symbols, the meaning of the lines is then chosen. This is the case for the "firmness dissolves softness" of the Solve hexagram and the "softness encounters firmness" of the Pair hexagram. Sometimes the complete hexagram refers to a function. For example, "something is lowered into the water and brings the water up: Well," and "above the wood, there is fire: Tripod." In the case of the Tripod hexagram, the symbol is also constituted from the shape of the hexagram. Sometimes the shape of the hexagram constitutes its symbol. For example, "below the mountain, there is thunder: Feed," but if "there is something at the center of the jaws," the hexagram is called Bite Down. So much for the meaning of the complete hexagrams. As for "firmness is above and softness below,"[3] or "there is taking from those above and adding to those below,"[4] these statements signify either that firmness occupies a position above and softness occupies a position below or that there is a taking from those above and an adding to those below. The *Judgment* is speaking about what completes the hexagram. It does not signify that something has risen, fallen, or reached the center within the hexagram. For example, the *Judgment* says of the Fight and No Fault hexagrams that "firmness arrives." How could it have arrived from the upper trigram substance?[5] Generally when a soft line occupies the fifth position, the *Judgment* will say that "softness advances and travels upward." Soft lines occupy positions below, but in this case it occupies the position of respect, which is to advance and ascend. It does not signify that it ascends from the lower trigram substance. The alteration of the hexagram always begins from the Lead and Yield trigrams. Earlier intellectuals could not attain this understanding, and this is why they said that the Dress hexagram is rooted in the Free hexagram. Since the Free hexagram is constituted by putting a Yield trigram on top of a Lead trigram, how could the Free hexagram be a cause and principle of alteration? The lower Cast trigram is rooted in a Lead trigram whose central line alters to complete the Cast trigram. The upper Calm trigram is rooted in a Yield trigram whose top line alters to complete the Calm trigram. The Cast trigram is inside, and this is why the *Judgment* says that "softness arrives." The Calm trigram is on top, and this is why it says that "firmness ascends." It does not ascend from the lower trigram substance. The Lead and Yield trigrams alter and constitute their six children. The eight trigrams are put one on top of the other to constitute the sixty-four hexagrams. All are caused by the alterations of the Lead and Yield trigrams.

The *Symbol* says: "Below the mountain, there is a fire: Dress. Noble people use it to shed light on their numberless acts of government, but they do not dare to hold trials." The mountain is where grasses, trees, and a hundred other things gather and live. When the fire is below it and illuminates what is above, the numberless kinds of thing all receive its bright light, which constitutes the symbol of the Dress or ornament hexagram. Noble people gaze on this symbol—"below the mountain, there is a fire" that sheds light or illuminates—so as to correct and shed light on their numberless acts of government, and to complete the order of pattern and enlightenment. They do not have the purpose and daring "to hold trials." Rulers bring about caution in those who hold trials. How could they rely on their own enlightenment, and treat their own employment lightly? The *Symbol* refers to whose who employ the heart of a sage, and its warning is deep. What it chooses as the symbol is only that "below the mountain, there is a fire" that sheds light on and illuminates the numberless things. Concerning the employment of this light, it warns that the Dress hexagram also has the meaning of not daring to hold trials. Those who hold trials employ without qualification the case's inclination and reality. If they have only its pattern and ornament, then they have not grasped its inclination. This is why they do not dare to employ the pattern when holding trials.

The initial "nine" line: it dresses its toes. It abandons the carriage and goes on foot. The initial "nine" line uses *yang* firmness to occupy the enlightenment trigram substance, it is placed at the bottom, and it refers to noble people who possess the virtues of firmness and enlightenment but are at the bottom. Noble people on a terrain without position can have no influence on the world. They can only dress and ornament their own actions, and that is all. The word "toes" is chosen because their actions are at the bottom. Noble people correct the way of ornament, make their actions straightforward, and keep guard over their reins and their placement in accordance with duty. Their actions are not reckless. If something is not proper to their duty, they will abandon their carriage or chariot and serenely travel on foot. The crowd is disappointed by this, but noble people consider it to be their dress. The meaning of the statement "it abandons the carriage and goes on foot" is chosen at the same time because of the closest line and because of its corresponding line. The initial line is close to the second, but it corresponds to the fourth. Its correspondence to the fourth is straightforward, but its agreement with the second is not straightforward. Since the firmness and enlightenment of the "nine" line keep guard over its duty, it does not agree with the nearby second line, but corresponds to the faraway fourth line. It abandons what is easy and attends to what is difficult, as though it "abandons the carriage" and travels "on foot." To keep guard over one's reins and duty is the dress of noble people. This is why the dress of noble people is a disappointment to the customs of the times, while what is esteemed by the customs of the times is poverty to noble people.[6] It speaks of a "carriage" and going "on foot" because it is concerned with the meaning of "toes" and "travel." **The *Symbol* says: "'It abandons the carriage and goes on foot': its duty is not to ride."** To abandon the carriage and travel on foot mean that its duty is that it should not ride. If the initial line corresponds to the fourth, it is straightforward, but if it attends to the second, it is not straightforward. It abandons the ease of the nearby second line and attends to the difficulty of the fourth: "It abandons the carriage" and travels "on foot." The dress of noble people is to keep guard over their duty, and that is all.

The second "six" line: it dresses its beard. Although the Dress hexagram is constituted by the alteration of two lines, it is the meaning of pattern and enlightenment that carries more weight.[7] The second line is really the master of the Dress hexagram, and this is why the line statement speaks about the way of the Dress hexagram. The ornamentation of things cannot make great alterations to their disposition. It is only because there is the disposition that ornament is attached to it, and this is why the meaning of the beard is chosen. The beard follows the movement of the jaws. Its movement and stopping are bound entirely to that from which it hangs, just as goodness and badness are not caused by one's dress. The pattern and enlightenment of the second line are nothing but dress and ornamentation. Their goodness and badness are bound to its disposition. **The *Symbol* says: "'It dresses its beard': it ascends together with those above."** The symbol of the beard signifies that this line ascends at the same time as the line above it. Its movement follows the line above it—that is, its movement and stopping are bound entirely to that from which it hangs, as when one attaches ornament to something. It is only because there is the disposition that one can dress it, while goodness and badness are in the disposition.

The third "nine" line: it is like something dressed, like something glistening. Endless purity brings good fortune. The third line is placed in the limit position of pattern and enlightenment, between two *yin* lines—the second and the fourth—and they are placed so as to dress each other. It refers to the abundance of the Dress hexagram, and this is why the line statement says that "it is like something dressed." The word "like" here is just a grammatical particle. When dress and ornamentation are abundant, one is brightly colored, soaking in grace. This is why it says that it is "like something glistening." When bright coloration is abundant, one is soaking in grace, as when the *Book of Poetry* says

that "the does shimmer, and shimmer again."[8] "Endless purity brings good fortune": there is no straightforward correspondence between the third line and
the second and fourth lines, but they are close to each other and complete each
other's dress. This is why it gives a warning about constant or endless purity
and straightforwardness. To dress is to ornament, and in an affair of dress and
ornament it is difficult to be constant. This is why endless purity will bring
good fortune. The third and the fourth lines dress each other, and further, the
third descends to be close to the second, so that two soft lines are here giving
their pattern to a single firm line. The lines above and below interact with and
dress it, which constitutes an abundance of dress. **The *Symbol* says: "The good
fortune of endless purity: in the end, no one usurps it."** As for those whose
ornamentation is neither constant nor straightforward, other people will usurp
and insult them. This is why the line statement warns that if it can be endlessly
straightforward, there will be good fortune. If its dress were already constant and
straightforward, who could usurp it?

**The fourth "six" line: it is like something dressed, like something gray. The
plain horse is like something soaring. If there are no bandits, there will be
a marriage.** The fourth line corresponds straightforwardly to the initial line,
which indicates that they dress each other. It is proper that they be "like something dressed" at their root, but they are separated by the third line. This is why
they do not obtain their dress, and are "like something gray." To be gray is to
be plain, when one has not yet obtained one's dress. The word "horse" refers
to something that moves in a position below. They have not yet obtained their
dress, and this is why the line statement calls the initial line a "plain horse."
Its tendency is to attend to its straightforwardly corresponding line as though
it were flying, and this is why it is said to be "like something soaring." If they
were not separated by the hostile bandit—the third "nine" line—they would
successfully marry and become related to each other. That on which one rides,
and which moves below one, is symbolized by the horse. The initial and fourth
lines correspond straightforwardly and will necessarily obtain a relationship in
the end. At the beginning, however, they are separated by something between
them. **The *Symbol* says: "The fourth 'six' line: it is doubtful that its position
is proper for it. 'If there are no bandits, there will be a marriage': in the end,
there is no resentment."** The fourth is far away from the initial line, and the
third is secure in the space between them—it is doubtful that such a position
is proper for it. Although the third line's hostile bandit is what separates them,
and they have not yet acquired a marital relationship, they are nonetheless in
straightforward correspondence. This principle will lead their duty straight to

victory, so that they will necessarily acquire alignment in the end. This is why the *Symbol* says that, "in the end, there is no resentment." To be resentful is to hate. They will dress each other in the end, and this is why there is no hatred or resentment between them.

The fifth "six" line: it is dressed in the garden on the summit. The bolts of silk are cut, and cut again. There is dismay but good fortune in the end. The fifth "six" line uses the disposition of *yin* softness, and is profoundly close to the top "nine" line—that is, a worthy person of *yang* firmness. This *yin* line is close to the *yang* line and is not bound by any corresponding line. Because it attends to it, it receives its dress from the top "nine" line. Since antiquity, people have provided obstacles to guard their states, and this is why ramparts and fortifications were often seated on summits and hilltops. The word "summit" signifies something outside and nearby but also lofty, and "garden" refers to tended earth very near to the ramparts and the district, but also outside and nearby. And so "garden on the summit" signifies something outside and nearby, and points to the top "nine" line. Although the fifth "six" line occupies the position of the ruler, its power of *yin* softness is not sufficient for it to guard itself. It is close to the *yang* firmness of the top line, and its tendency is to attend to it. It obtains its dress from a worthy person who is close but outside: "It is dressed in the garden on the summit." If it can receive its dress from the top "nine" line, it will also be portioned out and controlled, just like bolts of silk that are "cut, and cut again." In such a case, although it is soft and weak, and cannot guard itself, which may bring some small dismay, it can nonetheless attend to this person, complete the task of the Dress hexagram, and obtain good fortune in the end. To be "cut, and cut again," refers to the condition of being snipped, apportioned, divided, and sliced. When silk is not yet to be employed, it is rolled into bolts, and this is why the line statement refers to "bolts of silk." To control their being made into clothing one must snip, apportion, divide, slice, and "cut, and cut again." The "bolts of silk" are a metaphor for the root disposition of the fifth "six" line, and to be "cut, and cut again" signifies that it is snipped and crafted by someone so as to complete its function. What it owes to this person is not the same as in the Blind hexagram. The Blind hexagram does not speak of dismay because, in fact, it is fitting that the child be blind and dependent on another person. If it is not a child or immature, and yet it still owes its dress to another person, it should be dismayed. Nonetheless, it will feast on its accomplishment in the end, which constitutes good fortune. **The *Symbol* says: "The good fortune of the fifth 'six' line: it is happy."** To be able to attend to someone so as to complete the task of the Dress hexagram, and to feast on one's good fortune and beauty—this is to be happy.

The top "nine" line: its dress is plain. There is no blame. The top "nine" line is the limit of the Dress hexagram. To be at the limit of dress and ornamentation is to become lost in flowery falsehoods. If it can isolate its disposition by making its dress plain, it will not be blamed for excess or loss. The word "plain" refers to simplicity. If it values the simplicity of its disposition, then it will not lose its root and actuality. To value the simplicity of one's disposition does not signify to be without ornamentation but to refrain from producing a flower that has no reality. **The *Symbol* says: "'Its dress is plain. There is no blame': those above acquire the object of their tendencies."** "Its dress is plain. There is no blame": by being above, it acquires what it tends toward. The top "nine" line's acquisition of the object of its tendencies indicates that it is at the top, that its pattern and softness complete the task of the Dress hexagram, and also that the ruler referred to by the fifth "six" line receives its dress. This is why, although it occupies a terrain without a position, in reality it officiates over the task of the Dress hexagram, which indicates that it acquires the object of its tendencies. In other hexagrams, the occupation of the limit position refers to something different. When it is already at the top, acquires the object of its tendencies, and places itself at the limit of the Dress hexagram, it is about to be blamed for a flowery falsehood and a loss of reality. This is why the line statement warns it to use the simplicity of its disposition, so that there will be no blame. That is, its ornamentation should not become excessive.

23. WEAR (BO 剝)

The *Sequence of the Hexagrams* says: "Those who dress up are ornamented. When ornamentation has been brought about, the regulations for progress will be exhausted. This is why the Wear hexagram is next." As for things that have reached the point of pattern and ornamentation, they are at the limit of progress. Anything that reaches its limit must reverse itself. This is why, when the Dress hexagram reaches its end, the Wear hexagram begins. The hexagram consists of five *yin* lines and one *yang* line. At its beginning, *yin* is born at the bottom. Step by step, it grows until it reaches the limit of abundance. The group of *yin* lines wears away the *yang* line and makes it disappear, and this is why they constitute the Wear hexagram. Concerning the two trigram substances, one may remark that "the mountain is dependent on the earth." The mountain ascends to a lofty place above the earth, but it is also dependent on the earth, which symbolizes crumbling and wearing away.

Wear: there is no profit. It has a long journey. In the moment of the Wear hexagram, a group of *yin* lines is growing and becoming abundant, while the *yang* lines are worn away and disappear. A crowd of small people wear away and deprive the noble people. This is why the noble people have "no profit" and "a long journey." It is proper for them simply to make their speech lowly and to obscure their traces. If they follow the moment by disappearing into a place of rest, they will avoid the harm of small people.

The *Judgment* says: "To wear is to wear away. Softness alters firmness. 'There is no profit. It has a long journey': small people are growing." "To wear is to wear away": what is signified by the *bo* character of "wear" is deterioration. "Softness alters firmness": softness is growing, and firmness is altering. At the summer solstice, a single *yin* line is born, and it grows step by step. If one *yin* line is growing, then one *yang* line is disappearing. At the beginning of October, it has reached its limit and completes the Wear hexagram.[1] This is a case of *yin* softness altering *yang* firmness. The *yin* lines refer to the way of small people facing its growth and abundance. In the Wear hexagram, they have made the *yang* lines disappear, and this is why, for noble people, "there is no profit" in making a journey. **"To be submissive and come to a stop is to gaze on the symbol. Noble people value their disappearing and coming to rest, the full and the empty, the action of heaven."** When noble people are faced with the moment of the Wear hexagram, they recognize that they should not make a journey. By submitting to the moment and coming to a stop, they are able to gaze on the symbol of the Wear hexagram. The hexagram symbolizes being submissive and coming to a stop, which is how to place oneself on the way of the Wear hexagram. It is proper for noble people to gaze on it and give substance to it. "Noble people value their disappearing and coming to rest, the full and the empty, the action of heaven": the principle of disappearing and coming to rest, or the full and the empty, persists in the hearts of noble people, and they are capable of submitting to it, which is to align with the action of heaven. The principle of things includes disappearance and scarcity, coming to rest and growth, fullness and satiety, and emptiness and taking away. If one submits to it, then there will be good fortune, but if one rebels against it, there will be misfortune. By following the moment and valuing true-heartedness, noble people manage the affairs of heaven.

The *Symbol* says: "The mountain is dependent on the earth: Wear. Those above use it to benefit those below and to make them contented where they reside." The Calm trigram is put on top of the Yield trigram: "The mountain is dependent on the earth." The mountain ascends to a lofty place above the earth, but it also depends on the earth, which symbolizes ravaging and wearing away. The phrase "those above" signifies those who rule and occupy positions above other people. They gaze on the symbol of the Wear hexagram, and they bring benefits and certainty to those below, making them contented with the positions they occupy. Those below are the root of those above. There has never yet been something whose institution and root were certain that was nonetheless capable of wearing away. This is why the wearing away of those above will necessarily come from those below. If those below are wearing away, then those above will be in peril. If those above other people recognize that the principle of things is like this, they will bring contentment and nourishment to the people. They will bring benefits to their root, and so it will be content with the position it occupies. The *Book of History* says: "The people are the only root of kingdoms. If the root is certain, then the kingdom will be serene."[2]

The initial "six" line: it wears away the bed by the legs. To demean purity brings misfortune. The wearing away of *yang* by *yin* ascends from the bottom. The bed is chosen as symbol because it is where the body is placed. It wears away from the bottom, and will reach the body step by step. "It wears away the bed by the legs"—that is, it wears away the legs of the bed. Wearing away begins from the bottom, and this is why the line statement refers to wearing away the legs. As *yin* advances from the bottom step by step, purity and straightforwardness will be demeaned and disappear, which is the way of misfortune. The word "demean" refers to negation, and signifies that the way of straightforwardness is disappearing or vanishing. *Yin* wearing away *yang*, or softness altering firmness—such is the case when the crooked are invading the straightforward, or when small people are making noble people disappear. Their misfortune should be recognized. **The *Symbol* says: "'It wears away the bed by the legs': so as to destroy what is below."** The legs of a bed are chosen as the symbol because *yin* is invading and consuming *yang* at the bottom. The word "destroy" indicates that it is consumed. When *yin* destroys the way of straightforwardness, it ascends from the bottom.

The second "six" line: it wears away the bed by the beams. To demean purity brings misfortune. The word "beam" refers to what divides or separates those above from those below, which in this case is the bed frame. As *yin* advances step by step, and its wearing away has ascended to reach the beams, straightforwardness is even more demeaned, adding to its extreme misfortune. **The *Symbol* says: "'It wears away the bed by the beams': they do not yet possess agreement."** As *yin* is invading and wearing away *yang*, and it acquires additional abundance so that it reaches the point of wearing away the beams, this happens because *yang* does not yet possess anything with which it corresponds or agrees. As small people are invading and wearing away noble people, if someone were to agree with the noble people, they could be victorious over the small people and could not be harmed. It is only because no one agrees with them that they are demeaned, and there is misfortune. Since they are faced with a moment of disappearance and wearing away, and they have no disciples to agree with them, how could they persist by themselves? The *Symbol* says: "They do not yet possess agreement." When the wearing away is not yet abundant, those who "possess agreement" may still be victorious over it. The idea shown to people here is deep.

The third "six" line: it wears away. There is no blame. In the moment when a crowd of *yin* lines is wearing away the *yang* line, the third line is the only one to occupy a firm position and correspond to a firm line. In this respect, it differs from the *yin* lines above and below it. Its tendency is to attend to straightforwardness and, in the moment of the Wear hexagram, this constitutes the absence of blame. If what the third line does may be called good, why does the line statement not remark that there is good fortune? Response: the group of *yin* lines has started to wear away the *yang* line, and the crowd of small people has started to harm the noble people. Although the third line attends to straightforwardness, its propensity is isolated and weak, and its corresponding line is on a terrain without a position. In such a moment, it is difficult to avoid the result, so how could it acquire good fortune? Its meaning is only that "there is no blame." It remarks that "there is no blame" as a means of persuasion. **The *Symbol* says: "'It wears away. There is no blame': it loses sight of those above and below."** The third line occupies a position in the Wear hexagram, and yet "there is no blame." Concerning its placement, it is not the same as the various *yin* lines above and below it. That is, these lines of the same kind have lost sight of each other. For those placed on the way of the Wear hexagram, this constitutes the absence of blame. Such was the case of Lu Qiang in the Eastern Han dynasty.[3]

The fourth "six" line: it wears away the bed by the skin. There is misfortune. The Wear hexagram begins with the legs of the bed, and step by step reaches the skin. The word "skin" refers to the outside of the body. The body is about to be destroyed, and its misfortune should be recognized. The growth of *yin* is already abundant, the wearing away of *yang* is already extreme, and the way of purity is already disappearing. This is why the line statement no longer remarks that purity is demeaned, but goes straight to remarking on its misfortune. **The *Symbol* says: "'It wears away the bed by the skin': disaster is quite near."** The fifth is the position of the ruler, and the wearing away already extends to the fourth position. Concerning human beings, this refers to the wearing away of their skin. When wearing away extends to the skin, the body is about to vanish. It is "quite near" to affliction and disaster.

The fifth "six" line: it strings the fish, and someone in the palace is favored. Nothing is without profit. The wearing away extends to the position of the ruler, which is the limit of wearing away, and its misfortune should be recognized. This is why the line statement no longer remarks on wearing away but provides another meaning, opening the door for small people to relocate to the good. The fifth is the master of the group of *yin* lines, while a fish is a *yin* thing, and this is why it constitutes the symbol here. The fifth can make the group of *yin* lines submit to a sequence, just as when one "strings the fish." However, since it obtains the favor or love of the single *yang* line above it, as though it were "someone in the palace," nothing will be without profit. The phrase "someone in the palace" refers to people within the palace, such as wives, concubines, servants, and auxiliaries. Because it is speaking about a *yin* line, it chooses the meaning of obtaining favor or love. There is only one *yang* line above it, while the crowd of *yin* lines possesses the way of submitting and attending to it, and this is why it reveals this particular meaning. **The *Symbol* says: "'Someone in the palace is favored': in the end there is no resentment."** The group of *yin* lines has been wearing away the *yang* line and making it disappear, and it has now reached its limit. If the fifth "six" line can be the elder administrator over the group of *yin* lines, it will place itself at their head and submit them to a sequence. However, since it obtains the favor or love of the *yang* line, in the end there will be no excess or resentment. When the wearing away is about to end, the line statement turns to the revelation of this meaning. The intention of the sage, whose depth is extreme, is to persuade people to relocate to the good.

The top "nine" line: the large fruit is not eaten. Noble people acquire carriages, while small people wear away their huts. The various *yang* lines have already disappeared, and the Wear hexagram is exhausted. The top "nine" line is the only one that still persists, like a large and great fruit that is not for eating, but will soon see its way to the principle of rebirth.[4] If the top "nine" were also altered, then the hexagram lines would be uniformly *yin*, but there is no principle by which *yang* may be exhausted. If it is altered at the top, then it will be born at the bottom. There is no moment between these two that can embrace its rest. The sage reveals and sheds light on this principle so as to show that the way of *yang* and noble people cannot vanish. Someone asks: when the Wear hexagram is exhausted, it will constitute the uniform *yin* lines of the Yield hexagram. How could there still be *yang* lines? Response: concerning the matching of the hexagrams to the months, one may remark that the tenth is the proper month of the Yield hexagram. Concerning the disappearing and coming to rest of the *qi*, one may remark that the wearing away of the *yang qi* constitutes the Yield hexagram, while the arrival of the *yang qi* constitutes the Turn hexagram. *Yang* never tastes exhaustion. When its wearing away is exhausted at the top, it returns to be born at the bottom. This is why the tenth month is called the month of *yang*, out of fear that someone may wonder whether there is no *yang*.[5] *Yin* is also like this, although the sage does not remark on it. In the moment when the way of *yin* is abundant and at its limit, its disorder should be recognized. When its disorder is at its limit, it is proper to reflect on order, and this is why the hearts of the crowd aspire to bear noble people as their load: "Noble people acquire carriages." And so the "Without a Wind" and "Descending from the Spring" poems in the *Book of Poetry* occupy the end of their sections, and bring about an alteration.[6] Since there is already such a principle, it is also the case that, in the hexagrams, the crowd of *yin* lines is the ancestor of the *yang* lines, and is symbolized by the bearing of a shared load. "Small people wear away their huts": in the case of small people facing the limit of the Wear hexagram, they will wear away their huts, and there is no place that will embrace them. The line statement is no longer discussing the *yin* and *yang* lines, but remarks on small people placed at the limit of the Wear hexagram, when the wearing away extends to "their huts." The word "hut" is chosen to symbolize being at the top. Someone asks: when *yin* or *yang* is disappearing, it must wait to be exhausted, and afterward it will return to be born at the bottom. How can this top line have the meaning of returning to birth? And why does the line statement for the top "six" line of the Solve hexagram remark that "in the end there is misfortune"? Response: the top "nine" line occupies the position at the limit of the Wear hexagram. There is only one *yang* line at the top, but there is no principle by which *yang* may be exhausted. This is why it sheds light on the meaning of returning to be born, to show that the way of noble people may not vanish. In the Solve hexagram, *yang* is making *yin* disappear. *Yin* refers to the way of small people, and this is why the line statement remarks only on its disappearing or vanishing. What use would there be in further remarking that it has the principle of returning to be born? **The *Symbol* says: "'Noble people acquire carriages': the people bear them as their load. 'Small people wear away their huts': in the end they should not be employed."** When the way of straightforwardness has reached the limit of its disappearing and wearing away, people will return to reflecting on order. This is why the people serve and bear the *yang* firmness of noble people. Since small people may be placed at the limit of the Wear hexagram, the *Symbol* refers to the depletion of small people: "In the end they should not be employed." It is not saying that this "nine" line refers to small people, but that, at the moment when the Wear hexagram is at its limit, the case of small people is like this.

24. TURN (*FU* 復)

The *Sequence of the Hexagrams* says: "Things cannot, in the end, be exhausted. When they are worn away and depleted at the top, they revert to the bottom. This is why the Turn hexagram is next." There is no principle by which things are worn away to exhaustion. This is why, when they are worn away to the limit, they will arrive at the turning point. If they reach the limit of *yin*, then *yang* will be born. If *yang* is worn away to its limit at the top, then it will return to be born at the bottom. If it is depleted at the top, it will revert to the bottom, and so the Turn hexagram succeeds the Wear hexagram. As for the hexagram, a single *yang* line is born below five *yin* lines. *Yin* has reached its limit, and now *yang* is returning. In the year's tenth month, *yin* has reached the limit of its abundance. On the winter solstice, a single *yang* line returns to be born at the center of the earth. This is why these lines constitute the Turn hexagram.[1] *Yang* refers to the way of noble people. When *yang* has reached the limit of its disappearance, it reverses itself and returns. When the way of noble people has reached the limit of its disappearance, it returns and grows. This is why the hexagram has the meaning of reversion to the good.

Turn: there is progress. It goes out and enters without illness, and friends arrive. There is no blame. "Turn: there is progress": when the return has been made, there will be progress. The *yang qi* returns to be born at the bottom. Step by step it makes progress toward abundance. It gives birth to and cultivates the ten thousand things. The way of noble people has returned, and so, step by step, it will make progress and develop, and gratify the world. This is why the Turn hexagram possesses the principle of progress and abundance. "It goes out and enters without illness": "It goes out and enters" signifies that it is born and grows. To return and be born on the inside is to enter, while to grow and advance on the outside is to go out. The judgment says first that "it goes out" because this makes the spoken sentence flow better. A *yang* line has been born, but it is not in the outer trigram. It arrives in the inner trigram, and this is why the judgment says that it "enters." At the beginning and birth of things, their *qi* is extremely minimal, and this is why there are often blockages and hardships. At the beginning and birth of *yang*, its *qi* is extremely minimal, and this is why there are often bruises and breaks. When *yang* is revealed in the springtime, it is broken by the coldness of *yin*, as anyone who gazes at the grasses and trees at dawn or dusk will be able to see. "It goes out and enters without illness": this signifies that *yang*, though minimal, has been born and is growing, and nothing will harm it. Since nothing harms it, and it advances step by step to arrive with others of its kind, then they are about to make progress toward abundance. This is why "there is no blame." Concerning *qi*, the word "blame" signifies that it strays and wavers; concerning noble people, the word "blame" signifies that their path is restricted and choked, and that they cannot exhaust their principle. Those who face the return of *yang* may be able to make it ill, but they certainly cannot stop its return. They can only hinder and hamper it. Here the powers of the trigrams have the meaning of being without illness, which is the best that the way of returning can do. A single *yang* line begins and is born. It is extremely minimal, and it is certainly not yet capable of victory over the group of *yin* lines, which would reveal and give birth to the ten thousand things. It must wait for the arrival of the various *yang* lines, and afterward it will be able to bring the task of birth to completion without straying or wavering. It will use the arrival of its friends, and there will be no blame. The *qi* of the three *yang* months—December, January, and February—gives birth to and completes the ten thousand things.[2] This task belongs to the crowd of *yang* lines. If it were the way of noble people, it would have already disappeared and now be returning. How could it be victorious from the start over small people? It must wait for friends of its own kind to become abundant step by step, and then they will be able to join forces and be victorious. **It reverses itself and returns to its way. In seven days, it will arrive at the turning point. There are profit and a long journey.** The judgment is signifying the way of disappearance and growth. "It reverses itself and returns" to reach the point of recurrence. When the disappearance of *yang* has reached a period of "seven days," then "it will arrive at the turning point." The Pair hexagram refers to the beginning of *yang*'s disappearance. It is the first of the seven alterations that complete the Turn hexagram, and this is why the judgment says "seven days," to signify the seven modifications. The judgment of the Watch hexagram says that "when the eighth month is reached, there will be misfortune," which signifies that the growth of *yang* over eight months reaches the point when *yin* begins to grow. If *yang* is advancing, then *yin* is retreating. If the way of noble people is growing, then the way of small people is disappearing. This is why "there are profit and a long journey."

The *Judgment* says: "'Turn: there is progress': firmness reverses itself. There are movement and submission in its action. As a result, 'it goes out and enters without illness, and friends arrive. There is no blame.'" "Turn: there is progress" signifies that "firmness reverses itself," and so "there is progress." *Yang* firmness reaches the limit of its disappearance and arrives at its reversal. Since it has arrived at the point of reversal, it grows and becomes abundant step by step; it makes progress and develops. "There are movement and submission in its action. As a result, 'it goes out and enters without illness, and friends arrive. There is no blame'": concerning the powers of the trigrams, the *Judgment* remarks on the result they will bring about. The lower trigram refers to movement and the upper trigram to submission: "There are movement and submission in its action." *Yang* firmness reverses itself, and its movement is submissive. "As a result, 'it goes out and enters without illness, and friends arrive. There is no blame.'" The arrival of friends also refers to its submissive movement. **"'It reverses itself and returns to its way. In seven days, it will arrive at the turning point': this is the action of heaven. 'There are profit and a long journey': this is the growth of firmness. In turning, does one not see the heart of heaven and earth?"** Its way is to reverse itself and turn back, to make the journey and arrive: its disappearance recurs, and its coming to rest recurs. "In seven days, it arrives at the turning point": such is the revolution of heaven and earth.[3] It is the principle of heaven that disappearance and growth are causes of each other. *Yang* firmness, the way of noble people, is growing, and this is why "there are profit and a long journey." A single *yang* line has returned at the bottom, and so the heart of heaven and earth is to give birth to things. Earlier intellectuals all considered tranquility to be seeing the heart of heaven and earth.[4] In fact, they did not recognize that the heart of heaven and earth is the impetus of movement. As for those who do not know the way, how could they understand it?

The *Symbol* says: "Thunder is at the center of the earth: Turn. The first kings used it to lock the gates on the solstice. Merchants on the march did not travel. The princes did not inspect the regions." Thunder occurs when *yin* and *yang* approach each other and bring their sound to completion. It is proper that *yang*, when still minimal, cannot yet reveal itself. "Thunder is at the center of the earth": this is the moment when *yang* begins to return. When *yang* begins and is born at the bottom, it is extremely minimal. If it is contented and tranquil, it will afterward be able to grow. It was proper for the first kings, who submitted to the way of heaven, to be content and tranquil on the solstice, when *yang* begins and is born, so as to nourish it. This is why they "locked the gates," and kept "merchants on the march" from traveling. Those who rule do not inspect or look into the four regions. They gaze on the symbol of the Turn hexagram and submit to the way of heaven. Concerning the body of a single person, this is also the case. It is proper to be content and tranquil, so as to nourish one's *yang qi*.

The initial "nine" line: it returns from not far away. It does not extol regret. There are primacy and good fortune. The Turn hexagram refers to the reversal, arrival, or return of *yang*. *Yang* refers to the way of noble people, and this is why the Turn hexagram has the meaning of reverting to the good. The initial line is *yang* and firm, and it arrives and returns. It is placed in the initial position of the hexagram, at the very first part of the return. This is to return "from not far away." It lost something, and afterward returned to it. If it had not lost it, how could it possess a return? It is only because its return was "not far away" from its loss that it does not reach the point of regret. This is a great good, and there is good fortune. It is fitting that the *zhi* character of "extol" be voiced as a *di* character and have the meaning of "achieve."[5] The *Jade Chapters* says that it means "become suited to," but the meaning is still the same.[6] "It does not extol regret": this indicates that it does not reach the point of regret. A line statement in the Pit hexagram says: "It has extolled what is level. There is no blame."[7] This signifies that it has reached what is level. Fuzi says that the excess of Yanzi, which is without form or clarity, is "incipient in its degree," indicating that "it does not extol regret."[8] If an excess does not yet have a form, and one is already modifying it, how could it be a source of regret? As for those who are incapable of centrality without exhortation, but whose desires do not overshoot the statutes, theirs is a case of excess. Nonetheless, they are enlightened and firm, and this is why they do not taste the failure to recognize anything that is not good. Since they recognize it, they also do not taste the failure to hastily modify themselves, and this is why they do not reach the point of regret, which is to return "from not far away." Concerning the word "extol," Lu Deming endorses this pronunciation, and the *Jade Chapters*, the *Pattern and Sequence of the Five Classics*, and the *Discerning the Pronunciation of the Various Classics* also see it in this fashion.[9] **The *Symbol* says: "'It returns from not far away': it corrects itself."** "It returns from not far away": this is the way noble people correct themselves. It is none other than the way of learning and asking questions. It is simply to recognize what is not good, and then to modify oneself quickly so as to attend to the good, and that is all.

The second "six" line: a restrained return brings good fortune. Although the second line is *yin*, it is placed with centrality and straightforwardness, and it is quite close to the initial line. Its tendency is to attend to the *yang* line—that is, it can descend "into humaneness." This is the restraint and beauty of the Turn hexagram. The return here is a return to ritual. If it returns to ritual, then it will become humane. The initial line is the returning *yang* line, which is returning to humaneness. The second line is close to it, and descends to it, and so there will be beauty and good fortune. **The *Symbol* says: "The good fortune of a restrained return: it descends into humaneness."** The good fortune in the restraint and beauty of the return is constituted by its descent "into humaneness." The word "humaneness" refers to the public world and to the root of goodness. The initial line returns to humaneness and the second line can relate and descend to it. As a result, there is good fortune.

The third "six" line: a frequent return brings danger, but no blame. The third line uses *yin* restlessness to place itself at the limit of the movement trigram. Its returns are frequent and numerous because it cannot be certain. A return is estimable when it is contented and certain. Those who frequently return are also frequently lost again, indicating that they are not contented with their return. To return to the good and routinely lose oneself again is a perilous way. The sage is opening the door to the way of relocating to the good, putting the return together with the peril of routinely losing oneself. This is why he says that it "brings danger, but no blame." He cannot be using the frequency of loss to give a warning about the return. There is peril in frequently losing oneself, but how could there be blame in routinely returning? The excess is in the loss and not in the return. **The *Symbol* says: "The danger of a frequent return: it means that there is no blame."** Those who frequently return are also frequently lost again. Although they are imperiled and endangered, their return to the good nonetheless means that "there is no blame."

The fourth "six" line: it travels to the center and returns alone. It is very fitting that the meaning of this line statement be delineated and explored. The fourth line has traveled to the center of the group of *yin* lines, and it alone is capable of the return. It places itself in a straightforward position, and it corresponds to the line of *yang* firmness below it. Its tendency may be said to be good, but it does not say that there is either good or bad fortune. In fact, the fourth line uses softness to occupy a position within the group of *yin* lines. The initial line is extremely minimal at its starting point, and is not sufficient for them to support each other. There is no principle by which it may make the crossing, and this is why the sage simply notes that it can return alone. He does not want to say that there will necessarily be misfortune because it attends to the way alone. Someone asks: if this is the case, why does he not say that there is no blame? Response: since the line uses *yin* to occupy a *yin* position, and is extremely soft and weak, in the end it will not be able to make the crossing, even if its tendency is to attend to the *yang* line. This is why he does not say that there is no blame. **The *Symbol* says: "'It travels to the center and returns alone': it attends to the way."** The *Symbol* notes that it "returns alone" because it attends to the good way of *yang* firmness and noble people.

The fifth "six" line: its return is truehearted. There are no regrets. The fifth "six" line uses the virtues of centrality and submissiveness to place itself in the position of the ruler. It can be "truehearted" and devoted in its return to the good, and this is why "there are no regrets." Although at its root this is a good statement, there is also a warning at its center. In the moment when *yang* starts to return and is still minimal, those who use softness to occupy the position of respect, and who have no one below them to help in their return, will not yet be able to bring about progress or good fortune. They can be without regrets, and that is all. **The *Symbol* says: "'Its return is truehearted. There are no regrets': it uses centrality to test itself."** To use the way of centrality is to bring oneself to completion. The fifth line uses *yin* to occupy the position of respect, its placement is central, and it belongs to the submission trigram substance. It can make its tendency truehearted and devoted. If it uses the way of centrality to bring itself to completion, it will be able to be without regret. To bring oneself to completion here signifies to complete the virtues of centrality and submissiveness.

The top "six" line: a confused return brings misfortune. There are disasters and mistakes. It employs the action of the troops, but in the end there is a great defeat. Because of the state, there is misfortune for the ruler. It reaches the point of ten years without taking the field. It uses *yin* softness to occupy the end position of the Turn hexagram and refers to those who are confused and do not return in the end. They do not return because they are confused, and their misfortune should be recognized. "There are disasters and mistakes": the word "disasters" refers to heavenly disasters, which arrive from outside oneself, while the word "mistakes" refers to one's own excess, caused by one's own work.[10] Since they are confused and do not return to the good, their own movements will all involve excess and loss. Disasters and afflictions will also come from outside them, but in fact they themselves have provoked them. The way of confusion is to make no return, and it can have no influence. If "it employs the action of the troops," then "in the end there is a great defeat." If they are used by the state, then there will be "misfortune for the ruler." The phrase "ten years" refers to the end of the number series. "It reaches the point of ten years without taking the field": this signifies that it cannot travel in the end. Since its way is confused, at what moment could it travel? **The *Symbol* says: "The misfortune of a confused return: it reverses the way of the ruler."** Those who return will align with the way. Since it is confused in its return, "it reverses the way," and its misfortune should be recognized. "Because of the state, there is misfortune for the ruler": this signifies that it reverses the way of the ruler. Rulers occupy the top position and set the crowd in order. It is proper that they attend to the good of the world. If they are confused in their return, they reverse the way of the ruler. This does not stop at the ruler—people in general who are confused in their return will reverse the way, and will possess misfortune.

25. NO FAULT (*WUWANG* 無妄)

The *Sequence of the Hexagrams* says: "Someone who turns back will have no faults, and this is why the No Fault hexagram is next." To turn back is to revert to the way. Those who have turned back to the way will align with the straightforward principle and have no faults. This is why, after the Turn hexagram, the No Fault hexagram is next. As for the trigrams, the Lead trigram is above, and the Shake trigram below. To shake is to move. Those who move in accord with heaven will have no faults, while those who move in accord with human desires will be at fault. How great is the meaning of the No Fault hexagram!

No Fault: there are primacy and progress, profit and purity. What is not straightforward will make mistakes. There is no profit in a long journey. Those who have no faults are extremely sincere, and those who are extremely sincere are on the way of heaven. As heaven transforms and cultivates the ten thousand things, they are born and live without becoming depleted. "Each makes its nature and mandate straightforward," which is to have no faults.[1] If people can align with the way of the No Fault hexagram, they will, as the *Remarks* says, "align their virtue with heaven and earth."[2] The No Fault hexagram possesses the principle of great progress. If noble people put the way of the No Fault hexagram into action, they will be able to bring about great progress. The No Fault hexagram refers to the way of heaven, but the judgment is remarking on the way of the No Fault hexagram with reference to people. "Profit and purity": if the way of the No Fault hexagram is considered as a law, its profit lies in purity and straightforwardness. Those who lose their purity and straightforwardness will be at fault. Although their hearts may not be crooked, if they do not align with the straightforward principle they will be at fault, and then they will have crooked hearts. This is why the judgment says that what is not straightforward will constitute an excess or mistake. It is not fitting for those who are already without fault to make a journey. If they make a journey, then they will be at fault.

The *Judgment* says: "No Fault: firmness arrives from the outside and becomes master on the inside." The *Judgment* is referring to the initial "nine" line. The initial line of the Yield trigram has altered to constitute the Shake trigram: a firm line from the outside has arrived. This initial line is both the master of the Shake trigram and the cause of hexagram's completion. This is why the initial line is the master of the No Fault hexagram. Those who make use of heaven in their movement are without fault. This movement makes use of heaven, and so it is the master. The use of firmness to alter softness symbolizes the use of straightforwardness to drive out faults. Further, a firm and straightforward line is the "master on the inside," which also gives the meaning of the No Fault hexagram. A "nine" line occupies the initial position, which is straightforward. "There are movement and vigor. It is firm, central, and corresponds. It makes great progress by its straightforwardness, which is the mandate of heaven." The lower trigram refers to movement and the upper trigram to vigor, which indicates that the movement is firm and vigorous. Firmness and vigor are the substance of the No Fault hexagram. "It is firm, central, and corresponds": the fifth line makes use of firmness to occupy a central and straightforward position. The second line, in its turn, corresponds to it with centrality and straightfor-wardness. This indicates that they have submitted to principle and are without fault. This is why their way "makes great progress" and develops, and there are purity and straightforwardness, which are "the mandate of heaven." The "man-date of heaven" signifies the way of heaven, which is also signified by the No Fault hexagram. "'What is not straightforward will make mistakes. There is no profit in a long journey': how could the journey be without fault? What the mandate of heaven will not uphold—how could it be done?" What is signi-fied by the No Fault hexagram is straightforwardness, and that is all. If there is a small loss of straightforwardness, then there will be an excess, which is a fault. "What is not straightforward": this, in fact, signifies the cause of its journey. If it had no faults, there would be no journey, so what cause would there be of "what is not straightforward"? Those who have no faults are in line with the straight-forward principle. If they go on to make a journey, what will it get them? They will be at fault in whatever place they enter. If they make the journey, they will upend the principle of heaven. What the way of heaven will not uphold—"how could it be done?"

The *Symbol* says: "Below heaven, thunder travels: things are brought together without fault. The first kings used it in lushly responding to the moments

and cultivating the ten thousand things." When thunder travels through the world, *yin* and *yang* interact harmoniously. They approach each other and bring their sound to completion. In this, they disturb what is hibernating and stored away, they dust off the sprouts, and they reveal and give birth to the ten thousand things. Concerning what is granted to them and what brings them together, whether they are colossal or tiny, aloft or below, "each makes its nature and mandate straightforward."[3] They neither stray nor are at fault: "Things are brought together without fault." The first kings gazed on this symbol—"below heaven, thunder travels," revealing, giving birth, granting, and bringing together—and by "lushly responding to the moments" of heaven, they nourished and cultivated the ten thousand things. They made each to acquire what is fitting for it, just as heaven is without fault in what it brings together. The word "lushly" refers to an abundance. When the *Symbol* remarks on their "lushly responding," it is close to remarking on the example of abundantly "acting on the waters."[4] The phrase "responding to the moments" signifies submitting to and aligning with the moments of heaven. The way of heaven gives birth to the ten thousand things, and "each makes its nature and mandate straightforward" without fault. Those who are kings give substance to the way of heaven by nourishing and cultivating the people and even the insects, grasses, and trees, making each acquire what is fitting for it. This is the way of responding to the moments and cultivating things.

The initial "nine" line: it has no faults. Making a journey brings good fortune. This "nine" line uses *yang* firmness to become the master of the inner trigram, and is symbolized by someone who "has no faults." It uses firmness and fullness to alter softness and occupy a position in the inner trigram, and it refers to those with centrality, sincerity, and no faults. If it makes the journey without any faults, how could there be a place without good fortune? The hexagram judgment remarks that "there is no profit in a long journey," which signifies that those who have no faults should not make a journey. If they become excessive, they will be at fault. But the line statement remarks that "making a journey brings good fortune," which signifies that those who use the way of the No Fault hexagram in their action will bring good fortune. **The *Symbol* says: "'It has no faults' and makes a journey: it acquires the object of its tendencies."** When the No Fault hexagram is used in making a journey, there is nothing that will not acquire the object of its tendencies. In fact, there is nothing that sincerity cannot move. Those who use it to correct themselves will make themselves straightforward; those who use it to set their affairs in order will bring principle to their affairs; those who use it to watch over other people will affect and transform them. They will make no journey without acquiring the object of their tendencies.

The second "six" line: without plowing, it obtains something. Without fallowing, it harvests something. There is profit in a long journey. In general, there is no fault in the spontaneity of principle, but there is fault in what people want to do.[5] This is why the line statement uses plowing, obtaining, fallowing, and harvesting as examples. The second "six" line occupies the central position and acquires straightforwardness, it corresponds to the central and straightforward fifth line, it occupies a position in the movement trigram substance, it is soft and submissive, its movement is able to submit to something central and straightforward, and it refers to those who have no fault. This is why it speaks of its meaning as the limit of having no fault. One plows when one begins to farm, and something is obtained only at its completion and end. A field in its first year is said to be fallowed, and in its third year it is said to be harvested. To obtain something without plowing first, or to harvest something without fallowing first, signifies that this state of affairs is not created ahead of time. The state of affairs is caused by a principle that is proper and spontaneous. If the affair were created ahead of time, it would be the production and doing of the human heart and would have faults. If the cause of the affair is proper and spontaneous, it is submissive to principle and corresponds to the thing at hand, and is without fault. Such is the case when something is obtained or harvested. In fact, those who plow will necessarily obtain something, and those who fallow will necessarily harvest something. Such is the certain and spontaneous principle of this affair. It is not the creation or production of the heart and intention.[6] Someone asks: when sages control and produce profit for the world, the impetus is always something that they themselves have created. How is this not a fault? Response: sages follow the moment in what they control and produce, aligning with what is fitting for the climate or *qi*. They have never tasted the opening of a door before the right moment. If there were no waiting for the right moment, a single sage would be sufficient to exhaust every deed. Why would one wait for the successive productions of the sages to pile up? The moment is the impetus of the affair, and what the sage does follows the moment. **The *Symbol* says: "'Without plowing, it obtains something': it is not yet wealthy."** The phrase "not yet" indicates "not necessarily," as when the *Symbol* of the Watch hexagram says that "it does not yet submit to the mandate."[7] When one obtains something without plowing, or harvests something without fallowing, the cause of this state of affairs is proper and spontaneous. Those who have plowed will necessarily obtain something and those who have fallowed will necessarily bring the harvest to completion, but they do not necessarily do this for the wealth to be obtained or harvested. Those who plow and fallow at the beginning provide a heart that lies in the search for obtaining and harvesting something, so that they may become "wealthy." If they do this because of their heart's desires, then they are at fault.

The third "six" line: it is the disaster of no faults. Sometimes the cow is bound up and the traveler acquires it. It is a disaster for the people of the district. The third line uses *yin* softness without centrality or straightforwardness, which is a fault. Further, its tendency is to correspond to the top line, which refers to desire and is also a fault. Concerning the way of the No Fault hexagram, these constitute "disaster" and harm. When people are at fault in their movement, it is because they have desires. Whatever they acquire through their faulty movement will also necessarily be lost again. Although they may acquire what is profitable for them, their loss is already great if there is a fault in their movement. What will be the case when it is followed by misfortune and regret? When knowledgeable people see that their acquisition has faults, they recognize that their loss will necessarily be proportionate with it. This is why the sage, taking the third "six" line as the symbol of having faults, reveals and sheds light on its principle by saying: "It is the disaster of no faults. Sometimes the cow is bound up and the traveler acquires it. It is a disaster for the people of the district." He is remarking that the fault in the case of the third line is the disaster and harm of the No Fault hexagram. Provided that there is an acquisition, its loss will immediately follow. For instance, "sometimes the cow is bound up." The word "sometimes" here signifies that it may only sometimes be provided. Sometimes the cow is bound up or acquired, but then the traveler acquires it and considers it an acquisition. It is a disaster for the people of the district to lose their cow. Now suppose that the people of the district bind or acquire a horse, while the traveler loses the horse—this, too, is a disaster. He is remarking that what is acquired will also be lost, and so it is not sufficient to consider it merely as an acquisition. The line statement refers to the "traveler" and "people of the district" only to remark that what is acquired will also be lost, and says nothing concerning them in themselves. The blessing of a faulty acquisition is also followed by disaster. When the acquisition is a faulty acquisition, it may also be called loss and should certainly not be considered an acquisition. If people can recognize this, they will not be at fault in their movement. **The *Symbol* says: "'The traveler' acquires the cow: it is a disaster for 'the people of the district.'"** When "'the traveler' acquires the cow," "it is a disaster for 'the people of the district.'" If what is acquired will also be lost, how could it be considered an acquisition?

The fourth "nine" line: there may be purity and no blame. The fourth line is *yang* and firm, it occupies a position in the Lead trigram substance, it does not correspond to or agree with any line, and it refers to those who have no fault. Since it is firm and without anything private, how could it have a fault? Since it "may" keep guard with "purity" and certainty, there is "no blame" for it. How can a "nine" line occupying a *yin* position acquire straightforwardness? Response: were a *yang* line occupying a position in the Lead trigram substance to place itself in a firm position, it would become excessive. If it were excessive, then it would be at fault. Since it occupies the fourth position, it does not tend to value firmness. The statements "there may be purity" and "there is profit in purity" are not the same. "There may be purity" signifies that here, where it has placed itself, it may keep guard with purity and certainty. "There is profit in purity" signifies that there is profit in this purity. **The *Symbol* says: "'There may be purity and no blame': it possesses it with certainty."** If it keeps guard with purity and certainty, there is "no blame."

The fifth "nine" line: it is an illness without fault. Without medicine, there is happiness. This "nine" line uses centrality and straightforwardness, the position of respect is proper for it, a lower line submits and corresponds to it with centrality and straightforwardness, and it may be said to have no fault at all. There is nothing that it may attach to its way. The word "illness" refers to a defect. Since the fifth "nine" line has no faults, it is like someone ill who is set in order "without" the use of "medicine." As a result, "there is happiness." When people are ill, they use medicine and the needles to assault and drive out their crookedness, while nourishing their straightforwardness.[8] If their substance or *qi* is peaceful and harmonious, without any illness or defect at its root, and yet they assault it and set it in order, they will harm their straightforwardness. This is why, if it is "without medicine," then "there is happiness." "There is happiness" signifies that the illness makes itself vanish. What is here called "an illness without fault" signifies something that will not be set in order if it is set in order, something that will not be attended to if it is administered, and something that will not be reformed if it is transformed. The fault here is the "illness without fault." As instances of this, Shun had the Miao tribe, the Duke of Zhou had Guan and Cai, and Confucius had Shusun Wushu.[9] If there is already no fault, and yet there is an illness, it is proper that one treat it like an illness without fault, since it is not sufficiently distressing. Those who succeed in assaulting and setting themselves in order will adapt their being without fault and relocate it to a fault. The fifth line has placed itself in the limit position of the No Fault hexagram, and this is why it is only warned about movement. If it moves, then it will be at fault. **The Symbol says: "The medicine for those 'without fault': it should not be tested."** When people have faults, they will necessarily be corrected and modified by principle. If they already have no faults, and yet medicine is used to set them in order, they will come to be at fault instead. Why should it be employed? This is why the *Symbol* says that "it should not be tested." To test something is to employ it temporarily, as when one is said to have a little taste of something.

The top "nine" line: it has no faults. In acting, it makes mistakes. There is no long-term profit. The top "nine" line occupies the end position in the hexagram and refers to the limit of the No Fault hexagram. Those who act when at their limit will exceed their principle. If they exceed their principle, then they are at fault. This is why, when the top "nine" line acts, there are excesses and "mistakes," and "no long-term profit." **The Symbol says: "In acting, there are no faults: there is the disaster of depletion."** When the No Fault hexagram has reached its limit but attaches a further advance to it, this constitutes a fault. It constitutes disaster and harm by reaching its limit and depletion.

26. GREAT HERD (*DAXU* 大畜)

The *Sequence of the Hexagrams* says: "Those who have no faults may afterward herd other people, and this is why the Great Herd hexagram is next." To be without fault is to possess reality, and this is why they may herd or gather others. And so the Great Herd hexagram succeeds the No Fault hexagram. As for the trigrams, the Calm trigram is above and the Lead trigram below. Heaven is present, but at the center of the mountain, which symbolizes the extreme greatness of what is herded. The *xu* character of "herd" refers to stopping, but also to gathering. If things are stopped, they are also gathered. If one chooses to consider the symbol—"heaven is at the center of the mountain"—then the hexagram refers to what is collected into a herd. If one chooses to consider the stopping of the Lead trigram by the Calm trigram, then the hexagram refers to what is herded by being stopped. There is stopping, and afterward there is accumulation, and this is why stopping is the meaning of the herd hexagrams.

Great Herd: there is profit in purity. Not to eat with the family brings good fortune. There is profit in traversing a great stream. Nothing is greater than heaven, and yet it is at the center of the mountain. The Calm trigram is above, and it stops the Lead trigram below. They symbolize the extreme greatness of what is collected into a herd. In the case of people, this is the learning or art of the way and virtue, which replenishes and accumulates inside them. This is the greatness of what is herded. In general, what is gathered into a herd is always and without qualification spoken of as great. As for people collected into a herd, it is fitting that they acquire the straightforward way, and this is why the judgment says that "there is profit in purity." As for the fact that their impetus is different and their learning is partial, there are many people in the herd, and there will certainly be some that are not straightforward. When the way and virtue have replenished them and accumulated inside them, it is fitting that they occupy positions above, so that they can feast on wages from heaven and use them to influence the world. Then it will not be the good fortune of one person alone but the good fortune of the world. Were they to deplete their own place and need to eat with their family, they would lack the way. This is why "not to eat with the family brings good fortune." If the herd has become great, it is fitting that it influence the moment so as to cross through the hardships and obstacles of the world. This is the function of the great herd, and this is why "there is profit in traversing a great stream." The judgment only remarks on the meaning of the Great Herd hexagram as a whole, while the *Judgment* goes on to remark on the powers and virtues of the trigrams. As for the various lines, they only have the meaning of herding by stopping. In fact, the substance and way of the *Book of Changes* is to follow what is fitting. It makes its choices based on what will shed light and what is nearby.

The *Judgment* says: "Great Herd: there are firmness and vigor, devotion and reality, radiance and brightness. Each day it renews its virtue." The *Judgment* is remarking on the powers and virtues of the trigrams. The substance of the Lead trigram is firmness and vigor, and the substance of the Calm trigram is devotion and reality. When human powers are firm and vigorous, devoted and real, then what they herd will be capable of greatness, of replenishment and reality, and will possess radiance and brightness. Since their herding does not cease, their virtues will be renewed each day. **"Firmness is above and values the worthy. It can put a stop to vigor. Its straightforwardness is great."** "Firmness is above": this indicates that a *yang* line occupies the top position. This *yang* and firm line occupies a position above the position of respect, which means that it "values the worthy." What stops occupies a position above what is vigorous, which means that it "can put a stop to vigor." If those who put a stop to vigor do not possess great straightforwardness, how can they make use of *yang* firmness to respect and value the virtues of the worthy from their position at the top? What is able to stop extreme vigor is always the way of great straightforwardness. **"'Not to eat with the family brings good fortune': it nourishes worthy people. 'There is profit in traversing a great stream': it corresponds to heaven."** It is fitting for the people of the Great Herd hexagram to apply the influence of the herd to sustaining the world. This is why "not to eat with the family brings good fortune." This signifies that they occupy the position of heaven, and feast on wages from heaven. When the state "nourishes worthy people," worthy people will acquire the way of action. "There is profit in traversing a great stream": this signifies that it is fitting for people with a great grasp, who have collected things into a herd, to cross through the hardships and obstacles of the world. The *Judgment* goes on to reveal and shed light on the powers of the trigrams, saying that they can traverse the great stream because they correspond to heaven. The fifth "six" line is the ruler, and it corresponds to the central line of the Lead trigram below it. It is the ruler of the Great Herd hexagram, but it corresponds to the Lead trigram in its action. Its action is capable of corresponding to heaven, and there is no hardship or obstacle that it cannot cross through. How could the case be otherwise?

The *Symbol* says: "Heaven is at the center of the mountain: Great Herd. Noble people often use it to understand the words, journeys, and actions of those who came earlier, so as to herd their virtues." Heaven is extremely great, and yet it is at the center of the mountain, which symbolizes the herding of something extremely great. Noble people gaze on this symbol so as to give greatness to what they have collected into a herd. What people collect into a herd is made great by learning, by often hearing of the words and actions of the sages and worthies of early antiquity. They assess these traces so as to gaze on their function, they examine their words so as to seek their heart, and they acquire an understanding of them so as to herd and complete their virtues. This is the meaning of the Great Herd hexagram.

The initial "nine" line: there is danger, and profit in its cessation. In the Great Herd hexagram, the Calm trigram stops or herds the Lead trigram. This is why the meaning of being stopped by something is chosen for all three line statements of the Lead trigram, and the meaning of stopping something is chosen for all three line statements of the Calm trigram. The initial line makes use of *yang* firmness, it belongs to the vigor trigram substance, it occupies the position at the bottom, and it refers to those who will necessarily advance upward. Since the fourth "six" line is above it, and herds or stops it, how could it become the enemy of the higher line by acquiring the propensity for a position? Were the initial line to confront it by advancing, there would be peril and danger. This is why there is "profit in its cessation," and in not advancing. In other hexagrams, the straightforward correspondence of the fourth and initial lines indicates that they support each other, but in the Great Herd hexagram their correspondence indicates that one stops or herds the other. Since the top and third lines are both *yang*, their tendencies are aligned. In fact, the *yang* lines are both things that advance upward, and this is why they symbolize those who possess the same tendencies and do not have the meaning of stopping each other. The *Symbol* says: "'There is danger, and profit in its cessation': it does not confront disaster." If something is perilous, its cessation is fitting. One should not confront disaster and peril by acting. If one advances without measuring one's propensity, there will necessarily be a disaster.

The second "nine" line: the carriage throws its crossbars. The second line is herded or stopped by the fifth "six" line—its propensity is such that it should not advance. Since the fifth line has the propensity of a position above, how could it be confronted? Although the second line belongs to a trigram substance that is firm and vigorous, it nonetheless places itself so as to acquire the way of centrality, and this is why it loses nothing whether it advances or stops. Although it tends to advance, if it measures the inability of its propensity, it will stop without traveling. It is like a chariot or carriage with its wheels or crossbars omitted or removed, which signifies that it cannot travel. **The *Symbol* says: "'The carriage throws its crossbars': there is no resentment in centrality."** "The carriage throws its crossbars" and does not travel. In fact, it places itself so as to acquire the way of centrality, and its movement does not lose what is fitting. This is why there is neither excess nor resentment. Nothing is so good as the goodness of firmness and centrality. Softness and centrality will not reach the point of excessive softness, but in firmness and centrality there are both centrality and power. The initial "nine" line is placed so that it does not acquire centrality, and this is why its line statement warns that there is peril and that cessation is fitting. The second line has acquired centrality, so that whether it advances or stops it will neither stray nor become excessive. This is why the *Symbol* says only that "the carriage throws its crossbars," which signifies that it cannot travel. Since it cannot travel, "there is no resentment." The initial and second lines, belonging to the Lead trigram substance, are firm and vigorous, but this is not sufficient for them to advance. The fourth and fifth lines are *yin* and soft, yet they are capable of stopping them. The abundance or scarcity of the moment, the strength or weakness of one's propensity—it is fitting for students of the *Book of Changes* to understand them deeply.

The third "nine" line: the fine horse pursues it. There is profit in hardship and purity. Each day it safeguards the carriages and bulwarks. There is profit in a long journey. The third line is at the limit of firmness and vigor. The *yang qi* of the top "nine" line is also something that advances upward. Further, it is placed at the limit of the Herd hexagram and reflects on its alteration, so that it does not herd the third line and their tendencies are the same. They correspond to each other in order to advance. The third line uses the powers of firmness and vigor, and the top line advances by aligning with its tendencies. Their advance is like the galloping or pursuit of a "fine horse," a statement that indicates its rapidity. Although it has the propensity to advance rapidly, it should not rely on the vigor of its power and its correspondence with the top line, forgetting to be perfectly cautious. This is why it is fitting to treat its affairs as hardships and difficulties, and to bring about the way of purity and straightforwardness. The word "carriages" refers to things whose function is travel, and "bulwarks" are a means of defending oneself. It is proper for it each day, or ordinarily, to safeguard and put into practice its chariots and carriages, as well as its defenses and bulwarks. In such a case, "there is profit in a long journey." The third line belongs to the Lead trigram substance and occupies a straightforward position, so that it can be pure. It is proper that it make a keen advance, and this is why the line statement warns it to recognize the difficulty and not lose its purity. Since its tendency is to be keen in its advance, there are moments when it will lose something, even if it is firm and enlightened. It will acquire nothing without this reproof. **The *Symbol* says: "'There is profit in a long journey': it aligns its tendencies with those above."** "There is profit in a long journey" because the third and top lines align their tendencies. The *yang* nature of the top "nine" line is to advance upward. It is already at the limit of the Herd hexagram, and this is why it does not herd the third line below it, but they align their tendencies and advance upward.

The fourth "six" line: it is the horn guards of the young cow. There are primacy and good fortune. Concerning this position, one may remark that the fourth corresponds to the initial line below it, which refers to herding the initial line. The initial line occupies the bottom position, and is the minimum of *yang qi*. Since it is minimal and herded, it is easily controlled, as when horn guards are attached to a young cow. This is a great good and good fortune. The line statement is discussing the overall way of the Herd hexagram, in which the fourth line belongs to the Calm trigram substance, occupies a position above, and has acquired straightforwardness. It uses the virtue of straightforwardness to occupy the position of the great minister and refers to those who face command over the Herd hexagram. Great ministers are given command to herd or stop the crooked hearts of the rulers above them, and to herd or stop the bad people of the world below them. Initially, the badness of people can easily be stopped, but if it has become abundant, and they "enact prohibitions afterward, they will be flouted and defied, and they will find it difficult to be victorious."[1] This is why, when the badness of those above has become extreme, they cannot avoid drawing back from and brushing off even the sages who have saved them. When the badness of those below has become extreme, they cannot avoid punishment and execution, even when the sages have set them in order. Such is not the case when they are stopped at their initiation, as when horn guards are attached to a young cow. Then "there are primacy and good fortune." The nature of a cow is to prod or pierce things with its horns, and this is why horn guards are used to control it. Were the horn guards attached to it while it was still a young calf, when its horns were just beginning to grow, and its nature of prodding or piercing was as yet unrevealed, then it would be easy to avoid injury. In the case where the fourth "six" line can herd or stop the badness of those above and below early, when it is not yet revealed, there will be the good fortune of a great good. **The *Symbol* says: "In the fourth 'six' line, 'there are primacy and good fortune': there is happiness."** If the badness of the world is stopped when it is already abundant, those above will labor to control it with prohibitions and those below will be injured by being punished and put to death. This is why, if it is herded and stopped early, when it is minimal and small, there will be the good fortune of a great good. There is no labor and no injury, and this is why they may be happy. The herding of the initial line by the fourth is such a case, and the herding of the higher line is also like this.

The fifth "six" line: it is the tusks of the castrated pig. There is good fortune. The fifth "six" line occupies the position of the ruler. It stops and herds the crookedness and badness of the world. As for the crowd of countless millions, who reveal a heart of crookedness and desire, if the rulers want to control it by force, however profound their laws and severe their punishments, they will not be capable of victory. As for things, they are to be rallied and marshaled, while affairs are to be manipulated and made to converge. When sages acquire and wield this opportunity, they look at the hearts of the countless millions as one heart. When they put it on the way, it travels, and when they stop it, it is checked. This is why they are able to bring order without labor, just as they would in the case of "the tusks of the castrated pig." A pig is a firm and restless thing, and its tusks make it fierce and bring it profit. Those who control its tusks with strength employ force and labor without being able to stop its restlessness and ferocity. They may bind or anchor it, but they will not be able to alter it. Were they to castrate it so as to drive out these propensities, then although its tusks would persist, its firmness and restlessness would be stopped. To employ something like this would bring good fortune. If noble people reveal the meaning of the castrated pig and recognize that the badness of the world may not be controlled by force, they will examine how to manipulate it, and will wield the opportunity to choke off and sever its root and origin. This is why they do not presume to punish with severe or steep penalties, and yet the badness stops by itself. Take the case of stopping theft. The people have a heart of desire, and will move when they see profit. If no one knows how to teach them, and they are oppressed with hunger and cold, then, although they may be influenced each day by punishments and killings, how could anyone be victorious over the hearts of the countless millions who desire profit? Those who are sages recognize the way to bring them to a stop. They do not value authority and punishment but correct their government and teaching. If they make people take up the vocations of farming and silk production, and recognize the way of honesty and dishonesty, then "no one will steal despite its rewards."[2] This is why the way to stop badness is to recognize its root, acquire an opportunity, and that is all. It is, on the one hand, not to punish severely, and on the other, to correct one's government. In a similar case, those distressed when a pig profits by its tusks do not control the tusks but castrate its propensity. **The Symbol says: "The good fortune of the fifth "six" line: there is delight."** If those above do not recognize the method for stopping badness and punish with severity, considering the desires of the people to be enemies, their injuries will be extreme and they will accomplish nothing. Were they to recognize its root, they would possess the way to control it. In that case, customs would be reformed without labor and without injury, which is the blessing and delight of the world.

The top "nine" line: what is the high road of heaven? There is progress. I have heard teacher Hu say that the phrase "what is" was erroneously attached to the line statement, which should read: "There is progress on the high road of heaven."[3] When affairs reach their limit, they reverse themselves. This is a constant principle, and this is why there is progress at the limit of the Herd hexagram. The herd in the Small Herd hexagram is small, and this is why it is completed at the limit of the hexagram. The herd in the Great Herd hexagram is great, and this is why it is scattered at the limit of the hexagram. It is proper that there be alteration when the limit has been reached, and further, it is the nature of *yang qi* to travel upward. This is why it succeeds at being scattered. The "high road of heaven" is heaven's path and signifies a center that is empty and hollow. The *qi* of the clouds and birds in flight come and go on it, and this is why it is called the "high road of heaven." Progress on the high road of heaven signifies progress and development that are vast and voluminous, without any concealment or hindrance. This is an alteration from the way of the Herd hexagram. An alteration is progress, but it is not progress on the way of the Herd hexagram. **The Symbol says: "'What is the high road of heaven?': a way of great travel."** What is signified by the phrase "high road of heaven"? Because it does not stop or hamper anything, it is the way or path of great development and travel. The phrase "high road of heaven" is not ordinarily used, and this is why the *Symbol* takes the specific form of a question, asking what is signified by the phrase "high road of heaven." Because it is the way or path of great development and travel, it is chosen for a condition of hollowness and spaciousness. The *Symbol* uses the phrase "what is," and this is why it was also erroneously attached to the line statement.

27. FEED (*YI* 頤)

The *Sequence of the Hexagrams* says: "After things are herded, they may be nourished, and this is why the Feed hexagram is next." As for things that have been gathered into a herd, they must have something with which to nourish themselves. If they are without nourishment, then they will not be able to persist or come to rest. And so the Feed hexagram succeeds the Great Herd hexagram. As for the trigrams, the Calm trigram is above and the Shake trigram below. There are two *yang* lines, one at the top and one at the bottom, and they enclose four *yin* lines at their center. What is above stops and what is below moves; the outside is full and the center is empty—these are symbols of the upper and lower jaws. To feed is to nourish, and so what the human mouth eats and drinks also nourishes the human body. This is why the name of the hexagram is Feed. When the sage provided this hexagram, he unfolded the meaning of nourishment. Its greatest extreme is when "heaven and earth nourish" and cultivate "the ten thousand things. Sages nourish worthy people so that they will extend themselves to the ten thousand people." Concerning people, the nourishment of life, nourishment of form, nourishment of virtue, and nourishment of people all belong to the way of feeding and nourishing. Life is nourished by movement and rest, by reining in and letting out; form is nourished by eating, drinking, and wearing clothes; virtue is nourished by authority and ceremony, by action and duty; people are nourished by unfolding themselves so that they can extend themselves to other things.

Feed: purity brings good fortune. It gazes on the feeding. It seeks to fill its own mouth. Those who make use of straightforwardness on the way of the Feed hexagram will have good fortune. Whether people are nourishing their bodies, nourishing their virtue, nourishing other people, or being nourished by other people, if they use the way of straightforwardness, they will have good fortune. When the creation and transformation of heaven and earth nourish and cultivate the ten thousand things, each of them acquires what is fitting for it. This, too, is straightforwardness, and that is all. "It gazes on the feeding. It seeks to fill its own mouth": if it gazes on what feeds other people, together with the way of seeking to fill its own mouth, then it will be able to see both goodness and badness, both good and bad fortune.

The *Judgment* says: "'Feed: purity brings good fortune': if it nourishes with straightforwardness, there will be good fortune. 'It gazes on the feeding': it gazes on what it is that feeds. 'It seeks to fill its own mouth': it gazes on what feeds it." "Purity brings good fortune": if what nourishes is straightforward, then there will be good fortune. The phrase "what nourishes" signifies the people that nourish but also the way of nourishing people. "It seeks to fill its own mouth": this signifies seeking the way of nourishing one's own body. If all these cases make use of straightforwardness, there will be good fortune. **"Heaven and earth nourish the ten thousand things. Sages nourish worthy people so that they will extend themselves to the ten thousand people. How great is the moment of the Feed hexagram!"** The sage is remarking on the way of the Feed hexagram at its limit, and applauding its greatness. Concerning the way of heaven and earth, it is to nourish and cultivate the ten thousand things. The way to nourish and cultivate the ten thousand things is to be straightforward, and that is all. Concerning sages, they nourish the powers of the worthy and share the position of heaven with them. They make them eat of their wages from heaven, and enable them to influence and gratify the world. This is to "nourish worthy people so that they will extend themselves to the ten thousand people": they nourish worthy people and so they nourish the ten thousand people. As for the crowd of sundry things between heaven and earth, none of them can live without nourishment. Sages apportion and complete the way of heaven and earth, and they assist with what is fitting for heaven and earth, so as to nourish the world. Right down to the birds, beasts, grasses, and trees, everything has a government that nourishes it. Their way matches that of heaven and earth, and this is why Fuzi, while unfolding the way of the Feed hexagram and applauding the accomplishments of heaven, earth, and the sages, goes on to say: "How great is the moment of the Feed hexagram!"[1] Sometimes he says "the meaning," sometimes he says "the function," and sometimes he stops at saying "the moment," referring to what is great about it. Concerning the life and nourishment of the ten thousand things, it is the moment that is great, and this is why he says "the moment."

The *Symbol* says: "Below the mountain, there is thunder: Feed. Noble people use it to be cautious in the words they speak. They rein in their eating and drinking." Concerning the two trigram substances, one may remark that "below the mountain, there is thunder." Thunder shakes at the bottom of the mountain, and the living things of the mountain all move their roots and reveal their sprouts, which symbolizes nourishment. Concerning the meaning of the upper and lower trigrams, one may remark that the Calm trigram refers to stopping and the Shake trigram to movement. There are stopping above and movement below, which symbolizes the upper and lower jaws. Concerning the form of the hexagram, one may remark that there are two *yang* lines, one at the top and one at the bottom, and they enclose four *yin* lines at their center. The outside is full and the center is empty, which symbolizes the jaws of the mouth. The mouth is what nourishes the body, and this is why, when noble people gaze on the symbol of nourishing one's body, they are "cautious in the words they speak" so as to nourish their virtue, and they "rein in their eating and drinking" so as to nourish their substance. The *Symbol* says this not only because the mouth is chosen as the meaning of the nourishment hexagram, but also so as to bind together affairs that are extremely near with those that are extremely great—none of which exceeds eating and drinking on the one hand, and the words that one speaks on the other. As the words that one speaks are in line with the person, so all the general mandates, decrees, government, and teaching that go out from the person are in line with the world. Those who are cautious here will necessarily be proper and without loss. As eating and drinking are in line with the person, so all the general commodities, supplies, resources, and functions that nourish the person are in line with the world. Those who rein themselves in here will be suitable, fitting, and without injury. The way of unfolding nourishment is never otherwise, whether it is a case of nourishing virtue or nourishing the world.

The initial "nine" line: you abandon your spiritual turtle. You gaze on me and flex your jaws. There is misfortune. The initial "six" line of the Blind hexagram refers to those who are blind, but the line statement remarks on the masters of bringing revelation to blindness. The initial "nine" line of the Feed hexagram also uses language borrowed from outside the line. The word "you" signifies the initial line. "You abandon your spiritual turtle," and then "you gaze on me and flex your jaws." The word "me" provides the opposite of "you." What makes the initial line flex its jaws is the fourth line, but it is not the fourth line that is speaking. The word "you" is simply borrowed and provided here. The *yang* substance of the "nine" line is firm and enlightened, and its power and wisdom are sufficient to nourish straightforwardness. The turtle is capable of swallowing and breathing without eating. The phrase "spiritual turtle" is a metaphor for enlightenment and wisdom, and indicates that it should not seek nourishment outside itself. Although it has such a power, it nonetheless uses *yang* to occupy a position in the movement trigram substance during the moment of the Feed hexagram. It seeks to feed, which is what people desire. It corresponds to the fourth line above it, it cannot guard itself, its tendency is to travel upward, and it refers to those who enjoy what they desire and flex their jaws. When the heart has moved, it will necessarily lose sight of itself. Since it is confused by desire and has lost sight of itself, using *yang* to attend to *yin*, is there any place that it will not reach? As a result, "there is misfortune." The phrase "flex your jaws" refers to flexing and moving the upper and lower jaws. When people see food and desire it, they move their jaws and drip saliva. This is why it is considered the symbol. **The *Symbol* says: "'You gaze on me and flex your jaws': they are neither sufficient nor esteemed."** This "nine" line belongs to the movement trigram substance. The phrase "flex your jaws" signifies that it enjoys *yin* and tends to move. If what moves it is desire, it will necessarily lose sight of itself in the end, despite possessing the powers of firmness, vigor, enlightenment, and wisdom. This is why its powers are "neither sufficient nor esteemed." What people esteem in those who are firm is their capacity to set themselves up without being contracted by desire; what they esteem in those who are enlightened is their capacity to illuminate without losing their straightforwardness. If what they desire bewilders them, and they lose their straightforwardness, of what use is their possession of firmness and enlightenment? They should be considered impoverished.

The second "six" line: it upsets the feeding and shakes off tradition. It feeds on the summit. Taking the field brings misfortune. A woman cannot put herself in place but must attend to a man. The *yin qi* cannot set itself up alone but must attend to the *yang qi*. The *yin* softness of the second line cannot nourish itself but waits for its nourishment from other people. The son of heaven nourishes the world, while each of the various marquises nourishes a single state. Ministers are fed by wages from the ruler above them, and the people depend on the nourishment of the "pastoral agents."[2] Those below are always nourished by those above—this is the straightforward principle. Since the second line is unable to nourish itself, it must seek its nourishment from *yang* firmness. If it were to seek it from the initial line below, this would upset things or get them backward. This is why the line statement says: "It upsets the feeding." To upset things is to shake off or draw back from the traditional and constant, and to be unable to act. Were it to seek its nourishment on the summit, its journey would necessarily bring about misfortune. The word "summit" refers to something lofty and outside, and signifies the top "nine" line. The hexagram has only two *yang* lines. It should not upset the feeding with the initial line, but if it seeks to be fed by the top "nine" line, its journey will bring misfortune. In the moment of the Feed hexagram, lines that correspond to each other also nourish each other. If it makes the journey to seek nourishment from the top line, which does not correspond to it, then its movement is at fault rather than on the way. As a result, there will be misfortune. If it upsets the feeding, then it "shakes off tradition." It does not obtain "your" nourishment but is at fault in seeking it from the top line. If it makes this journey, then it will acquire misfortune. Today there are people whose powers are not sufficient to nourish themselves. If they see that those above have sufficient propensity and force to nourish people, but they are not of their class or kind, and yet they are at fault in making the journey to seek them out, they will choose to be disgraced and will acquire misfortune. In other hexagrams, when the second "six" line is central and straightforward, it often possesses good fortune. Why does it possess misfortune here? Response: it is the moment for such a case. *Yin* softness is insufficient to nourish itself, and neither the initial nor the top line agrees with it. This is why, if it makes the journey to seek them, it will upend its principle and acquire misfortune. **The *Symbol* says: "'The second 'six' line. Taking the field brings misfortune': in traveling it loses its own kind."** If it takes the field and attends to the top line, there will be misfortune, because they are not of the same kind. If it makes the journey to seek it and "loses its own kind," it is fitting that it acquire misfortune. The word "traveling" refers to making a journey.

The third "six" line: it shakes off the feeding. Purity brings misfortune. For ten years it is without employment. There is no long-term profit. Concerning the way of the Feed hexagram, those who are straightforward will have good fortune. The third line uses the disposition of *yin* softness and places itself without centrality or straightforwardness. Further, it is at the limit of the movement trigram, and it refers to those whose movement is soft, crooked, and without straightforwardness. Since this is how they nourish others, they will shake off or draw back from the straightforward way of the Feed hexagram. As a result, there will be misfortune. If they were to acquire straightforwardness in their feeding, then everything they nourished would have good fortune. Whether they sought their own nourishment or to nourish other people, they would be aligned with their duty. When they nourished themselves, they would bring their virtue to completion. The third line shakes off or draws back from the straightforward way, and this is why the line statement warns that "for ten years it is without employment." The number ten is chosen because it is the end of the number series. It signifies that it should not be employed in the end. There is no journey it can make that will be profitable. **The *Symbol* says: "'For ten years it is without employment': its way is greatly upended."** The reason the line statement warns that it should not be employed in the end is that, by means of the way of what it causes to happen, it is "greatly upended" concerning duty and principle.

The fourth "six" line: it upsets the feeding. There is good fortune. The tiger looks at it intently, and intently again. Its desire is for pursuit, and pursuit again. There is no blame. The fourth is the position of the great minister, above other people, and this "six" line uses *yin* to occupy it. If *yin* softness is insufficient to nourish itself, what will be the case when it nourishes the world? The initial "nine" line uses *yang* firmness to occupy the bottom position and refers to worthy people in positions below. It corresponds to the fourth line, while the fourth line, being soft, submissive, and straightforward, is able to submit to the initial line. That is, it depends on the nourishment of the initial line. Submission is when those above nourish those below, but this line seeks its nourishment from a line below it. It upsets things or gets them backward, and this is why the line statement says that it "upsets the feeding." Nonetheless, since it does not achieve victory by its own command, it seeks out worthies in positions below. If it submits and attends to them in crossing through its affairs, the world will acquire its nourishment. It will not have the blame of a vast defeat, and this is why there will be good fortune. As for those who occupy positions above, they must possess power and virtue, authority and hope, so that the people below will respect and tremble before them. In such a case, they will put their affairs into action and the hearts of the crowd will obey and attend to them. If those below are sometimes at ease with those above, then their government will go out, but people will draw back from it. They will apply the influence of punishment, but hatred will arise. To treat confrontational usurpers lightly is the cause of disorder. Although the fourth "six" line can submit and attend to *yang* firmness, and it does not neglect the mission of its fellow line, its disposition or root is nonetheless *yin* and soft, and its making the crossing depends on other people. Other people treat it lightly, and this is why it must nourish its authority and severity. If it looks "intently, and intently again," like the tiger, then it will be able to give weight to its substance and appearance so that those below will not dare to be at ease with it. Further, those who attend to other people must do so with constancy. Were there sometimes a space between them, so that the one did not succeed the other, their government would be defeated. The phrase "its desire" signifies what they require to function, which must be "pursuit, and pursuit again," so that they succeed each other without fatigue. In such a case, they will be able to cross through their affairs. Were they to choose other people without this succession, they would be trapped and depleted. But they have authority and severity, and their influence is not depleted, and this is why they can be without blame. When the second line upsets the feeding, it shakes off tradition, but when the fourth line does it, there is good fortune. Why is this? Response: the second line is higher, but it seeks its nourishment from the line below it. The lower line does not correspond to it in kind, and this is why "it shakes off tradition." If it were the fourth line, it would occupy a position above, "the esteemed" would "descend to the impoverished," and it would make worthy people in positions below into its "causes," so that they could put their way into action.[3] The tendencies of those above and below would correspond to each other, and would influence the people—what could be more fortunate than this? From the third line on down, it refers to nourishing one's substance through the mouth; from the fourth line on up, the meaning is of nourishing one's virtue. A ruler who is supplied and nourished by a minister, or someone in a position above who depends on the nourishment of those below—in both cases, it is virtue that is nourished. **The *Symbol* says: "The good fortune of upsetting the feeding: the brightness of those above has an influence."** It upsets it or gets it backward while seeking nourishment, and so there is good fortune. In fact, it acquires the correspondence of a line that is *yang* and firm so that it may cross through the affair. It acquires for itself the virtue and influence of someone occupying a position above, and its brightness and enlightenment blanket the world. What great good fortune!

The fifth "six" line: it shakes off tradition. To occupy a position with purity brings good fortune. It should not traverse a great stream. The fifth "six" line in the moment of the Feed hexagram occupies the position of a ruler who nourishes the world. Nonetheless, its disposition of *yin* softness does not have sufficient power to nourish the world. Above it are worthy people of *yang* firmness, and this is why it submits and attends to them. Its sustaining the world depends on their nourishment. A ruler is someone who nourishes other people, but here it is someone who depends on the nourishment of other people. This is to draw back from or "shake off tradition" or what is constant. Because of its own insufficiency, it submits and attends to worthy teachers and tutors. The top position is that of the teachers and tutors. It must occupy and guard its position with purity and certainty, and devote itself to being believable and worthy of appointment, and then they will assist and aid it, and its grace will be extended to the world. This is why there is good fortune. Those with the disposition of *yin* softness do not have natures that are pure and firm. This is why the line statement warns that if they can "occupy a position with purity," there will be "good fortune." As for those with the power of *yin* softness, although they can delegate command to firm and worthy people, on whom they then depend, and they can retrace their steps in a moment of peace, they should not be placed in hardship and difficulty on the border where alteration occurs. This is why it says that they "should not traverse a great stream." If King Cheng, whose powers did not reach the extremity of softness and weakness, was almost not preserved by the Duke of Zhou when he faced the disorder of Guan and Cai, what will the case be like for those below? This is why the *Book of History* says that "the king did not dare to accuse the duke."[4] He depended on the two dukes, and made himself believable in the end. This is why those on the border of a hardship and obstacle should not be relied on unless they are masters of firmness and enlightenment, though sometimes they cross through the hardship and obstacle because nothing else can be done. By revealing this meaning, it gives a deep warning to those who rule. As for the top "nine" line, it accords with the way of ministers who bring about the exhaustion of their loyalty, and this is why it does not say the same thing. **The *Symbol* says: "The good fortune of occupying a position with purity: it submits and attends to those above."** "The good fortune of occupying a position with purity": this signifies that it can submit and attend with solidity and certainty to the worthy people referred to by the top "nine" line, so that it may nourish the world.

The top "nine" line: it is the cause of feeding. Danger brings good fortune. There is profit in traversing a great stream. The top "nine" line uses the virtue of *yang* firmness and occupies a position with command over teaching and tutoring. The ruler referred to by the fifth "six" line attends to it with softness and submissiveness, and depends on its nourishment. It refers to those who face command over the world, and to those who are the cause of the world's nourishment. To be a minister and faced with such command, one must constantly cherish one's peril and danger, and then there will be good fortune. In the cases of Yi Yin and the Duke of Zhou, how could they be without the taste of worry, diligence, alarm, and trembling? This is why they acquired good fortune in the end. As for rulers whose power is insufficient, they delegate command to those on whom they then depend. It is fitting for those who face great command over the world to drain their power and force, so as to cross through the hardship and peril of the world and bring the order and contentment of the world to completion. This is why the line statement says that "there is profit in traversing a great stream." When they acquire a rule that is unqualified like this, and when they receive a command that is weighty like this, if they do not cross through the hardship and peril of the world, how could they be sufficiently renowned or faithful in their appointment or encounter to be called worthy? It is proper that they exhaust their sincerity and drain their force without being concerned or apprehensive. Nonetheless, they should not forget to be careful of the danger. **The *Symbol* says: "'It is the cause of feeding. Danger brings good fortune':** **there is great delight."** If those who, like the top "nine" line, face a great command can be alarmed and trembling like this, the world will be blanketed with their virtue and grace. In such a case, "there is great delight," and blessings.

```
          ䷛
```

28. GREAT EXCESS (*DAGUO* 大過)

The *Sequence of the Hexagrams* says: "To be fed is to be nourished. Someone without nourishment will not be able to move, and this is why the Great Excess hexagram is next." In general, after things are nourished, they can be brought to completion. Once they are complete, they can move, and once they move, they become excessive. And so the Great Excess hexagram succeeds the Feed hexagram. As for the trigrams, the Joy trigram is above and the Low trigram below. "The lake" is above the tree and "destroys the tree." The word "lake" refers to what soaks into and nourishes the tree. Here it reaches the point of destroying and consuming the tree, which is the meaning of the Great Excess hexagram. A great excess is an excess of *yang*, and this is why the hexagram refers to a greatness that is excessive, or the greatness of those who are excessive, together with great affairs that are excessive. The way and virtue possessed by sages and worthies, as well as their task and vocation, greatly exceed those of other people but, in general, affairs that greatly exceed the ordinary are also like this. As for the sages who exhaust the human way, they do not exceed their principle, but use the world's straightforward principle in their control over states of affairs. When they are improving their employment of the moment, if they exceed the center slightly, then they will grasp it. Such is the case of being "excessively modest when doing something, excessively sorrowful when deprived of something, and excessively thrifty when employing something."[1] In fact, there is a small excess in their improvement, but they can afterward extend themselves to the center, and so they are employing a search for the center. What is here called "great excess" is greater than ordinary affairs, but it is not in excess of the principle. It is only because it is great that it is not seen as ordinary. It is seen as great by comparison with the ordinary, and this is why it is called "great excess." The examples of Yao and Shun abdicating the throne, or Tang and Wu making their attack, are all the result of the way.[2] The way is never other than the center, and never other than the ordinary, but the people of the times see it as extraordinary. This is why it is said to greatly exceed the ordinary.

Great Excess: the ridgepole is warped. There is profit in a long journey, and also progress. In the Small Excess hexagram, there is an excess of *yin* lines at both the top and the bottom. In the Great Excess hexagram, there is an excess of *yang* lines at the center. Because there is an excess of *yang* lines at the center, both the top and the bottom are weak. This is why the judgment refers to the symbol of the warped ridgepole. It chooses the ridgepole because of its impressive weight. When four *yang* lines are gathered at the center of a hexagram, they may be said to have weight. The symbol of the ridgepole is chosen for both the third and the fourth "nine" lines, which signifies their weighty command. The word "warped" is chosen because both the root and the branches of the hexagram are weak. The center is strong, but the root and branches are weak. As a result, the hexagram is warped. The *yin* lines are weak, while the *yang* lines are strong. Noble people are in abundance, while small people are scarce. This is why "there is profit in a long journey, and also progress." Today, people call the ridgepole a crossbeam.

The *Judgment* says: "Great Excess: the greatness is excessive." "The greatness is excessive" signifies that *yang* is excessive. In the case of affairs, it refers to the greatness of the affairs that are excessive, as well as to the greatness of their excess. **"'The ridgepole is warped': the root and the branches are weak."** The *Judgment* is saying that the two *yin* lines, at the top and bottom of the hexagram, are scarce and weak. If the *yang* lines are abundant, then the *yin* lines will be scarce. This is why it refers to a greatness that is excessive. In the case of the Small Excess hexagram, the *Judgment* says that "the smallness is excessive," indicating that *yin* is excessive. **"Firmness is excessive but central. There are lowliness and the act of enjoyment. 'There is profit in a long journey,' and 'progress.'"** The *Judgment* is remarking on what is good about the powers of the trigrams. Although the firm lines are excessive, the second and fifth lines have both acquired centrality. That is, they have placed themselves without losing the way of centrality. The Low trigram is below and the Joy trigram above. This is to put the way of lowliness, submissiveness, harmony, and enjoyment into action. At the moment of the Great Excess hexagram, the way of centrality, lowliness, and enjoyment is put into action. This is why "there is profit in a long journey," and so there can be "progress." **"How great is the moment of great excess!"** In the moment of the Great Excess hexagram, one's affairs are extremely great, and this is why the *Judgment* applauds it, saying how great it is. For example, setting up a great affair that is out of the ordinary, mustering the great accomplishment of a hundred generations, or severing what is customary so as to bring great virtues to completion—these are all affairs of the Great Excess hexagram.

The *Symbol* says: "The lake destroys the tree: Great Excess. Noble people use it to set themselves up alone and are not troubled. They flee the times without despair." The word "lake" refers to what soaks into and nourishes the tree. Here it reaches the point of destroying and consuming the tree, and so its excess is extreme. This is why it refers to the Great Excess hexagram. When noble people gaze on the symbol of the Great Excess hexagram, they use it to set up actions that greatly exceed those of other people. Noble people greatly exceed other people because they can "set themselves up alone and are not troubled," and "flee the times without despair." When the world wrongs them, they are not concerned: they set themselves up alone and are not troubled. Though the times do not see or recognize them, they are without regret: "They flee the times without despair." In a case like this, they will afterward be able to guard themselves, and so they will greatly exceed other people.

The initial "six" line: the pad employs plain rushes. There is no blame. The initial line makes use of *yin* softness, it belongs to the Low trigram substance, it is placed at the bottom, and it refers to those with an excess of trembling and caution. The use of softness in the bottom position is symbolized by the employment of rushes to pad something. If one does not lay things on the earth but pads them with rushes, this is an excess of caution, and so there will be no blame. Although rushes are meager things, they may become weighty by their employment, since their employment can bring the way of reverence and caution to completion. As for those who guard this art with caution in their action, how could they lose anything? Such is the employment of the Great Excess hexagram. The *Appended Statements* says: "One may lay things on the earth, but if one employs rushes to pad them, what blame could there be? This is the extremity of caution. As for rushes, they are meager things that may become weighty by their employment. Those who use this art with caution on their journey will never lose anything."[3] It is remarking on the extremity of reverence and caution. Although rushes are extremely meager things, they can nonetheless become extremely weighty by their employment. The way of weight and caution is to use them as pads for offerings—this is a weighty employment for them. If people are excessive in their reverence and caution, there will be no difficulty and they will be able to preserve their contentment without excess. Were they able to use caution in this way, unfolding it when they act in their affairs, they would not lose anything. **The *Symbol* says: "'The pad employs plain rushes': there is softness at the bottom."** Concerning the way of using *yin* softness to place oneself in a humble position below, nothing is more proper than to be excessively reverent and cautious, and that is all. "There is softness at the bottom": this refers to the symbol of using rushes to pad something. It is the way of reverence and caution.

The second "nine" line: the dry poplar gives birth to weeds. The old man acquires a young wife. Nothing is without profit. When a great excess of *yang* draws it close to *yin*, they will align. This is why the second and the fifth lines are both symbolized by giving birth. It is proper that the second "nine" line, at the initiation of the Great Excess hexagram, acquire centrality and occupy a soft position. It is profoundly close to the initial line, and they agree with each other. Since the initial line has drawn quite close to the second, the second in turn will no longer correspond to the higher line, and their agreement with each other should be recognized. It refers to people who are excessively firm, but who can place themselves at the center, and who employ softness to make the crossing together. If they were merely excessively firm, there would be nothing they could do—such is the case of the third "nine" line. But if they acquire centrality and employ softness, they will be able to complete the task of the Great Excess hexagram—such is the case of the second "nine" line. The word "poplar" refers to a thing that is easily affected by *yang qi*. If the *yang qi* becomes excessive, then it will dry out. The dry poplar has withered, and now in turn it gives birth to weeds. The *yang qi* is excessive, but it has not yet reached its limit. In the second "nine" line, the *yang qi* has become excessive, but it agrees with the initial line, and it is symbolized by the old man who acquires a young wife. If the old man acquires a young wife, they will be able to bring the task of birth and cultivation to completion. The second line acquires centrality, occupies a soft position, and agrees with the initial line. This is why it can, in its turn, give birth to weeds, without the loss that comes at the limit of excess: "Nothing is without profit." In the Great Excess hexagram, it is good when a *yang* line occupies a *yin* position, which is the case for the second and fourth lines. The line statement does not remark on the good fortune of the second line. It remarks that "nothing is without profit" at the start, which does not prematurely reach the point of good fortune. The word "weeds" refers to roots. In his petition *On the Right to Advance*, Liu Kun says: "A complexity of flowers is born from the dry wildings,"[4] where the phrase "dry wildings" signifies dry roots. Zheng Xuan, in his commentary on the *Book of Changes*, also treats the word "wildings" as the same as "weeds."[5] **The *Symbol* says: "The 'old man' and the 'young wife': their agreement with each other is excessive."** When an old man enjoys a young woman, and the young woman submits to the old man, their agreement with each other exceeds their ordinary roles. It signifies the harmony of the second "nine" line and the initial "six" line—that is, *yin* and *yang*—in an agreement with each other that exceeds what is ordinary.

The third "nine" line: the ridgepole is warped. There is misfortune. As for those who occupy the moment of the Great Excess hexagram, they are mustered to tasks of great excess, and they set up affairs of great excess. If their firmness and softness do not acquire centrality, or if they choose not to be assisted by other people, they will not be capable of them. If they are excessively firm and strong, they will be unable to be the same as ordinary people in their ordinary tasks, and will at the same time be unable to set themselves up alone. What will the case be like for affairs of great excess? Since those with the power of sages will necessarily choose to be assisted by other people even in small affairs, this should also be recognized in the case of those facing great command over the world. The third "nine" line makes use of *yang* in the moment of great excess, it uses firmness to occupy a position by itself, it does not acquire centrality, and it refers to those with an extreme excess of firmness. If those with an extreme excess of firmness make a move, they will draw back from centrality and harmony, and will brush off the hearts of the crowd. How could they face command over the Great Excess hexagram? This is why they are not victorious in their command, like warped ridgepoles that cause the collapse and defeat of the house. As a result, "there is misfortune." The ridgepole is chosen as their symbol because they are without assistance and cannot be victorious in their weighty command. Someone asks: since the third line belongs to the Low trigram substance and corresponds to the top line, why not employ a symbol that is soft? Response: when remarking on the *Book of Changes*, it is estimable to understand the weight or lightness of the propensities, and the alteration or change of the moments. The third line employs firmness while occupying a position that is excessive. When lowliness has come to an end and is altering, how could one employ the meaning of softness? The correspondence of the lines signifies that their tendencies attend to each other. When the third line is starting to become excessively firm, will the top line be able to bind up its tendency? **The *Symbol* says: "The misfortune of a warped ridgepole: there can be no assistance."** If it is excessively firm and strong, it will not be able to acquire anything from other people, and they will also not be able to relate to or assist it.[6] It is like a ridgepole that is warped or broken and cannot be propped up or assisted. The ridgepole is properly at the center of the house, and nothing may be attached to help it: "There can be no assistance."

The fourth "nine" line: the ridgepole is ample. There is good fortune. If it possesses another, there is dismay. The fourth line occupies a position near the ruler and refers to those who face command over the Great Excess hexagram. To occupy a soft position indicates that it is able to employ softness in making the crossing. Since it is not excessively firm, it will be able to be victorious in its command, like a ridgepole that is ample and raised up. As a result, there will be "good fortune." The phrase "ample and raised up" is chosen to mean that it does not descend because of warping.[7] In the moment of the Great Excess hexagram, one cannot make the crossing without *yang* firmness. Since it uses firmness to place itself in a soft position, it has acquired what is fitting. If it were to go on and correspond to the *yin* of the initial "six" line, it would be excessive. Its firmness and softness have acquired what is fitting, but its tendency is to correspond to the *yin* line: "It possesses another." If it possesses another, it possesses a burden on its firmness. Although it does not yet reach the point of great harm, there should still be dismay. In fact, in the moment of the Great Excess hexagram, it is movement that causes the excess. The phrase "it possesses another" signifies that it possesses another tendency, while "dismay" has the meaning of insufficiency, and signifies that it should lessen it. Someone asks: when the second line is close to the initial line, "nothing is without profit," but when the fourth line corresponds to the initial line, "there is dismay." Why is this? Response: the second is close to the initial line while acquiring centrality, which means that they use softness to make the crossing together. The fourth corresponds straightforwardly to the initial line, and so their tendencies are bound to each other. Since a "nine" line occupies the fourth position, firmness and softness have acquired what is fitting. If it were guided and bound by the *yin* line, doing harm to its firmness, then there should be dismay. **The *Symbol* says: "The good fortune of an ample ridgepole: it does not warp at the bottom."** If the ridgepole is ample and raised up, there will be good fortune. It is not warped or twisted at the bottom, which signifies that it does not descend to bind itself to the initial line.

The fifth "nine" line: the dry poplar gives birth to flowers. The old woman acquires a young husband. There is neither blame nor praise. The fifth "nine" line faces the moment of the Great Excess hexagram, and it uses centrality and straightforwardness at its root to occupy the position of respect. Nonetheless, it has no corresponding line to help it from below, and it certainly cannot complete the task of the Great Excess hexagram. It is close to the *yin* line at the limit of excess above it, and they make the crossing together, just like a "dry poplar" that "gives birth to flowers." When the dry poplar has given birth to roots or weeds below it, it can return to life, just like the *yang* line of the Great Excess hexagram that is mustered to bring the affair or task to completion. If it gives birth to flowers or foliage above it, they will not add anything to its dryness even after they are revealed. The top "six" line, a *yin* line at the limit of excess, refers to the "old woman." Although the fifth line is not young, when it draws close to the old woman it becomes mighty. The fifth does not depend on the top line for anything, and this is why the old woman is said to acquire it instead. When a *yin* line at the limit of excess crosses through it together with a *yang* line, it is not considered to be adding nothing to itself. Even though there is nothing criminal or blameworthy about a young husband acquiring an old woman, it is peculiar and there is nothing beautiful about it. This is why the line statement says that "there is neither blame nor praise." The *Symbol*, in turn, remarks that this "may be uncouth." **The *Symbol* says: "'The dry poplar gives birth to flowers': how should it continue? An 'old woman' and a 'young husband': this, too, may be uncouth."** The dry poplar does not give birth to roots but to flowers. Since it will return in its cycle to dryness, how could this continue? When an old woman acquires a young husband, how could they complete the task of birth and cultivation? "This, too," is why it "may be uncouth."

The top "six" line: it traverses the excess and destroys its crown. There is misfortune, but no blame. The top "six" line uses *yin* softness to place itself at the limit of excess and refers to small people at the limit of exceeding what is constant. In the case of small people, what is signified by the phrase "great excess" is not that they can manage affairs that greatly exceed those of other people; its reference goes straight to how they exceed what is constant and surpass their principle. They are not anxious that they might vanish or be in peril but walk over obstacles and tread on afflictions, and that is all. It is as though they were traversing an excess of water, and reached the point of destroying or consuming their crown—their misfortune should be recognized. Small people bring afflictions on themselves by their insane restlessness and, in fact, this is fitting. How could they turn around and resent anyone? This is why the line statement says that there is "no blame," remarking that they themselves have done it, and there is no one else for them to hate and blame. It chooses the meaning of traversing because the trigram symbol is the lake. **The *Symbol* says: "'It traverses the excess' and 'there is misfortune': it should not blame anyone."** When it "traverses the excess" and reaches the point of drowning, it has done this to itself. There should not be any blame—that is to say, there is no one else for it to hate and blame.

29. DOUBLE PIT (*XIKAN* 習坎)

The *Sequence of the Hexagrams* says: "Things cannot, in the end, be excessive, and this is why the Pit hexagram is next. A pit is a snare." There is no principle by which things can be ceaselessly excessive. When they reach the limit of excess, they will necessarily be ensnared, and so the Pit hexagram succeeds the Great Excess hexagram. The *xi* character of "double" signifies "repeated." In the other hexagrams, even when there is repetition, the hexagram judgment does not attach this word. Only in the case of the Pit hexagram does it attach the word "double," so that one may see the repetition of the obstacle. When there is another obstacle at the center of an obstacle, its meaning is great. At the center of the trigram, there is a *yang* line, while above and below it are two *yin* lines. *Yang* lines are full, while *yin* lines are empty. In the upper and lower trigrams—it does not matter which—a single *yang* line is snared at the center between two *yin* lines, and this is why these lines have the meaning of a pit or snare. When a *yang* line occupies the center between two *yin* lines, it refers to a snare, but when a *yin* line occupies the center between two *yang* lines, it refers to a connection. In general, when a *yang* line is at the top, it symbolizes stopping; when it is at the center, it symbolizes a snare; when it is on the bottom, it symbolizes movement. When a *yin* line is at the top, it symbolizes enjoyment; when it is at the center, it symbolizes a connection; when it is at the bottom, it symbolizes lowliness. A snare constitutes an obstacle. To double is to repeat, as when it is said that "they double their learning," or "they double their review."[1] It always has the meaning of repetition and return. "A pit is a snare": it is remarking that the hexagram concerns the way of placing oneself in obstacles and difficulties. The Pit trigram also refers to water. The single line that begins at the center is the first of those to possess life, and this is why the trigram refers to water. It is also because the substance of water is something that ensnares.

Double Pit: it is trustworthy. The heart alone makes progress. There is something valuable in its action. A *yang* line is full at its center, indicating that its center is trustworthy and believable. "The heart alone makes progress": the heart alone is sincere and unified, and this is why it can make progress and develop. Extreme sincerity can develop "through metal and stone, and tread both fire and water."[2] How could it be unable to make progress through obstacles and difficulties? "There is something valuable in its action": this signifies that it puts its sincerity and unity into action, and is able to go out from the obstacle. It is capable of being excellent and valuable, which signifies that it "will accomplish something." If it had not acted, then it would be constantly at the center of the obstacle.

The *Judgment* says: **"Double Pit: the obstacle is repeated. Water flows but does not fill. It acts within the obstacle, but no one loses belief in it."** The phrase "double pit" signifies that "the obstacle is repeated." The Pit trigram is both above and below—there are two obstacles, one on top of the other. The line statement of the initial "six" line says "the abyss of the pit." That is, at the center of the pit, there is another pit: "The obstacle is repeated." "Water flows but does not fill": the *yang* line has moved to the center of the obstacle, and has not yet gone out from the obstacle. It has the flowing action belonging to the nature of water, but it has not yet filled the pit. If the pit were already full, then it would go out from the pit. "It acts within the obstacle, but no one loses belief in it": a line that is *yang* and firm, with its center filled in, occupies the center of the obstacle. This is to act within the obstacle without losing one's believability. The center of the pit is filled in, and the water is already at its bottom—both of these mean to be believable and trustworthy. "**'The heart alone makes progress': because of its firmness and centrality.**" Only the heart of the trigram can make progress and develop, because of its firmness and centrality. Its center is filled in, which is the symbol of being trustworthy. Concerning the way of extreme sincerity, where will it not develop? If it puts the way of firmness and centrality into action, then it will be able to cross through the obstacle and difficulty, and will make progress and develop. "**There is something valuable in its action': if it makes the journey, it will accomplish something.**" If it puts the powers of firmness and centrality into its journey, then "it will accomplish something." This is why it is capable of being excellent and valuable. Were it to stop without acting, it would be constantly at the center of the obstacle. Being able to act while in a pit may be considered an accomplishment. "**No one can rise above the obstacle of heaven. The obstacles of earth are mountains, streams, summits, and hills. Kings and dukes provide obstacles to guard their** states. How great are the moment and function of the Pit hexagram!" A height that no one can rise above is the "obstacle of heaven"; "mountains, streams, summits, and hills" are the "obstacles of earth"; "kings and dukes" are the rulers. Gazing on the symbol of the Pit hexagram, they recognize obstacles that cannot be surmounted. This is why they provide ramparts, earthworks, trenches, and pools as obstacles, to guard their states and preserve their people. This is the moment when the obstacle has its function. Its function is extremely great, and this is why the *Judgment* applauds its greatness. Mountains, rivers, ramparts, and pools are provided as the greatest of obstacles. Distinguishing the respected from the humble, dividing the esteemed from the impoverished, shedding light on the degrees of authority, differentiating their things and colors—these generally restrict and sever off usurpers and poachers, their perimeters separate those above from those below, and they all give substance to the function of obstacles.

The *Symbol* says: "The rolling water is extreme: Double Pit. Noble people use it to make their virtuous action constant. They double the affair of their teaching." The Pit trigram refers to water, and the flow of water becomes extreme by perpetually rolling. Here the two Pit trigrams double each other, which symbolizes the flow of water perpetually rolling. From trickles and drips, the flow of water becomes inches and feet across, eventually reaching the point of becoming rivers and oceans, doubling its roll without being abrupt. Its propensity causes it to go downward, and because this is so constant, people believe in it. This is why, when noble people gaze on the symbol of water or the pit, they choose to see its constancy, and they "make their virtuous action constant" and continuous. If the virtuous action of people is not constant, it will become false. This is why it is proper that they be like the constancy of water. When they choose to see how it receives a doubling of its roll, they double or mature the affairs of their teaching and decrees. As for the revelation of their government, and the action of their teaching, they must make the people mature by hearing and listening to it. Afterward, they will be able to attend to it,[3] and this is why noble people give "three decrees and five reports" on it.[4] Were they to inform the people abruptly, without providing examples, being quick to reproach them, they would not be capable of anything, even if they imposed severe punishments as a barrier. This is why it is proper that they be like the doubled roll of water.

The initial "six" line: there is a double pit. It enters into the abyss of the pit. There is misfortune. The initial line uses *yin* softness to occupy the bottom position in the pit or obstacle hexagram; it is soft and weak, without support, and it does not acquire a place that is proper for it. It will not be able to go out from the obstacle, but will only add to the snares in the depth of the obstacle. The word "abyss" here refers to a snare placed at the center of the pit. Since it is already at the center of the double pit, it enters further into the abyss of the pit, and its misfortune should be recognized. **The *Symbol* says: "'There is a double pit,' and it enters the pit: to lose the way brings misfortune."** Because of the double pit, it enters further into the abyss of the pit, which is "to lose the way." As a result, there is misfortune. If it can go out from the obstacle, it will not lose the way.

The second "nine" line: in the pit there is an obstacle. It seeks what is small and acquires it. The second line faces the moment of the pit or obstacle, and it is snared between the two *yin* lines above and below it. It has reached a terrain with an obstacle: "There is an obstacle." Nonetheless, with the powers of firmness and centrality, it may make its own small crossing even if it cannot yet go out from the center of the obstacle. It does not, like the initial line, reach the point of adding to the snare and entering the depth of the obstacle: "It seeks what is small and acquires it." Noble people can preserve themselves when placed in obstacles and difficulties because they are firm and central, and that is all. Since they are firm, their power is sufficient to safeguard them; since they are central, their movement does not lose sight of what is fitting. **The *Symbol* says: "'It seeks what is small and acquires it': it does not yet go out from the center."** When it faces being snared by two *yin* lines on a terrain with an obstacle, it uses the powers of firmness and centrality so as not to be snared in the depth of the obstacle: "It seeks what is small and acquires it." Nonetheless, it cannot yet go out from the obstacle at the center of the Pit trigram.

The third "six" line: There is a pit, and a pit again, for those who arrive. There is an obstacle but also a pillow. It enters into the abyss of the pit. It should not be employed. The third "six" line in the moment of the pit or snare uses *yin* softness to occupy a position without centrality or straightforwardness. It has not placed itself well, and it is incapable either of advancing, retreating, or occupying its position. If it arrives at a lower position, it will enter the center of the obstacle, while if it ascends, the obstacle will repeat itself. Whether it retreats—that is, arrives—or advances, there will be an obstacle. This is why the line statement says that "there is a pit, and a pit again, for those who arrive." Whether it advances or retreats there will be an obstacle, and there is also an obstacle in the position it occupies. The word "pillow" signifies something that props one up, or on which one relies. It occupies a position in the obstacle hexagram, and it places itself only by propping itself up or relying on something else, which indicates its extreme discontent. To be placed like this only adds to its entry into the depth of the obstacle, and this is why it says that it "enters into the abyss of the pit." The way in which the third line places itself should not be employed, and this is why it warns that "it should not be employed." **The Symbol says: "'There is a pit, and a pit again, for those who arrive': in the end, it accomplishes nothing."** Whether it advances or retreats there will be an obstacle, and further, it is not contented where it is placed. Were it to employ this way, it is proper that it would add to its entry into the obstacle. How could it accomplish anything in the end? If the use of *yin* softness to place oneself without centrality or straightforwardness brings about regret and blame even on a terrain of peace and ease, what will the case be like when one is placed in an obstacle? An obstacle is something that people want to go out from. They must acquire the way, and then they will be able to depart from it. If they lose their way when seeking to depart from it, they will add to the trap and to their depletion. This is why the sage warns that a placement like that of the third line "should not be employed."

The fourth "six" line: there are a goblet, wine, and twin tureens. It employs a pot and accepts conjunction by the window. In the end, there is no blame. The fourth "six" line is *yin* and soft, it has no help below it, and it refers to those who cannot cross through the obstacles of the world. It is in a lofty position, and this is why the line statement remarks on the way for ministers to place themselves in obstacles. It is proper that ministers facing the moment of obstacles and difficulties be nothing but extremely sincere, so that they seem believable to their rulers. If their interaction is to be certain, there should be no space between them. Further, if they can open and enlighten the hearts of the rulers, they should be preserved and without blame. As for those who desire the devotion and belief of those above, it is proper that they do nothing but exhaust their disposition and reality, and that is all. Complicated ceremonies and valuable ornaments are nothing like the ritual of the Yan feast, and this is why it uses the Yan feast as an example.[5] It is remarking that it is not proper to value superfluous ornament, but only to make use of one's disposition and reality. What is employed is the wine of a single goblet, and the food of two tureens. An earthenware pot is used as the vessel, which refers to the extremity of one's disposition. When one's disposition and reality are like this, what is still required is to accept "conjunction by the window." The phrase "accepts conjunction" signifies that it advances and is knotted to the way of the ruler, and "window" means an opening and communication. Houses are dim, and this is why windows are provided, so as to communicate the light. The phrase "by the window" remarks that it places itself so that the light may be communicated. In this case, it is the heart of the ruler that is placed in the light. The *Book of Poetry* says: "Heaven serves as a window for the people, acting like the pipe and the flute."[6] The Duke of Mao explains that "window" here refers to the way, but it also signifies an opening and communication.[7] When ministers use the way of loyalty and believability in knotting themselves to the heart of the ruler, they must come to a place of light, and then they will be able to enter it. In the human heart, there are places of concealment and places of communication. The places of concealment are dim, while the places of communication are light. It is proper that they approach its places of light and inform them, and then it will be easy if they seek to be believed. This is why it says that it "accepts conjunction by the window." If they can be like this, they will acquire no blame in the end, even in a moment of hardship and obstacles. Take the case where the heart of the ruler is concealed in barren pleasures, but this is the only reason it is concealed. Although one may forcefully condemn the wrongfulness of barren pleasures, what will this do for the fact that it does not see? One must approach the heart of the ruler in affairs where there is no concealment, unfolding and extending it to the others, and then one will be able to awaken it. Since antiquity, those who can remonstrate with their rulers have never had an effect on anything but what is enlightened in them. This is why, in the great majority of cases, those who make a straight accusation with strength and ferocity simply make them stubborn, while those who speak with mild, beneficent, and enlightened arguments are more often able to act. For instance, Gaozu of the Han dynasty loved Qi Ji and was about to change the identity of the crown prince—this is where he was concealed.[8] The group of ministers who contended with him was a great crowd. He was not without enlightenment on the duties of children born from the first wife and from concubines, or on the sequence of older and younger children, and so what could they do for what he had concealed and not examined? As for the four old men, Gaozu simply recognized their worth and put weight on it. This was where his heart was enlightened and not concealed. This is why, if one has an effect where the heart is enlightened and extends it to other affairs, its awakening will be like turning over one's hand.[9] As for the force of the four old men, how could it be equal to Zhang Liang or the group of dukes, dignitaries, and scholars of the world? As for the ardency of their remarks, how could it be equal to Zhou Chang or Shusun Tong? Nonetheless, Gaozu did not attend to the latter but to the former, because the latter assaulted him where he was concealed, which is different from approaching him where he was enlightened. A further instance is Dowager Queen Zhao, who loved her younger son, the prince of Chang'an, and was not willing to make him a hostage of the Qi state.[10] The concealment in this case lies in her private love.

Although her great ministers strongly remonstrated with her, she became day by day more concealed from them. How could she listen? Her love of her son and her desire to make his wealth and esteem continuously grow were where her heart was enlightened. This is why Chu Long, Commander of the Left, had an effect where she was enlightened and directed her by planning for her son's continuous growth. This is why she listened to him as though she were an echo. It is not only when informing rulers that one should be like this; it is also the case for teachers. As for teachers, they must approach people where they are already grown, and where they are grown is where their hearts are enlightened. They enter their hearts by attending to where they are enlightened, and afterward they unfold and extend them to other things. This is signified by Mencius when he says that "they bring virtue to its completion and power to its attainment."[11] **The *Symbol* says: "'There are a goblet, wine, and twin tureens': firmness and softness border each other."** The *Symbol* only brings up the head of the statement—the case is often like this. "There are a goblet, wine, and twin tureens": this refers to the extremity of one's disposition and reality. If the way that "firmness and softness border" or respond to "each other" can be like this, they may be preserved without blame to the end. The interaction between rulers and ministers can be certain and constant when it has sincerity and reality, and that is all. The words "firmness" and "softness" point to the fourth and fifth lines, and signify the border or interaction between rulers and ministers.

The fifth "nine" line: the pit is not filled. It has extolled what is level. There is no blame. The fifth "nine" line is at the center of the pit, indicating that it is not filled. If the pit were filled, the ground would be level and the fifth line would go out from it. It is fitting that the *zhi* character of "extol" be pronounced as a *di* character and have the meaning of "achieve." A line statement in the Turn hexagram says that "it does not extol regret."[12] It must achieve what is already level, and then there will be no blame. Since it says that it "is not filled," it is not yet level. It is still at the center of the obstacle and does not yet acquire "no blame." Because the powers of the fifth "nine" line are firmness and centrality, and it occupies the position of respect, it is fitting that it be able to cross through the obstacle. Nonetheless, it has no help below it. The second line is snared at the center of the obstacle and cannot yet go out from it, and the remaining lines are all soft and *yin*, without the power to cross through the obstacle. Even if the rulers had this power, how could they cross through the obstacles of the world alone? Those who occupy the position of the ruler without being able to bring the world out from the obstacles will be blamed. They must extol what is already level, and then they will acquire no blame. **The *Symbol* says: "'The**

pit is not filled': its centrality is not yet great." The powers of the fifth "nine" line are firmness and centrality, and it has acquired the position of respect. It is proper that it cross through the obstacles and difficulties of the world, but it is still the case that "the pit is not filled." It is not yet able to level out the obstacles and difficulties. This is a case in which the way of firmness and "centrality is not yet" bright and "great." In a moment of obstacles and difficulties, how will rulers and ministers be able to make the crossing if their forces are not allied? The way of the fifth line is not yet great because it has no minister. If the way of the ruler cannot cross through the obstacles and difficulties of the world, it is not yet great—that is, it is not yet proportioned to its position.

The top "six" line: it is bound with an elegant cord. It is dumped in a thorny thicket. Three years without acquisition bring misfortune. The top "six" line uses *yin* softness to occupy the limit position in the obstacle hexagram, and it refers to the depth of the snare. The line statement chooses trial and imprisonment to exemplify being in the depth of the snare, as when one is "bound" or trussed with "an elegant cord" and confined or "dumped" at the center of a thorny thicket. A line that is *yin* and soft in the depth of the snare will be unable to go out from it. This is why it says that it reaches the point of continuing for three years without being able to avoid it. Its misfortune should be recognized. **The *Symbol* says: "The top 'six' line loses the way: this is the misfortune of 'three years.'"** To use *yin* softness to place oneself on the terrain at the limit of the obstacle—this is to lose the way. This is why its misfortune reaches the point of continuing for three years. It continues for three years without being able to avoid it, and so the line statement says that there will be misfortune in the end. To remark on the continuity of something, the line statements sometimes use the number ten and sometimes the number three, always following the state of affairs. Here it is snared by a trial that goes on for three years, indicating that it is continued to its limit. In the other hexagrams that remark on a number of years, in each case it is according to the state of affairs. For instance, "it does not begin for three years," or "after ten years, she will be betrothed."[13]

30. CAST (*LI* 離)

The *Sequence of the Hexagrams* says: "A pit is a snare. Those who are ensnared must connect themselves to something, and this is why the Cast hexagram is next. To cast is to make a connection." Those who are snared at the center of an obstacle and difficulty must depend on and connect themselves to something—this is a spontaneous principle. And so the Cast hexagram succeeds the Pit hexagram. To cast is both to make a connection and to shed light. The hexagram judgment chooses a *yin* line connected to *yang* lines above and below it to mean dependence and connection. It chooses an empty line at the center to mean the shedding of light. The Cast trigram refers to fire, since the substance of fire is empty, but it connects to things and sheds light on them. The trigram also refers to the sun, again by symbolizing emptiness and the shedding of light.

Cast: there are profit, purity, and progress. It herds the female cattle. There is good fortune. "To cast is to make a connection." None of the ten thousand things is without connection to anything else. If something has a form, then it will have a connection. In the case of people, they will be connected to the people with whom they relate and on whom they depend. They will also be connected to the way that they cause to come about and to the affairs of which they are the masters. When people are making connections, their profit lies in purity and straightforwardness. If they acquire straightforwardness, then they will be capable of progress and development. This is why the judgment says: "Cast: there are profit, purity, and progress." "It herds the female cattle. There is good fortune": the nature of cattle is submissive, and in this case they are female, which indicates extreme submissiveness. Those who have depended on and connected with what is straightforward must be able to submit to the way of straightforwardness, as female cattle do, and then there will be good fortune.

"It herds the female cattle": this signifies that it nourishes the virtue of submissiveness. The virtue of submissiveness in people is brought to completion by nourishment. If they have connected themselves to what is straightforward, it is proper that they use nourishment and practice so as to bring the virtue of submissiveness to completion.

The *Judgment* says: "To cast is to make a connection. The sun and moon are connected to heaven. The hundred grains, plants, and trees are connected to the earth." "To cast is to make a connection": the *li* character of "connection" signifies dependency. In the case of "the sun and moon," they are "connected to heaven." In the case of "the hundred grains, plants, and trees," they are "connected to the earth." Of the ten thousand things, none is without connection to something. Between heaven and earth, there is nothing that is without connection. In the case of people, it is proper to scrutinize their connections. If these connections acquire straightforwardness, then they will be able to make progress. **"The light is repeated. By connecting itself with straightforwardness, it transforms and completes the world."** The *Judgment* is remarking on the powers of the trigrams. The Cast trigram is both above and below—the lights are put one on top of the other. The fifth and second lines both place themselves with centrality and straightforwardness: they are connected "with straightforwardness." The ruler and minister, or those above and below, both possess the virtue of enlightenment and are placed with centrality and straightforwardness. They can transform the world and bring the customs of pattern and enlightenment to completion. **"Softness is connected with centrality and straightforwardness. This is why there is 'progress.' As a result, 'it herds the female cattle. There is good fortune.'"** The second and fifth lines use softness and submissiveness to connect themselves with centrality and straightforwardness, and so they can make progress. When people can nourish extreme submissiveness so as to connect themselves with centrality and straightforwardness, "there is good fortune." This is why the judgment says: "It herds the female cattle. There is good fortune." Someone asks: the second line is central and straightforward, but the fifth line uses *yin* to occupy a *yang* position. How can it have acquired straightforwardness? Response: what casts is the master of its connections. The fifth is the position of centrality and straightforwardness. When a "six" line connects itself with a straightforward position, it becomes straightforward. When students recognize the meaning of the moment and do not lose sight of what is weighty and what is light, they will be able to speak about the *Book of Changes*.

The *Symbol* says: "The light twice produces a cast. Great people use it successively to shed light on and illuminate the four regions." If the *Symbol* had said "two lights," there would be two lights, and no one would see the meaning of successively shedding light. This is why it says: "The light twice"—that is, the light is repeated, or occurs twice—signifying that the casts succeed each other. The phrase "produces a cast" indicates that the light twice constitutes a cast, which means "successively to shed light." The Shake and Low hexagrams choose this meaning for the terms "rolling" and "following," and there are others of this kind.[1] Nonetheless, the meaning of the Cast hexagram carries the most weight. When it remarks on "great people" who are great because of virtue, they are sages; when they are great because of their positions, they are kings. Great people gaze on the symbol of casts of light succeeding each other, and they use the enlightenment and virtue of successive generations to illuminate and watch over the four regions. In the great majority of cases when lights succeed each other, it is a successive shedding of light. It has brought up the greatest case, and this is why it remarks on a successive illumination inherited over the ages.

The initial "nine" line: it walks in error. If it is reverent, there will be no blame. A *yang* line will certainly prefer to move, and, further, this one occupies the bottom position and belongs to the Cast trigram substance. If a *yang* line occupies the bottom position, it will desire an advance. The nature of the Cast trigram is to flame upward. Its tendency is to connect with something above it, and it is about to move restlessly. "It walks in error": this signifies that there is error in its interaction. Although it has not yet advanced, there are already traces of this movement. If it moves, it will lose the role of occupying the bottom position, and there will be blame. Nonetheless, its powers are firmness and enlightenment. If it recognizes its duty by being "reverent" and cautious, it will not reach the point of blame. The initial line is at the bottom and has no position. If it sheds light on its own advance and retreat, then it is on the way of connection. Since its tendency is to move, if it cannot be reverent and cautious, then its movement will be faulty. In such a case, it will not shed light on its connection, and there will be blame. **The *Symbol* says: "'It is reverent' but 'it walks in error': it eludes blame."** "It walks in error," but it desires movement. It knows how to be reverent and cautious, and it does not dare to advance. And so, it seeks to elude or avoid excess and blame. It occupies its position with enlightenment and firmness, and this is why it knows how to elude them. If it were not firm and enlightened, its movement would be faulty.

The second "six" line: the cast is yellow. There are primacy and good fortune. The second line occupies the central position and acquires straightforwardness: it is connected to centrality and straightforwardness. The word "yellow" refers to the color of centrality and the beauty of pattern. Pattern, enlightenment, centrality, and straightforwardness constitute an abundance of beauty. This is why the line statement says that "the cast is yellow." It uses the virtues of pattern, enlightenment, centrality, and straightforwardness to ascend and become the same as the ruler of pattern, enlightenment, centrality, and submissiveness. When its enlightenment is like this, and its connection is like this, there is the good fortune of a great good. **The *Symbol* says: "'The cast is yellow. There are primacy and good fortune': it acquires the way of centrality."** The reason "there are primacy and good fortune" is that "it acquires the way of centrality." The *Symbol* does not say that it is straightforward because, in the Cast hexagram, centrality carries more weight. Its pattern and enlightenment are brought to completion by centrality, and its straightforwardness lies in this centrality.

The third "nine" line: the cast is from the setting sun. If it does not drum on a pot and sing, then it will lament its great old age. There is misfortune. The eight uniform hexagrams all have the meaning of their two trigram substances. In the Lead hexagram, the inner and outer trigrams both refer to vigor. In the Yield hexagram, the upper and lower trigrams both refer to submissiveness. In the Shake hexagram, authority and shaking succeed one another. In the Low hexagram, the upper and lower trigrams submit to and follow each other. In the Pit hexagram, the obstacles are repeated and double each other. In the Cast hexagram, two lights successively illuminate. In the Calm hexagram, the inner and outer trigrams both refer to stopping. In the Joy hexagram, the one and the other trigram enjoy each other. The meaning of the Cast hexagram is greatest when it concerns human affairs. The third "nine" line occupies the end position of the lower trigram substance. It is the moment when the earlier light is about to be exhausted, and it is proper that the later light succeed it. It refers to the beginning and end of human beings, and to the reform and change of the moments. This is why "the cast is from the setting sun"—that is, the light is from the sun that is setting and descending. If it is setting, then it is about to be consumed. Concerning principles, one may remark that the abundant will necessarily become scarce, and what has begun will necessarily end—this is the constant way. Those who have attained this take pleasure in submitting to principle. A "pot" is a vessel for ordinary employment. To "drum on a pot and sing" is to take pleasure in the ordinary. Someone unable to act like this will consider "great old age" to be a reason for lamentation or worry, which constitutes "misfortune." The phrase "great old age" refers to one's collapse and consumption. When people are at their end or are exhausted, those who have attained this will recognize the constant principle. They will take pleasure in heaven, and that is all. All their encounters with ordinary things will be pleasurable, as in the case of those who "drum on a pot and sing." As for those who have not attained this, they will fear what lasts, and will be melancholy as they approach their exhaustion. They will lament their "great old age," which constitutes their misfortune. Such are the ways of placing oneself in life and death. The phrase "old age" is the same as "fading away." **The *Symbol* says: "'The cast is from the setting sun': how could it continue?"** When the sun has collapsed and set, how could its light continue? The enlightened recognize that this is the case, and this is why they seek people to succeed them in their affairs. They retreat to a place where they can restrain themselves, they content themselves with the ordinary, and they place themselves submissively. How could this be sufficient to constitute misfortune?

The fourth "nine" line: its arrival is like a blast, like a burn, like death, and like desertion. The fourth "nine" line, cast off from the lower trigram substance, has risen to the higher substance. It initiates the succeeding light, and this is why the line statement remarks on the meaning of succession and service. It is in a position above and near the ruler, which is the terrain for succession and service. It uses *yang* to occupy a position in the Cast trigram substance, and it places itself in the fourth position, which is to be firm and restless, without centrality or straightforwardness. It is also the repetition of a firm line. It is without straightforwardness, and it has a propensity to be abundantly firm: "Its arrival is like a blast." It refers to those whose succession is not good. As for those who succession is good, they must possess the sincerity of lowliness and abdication. This is the way to submit and to serve, as in the case of Shun and Qi.[2] In the present case, the fourth line's "arrival is like a blast"—that is, it has lost the way of good succession. Further, it serves the fifth "six" line, a ruler of *yin* softness, and the propensity of its firmness is to be abundant, to usurp it, and to glow. Its *qi* flares like a burn, and this is why it says: "Like a burn." When the action of the fourth line is not good, as in this case, it must be afflicted and harmed, and this is why it says: "Like death." Those who lose sight of the duties of succession and inheritance, and the way of serving those above, always possess the virtue of rebellion. They are deserted and abandoned by the crowd, and this is why it says: "Like desertion." When they reach the point of death and desertion, they are already at the limit of their affliction, and this is why it does not appear to remark on their misfortune. **The *Symbol* says: "'Its arrival is like a blast': no place will embrace it."** They usurp the ruler above them without submitting to the one they serve. People detest them and the crowd deserts them. There is no place in the world that will embrace them.

The fifth "six" line: it is as though it sobbed tears, as though it were distraught and lamenting. There is good fortune. The fifth "six" line occupies the position of respect and guards its centrality. It has the virtues of pattern and enlightenment, and may be called good. Nonetheless, it uses softness to occupy a position above, and it has no help below it. It is alone between the firm and strong lines to which it is connected and on which it depends—its propensity is perilous and troubling. It has only its enlightenment, and this is why it can be deeply trembling and troubled, and can reach the point of sobbing "tears." The depth of its worry and apprehension reaches the point of being "distraught and lamenting," and so it can preserve its good fortune. Phrases like "sobbed tears" and "distraught and lamenting" remark on the limit or depth of worry and trouble. This is the proper moment for them. It uses pattern and enlightenment to occupy the position of respect, and it knows how to possess such worry and trembling. This is why it will acquire good fortune. Were it to rely on its own virtues of pattern and enlightenment while connected to centrality and straightforwardness, being so free that it was not troubled, how could it preserve its good fortune? **The *Symbol* says: "The 'good fortune' of 'the fifth 'six' line': it is cast upon the king and the duke."** The "good fortune of the fifth 'six' line" is that it connects itself to and acquires the straightforward position of the king and the duke. It accords with the propensity of the top line, and its enlightenment examines affairs and their principles. It is constrained to be trembling, troubled, worried, and deliberative, and so it will be capable of good fortune. If such were not the case, how could it be contented?

The top "nine" line: the king employs it to go out and take the field. It possesses excellence. This "nine" line uses *yang* to occupy the top position, it is at the end of the Cast hexagram, and it refers to the limit of firmness and enlightenment. Being enlightened, it is able to illuminate; being firm, it is able to make decisions. The ability to illuminate is sufficient for the examination of crookedness and badness; the ability to decide is sufficient for the actions of authority and punishment. This is why it is fitting that "the king employs it." In such a case, when its firmness and enlightenment distinguish the crookedness and badness of the world, and it acts to "take the field" and attack them, it will possess an accomplishment of "excellence" and beauty. To take the field and attack is to employ the greatest form of punishment. **It breaks their heads. It obtains nothing uncouth. There is no blame.** As for the limit of enlightenment, nothing is so minimal that it is not illuminated, while the limit of decisiveness has neither tolerance nor lenience. Those who do not conjoin themselves to the center will be injured by the severity of their examination. If those who drive out the badness of the world exhaustively study what is becoming infected step by step with iniquity and error, how may they victoriously put it to death? The injury inflicted by their savagery will also be extreme, and this is why it is proper to break or choose only the chiefs and "heads." If those that they hold or obtain are not from among the uncouth, they will not be blamed for savagery and violence. The *Book of History* says: "When I annihilate the chiefs of the insurrection, I will not set in order those who were coerced to attend to them."[3] **The *Symbol* says: "'The king employs it to go out and take the field': he makes the kingdoms straightforward."** The king employs the virtues of this top "nine" line, using its enlightenment to illuminate and its firmness to make decisions. He examines and expels the badness of the world, and so he "makes the kingdoms" and states "straightforward," and sets them in order. To be firm and enlightened is the way to occupy a position above.

Part Two

31. STIR (*XIAN* 咸)

The *Sequence of the Hexagrams* says: "First there are heaven and earth, and then there are the ten thousand things; first there are the ten thousand things, and then there are men and women; first there are men and women, and then there are husband and wife; first there are husband and wife, and then there are father and son; first there are father and son, and then there are ruler and minister; first there are ruler and minister, and then there are those above and below; first there are those above and below, and then there are ritual and duty, where they intersect." Heaven and earth are the root of the ten thousand things, while husband and wife are the beginning of human kinship, and so the first part of the *Book of Changes* has the Lead and Yield hexagrams at its head, while the second part has the Stir hexagram, succeeded by the Last hexagram, at its head. Heaven and earth are two things, and this is why the way of heaven and earth is divided into two hexagrams. Men and women interact and align, and become husbands and wives. This is why the Stir and Last hexagrams, both of them composed of two aligned trigram substances, have husbands and wives as their meaning.[1] "To stir is to affect," and so it has enjoyment as its master; to last is to be constant, and so it has straightforwardness as its root. The way of enjoyment will by itself possess straightforwardness, while the way of straightforwardness will certainly possess enjoyment. "There are lowliness and movement. All the firmness corresponds to all the softness," which constitutes enjoyment.[2] As for the trigrams of the Stir hexagram, the Joy trigram is above and the Calm trigram below. They refer to a young woman and a young man.[3] The affection of men and women for each other is never so deep as when they are young, and this is why two young people are symbols of the Stir hexagram. The Calm trigram substance refers to real devotion. The stopping referred to by the trigram means sincerity and probity. The man tends to descend and interact out of real devotion, while the woman's heart enjoys it and corresponds to the man from above. The affection of the man comes first—that is, the man first has a sincere affection, and then the woman enjoys it and corresponds to him.

Stir: there are progress, profit, and purity. The choice of a woman brings good fortune. "To stir is to affect": the judgment does not speak of affection, but the Stir hexagram has both meanings. Men and women interact and affect each other. Of the things that affect each other, none are so extreme as men and women when they are young. In general, rulers and ministers, those above and below, and the rest of the ten thousand things all have a way to affect each other. If things affect each other, they possess the principle of progress and development. If rulers and ministers can affect each other, it is because the way of rulers and ministers is developing. If those above and below can affect each other, then the tendencies of those above and below will develop. One can go on to fathers and sons, husbands and wives, blood relations, and friends. If their inclinations or intentions affect each other, then there will be harmony and submissiveness, or progress and development. Affairs and things are always like this, and this is why the Stir hexagram has the principle of progress. "Profit and purity": concerning the way of affecting each other, the profit lies in straightforwardness. Those who do not make use of straightforwardness will enter into bad acts. For instance, husband and wife may use license and debauchery, ruler and minister may use flattery and enjoyment, and those above and below may use crookedness and crassness—in all these cases, they affect each other without making use of straightforwardness. "The choice of a woman brings good fortune": the judgment is remarking on the powers of the trigrams. In the hexagram, "there is softness above and firmness below. Their two kinds of *qi* affect and correspond to each other, so that they may be together. There are stopping and enjoyment," which has this meaning: "The man puts himself below the woman." Given that this is the meaning, if there is "the choice of a woman," then they will acquire straightforwardness and there will be good fortune.

The *Judgment* says: "To stir is to affect. There are softness above and firmness below. Their two kinds of *qi* affect and correspond to each other, so that they may be together. There are stopping and enjoyment. The man puts himself below the woman. This is to make use of 'progress, profit, and purity. The choice of a woman brings good fortune.'" The meaning of the Stir hexagram is affection. Concerning the hexagram, a soft line ascends and a firm line descends. The soft line ascends to alter a firm line and complete the Joy trigram, while the firm line descends to alter a soft line and complete the Calm trigram.

The *yin* and *yang* lines interact with each other, which has the meaning of men and women interacting and affecting each other. Further, the Joy or woman trigram is on top, while the Calm or man trigram occupies the bottom, which also refers to "softness above and firmness below." *Yin* and *yang*, "their two kinds of *qi*," affect each other and correspond to each other, so that they harmonize and align. The clause "so that they may be together" refers to this. "There are stopping and enjoyment": to be stopped by enjoyment constitutes an intention of solidity and probity. The Calm or stopping trigram is at the bottom, referring to a descent made with devotion and sincerity, and the Joy or enjoyment trigram is at the top, referring to a correspondence made with harmony and enjoyment. When "the man puts himself below the woman," this is the extremity of harmony. When they affect each other in this way, they can make progress and develop as a result, and they will also acquire straightforwardness. When "the choice of a woman" is like this, there will be "good fortune." In the great majority of cases where the powers of the trigrams are like this, the profit in the way of affecting each other will lie in straightforwardness. **"Heaven and earth affect each other and the ten thousand things are transformed and born. Sages affect the human heart and the world is harmonious and peaceful. If one gazes on those that affect, the inclinations of heaven, earth, and the ten thousand things may be seen."** The *Judgment* has already remarked on the meaning of men and women affecting each other. Now it turns to unfolding the way of affection at its limit, so as to exhaust the principle of heaven and earth and the function of the sage. When the two kinds of *qi*, heavenly and earthly, affect each other, they transform and give birth to the ten thousand things. Sages make their sincerity extreme so as to affect the hearts of the countless millions, and "the world is harmonious and peaceful." And so the hearts of the world are harmonious and peaceful, because the sages have affected them. If one gazes on the principle by which heaven and earth interact and affect each other, transforming and giving birth to the ten thousand things, and the way by which "sages affect the human heart," bringing about harmony and peace, then "the inclinations of heaven, earth, and the ten thousand things may be seen." As for the principle of mutual affection, those who know the way may gaze on it in silence.

The *Symbol* says: "Above the mountain, there is a lake: Stir. Noble people use it to receive people with emptiness." The nature of the lake is to soak into what is below it, while the nature of earth is to receive what soaks into it. The lake is above the mountain, and its soaking develops and pervades it step by step. This is how things with two kinds of *qi* mutually affect each other. When noble people gaze on the symbol of the mountain and lake *qi* developing, they empty out their center so as to receive people. As for people whose centers are empty, they can be receptive, but nothing can enter those who are full. Those with empty centers are non-selves.[4] When the center has no private master, there is no affection that will not be mutual. Those who calculate what they will embrace, or who select what they will align with and receive, are not on the way of the sage, whose affections must be mutual.

The initial "six" line: it stirs its big toe. The initial "six" line is at the bottom of the lower trigram, and it affects the fourth line. Since it is minimal, being placed in the initial position, and its affection is not yet deep, how could it move people? This is why it is like the movement of the big toe, which is not sufficient for the person to advance. The "big toe" is the greatest digit on the foot. In the affection of people for each other, there are differences of shallowness and depth, or of lightness and weight. Those who understand the propensity of the moment will not lose what is fitting when they place themselves. **The *Symbol* says: "'It stirs its big toe': it tends toward the outside."** The movement of the initial line's tendency affects the fourth, and this is why the *Symbol* says that it is "toward the outside." Although its tendency is to move, it does not yet affect anything deeply—it is just like the movement of the big toe, which is not sufficient for the person to advance.

The second "six" line: it stirs its calf. There is misfortune, but good fortune in occupying a position. The second line uses *yin* to occupy a position in the lower trigram, and it corresponds to the fifth, which is why the line statement provides the warning about stirring its calf. The calf is between the foot and the belly. When one travels, it is the first to move. For raising the foot, there is nothing like the calf setting itself in motion. If the second line does not guard the way by waiting for those above to seek it out but moves itself like the calf, it will lose itself, being restless and at fault, and so there will be misfortune. If it is contented with the position it occupies and does not move, but waits for those above to seek it out, it will acquire the way of advancing and retreating, and there will be good fortune. The second line refers to people of centrality and straightforwardness. It is only because this is the Stir hexagram, and because it corresponds to the fifth line, that the line statement gives this warning. It says in turn that there is "good fortune in occupying a position." If it is contented with its role and does not set itself in motion, there will be good fortune. **The *Symbol* says: "Although 'there is misfortune,' there is 'good fortune in occupying a position': if it is submissive, there will be no harm."** The second line occupies the center and has acquired straightforwardness, its corresponding line is also central and straightforward, and its powers are good at their root. It is only because this is the moment of the Stir hexagram, and because it corresponds to those above with its soft disposition, that the line statement warns of the misfortune that comes from moving first to seek the ruler. If it guards itself in the position it occupies, there will be good fortune. The *Symbol* in turn sheds some light on this, saying that the warning is not to avoid acquiring affection for each other, but only that there will be no harm if it submits to principle—that is, if it guards the way and is not the first to move.

The third "nine" line: it stirs its thigh. It holds to what it follows. Making a journey brings dismay. The third "nine" line uses *yang* to occupy a firm position, it has the power of *yang* firmness, it is the master of the inner trigram, and it occupies the top of the lower trigram. It is fitting for it to acquire the way of straightforwardness for itself so that it may affect other things, but what it corresponds to is the top "six" line. The *yang* line prefers the top line and enjoys it, while the top *yin* line occupies the limit position of the affection or enjoyment trigram, and this is why the third is affected by and attends to it. The thigh is below the body and above the foot and can do nothing by itself. It moves by following the body, and this is why it is considered the symbol. The line statement is saying that the third "nine" line cannot be its own master, but moves by following other things, just like the thigh. What it holds to and guards is the thing that it follows. Its power of *yang* firmness is affected by and follows what it enjoys. If one makes a journey in a case like this, there should be disappointment and dismay. **The *Symbol* says: "'It stirs its thigh': it, too, is not in its place. It tends to follow other people: it holds to those below."** The *Symbol* says "it, too," because, in fact, the statements of the *Symbol* and the *Book of Changes* were not originally interspersed. It was in one place of its own, and this is why the ideas of the *Symbol* statements for the various lines refer to each other.[5] Here it says "it, too" in reference to its statement about an earlier line. Earlier it said: "'It stirs its big toe': it tends toward the outside. Although 'there is misfortune,' there is 'good fortune in occupying a position': if it is submissive, there will be no harm." "'It stirs its thigh': it, too, is not in its place": the two previous *yin* lines both move by affecting others. Although the third is a *yang* line, it, too, is like this, and this is why it says that "it, too, is not in its place." The phrase "not in its place" signifies movement. It has the disposition of *yang* firmness, but it cannot be its own master. On the contrary, "it tends to follow other people," because what it wields or holds to is extremely humble and in a position below.

The fourth "nine" line: purity brings good fortune. Regrets vanish. It wavers, and wavers again, whether it arrives or makes a journey. Friends are attentive

to your reflections. Affection is what moves people, and this is why nearly all the line statements choose the human body as their symbol. The big toe is chosen because it is at the bottom and moves minimally, the calf is chosen because it moves first, and the thigh is chosen because it follows other things. Nothing is chosen for the fourth "nine" line, and so it goes straight to remarking on the way of affection. It does not remark that "it stirs its heart," because affection is itself the heart. The fourth line is at the center and occupies a position above, which is the proper position of the heart, and this is why it is the master of affection and why the line statement remarks on the way of affection. If it is pure and straightforward, there will be good fortune and regrets will vanish. If its affection is not straightforward, then there will be regrets. Further, the fourth line belongs to the enjoyment trigram substance, it occupies a *yin* position, and it corresponds to the initial line. This is why it warns about purity on the way of affection, so that nothing will be other than mutual. If it has private bonds, these will do harm to the mutual affection and there will be regrets. When sages affect the hearts of the world, they are like the cold and heat or the rain and sunlight. Nothing is other than mutual, and there is nothing that does not correspond to them, because they are pure, and that is all. The word "purity" signifies the empty center and the non-self. "It wavers, and wavers again, whether it arrives or makes a journey. Friends are attentive to your reflections": if its purity is unified, it will have no affection that is not mutual. But if, in its journeys and arrivals, "it wavers, and wavers again" like this, and employs its private heart to affect other things, then it can move and affect those to whom its reflections are extended while being unable to affect those to whom they are not extended. This is the case of "friends" or those of its kind who are "attentive" to its "reflections." Since it is bound by a private heart and has mastered only one corner or one affair, how could it have such latitude that nothing is other than mutual? The *Appended Statements* says: "As for the world, what are its reflections? What are its apprehensions? The world is wedded to the same thing, though it comes by peculiar paths. When one thing is brought about, it prompts a hundred apprehensions. As for the world, what are its reflections? What are its apprehensions?"[6] Fuzi is prompted by the Stir hexagram to discuss the way of mutual affection to its limit.[7] When one uses a private heart of reflection and apprehension to affect things, the number of things affected will shrink. Since the principle of the world is one, although its paths are peculiar, they are all wedded to the same thing. Although it has a hundred apprehensions, they bring about only one thing. Although things may have ten thousand peculiarities and affairs may have ten thousand alterations, they are one when united, and none of them can draw back. This is why, if one's intentions are pure, one will deplete the world and no affection will be other than mutual. This is why it says: "As for the world, what are its reflections? What are its apprehensions?" If one employs a private heart of reflection and apprehension, how could anything not be other than mutual? "When the sun goes on a journey, the moon arrives, and when the moon goes on a journey, the sun arrives. Light is born as the sun and moon supplant each other. When the cold goes on a journey, the heat arrives, and when the heat goes on a journey, the cold arrives. The year is completed as the cold and heat supplant each other. To go on a journey is to contract, while to arrive is to expand.[8] Profit is born as contraction and expansion affect each other." This passage uses journey and arrival, or contraction and expansion, to shed light on the principle that they "affect and correspond." When the *Judgment* says that they "affect and correspond," it signifies that what has contracted will expand and what has expanded will contract. This is why the *Appended Statements* says that "light is born as the sun and moon supplant each other," and "the year is completed as the cold and heat supplant each other." It is completed because they perform their function, and this is why it says that "profit is born as contraction and expansion affect each other." To affect is to move, and where there is affection, there will necessarily be correspondence. In general, where there is movement, it is entirely constituted by affection, and where there is affection, there will necessarily be correspondence. What corresponds becomes in its turn what affects, and what affects becomes in its turn what corresponds, and so this goes on ceaselessly. "The inchworm contracts so that it may seek expansion. The dragon and the snake hibernate so that they may preserve their bodies. The meaning of the essence enters the spirit so that it may bring about its function. The function of profit is to make the body contented so that it may make its virtue venerable. Those whose journey exceeds this point do not yet know anything." The foregoing passage is speaking about the principle of contraction and expansion, but it chooses particular things to shed light on it. When the inchworm travels, it first contracts and afterward expands. In fact, if it did not contract, it would not expand, and once it has expanded, it will contract again. Those who gaze on the inchworm will recognize the principle of affection and correspondence. Dragons and snakes store themselves away to preserve and rest their bodies, and afterward they can quickly rouse themselves. If they did not hibernate, they could not rouse themselves. Movement and rest affecting each other—this is contraction and expansion. Noble people hide in their hearts "the meaning of the essence" and minimum. It enters their spirit mysteriously "so that it may bring about its function." To hide the essence and minimum in one's heart is to accumulate it, while to bring about its function is to have an influence. Accumulation together with influence—this is contraction and expansion. "The function of profit is to make the body contented so that it may make its virtue venerable": this refers to the preceding text about bringing about its function, and remarks that there is profit in its influence and function. By making the place of its body contented, it makes its virtue and vocation venerable and great. If what acts is aligned with principle, its affairs will be straightforward and its body will be contented. The ability of sages to manage affairs is exhausted in this, and this is why it says that "those whose journey exceeds this point do not yet know anything." "To deplete the spirit and to recognize its transformations is the abundance of virtue": the *Appended Statements* has already said that "those whose journey exceeds this point do not yet know anything," and now it goes on to end with these words. It is saying that to deplete and bring to its limit the extreme mystery of the spirit, and to recognize the way of transformation and cultivation, is the extreme abundance of virtue. There is nothing further to be said. **The *Symbol* says: "'Purity brings good fortune. Regrets vanish': its affection is not yet harmful. 'It wavers, and wavers again, whether it arrives or makes a journey': it is not yet bright or great."** If it is pure, then there will be good fortune and regrets will vanish. It does not yet constitute the private affection that harms, but if it is bound by a private correspondence, then it will harmed by its affection. "It wavers, and wavers again, whether it arrives or makes a journey": if it uses a private heart to affect someone, then the way of affection will shrink, and this is why the *Symbol* says that "it is not yet bright or great."

The fifth "nine" line: it stirs its dorsum. There are no regrets. A "nine" line occupies the position of respect. It is proper that it use extreme sincerity to affect the world, but it corresponds to the second line and is close to the top line. Were it to bind itself to the second and enjoy the top line, it would shrink into the shallows of partiality and privacy. Since this is not the way of the ruler, how could it affect the world? The word "dorsum" refers to the muscles of the back. It refers to what is at the back of the heart and to what is unseen. The line statement is remarking that if it can turn its back on its private heart, or if it can affect those that it does not see and enjoy, then it will acquire the straightforwardness of a ruler who affects the world, and there will be no regrets. **The *Symbol* says: "'It stirs its dorsum': it tends toward the branches."** The *Symbol* is warning that it must be made to turn its back on its heart or to stir its dorsum, but it persists in having a heart for the shallows and the branches. It is bound to the second line and enjoys the top line, which is to be affected by private desires.

The top "six" line: it stirs its jowls, cheeks, and tongue. The top line is *yin* and soft, belongs to the enjoyment trigram substance, and is the master of the enjoyment trigram. Further, it occupies the limit position of the affection hexagram—this is to be at the limit of wanting to affect things. This is why it cannot affect things with extreme sincerity, as may be revealed and seen in the space of its mouth and tongue. Such being the ordinary attitude of small people and women, how could they move other people? The line statement does not go straight to speaking of the mouth, but it does speak of the "jowls, cheeks, and tongue." It is just as when people today use the word "mouth" to signify either excessive speech or closed lips. It speaks of the cheeks and tongue because the jowls, cheeks, and tongue are all employed in speech. **The *Symbol* says: "'It stirs its jowls, cheeks, and tongue': it speaks with a frothing mouth.** It is only extreme sincerity that can affect people. As for those who use softness to speak with a frothing and flapping of the mouth and tongue, how could their words and speech be capable of affecting anyone?

32. LAST (*HENG* 恆)

The *Sequence of the Hexagrams* says: "The way of husband and wife should not be without continuity, and this is why the Last hexagram is next. To last is to continue." The Stir hexagram refers to the way of husband and wife. Husband and wife do not alter to the end of their lives, and this is why, after the Stir hexagram, the Last hexagram is next. In the Stir hexagram, a young man is below a young woman. When the man is below the woman, it means that the man and woman interact and affect each other. In the Last hexagram, a grown man is above a grown woman.[1] The man is in the position of respect and the woman is humble, which is the constant way of husbands and wives in the home. If one discusses the inclination to interact and be affectionate, it is the young that have such an intimate relationship. If one discusses the sequence of respect and humility, it is the fully grown that are properly prudent and straightforward. This is why the Joy and Calm trigrams constitute the Stir hexagram, while the Shake and Low trigrams constitute the Last hexagram. The man is above the woman. The man moves on the outside, while the woman is submissive on the inside, which is the constant human principle. This is why they constitute the Last hexagram. Further, "firmness is above and softness below. Thunder and wind agree with each other. There are lowliness and movement," and firmness and softness correspond to each other—all of these have the meaning of the Last hexagram.

Last: there are progress and no blame. There are profit and purity. There is profit in a long journey. To last is to be constant and continue. The way of lasting is capable of progress and development. If something lasts, and it can make progress, then there will be no blame. If it lasts, and it cannot make progress, then it is not on the way of being able to last, and it will be blamed. For instance, when noble people last in the good, they are on the way of what can last. When small people last in the bad, they have lost the way of what can last. And so what lasts can make progress, and this is because of its purity and straightforwardness. This is why the judgment says: "There are profit and purity." As for what is signified by the Last hexagram, it signifies the way of being able to last and continue, not guarding a single corner without knowing how to alter. This is why "there is profit in a long journey." It is only because it makes a journey that it can last. If it had just one determination, then it would not be capable of constancy. Further, since this is the way of constancy and continuation, how could a journey not bring profit?

The *Judgment* says: "To last is to continue." The meaning of the Last hexagram is to grow and to continue. **"Firmness is above and softness below. Thunder and wind agree with each other. There are lowliness and movement. All the firmness corresponds to all the softness: Last."** There are four powers of the trigrams that complete the meaning of the Last hexagram. "Firmness is above and softness below": this signifies that the initial line of the Lead trigram ascends to occupy the fourth position, while the initial line of the Yield trigram descends to occupy the initial hexagram position: the firm line is above and the soft line below. Since the two lines have changed their places, they have completed the Shake and Low trigrams. The Shake trigram is above and the Low trigram below—this, too, is signified by "firmness is above and softness below." Firmness places itself at the top and softness occupies the bottom, which is the way of the Last hexagram. "Thunder and wind agree with each other": the shaking of thunder is revealed by the wind. The two require each other, and their interaction is helpful to the propensities of each. This is why the *Judgment* says that they "agree with each other," which is how they are constant. "There are lowliness and movement": the Low or submissiveness trigram is below, and the Shake or movement trigram is above. Together they constitute "lowliness and movement." The creation and transformation brought about by heaven and earth is lasting and continuous without ceasing, only because there are submissiveness and movement, and that is all. "Lowliness and movement" are the way of being constant and continuous. If there were movement without submission, how could it be constant? "All the firmness corresponds to all the softness": the firm and soft lines of each trigram all correspond to each other. That firmness and softness correspond to each other is a constant principle. These four powers are the way to last, and so they constitute the Last hexagram. **"'Last: there are progress and no blame. There are profit and purity': it continues on its way."** The way of the Last hexagram can bring about progress and be without excess or blame, but it is fitting for what lasts to acquire straightforwardness. If it loses straightforwardness, it cannot be on the way of the Last hexagram. This is why the *Judgment* says: "It continues on its way." The phrase "its way" refers to the straightforward way of what can last. If its virtues do not last, or it lasts without being straightforward, it will not be capable of progress, and there will be blame. **"The way of heaven and earth is to last and continue without ceasing."** Heaven and earth do not cease because, in fact, they possess the way "to last and continue." Anyone who can last on the way of what can last will align with the principle of heaven and earth. **"'There is profit in a long journey': if there is an end, then there is a beginning."** The principle of the world is that nothing can last without movement. Those who move will come to an end and return to their beginning, and so they will last and not be depleted. In general, although the things given birth by heaven and earth may be as solid and beneficial as mountain peaks, they cannot be without alteration. This is why things that last are not said to have a single determination. If they had a single determination, they would not be able to last. They can only follow the moment, alter, and change, which is the constant way. This is why the judgment says that "there is profit in a long journey." It sheds light on this aspect of the principle to trouble anyone who has become mired in the ordinary. **"Because the sun and moon acquire heaven, their illumination can continue. Because the four seasons alter and transform, their completion can continue. Sages continue on their way, and the transformations of the world are completed. If one gazes on those that last, the inclinations of heaven, earth, and the ten thousand things may be seen."** This is the limit of the *Judgment*'s remarks on the constant principle. The "sun and moon" have *yin* and *yang* as their essence and *qi*. It is only by submitting to the way of heaven that they make their journey and arrival, or wax and wane, and this is why "their illumination can continue" without ceasing. To "acquire heaven" is to submit to the principle of heaven. The "four seasons" have *yin* and *yang* as their *qi*. That they journey and arrive, "alter and transform," and bring the ten thousand things to birth and completion, is also because they "acquire heaven." This is why they are constant, continuous, and without ceasing. Sages use the way of constancy and continuity to bring constancy to their actions, and to complete the beautiful customs that will transform the world. "If one gazes on those that last"—this signifies that one gazes on the principle by which the sun and moon continuously illuminate, the four seasons are continuously completed, and the reason the way of sages is constant and continuous. If one gazes on this, then the inclinations and principles of "heaven, earth, and the ten thousand things may be seen." The way by which heaven and earth are constant and continuous, and the principle by which the world is constant and continuous—how could those who do not know the way understand them?

The *Symbol* says: "There are thunder and wind: Last. Noble people use it to set themselves up without changing their region." Noble people gaze on the symbol of thunder and wind agreeing with each other and completing the Last hexagram, and they make their virtue constant and continuous. They "set themselves up" on the way of great centrality, which is constant and continuous, without altering or "changing their region" or place.

The initial "six" line: it digs into what lasts. Purity brings misfortune. There is no long-term profit. The initial line occupies the bottom position and corresponds straightforwardly to the fourth. It refers to soft and dim people who can guard what is constant but cannot set a measure to their own propensities. The fourth line belongs to the Shake trigram substance, its nature is *yang*, it uses firmness to occupy a lofty position, and its tendency is to ascend and not to descend. Further, it is separated from the initial line by the second and third, and so it differs from the constant by tending to correspond to it. The initial line "seeks out" and puts its hope in "depth"—that is, it knows how to be constant without knowing how to alter. The phrase "digs into" refers to deepening. "It digs into what lasts" signifies that it seeks out the depth of what lasts. It guards what is constant without setting a measure to its propensities, it seeks out and hopes for the depth of those above, and it guards this with solidity and certainty—this is the way of misfortune. When it becomes mired in the ordinary like this, there is no profitable journey to be made. The poison of the times is that people bring about regret and dismay by putting their hope in what is old and simple, which is also indicated by "it digs into what lasts." It already tends to seek out the depth of those above—that is, it cannot last and be contented with its place. When what is soft and minimal is not lasting or contented with its place, this, too, will bring about the way of misfortune. In general, the initial and final positions of a hexagram are respectively terrains of shallowness and depth, of the minimal and the abundant. To be at the bottom and seek depth is another failure to recognize the moment. **The *Symbol* says: "'It digs into what lasts' and brings about misfortune: at the beginning, it seeks out depth."** It occupies the beginning of the Last hexagram, but it "seeks out" and puts its hope in the "depth" of those above—that is, it recognizes what is constant without knowing how to set a measure to its extreme propensities. As a result, there is misfortune, and its *yin* dimness does not acquire a fitness for what lasts.

The second "nine" line: regrets vanish. The meaning of the Last hexagram is that the way of constancy is to occupy a straightforward position. This "nine" line is *yang* but it occupies a *yin* position, which does not accord with the constant principle. Since it places itself without constancy, at root it is proper that there be regrets. But the second "nine" line uses the virtue of centrality and corresponds to the fifth, and the fifth also occupies a central position. It is at the center and it corresponds to a line with centrality, so that both its place and its movement acquire centrality—this is to be capable of lasting and continuing to be at the center. If it can last and continue to be at the center, it will not lose its straightforwardness. Centrality carries more weight than straightforwardness. If something is at the center, then it will be straightforward, while the straightforward will not necessarily be at the center.[2] The second "nine" line uses the virtues of firmness and centrality, and it corresponds to a line with centrality. Its virtues are victorious and sufficient to make its regrets vanish. When people can understand the lightness or weight of a propensity, then they can speak about the *Book of Changes*. **The *Symbol* says: "In the second 'nine' line, 'regrets vanish': it can continue at the center."** The reason its regrets vanish is because "it can" last or "continue at the center." When people can last or continue at the center, it is the goodness of their virtue that puts a stop to their regrets and makes them vanish.

The third "nine" line: its virtue does not last. Sometimes it is served with disappointment. Purity brings dismay. The third is a *yang* line, it occupies a *yang* position, and it is placed so as to acquire its position—that is, it is placed with constancy. Its tendency, however, is to attend to the top "six" line. Not only do these *yin* and *yang* lines correspond to each other, but the wind attends to the thunder. And so it is in a lasting place, but it does not place itself there, and it refers to someone who does not last. Since its virtue does not last, it will sometimes be served with disappointment and disgrace. The phrase "sometimes it is served" signifies that there are moments when this happens. "Purity brings dismay": if it keeps guard with certainty over what does not last as though it were what lasts, how could there not be disappointment and dismay? **The *Symbol* says: "'Its virtue does not last': no place will embrace it."** When people have not lasted, what place will embrace them? When it is proper for them to be placed on a terrain, and they have not been able to last there because they did not seize their place, how could they last? These are the people who do not last, who have no place that will embrace them.

The fourth "nine" line: the field has no game. It uses *yang* to occupy a *yin* position, and so its place is not its position. Since it does not place itself in its place, how will it add to itself even if it is constant? If people acquire the way in what they do, then they will continue and complete their tasks. If they do not acquire the way, how will they add to themselves even if they continue? This is why the line statement, taking the field as its metaphor, remarks that occupying the fourth position with a "nine" line is like hunting in the fields without obtaining the wild game, even though it may be lasting and continuous. It signifies that it employs its force ineptly without accomplishing anything. **The Symbol says: "It continues, but not in its position: how could it acquire the game?"** Its place is not its position. Even if "it continues," how could it acquire anything? The field is taken as a metaphor, and this is why the *Symbol* says: "How could it acquire the game?"

The fifth "six" line: if its virtue lasts, there is purity. The wife brings good fortune, but the husband brings misfortune. The fifth line corresponds to the second, it makes use of *yin* softness to correspond to *yang* firmness, it occupies the center, and its corresponding line is also central. This is how *yin* softness becomes straightforward, and this is why, if its virtue lasts and continues, "there is purity." As for considering submissiveness and attentiveness to be what lasts, this is the way of the wife. It constitutes the purity of the wife, and this is why there is good fortune. Were the husband to consider submitting and attending to another person as what lasts, he would lose his straightforward *yang* firmness, and there would be misfortune. The fifth is the position of the ruler, but the line statement does not remark on the way of the ruler. If the meaning of the fifth "six" line is misfortune for the husband, what would the case be like for the way of the ruler? In other hexagrams, when a "six" line occupies the position of the ruler and corresponds to a firm line, it does not yet constitute a loss, but this is the Last hexagram, and this is why it cannot be the case. How could the way of the ruler consider softness and submission as what lasts? **The Symbol says: "In the wife, 'purity brings good fortune': in the end, she attends to one man. In the husband are control and duty: attending to the wife brings misfortune."** In a wife, to be like the fifth line attending to the second constitutes straightforwardness and good fortune. The straightforwardness of the wife lies in her attentiveness, and her virtue is submissiveness. It is proper that she guard herself to the end by attending "to one man." Duty and control are in the husband. The way of "attending to the wife" will bring him "misfortune."

The top "six" line: dusting itself off is what lasts. There is misfortune. This "six" line occupies the limit position in the Last hexagram, at the end of the Shake trigram. Being at the limit of the Last hexagram, it is not constant; being at the end of the Shake trigram, it has reached the limit of its movement. It uses *yin* to occupy the top position, and it is not content with its place. Further, *yin* softness cannot guard itself with solidity and certainty, which also gives the meaning of inconstancy. This is why "dusting itself off is what lasts"—that is, it considers dusting itself off as what lasts. To dust oneself off is to move rapidly, as when one dusts off clothing or books. The idea is of a tremulous, jittery, or revolving movement. When something is at the top, does not rein in its movement, and considers this as what lasts, its misfortune is fitting. **The *Symbol* says: "'Dusting itself off is what lasts' at the top: its failure to accomplish anything is great."** The way of occupying the top position necessitates that it possess the virtue of the Last hexagram, and then it will be able to accomplish something. Were its movement to be restless and inconstant, how could it bring anything to completion? If it occupies the top position without being constant, its misfortune will be extreme. The *Symbol* further remarks that it cannot complete or set up anything, and this is why it says: "It greatly fails to accomplish anything."

33. FLEE (*DUN* 遯)

The *Sequence of the Hexagrams* says: "To last is to continue. Things cannot continually occupy their places, and this is why the Flee hexagram is next. To flee is to retreat." As for what continues, it will also depart—it is by principle that they require each other. And so the Flee hexagram succeeds the Last hexagram. "To flee is to retreat," but it also signifies to evade and to depart from somewhere. As for the trigrams, "below heaven, there is a mountain." Heaven is a thing that is above, and the nature of *yang* is to advance upward. A mountain is a thing that is lofty and rises up but, despite having a form that is lofty and rises up, its trigram substance refers to stopping. The hexagram is symbolized by a thing that climbs upward but stops without advancing, while heaven advances upward and departs from it. Those below are climbing up while those above are departing, which is to flee and draw back from them. This is why the hexagram has the meaning of fleeing and departing. Its two *yin* lines are born at the bottom. *Yin* is growing and will soon become abundant, while *yang* is disappearing and retreating. Small people are becoming abundant step by step, while noble people retreat and evade them. This is why these lines constitute the Flee hexagram.

Flee: there is progress. There are a small profit and purity. The Flee hexagram refers to the growth of *yin* and the disappearance of *yang*. It is the moment when noble people flee and store themselves away. Noble people retreat and store themselves away so that their way may expand. If their way does not contract, this itself will constitute progress, and this is why fleeing may have progress as its result. In the case of affairs, too, there can be progress because there has been flight and evasion. Although this is the moment when the way of small people grows, noble people recognize it while it is still incipient and retreat to evade it, which is certainly good. Nonetheless, not all states of affairs are equal, and the moments of disappearing and coming to rest are necessarily not the same. *Yin* softness has started to grow, but it has not yet reached the point of extreme abundance. Noble people value the way of lingering, and lingering again, until they bring about their force. They are not capable of great purity, and so they value the profit of a small purity.

The *Judgment* says: "'Flee: there is progress': if it flees, there will be progress." In the moment when the way of small people is growing, noble people flee and retreat, and this is the progress of their way. Noble people flee and store themselves away, and so their way expands. The *Judgment* is remarking here on the way to place oneself when fleeing. From the point at which it says that "the position of firmness is proper for it, and it corresponds to something," and so on, it will discuss the moment and the powers of the trigrams, and will value the principle by which one is capable of doing something. "The position of firmness is proper for it, and it corresponds to something. It acts in agreement with the moment." Although this is the moment of the Flee hexagram and noble people are placed here, it does not yet mean that they must flee. The fifth line uses the virtue of *yang* firmness to place itself in a position of centrality and straightforwardness, and further, it corresponds to the second "six" line below it with centrality and straightforwardness. Although this is the moment when *yin* is growing, the powers of the trigrams are such that it is proper and valuable for it to follow the moment in its disappearing and coming to rest. Were it able to bring about its force—not without extreme sincerity—and exhaust itself in aiding and wielding its way, it would not yet have to flee and store itself away without doing anything. This is why the *Judgment* says: "It acts in agreement with the moment." "'There are a small profit and purity': it is gradual in its growth. How great are the moment and the meaning of the Flee hexagram!" When faced with a moment when *yin* is growing, one can have no great purity, but should value "a small profit and purity." In fact, the growth of *yin* is necessarily gradual and step by step, and cannot quickly become abundant. Noble people value the small purity that their way can possess, which is signified by "a small profit and purity." They are aiding and wielding it, which results neither in success nor in vanishing away. The Flee hexagram refers to the growth of *yin* at its beginning. Noble people recognize it when it is minimal, and this is why a deep warning is proper here. The intention of the sage is that one should not yet be ready to cease quickly, and this is why the *Judgment* teaches that "it acts in agreement with the moment. 'There are a small profit and purity.'" When sages and worthies are in the world, although they recognize that the way is about to be neglected, how could they be willing to sit and look at this disorder without saving people from it? They must trifle with trifles and bring about their force in the space before the limit is reached. They must put their strength into the scarcity of the one side, and their hardship into the advance of the other. They must map out a temporary contentment if they are to get anything done. This was the little that Confucius and Mencius did, as well as the Han dynasty's Wang Yun and the Jin dynasty's Xie An.[1] If there is a way that can make alterations, or a principle that can make progress, the *Judgment* does not presume to remark further on it. This is the way to place oneself in the moment of the Flee hexagram, and this is why the sage applauds the greatness of its moment and meaning. Whether it is continuous or brief, its meaning is great in either case.

The *Symbol* says: "Below heaven, there is a mountain: Flee. Noble people use it to go far away from small people. They do not detest them, but they are severe." "Below heaven, there is a mountain": the mountain rises from below, but it stops, while heaven advances above it. They draw back from each other, and this is the symbol of flight and evasion. When noble people gaze on this symbol, they use it to evade and "go far away from small people." Concerning the way of going far away from small people, if there is disgust in their voice and danger in their countenance, this is well-suited and sufficient to bring about hatred and wrath toward them. If they are only sympathetic, solemn, authoritative and severe, and make the others know how to be reverent and trembling, this will take them far away spontaneously.

The initial "six" line: in fleeing at the tail there is danger. It should not be employed. It has a long journey. In other hexagrams, the bottom is the initial position, but in the Flee hexagram it refers to making a journey or fleeing. What goes before is the first to advance, and this is why the initial line is referred to as "the tail." The word "tail" refers to a thing that goes afterward. If those who flee extend themselves to what goes afterward, they will be in peril. Since the initial line uses softness to place itself in a minimal position, it is already going afterward, and it should not make the journey. If it makes the journey, there will be peril. The minimal is easy to obscure and store away, but in a journey there is already peril. If it is not like this, if it does not make the journey, then there will be no disaster. The *Symbol* says: "The danger of fleeing at the tail: if it does not make the journey, how could there be a disaster?" To see the incipient and be the first to flee is certainly good, but to flee at the tail is a perilous way. In a journey there is already peril, but if it is not like this, if it does not make the journey but obscures and stores itself away, it will be able to avoid disaster. This is because it places itself in a minimal position. Many people of antiquity placed themselves in minimal positions—that is, at the bottom—and concealed themselves from the disorder of the times, rather than departing from them.

The second "six" line: it holds them, employing the hide of a yellow cow. None of them is called victorious. The second line corresponds straightforwardly to the fifth. Although this is the moment for them to draw back and flee from each other, the second uses centrality and straightforwardness to submit and correspond to the fifth, and the fifth uses centrality and straightforwardness to relate to and align with the second: their interaction is certain in itself. Yellow is the color of centrality, a cow is something submissive, and a hide is something solid and certain. The second and fifth lines use the way of centrality, straightforwardness, and submission to agree with each other. Their certainty is comparable to holding or binding something with the hide of a cow. "None of them is called victorious": this signifies that the certainty of their interaction should not be remarked on as victorious. They are in the moment of the Flee hexagram, and this is why there is a limit to what it can say. **The *Symbol* says: "'It holds them,' employing a yellow cow: it makes its tendencies certain."** Those above and below are knotted to each other with certainty, using the way of centrality and submission. The tendencies of their hearts are extremely solid, as though they held something with the hide of a cow.

The third "nine" line: it is bound while it flees. There are illness and danger. The herding of ministers and concubines brings good fortune. The tendency of *yang* is to enjoy *yin*. The third line is quite close to the second—that is, "it is bound" to the second. Flight is estimable when one goes far away quickly. Since this line is bound to or burdened by something, how could it go quickly or far away? It is harmed in its flight, and this is why there is "illness." It does not flee quickly, and so it is in peril. As for "ministers and concubines" or small people and women, to cherish them with kindness is not to recognize one's duty, but if one relates to and loves them, they will be loyal to those above.[2] The private kindness of a bond of longing is the way to cherish small people and women, and this is why those who herd and nourish their ministers and concubines will have the good fortune of acquiring their hearts. Nonetheless, the case of noble people waiting on small people is not like this. The third line does not correspond straightforwardly to the second. They relate to each other with intimate closeness, which is not the way that noble people wait on others. If they were to make use of straightforwardness, then, although bound to each other, they would not acquire an illness because of it. Such was the case of the first master of Shu, who was not so cruel as to desert his scholars and the people.[3] Although he was in peril, there was no blame. **The *Symbol* says: "The danger**

of being bound while it flees: there are illness and weariness. 'The herding of ministers and concubines brings good fortune': it should not be a great affair." Those who flee while bound to or burdened by something will necessarily be trapped and wearied, which will bring them into peril. If they are ill, this will weary them, and in fact, their force will also be insufficient. If they use a heart of intimate love to herd and nourish their ministers and concubines, then there will be good fortune. How could a "great affair" be proper here?

The fourth "nine" line: it prefers something and flees. Noble people bring good fortune, but small people are lacking. The fourth and initial lines are in straightforward correspondence—that is, they have something they prefer or love. Although noble people have something they prefer or love, if it is proper and dutiful for them to flee, they have no doubts about departing. This is signified in the passage where "they conquer themselves and return to ritual."[4] They control their desires with the way, and so there is good fortune. If they were small people, they would not be able to place themselves in accord with their duty, but would be intimate with what they preferred and guided by the private. They would reach the point of ensnaring and disgracing themselves, and would not be able to put it in the past. This is why "small people are lacking." The word "lacking" refers to what is not good. The fourth line, as part of the Lead trigram substance, can be firm and decisive. Because it is placed in a *yin* position and is bound to something, the sage provides a warning about small people, fearing their loss of straightforwardness. **The *Symbol* says: "Noble people prefer something and flee: 'small people are lacking.'"** Although there is something that noble people prefer, they are still able to flee, and so they do not lose sight of their duty. If they were small people, they would not be capable of victory over their private intentions and would reach the point of not being good.

The fifth "nine" line: its fleeing is excellent. Purity brings good fortune. The fifth "nine" line is central and straightforward, and it refers to an excellent and beautiful flight. It places itself on the way of acquiring centrality and straightforwardness. At some moments it stops and at some moments it acts, which is what excellence and beauty signify. This is why it is pure and straightforward, and there will be good fortune. The fifth "nine" line is not bound to anything— that is, it is not bound to its corresponding line. Nonetheless, it places itself with centrality and straightforwardness just like the second line. In such a case, their hearts and tendencies will never be other than central and straightforward, whether they are stopped or in movement. They will get lost in no private bond, and this constitutes their excellence. Concerning the *Judgment*, it is remarking on the overall moment of the Flee hexagram, and this is why it says "it acts in agreement with the moment. 'There are a small profit and purity.'" It values the intention of making the crossing and fleeing. But when it reaches the fifth line, the flight is almost at its limit, and this is why it remarks only on placing oneself in flight with centrality and straightforwardness. Fleeing is not an affair for rulers, and this is why it does not remark on the fifth as the position of the master or ruler. Nonetheless, when rulers evade or go far away from something, they, too, are fleeing and are to be central and straightforward, and that is all. **The Symbol says: "'Its fleeing is excellent. Purity brings good fortune': its tendencies are straightforward."** If its tendencies are straightforward, its movement will necessarily be because of its straightforwardness. As a result, it will possess the excellence of the Flee hexagram. Since it occupies a central position and so acquires straightforwardness, its correspondence will be central and straightforward. This is to have straightforward tendencies, and so there will be good fortune. Whether people flee or stop, they are only to make their tendencies straightforward, and that is all.

The top "nine" line: its fleeing is fat. Nothing is without profit. The word "fat" refers to the idea of being replete with great tolerance and generosity. To flee is simply to drift off and recede far away. It is good not to be lazy or bound to anything. The top "nine" line, as part of the Lead trigram substance, is firm and decisive. It is in the trigram's outer position and it is not bound to any line below it, so it can flee far away unburdened by anything. This may be called the span of its tolerance and the surplus of its generosity. The Flee hexagram refers to the moment of depleting and trapping. To place oneself well here is to be "fat." When one flees like this, how could anything be without profit? **The Symbol says: "'Its fleeing is fat. Nothing is without profit': there is no place for doubt."** Concerning fleeing far away, there is no place for doubt or laziness. In fact, since it is in the outer trigram, it is already far away. Since it has no corresponding line, it is unburdened by anything. This is why the *Symbol* refers to a firm resolution without any doubt.

34. GREAT MIGHT (*DAZHUANG* 大壯)

The *Sequence of the Hexagrams* says: "To flee is to retreat. Things cannot flee to the end, and this is why the Great Might hexagram is next." Flight has the meaning of withdrawal and departure, while might has the meaning of advance and abundance. The Flee hexagram refers to the growth of *yin* and the flight of *yang*, while the Great Might hexagram refers to the might and abundance of *yang*. What has become scarce will necessarily become abundant. Disappearing and coming to rest[1] require each other, and this is why something that has fled will necessarily become mighty. And so the Great Might hexagram succeeds the Flee hexagram. As for the trigrams, the Shake trigram is above and the Lead trigram below. The Lead trigram refers to firmness and the Shake trigram to movement. The use of firmness and movement is the meaning of the Great Might hexagram. *Yang* firmness is great, and the growth of *yang* has already exceeded the center, so its greatness is mighty and abundant. Further, the authority of thunder shakes and "is above heaven," which is also the meaning of the Great Might hexagram.

Great Might: there are profit and purity. For those on the way of the Great Might hexagram, the profit lies in purity and straightforwardness. Those who possess great might without acquiring straightforwardness will act with strength and ferocity, and that is all. This is not the might and abundance that belong to the way of noble people.

The *Judgment* says: "Great Might: what is great is mighty. Firmness makes use of movement, and this is why there is might." "What is great is mighty": this signifies the reason it is called the Great Might hexagram. The *yin* lines are becoming smaller, while the *yang* lines are becoming greater. The growth of *yang* has become abundant, which indicates that "what is great is mighty." The lower trigram refers to firmness and the upper trigram to movement. The movement has the extreme firmness of the Lead trigram, and this is why these trigrams constitute the Great Might hexagram. It indicates that "what is great is mighty," but it also refers to the greatness of what is mighty. "'**Great Might: there are profit and purity': what is great is straightforward. When one's straightforwardness is great, the inclinations of heaven and earth may be seen.**" Since what is great has become mighty, it will profit from purity and straightforwardness. Those who are straightforward and great are on the way. When the principle that "straightforwardness is great" has reached its limit, then "the inclinations of heaven and earth may be seen." The way of heaven and earth is constant and continuous without ceasing. It is extremely great and extremely straightforward. Those who learn the principle that "straightforwardness is great" with a heart of silent understanding may develop. The *Judgment* does not say "great straightforwardness" but "straightforwardness is great," fearing that someone may wonder whether they are a single state of affairs.

The *Symbol* says: "Thunder is above heaven: Great Might. Noble people use it to walk only when it is according to ritual." When thunder shakes above heaven, it is great and mighty. When noble people gaze on the symbol of the Great Might hexagram, they use it to put their might into action. Noble people never have such great might as when they "conquer themselves and return to ritual."[2] As someone said in antiquity: "To be victorious over oneself may be called strength."[3] When the *Doctrine of Centrality* says that "they harmonize without flowing away" and "they are set up at the center and delegate nothing," it is saying in both cases that exclamations like "How strongly they improve!" "They charge into cauldrons and fire!" and "They tread on bared knives!" are possible for the courage of warlike men.[4] But to reach the point that they "conquer themselves and return to ritual" is not possible for anything but the great might of noble people. This is why the *Symbol* says: "Noble people use it to walk only when it is according to ritual."

The initial "nine" line: there is might in the toes. Taking the field brings misfortune. It is trusted. The initial line is *yang* and firm, it belongs to the Lead trigram substance, it is placed at the bottom, and it refers to those who are mighty in their advance. It is at the bottom and it employs its might: "There is might in the toes." The word "toes" refers to things that are at the bottom and advance when they move. This "nine" line is at the bottom and employs its might, yet it does not acquire the center. As for those who use firmness to place themselves in the Might hexagram, if they may not act even when they occupy positions above, what will the case be like when they are at the bottom? This is why "taking the field brings misfortune." "It is trusted": to be trusted is to be believed and signifies that it will necessarily acquire misfortune if it uses its might to make a journey. **The *Symbol* says: "'There is might in the toes': trust that it is depleted."** It is at the very bottom, and it employs might in order to act. One must necessarily believe that it will be depleted and trapped, and there will be misfortune.

The second "nine" line: purity brings good fortune. Although the second line uses *yang* firmness to face the moment of the Great Might hexagram, it nonetheless occupies a soft position and is placed at the center of the trigram. This indicates that firmness and softness have acquired the center, but they are not excessive in their might. They have acquired purity and straightforwardness, and there will be good fortune. Someone asks: is it not the case that the purity of a "nine" line occupying the second position constitutes a warning? Response: the *Book of Changes* chooses as its meaning whatever will bring victory. This line makes use of *yang* firmness, it belongs to the vigor trigram substance, it faces the moment of the Great Might hexagram, and it places itself so as to acquire the way of centrality—it is not without straightforwardness. If it were the fourth line, then it would be warned about its lack of straightforwardness. When people can understand what is light and what is weighty in the moment and its meaning, then they may study the *Book of Changes*. **The *Symbol* says: "In the second 'nine' line, 'purity brings good fortune': it makes use of centrality."** The reason its purity and straightforwardness will bring about good fortune is that it has acquired the way of centrality. If it does not lose its straightforwardness when it is at the center, what will the case be like when it is *yang* and firm, and belongs to the Lead trigram substance?

The third "nine" line: small people employ might, while noble people employ belittlement. Purity brings danger. The ram has pierced the hedge, and its horns are crippled. The third "nine" line uses firmness to occupy a *yang* position, it is placed in the Might hexagram, and further, it faces the end of the Lead trigram substance, which is the limit of might. As for those at the limit of might, if they are small people, they will "employ might," but if they are noble people, they will "employ belittlement." Small people value force, and this is why they employ their might and courage. The tendencies of noble people are firm, and this is why they employ belittlement. To belittle is to negate, as though one were to speak demeaningly. Because of its extreme firmness, it is demeaning when it looks at states of affairs, and there is nothing that causes it to be jealous or scared. People are said to be "noble people" or "small people" concerning a specific terrain, as in the following passage: "Noble people who have courage but not a sense of duty will become disorderly."[5] When firmness and softness acquire the center, they will neither break nor contract. Their influence on the world will never be other than fitting. Were they to have a great excess of firmness, then they would not have the virtues of harmony and submissiveness. There would be numerous injuries and no agreement. To guard one's purity and certainty like this is a perilous way. In general, things are never without the employment of their might: teeth bite, horns pierce, and hooves kick. The might of a sheep is in its head, and if it is a ram, it will be happy to pierce others with it. This is why it was chosen as the symbol. A sheep will be happy to pierce a hedge or fence when the hedge or fence is before its face. In fact, it will necessarily pierce what it faces, and it is happy to employ its might like this. It will necessarily cripple and trap its horns, just like people who value firmness and might. They will necessarily employ it on what they face, and so they will necessarily reach the point of becoming bruised and trapped. When the might of the third line is extreme like this, how could it not reach the point of misfortune? Response: when one acts like the third line, one's journey will be sufficient to bring about misfortune, but the line statement is speaking only about the start of its peril. This is why it does not yet extend itself to misfortune. In general, if something may bring about misfortune but has not yet reached it, it will say that there is danger. **The *Symbol* says: "'Small people employ might': noble people belittle it."** In the case of small people, they will employ the force of their strength and might. In the case of noble people, they will employ belittlement. Their tendency and *qi* are firm and strong, and they are demeaning when they look at states of affairs. There is nothing that concerns or scares them.

The fourth "nine" line: purity brings good fortune. Regrets vanish. The hedge is dissolved and does not cripple it. There is might in the crossbars of the great carriage. In the fourth line, *yang* firmness has grown into abundance, its might has already exceeded the center of the hexagram, and it refers to the extremity of might. Nonetheless, when it occupies the fourth position, it is without straightforwardness. In the moment when the way of noble people has started to grow, how could anyone be without straightforwardness? This is why the line statement warns that if it is pure, there will be good fortune and regrets will vanish. In fact, in the moment when their way has started to grow, a small loss will harm their propensity to make progress and advance, which indicates that they will have regrets. In other hexagrams, when a weighty and firm line occupies a soft position, it will not necessarily be other than good. Such is the case for the

Great Excess hexagram. There is a hedge, and so there is a hardship or cause of separation. When the hedge or fence is dissolved or opened up, it will not cripple or trap one's might. When a carriage is lofty and great, and its wheels and crossbars are strong and mighty, the profit in its travel should be recognized. This is why it says: "There is might in the crossbars of the great carriage." The term "crossbars" refers to the place where the wheels are attached. The defeat of a carriage will be constant when its crossbars are broken. When the crossbars are mighty, the carriage is strong. It says that the crossbars are mighty to signify that its advance is mighty. The crossbars are the same as the spokes.[6] **The *Symbol* says: "'The hedge is dissolved and does not cripple it': it values a journey."** The growth of *yang* firmness will necessarily reach its limit. Although the fourth line is already abundant, its journey has nonetheless not yet come to a stop. When *yang* reaches the point of abundance, it employs its might to advance, and this is why there is nothing that faces it. The hedge has dissolved or opened up and does not cripple or trap it—such is its force. "It values a journey": it advances without ceasing.

The fifth "six" line: it is deprived of the sheep while at ease. There are no regrets. A group of sheep that is traveling and happy to pierce anything is the symbol of the various *yang* lines advancing together. The four *yang* lines start to grow and advance together, while the fifth line uses its softness to occupy a position above them. Were it to control them by force, its victory would be difficult and there would be regrets. But if it waits on them with harmony and ease, the group of *yang* lines will be unable to employ its firmness. This is to be deprived of one's might by harmony and ease. In a case like this, there should be no regrets. Concerning its position, one may remark that the fifth line is straightforward; concerning its virtue, one may remark that it is central. This is why it can employ the way of harmony and ease to make even a group of *yang* lines unable to employ its might. **The *Symbol* says: "'It is deprived of the sheep while at ease': its position is not proper for it."** The reason it must employ softness and harmony is that it uses *yin* softness to occupy the position of respect. Were it to use *yang* firmness, centrality, and straightforwardness to acquire the position of respect, those below it would not be mighty. The position of the fifth "six" line is not proper for it, and this is why the line statement provides the meaning of being "deprived of the sheep while at ease." Nonetheless, in the great majority of cases, firmness should not be employed to set the might of others in order. As for the propensities of rulers and ministers, or those above and below, they are not equivalent to each other. If the aptitude of the rulers is sufficient to control those below, then although the latter may be strong, mighty, domineering, and insolent, they are not sufficient to be called "mighty." It is only when the propensity of the rulers has something insufficient about it that, afterward, they will necessarily be said to have set the might of the others in order. This is why the way of setting might in order should not make use of firmness.

The top "six" line: the ram has pierced the hedge. It cannot retreat, and it cannot succeed. There is no long-term profit. If there is hardship, there will be good fortune. The ram is chosen because it employs might, and this is why it can also refer to a *yin* line. This "six" line uses *yin* to place itself at the end of the Shake trigram, and it faces the limit of the Might hexagram—its excess should be recognized. Just like a ram piercing a hedge or fence, if it advances, the hedge will hamper its body, while if it retreats, the hedge will interfere with its horns. Advance and retreat are both impossible. Its root power is *yin* softness, and this is why it cannot be victorious over itself and do its duty: "It cannot retreat." When people of *yin* softness are at their limit, they may have hearts that can employ might, but they will necessarily be incapable of bringing this might to its end. Because of their bruises, they will necessarily wane: "It cannot succeed." When they are placed like this, there is no journey they can make that will be profitable. *Yin* softness is placed in a position of might, but it cannot guard itself with certainty. Were it to encounter hardships and traps, it would necessarily lose its might. If it loses its might, it will acquire the contrary role of softness and weakness: "If there is hardship," it will acquire "good fortune." If it employs its might, then there will be no profit, but if it recognizes its hardship and places itself in a soft position, then "there will be good fortune." It occupies the end of the Might hexagram, and so it has the meaning of alteration. **The Symbol says: "'It cannot retreat, and it cannot succeed': it has not delineated anything. 'If there is hardship, there will be good fortune': the blame does not grow."** This is not its place, but it is placed here anyway, and this is why it can neither advance nor retreat. In placing itself here, "it has not delineated anything" cautiously. "If there is hardship, there will be good fortune": this soft line encounters hardship and difficulty, and further, it occupies the end of the Might hexagram. It is proper that it alter itself. If it alters itself, then it will acquire its role, its excess and blame will not grow, and there will be good fortune.

35. LIFT (*JIN* 晉)

The *Sequence of the Hexagrams* says: "Things cannot be mighty to the end, and this is why the Lift hexagram is next. To lift is to advance." The principle is that, when things are without might, they come to a stop in the end. What is already abundant and mighty will necessarily advance, and so the Lift hexagram succeeds the Great Might hexagram. As for the trigrams, the Cast trigram is above the Yield trigram: "Light goes out above the earth." When the sun goes out onto the earth, it rises and adds to its light, and this is why it is the symbol of the Lift hexagram. In the Lift or advance hexagram, the idea is to make one's light bright and one's greatness abundant. In general, things become abundant step by step, and this is their advance. This is why the *Judgment* says: "To lift is to advance." Among the hexagrams, there are those that possess the virtues and there are those that lack the virtues—the judgment follows what is fitting for them. When the judgment of hexagrams other than Lead and Yield says "there are primacy and progress," these hexagrams certainly possess them. When it says "there are profit and purity," something is not sufficient, and yet these hexagrams may still accomplish something. When two hexagrams are not described with the same virtues—as in the case of the Hide and Step hexagrams—it may be seen that the virtues follow the hexagram. The Lift hexagram refers to abundance, and so its judgment lacks the virtues, as possessing them would have no function. The enlightenment of the Lift hexagram is abundant, and this is another reason the judgment does not remark that there is progress. There is submissiveness toward the greatly enlightened, and so the *Judgment* does not employ a warning about straightforwardness.

Lift: the marquis of health employs them and bestows a bountiful number of horses. In a day, they receive three responses. The Lift hexagram refers to a moment of advance and abundance. There is great enlightenment in the upper trigram. The substance of the lower trigram, the symbol of the various marquises who serve the king, submits to and depends on it. This is why it is considered "the marquis of health." The marquis of health is the marquis of order and contentment. Those below can possess the same virtues as those above, who are greatly enlightened, by submitting to and depending on the marquis of order and contentment. This is why they receive such numerous favors— that is, he bestows on them a large crowd of horses. Carriages and horses are weighty tributes, and a "bountiful number" is a large crowd. Not only is there the benefit of what he bestows on them, but there is also the ritual of seeing and relating to him. In the course of a day, they reach the point of receiving three responses—the judgment is remarking that the favor they encounter is extreme. The Lift hexagram refers to a moment of advance and abundance. Those above are enlightened, and those below are submissive: rulers and ministers make an acquisition of each other. Concerning those above, one may remark that they advance to the point of enlightenment and abundance; concerning ministers, one may remark that they advance and rise to loftiness and clarity, to receive bright favors.

The *Judgment* says: "To lift is to advance. Light goes out above the earth. There are submission and a connection to the great light. Softness advances and travels upward. As a result, 'the marquis of health employs them and bestows a bountiful number of horses. In a day, they receive three responses.'" "To lift is to advance": the light advances and becomes abundant. Light goes out onto the earth, is added to, advances, and becomes abundant, and this is why the trigram belongs to the Lift hexagram. The reason it is not called the Advance hexagram is that the *jin* character of "advance" refers to going forward and cannot contain the meaning of light and abundance. "Light goes out above the earth": the Cast trigram is above the Yield trigram. The Yield trigram is connected to the Cast trigram so that it may submit and connect itself to its great light. Ministers with the virtue of submissiveness ascend to and depend on rulers with great enlightenment. "Softness advances and travels upward": in general, when the Cast trigram is on top and a soft line occupies the position of the ruler, the *Judgment* will often say "softness advances and travels upward," as in the case of the Bite Down, Split, and Tripod hexagrams. The fifth "six" line uses softness to occupy the position of the ruler. It is enlightened, but there are also "submission and a connection," which means that it can wait on those below by favoring them with an encounter and a profound relationship. As a result, "the marquis of health employs them and bestows a bountiful number of horses. In a day, they receive three responses." Rulers of great enlightenment bring contentment to the world. The various marquises can submit to and depend on the enlightened virtue of the son of heaven. He is the marquis who brings health to the people and contentment to the states, and this is why he is called "the marquis of health." As a result, he feasts them, favors them, and bestows on them the ritual of seeing and relating to him. In the space of a day, they are seen and responded to three times by the son of heaven. It does not say "duke" or "dignitary," but "marquis." The son of heaven brings order to those above, while the various marquises bring order to those below. The lower trigram is the symbol of the various marquises, who submit to and depend on rulers of great enlightenment.

The *Symbol* says: "'Light goes out above the earth': Lift. Noble people use it to illuminate their own enlightened virtue." To illuminate is to shed light on something. The Zuo commentary says: "It illuminates virtue and chokes off those who draw back," which is to illuminate the standard of measurement.[1] When noble people gaze on the symbol of light going out above the earth and adding to the abundance of light, they "illuminate their own enlightened virtue." By driving out concealment and bringing about knowledge, they illuminate the enlightened virtue in themselves; by shedding light on the enlightened virtue in the world, they illuminate the enlightened virtue outside of them. They shed light on the enlightened virtue in themselves, and this is why the *Symbol* says that they "illuminate their own enlightened virtue."

The initial "six" line: it is as though lifted up, as though bruised. Purity brings good fortune. It belittles its trustworthiness. Generosity is without blame. The initial line occupies the bottom of the Lift hexagram and refers to the beginning of the advance. "It is as though lifted up," which is to rise and advance, but "as though bruised," which is to be impeded and in retreat. Concerning the beginning of the advance, the line statement remarks that, whether the advance is successful or unsuccessful, there will be good fortune as long as it acquires straightforwardness. "It belittles its trustworthiness": since it is at the bottom and begins to advance, how could those above see it deeply and believe in it? If those above do not yet see and believe in it, it is proper that it be contented at its center and guard itself. It should have a balanced appearance and be tolerant and generous, without agitatedly seeking to make those above believe in it. If its heart is ardent in its desire to make them believe in it but it is not doing its best, so that it loses its guard, it will still get worked up enough to injure its duty. Both are blameworthy, and this is why "generosity is without blame." This is the way noble people place themselves in their advances and retreats. The *Symbol* says:

"'It is as though lifted up, as though bruised': it does nothing but act straightforwardly. 'Generosity is without blame': it has not yet received the mandate."
It does not advance, it is not impeded, and it merely "does nothing but" put the
way of straightforwardness into action. If it is tolerant and generous, there will
be no blame. It wants to advance at the beginning because its position is not yet
proper for it. The advances and retreats of noble people are sometimes delayed
and sometimes rapid, but they only do what is proper to their duty and they
never taste a lack of generosity. The sage feared that people who came afterward
would not attain the meaning of tolerance and generosity and would consider
the neglect of their mission and loss of their guard as generosity when they occupied positions. This is why he says especially that if the initial "six" line is
generous, then there will be no blame because, at the beginning of its advance,
it has not yet received its proper mandate, mission, or command. If it were to be
a governor or guardian, those above would not believe in it, it would lose sight
of its mission, and it would not occupy its position for a single day. Nonetheless,
affairs are not all of one variety. Whether they are continuous or rapid depends
only on the moment, and it embraces a million things that must also be done.

**The second "six" line: it is as though lifted up, as though anguished. Pu-
rity brings good fortune. It will soon receive secure blessings from its queen
mother.** The second "six" line is below, it has no corresponding or supporting
line above it, it uses the virtues of centrality, straightforwardness, softness, and
harmony, and it does not have the strength to advance. This is why there may be
worry and anguish in its advance, which signifies that its advance will be difficult. Nonetheless, if it guards its purity and straightforwardness, it is proper that
it acquire good fortune. This is why the line statement says that "it is as though
lifted up, as though anguished. Purity brings good fortune." The phrase "queen
mother" refers to one's grandmother. Here it signifies the most respected of the
yin lines, and so it points to the fifth "six" line. The second line guards itself
with the way of centrality and straightforwardness. Although it has no corresponding or supporting line above it, and it cannot itself advance, its virtues of
centrality and straightforwardness will nonetheless continue and will necessarily be on display. It is proper that people above seek it out. In fact, the fifth "six"
line or ruler of great enlightenment has the same virtues, and it is necessary and
proper that it seek it out, attaching favor and a wage to it: it receives "secure
blessings from its queen mother." The word "secure" here refers to their greatness. **The *Symbol* says: "'It will soon receive secure blessings': it uses centrality
and straightforwardness."** "It will soon receive secure blessings": "It uses" the
way of "centrality and straightforwardness." If people can guard the way of cen-

trality and straightforwardness, they will necessarily make continuous progress. In a case where those above possess great enlightenment and their virtues are the same, they will necessarily receive great blessings.

The third "six" line: the crowd allows it. Regrets vanish. This "six" line occupies the third position and does not acquire centrality and straightforwardness, so it is fitting that there be regrets and blame. On the other hand, the third line is in the top position of the submission trigram substance, and it refers to someone whose submissiveness has reached its limit. These three *yin* lines are all submissive to those above. When the third line submits to those above, its tendency is the same as that of the crowd. "The crowd allows" and attends to it, and so its "regrets vanish." Since it has the tendency of submitting to those above and to the enlightened, and since the crowd allows and attends to it, what could be without profit for it? Someone asks: does it acquire what is good not because it is central or straightforward but because it is the same as the crowd? Response: what the crowd allows will necessarily be extremely proper. In a case where it also submits to the great enlightenment of those above, how could it be other than good? As a result, its regrets vanish. In fact, what it has lost from not being central and straightforward vanishes. Someone of antiquity says: "Those who skillfully attend to the crowd will align with the heart of heaven."[2] **The *Symbol* says: "In its tendency, 'the crowd allows it': it travels upward."** "It travels upward": it ascends to submit and connect itself to great enlightenment. It ascends to attend to a ruler of great enlightenment, and its tendency is the same as that of the crowd.

The fourth "nine" line: it is lifted up as though it were a squirrel or rat. Purity brings danger. This "nine" line occupies the fourth position, which does not belong to it. To occupy a position that does not belong to one is to greedily seize the position. Since it greedily places itself in a lofty position, it has no place of contentment. Further, it has the same virtue as the top line, and so it submits and connects itself to the top line. There are three *yin* lines together below it, and yet its propensity is necessarily to advance upward. This is why its heart trembles with jealousy. A greedy and trembling person is like a squirrel or rat, and this is why the line statement says that "it is lifted up as though it were a squirrel or rat." It is greedy because it does not accord with its position, and it persists in a heart that trembles with jealousy. If it guards its purity and certainty here, its peril should be recognized. When it remarks that "purity brings danger," it opens up a way of modifying it. **The *Symbol* says: "'As though it were a squirrel or rat. Purity brings danger': its position is not proper for it."** Worthy people use the virtue of straightforwardness, and so it is fitting that they be in lofty positions. If those who are not straightforward are placed in lofty positions, there is not yet an accord between them. Since they are greedy and troubled by loss, they are people who tremble. When they place themselves with certainty on this terrain, their peril should be recognized.

The fifth "six" line: regrets vanish. Whether it loses or acquires it, it has no anxiety. Making a journey brings good fortune. Nothing is without profit. This "six" line uses softness to occupy the position of respect. At root, it is proper for it to have regrets. It makes use of great enlightenment, and those below all submit to and depend on it. This is why it makes its regrets vanish. Since it has the same virtue as those below, and they submit to and depend on it, it is proper for it to unfold their sincerity and appoint them to command. This will exhaust the powers of the crowd and develop the tendencies of the world. It does not give the command to its own enlightenment, and it is not anxious about loss or acquisition. If it makes a journey in a case like this, there is "good fortune" and "nothing is without profit." As for the fifth "six" line—referring to a ruler of great enlightenment—it is not distressed at its inability to illuminate and shed light; it is distressed at an excessive employment of light. If it reaches the point of examining, and examining again, it will lose the way of appointing others to command. This is why the line statement warns: "Whether it loses or acquires it, it has no anxiety." As for those who do not examine their private intentions and partiality when delegating command, they will conceal themselves. How could it be proper for those who exhaust what is public in the world to employ an examination of what is private? **The *Symbol* says: "'Whether it loses or acquires it, it has no anxiety': there is delight in making a journey."** It uses the virtue of great enlightenment, and those below come to depend on it. If it unfolds their sincerity and appoints them to command, then it will be able to complete the great task of the world. This is to have blessings and "delight" in "making a journey."

The top "nine" line: it lifts up its horn. It is only employed to attack the district. Danger brings good fortune and no blame. Purity brings dismay. The word "horn" refers to something firm that occupies the top. The top "nine" line uses firmness to occupy the limit position in the hexagram, and this is why it is symbolized by the horn. Those who use *yang* to occupy the top position are at the limit of firmness; the top of the Lift hexagram refers to the limit of the advance. To be at the limit of firmness is to be excessively strong and fierce, and to be at the limit of the advance is to lose oneself in restless agitation. To use firmness at the limit of one's advance is an extreme loss of centrality. There is nothing that should be employed, unless "it is only employed to attack the district," and then there will be "good fortune and no blame" despite the "danger." To attack the four regions is to set the outside in order, while to attack the district that one occupies is to set the inside in order. When the line statement remarks that it attacks the district, it signifies that its inside or self is set in order. When people set themselves in order, if they are at the limit of firmness, then they will guard the way and become more certain; if they are at the limit of their advance, then they will relocate to the good and move more rapidly. For instance, if the top "nine" line sets itself in order like this, then there will be good fortune and no blame even though it is injured by the danger. Severity and danger are not the way of contentment and harmony, but if it sets itself in order, then it will accomplish something. It says that "purity brings dismay" so as to exhaust this meaning. At the limit of firmness and the advance, even though it accomplishes something by setting itself in order, it is nonetheless without the virtues of centrality and harmony. This is why the way of purity and straightforwardness may bring dismay. Not to lose one's centrality and straightforwardness constitutes purity. **The *Symbol* says: "'It is only employed to attack the district': its way is not yet bright."** "It is only employed to attack the district": it has already acquired good fortune and no blame. The line statement then says that "purity brings dismay," which indicates that the way of purity is "not yet bright" and great. Concerning the straightforward principle, the *Symbol* remarks that there may still be dismay. As for the way that is already bright and great, it is not without centrality and straightforwardness, so how could there be excess? Since it is now making use of excessive firmness, its way is not yet bright and great, even though it accomplishes something by setting itself in order. This is why there may also be dismay. The sage is remarking on the way to exhaust what is good.

36. WASTE LIGHT (*MINGYI* 明夷)

The *Sequence of the Hexagrams* says: "To lift is to advance. Those who advance will necessarily have someone that they injure, and this is why the Waste Light hexagram is next. What is wasted is injured." As for an advance that does not cease, it will necessarily have someone that it injures—this is a spontaneous principle—and so the Waste Light hexagram succeeds the Lift hexagram. As for the trigrams, the Yield trigram is above and the Cast trigram below: "Light enters the center of the earth." The Waste Light hexagram is completed by reversing the Lift hexagram, and this is why their meanings are straightforwardly the reverse of each other. The Lift hexagram refers to enlightenment and abundance. It is the moment when an enlightened ruler is above, and a group of worthy people also advances. The Waste Light hexagram refers to darkness and dimness. It is the moment when a dim ruler is above, and the injuries of enlightened people are seen. The sun enters into the center of the earth: the light is injured, and there are darkness and dimness. This is why these trigrams constitute the Waste Light hexagram.

Waste Light: there are profit, hardship, and purity. When noble people are faced with the moment of the Waste Light hexagram, the profit lies in recognizing the hardship and difficulty, and in not losing their purity and straightforwardness. In this moment of darkness, dimness, hardship, and difficulty, they are able to avoid losing their straightforwardness, and so they will possess the enlightenment of noble people.

The *Judgment* says: "Light enters the center of the earth: Waste Light. There are pattern and enlightenment inside, but softness and submissiveness outside. When there is great difficulty because of blindness, King Wen makes use

of it." "Light enters the earth": its light is destroyed. This is why these trigrams constitute the Waste Light hexagram. The inner trigram is the Cast trigram, which symbolizes "pattern and enlightenment"; the outer trigram is the Yield trigram, which symbolizes "softness and submissiveness." As for people, they possess the virtues of pattern and enlightenment inside, while outside they are capable of softness and submissiveness. In the past, this was the case for King Wen, and this is why the *Judgment* says that "King Wen makes use of it." When faced with the darkness and dimness of Zhou in the moment of the Waste Light hexagram, King Wen possessed the virtues of pattern and enlightenment inside, while outside he was soft and submissive in managing the affairs of Zhou.[1] Because of the blindness, he confronted great difficulties, but he did not lose his inner enlightenment and sageliness, while outside he kept the affliction and distress sufficiently far away. Such was the way employed by King Wen, and this is why it says that "King Wen makes use of it." "'There are profit, hardship, and purity': it obscures its light. It has difficulty inside, but it can straighten out its tendencies. Jizi[2] makes use of it." In the moment of the Waste Light hexagram, there is profit in placing oneself in hardship and peril without losing one's purity and straightforwardness, which signifies the ability to obscure and store away one's light. Those who do not obscure their light will be afflicted and distressed, while those who do not guard their straightforwardness will be neither worthy nor enlightened. At the moment when Jizi faced Zhou, he placed himself inside the state and quite near the difficulty. This is why the *Judgment* says: "It has difficulty inside." Nonetheless, Jizi was able to store away and obscure his light, and to guard his straightforward tendencies. Such was the way employed by Jizi, and this is why it says that "Jizi makes use of it."

The *Symbol* says: "Light enters the center of the earth: Waste Light. Noble people use it to organize the crowds. They employ obscurity and shed light." They are enlightened, and so they illuminate others. There is nothing that noble people do not illuminate, but if they employ their light excessively, they will be injured by their own examinations. If they make great examinations, they will exhaust the state of affairs and they will be without a measure of "enclosure" and "immensity."[3] This is why, when noble people gaze on the symbol of light entering the center of the earth, they "use it to organize the crowds." They do not push the light of examination to its limit, but "employ obscurity," so that later they can embrace all things and harmonize with the crowds. The crowds relate to them and are contented. This is to employ obscurity so as also to shed light. Were they to give command to their own enlightenment, and leave nothing unexamined, they would not be victorious over illness and wrath. If they do not have the virtues of enclosing and embracing, or tolerance and beneficence, the inclinations of people will split away and be doubtful and discontented. When the way of organizing the crowds is lost, it is suitable that there be no enlightenment. The sages of antiquity provided a screen of trees to be set in front of them, desiring that light not be shed exhaustively on what is concealed.

The initial "nine" line: wasted light in flight dips its tail feathers. While traveling, noble people do not eat for three days. They have a long journey. Among the masters, there are remarks. The initial "nine" line belongs to the enlightenment trigram substance, it occupies the initial position in the Waste Light hexagram, and it sees the beginning of the injury. This "nine" line is *yang*, enlightened, and rises upward. This is why the symbol of "flight" is chosen. There are darkness and dimness above that injure the light of *yang* and prevent it from making its advance upward—this is to injure one's "tail feathers" while in flight. It sees that its tail feathers are injured, and this is why it "dips" or drops them. In general, when small people harm noble people, they harm what they use in their travels. "While traveling, noble people do not eat for three days": since noble people are enlightened and illuminated, they see affairs when they are minimal. Although the impetus for the injury may be seen at the beginning, it is not yet clear. Noble people can see it, and this is why they travel to depart from or evade it. The phrase "while traveling" signifies that noble people depart from their positions with wages to retreat and store themselves away. "Do not eat for three days": this is remarking that they are at the limit of their entrapment and depletion. If the affair is not yet clear, those who are placed in extreme hardship will not be able to see the incipient without enlightenment. As for recognizing the incipient, only noble people can see it. The crowd of people cannot understand it. This is why, at the beginning of the Waste Light hexagram, if they see the injury that is not yet clear and depart from it, anyone who follows the customs of the times will consider this wondrous and strange. This is why, if they have a suitable "journey" to make, then "among the masters, there are remarks." Nonetheless, noble people do not consider the fact that they seem strange to the customs of the times as a reason to delay or cast doubt on their travels. Were they to wait until the crowd of people had exhaustively understood it, the injury would already extend to them and they would not be able to depart. Xue Fang was considered enlightened for this reason, while Yang Xiong did not succeed in departing.[4] Someone asks: if the injury has reached the point at which the tail feathers dip, then the injury has already been brought to light. How could the crowd of people still not understand it? Response: the initial line refers to the beginning of the injury. The line statement says that "it dips its tail feathers" to signify that it has injured its means of flight. If this is the state of affairs, then it is not yet clear. Noble people see the incipient, and this is why they hasten to depart from it. The people who follow the customs of the times are not yet able to see it, and this is why they differ from them and consider them to be wrong. For instance, if Duke Shen and Duke Bai considered Mu Sheng as wrong to depart from the state of Chu, what will be the case for people who follow the customs of the times? They ridiculed his reproach of the king over a small ritual, without recognizing that the departure of Mu Sheng was to evade the affliction of rotting in prison. When faced with their remarks, he said: "If I had not departed, the people of Chu would have pilloried me in the marketplace."⁵ Although they were both intellectuals, he considered their remarks to be excessive and extreme. A further instance is Yuan Hong, when the "affair of the faction" was about to arise. When it arose that scholars of renown and virtue were starting to be put to the sword, he alone hid himself in an earthen room. This is why people considered him as living like the insane, but he finally avoided the affliction of the suppression of the faction.⁶ When one makes a journey, and there are remarks among other people, why is that so strange? **The *Symbol* says: "'While traveling, noble people': they do their duty rather than eat."** Noble people flee and store themselves away when they are trapped and depleted—it is dutiful and proper in such a case. They do this only when it is proper to their duty, and this is why they are contented with their place and do not despair, even though they are not able to eat.

The second "six" line: there is wasted light. Its left thigh wastes away. It employs the might of the horse to rescue itself. There is good fortune. The second "six" line uses the power of extreme enlightenment, it acquires centrality and straightforwardness, and it belongs to the submission trigram substance. It places itself by submitting to the moment, which is the best it can do to place itself. Although noble people place themselves well, they nonetheless face the moment when small people who are *yin* and dull injure the enlightened, and they do not avoid being injured. But noble people place themselves according to the way, and this is why they cannot be deeply injured or harmed. In the end, they will be able to draw back and evade it. The foot is the means of traveling, while the thigh is above both the shin and the foot. Its employment in traveling is not very extreme, and further, things on the left are not readily employed. In the employment of hands and feet, those on the right are considered readier. It is only on the foot-drawn crossbow that one employs the left hand, and even here the right hand sets itself up as the root.⁷ "Its left thigh wastes away": this signifies that its traveling is injured or harmed, but it is not very extreme. Although such is the case, there will necessarily also be a way to avoid it. If it rescues itself by employing a horse of might and vigor, then it will succeed in rapidly avoiding it, and "there is good fortune." *Yin* dullness is what injures noble people, but they have a way to place themselves, and this is why their injury is not extreme. They have a way to rescue themselves, and this is why they succeed in swiftly avoiding it. If they employ a way of rescuing themselves that is not mighty, then their injury will be deep. This is why the line statement says that, if there is the might of the horse, then there will be good fortune. The second line uses enlightenment to occupy a lower position of *yin* dullness. The phrase "good fortune" here signifies that it avoids the injury and harm, and that is all. It does not signify that it should do anything during this moment. **The *Symbol* says: "The good fortune of the second 'six' line: there are submission and regulation."** The second "six" line acquires good fortune because it is placed submissively, and it possesses law and regulation. The word "regulation" signifies the way of centrality and straightforwardness. It can be submissive and acquire centrality and straightforwardness, and so it can preserve its good fortune even when placed in the moment when the enlightened are injured.

The third "nine" line: wasted light on the southern chase acquires a great head. It should not be swift, but it is pure. The third "nine" line is at the top of the Cast trigram and refers to the limit of enlightenment. Further, it advances while placed in a firm position. The top "six" line is at the top of the Yield trigram and refers to the limit of dimness. Extreme enlightenment occupies a position in the lower trigram and is at the top of the lower trigram, while extreme dimness is in the top position and places itself on a terrain of depletion and limitation. They straightforwardly correspond to each other as enemies and refer to the moment when enlightenment is about to drive out dimness. Since this is its meaning, it refers to the affairs of Tang and Wu.[8] The word "southern" refers to a region that is ahead and enlightened, and "chase" refers to the affair of hunting or driving out what is harmful. The phrase "southern chase" signifies that one advances ahead and expels what is harmful. It is proper to conquer it and obtain "a great head." The phrase "great head" signifies the top "six" line or the chief and head of the dim lines. The third and top lines correspond to each other straightforwardly and symbolize the conquering of extreme dimness by extreme enlightenment. "It should not be swift, but it is pure": this signifies that it puts the primary badness to death. When customs have long been infected with corruption, it cannot hastily reform them, but must go step by step. If it hastily reforms them, people will be shocked and troubled, and no one will be contented. This is why the "Announcement About Drunkenness" says: "It was only on the instruction of the Yin that the ministers and artisans got drunk with wine. In an everyday case, they should not be killed, but only given a provisional teaching,"⁹ and this should continue for a long period. When the *Book of History* says that "the remainder of these habits has not yet been exterminated," it indicates that these customs have permeated them step by step, and cannot be hastily reformed.¹⁰ This is why it says that "it should not be swift, but it is pure"—that is, what is straightforward should not be agitated. Although the top "six" line is not in the position of the ruler, it occupies the top position while at the limit of dimness. This is why it is considered the master of dimness and is signified by the phrase "great head." **The *Symbol* says: "The tendency of the southern chase: something great is acquired."** As for using the enlightenment of those below to expel the dimness of those above, their tendency is to drive out harm, and that is all. For instance, how could Tang and Wu of the Shang and Zhou dynasties have intended to bring profit to the world? If they acquire "a great head," this is to be able to drive out the harm and to acquire the great object of their tendencies. If they did not have such tendencies, then this would be an affair of upending and disorder.

The fourth "six" line: it enters the left side of the torso and obtains the heart of wasted light. It goes out from the courtyard of the gate. The fourth "six" line uses *yin* to occupy a *yin* position, it belongs to a trigram substance that is *yin* and soft, it places itself near the position of the ruler, and it refers to small people who are *yin* and crooked but who occupy lofty positions. They submit to the ruler with softness and crookedness. The fifth "six" line occupies the ruling position in the Waste Light hexagram and refers to the master of injury to the enlightened.¹¹ The fourth line submits and attends to it with softness and crookedness so as make their interaction certain. As for small people who manage the affairs of rulers, their alignment does not have a way that is clear and enlightened as its cause. They will necessarily use a way that is concealed and crass when knotting themselves to those above. It is proper that the right side be employed, and this is why it is considered a place of light and clarity. It is not proper that the left side be employed, and this is why it is considered a place of concealment and crassness. Everyone considers the right hand and foot as the one to be employed, and people today refer to the crass as "crassly left-handed"—that is, the left side is a place of concealment and crassness. Because of its way of concealment and crassness, the fourth line enters its ruler deeply. This is why the line statement says: "It enters the left side of the torso." That it enters the torso signifies that their interaction is deep. Their interaction is deep, and this is why one of them acquires the other's "heart." In general, when vile and crooked people seem believable to their rulers, it is because they strive for their hearts. If they do not strive for their hearts, how could their rulers not awaken to them? "It goes out from the courtyard of the gate": they already believe in them in their hearts, and afterward they put them into action on the outside. When crooked ministers manage the affairs of dim rulers, they will necessarily first blight their hearts, and afterward they can be put into action on the outside. **The *Symbol* says: "'It enters the left side of the torso': it obtains their hearts and intentions."** "It enters the left side of the torso": this signifies that it uses the way of crookedness and crassness to enter the rulers and acquire "their hearts and intentions." It acquires their hearts, and so they will not awaken to it in the end.

The fifth "six" line: this is Jizi's wasted light. Profit brings purity. The fifth is the position of the ruler. This is constant, but the meaning chosen by the *Book of Changes* alters and moves as it follows the moment. The top "six" line is placed at the top of the Yield trigram and at the limit of the Waste Light hexagram. *Yin* dimness has reached the limit of its injury to the enlightened. The fifth line is quite near it, and so the sage considers the fifth line as quite near people of extreme dimness. He sees that it has a duty to place itself there, and this is why he does not remark that this is the unqualified position of the ruler. The top "six" line is where *yin* dimness has reached the limit of its injury to the enlightened, and this is why it is considered the master of the Waste Light hexagram. The fifth line is quite near the master of injury to the enlightened. Were it to make its enlightenment clear, those who saw it would necessarily injure and harm it. This is why it is proper that it obscure and store itself away as Jizi did, and then it will be able to avoid the difficulty. Jizi was a former minister of the Shang dynasty and a relative with the same family name, and so he may be said to have been quite near to King Zhou. If he had not obscured his own enlightenment, he would necessarily have been afflicted. This is why he pretended to be insane during his enslavement, so that he could avoid harm. Although he obscured and stored away his enlightenment, he guarded his straightforwardness inside. This is why the *Judgment* says that "it has difficulty inside, but it can straighten out its tendencies," and so it may be called humane and enlightened. In the case of Jizi, he may be called "pure." The fifth line is *yin* and soft, and this is why it gives a warning by saying that "profit brings purity." This signifies that it is fitting to possess the purity and certainty of Jizi. If it were remarking on the way of the ruler, its meaning would still be like this. When rulers face the moment for enclosing themselves in obscurity, they, too, will dim their enlightenment on the outside and make their tendencies straightforward on the inside. **The**

***Symbol* says: "The 'purity' of Jizi: his enlightenment should not be put to rest."** Jizi obscured and stored himself away, but he did not lose his purity and certainty. Although he suffered distress and difficulty, his own enlightenment persisted and could not be destroyed or put to rest. Were he to press against the affliction and distress, he would succeed in losing what he had guarded. In this case, his enlightenment would vanish—that is, it would be destroyed and put to rest. Such was the case for people of antiquity like Yang Xiong.[12]

The top "six" line: it does not shed light but obscures. Initially it climbs to heaven, but afterward it enters the earth. This top line occupies the end position, it is the master of the Waste Light hexagram, and it is at the limit of the Waste Light hexagram. The top line is on a terrain of extreme loftiness. When a light is extremely lofty, it is proper at root that it illuminate even what is far away, but this light is already wasted and injured. This is why it does not enlighten but darkens and obscures. At root, it occupies a position of loftiness and enlightenment, and it is proper that it extend to what is far away: "Initially it climbs to heaven." Its light is wasted and injured, becoming dark and dim: "Afterward it enters the earth." The top line is at the end of both the Waste Light hexagram and the Yield or *yin* trigram, and so it refers to the limit of injury to the enlightened. **The *Symbol* says: "'Initially it climbs to heaven': it illuminates the four states. 'Afterward it enters the earth': it loses its regulation."** "Initially it climbs to heaven": when it sheds light while occupying a lofty position, it is proper that its illumination extend to the four regions. When it is injured, becoming dark and dim, it is a case when "afterward it enters the earth" and loses the way of enlightenment. "It loses its regulation": it loses its way.

37. FAMILY (*JIAREN* 家人)

The *Sequence of the Hexagrams* says: "What is wasted is injured. Those who are injured while outside will necessarily go back to their families. This is why the Family hexagram is next." As for those who are injured and trapped while outside, they will necessarily go back to the inside, and so the Family hexagram succeeds the Waste Light hexagram. The Family hexagram refers to the way of the family and the inside. The relationship of father and son, the duties of husband and wife, the sequence of respect and humility in the fully grown and the immature, the principle of straightforwardness and coherence, the meaning of devotion and kindness—these constitute the way of the family. As for the hexagram, the Low trigram is outside and the Cast trigram inside: "Wind goes out from fire." When fire burns, then the wind is born. The wind is born from fire, from the inside, and then it goes out. Going out from the inside is the symbol of extending oneself from the family to what is outside. The second and the fifth line are in the straightforward positions of men and women, one on the inside and the other on the outside, which constitutes the way of the family. There is enlightenment on the inside and lowliness on the outside, which is the way of placing oneself in the family. As for people who have various things in themselves, they can influence their family. If they take action within the family, then they will be able to apply it to the state and so will reach the point of bringing order to the world. The way of bringing order to the world is, in fact, the way of bringing order to the family, but unfolded and put into action on the outside. This is why the *Symbol* chooses the symbol of going out from the inside, which constitutes the meaning of the Family hexagram. Wen Zhongzi's book considers enlightenment on the inside and equality on the outside to be the meaning.[1] People of the past and present consider this to be a good interpretation, but it is wrong about the intention behind the choice of the symbol. When the *Explanation of the Trigrams* says "there is equality in the Low trigram," it is remarking that the ten thousand things are unpolluted and equal in their lowly starting point.[2] It is not saying that the Low trigram has equality as its meaning. It is just as when the *Explanation* says "there is clashing in the Lead trigram," even though the Lead trigram does not have clashing as its meaning.

Family: there is profit in the purity of women. Concerning the way of the family, there is profit in the straightforwardness of women. If women are straightforward, then the way of the family will be straightforward. When "the husband does what the husband should, and the wife does what the wife should, then the way of the family is straightforward," but the judgment says only that "there is profit in the purity of women." If the husband is straightforward, then his own person will be straightforward, but if the woman is straightforward, then the family will be straightforward. That men will be straightforward if women are straightforward should be recognized.

The *Judgment* says: "Family: women are positioned straightforwardly when they are inside. Men are positioned straightforwardly when they are outside. To make men and women straightforward is the great duty of heaven and earth." The *Judgment* is remarking on the powers of the trigrams. A *yang* line occupies the fifth position, in the outer trigram, while a *yin* line occupies the second position, placing itself in the inner trigram. The man and the woman have each acquired their straightforward positions. The way of the respected and the humble, or the inside and the outside, is in straightforward alignment with the great duty of heaven and earth, or *yin* and *yang*. **"The family has severe rulers. They are called the father and mother."** The way of the family must have rulers or elders that are respected and severe: "They are called the father and mother." Although a family is a small thing, if it has no one respected and severe, then filial piety and reverence will become scarce. If there are no rulers or elders, then the laws and measures will be neglected. If there are severe rulers, then "the way of the family is straightforward." The family is the standard for the state. **"When the father does what a father should, the son does what the son should, the older brother does what the older brother should, the younger brother does what the younger brother should, the husband does what the husband should, and the wife does what the wife should, then the way of the family is straightforward. If the family is straightforward, it will give determination to the world."** When father and son, older brother and younger brother, and husband and wife each have acquired their way, "the way of the family is straightforward." When the way of a single family is unfolded, it can extend to the world, and this is why "if the family is straightforward, it will give determination to the world."

The *Symbol* says: "Wind goes out from fire: Family. Noble people use it to make their remarks like things, and to make their actions lasting." The root of making the family straightforward is to make one's own person straightforward. Concerning the way of making one's own person straightforward, neither a single remark nor a single movement may be changed. When noble people gaze on the symbol of wind going out from fire, they recognize that the causes of affairs are first inside, and then go out. This is why their remarks will necessarily be like things, and their actions will necessarily be lasting. The word "thing" signifies a reality or state of affairs, while "lasting" signifies constant measures, laws, and standards. Their virtue and vocation are manifest on the outside because their remarks and actions are prudent on the inside. If their remarks are cautious and their actions are correct, their own persons will be straightforward and their families set in order.

The initial "nine" line: it safeguards and possesses a family. Regrets vanish. The initial line begins the way of the family. The *xian* character of "safeguard" signifies the defense of laws and measures. If those who set the beginning of the family in order can use laws and measures as defenses and safeguards, then they will not reach the point of regret. To bring order to the family is to bring order to a crowd of people. If they do not safeguard it with laws and measures, then people will surrender to the flow of their inclinations, and they will necessarily reach the point of having regrets. The sequence of the fully grown and the immature will be lost, the discrimination between men and women will be disordered, kindness will injure duty, kinship will harm principle, and there is no place they will not reach. But if they can use laws and measures to safeguard it at the beginning, this will not be the case. This is why "regrets vanish." This "nine" line, with its powers of firmness and enlightenment, refers to those who can safeguard their families. The line statement does not say that there are no regrets—there will necessarily be regrets when a group occupies a position—but it can use safeguards, and this is why they vanish. **The *Symbol* says: "'It safeguards and possesses a family': its tendencies do not yet alter."** It safeguards it at the beginning, when the "tendencies" or intentions of the family "do not yet alter" or move ahead. If it safeguards its straightforward tendencies when they have not yet flowed out or scattered, altered or moved, then it will not injure its kindness or lose sight of its duty. This is to place oneself well in the Family hexagram, and as a result, regrets vanish. If its tendencies alter and only afterward are set in order, it will often be injured, and it will have regrets.

The second "six" line: there is no long-term success. There is an oblation at the center. Purity brings good fortune. When people are placed in families—in the space between meat and bone, between father and son—in the great majority of cases their inclinations will be victorious over the rituals, and their kindness will strive with their duty. Only people who have set themselves up firmly will be able to avoid losing the straightforward principle to private love. This is why the great opportunity of the Family hexagram is to consider firmness as good, as in the case of the initial, third, and top lines. The second "six" line uses the power of *yin* softness and occupies a soft position, so it cannot bring order to the family. This is why "there is no long-term success," because there is nothing that it does or should do. As for the power of heroes, when they cannot guard themselves because they value an addictive inclination and love, what will the case be like for soft and weak people? Can they be victorious over the inclinations of their wives and children? As for the power of the second line, if it constitutes the way of the wife, then it is straightforward. To use softness and submissiveness, and to place oneself with centrality and straightforward-ness is the way of the wife. This is why, if "there is an oblation at the center," it will acquire straightforwardness, and there will be good fortune. Wives occupy positions at the center, and are the masters of oblations. This is why it says that "there is an oblation at the center." **The *Symbol* says: "The good fortune of the second 'six' line: it is submissive and lowly."** The second line uses *yin* softness to occupy a central and straightforward position and refers to those who can be submissive and attentive, humble and lowly. This is why it indicates that the purity of wives will bring good fortune.

The third "nine" line: the family is chided, and chided again. Regret at its danger brings good fortune. The wife and son giggle, and giggle again. In the end, there is dismay. The meaning of the phrase "is chided, and chided again" is not delineated by referring to the characters. One gazes on it using the inten-tion of the text and the meaning indicated by its sound. Its sound agrees in kind with "wails, and wails again," and further, the text intends to refer to those who are bolted up with agitation.[3] The third "nine" line is at the top of the inner trigram and refers to the master of bringing order to the inside. It uses *yang* to occupy a firm position, but it is not at the center. Although it has acquired straightforwardness, it is excessively firm. When those who bring order to the inside are excessively firm, they are injurious in their severity and agitation. This is why the family "is chided, and chided again" like this. Those who bring order to the family are excessively severe, and cannot avoid injuring it. This is why they will necessarily regret their severity and "its danger." It is kindness to one's flesh and blood that brings the victory, but they are excessively severe, and this is why there is regret. Although they regret their severity and its danger, they have not yet acquired the center, between tolerance and ferocity. Nonetheless, when the way of the family is equable and sober, and the human heart extols and trembles before it, this will bring something like the good fortune of the family. But if "the wife and son giggle, and giggle again," it will reach the point of disappointment and dismay in the end. In the hexagram, this line is not symbolized by the phrase "giggle, and giggle again." In fact, the line statement remarks on it as the opposite of the phrase "is chided, and chided again." It signifies that they lose themselves and surrender to indulgence rather than becoming excessive in their severity. The phrase "giggle, and giggle again" refers to putting no rein on one's laughter and pleasure. If they put no rein on their wallowing, they will bring about the defeat of the family in the end, and should be disappointed and dismayed. In fact, although an excess of severity and prudence cannot avoid injuring human inclinations, when laws and measures are set up, and kinship and principle are straightforward, then kindness and duty will both persist. But if they "giggle, and giggle again" without measure, this is what causes the neglect of laws and measures. When one causes the disorder of kinship and principle, how could the family be preserved? If they "giggle, and giggle again" to an extreme, they will bring about the misfortune of defeating the family. It speaks only of dismay, but if the dismay should become extreme, it will reach the point of misfortune. This is why it does not remark hastily on their misfortune. **The *Symbol* says: "'The family is chided, and chided again': it has not yet lost anything. 'The wife and son giggle, and giggle again': the family has lost its rein."** Although it "is chided, and chided again," the way of bringing order to the family has not yet become extreme. If "the wife and son giggle, and giggle again," this is to lack ritual and law, and to lose one's rein on the family. It indicates that the family will necessarily be disordered.

The fourth "six" line: the family is wealthy. There is great good fortune. The substance of this "six" line is lowly and submissive, and it occupies the fourth position. It has acquired a straightforward position or, rather, the position it has acquired is straightforward for it, which means that it is in a place of contentment. Since it is lowly and submits to the state of affairs—which causes the way of straightforwardness—it refers to those who are able to preserve the wealth that they possess. If those who occupy the way of the family can preserve the wealth that they possess, this constitutes "great good fortune." The fourth line is in a lofty position, and its line statement is the only one to speak of wealth. It is in the Family hexagram, and one may remark that its position is lofty, so it refers to the position of respect in the family. To be able to preserve the wealth that one possesses is to be able to preserve one's family. What great good fortune! **The *Symbol* says: "'The family is wealthy. There is great good fortune': it is submissive and holds a position."** It is lowly and submissive, and it occupies a straightforward position. Those who are straightforward, lowly, and submissive will be able to preserve the wealth that they possess. Wealth is the great good fortune of the family.

The fifth "nine" line: when the king appears, he will possess a family. He is without anxiety and has good fortune. The fifth "nine" line refers to the male, it is in the outer trigram, it is firm and placed in a *yang* position, it occupies the position of respect, and it is central and straightforward. Further, the corresponding line in the inner trigram is submissive and straightforward. This is what is best and most straightforward in bringing order to the family. "When the king appears, he will possess a family": the fifth is the position of the ruler, and this is why the line statement remarks on the king. The word "appears" refers to reaching something, which in this case is the limit of the way of having a family. As for the way of kings, they correct themselves so as to make the family equable. If the family is straightforward, the world will be orderly. Since antiquity, there has never been a sage-king who did not consider a modest self and a straightforward family to be the root. This is why, when the way of having a family has become extreme, the world will be set in order without worry or labor: "He is without anxiety and has good fortune." The fifth line refers to having a modest self on the outside, while the second line refers to having a straightforward family on the inside. When those on the inside and outside have the same virtues, they may be called "extreme." **The *Symbol* says: "'When the king appears, he will possess a family': they interact and love each other."** The way of the king appearing and possessing a family does not stop at being able to make it submit and attend to him, and that is all. He must bring it about that their hearts are transformed and aligned with sincerity. The husband loves the one who helps him on the inside, while the wife loves the one who punishes the family: "They interact and love each other." To be capable of this is to be like the consort of King Wen.[4] Those who correct themselves and set up laws, but do not yet transform the family, have not yet acquired the way by which "when the king appears, he will possess a family."

The top "nine" line: it is trustworthy, like someone in authority. In the end, there is good fortune. The top line is at the end of the hexagram, and completes the way of the family. This is why the line statement for this limit position remarks on the root of setting the family in order. Without extreme sincerity, one cannot bring about the way of setting the family in order. This is why one must be central, trustworthy, and believable, so that one can be constant and continuous, and then the crowd of people will transform themselves for the better. If those who do nothing by extreme sincerity cannot guard themselves with constancy, what will be the case when they want to do something to other people? This is why trustworthiness is considered the root of setting the family in order. As for those who bring order to their families, in the space of their inclination and love for their wives and children, if their compassion is excessive, then they will not be severe. If their kindness is victorious, then it will cover over their duty. This is why the distress of the family is constant when the rituals and laws are insufficient, bringing disdain and lethargy to life. If grown people lose their respect and severity, the young will forget to be modest and submissive, and there has not yet been such a case in which the family is not disordered. This is why there must be authority and severity, and then it will be possible that "in the end, there is good fortune." To preserve one's family in the end is to be two things, "trustworthy" and "like someone in authority," and that is all. This is why the end of the hexagram remarks on them. **The *Symbol* says: "The good fortune of being 'like someone in authority': it signifies reversion to oneself."** As for the way of setting the family in order, its root is considered to be making the self straightforward. This is why the *Symbol* says: "It signifies reversion to oneself." The line statement has said that, in bringing order to the family, it is proper that there be authority and severity. Fuzi returns to this point again and gives a warning, saying that it is first of all proper to be severe to oneself.[5] Those who do not first put their authority and severity into action on themselves will find that people hate them and do not obey. This is why he says that those who have the good fortune of being "like someone in authority" will be able to revert to themselves. This is what is signified by Mencius when he says: "If they do not travel the way themselves, it will not be traveled by their wives and children."[6]

38. SPLIT (*KUI* 睽)

The *Sequence of the Hexagrams* says: "When the way of the family is depleted, it will necessarily become fractured. This is why the Split hexagram is next. To split is to fracture." When the way of the family is depleted, it will be split up, fractured, cast off, and scattered. Its principle requires this to be the case, and this is why, after the Family hexagram, the Split hexagram is next. As for the trigrams, the Cast trigram is above and the Joy trigram below. The fire referred to by the Cast trigram is flaming upward, while the lake referred to by the Joy trigram is soaking downward. The two trigram substances draw back from one another, which is the meaning of the Split hexagram. Further, they refer to two women in their youth and middle age.[1] Although they "occupy the same position," each is wedded to a different man. That is, "they do not tend toward the same action," and this, too, constitutes the meaning of the Split hexagram.

Split: a small affair will bring good fortune. The Split hexagram refers to a moment of splitting, fracturing, casting off, and scattering, when there is no way of good fortune. But if one employs the goodness in the powers of the trigrams, even if placed in the moment of the Split hexagram, then "a small affair will bring good fortune."

The *Judgment* says: "Split: fire moves upward, while the lake moves downward. Two women occupy the same position, but they do not tend toward the same action." The *Judgment* first explains the meaning of the Split hexagram, then it remarks on the powers of the trigrams, and finally it remarks on the way to align with the Split hexagram and applauds the greatness of its moment and function. The nature of fire is to move upward, while the nature of the lake is to move downward. The natures of the two things are different and draw back from each other, and this is why they constitute the meaning of the Split hexagram. Although two women in their youth and middle age "occupy the same position," "they do not tend toward the same action," and this, too, constitutes the meaning of the Split hexagram. When the women were young, their place was the same, but now that they are grown, and each is suited to be wed, their tendencies are different. When one remarks that two things have split apart, their root must be the same. If their root were not the same, they could not split apart. **"There are enjoyment and a connection with enlightenment. Softness advances and travels upward. It acquires the center and corresponds to firmness. As a result, 'a small affair will bring good fortune.'"** Since the powers of the trigrams are like this, "a small affair will bring good fortune." The Joy trigram refers to enjoyment and the Cast trigram to connection and enlightenment. This is why the *Judgment* refers to enjoyment and submissiveness, as well as to dependency and "a connection with enlightenment." In general, when the Cast trigram is on top, and the *Judgment* wants everyone to see that a soft line occupies the position of respect, it says that "softness advances and travels upward." Such is the case for the Lift and Tripod hexagrams. Faced with the moment of splitting and fracturing, the fifth "six" line uses softness to occupy the position of respect. It possesses the goodness of enjoyment, submissiveness, connection, and enlightenment, and further, it has acquired the way of centrality, and it corresponds to a firm line. Although it cannot bring alignment to the splitting apart of the world or bring completion to the great affairs of the world, it can nonetheless make a small crossing: "A small affair will bring good fortune." The fifth line makes use of enlightenment and corresponds to a firm line, yet it cannot bring about great good fortune. Why is this? Response: the fifth line is *yin* and soft. Although it corresponds to the second line, this is the moment of the Split hexagram. The way by which they agree with each other cannot yet be deep and certain. This is why the second line must encounter "the master in the lane," and if the fifth line "bites through the skin," there will be no blame. At the moment when the world is split apart and scattered, there must be rulers and ministers of *yang* firmness, centrality, and straightforwardness, of extreme sincerity and allied forces, and these will afterward be capable of bringing about alignment. **"Heaven and earth are split apart, but their affairs are the same. Men and women are split apart, but their tendencies develop together. The ten thousand things are split apart, but their affairs are of a kind. How great are the moment and function of the Split hexagram!"** The *Judgment* unfolds how the principles of things are the same, so as to shed light on the moment and function of the Split hexagram. The way of sages is to align what has split apart. Seeing the sameness in things that are the same is the knowledge of the customs of the times. The sages shed light on how the principles of things are the same at their root, and so they can bring sameness to the world, harmonizing and aligning the ten thousand kinds of thing. They shed light on heaven and earth, men and women, and the ten thousand things. Heaven is lofty and the earth is below—their substances have split apart. Nonetheless, when *yang* has fallen and *yin* has risen, when they align with each other and complete the affairs of transformation and cultivation, they become the same.[2] Men and women have different dispositions—this is how they split apart. But when they tend to seek each other, they communicate with each other. The lives of things have ten thousand peculiarities—this is how they split apart. Nonetheless, when they acquire the harmony of heaven and earth, and receive their *yin* and *yang qi*, they are of each other's kind. Although things are different, their principles are the same at their root. This is why sages can bring sameness to the greatness of the world, to the crowd of living things in all their groups, and to the ten thousand peculiarities that split things apart and scatter them. To be placed in the moment of the Split hexagram, and to have the function of aligning what has split apart, is an extremely great affair. This is why it says: "How great," and so on.

The *Symbol* says: "Fire is above and the lake below: Split. Noble people make use of sameness and difference." "Fire is above and the lake below": the natures of these two things are different and draw back from each other, and so they symbolize splitting apart and casting off. When noble people gaze on the symbol of splitting apart and differentiating, they recognize what should properly be differentiated even at the center of the great sameness. As for the place and time of sages and worthies, they are constantly within the human principle, and are not other than the great sameness. But concerning making themselves the same as the customs of the times, there are moments when they alone are different. In fact, in maintaining the paradigm, they are the same, but in losing the customs of the times, they are different. Anyone not capable of the great sameness is someone who brings disorder to what is constant and brushes off the principle. Anyone not capable of being different alone is someone who follows custom and who practices what is wrong. They have the opportunity for sameness, but are capable of difference. This is what the *Doctrine of Centrality* says: "They harmonize without flowing away."

The initial "nine" line: regrets vanish. It is deprived of a horse. It does not pursue it, but the horse returns. It sees bad people, but there is no blame. A "nine" line occupies the initial position of the hexagram, which is the beginning of the split. In the moment of the Split or fracture hexagram, it makes use of firm movement at the bottom, and its regrets should be recognized. It is able to make them vanish because the fourth "nine" line above it also makes use of *yang* firmness. They split apart, cast each other off, and disagree, and yet those of the same kind also spontaneously align with each other. They are the same in being *yang* lines, they are the same in occupying bottom positions, and further, it is proper that their positions correspond to each other. Two *yang* lines do not at root correspond to each other, but they are in the Split hexagram, and this is why they align. Those above and below agree with each other, and this is why they can make their regrets vanish. In the Split hexagram, various lines correspond to each other. As for those that align, they will also split apart. If they were different at root, how could they split apart? It is only in the case of the initial and fourth lines that, although they do not correspond, they agree with each other because their virtues are the same. This is why they encounter each other. The word "horse" refers to a means of travel, and *yang* is what travels upward. These are the only lines in the Split hexagram that do not agree, and so the initial line cannot travel: "It is deprived of a horse." The fourth line has aligned with it, and so it can travel: "It does not pursue it, but the horse returns." The phrase "bad people" refers to those who are fractured and different from themselves. When "it sees" them, they encounter each other. Although those of the same virtues agree with each other when they face the moment of the Split hexagram, small people have nonetheless become a crowd of fractures and differences. Were it to desert them or sever itself from them, will not almost everyone in the world become hostile to the noble person? In a case like this, it will lose the meaning of "enclosure" and "immensity," and will bring about the way of misfortune and blame.[3] Further, how could it transform those who are not good, and make them align? This is why it will necessarily see "bad people, but there is no blame." The reason the sage-kings of antiquity were able to transform the vile and unfortunate into the good and fine, to reform hostile enemies into their ministers and people, is that they did not sever themselves from them. **The *Symbol* says: "'It sees bad people': it eludes blame."** In the moment of splitting apart and casting off, human inclinations fracture and draw back from each other. It seeks to harmonize and align them, but it is defective and does not bring this about. Were it to reject the bad people and sever itself from them, the crowd would soon become hostile to the noble person, and its affliction and blame would be extreme. This is why it must see them, and so it will avoid and evade their hatred and blame. If there is no hatred or blame, then the way of alignment will become possible.

The second "nine" line: it encounters the master in the lane. There is no blame. The second and fifth lines straightforwardly correspond, indicating that they agree with each other. Nonetheless, in the moment of the Split or fracture hexagram, the way of *yin* and *yang* corresponding to each other is becoming scarce, and the intention of firmness and softness repulsing each other is becoming victorious. If those who study the *Book of Changes* understand this, they will recognize what mutual alteration is. This is why it is proper that the second and fifth lines twist around and seek each other, even though their correspondence is straightforward. The second line uses the virtues of firmness and centrality to occupy a lower position, and corresponds to the fifth "six" line—the ruler, in other words—above it. Since their ways are aligned, they will act on their tendencies and complete the task of crossing through the Split hexagram. They occupy the moment of splitting apart and casting off, and their interaction is uncertain. It is proper that the second line twist around and seek an encounter with the fifth. It longs to be aligned with it, and this is why the line statement says that "it encounters the master in the lane." Since they are necessarily capable of alignment, there will afterward be no blame. When rulers and ministers split apart and cast each other off, their blame is great. The word "lane" refers to a path that twists around, and "encounter" signifies a chance convergence. It is proper that they twist around and seek each other, wishing to converge on and encounter each other, and be aligned together. The phrase "twisting around" signifies winding about on the way of the good when one is about to bring about alignment, and that is all. It does not refer to bending oneself up and contracting the way.[4] **The *Symbol* says: "'It encounters the master in the lane': it has not yet lost the way."** When rulers face the moment of the Split hexagram, their hearts are not yet aligned, and worthies and ministers are in positions below. They drain their force and exhaust their sincerity, wishing to make the rulers believe in and align with them, and that is all. They make their sincerity extreme in affecting and moving them, and they exhaust their force in aiding and constraining them. They shed light on duty and principle so as to become knowledgeable, they restrict and conceal their own bewilderment so as to make their intentions sincere, and they wind about like this so as to seek out alignment. Their "encounter" is not a chance rendezvous on a bending way, and the "lane" is not a crooked, crass, and twisting byway. This is why Fuzi specifically says that "'it encounters the master in the lane': it has not yet lost the way."[5] The phrase "not yet" indicates "not necessarily," and signifies that it will not necessarily lose the way.

The third "six" line: it sees the carriage dragged away and its oxen yoked. Someone is scalped and nosed. It has no initiation, but it has an end. If *yin* softness is not sufficient to set itself up in a moment of peace, what will the case be like when it is on the verge of being split apart and cast off? Since the third line occupies a position between two firm lines, it is not in a place of contentment—that it is seen as an invader and a usurper should be recognized. The third straightforwardly corresponds to the top line, and it wants to advance and align its tendencies with those at the top, but the fourth line hinders it ahead and the second line guides it from behind. Carriages and oxen are equipment for travel, but this carriage is dragged away and guided from behind, and these oxen are yoked and hindered ahead. The line behind it guides and drags it away, and that is all, but the line ahead of it confronts its advance with force. This is why it suffers a weighty injury from above, and it is the fourth line that injures it. "Someone is scalped and nosed": the word "scalp" refers to shaving the head, and "nose" refers to cutting off the nose. The third line attends to its straightforwardly corresponding line, but the fourth stops it by separating them. Although the third line is *yin* and soft, it is placed in a firm position, and it acts on its tendencies. This is why it advances by force to confront it, and is injured as a result. To remark that it is both scalped and nosed indicates that it suffers a weighty injury. The third line aligns with neither the second nor the fourth, and the moment of the Split hexagram itself has the meaning of nonalignment. It is suitable for it to align with the way of occupying a firm position and guarding its straightforwardness. Because of its straightforward correspondence, it will possess the principle of alignment in the end, at the limit of the Split hexagram. The two *yang* lines imperil it at the beginning: "It has no initiation." Afterward, it will necessarily acquire alignment: "It has an end." Those who are yoked attend to what controls them—that is, they attend to one's hand, which means that they are stopped when one holds them. **The Symbol says: "'It sees the carriage dragged away': its position is not proper for it. 'It has no initiation, but it has an end': it encounters firmness."** A "six" line occupies the third position, which is not straightforward. If it is not straightforward, then it will not be contented. Further, it is between two *yang* lines, and so it has hardships and perils like this, because "its position is not proper for it." "It has no initiation, but it has an end": in the end it will necessarily agree with the higher "nine" line. They will encounter each other and align: "It encounters firmness." When it aligns without straightforwardness, it is not yet so continuous that it will not be cast off. If it were to align using the way of straightforwardness, it would not in the end possess the principle of the Split hexagram. This is why worthy people submit to principle and act with contentment, while wise people recognize the incipient and guard it with certainty.

The fourth "nine" line: it splits apart in isolation. It encounters a primary man. Their interactions are based on trust. It is in danger, but there is no blame. The fourth "nine" line faces the moment of the Split hexagram, it does not occupy a position of contentment, it has no corresponding line, and it is between two *yin* lines. It refers to those who are split apart or cast off in an isolated place. Since it uses the virtue of *yang* firmness while facing the moment of splitting apart and casting off, and it sets itself up in isolation without agreeing with any other line, it will necessarily seek out and align with those who possess the same kind of *qi*: "It encounters a primary man." The word "man" is here a name for the *yang qi*, and "primary" refers to it as good. The initial "nine" line faces the initial moment of the Split hexagram, but it succeeds in being able to agree with those of the same virtue, and so it makes the regrets of the Split hexagram vanish. This is the best one can do when placed in the Split hexagram, and is why it is seen as a "primary man." It is as though it were said to be a "good scholar."[6] The fourth line, on the other hand, has exceeded the center, and so its splitting apart is already extreme and it does not possess the goodness of the initial line. The fourth and initial lines both use *yang* to place themselves at the bottom of a trigram, they occupy positions that correspond to each other, and they face the moment of splitting apart and fracturing. Each is without the support of a corresponding line, but they spontaneously relate to each other, since they possess the same virtues, and this is why they converge in an encounter. When those of the same virtue encounter each other, they must necessarily agree with each other in their extreme sincerity. "Their interactions are based on trust": each of them is trustworthy and sincere. If these two *yang* lines, one above and one below, align with each other in their extreme sincerity, how could they be incapable of acting at this moment? How could they be incapable of crossing through the peril? This is why, although it is placed in peril and danger, there is no blame. It faces the moment of splitting apart and casting off, it occupies an isolated position between two *yin* lines, and it is placed in a position that is not proper for it, so that there are peril and blame. But it "encounters a primary man" and "their interactions are based on trust," and this is why it acquires no blame. **The *Symbol* says: "'Their interactions are based on trust. There is no blame': it acts on its tendencies."** The initial and fourth lines are both *yang* and firm and refer to noble people facing the moment of splitting apart and fracturing. When those above and below interact with each other in their extreme sincerity, with allied tendencies and the same force, then they will be able to act on their tendencies. They will not stop at being without blame, and that is all. The hexagram statement remarks only that "there is no blame," but Fuzi attends to it further and sheds light on it, saying that they can act on their tendencies and save themselves from the moment of the Split hexagram.[7] In fact, when they use the powers of *yang* firmness possessed by noble people and assist each other in their extreme sincerity, what will they be unable to cross through? But it is only noble people who will be able to act on their tendencies.

The fifth "six" line: regrets vanish. Its fellow sectarian bites through the skin. In making a journey, what blame could there be? This "six" line uses *yin* softness while facing the moment of splitting apart and casting off, it occupies the position of respect, and its regrets should be recognized. Nonetheless, it has below it the worthy people referred to by the second "nine" line, which is *yang* and firm. They agree and correspond to it so as to assist and aid it, and this is why "regrets vanish." The phrase "fellow sectarian" refers to its faction and signifies its straightforward correspondence to the second "nine" line. The phrase "bites through the skin" refers to biting and chewing one's flesh and skin so as to enter more deeply. If those who face the moment of the Split hexagram do not make an entry that is deep, how will they be able to align with each other? Although the fifth line has the power of *yin* softness, the second line assists it with the way of *yang* firmness and enters it deeply, so that it can make the journey and possess delight. What blame or excess could there be? During the Zhou dynasty, when Cheng was in his immaturity and youth, the order of the king was flourishing and abundant.[8] When Liu Shan was in his darkness and weakness, it still had the propensity to be central and flourishing. This is because, in fact, they delegated command to worthies and sages as their assistants. Duke Ji and Kong Ming also made an entry that was deep.[9] **The *Symbol* says: "'Its fellow sectarian bites through the skin': if it makes a journey, there will be delight."** The line statement remarks only that if "its fellow sectarian bites through the skin," it will be able to make a journey and there will be no blame. The *Symbol*, in turn, unfolds and sheds light on the meaning of this. It remarks that, although this is the ruling line, its powers are not sufficient. If it were able to believe in and delegate command to worthy people as its assistants, who would make its way enter deeply into themselves, then something could be done. If this is the journey to be made, then there will be blessing and delight.

The top "nine" line: it splits apart in isolation. It sees a pig carrying filth. It bears a load of ghosts in a single carriage. First it draws the bow, and afterward it releases the bow. If there are no bandits, there will be a marriage. If it encounters rain on its journey, there will be good fortune. The top line occupies the end position of the hexagram and refers to the limit of the splitting apart.

A line that is *yang* and firm occupies the top position and refers to the limit of firmness. It is at the top of the Cast trigram and refers to the limit of the employment of enlightenment. Since this is the limit of the Split hexagram, it is opposed and repulsed, and aligns only with difficulty; since this is the limit of firmness, it is restless and violent, and "delineates nothing";[10] since this is the limit of enlightenment, it is excessive in its examination, and has many doubts. The top "nine" line has a straightforward correspondence to the third "six" line. In reality, it is not isolated, but its powers and nature are such that it splits apart and isolates itself. In the case of people, although they have their relations and factions, they have many doubts and suspicions concerning them. They are at fault in fracturing and casting off other living things. Although they are placed between the meat and bones of their relations and factions, they are constantly isolated and alone. Although the top line has a straightforward correspondence with the third, it nonetheless occupies the limit position of the Split hexagram, and there is nothing about which it is not doubtful. It sees the third line as the corruption and dirt of a pig that is also carrying mud and filth on its back. It may go to an extreme in detesting such a sight. When it has gone to an extreme in detesting it, its suspicions will bring its recriminating and detesting to their completion, as though it saw someone bearing a load of ghosts, enough to fill a single carriage. Ghosts are at root without form, but here it sees someone bearing a load of them in a single carriage. The line statement is remarking that it considers what is not as what is—its fault has reached its limit. When the principle of a thing has reached its limit, it will necessarily reverse itself. Things nearby may be used to shed light on this: when people go east, and reach the limit of the east, they will go west when they move. When people rise to a lofty height, and reach the limit of loftiness, they will descend when they move. When they have reached the limit, they will necessarily reverse themselves when they move. The top line is already at the limit of splitting apart and fracturing, and the third line places itself according to the straightforward principle. In the great majority of cases, when the loss of the way has reached its limit, it will necessarily revert to the straightforward principle. This is why the top line begins by doubting the third, but they will necessarily align in the end. "First it draws the bow": at the beginning it doubts and detests it, and wants to shoot it. But its doubt is a fault, and how could a fault be constant? This is why it will necessarily return to straightforwardness in the end. In reality, the third line is not detestable, and this is why "afterward it releases the bow" and does not shoot it. It is at the limit of the Split hexagram and it reverses itself, which is why it will agree with the third line and not turn to becoming a bandit or adversary: "There will be a marriage." The statement—"if there are no bandits, there will be a marriage"—is the same as elsewhere, but its meaning is peculiar to this hexagram.[11] When *yin* and *yang* interact and freely harmonize, they bring about the rain. At the beginning, the top line doubts the third and splits apart from it, but at the limit of the Split hexagram it is no longer doubtful and aligns with it. When *yin* and *yang* align and add to their harmony, they bring about the rain, and this is why the line statement says: "If it encounters rain on its journey, there will be good fortune." Since the word "journey" refers to a journey away from here, it signifies that, if they have aligned and added to their harmony, there will be good fortune. **The *Symbol* says: "The good fortune of encountering rain: a group of doubts vanishes."** The word "rain" refers to the harmony of *yin* and *yang*. They split apart at the beginning, but are able to harmonize at the end, and this is why "there will be good fortune." The reason they are able to harmonize is that "a group of doubts" is exhausted and "vanishes." They split apart at the beginning, and there is nothing they do not doubt. This is why the *Symbol* speaks of "a group of doubts." Since they align at the limit of the Split hexagram, every doubt vanishes.

39. LIMP (*JIAN* 蹇)

The *Sequence of the Hexagrams* says: "To split is to fracture. Those who fracture something will necessarily be in difficulties, and this is why the Limp hexagram is next. Those who limp are in difficulties." At the moment when people split and fracture something, they will necessarily limp and be in difficulties. And so the Limp hexagram succeeds the Split hexagram. The Limp hexagram has the meaning of an obstacle or hindrance, and this is why it refers to limping and being in difficulties. As for the trigrams, the Pit trigram is above and the Calm trigram below. The Pit trigram refers to an obstacle and the Calm trigram to stopping. "There is an obstacle ahead," and so one stops and cannot advance. Ahead, there is an obstacle or snare, while behind, there is a steepness or hindrance. This is why these trigrams constitute the Limp hexagram.

Limp: there is profit in the southwest, but no profit in the northeast. There is profit in seeing great people. Purity brings good fortune. The southwest is the region of the Yield trigram.[1] The Yield trigram refers to the earth, and its substance refers to submission and ease. The northeast is the region of the Calm trigram. The Calm trigram refers to the mountain, and its substance refers to stopping and an obstacle. In a moment of limping and difficulty, there is profit in submitting to placement on a terrain of peace and ease, but no profit in stopping on a terrain of peril and obstacles. Those who are placed with submission and ease will find their difficulties relieved, while those who are stopped by an obstacle will add to the extremity of their difficulties. In a moment of limping and difficulty, there must be sagely and worthy people who will be able to cross through the difficulties of the world. This is why "there is profit in seeing great people." Those who cross through difficulties must use the way of great straightforwardness, and keep guard with solidity and certainty. This is why, if

311

they are pure, there will be good fortune. In general, those who are placed in difficulties must guard their purity and straightforwardness. Even if this does not provide the means of setting them loose from the difficulty, they will not lose the virtue of straightforwardness. As a result, there will be good fortune. Were they to encounter a difficulty and be unable to keep guard with certainty, they would enter into crookedness and transgression. Even if they could recklessly avoid it, their virtue would still be bad. Those who recognize their duty and the mandate will do nothing.

The *Judgment* says: "A limp is a difficulty. There is an obstacle ahead." "A limp is a difficulty": the Limp hexagram refers to difficulty, just as the Lead hexagram refers to vigor. Were the *Book of Changes* simply referring to difficulty here, its meaning would not yet be sufficient. The Limp hexagram has the meaning of obstacles and hindrances, but the Block hexagram also has the meaning of difficulty, as does the Trap hexagram. The difficulty is the same in each of them, but their meanings are different. The Block hexagram is the beginning of the difficulty, when it has not yet developed; the Trap hexagram is the depletion of one's force; the Limp hexagram has the meaning of obstacles, hindrances, hardships, and difficulties—they are not the same. "There is an obstacle ahead": the Pit trigram is the obstacle ahead. The lower trigram stops and does not make an advance. This is why these trigrams constitute the Limp hexagram. **"To see the obstacle and be able to stop—this is knowledge!"** The *Judgment* is using the powers of the trigrams to remark on the way to place oneself in the Limp hexagram. The upper trigram refers to the obstacle and the lower trigram to the stopping. This is "to see the obstacle and be able to stop." If one confronts the obstacle and advances, there will be regret and blame. This is why it refers to knowledge, as what is beautiful about the ability to stop. When facing the moment of limping and difficulty, one can do nothing better than to stop. This is why the various lines, excepting the fifth and the second, all consider making a journey as losing something, but arriving as acquiring something. **"'Limp: there is profit in the southwest': if a journey is made, it will acquire the center. 'No profit in the northeast': its way is depleted."** In the moment of the Limp hexagram, there is profit in placing oneself with peace and ease. The southwest is the region of the Yield trigram, which refers to submission and ease. The northeast is the region of the Calm trigram, which refers to obstacles and hindrances.[2] The top "nine" line occupies the fifth position, and has acquired a position of centrality and straightforwardness. This is to make the journey and acquire a terrain of peace and ease, and this is why the judgment refers to profit. The fifth line occupies the center of the Pit or obstacle trigram, and yet it signifies peace and ease. In fact, its root is the Yield trigram. The Pit trigram is completed only because the fifth line makes a journey, and this is why the *Judgment* chooses "a journey is made" and "it will acquire the center" as its meaning. It does not choose the completed Pit trigram as its meaning. Those who face the Limp hexagram and stop on a terrain of perils and obstacles will add to the extremity of their limp. This is why there is "no profit in the northeast." "Its way is depleted": this signifies that their limp has reached its limit. "'There is profit in seeing great people': if a journey is made, it will accomplish something. Their position is proper, 'purity brings good fortune,' and the kingdom is straightforward." In the moment of limping and difficulty, those who are not sages or worthies will be incapable of crossing through the limping of the world, and this is why "there is profit in seeing great people." When great people are in their proper positions, they will complete the task of crossing through the limp: "If a journey is made, it will accomplish something." What is capable of crossing through the limping of the world is nothing but the way of great straightforwardness. Further, Fuzi chooses to remark on the powers of the trigrams, saying that the various lines of the Limp hexagram, excepting the initial line, are all in their proper and straightforward positions.[3] This is why they are pure and straightforward, and there will be good fortune. Although the initial "six" line makes use of *yin* to occupy a *yang* position, it is placed at the bottom, and this is also how a *yin* line may be straightforward. Those who use such a way of straightforwardness to make "the kingdom straightforward" will be able to cross through the limp. "How great are the moment and the function of the Limp hexagram!" For those placed in the moment of the Limp hexagram, who are on the way of crossing through the limp, its function is extremely great. This is why the *Judgment* says how great it is. How can the difficulties of the world be brought to peace and ease? A function may be called "great" when those who are not sages or worthies are incapable of it. To place oneself in submission to the moment, to calculate the obstacle and then act, to attend to the way of peace and ease—the cause of all these is the principle of extreme straightforwardness, which is the moment and function of the Limp hexagram.

The *Symbol* says: "Above the mountain, there is water: Limp. Noble people revert to themselves and correct their virtue." Above the steep hindrance of the mountain, there is water. The Pit or water trigram is the symbol of an obstacle or snare. Above and below there are obstacles and hindrances, and this is why these two trigrams constitute the Limp hexagram. When noble people gaze on the symbol of limping and difficulty, they "revert to themselves and correct their virtue." When noble people encounter hardships and hindrances, they will necessarily revert to seeking various things within themselves, and add to their self-correction. Mencius says: "Those who act to possess something, and yet make no acquisition, should revert to seeking various things within themselves."[4] This is why, when they encounter the hardships of the Limp hexagram, they must inspect themselves in their own persons. If they have lost something, will they not bring it back? This is how they "revert to themselves." If there is anything in them that is not yet good, they will modify it. If there is nothing missing in their hearts, they will exhort themselves further, which is how they "correct their virtue" by themselves. Noble people correct their virtue so as to await the moment, and that is all.

The initial "six" line: it limps on its journey. If it arrives, there will be praise. This "six" line occupies the initial position in the Limp hexagram. If it makes the journey and advances, it will add to and enter into the limp: "It limps on its journey." It faces the moment of the Limp hexagram, it makes use of *yin* softness, and it advances without support—it should be recognized that it limps. The phrase "it arrives" is opposed to "it makes a journey." It makes a journey if it advances upward, while it arrives if it does not advance. It stops and does not advance—this is to possess the beauty of seeing the incipient and recognizing the moment. Since it arrives, there will be praise. **The *Symbol* says: "'It limps on its journey. If it arrives, there will be praise': it is fitting to wait."** As for the initial line, at the start of the Limp hexagram, it will add to the limp if it advances, because this is not yet the moment when one should advance. This is why it is fitting to see the incipient and to stop so as to wait for the moment. When it should act, it will afterward act. Various line statements say that "it limps on its journey," and that it is good to arrive. Since this is the case, why do they not mean that it is going out from the limp? Response: those who make a journey during the Limp hexagram are limping. At the end of the Limp hexagram, there will be alteration, and this is why the top line already has the meaning of being "large."

The second "six" line: the king and his ministers are limping, and limping again. It is not for its own sake. The second line uses the virtues of centrality and straightforwardness, it occupies a position in the Calm trigram substance, and it refers to those who stop in central and straightforward positions. Because it corresponds to the fifth line, it refers to people of centrality and straightforwardness who are believed in and given command by rulers of centrality and straightforwardness. This is why the line statement calls them "the king and his ministers." Although those above and below have the same virtues, the fifth line faces the center of the "great limp." It brings force to bear on the moment of limping and difficulty, and so its hardship and limping reach their extreme. This is why they limp within their limp. Although the second line is central and straightforward, it uses the power of *yin* softness. How could it easily be victorious in its command? As a result, it limps within its limp. Its tendency is to sustain the ruler at the center of the limping and difficulty. It is "limping, and limping again," but this is "not for its own sake." Although it does not make itself victorious, its tendency and duty may be excellent. This is why it says that its loyalty and faithfulness are not for itself. Its power is not sufficient to cross through the Limp hexagram, but it may make a small crossing, and so it is proper that the sage refer to it as abundant and renowned, as a means of per-suading people. **The *Symbol* says: "'The king and his ministers are limping, and limping again': in the end, there is no resentment."** Although there are hardship and peril in the moment of the Limp hexagram, it nonetheless tends to cross through the difficulty with the ruler. Although it has not yet completed its task, it will nonetheless be without excess or resentment in the end. The sage chooses its tendency as the meaning of the line, saying that "there is no resent-ment," so as to persuade people to be loyal and faithful.

The third "nine" line: it limps on its journey. If it arrives, it will revert to some-thing. The third "nine" line uses firmness to occupy a straightforward position, it is placed at the top of the lower trigram substance, and it faces the moment of the Limp hexagram. The lines below it are all soft, and will necessarily rely on the third—it is what those below depend on. The third corresponds straightfor-wardly to the top line, but the top line is *yin* and soft, has no position, and is not sufficient to support it. This is why it will limp if it makes the journey upward. The phrase "it arrives" here indicates that it arrives below, and "it will revert" indicates that it will relocate or wed itself to something. The two *yin* lines below are happy with the third, and this is why its arrival is a reversion to its place, to a terrain of slight contentment. **The *Symbol* says: "'It limps on its journey. If it arrives, it will revert to something': those within are happy with it."** The *yin* lines of the inner trigram are in the lower positions. When *yin* softness faces the moment of the Limp hexagram, it cannot set itself up. This is why they both depend on the *yang* of the third "nine" line. They "are happy with it," and love it. In the Limp hexagram, when a "nine" line is placed in the third position, this indicates that it has acquired its place. Those who are placed in the Limp hexagram and acquire the hearts of those below will be able to seek content-ment. This is why its arrival is also considered its reversion. It is just like the word "wed" in the *Spring and Autumn Annals*.[5]

The fourth "six" line: it limps on its journey. If it arrives, it will be linked.
If it makes a journey, it will add to and enter the depth of the pit or obstacle:
"It limps on its journey." As for those who occupy positions in the moment of
limping and difficulty, they are placed in the same hardship and peril, and they
are the same in having unskilled tendencies. Further, the fourth line occupies
a position in the upper trigram, and it is the same as the line below it in acquiring a straightforward position. Further, it is close to the third line and relates
to it, while the second and the initial line are the same in kind and agree with
each other—this is to have the same tendency as those below, and to be the one
attended to and depended on by the crowd. This is why the line statement says
that "if it arrives, it will be linked." If it arrives, then it will link itself up and
align with the crowd of those below. Those who can align with the crowd will
acquire the way to place themselves in the Limp hexagram. **The *Symbol* says:**
"'It limps on its journey. If it arrives, it will be linked': it is proper that its posi-
tion have reality." The fourth line faces the moment of the Limp hexagram, it
occupies a position in the upper trigram, it arrives instead of making a journey,
and it has the same tendency as those below—this is certainly sufficient for
making an acquisition of the crowd. Further, it uses *yin* to occupy a *yin* position, and so it acquires reality. It uses sincerity and reality to agree with those
below, and this is why it can link itself up and align with them by descending to
them. The second and the third lines have also acquired reality, and even the
initial line uses *yin* to occupy a position below, which is its reality. They face the
same moment of distress, they use reality to interact with each other, and their
alignment should be recognized. This is why, "if it arrives, it will be linked,"
and "it is proper that its position" make use of reality. As for those placed in
the moment of limping and difficulty, how will they cross through it if they
are not sincere and real? The *Symbol* does not say that the proper position is
"straightforward," but that it has "reality." Sincerity and reality are the masters of
the interactions of those above and below, and the *Symbol* employs them when
each line is in its place.

The fifth "nine" line: it has a great limp. Friends arrive. The fifth line occupies
the position of the ruler, and is at the center of the limping and difficulty—this
is the "great limp" of the world. It is faced with a limp, and further, it is at the
center of an obstacle, which may also be considered a "great limp." It is in the
moment of the great limp, and it corresponds to the second line in the lower
trigram with centrality and straightforwardness—this is the arrival of its friends
and helpers. It faces the moment when the world limps, and it has acquired
ministers of centrality and straightforwardness to assist it. How could their help

be small? Its friends have arrived, and yet there is no good fortune. Why is this? Response: it is not yet sufficient to cross through the limp. Those who rule with *yang* firmness, centrality, and straightforwardness, and face the center of the great limp, will not be able to cross through the limping of the world if they do not acquire ministers of *yang* firmness, centrality, and straightforwardness to assist them. The centrality and straightforwardness of the second line are certainly helpful but, though they may desire the help of *yin* softness in crossing through the difficulties of the world, there is nothing it can do. Since antiquity, when sage-kings cross through the limping of the world, they have never yet brought this about without the help of worthy and sagely ministers. Such was the case for Tang and Wu, who acquired Yi and Lü.[6] There are also rulers whose centrality is ordinary, yet who acquire ministers of firmness and enlightenment, and so are able to cross through great difficulties. Such was the case when Liu Shan acquired Kong Ming, the Tang emperor Suzong acquired Guo Ziyi, and emperor Dezong acquired Li Sheng.[7] If the ruler is worthy and enlightened but the minister is not, then they will not be able to cross through the difficulties. This is why, generally, when a "six" line occupies the fifth position and a "nine" line occupies the second position, the one will often be a cause of help to the other, and they will accomplish something. Such is the case for the Blind and Free hexagrams, and others of this kind. If a "nine" line occupies the fifth position and a "six" line occupies the second position, what they accomplish will often be insufficient. Such is the case for the Block and Clog hexagrams, and others of this kind. In fact, when the ministers are worthier than the rulers, they will assist the rulers in what the rulers cannot do. When the ministers do not extend themselves to the level of the rulers, they will applaud and help them, and that is all. This is why they will not be able to complete any great task. **The *Symbol* says: "'It has a great limp. Friends arrive': it is reined by centrality."** The *peng* character of "friends" here refers to those of its kind. The fifth line has the virtues of centrality and straightforwardness, and the second line is also central and straightforward. Although this is the moment of the great limp, they have not lost their guard. They have made the limp itself to limp by corresponding to and helping each other. This is to make use of centrality and straightforwardness as one's rein. Although those above and below are central and straightforward, they have not made the crossing because the power of the ministers is insufficient. Since antiquity, how could there be only a few who kept guard over their rein and maintained their duty, but whose power was not sufficient to make the crossing? Such was the case for Li Gu and Wang Yun in the Han dynasty, and Zhou Yi and Wang Dao in the Jin dynasty.[8]

The top "six" line: it limps on its journey. If it arrives, it will be large. There is good fortune, and profit in seeing great people. This "six" line uses *yin* softness to occupy the limit position of the Limp hexagram. It makes the journey to brave the limit of the obstacle, and so "it limps." If "it arrives" instead of making the journey, attending to the fifth line and seeking out the third, it will acquire the help of *yang* firmness, and so it will be "large." Those on the way of the Limp hexagram will choke off peril and deplete anguish. The word "large" refers to greatness, and is a name for tolerance and generosity. Those who arrive will be tolerant and great, and their limp will be relieved. At the limit of the Limp hexagram, there is a way of going out from the limp. The top "six" line makes use of *yin* softness, and this is why it does not go out. If it acquires the help of *yang* firmness, it will be able to bring relief to its limp, and that is all. In the moment when the Limp hexagram is at its limit, the acquisition of relief constitutes good fortune. If there is no *yang* firmness, centrality, or straightforwardness, how could it go out from the limp? There is "profit in seeing great people": in the moment when the Limp hexagram is at its limit, those who see people of great virtue will be able to cross through the limp. The phrase "great people" here signifies the fifth line — this meaning is revealed by their closeness to each other. Since the fifth line possesses *yang* firmness, centrality, and straightforwardness, and occupies the position of the ruler, it is the "great people." Since the fifth line statement does not remark that its task is to cross through the limp, why is there profit for the top "six" line in seeing it? Response: the fifth line statement does not remark on this because it occupies the center of the pit or obstacle trigram, and it does not have the help of a line with *yang* firmness. This is why it cannot mean to cross through the limp. Since the top "six" line is at the limit of the Limp hexagram, and it sees people of great virtue, it can cross through the limp. This is why there is profit for it. The meanings chosen for each line are not the same. In the Block hexagram, for instance, the tendency of the initial "nine" line is straightforward, but in the second "six" line it is seen as a bandit. Various line statements here do not remark that there is good fortune; only the top line statement remarks that there is good fortune. Various lines here have acquired straightforwardness, and each has something good about it, but they are not yet able to go out from the limp. This is why they are not yet sufficient to constitute good fortune. Only the top line is placed at the limit of the Limp hexagram and acquires the tolerance and generosity that constitute good fortune. **The *Symbol* says: "'It limps on its journey. If it arrives, it will be large': it tends toward the inside. There is 'profit in seeing great people': it attends to what is esteemed."** The top "six" line corresponds to the third and attends to the fifth: "It tends toward the inside." Since the Limp hexagram has reached its limit and has a line to help it, it is "large," and there will be good fortune. This "six" line uses *yin* softness to face the limit of the Limp hexagram, it is profoundly near to a ruler of *yang* firmness, centrality, and straightforwardness, on whom it spontaneously tends to attend and depend, and it seeks to make the crossing. This is why there is "profit in seeing great people," which signifies that it attends to the esteemed fifth "nine" line. As a result, the *Symbol* says that it "attends to what is esteemed," fearing people will not recognize that the phrase "great people" is pointing to the fifth line.

40. LOOSE (*JIE* 解)

The *Sequence of the Hexagrams* says: "Those who limp are in difficulties. Things cannot be in difficulties to the end, and this is why the Loose hexagram is next." There is no principle by which things may be in difficulties to the end. When they reach the limit of their difficulties, they will necessarily be scattered. "To set loose is to scatter," and so the Loose hexagram succeeds the Limp hexagram. As for the trigrams, the Shake trigram is above and the Pit trigram below. The Shake trigram refers to movement and the Pit trigram to an obstacle. The movement is outside the obstacle, which refers to a going out from the obstacle. This is why these trigrams symbolize setting loose or scattering the distress and difficulties. Further, the Shake trigram refers to thunder and the Pit trigram to rain. Together, they refer to the production of thunder and rain. In fact, when *yin* and *yang* interact and affect each other, they harmonize smoothly and are slackened or scattered. This is why these trigrams constitute the Loose hexagram. The Loose hexagram refers to the moment when the distress and difficulties of the world are set loose and scattered.

Loose: there is profit in the southwest. When there is no journey to make, its arrival and return will bring good fortune. When it has a long journey, being prompt will bring good fortune. The southwest is the region of the Yield trigram. The substance of the Yield trigram is broad and great, peaceful and at ease. It is proper that the difficulty of the world start to be set loose, and that people begin to cast off hardship and bitterness. They should not bring about an order that is bothersome, exacting, severe, and agitated. It is proper for them to make the crossing with great tolerance and uncomplicated ease, for this is what is fitting. In such a case, people will cherish them in their hearts, and be contented. This is why "there is profit in the southwest." Tang expelled the tyranny of Jie and brought about a tolerant order, while King Wu put to death the violence of Zhou and opposed the government of the Shang dynasty.[1] Both of them attended to tolerance and ease. "When there is no journey to make, its arrival and return will bring good fortune. When it has a long journey, being prompt will bring good fortune." "There is no journey to make": this signifies that the difficulties of the world have already been set loose and scattered, and so there is nothing left to do. "It has a long journey": this signifies that there is still an affair that it is proper to set loose. As for the states of the world, their precepts, doctrines, laws, and measures must first be neglected and disordered, and this will afterward give birth to affliction and distress. When sages have set loose the difficulties, there will be contentment and peace, and no affairs to manage. "There is no journey to make" refers to this. It is proper to be corrected and return to the way of order, to make the precepts and doctrines straightforward, to shed light on the laws and measures, and to advance and return to the order of the earlier dynasties and enlightened kings. "Its arrival and return" refers to this. It signifies a reversion to the straightforward principle, which is the world's good fortune. "Its" is here just a grammatical particle.[2] Since antiquity, when sages and kings saved people from difficulties and gave them determinacy rather than disorder, they began to act neither too slowly nor too hastily. When people were already contented and determinate, they enacted an order that could continue and succeed them. From the time of the Han dynasty on down, when disorder has already been expelled, no one turns to grasp what the sages enacted. They follow the moment temporarily, anchored and constrained by it, and that is all. This is why they are unable to bring about complete goodness and order. In fact, they do not recognize the meaning of "its arrival and return." "When it has a long journey, being prompt will bring good fortune": this signifies that there is still an affair that it is proper to set loose. If someone acts early enough, this will bring good fortune. If it is proper to set the affair loose, but it has not yet been exhausted, then it has not been driven out early enough, and it will return to abundance. When a state of affairs returns to life because no one acted early enough, it will step by step become great. This is why "being prompt will bring good fortune."

The *Judgment* says: "Loose: there are movement and an obstacle. If it moves, it will avoid the obstacle: Loose." The Pit trigram refers to an obstacle and the Shake trigram to movement: "There are movement and an obstacle." If there were no obstacle, then there would be no difficulty. If there were no movement, then no one could go out from the difficulty. When one moves and goes outside the obstacle, this is to "avoid the obstacle" and difficulty, and this is why these trigrams constitute the Loose hexagram. "'Loose: there is profit in the south-west': if a journey is made, it will make an acquisition of the crowd." Concerning the way of being set loose from a difficulty, there is profit in breadth, greatness, peace, and ease. Those who use tolerance and ease to make the journey, the crossing, and the setting loose, will acquire and wed themselves to the heart of the crowd. "'Its arrival and return will bring good fortune': it will acquire the center." The *Judgment* does not say "there is no journey to make," omitting this part of the text. To save something from disorder, and to expel a difficulty, are the affairs of a single moment. If one is not yet capable of bringing the way of order to completion, one must wait to be set loose from the difficulty, and so "there is no journey to make." Afterward, one will arrive at and return to the order of the first kings. This is to acquire the way of centrality, which signifies that one has aligned with what is fitting. "'When it has a long journey, being prompt will bring good fortune': a journey will accomplish something." If it has something to do, "being prompt will bring good fortune." If it is early enough, then it will make the journey and accomplish something. If it is slackened, the bad will thrive and its harm will be deep. "When heaven and earth are set loose, they produce the thunder and rain. When the thunder and rain are produced, the hundred fruits, grasses, and trees all break out of their shells. How great is the moment of the Loose hexagram!" The *Judgment* has already shed light on the way to place oneself in the Loose hexagram. Now it remarks that heaven and earth are set loose, so that the greatness in the moment of the Loose hexagram may be seen. When the heavenly *qi* and the earthly *qi* are opened up and scattered, they interact with and affect each other, and smoothly harmonize, which brings the thunder and rain to completion. "When the thunder and rain are produced," the ten thousand things are all born, revealed, and "break out of their shells." Heaven and earth complete their tasks because they have been set loose, and this is why it applauds the moment of the Loose hexagram as great. Those who are kings take the way of heaven as their law, act with tolerance and lenience, apply the influence of their kindness and favor, nourish and cultivate the million people, and reach even to the species of insects, grasses, and trees. They submit to the moment of the Loose hexagram, and align with the virtue of heaven and earth.

The *Symbol* says: "'Thunder and rain are produced': Loose. Noble people use it to pardon excess and to be lenient with crime." When heaven and earth are set loose and scattered, they bring the thunder and rain to completion. This is why the production of thunder and rain refers to the Loose hexagram. This statement is not the same as "the light twice produces a cast."[3] To pardon is to explain away, while to be lenient is to be tolerant. In cases of excess or loss there should be pardon, but if there is pardon for the criminal and bad, then one has not done one's duty. This is why there is lenience, and that is all. When noble people gaze on the symbol of thunder and rain produced and set loose, they give substance to its revelation and cultivation by applying the influence of their kindness and humaneness; they give substance to its being set loose and scattered by acting tolerantly and by explaining things away.

The initial "six" line: there is no blame. This "six" line occupies the initial position in the Loose hexagram. The moment of the Loose hexagram has put it in distress and difficulty, but it uses softness to occupy a firm position, and it uses *yin* to correspond to *yang*. As a result, it is a soft line that can also mean firmness. Since there are no distress and difficulty, it has placed itself so as to acquire what is fitting for both firmness and softness. The distress and difficulty have been set loose, it is contented and serene with no affairs to manage, and it places itself so as to acquire only what is fitting. As a result, "there is no blame." It is fitting for those who face the initial point of the Loose hexagram to restrain themselves and rest in contentment and tranquility. This idea is shown by the brevity of the line statement. **The *Symbol* says: "Firmness borders softness: it means that 'there is no blame.'"** The initial and fourth lines correspond to each other—that is, a firm and a soft line border and respond to each other. When firmness and softness border each other, they acquire what is fitting for them. Since the difficulty has been set loose, and they place themselves so that firmness and softness acquire what is fitting, "it means that 'there is no blame.'"

The second "nine" line: while in the field, it obtains three foxes. It acquires a yellow arrow. There are purity and good fortune. The second "nine" line uses *yang* firmness to acquire the power of centrality, it corresponds to the ruler or fifth "six" line above it, and it refers to those employed in the moment. There is constantly a crowd of small people in the world, but when rulers of firmness and enlightenment are above it, their enlightenment is sufficient to illuminate it, their authority is sufficient to trouble it, and their firmness is sufficient to decide for it. This is why small people do not dare to employ their inclinations, but they still constantly persist as a lesson or a warning. One must apprehend whether they have the space to do harm to the straightforward. The fifth "six" line uses *yin* softness to occupy the position of respect, and so its enlightenment is easily concealed, its authority is easily confronted, and its decisiveness bears no fruit and is easily bewildered. Any small person who draws near it will convert its heart. In a case where the difficulty is starting to be set loose and beginning to be set in order, the alteration is particularly easy. Since it is proper that the second line be employed, it necessarily requires the ability to drive out the small people, and then it will be able to make the heart of the ruler straightforward and put the way of firmness and centrality into action. The phrase "in the field" refers to an affair that drives out what is harmful, while "foxes" are crooked and flattering beasts. "Three foxes" points to the hexagram's third *yin* line, which refers to the small people of the moment. "Obtains" signifies that it can alter and transform or expel and drive them out, just like someone who obtains three foxes while in the field. If it obtains them, then it will acquire the way of centrality and straightness, it will become pure and straightforward, and there will be good fortune. "Yellow" refers to the color of centrality, and an "arrow" is something straight, so the "yellow arrow" signifies centrality and straightness. If the crooked group is not driven out, but finds an entry into the heart of the ruler, then no one will put the way of centrality and straightness into action. Such is the case of Huan and Jing, who did not drive out Wu Sansi.[4] **The Symbol says: "In the second 'nine' line, 'there are purity and good fortune': it acquires the way of centrality."** The phrase "purity and good fortune" signifies that "it acquires the way of centrality." Those who expel or drive out the crooked and bad will make the way of centrality and straightness to be put into action. As they become straightforward, there will be good fortune.

The third "six" line: those who carry are those who ride. They are brought to the point of reaching bandits. Purity brings dismay. The third "six" line is *yin* and soft, and it occupies the top position in the lower trigram. It is not placed in its own position, just like small people who ride in carriages even though it is fitting that they carry and haul them from below. Their place does not accord with them, but will necessarily bring itself "to the point of reaching bandits" or strife. Even if they do something straightforward, they should still be scorned and dismayed. When small people steal positions of abundance, even if they are exhorted to make their affairs straightforward, their *qi* and disposition are still humble and belong at the bottom. At root they are not things that belong above, and in the end they should be dismayed. Were they capable of great straightforwardness, what would the case be like? Response: *yin* softness is not capable of great straightforwardness. Were they capable of it, this would transform them into noble people. It is fitting that the third line or the small person of *yin* softness be at the bottom, but it has placed itself at the top of the lower trigram, just like small people who ride even though it is fitting that they carry. It is proper that it bring on the bandits or strife. If small people steal positions in the moment when the difficulty is set loose, they will in turn bring on the bandits. **The Symbol says: "'Those who carry are those who ride': it can still be uncouth. I**

myself bring on the weapons: who else could be blamed?" When the people who carry and haul are riding in the carriages, it should be considered uncouth and bad. If their place does not accord with them, and their virtue is not proportioned to their vessel, then they will bring on the bandits or "weapons." Since they themselves have chosen to provoke them, "who else could be blamed?" In his *Appended Statements*, the sage sheds further light on the way of bringing on the bandits, saying that "the authors of the *Book of Changes* knew about robbery!"[5] Robbery comes about because of a quarrel between riders. If they did not quarrel and break up, how could the robbers confront them? To carry the carriage is an affair for small people, while noble people ride in it as their vessel. Small people who ride in the vessel of noble people cannot be contented with anything. This is why robbers ride in on their quarrel and strive with them. When small people occupy the positions of noble people, they cannot be ready for anything. This is why, in their presumption and satisfaction, they will be lethargic and usurp those above, and be violent and invade those below. If robbers are around, they will ride in on their excess and badness, and attack them. To attack here simply means to give voice to their crimes, and robbers are those who reach the point of leveling them with violence. To treat the storehouse of one's resources and commodities lightly and lethargically is to teach or instruct the robbers, making them choose one. The young woman who appears tender and seductive is teaching or instructing the licentious, and making them do violence to her. Small people who ride in the vessel of noble people are provoking robbers and making them strive against them. All these significations of "I myself" are chosen by the *Symbol*.

The fourth "nine" line: it sets loose the big toe. Its friends are reached. They are trustworthy. The fourth "nine" line uses the power of *yang* firmness, it occupies a position in the upper trigram, it serves the ruler or fifth "six" line, and it refers to the great minister. It corresponds to the initial "six" or *yin* line below it. The "big toe," as something minimal and at the bottom, signifies the initial line. Since it occupies a position in the upper trigram and relates to small people, worthy people and straightforward scholars will retreat far away from it. If it ousts and drives out the small people, then the faction of the noble people will advance, and they will treat each other with sincerity. If the fourth line can set loose or drive out the *yin* softness of the initial "six" line, then the "friends" of noble people with their *yang* firmness will arrive or be "reached," and will align with them in their sincerity. If it does not set loose or drive out the small people, then it has not yet reached the point of being sincere in itself. How could it acquire other trustworthy people? The initial "six" line corresponds to it, and this is why what is set loose may be called far away. **The *Symbol* says: "'It sets loose the big toe': its position is not yet proper for it."** Although the fourth line is *yang* and firm, it nonetheless occupies a *yin* position, and one may wonder whether its straightforwardness is insufficient. Were it to relate and draw close to small people, it would necessarily lose its straightforwardness. This is why the line statement warns that it must set loose "the big toe." The noble people will be able to arrive only afterward, so that it has not yet placed itself in a position that is "proper for it." The Loose hexagram has the casting off of alignment as its root. This line must set loose the big toe, and afterward it will have friends who are trustworthy. In fact, when noble people interact, if small people appear in the space between them, this is because the noble people have not yet reached the point of sincerity.

The fifth "six" line: noble people alone are setting them loose. There is good fortune. They trust the small people. The fifth "six" line occupies the position of respect, it is the master of the Loose hexagram, and it refers to the ruler who sets others loose. The line statement is remarking on the communication of noble people. Those to whom noble people relate and draw close will necessarily also be noble people; those whom they set loose and drive out will necessarily be small people. This is why, if "noble people alone are setting them loose," then "there is good fortune." If small people are driven out, then noble people will advance. How could their good fortune be greater? The phrase "they trust" would be phrased by people of the times like this: "They see and evaluate." What they should evaluate is the small people. If the faction of small people is driven out, this is because noble people are able to set them loose. If small people are driven out, then noble people will themselves advance, they will themselves put the way of straightforwardness into action, and the world not will not need to be set in order. **The *Symbol* says: "'Noble people alone are setting them loose': small people retreat."** When noble people set something loose, it signifies that small people retreat and depart. If small people depart, then the way of noble people is put into action. As a result, there is good fortune.

The top "six" line: the duke is employed to shoot a falcon above the lofty battlement. He obtains it. Nothing is without profit. The top "six" line is on a lofty and respected terrain, but it is not the position of the ruler. This is why the line statement calls it a "duke," but it is remarking only on the one who sets things loose in the end. A "falcon" is a thing that preys on others and harms them, and it symbolizes the harmful small people. The "battlement" is the perimeter between those inside and outside the city wall. If the harm were done on the inside, this would not yet be the moment of setting it loose. If it were to go outside

the battlement, then there would be no harm at all. What could there be to set
loose? This is why it is above the battlement, when it has been cast off from the
inside but has not yet departed. It says "lofty" so that one may see the severity of
this defensive perimeter. What has not yet been driven out is at the top or limit
of the Loose hexagram. In the moment of the limit of the Loose hexagram, it
alone has not yet been set loose, which indicates the solidity and strength of its
harm. The top line occupies the limit position in the Loose hexagram, when
the way of setting loose is already extreme, and its tools are already complete.
This is why it is able to shoot and obtain it. Since it "obtains it," the distress of
the world is already set loose and exhausted. What could be "without profit"?
In his *Appended Statements*, Fuzi expands on this meaning, saying that "the
word 'falcon' refers to a game animal, the bow and arrows are tools, and it is a
person that shoots it. Noble people store their tools on their bodies, they wait for
the moment, and then they move. How could anything be 'without profit' for
them? Their movement is not tied to anything, and so they go out and obtain
something. It is saying that they only move when their tools are complete."[6] A
thing that preys on others and harms them is above the city wall. If they were
without their tools, or if they revealed them without waiting for the moment,
how could they obtain anything? The tools here are what one uses on the way
of setting things loose. The moment here is when it is proper that the affair be
set loose, and when the way of setting it loose has been reached. They move in
such a case, and this is why they are not tied or knotted to anything. When they
reveal their tools, nothing is without profit. To be tied or knotted to something
signifies to be hindered or hampered. In this passage, the sage reveals and sheds
light on the meaning of storing one's tools and waiting for the moment. As for
the action of one person reaching the affairs of the world, if he does not have his
tools and does not move using the moment, he will be tied up and choked by
small affairs and deficient and defeated in great affairs. Since antiquity, people
have been happy to do what does not complete their task or what upsets and
overturns it—both of them have these as their causes. **The *Symbol* says: "'The
duke is employed to shoot a falcon': he is upended, but sets it loose."** If it
reaches the end of the Loose hexagram without setting anything loose, it is
greatly "upended" and disordered. It shoots it, and so "sets it loose." If it is set
loose, then the world will be at peace.

41. TAKE (SUN 損)

The *Sequence of the Hexagrams* says: "To set loose is to slacken. What is slackened will necessarily lose something. This is why the Take hexagram is next." What is compliant or slackened will necessarily lose something. If it is lost, it has been taken away, and so the Take hexagram succeeds the Loose hexagram. As for the trigrams, the Calm trigram is above and the Joy trigram below. The substance of the mountain is lofty, while the substance of the lake is deep. The more one lowers what is deep, the more one adds to the loftiness above, which has the meaning of taking from what is below and adding to what is above. Further, the lake is at the bottom of the mountain. Its *qi* develops as it ascends and soaks into the grasses, trees, and a hundred other things—this is to take from what is below and add to what is above. Further, the lower trigram refers to joy or enjoyment. Its three lines each correspond to a line in the upper trigram— this is to enjoy honoring those above, which again has the meaning of taking from what is below and adding to what is above. Further, the Joy trigram below is a complete Joy trigram because of an alteration in the third "six" line, while the Calm trigram above is a complete Calm trigram because of an alteration in the top "nine" line. The root of the third line is firm, but it brings a soft line to completion; the root of the top line is soft, but it brings a firm line to completion. This again has the meaning of taking from what is below and adding to what is above. If something were taken from what is above and added to what is below, this would be the Add hexagram. Since something is chosen from what is below and added to what is above, it is the Take hexagram. In the case of people, when the influence and grace of those above are extended to those below, they are adding to them. When they choose something from those below so as to benefit themselves, they are taking from them. In the example of an earthen fortification, if one takes from its upper part so as to toughen and benefit its foundation and root, then its upper and lower parts will certainly be contented. How could this not be a case of addition? But if one chooses something from its lower part so as to increase the loftiness of its upper part, then the peril of a crash will be extreme. How could this not be a case of taking away? This is why the Take hexagram has the meaning of taking from what is below and adding to what is above, while the Add hexagram is the reverse of this.

Take: it is trustworthy. There are primacy and good fortune, and no blame. It may be pure. There is profit in a long journey. The *sun* character of "take" refers to decrease. In general, a taking away that restricts some excess so as to approach duty and principle is entirely on the way of the Take hexagram. Those who are on the way of the Take hexagram must be trustworthy and sincere, which signifies their extreme sincerity and submission to principle. If they submit to principle when taking away, there will be great goodness and good fortune. Those who neither exceed nor stray in their taking away "may be pure" and certain. They will act with constancy, and "there is profit" in any journey that they make. People sometimes take away too much, sometimes not enough, and sometimes they are inconstant.[1] None of these align with the straightforward principle, and so they are not trustworthy. If they are not trustworthy, there will be blame rather than good fortune. Those who cannot be on the way of purity will not be able to act. **What should be employed? Two tureens should be employed at the feast.** In the Take hexagram, one takes away the excess so as to approach the center. One takes away the superfluous branches so as to approach the root and reality. Sages consider serenity and thrift to be the root of ritual. This is why, when the judgment is revealing and shedding light on the meaning of the Take hexagram, it remarks on a feast and libation. In the ritual of a feast and libation, the pattern is extremely complicated. Nonetheless, sincerity and reverence are considered its root. There are many ceremonies and things to be perfected, and so people come to ornament this heart of sincerity and reverence. When their ornament exceeds their sincerity, they will become false. If they take away from their ornament, their sincerity will persist, and this is why the judgment says: "What should be employed? Two tureens should be employed at the feast." If the conjunction of two tureens should be employed at the feast and sacrifice, then the remarks of the judgment concern sincerity, and that is all. It remarks that sincerity constitutes the root. Harm to the world has no other cause than the victory of the branches. The roots of steep eaves and engraved panels are palaces and houses; the roots of pools filled with wine and forests of meat are eating and drinking; the roots of licentious brutality and savage cruelty are punishments and penalties; the roots of depleting soldiers and grievous war are campaigning and taking the field. In general, the roots of all excessive human desires lie in presenting nourishment. When they flow too far, they become harmful. The first kings controlled their root, which is the heavenly principle. Later generations flowed into the branches, which are human desires. The meaning of the Take hexagram is to take away from human desires so as to return to the heavenly principle, and that is all.

The *Judgment* says: "Take: there is taking from those below and adding to those above. Its way is to travel upward." What makes the Take hexagram to be the Take hexagram is the "taking from those below and adding to those above." Something is chosen from what is below and added to what is above, and this is why the *Judgment* says: "Its way is to travel upward." As for "taking from those above and adding to those below," this constitutes the Add hexagram, while "taking from those below and adding to those above" constitutes the Take hexagram. If one takes from the foundation and root so as to become lofty, how could this be called "adding"? **"If it takes something away, 'it is trustworthy. There are primacy and good fortune, and no blame. It may be pure. There is profit in a long journey.'"** The *Judgment* says that those who take things away with extreme sincerity will possess the primacy and good fortune of the four quoted sentences. They will exhaust what is good about the way of the Take hexagram. **"'What should be employed? Two tureens should be employed at the feast': this is the moment to which two tureens correspond. It is the moment for taking from firmness and adding to softness."** Fuzi gives a specific explanation of "what should be employed? Two tureens should be employed at the feast."[2] The hexagram judgment is straight and uncomplicated, signifying that it is proper to take away and drive out superfluous ornamentation. It is saying: how could this be employed, since two tureens should be used at the feast? That is, it is saying that one should benefit the root and take from the branches. Fuzi fears that later generations will not attain this—that is, they will not succeed in considering it proper to exhaust and drive out pattern and ornament. This is why he delineates it in his remarks. What has a root will necessarily also have branches; what has a reality will necessarily also have a pattern. None of the world's ten thousand affairs is otherwise: "What has no root cannot set itself up. What has no pattern cannot act."[3] Fathers and sons are the masters of kindness, and so they must also possess the substance of severity and submissiveness. Rulers and ministers are the masters of reverence, and so they must also possess the ceremonies of serving and responding. When ritual abdicates but persists on the inside, it is waiting for authority and ceremony, and afterward it will act. Respect and humility have their sequence, and there is no thing, color, or standard that should not be discriminated. Pattern and reality must agree with each other, and there should be no gap between them. When pattern has become victorious, and the branches have become superfluous, when their root is far away and they are deprived of reality, then one faces the moment of the Take hexagram. This is why the judgment asks what should be employed, and says that two tureens will be sufficient for making offerings with sincerity. This signifies that it is proper to busy oneself with reality and take away from one's ornamentation. Fuzi fears that people may become mired in these remarks, and this is why he turns to shed light on them, saying that it is proper to employ the disposition of two tureens according to the moment. One should not employ them when there is nothing on which to employ them. He is saying that it is wrong to take away from pattern and ornamentation when they are not yet excessive, or if the taking away reaches the point of excess and extremity. "It is the moment for taking from firmness and adding to softness," when firmness is excessive and softness is insufficient. The Take and Add hexagrams both take away from firmness and add to softness. They must submit to the moment in their action. It is wrong to take from or add to something when it is not the proper moment for it. **"Taking and adding, filling and emptying—they act in agreement with the moment."** Whether taking or adding, whether filling or emptying, one merely follows the moment, and that is all. To take away from the excessive and add to the insufficient, to fill what has become less and empty what has become full—"they act in agreement with the moment."

The *Symbol* says: **"Below the mountain is a lake: Take. Noble people use it to admonish wrath and obstruct desire."** "Below the mountain is a lake," whose *qi* develops, ascends, and soaks into it. It is just like deepening those below so as to increase one's loftiness. Both are symbols of taking away from those below. When noble people gaze on the symbol of the Take hexagram, they take away from themselves. Concerning the way of correcting oneself, it is proper to take away only wrath and desire. This is why they admonish or warn against their own wrath and anger, and they obstruct or choke off their own intentions and desires.

The initial "nine" line: when the affair has ceased, it makes a quick journey. There is no blame. It considers how to take from itself. The meaning of the Take hexagram is that something is taken from firmness and added to softness. That is, it is taken from the lower trigram and added to the upper trigram. The initial line uses *yang* firmness and corresponds to the fourth, while the fourth uses *yin* softness and occupies a position above—it depends on what the initial line adds to it. When those below add to those above, it is proper that they not consider what they take from themselves to be their own accomplishment. When they have added to those above and "the affair has ceased," they rapidly depart and do not occupy a position of accomplishment. As a result, "there is no blame." Were they to feast on the beauty of the completed task, they would not be taking from themselves and adding to those above. This is blameworthy for anyone on the way of those below. The *yin* softness of the fourth depends on the initial line, and this is why it listens to the initial line. It is proper that the initial line consider and measure what is fitting, taking from itself and adding to the other line. If it exceeds this point or does not extend itself far enough — neither of these is something it should do. **The *Symbol* says: "'When the affair has ceased, it makes a quick journey': it values the alignment of its tendencies."** The valuable is what is in a position above; what should be venerated and employed at the moment is the valuable. The initial line values the alignment of its tendencies with the higher line. When the fourth depends on the initial line, and the initial line adds to the fourth, there is the "alignment of its tendencies" with the higher line.

The second "nine" line: there is profit in purity. Taking the field brings misfortune. It does not take from but adds to it. The second line makes use of firmness and centrality, it faces a moment of firmness in the Take hexagram, it occupies a soft position in the enjoyment trigram substance, and it corresponds to the fifth "six" line or ruler of *yin* softness above it. Since it uses softness and enjoyment in corresponding to the higher line, it loses the virtues of firmness and centrality. This is why the line statement warns that profit lies in purity and straightforwardness. The phrase "taking the field" refers to acting. If it casts off its centrality, then it will lose its purity and straightforwardness, and there will be misfortune. If it guards its centrality, then it will be pure. "It does not take from but adds to it": if it "does not take from" its own firmness and purity, then it will be able to add to the higher line, and so it "adds to it." Were it to lose its firmness and purity by employing softness and enjoyment, this would be suitable and sufficient for it to take from itself, and that is all. It would not be taking from itself and adding to the higher line. As for the stupid people of the times, although they do not have crooked hearts, the only thing they know about loyalty is to drain their force in submission to those above. In fact, they do not know the meaning of "it does not take from but adds to it." **The *Symbol* says: "In the second 'nine' line, 'there is profit in purity': it makes centrality its tendency."** This "nine" line occupies the second position, which is not straightforward, and it places itself in the enjoyment trigram, which is not firm. It would be good for it to acquire centrality. Were it to guard the virtue of centrality, how could it not be good? How could it be at the center without also being straightforward? How could it be at the center and yet also be excessive? When the second line statement says that "there is profit in purity," it signifies that centrality is to be considered its tendency. If its tendency persists at the center, then it will make itself straightforward. In the great majority of cases, centrality carries more weight than straightforwardness. Those who are central will also be straightforward, but those who are straightforward will not necessarily be at the center.[4] Those who can guard their centrality will make an addition to those above.

The third "six" line: if three people act, one person will be taken away. If one person acts, a friend will be acquired. To take here refers to taking from what has a surplus, while to add refers to adding to what is insufficient. The phrase "three people" signifies the three *yang* lines of the lower trigram and the three *yin* lines of the upper trigram. Since the three *yang* lines have the same action, the third "nine" line is taken away and added to the upper trigram. Since the three *yin* lines have the same action, the top "six" line is taken away so as to become the third line: "If three people act, one person will be taken away." When the softness of the top line is changed to firmness, it is said to be taken away, but the line statement remarks only that this one line is decreased. Although the top and third lines correspond to each other at their root, because these two lines rise and fall to complete a single trigram each, they agree with the two lines in their new trigrams. The initial and the second line are both *yang*, while the fourth and the fifth are both *yin*. They draw close to each other because their virtues are the same. Since the third corresponds to the top line, and they agree with the two lines in their new trigrams, their tendencies are unqualified and in every case "a friend will be acquired." Although the third line is close to the fourth, they nonetheless belong to different trigram substances, the third corresponds to the top, and their actions are not the same. If there are three people, then one person is taken away, but if there is one person, then a friend is acquired. In fact, the world is never without duality. When unity and duality oppose and wait on each other, they constitute the root of birth and life. Three is a surplus, and so it is proper that one be taken away. This is the great meaning of the Take and Add hexagrams. In the *Appended Statements*, Fuzi goes further to exhaust this meaning, saying that "when heaven and earth interweave and tangle, the ten thousand things are transformed and distilled. When male and female combine their essences, the ten thousand things are transformed and born. The *Book of Changes* says: 'if three people act, one person will be taken away. If one person acts, a friend will be acquired.' It is remarking that unity will be brought about."⁵ The phrase "interweave and tangle" refers to a condition of profound interaction. When the heavenly and earthly *qi* have a profound inter-action, they give birth to the transformation and distillation of the ten thousand things. The word "distillation" signifies a concentrated benefit. Their benefit is concentrated, as though they had a single essence. When the male and female essence and *qi* interact and combine, they transform and give birth to the ten thousand things. It is only because their essence and distillation are unquali-fiedly one that they are able to give birth. There is one *yin* and one *yang*—how could there be three? This is why, if there are three, it is proper that one be taken away. It is remarking that an unqualified unity is brought about. In all the space between heaven and earth, it is proper that nothing exceed this taking and adding in its enlightenment and greatness. **The *Symbol* says: "'One person acts': if there are three, it is doubtful."** "One person acts" and one person is acquired—that is, "a friend will be acquired." Were three people to act, "it is doubtful" that they would agree. It is proper and according to principle that one of them depart or be taken away, so as to take away the surplus.

The fourth "six" line: it takes from its illness. If this is made to happen quickly, then it will possess happiness. There is no blame. The fourth line uses *yin* soft-ness to occupy a position in the upper trigram, and it corresponds to the *yang* firmness of the initial line. It corresponds to a firm line in the moment of the Take hexagram, and it can take from itself so that it may attend to *yang* firm-ness—that is, it takes from what is not good and attends to what is good. The fourth line adds to the initial line, taking from its softness and adding to the firm line, which is to take from what is not good. This is why the line statement says that "it takes from its illness." The *ji* character of "illness" here signifies a defect that is not good. If it takes away from what is not good, and this is made to happen "quickly" or rapidly, then it will "possess happiness" and "there is no blame." When something excessive is taken from people, their only distress is that it is not done rapidly. If it were done rapidly, they would not reach the point of a deep excess, and they could be happy. **The *Symbol* says: "'It takes from its illness': it can also be happy."** What makes it ill is taken away, and so it can certainly be happy. The *Symbol* says "also," which is just a particle of speech.

The fifth "six" line: sometimes ten friends add to it. None of the turtles is ca-pable of drawing back. There is primary good fortune. The fifth "six" line is in the moment of the Take hexagram, it uses centrality and submissiveness to oc-cupy the position of respect, and it empties its center so as to correspond to the *yang* firmness of the second line. It refers to rulers who can empty their centers and take from themselves so as to submit and attend to worthy people below them. If they can be like this, who in the world will not take from themselves and exhaust themselves so as to "add to it"? This is why, if there is sometimes the affair of adding to it, then "ten friends" will help it. The word "ten" indicates a crowd, and "turtles" are things that resolve right and wrong, or good and bad fortune. What the crowd discusses publicly will necessarily align with the straightforward principle, and even the "turtles" and yarrow stalks cannot draw back. A case like this may be called the good fortune of a great good. Someone of antiquity says that "those who skillfully attend to the crowd will align with the heart of heaven."[6] **The *Symbol* says: "In the fifth 'six' line, 'there is primary good fortune': there is sustenance from above."** The reason it acquires "primary good fortune" is that it can exhaust what the crowd of people sees and align with the principle of heaven and earth. This is why blessings and "sustenance" fall "from" heaven "above."

The top "nine" line: it does not take from but adds to it. There is no blame. There are purity and good fortune. There is profit in a long journey. It acquires a minister but not a family. The general meaning of the Take hexagram is threefold: to take one's self away and attend to other people; to take from oneself so as to add to other people; to put the way of the Take hexagram into action so as to take from other people. To take one's self away and attend to other people is to adapt to one's duty; to take from oneself so as to add to other people is to extend one's self to things; to put the way of the Take hexagram into action so as to take from other people is to put one's duty into action. Each of them has its moment, but the line statement chooses to remark only on the greatest of them. As for the fourth and fifth, taking one's self away and attending to other people was chosen for these two lines. For the three lines of the lower trigram substance, taking from oneself so as to add to other people was chosen. The function of the moment of the Take hexagram is to put the way of taking into action so as to take what it is proper to take from the world. In the case of the top "nine" line, the meaning of putting the Take hexagram into action was not chosen. This "nine" line occupies the end position in the Take hexagram, it is at the limit of the taking away, and it is in the proper position for alteration. It uses *yang* firmness to occupy the top position. Were it to employ firmness to take from or pare down the lines below it, then it would not be on the way of those above and its blame would be great. Since it does not put the Take hexagram into action, but alters and uses the way of *yang* firmness to add to the lines below, then "there is no blame" and it acquires both straightforwardness and good fortune. In a case like this, it is fitting that it make the journey. If it makes the journey, then it will add to them. If those above do not take from those below, but are able to add to them, who in the world will not obey and attend to them? The crowd of those who obey and attend has neither inside nor outside, and this is why it says that it "acquires a minister but not a family." The phrase "acquires a minister" signifies that it acquires the hearts of people who wed themselves and are obedient to it, and "not a family" signifies that there is no boundary between near and far or inside and outside. **The *Symbol* says: "'It does not take from but adds to it': it acquires the great object of its tendencies."** It occupies the top position, and it does not take from those below, but adds to them. Such are the noble people who acquire "the great object" by putting their tendencies into action. The sole tendency of noble people is to add to other people, and that is all.

42. ADD (*YI* 益)

The *Sequence of the Hexagrams* says: "If something is ceaselessly taken away, it must also be added back. This is why the Add hexagram is next." Abundance and scarcity, taking from and adding to, are like tracing a circle. When something has been taken away to its limit, it must be added back. This is a spontaneous principle, and so the Add hexagram succeeds the Take hexagram. As for the trigrams, the Low trigram is above and the Shake trigram below. Thunder and wind are two things that add to each other. When the wind is relentless, there will be sudden thunder; when the thunder is terrible, there will be angry wind.[1] The two help out and add to each other, and so they constitute the Add hexagram. These remarks concern the trigram symbols. But the two trigrams, Low and Shake, are both brought to completion by an alteration in the bottom line. When the *yang* line alters and becomes *yin*, it results in the Take hexagram. When the *yin* line alters and becomes *yang*, it results in the Add hexagram. A line is taken from the upper trigram and added to the lower trigram. It is taken from what is above and added to what is below, and so this alteration constitutes the Add hexagram. These remarks concern the meaning of the hexagram. If those below are benefited, then those above will be contented, and this is why an addition to those below constitutes the Add hexagram.

Add: there is profit in a long journey. There is profit in traversing a great stream. In the Add hexagram, one adds to the way of the world, and this is why "there is profit in a long journey." Concerning the way of the Add hexagram, one must cross through obstacles and difficulties, and so "there is profit in traversing a great stream."

The *Judgment* says: "Add: there is taking from those above and adding to those below. The people enjoy it without boundaries. Those above are

descending below. Their way is great and bright." The *Judgment* is remarking on both the meaning of the hexagram and the powers of the trigrams. This
is the Add hexagram because "there is taking from those above and adding to
those below." If "there is taking from those above and adding to those below,"
then there will be no boundary to the people's enjoyment, which signifies that
it is neither depleted nor at its limit. When those above diminish themselves
and descend to those below, the greatness and brightness of their way will be
clear. A *yang* line has descended to occupy the initial position, while a *yin* line
has ascended to occupy the fourth position, which means that "those above
are descending below." "**'There is profit in a long journey': in centrality and
straightforwardness, there is delight.**" The fifth line uses *yang* firmness, centrality, and straightforwardness to occupy the position of respect, and the second
line corresponds to it with centrality and straightforwardness. As a result, the
way of centrality and straightforwardness is added to the world, and the world
receives its blessing and delight. "**'There is profit in traversing a great stream':
the way of the tree is to act.**" When the way of the Add hexagram is within the
borders of peace and constancy, when there are no affairs to manage, it makes
an addition that is somewhat small. When it faces hardship, peril, obstacles,
and difficulties, then what it adds is extremely great, and this is why "there is
profit in traversing a great stream." Crossing through hardships and obstacles
is the moment when the way of the Add hexagram is greatly put into action.
The character for "Add" here has erroneously been made into "tree." Perhaps
someone thought that, because the Low trigram is above and the Shake trigram
below, the *Judgment* says "the way of the tree," but this is wrong. "**Add: there
are movement and lowliness. It advances daily without boundaries.**" Further,
the *Judgment* uses the two trigram substances to remark on the powers of the
trigrams. The lower trigram refers to movement and the upper trigram to lowliness: "There are movement and lowliness." If the movement on the way of the
Add hexagram is lowly and submissive to principle, then its addition "advances
daily" and its breadth will be great, having no boundary or perimeter. If its
movement were not submissive to principle, how could it bring any great addition to completion? "**Heaven sheds its influence and the earth gives life. Its addition is without a region.**" Using the accomplishments of heaven and earth,
the *Judgment* remarks on the greatness in the way of the Add hexagram. Sages
give it substance so that they can add to the world. The way of heaven supplies
the beginning, and the way of earth gives life to things. "Heaven sheds its influence and the earth gives life": they transform and cultivate the ten thousand
things. "Each makes its nature and mandate straightforward," and "its addition"
may be said to be "without a region." A region is where something is. Those

who have regions will also have calculated their perimeters. The phrase "without a region" signifies that one is broad and great, without depletion or limit. How could the addition made by heaven and earth to the ten thousand things be depleted or have a border? **"In general, concerning the way of the Add hexagram, it acts in accordance with the moment."** The addition made by heaven and earth is not depleted because it is principle, and that is all. When sages bring profit and addition to the way of the world, they correspond to the moment and submit to principle. They align with heaven and earth, and act "in accordance with the moment."

The *Symbol* says: "There are wind and thunder: Add. When noble people use it to see something good, they relocate to it. When there is excess, they modify themselves." When the wind is relentless, there will be sudden thunder; when the thunder is terrible, there will be angry wind. These are two things that add to each other. When noble people gaze on the symbol of wind and thunder adding to each other, they seek to add to themselves. Concerning the way of the Add hexagram, nothing is like seeing the good and relocating to it, or modifying oneself when there is excess. If they see the good and can relocate to it, they can exhaust the goodness of the world. If they can modify themselves when there is excess, there will be no excess. Such an addition to a person is greater than any other.

The initial "nine" line: there is profit in employing deeds and producing great things. There are primacy and good fortune. There is no blame. The initial "nine" line is the master of the Shake or movement trigram and has an abundance of *yang* firmness. It occupies a moment in the Add hexagram, and its power is sufficient for adding to things. Although it occupies the very bottom, it corresponds to the great minister or fourth "six" line above it. The fourth line is the master of the Low or submission trigram, and is capable of both lowliness toward the ruler above it and submission to the powers of worthy people below it. The bottom line cannot do anything, but since it corresponds and attends to the higher line, it is fitting that it assist the higher line with its way. It produces a great addition to the affairs of the world: "There is profit in employing deeds and producing great things." It occupies a position below and is employed by those above to put its tendencies into action. Because of its deeds, there must necessarily be a great good and good fortune, and so there will be neither excess nor blame. If it is incapable of "primacy and good fortune," then not only will it have its own share of blame, but it will burden those above, and so those above will also be blamed. Since it is at the very bottom and faces a great command, a small good will not be of sufficient heft. This is why there must be primacy and good fortune, and afterward there will be no blame. **The *Symbol* says: "'There are primacy and good fortune. There is no blame': those below do not have beneficial affairs."** At root, it is not proper for those below to place themselves so as to have beneficial affairs. The phrase "beneficial affairs" refers to affairs of weight and greatness. If those above give it command, so that it faces great affairs, it must be able to cross through the great affairs and bring about primacy and good fortune, which is to be without blame. If it can bring about primacy and good fortune, then those above have given it command from their knowledge of people. It is proper that it be victorious in its command. If such is not the case, then those above and below will both be blamed.

The second "six" line: sometimes ten friends add to it. None of the turtles is capable of drawing back. Endless purity brings good fortune. The king employs a feast for the lord. There is good fortune. The second "six" line is placed with centrality and straightforwardness and its trigram substance is soft and submissive, which symbolizes the possession of an empty center. When people place themselves on the way of centrality and straightforwardness, they seek to add to it by emptying their centers. If they can submit and attend to the world, who would not aspire to inform them and add to them? Mencius says: "When officials prefer what is good, then everyone between the four seas will come, treating a thousand miles as a light distance, to inform them about what is good."[2] If the officials are satiated, they will receive nothing, but if they are empty, then things will come to them—this is a spontaneous principle. This is why, if there is "sometimes" an affair to which it may make an addition, then a crowd of "friends" will help and "add to it." The number ten refers to a crowd. What the crowd takes to be right is extremely proper to principle. The word "turtles" refers to a prognostication of good and bad fortune, which distinguishes what is right and wrong in things. The line statement is remarking that, when something is extremely right, the turtles cannot draw back. "Endless purity brings good fortune": it is remarking on the power of the second "six" line. The second line is central and straightforward, its center is empty, and it refers to those who can acquire the addition of a crowd of people. Nonetheless, its root or disposition is *yin* and soft. This is why it is warned about constant and endless purity and certainty, so that there will be good fortune. If those on the way of seeking addition do not possess endless purity, how can they keep guard over themselves? In the fifth "six" line of the Take hexagram, there are "ten friends," "turtles," "primacy," and "good fortune." In fact, that line occupies the position of respect and takes away from itself. It corresponds to the firm line below it, and it uses softness to occupy a firm position. Softness here constitutes emptiness and receptivity, while firmness constitutes certainty and the guarding of oneself. This is the best one can do when seeking addition, and this is why there are primacy and good fortune. The second "six" line's center is empty, and it seeks addition, but it also corresponds to a line that is *yang* and firm, and it uses softness to occupy a soft position. One may wonder whether its addition is not yet certain. This is why it is warned to be capable of constant and endless purity and certainty, and then there will be good fortune. "The king employs a feast for the lord. There is good fortune": since the second line has an empty center and is capable of endless purity, if it employs a feast for the lord, it is proper that it obtain good fortune. In cases where it agrees with other people or responds to things, will the intention of this statement not be developed? If it seeks an addition from other people, will they not correspond to it? Sacrifices to heaven are an affair for the son of heaven, and this is why it says that the king employs them. **The *Symbol* says: "'Sometimes ten friends add to it': they arrive from the outside."** If it is already central and straightforward, with an empty center, and can receive what is good from the world while guarding itself with certainty, then it will possess the affair of adding to itself. A crowd of people "arrive from the outside" and add to it. Someone says: if they arrive from the outside, how could this not signify the fifth line? Response: since the second line is central and straightforward, with an empty center, who in the world would not aspire to add to it? It corresponds straightforwardly to the fifth line, which certainly has something at its center.

The third "six" line: in adding to itself, it is employed in an affair of misfortune. There is no blame. It is trustworthy. It acts with centrality. It informs the duke by employing the seal. The third line occupies the top position in the lower trigram and refers to those who are above the people, and who keep guard over the decrees. It occupies a *yang* position, corresponds to a firm line, places itself at the limit of the movement trigram, occupies a position above the people, is firm in its resolution, and has addition as its purpose. If addition is its purpose and "it is employed in an affair of misfortune," then "there is no blame." The phrase "affair of misfortune" signifies an affair of extraordinary distress and difficulty. Since the third line occupies the top position in the lower trigram, and it is proper for those below to serve and report to those above, how could it give itself command and poach the addition for itself? Only in an affair of extraordinary distress and difficulty should it calculate what is fitting and correspond to it in the end. Then it will be aroused without being concerned for its own body, and will use its force to protect the people. This is why there is no blame. When those below give themselves unqualified command, those above

will necessarily make themselves ill with jealousy. Although it uses its duty in
what it does to face misfortune and difficulty, it must nonetheless be trustworthy and sincere, and align with the way of centrality in what it does. Then its
sincere intentions will be communicated to those above, and those above will
believe in and agree with it. To do something unqualified without the extreme
sincerity of doing it for those above or out of love for the people—this should
certainly not be done. Although it may possess sincere intentions, to do something without aligning with the action of centrality—this should also not be
done. The word "seal" refers to a thing that communicates one's believability.
As the *Book of Rites* says, "great officials hold the seal, which makes explicit
that they are to be believed."[3] In the sacrifices and libations of the court and
of wedlock, one generally employs a jade seal, which communicates that one
has attained sincerity and believability. Those who possess sincerity and trustworthiness by acquiring the way of centrality will be able to make those above
to believe in them—this is like the case where it "informs the duke" or those
above "by employing" the jade "seal." Its trustworthiness is able to communicate with and attain those above. When those below are on the way of doing
something, it is certainly proper that they be trustworthy and act with centrality.
Further, the third line is *yin* and without centrality, and this is why the line
statement reveals this meaning. Someone says: since the third line is *yin* and
soft, how will it acquire firmness of purpose and command over affairs as its
meaning? Response: although the root and disposition of the third line is *yin*,
it nonetheless occupies a *yang* position—that is, it places itself with firmness.
It also corresponds to a firm line, and so it tends toward firmness. It occupies
the limit position in the movement trigram, and so there is firmness of purpose
in its action. How could it be without firmness of purpose when it acts to add
something in this case? The *Book of Changes* considers what will bring victory
here as its meaning, and this is why it does not discuss the root and disposition
of the line. **The *Symbol* says: "'In adding to itself, it is employed in an affair
of misfortune': it will certainly possess it."** The third "six" line is the only one
in the Add hexagram that, should it be "employed in an affair of misfortune,"
will possess it with certainty. This signifies that it gives itself command over the
affair with unqualified certainty. It is proper that those who occupy positions below report to and serve those above. If they have unqualified command over an
affair, they should do nothing but save the people from misfortune and disaster,
and rescue them from the hardship and agitation of the moment. They place
themselves with the aptitude and fitness to be a cause of alteration in their hardship and agitation, and this is why they acquire no blame. Were this a moment
of peace, they should not do it.

The fourth "six" line: if it acts with centrality, it will inform the duke and he will attend to it. There is profit in being employed as someone reliable. It relocates the state. The fourth line faces the moment of the Add hexagram, it places itself in a position near the ruler, it occupies a straightforward position, it uses softness and lowliness to assist those above, and it submits and corresponds to the *yang* firmness of the initial line below it. In a case like this, it can make an addition to those above. And yet it places itself without acquiring centrality, and further, it corresponds to a line that is not central, which indicates that its centrality is not sufficient. This is why the line statement says that if its action acquires the way of centrality, then it will be able to make an addition to the rulers above it. It will inform those above and they will believe in and attend to it. It uses a trigram substance that is soft and lowly, and it does not wield it with any special firmness. This is why "there is profit in being employed as someone reliable." To relocate the state as someone reliable is to be relied or depended on by those above. The phrase "relocate the state" refers to movement with submission to those below. It relies on a ruler of firmness and centrality above it, and brings about an addition to it; it submits to the power of *yang* firmness below it so as to put its affairs into action: "There is profit in being employed" like this. Since antiquity, when the people of states and districts are not contented with the positions they occupy, they relocate. To relocate the state is to move with submission to those below. **The *Symbol* says: "'It will inform the duke and he will attend to it': its tendency is to add."** The line statement says only that if it acquires the action of centrality, then it will inform the duke and he will obtain or attend to it. The *Symbol* sheds light on this by saying that when it informs the duke and he obtains or attends to it, it is informing him out of a tendency to add to the world. If its tendency is to add to the world, those above must believe in and attend to it. When it manages the affairs of rulers, it will not be distressed if those above do not attend to it, but it will be distressed if its tendency is not sincere.

The fifth "nine" line: it is trustworthy. Its heart is favorable. No one asks about it. There are primacy and good fortune. It is trustworthy. My virtue is favorable. The fifth line occupies the position of respect with *yang* firmness, centrality, and straightforwardness. Further, it corresponds to the second "six" line with centrality and straightforwardness, and it puts its addition into action—how could there be no profit in this? It makes use of *yang* fullness at its center, which is the symbol of trustworthiness. It makes use of the virtue, power, and position of the fifth "nine" line, and its center or heart is extremely sincere. When it favors or adds to things, its extreme goodness and great good fortune should be recognized without asking about it. This is why the line state-ment says: "No one asks about it. There are primacy and good fortune." People who rule occupy positions that acquire and bring things about; they wield an aptitude that may bring things about. Were they to add to the world with their extreme sincerity, the world would receive great blessings, and its "primacy and good fortune" would not be just borrowed words. "It is trustworthy. My virtue is favorable": when people who rule add to the world with their extreme sincer-ity, no one in the world will be without extreme sincerity, love, and adoration, considering the virtue and grace of the rulers to be kindness and favor. **The Symbol says: "'It is trustworthy. Its heart is favorable': 'no one asks about it.' 'My virtue is favorable': it acquires the great object of its tendencies."** When people who rule possess a heart that is extremely sincere, favorable, and that adds to the world, their primacy and good fortune are not just borrowed words. This is why the *Symbol* says that "no one asks about it." When the world is extremely sincere and cherishes "my virtue" as something "favorable"—this is for its way to be put greatly into action, and for the tendencies of the ruler to acquire something.

The top "nine" line: it does not add to it but sometimes strikes it. Its heart is not set up to last. There is misfortune. The top line occupies a terrain with-out a position and refers to those who do not act so as to add to people. It uses firmness to place itself at the limit of the Add hexagram and refers to those at the extreme of seeking addition. It corresponds to a *yin* line and refers to those who choose to add nothing good to themselves. The crowd of people is all the same in desiring profit. Their unqualified desire to add to themselves does great harm. If their desire is extreme, they will darken and conceal themselves, forgetting duty and principle. At the limit of their search there will be invasion and strife, bringing about hostility and hatred. This is why Fuzi says: "Those whose actions surrender themselves to profit will often bring about hatred."[4] And Mencius says: "Those who put profit first will not be sated without strife."[5] Such is the deep warning of sages and worthies. This "nine" line uses firm-ness at the limit of seeking addition. The crowd of people shares in detesting it, and this is why "it does not add to it but sometimes" assaults or "strikes it." "Its heart is not set up to last. There is misfortune": the sage warns people that their hearts should not persist in unqualified profit, saying that not to last like this is the way of misfortune. It is proper to modify it quickly. **The Symbol says: "'It does not add to it': its statements are partial. 'But sometimes strikes it': it comes from the outside."** Principle is the most public thing in the world, while profit is what the crowd of people is the same in desiring. Were it to make its heart public, it would not lose its straightforward principle, it would agree with the crowd, and their profit would be the same. If people were not invaded by it, then they would also desire agreement with it. But if it is cut off from them by its preference for profit, concealed by its own private things, and seeking to add to itself by taking from other people, then people will also agree with it in forceful contention. This is why no one is willing to "add to it," but everyone strives against it and "strikes it." The *Symbol* says that "it does not add to it" indicates that "its statements" are not for others but "partial" to itself. If it were not partial to itself but aligned with the public way, then other people would also add to it. Why would they strike it? Since it has reached the extreme limit of seeking addition from other people, they all detest it and want to assault it. This is why the phrase "it strikes it" indicates that "it comes from the outside." When people are good, everyone outside them will correspond to them, even if they are a thousand miles away. This is the case of the second "six" line, which is central, straightforward, and empties itself, and those who add to it come from the outside. If it were not good, everyone outside it would draw back from it, as far as a thousand miles away. This is the case of the top "nine" line, which is at the limit of seeking addition, and those who strike it come from the outside. The *Appended Statements* says: "Noble people make themselves contented before they move; they set their hearts at ease before they speak; they make their interactions with others determinate before seeking anything from them. Noble people make themselves correct on these three points, and this is why they are whole. If their movement brings peril, the people will not agree with them; if their speech brings trouble, the people will not correspond to them; if they do not interact with those from whom they seek something, the people will not agree with them. If no one agrees with them, they will reach the point of injury. The *Book of Changes* says 'it does not add to it, but sometimes strikes it. Its heart is not set up to last. There is misfortune.'"[6] Noble people make use of this way in everything they do, whether it be their remarks, movement, or seeking, and so their goodness is intact. If such were not the case, they would be choosing injury and there would be misfortune.

43. SOLVE (*GUAI* 夬)

The *Sequence of the Hexagrams* says: "If something ceaselessly adds to itself, it will necessarily be dissolved. This is why the Solve hexagram is next. The Solve hexagram refers to dissolution." When something reaches the limit of adding to itself, it will necessarily be dissolved, and afterward stop. There is no principle of constant addition. "If something ceaselessly adds to itself," it must also cease, which is to dissolve. And so the Solve hexagram succeeds the Add hexagram. As for the trigrams, the Joy trigram is above and the Lead trigram below. Concerning the two trigram substances, one may remark that a lake is a gathering of waters. Here it ascends to a place of extreme loftiness, which symbolizes diffusion and dissolution. Concerning the lines, one may remark that the five *yang* lines below are growing and about to reach their limit. The single *yin* line above is disappearing and about to exhaust itself. The crowd of *yang* lines advances upward. It dissolves and drives out the single *yin* line, and so they constitute the Solve hexagram. The Solve hexagram has as its meaning a firmness that dissolves. The crowd of *yang* lines advances to dissolve and drive out the single *yin* line. It is the moment when the way of noble people grows, while small people are disappearing, becoming scarce, and about to exhaust themselves.

Solve: it discloses it in the king's court. The call is trustworthy, but there is danger. At the moment when small people are starting to become abundant, the way of noble people is not yet victorious. How could they clarify and use the way of straightforwardness to dissolve and drive them out? This is why they enclose themselves in obscurity and await their moment. Step by step, they plan out a way to make them disappear. At present, when the small people have already become scarce and minimal, and the way of noble people is abundant, it is proper for them to clarify it and put it into action in the public court. People will become enlightened, and recognize what is good and what is bad. This is why the judgment says: "It discloses it in the king's court." To be trustworthy is to be believable at one's center—to make one's intentions sincere—and the word "call" refers to a mandate given to the crowd. Although the way of noble people is growing abundant, they do not dare forget to perfect a warning. This is why they are extremely sincere in giving the mandate to the crowd, so that it will recognize and value the way when there is peril. Although they are becoming extremely abundant, while the dissolution of the others has made them extremely scarce, if the former are at ease and unperfected, they will regret their "absence of deliberation."[1] This is to value the principle when there is peril. Their hearts must be warned and troubled, and then they will be without distress. The intention of the warning provided by the sage is deep. **It informs its own district. There is no profit in approaching weapons. There is profit in a long journey.** Noble people bring order to what is not good in small people. To be victorious over it and to reform it, they must use the way of their own goodness. This is why the sages who put disorder to death must first correct themselves. This was the case for Shun when he "promulgated pattern and virtue."[2] The *yi* character of "district" refers to what is private. "It informs its own district": this indicates that it sets itself in order first. It uses the abundant crowd of *yang* lines to dissolve the single *yin* line. It has a surplus of force and certainty, but it should not bring its firmness to the limit and reach the point of great excess. If it becomes greatly excessive, it will be like the bandits of the Blind hexagram's top "nine" line. The use of weapons and soldiers is an affair for the strong and warlike. "There is no profit in approaching weapons": this signifies that it is not fitting to value the mighty and warlike. The word "approaching" refers to attending to something. Those who attend to their weapons value the warlike. "There is profit in a long journey": although the *yang* lines are abundant, they have not yet reached their limit at the top of the hexagram. Although the *yin* line is minimal, it is still present, and has not yet been driven out. This is a case where small people still persist, and the way of noble people is not yet extreme. This is why it is fitting to advance and make a journey. Not valuing the firm and warlike, while adding to and advancing in one's way—this is how to be good in the Solve hexagram.

The *Judgment* says: "To solve is to dissolve. Firmness dissolves softness. There are vigor and enjoyment, resolution and harmony." The Solve hexagram has the meaning of dissolution. The five *yang* lines are dissolving the single *yin* line at the top. "There are vigor and enjoyment, resolution and harmony": the *Judgment* uses the two trigram substances to remark on the powers of the trigrams.

The lower trigram refers to vigor and the upper to enjoyment—this is to be vigorous and capable of enjoyment, to be resolved and capable of harmony, which is the best one can do in the Solve hexagram. The enjoyment of the Joy trigram refers to harmony. "'**It discloses it in the king's court': softness rides the five firm lines.**" Although softness is disappearing, it nonetheless occupies a position above five firm lines, as though to symbolize riding and usurping. It is *yin* and it is riding on *yang*, which is to have no principle at all. Since the propensities of noble people are already sufficient to drive it out, it is proper to make clear and disclose its crimes in the great hall of the king's court, so that the crowd will recognize what is good and what is bad. "'**The call is trustworthy, but there is danger': when in peril, it is bright.**" To be exhaustively sincere and believable when giving the mandate to the crowd, and to know how to be imperiled and troubled—this is the way of noble people. It has nothing to deliberate about, and is bright and great. "'**It informs its own district. There is no profit in approaching weapons': what it values is depleted.**" It is proper first to set oneself in order. It is not fitting to put unqualified value on the firm and warlike. What those who approach weapons value will reach the point of being limited and depleted. In the moment of the Solve hexagram, "what it values" signifies the firm and warlike. "'**There is profit in a long journey': firmness is growing and coming to its end.**" Although *yang* firmness is abundant, its growth has not yet come to its end. There is still the one *yin* line, and it is proper to dissolve and drive it out. The way of the noble people will then be uniform and one, and no harm will come to it. This is the end toward which firmness is growing.

The *Symbol* says: "**The lake ascends to heaven: Solve. Noble people use it to extend the influence of their wages to those below. If they occupy positions of virtue, they will be jealous.**" A lake is a gathering of waters. Here it "ascends to heaven," a place of extreme loftiness, and this is why it symbolizes the Solve hexagram. When noble people gaze on the symbol of a lake that is dissolved in its ascent, and that is concentrated and condensed in its descent, they "extend the influence of their wages to those below." This signifies that the influence of their wages is extended like a lake to those below. When they gaze on the symbol of dissolution and diffusion, "if they occupy positions of virtue, they will be jealous." To occupy a position of virtue signifies that they are contented when placed in virtue, and have joined themselves to it. To be jealous is to defend, and signifies that, having joined themselves to it, they set up defenses and prohibitions. If they have defenses and prohibitions, they will not be diffused and scattered. Wang Bi makes "jealous" into "enlightened and jealous," and also "developing."[3] But the *Symbol* does not say that the lake is above heaven. It says only that "the lake ascends to heaven." If it ascends to heaven, then it does not intend to reach contentment but has the propensity to dissolve and diffuse. If it had said that it is above heaven, this statement would indicate contentment.

The initial "nine" line: there is might in the toes that go ahead. A journey without victory is blamed. The "nine" line is *yang* and belongs to the Lead trigram substance. It is a firm and vigorous thing at the top, but here it is at the bottom, occupying a moment of resolution, and refers to those who advance ahead because of their might. The phrase "toes that go ahead" signifies that its act is to advance. When people resolve to act, if their action is fitting, then their resolution is like this; if their journey is not fitting, then their resolution is excessive. This is why "a journey without victory is blamed." Those who make journeys in the moment of the Solve hexagram will make resolute journeys. This is why the line statement remarks on carrying the victory. It is a "nine" line, it occupies the initial position, it is mighty in its advance, and it refers to those who move restlessly. This is why there is the warning about being "without victory." Although the *yin* line is about to exhaust itself, its own movement is restless. It is fittingly blamed for being without victory, since it has not accounted for the other line. **The *Symbol* says: "'Without victory,' it makes a journey: there is blame."** When people act, they must measure whether a state of affairs may be brought about, and only afterward resolve on it. Then they will be without excess. If there is no principle by which they can be victorious, yet they make the journey anyway, their blame should be recognized. In general, when "there is blame" for actions, it is because someone was excessively resolved on them.

The second "nine" line: it is careful and calls out. In the evening, there are weapons but no anxiety. In the Solve hexagram, the moment when the *yang* lines are dissolving the *yin* line and noble people are dissolving small people, they should not forget to perfect its warning. In the moment when the growth of *yang* is about to reach its limit, the second line is placed at the center and occupies a soft position. It is not excessively firm, and it is capable of knowing how to perfect the warning, which is the best one can do when placed in the Solve hexagram. It cherishes its alarm and care on the inside, and it gives a severe reproof or call on the outside. Although "in the evening" there are the "weapons" of soldiers, there should still be "no anxiety." **The *Symbol* says: "'There are weapons but no anxiety': it acquires the way of centrality."** "In the evening" there are the "weapons" of soldiers, and so it should be extremely troubled. It should, nonetheless, be without anxiety, because it has placed itself well. It has acquired "the way of centrality," and further, it knows how to be careful and troubled, and it has perfected the warning. How could the affair be sufficient to make it anxious? When a "nine" line occupies the second position, it will not be straightforward even though it has acquired centrality, so how could it be considered to be in the best position? Response: the *yang* lines are dissolving the *yin* line and noble people are dissolving small people. Since it has acquired centrality, how could it not be straightforward? To recognize the moment and understand its propensities—this is the great rule for studying the *Book of Changes*.

The third "nine" line: there is might in the malars, and misfortune. Noble people solve, and solve again. If it acts alone, it encounters rain and seems to glisten with frustration. There is no blame. This line statement has strayed into error. Duke Hu of Anding has modified the text to say: "There is might in the malars, and misfortune. If it acts alone, it encounters rain and seems to glisten with frustration. Noble people solve, and solve again. There is no blame."[4] One should not be contented with this. It is proper for it to say: "There is might in the malars, and misfortune. If it acts alone, it encounters rain. Noble people solve, and solve again. It seems to glisten with frustration. There is no blame."[5] The Solve or resolve hexagram refers to a moment when firmness and vigor are valued. The third line occupies the top position in the lower trigram substance, and further, is placed at the limit of the vigor trigram substance. It refers to those who are firm and purposeful in their resolve. The word "malars" refers to the cheekbones, which are at the top, but not yet at the upper limit. The third line occupies the top position in the lower trigram substance. Although it is at the top, it is not yet at the very top. There is a ruler above it, but it delegates command to its own firm resolution: "There is might in the malars," and it is on the way of "misfortune." "If it acts alone, it encounters rain": the third line corresponds straightforwardly to the top "six" line. In the moment when the group of *yang* lines shares in starting to dissolve the single *yin* line, the third line corresponds to it in private. This is why "it acts alone" and does not agree with the crowd of lines that are the same as it. It agrees with the top "six" line, with the result that *yin* and *yang* harmonize and align, and this is why it says that "it encounters rain." When there are remarks on rain in the *Book of Changes*, it always signifies that *yin* and *yang* are in harmony. It is the moment when the way of noble people is growing, and is dissolving and driving out the small people. This line alone agrees and harmonizes with them, and its wrongness should be recognized. Only noble people placed in such a moment will be able to "solve, and solve again," which signifies that they solve their own solution. That is, they are purposeful and resolved on their decision. Although the third agrees with the top line in private, it is proper for it to go far from it, and to sever it. Were the other line to see it as glistening with corruption, it would take on a countenance of frustration and disgust. When the case is like this, there will be no excess or blame. Since the third line belongs to the vigor trigram substance and is placed in a straightforward position, it will not necessarily lose itself like this. And so, its meaning is to be considered simply as a teaching. The text of the line statement became erroneously tangled because there are the phrases "it encounters rain" and "it seems to glisten," and this is why someone erroneously considered them to be linked.[6] **The *Symbol* says: "'Noble people solve, and solve again': in the end there is no blame."** When one is guided and manacled by a private preference, this is because one has no resolution. Noble people agree and draw close to others out of duty, and so their resolutions are the proper resolutions. This is why, in the end, they do not reach the point of being blamed.

The fourth "nine" line: the buttocks have no skin. It is uncomfortable to travel. It is guided like a sheep. Regrets vanish. It hears the remarks but does not believe them. "The buttocks have no skin": it is not contented in the position that it occupies. "It is uncomfortable to travel": it does not go ahead with its advance. "It is uncomfortable": it advances into a condition of difficulty. The fourth "nine" line uses *yang* to occupy a *yin* position, and so its firmness and resolve are insufficient. If it wants to stop, the crowd of *yang* lines below it will advance together, and so its propensity will not be contented. It is as though its buttocks were injured, and could not be contented with occupying a position. Though it desires travel, it has lost its firmness and might by occupying a soft position, and it will be unable to make a strong advance. This is why "it is uncomfortable to travel." "It is guided like a sheep. Regrets vanish": sheep are things that travel in a group. The word "guided" means to be coaxed and cajoled. The line statement is remarking that, were it to strengthen itself and be guided and coaxed to attend to the group of travelers, then it would be able to make its regrets vanish. It has, however, placed itself in a soft position, and so it will necessarily be incapable of this. Although it is made to hear these remarks, it will necessarily be incapable of believing or employing them. As for those who are excessive but can modify themselves, they both hear what is good and can employ it. To conquer oneself so as to attend to one's duty—only the firm and enlightened are capable of this. In other hexagrams, when a "nine" line occupies the fourth position, its loss has not yet reached such an extreme. But in the Solve hexagram, it occupies a soft position and its harm is great. **The *Symbol* says: "'It is uncomfortable to travel': its position is not proper for it. 'It hears the remarks but does not believe them': its awareness is not enlightened."** A "nine" line is placed in a *yin* position, which is not proper. It uses *yang* to occupy a soft position, and so it loses its firmness and resolution. This is why it cannot make a strong advance: "It is uncomfortable to travel." After firmness has become capable of enlightenment, if it occupies a soft position, it relocates and loses the straightforwardness of its nature. How could it return to enlightenment? This is why "it hears the remarks" but cannot "believe them." In fact, it is not enlightened in its awareness or hearing.

The fifth "nine" line: the shore weed solves it, and solves it again. This is the action of centrality. There is no blame. Although the fifth line is *yang*, firm, central, and straightforward, and occupies the position of respect, it is nonetheless quite near to the top "six" line. The top "six" line belongs to the enjoyment trigram substance, and is the hexagram's single *yin* line, which is what *yang* draws close to. The fifth line is the master of dissolving *yin*, and yet it is close to it, and so its blame is great. This is why it must be resolute in its resolution, just like the shore weed. It will then have the virtue of acting with centrality, and there will be no blame. "The action of centrality" refers to the way of centrality. Shore weed these days is called "horse tooth weed." Those who dry it find it difficult to dry, indicating that it is affected by a quantity of *yin qi*. It is also brittle and easy to break. If the fifth line is like the shore weed then, even if it is affected by the *yin* line and changes its resolution and decision, it will act with centrality and there will be neither excess nor blame. If this is not the case, then it will lose its centrality and straightforwardness. As something affected by quantities of *yin*, the shore weed refers to a change of decision, and this is why the line statement chooses it as a symbol. **The *Symbol* says: "'This is the action of centrality. There is no blame': its centrality is not yet bright."** The line statement says that it "solves it, and solves it again," indicating that in "the action of centrality there is no blame." The *Symbol* returns to it and exhausts its meaning, saying that "its centrality is not yet bright." As for people with straightforward hearts and sincere intentions, they can take the way of centrality and straightforwardness to its limit, and be replete or filled with radiant brightness. The heart of the fifth line has a closeness to something, but duty will not allow it, and so it dissolves it. Although it is acting on the outside line, it has not lost the meaning of centrality and straightforwardness, and there can be no blame. Nonetheless, the way of centrality has not yet acquired brightness and greatness. In fact, when the hearts of people desire only one thing, they will cast off the way. Fuzi shows through this passage the depth of his intentions concerning people.[7]

The top "six" line: it does not call out. In the end, there is misfortune. The growth of the *yang* lines is about to reach its limit, while the disappearance of the *yin* line is about to be exhausted. The single *yin* line is placed on a terrain of limit and depletion. It refers to the crowd of noble people acquiring their moment, and dissolving and driving out the small people, who are imperiled and at their limit. Their propensity must necessarily disappear and be exhausted, and this is why the line statement says that they do not shout or call out, because they are trembling and troubled. In the end, there will necessarily be misfortune. **The *Symbol* says: "The misfortune of not calling out: in the end, it should not grow."** The way of noble people with *yang* firmness is advancing and adding to its abundance, while the way of small people is already at its limit and depletion, and is spontaneously disappearing and vanishing. How could it continuously grow? Even if it shouted or called out, it could do nothing, and this is why the *Symbol* says: "In the end, it should not grow." Earlier intellectuals saw in the course of the hexagram "the call is trustworthy" and "it is careful, and calls out," and they wanted to consider "it does not call out" as "it does not call out" where "call" is pronounced with a departing tone.[8] In this case, it would signify that it does not employ anyone further with a call or decree, which is wrong. What is the harm in pronouncing the same character twice with a departing tone and once with a level tone in the course of a single hexagram? And yet the majority of all those who read the *Book of Changes* are doubtful about this. Someone asks: although sages greatly detest the world, they have not yet tasted the necessity of severing themselves from it. But now the line statement says straight out that they do not "call out," which signifies that there will necessarily be misfortune. How can this be? Response: the Solve hexagram refers to the moment when the way of small people is disappearing and vanishing. In dissolving or driving out the way of small people, how could it be necessary to exhaust them or to put them all to death? If they are made to alter and reform, the way of small people will vanish. The vanishing of their way is their misfortune.

44. PAIR (GOU 姤)

The *Sequence of the Hexagrams* says: "To solve is to dissolve. When one thing has been dissolved, something else will necessarily be encountered. This is why the Pair hexagram is next. To pair is to bring about an encounter." To dissolve is to cut off. The dissolution and cutting off of one thing will bring about an encounter and alignment with something else. If things were already aligned at their root, how could they encounter each other? And so the Pair hexagram succeeds the Solve hexagram. As for the trigrams, the Lead trigram is above and the Low trigram below. Concerning the two trigram substances, one may remark that the wind is traveling below heaven. Below heaven are the ten thousand things. The wind in its travels never avoids passing through and piercing them, which is the symbol of encountering. Further, a single *yin* line begins and is born at the bottom. *Yin* is what encounters *yang*, and this is why these lines constitute the Pair hexagram.

Pair: the woman is mighty. It should not employ or choose the woman. This is the beginning and birth of a single *yin* line. It has come to be, and is growing, and step by step it will become abundant—that is, the woman is about to grow and become mighty. If *yin* grows, then *yang* will disappear; if women become mighty, then men will become weak. This is why the judgment warns that "it should not employ or choose" a woman who is like this. Those who choose women desire that they be soft and harmonious, submissive and attentive, so that the way of the family will be completed. In the Pair hexagram, *yin* has just started to advance. Step by step it will become mighty and be the enemy of *yang*. As a result, it should not be chosen. If women become mighty step by step, both women and men will lose their straightforwardness, and the way of the family will be defeated. Although the Pair hexagram's single *yin* line is ex-

354

tremely minimal, it nonetheless has a way to become mighty step by step, and so the judgment gives a warning about it.

The *Judgment* says: "To pair is to bring about an encounter. Softness encounters firmness." The meaning of the Pair hexagram is to encounter. These lines constitute the Pair hexagram because softness encounters firmness. A single *yin* line has just started to be born. It is at the beginning of its encounter with *yang*. "'It should not employ or choose the woman': they should not grow together." A single *yin* line is already born. Step by step it will grow and become abundant. When *yin* becomes abundant, *yang* becomes scarce. Those who choose women desire that their growth be continuous and that they bring the family to completion, but here, *yin* is becoming abundant step by step, and is about to be victorious over the disappearing *yang*. How could their growth together be continuous? In general, when "young women and small people," or the Yi and Di tribes, have the reckless propensity to become abundant step by step—how could one be together with them continuously?[1] This is why the *Judgment* gives a warning not to "employ or choose" a woman who is like this. "Heaven and earth encounter each other. The sundry things are stirred to arrange themselves." *Yin* begins and is born below. *Yin* and *yang* encounter each other: "Heaven and earth encounter each other." If *yin* and *yang* did not interact or encounter each other, the ten thousand things would not be born. If heaven and earth encounter each other, they will transform and cultivate the numberless kinds of thing. "The sundry things are stirred to arrange themselves": the ten thousand things are arranged and enlightened. "The encounter of firmness is central and straightforward. The action of the world is great." The *Judgment* is remarking on the powers of the trigrams. The fifth and second lines both use *yang* firmness to occupy positions that are central and straightforward: they encounter each other with centrality and straightforwardness. The rulers acquires ministers of firmness and centrality, and the ministers encounter rulers of centrality and straightforwardness. The rulers and ministers use *yang* firmness in encounters that are central and straightforward. Their way can be put into great action in the world. "How great is the moment and the meaning of the Pair hexagram!" The *Judgment* applauds the moment of the Pair hexagram, as well as the meaning of the Pair hexagram, for their extreme greatness. If heaven and earth do not encounter each other, then the ten thousand things will not be born; if rulers and ministers do not encounter each other, then the order of government will not flourish; if sages and worthies do not encounter each other, then their way and virtue will not make progress; if affairs and things do not encounter each other, then they will not bring their task and function to completion. The moment and meaning of the Pair hexagram are both extremely great.

The *Symbol* says: "Below heaven, there is wind: Pair. The princes use it to apply the influence of their mandate and to inform the four regions." The wind travels below heaven, and there is nothing it does not encompass. Here it refers to rulers and princes. When they gaze on the symbol of entirely encompassing, they apply the influence of their mandate and decree, and they encompass and inform the four regions. "The wind travels above the earth" and "below heaven, there is wind" both symbolize entirely encompassing the numberless things.[2] If it travels above the earth to pierce entirely the ten thousand things, then it symbolizes the passing through, experiencing, gazing, and inspecting that occur in the Gaze hexagram. If it travels below heaven to encompass entirely the four regions, then it symbolizes the revealing and applying the influence of one's mandate and decree that occur in the Pair hexagram. The various *Symbol* passages sometimes name the first kings, sometimes the princes, and sometimes the nobles and great people. When they name the first kings, it is because the first kings set up the laws and controls that would establish their states. For instance, they produced music and inspected the regions; they prescribed laws to lock their gates; they cultivated things and held feasts for the lords.[3] When they name the princes, it is because of what princes and kings do. For instance, they are resourceful at bringing the way of heaven and earth to completion, and they "apply the influence of their mandate" and "inform the four regions." "Noble people" is a name common to those above and below, and "great people" is a name common to kings and dukes.

The initial "six" line: it is bound to a metal brake. Purity brings good fortune. If it has a long journey, it will see misfortune. The crippled sow aimlessly paces about. In the Pair hexagram, *yin* begins and is born, and is about to grow. When a single *yin* line is born, it will grow and become abundant step by step. As *yin* is growing, *yang* is disappearing. When the way of small people grows, it is proper to control them at the moment when they are minimal and have not yet become abundant. The word "brake" refers to a thing that stops carriages. When made of metal, it is extremely solid and strong. It is stopped by a metal brake, and further, it is bound to it, which makes it certain that it will stop. Since its certain stopping makes it unable to advance, there will be good fortune for the way of *yang* firmness, purity, and straightforwardness. If it were made to advance or go on a journey, it would become abundant step by step and would do harm to *yang*—this is to "see misfortune." "The crippled sow aimlessly paces about": the sage repeats his warning, remarking that, although *yin* is extremely minimal, one should not be oblivious to it. The word "sow" refers to a thing of *yin* restlessness, and this is why it is the case referred to here. The sow is crippled and weak. Although it is not yet able to be strong and fierce, its center or heart is nonetheless set on aimlessly pacing about. The phrase "aimlessly paces about" refers here to jumping back and forth. *Yin* is minimal and at the bottom of the hexagram, and may be called "crippled," but its center or heart is constantly set on making *yang* disappear. The ways of noble people and small people are different. Although small people are minimal and weak at the moment, they have never yet tasted a heart that is not harmful to noble people. If one defends against the minimal, it will not be able to do anything. **The Symbol says: "'It is bound to a metal brake': the way of softness guides it."** To be guided is to be drawn and to advance. *Yin* begins and is born, and advances step by step, which is how the way of softness starts to be guided. If it is bound to a metal brake, this will stop its advance. If it does not advance, it will not be able to make the straightforward way disappear, and so "purity brings good fortune."

The second "nine" line: the container has a fish in it. There is no blame. There is no profit in a visitor. "To pair is to bring about an encounter": the second line is profoundly close to the initial line and refers to those who encounter each other. In some other hexagrams, the initial line corresponds straightforwardly to the fourth, but in the Pair hexagram this encounter carries the most weight. Unqualified unity is the master of those on the way of encountering one another. The firmness and centrality of the second line indicate that its encounter will be certain and sincere. Nonetheless, the initial line is *yin* and soft, and a group of *yang* lines is above it. Further, it corresponds to one of them, and its tendency is to seek it out. A disposition of *yin* softness is seldom capable of purity and certainty. The second line will find it difficult to acquire a sincere heart from the initial line. When it encounters it without acquiring a sincere heart, the way of the encounter will be fractured. The word "container" here refers to a sack made from hemp, and the word "fish" refers to a *yin* thing that is beautiful. What *yang* enjoys in *yin* is its beauty, and this is why the line statement chooses the symbol of the fish. If the second line can herd the initial line with certainty, like a hempen container that has a fish in it, then "there is no blame" in their encounter. The word "visitor" refers to the arrival of an outsider. "There is no profit in a visitor": how could a fish in a hempen container be extended to a visitor? This signifies that it should not be extended further to people outside. It is proper that the way of encounter possess unqualified unity. If two are encountered, it will mix things up. **The *Symbol* says: "'The container has a fish in it': its duty is not to extend it to the visitor."** The encounter between the second and initial lines should not be made to include a second line from the outer trigram. It is proper that it be like the hempen container having a fish in it. The fish is in the hempen container—that is, "its duty is not to extend it" to visitors and guests.

The third "nine" line: the buttocks have no skin. It is uncomfortable to travel. There is danger but no great blame. The second and initial lines have already encountered each other. The third enjoys the initial line, and is profoundly close to the second, so it is not in a place of contentment. Further, the second line is jealous of and detests it. It is not contented with the position it occupies, just like buttocks that have no skin. Since it is already not contented with its place, it is proper for it to depart. It occupies a position in the moment of the Pair hexagram, and so its tendency is to seek an encounter. There is one *yin* line below it, and this is what it desires. This is why, although it is not contented with the position it occupies, travel will make it even more uncomfortable. Discomfort is a condition that makes it difficult to advance, and signifies that it cannot hastily abandon its position. Nonetheless, the third line is firm and straightforward, and is placed in the Low trigram, which means that it will not be confused in the end. If it recognizes what is not straightforward for it, if it cherishes its peril and trouble, and does not dare to be at fault in its movement, then it will be able to be without "great blame." Since its duty is not to seek an encounter, there is certainly blame already, but if it recognizes its peril and stops, then it will not reach the point of becoming great. **The *Symbol* says: "'It is uncomfortable to travel': its travel is not yet guided."** At the beginning, its tendency is to seek an encounter with the initial line. This is why it lingers, and lingers again, and its travel is not yet guided—that is, it does not rush into travel. But it has recognized its peril and is modifying itself, and this is why it has not yet reached the point of great blame.

The fourth "nine" line: the container has no fish in it. Misfortune arises. Containers are what herd other things into sacks, and a fish is something beautiful. The fourth corresponds straightforwardly to the initial line. It is proper that they encounter each other, but the initial line has already been encountered by the second. The fourth has lost anything to encounter, like a container that has no fish in it. What it once possessed has vanished. The fourth line faces the moment of pairing or encountering, it occupies a position in the upper trigram, and it has lost what is below it. It is cast off by those below because it has lost its own virtue. The fourth line has lost them because it is neither central nor straightforward. Since it is neither central nor straightforward and it has lost the people, there will be misfortune. Someone says: the initial line attends to the second because they are close to or near each other. How could this be the crime of the fourth line? Response: the line statement is remarking on the fourth line, and it means that it is proper to blame it. It cannot preserve those below, which is why it is on the way to losing them. If those above were not on the way of loss, how could those below cast them off? The way of encounter is always like this, whether it concerns rulers and ministers, the people and their masters, husband and wife, or friends. The fourth line has split off from those below, and this is why it is remarking on the people and their masters. When those below have cast off those above, there will necessarily be misfortune and alteration. The word "arises" signifies that something is about to be born. The hearts of the people have already cast it off, and this is about to produce difficulties. **The *Symbol* says: "The misfortune of having no fish: it is far from the people."** Those below cast it off because it has itself brought something about. "It is far from the people": it has made itself far from them. Since it is above, it is able to make them cast it off.

The fifth "nine" line: it uses the medlar to contain the melon. If it encloses its arrangement, something falls from heaven. The fifth "nine" line, too, has no corresponding line below it, and so there is no encounter. Nonetheless, it has acquired the way of encounter, and this is why there will necessarily be an encounter in the end. As for encounters between those above and below, they occur because they seek each other. The word "medlar" refers to a lofty tree with great leaves. To be in a lofty place and of great substance, and to be able to contain other things, is to be a medlar. To be beautiful and full, but placed below, is to be a melon. Because it is beautiful and occupies a position below, it symbolizes worthy people who are ensconced in minimal positions. The fifth "nine" line occupies the position of respect or of the ruler, but it seeks the powers of worthy people below it. Although it is extremely lofty, it seeks those who are at the very bottom, just as the leaves of the medlar may be used to contain a melon. It can diminish and contract itself like this, and further, it collects the virtues of centrality and straightforwardness inside itself, and is replete and full, arranged and beautiful. When rulers are like this, they will not be without an encounter with what they seek. Although they may contract themselves to seek the worthy, if their virtue is not straightforward, worthy people will not do even a little for them. This is why they must enclose and herd their arrangement and beauty. If they have accumulated extreme sincerity on the inside, "something falls from heaven," like a cloud that falls from heaven. The line statement is remarking that they will necessarily acquire something. Since antiquity, when rulers of extreme sincerity have diminished and contracted themselves, using the way of centrality and straightforwardness, and seeking the worthy people of the world, they have not been without an encounter. When Gaozong was affected by dreams in his sleep, and when King Wen encountered the fisherman—both of them put this way into action.[4] **The *Symbol* says: "The fifth 'nine' line 'encloses its arrangement': it is central and straightforward."** The phrase "encloses its arrangement" signifies that it encloses and collects the virtues of centrality and straightforwardness. If its virtue is replete and full, then it will complete its arrangement and become radiantly bright. **"'Something falls from heaven': its tendencies do not abandon the mandate."** The word "mandate" refers to the principle of heaven, and "abandon" refers to drawing back. It is extremely sincere, central, and straightforward, it contracts itself and seeks the worthy, and it persists in aligning its tendencies with the principle of heaven. As a result, "something falls from heaven," and it will necessarily acquire something.

The top "nine" line: it pairs its horns. There is dismay but no blame. To be extremely firm and in the top position is to be a horn. This "nine" line uses firmness to occupy the top position, and this is why it is symbolized by a horn. When people encounter each other, they attend to each other by diminishing and contracting themselves. They respond to each other by harmonizing and submitting, and this is why they are able to align. This top "nine" line is lofty and proud, and its firmness has reached its limit—who could agree with it? When people like this seek an encounter, there should certainly be dismay. If they themselves are like this, and other people are far away from them, this is not the crime of the other people. They have brought it about by themselves, and this is why the blame can be wedded to no one. **The *Symbol* says: "'It pairs its horns': those above are depleted and dismayed."** It is already in the place of depletion—that is, the top—and its firmness has reached its limit. This is the case when "those above are depleted" and bring about dismay. If someone uses the limit of firmness to occupy a lofty position, and still seeks an encounter—how could this be anything but difficult?

45. MEET (*CUI* 萃)

The *Sequence of the Hexagrams* says: "To pair is to bring about an encounter. Things encounter one another, and afterward they gather. This is why the Meet hexagram is next. A meeting is a gathering." When things converge and encounter one another, they complete a group, and so the Meet hexagram succeeds the Pair hexagram. As for the trigrams, the Joy trigram is above and the Yield trigram below. "The lake," which is a gathering of waters, "ascends above the earth," and this is why it symbolizes the Meet hexagram. The *Symbol* does not remark that the lake is above the earth, but says that "the lake ascends above the earth." Since it remarks that it "ascends above the earth," it means that it gathers in a certain region.

Meet: there is progress. When the king appears, he will possess a temple. The king is on the way of gathering and bringing about a meeting of the world. When he reaches the point of possessing a temple, he will be at his limit. The group of living things may be extremely crowded, but it can admire and wed itself to a single thing. The human heart "does not recognize its village," but its sincerity and reverence can be brought about.[1] "Ghosts and spirits may not be measured," but their arrival and tarrying can be brought about.[2] There is not just one way to make the hearts of people in the world meet and align with each other, to rally and marshal their crowd of tendencies, but the greatest of these does not exceed the ancestral temple. This is why, when the king is on the way of bringing about a meeting of the world, and reaches the point of possessing a temple, the way of the Meet hexagram will be at its extremity. The performance of sacrifices and libations is rooted in the human heart. Sages control the rituals so as to bring their virtue to completion. This is why jackals and otters are capable of sacrifices, because they possess such a nature.[3] After the word "Meet," the judgment puts "there is progress," which is a distortion of the text. The word "progress" occurs below, but it is not the same as in the Ebb hexagram. If this were the Ebb hexagram, the judgment would remark first on the powers of the trigrams, but in the Meet hexagram it remarks first on the meaning of the hexagram. The statements of the judgment are extremely enlightening. **There is profit in seeing great people. There is progress, and profit in purity.** Those who gather the world must acquire great people to set it in order. When people are gathered, there will be disorder; when things are gathered, there will be contention; when affairs are gathered, there will be chaos. If there are no great people to set them in order, their meeting will bring about contention and disorder as its result. If they do not meet straightforwardly, the gathering of people will be reckless when aligned, and the gathering of resources will be upended when entered into. How could progress be made? This is why there is "profit in purity." **To employ great livestock brings good fortune. There is profit in a long journey.** The Meet hexagram refers to a moment of thickness and benefit. What is employed must be fitting and proportioned to it, and this is why "to employ great livestock brings good fortune." Of affairs, none is as weighty as the sacrifice, and this is why the judgment remarks on a sacrifice and feast. Those who ascend to interact with ghosts and spirits, or who descend in response to the people and things — they may employ a hundred things, but all of them will be like this. When they face the moment of the Meet hexagram, and their interaction makes use of beneficial things, then they will have the good fortune to feast on thickness and wealth. No one in the world will be without the same pleasure in this wealth. Were it the moment for benefit, and yet their interaction made use of meager things, then their feast would not be thick and beautiful. The world would not agree with them, and regret and dismay would be born. But, in fact, they follow the fitness of the moment and submit to principle in their actions. This is why the *Judgment* says: "It submits to the mandate of heaven." As for those who are not capable of doing anything, their force is insufficient. They face the moment of the Meet hexagram, and this is why "there is profit in a long journey." In the great majority of cases, when marshaling some work of art or setting up some state of affairs, one will hold in esteem the moment when it should be done. Those who meet first and afterward employ things will, as a result, be generous in their movement. Such is the principle of heaven.

The *Judgment* says: "**A meeting is a gathering. There are submission and enjoyment. Firmness is central and corresponds, and this is why there is a gathering.**" The meaning of the Meet hexagram is a "gathering." "There are submission and enjoyment": the *Judgment* is remarking on the powers of the trigrams. The enjoyment trigram is above and the submission trigram below. Those above use the way of enjoyment on the people, submitting to the human heart; those below enjoy the government and decrees of those above, submitting and attending to those above. Those above and below already have submission and enjoyment, and further, a line with *yang* firmness places itself in a central and straightforward position. It corresponds to and helps those below. The case is like this, and "this is why there" can be "a gathering." If those who desire the meeting of the world do not have powers like this, they will not be capable of it. "'**When the king appears, he will possess a temple': he will bring about filial piety and a feast.**" The way of the king is to meet the human heart. He reaches the point of establishing or setting up the ancestral temple, and so he brings about the sincerity that lies in "filial piety and a feast." Sacrifices and libations are where the human heart exhausts itself. This is why, for meeting the heart of the world, there is nothing like filial piety and a feast. The way of the king is to meet the world. When he reaches the point of possessing a temple, he is at his limit. "'**There is profit in seeing great people. There is progress': there is a gathering because it is straightforward.**" In the moment of the Meet hexagram, those who see great people will be capable of progress. In fact, their gathering will use the way of straightforwardness. If they see great people, then their gathering will use the way of straightforwardness. If they acquire straightforwardness, then they will make progress. If the Meet hexagram did not use straightforwardness, how could it make progress? "'**To employ great livestock brings good fortune. There is profit in a long journey': it submits to the mandate of heaven.**" The phrase "to employ great livestock" refers to the preceding text—"he will possess a temple"—and is remarking on the feasts and libations. In general, there is no affair that is not like this. In the moment of thickness and gathering, it is proper for those who interact with things to be beneficial, and to portion out what is fitting for them. When things combine their forces by gathering together, they should be able to do something, and this is why "there is profit in a long journey." Such is always the principle of heaven, and this is why the *Judgment* says: "It submits to the mandate of heaven." "**If one gazes on what gathers, the inclinations of heaven, earth, and the ten thousand things may be seen.**" "If one gazes" on the principle of the Meet hexagram, one should be able to see "the inclinations of heaven, earth, and the ten thousand things." What is generally the case for the transformation and cultivation of heaven and earth, as well as the birth and completion of the ten thousand things, is that they are all gatherings. The principle of being and not being, of movement and tranquility, of ending and beginning, is gathering and scattering, and that is all.

This is why, "if one gazes on what gathers, the inclinations of heaven, earth, and the ten thousand things may be seen."

The *Symbol* says: "The lake ascends above the earth: Meet. Noble people use it to repair their weapons and tools. They warn against an absence of deliberation." "The lake ascends above the earth": this symbolizes a meeting or gathering. When noble people gaze on the symbol of the Meet hexagram, they "use it to repair" and bring order to "their weapons and tools." They employ warnings to perfect people against "an absence of deliberation." In general, when things meet each other, no one deliberates about or takes the measure of their affairs, and this is why there is contention in the gathering of the crowd, and strife in the gathering of things. In the great majority of cases where people have gathered, there are many factors. This is why they give a warning after gazing on the symbol of the Meet hexagram. The word "repair" signifies to make something uncomplicated and orderly, to drive out decay and badness. They repair what they have gathered, and so they "warn against an absence of deliberation."

The initial "six" line: it is trustworthy, but not in the end. Sometimes there is disorder, and sometimes a meeting. If it calls out, one handful will be laughing. It is without anxiety. In making a journey, there is no blame. The initial line corresponds straightforwardly to the fourth—that is, they are trustworthy at their root in attending to each other. It is nonetheless facing the moment of the Meet hexagram, and three of the *yin* lines are gathered in one place. These soft lines do not guard the reins of their straightforwardness. If it abandons its straightforwardly corresponding line and attends to those of its own kind, then "it is trustworthy, but not in the end." "Sometimes there is disorder"—there is a bewilderment or disorder in the heart—"and sometimes a meeting"—a gathering with those of the same kind. If the initial line guards its straightforwardness, and does not attend to them but calls out and shouts, seeking its straightforwardly corresponding line, then "one handful" will laugh at it. "One handful" is the customary phrase for "one party," and signifies that the crowd considers it laughable. If it can be "without anxiety," and make the journey to attend to the line of *yang* firmness to which it straightforwardly corresponds, then there will be no excess or blame. If such is not the case, then it will enter the group of small people. **The *Symbol* says: "'Sometimes there is disorder, and sometimes a meeting': its tendencies are disordered."** Its heart and tendencies are bewildered and disordered by those of the same kind. This is why there is "sometimes a meeting" with the group of *yin* lines. If it cannot keep guard with certainty, then the small people will bewilder and disorder it, and it will lose its straightforwardness.

The second "six" line: if it is drawn, there will be good fortune and no blame. If it is trustworthy, there will be profit in employing the lesser seasonal sacrifice.[4] The initial line is *yin* and soft, and it is neither central nor straightforward. It is feared that it will be unable to be trustworthy in the end, and this is why the line statement warns it to do something about its powers. Although the second line is *yin* and soft, it has acquired centrality and straightforwardness, and this is why the line statement gives a warning that is no more than minimal. In general, when a line statement concerns the two impetuses of acquisition and loss, whether it gives a law or a warning, what it provides in each case follows the powers of the line. "If it is drawn, there will be good fortune and no blame": those who are drawn guide each other. When people interact, if they seek each other out, they will align, but if they wait for each other, they will be cast off. The second line corresponds straightforwardly to the fifth, and so it is proper that they meet, but they are far from each other, and further, the second is between the grouped *yin* lines. They must guide and draw each other, and then they will acquire a meeting. The fifth line occupies the position of respect, and possesses the virtues of centrality and straightforwardness. The second line also uses the way of centrality and straightforwardness in making the journey to their meeting, and so there is harmony and alignment between ruler and minister. As to what they share in bringing about, how could it be calculated? As a result, "there will be good fortune and no blame." "When there is no blame, one's goodness alleviates one's excess."[5] If the second and fifth lines did not draw each other, there would be excess. "If it is trustworthy, there will be profit in employing the lesser seasonal sacrifice": to be trustworthy is to be believable at one's center and sincere in what one says. The "lesser seasonal sacrifice" is the most uncomplicated and meager of the sacrifices. When the sacrifice is coarse and meager, one does not value the perfection of the things employed, but uses one's sincere intentions to go straight to an interaction with spiritual enlightenment. "If it is trustworthy": this signifies that, if it is trustworthy, it will not need to employ pattern and ornamentation. It will use its extreme sincerity to interact without qualification with those above. It remarks on the lesser seasonal sacrifice to signify that one offers one's sincerity, and that is all. If those above and below value ornamentation when gathering each other, they are not yet sincere. In fact, if there is reality at their center, they will not borrow ornamentation for the outside—this is the meaning of "employing the lesser seasonal sacrifice." Trust and belief are the roots of the Meet hexagram. It is not only the gathering of ruler and minister but more generally any gathering of the world that lies in sincerity, and that is all. **The *Symbol* says: "'If it is drawn, there will be good fortune and no blame': its center is not yet altered."** In the moment of the Meet hexagram, the acquisition of a gathering is considered to be good fortune. This is why the fourth "nine" line acquires a meeting of those above and below. Although the second and fifth lines are in straightforward correspondence, they are nonetheless in different places with space between them. It is proper that they meet, but they have not yet aligned. This is why, if they can draw each other into a meeting, "there will be good fortune and no blame." Because they possess the virtues of centrality and straightforwardness, they do not reach the point of modification and alteration too hastily. If they alter, they will not draw each other. Someone asks: the second line already possesses the virtues of centrality and straightforwardness, and yet the *Symbol* says that it "is not yet altered," which does not seem to be a sufficient statement. Why is this the case? Response: the *yin* lines are close together and grouped in one place. They have gathered those of their kind. The second line faces the moment of the Meet hexagram, and it occupies a position between them. It can guard itself and does not alter, but it is far away from the straightforwardly corresponding line that it requires. If a firm line were set up here, it would be capable of it. The second line, with its power of *yin* softness, and using the virtues of centrality and straightforwardness, should only long to avoid reaching the point of alteration. This is why this idea is enclosed in the *Symbol*'s warning about how to persist.

The third "six" line: it is like a meeting, like lamentation. There is no long-term profit. If it makes the journey, there will be no blame, but some small dismay. The third line refers to people of *yin* softness, without centrality or straightforwardness. They may seek to meet other people, but no one will agree with them in their search. It may seek the fourth line, but this is not its straightforwardly corresponding line, and is not one of its kind. As a result, the fourth line will desert it, because it is not straightforward. It may agree with the second line, but the second is itself in straightforward correspondence with the fifth. As a result, the second line will not agree with it, because it is not straightforward. This is why, if it desires something "like a meeting," people will desert and sever themselves from it, and it will be "like lamentation." It will not obtain a meeting, but only lamentation and animosity. Those above and below do not agree with it, and so nothing is profitable for it. If it would only make the journey and attend to the top "six" line, then it would acquire its meeting, and there would be no blame. Although the third and the top lines do not straightforwardly correspond as *yin* and *yang*, nonetheless, in the moment of the Meet hexagram, those of one kind attend to each other. These lines both use softness to occupy the top position in their trigrams. Though they do not agree, they occupy terrains that correspond to each other, and they are top lines placed at the limit of the enjoyment and submission trigrams. This is why they will acquire a meeting, and there will be no blame. The way of the *Book of Changes* is not constancy, but alteration and movement. This is what people ought to understand. Such being the case, why is there also "some small dismay?" The third line begins by seeking to meet with the fourth and the second, but it does not obtain them, so afterward it makes the journey and attends to the top "six" line. When people move like this, although they may acquire what they seek, there should also be some small disappointment and dismay. **The *Symbol* says: "'If it makes the journey, there will be no blame': there is lowliness at the top."** The top lines occupy the limit positions in the softness and enjoyment trigrams. If the third line "makes the journey, there will be no blame." The top "six" line is lowly and submissive, and will receive it.

The fourth "nine" line: there are great good fortune and no blame. The fourth line faces the moment of the Meet hexagram, and it is close to the fifth "nine" line, which refers to the ruler, so that it brings about the gathering of rulers and ministers. It is also close to the group of *yin* lines in the lower trigram substance below it, and so it brings about a gathering of the people below. It brings about a gathering of those above and below, which one may say is good. Nonetheless, the fourth line makes use of *yang* to occupy a *yin* position, which is not straightforward. Although it has brought about a gathering of those above and below, it must still acquire "great good fortune," and afterward there will be "no blame." The word "great" means that it entirely encompasses all things. If there is nothing that it does not encompass, it will afterward be great. If there is nothing that is not straightforward, there will be great good fortune, and if there is great good fortune, there will be no blame. As for the gathering of those above and below, it is certainly not always brought about because of the way of straightforwardness. Since antiquity, a way that is bent and without principle has often made an acquisition of the ruler. In fact, a way that is bent and without principle has also sometimes made an acquisition of the people. Such was the case for Chen Heng of the Qi kingdom and the Ji clan of the Lu kingdom.[6] Nonetheless, did their acquisition constitute great good fortune? Was their acquisition without blame? This is why the fourth "nine" line must be capable of great good fortune, and afterward there will be no blame. **The *Symbol* says: "'There are great good fortune and no blame': its position is not proper for it."** Because "its position is not proper for it," one may wonder whether it is not yet capable of exhausting what is good. This is why the line statement says that it must acquire great good fortune, and afterward there will be no blame. If it does not exhaust what is good, how will it acquire great good fortune?

The fifth "nine" line: at the meeting, it grasps its position. There is no blame. No one is trustworthy. There are primacy, endlessness, and purity. Regrets vanish. The fifth "nine" line occupies a position respected by the world, it meets the crowd of the world, and it rules and watches over it. It is proper that it make its position straightforward, and that it correct its virtue. It uses *yang* firmness to occupy the position of respect, and so it is proportioned to its position—that is, "it grasps its position." It has acquired the way of centrality and straightforwardness, and is without excess or blame. In such a case, when there are those who do not believe in and are not yet wedded to it, it is proper that it revert to itself and correct its virtues of "primacy, endlessness, and purity." Then no one will reflect on disobedience, and "regrets vanish." The people wed themselves to primacy, endlessness, and purity, which are the virtues of the rulers. This is why the way of drawing close to the world, and the way of meeting the world, both lie in these three virtues. Since the king has grasped his position, and further, has grasped his virtues, he is central and straightforward, and there is no excess or blame. But in the world there are still some who do not believe in or obey him, who are not wedded to or dependent on him. In fact, his way is not yet bright and great, and the way of primacy, endlessness, and purity is not yet extreme. He is correcting his virtue so that he may arrive at this point. It was like this when the Miao people rebelled against the mandate—Lord Shun simply augmented and promulgated his pattern and virtue.[7] The virtue of Shun was never other than extreme, but it was different toward those far away and those nearby, toward the darkened and the enlightened. This is why there was a time before they were wedded to him, and a time after. Since they were not yet wedded to him, it was proper that he correct his virtue. The word "virtue" signifies the way of primacy, endlessness, and purity. The word "primacy" refers to being the head or the elder. The virtue of the rulers goes out at the head of the numberless things, since rulers are the elders within the group of living things. Sometimes it means to be greatly respected, and sometimes it means to be the master of the whole. If they are also lasting and endless, and pure and certain, then it will develop into spiritual enlightenment. They will brighten everything between the four seas, and no one will think about disobeying. It will not be the case that "no one is trustworthy," and its "regrets" will "vanish." The word "regrets" signifies that "its tendencies are not yet bright," and that its heart is not yet appeased. **The *Symbol* says: "'At the meeting, it grasps its position': its tendencies are not yet bright."** The *Symbol* brings up the earlier part of the line statement. Concerning the tendencies of kings, they must desire that their sincerity and believability be manifest to the world. When there is affection, it must be communicated, so that nothing enclosed in the kinds of living thing will not cherish and wed itself to them. If they value something, and yet "no one is trustworthy," this is because their "tendencies are not yet bright" and great.

The top "six" line: it shows grief and sobs tears. There is no blame. This "six" line is the master of the enjoyment trigram and refers to small people of *yin* softness, who enjoy the lofty position in which they place themselves. Who in the world would be willing to agree with them? When they seek a meeting, and there are none who agree with them, they are depleted to the point that they show grief and sob tears. The phrase "shows grief" refers to grief and lamentation. They have been severed from other people, and they themselves are the cause. They themselves have chosen this—who else could be blamed? When other people detest them, and sever themselves from them, and they do not know what to do, they will fall like the harvest and reach the point of lamentation and sobbing. This is the actual inclination and condition of small people. **The *Symbol* says: "'It shows grief and sobs tears': it is not yet content to be above."** When small people place themselves, they ordinarily lose what is fitting for them. They are already greedy, attentive to their desires, and cannot content themselves with the terrain they have selected. When they reach the point of trapping and depleting themselves, they are thoroughly upset and do not know what to do. This "six" line sobs tears because, in fact, it is not contented with its place above. Noble people are cautious in placing themselves. If a position is not in accord with their duty, they will not occupy it. If it is not felicitous, but possesses perils and traps, they will content themselves as though they were free, and will not burden their hearts. When small people are not contented with occupying the position they have selected, they will ordinarily not walk in accord with it. When this extends to the point at which it depletes and oppresses them, they will fall like the harvest in their restlessness and frustration. Having reached the extreme, they will sob tears, and should be disappointed. The phrase "not yet"—or as it is customarily said, "not yet ready"—indicates that this does not happen hastily.[8] They are not yet ready to be capable of contentment in their position above. They are *yin* and occupy positions above, placed in isolation with no one who agrees with them, and are no longer in accord with their positions. How could they be contented?

46. RISE (*SHENG* 升)

The *Sequence of the Hexagrams* says: "A meeting is a gathering. To be gathered and then to ascend is signified by the word 'rise,' and this is why the Rise hexagram is next." The accumulation and gathering of things adds to their loftiness and greatness. This is "to be gathered and then to ascend," and is why they constitute the Rise hexagram. And so it succeeds the Meet hexagram. As for the trigrams, the Yield trigram is above and the Low trigram below. The tree is below the earth, which indicates that "at the center of the earth, a tree is born." If a tree is born at the center of the earth, it will grow and add to its loftiness. This is the symbol of the Rise hexagram.

Rise: there are primacy and progress. It employs the sight of great people and is without anxiety. If it takes the field in the south, there will be good fortune. To rise is to advance and ascend. To rise or ascend has the meaning of progress, and uses what is good about the powers of the trigrams. This is why "there are primacy and progress." Those who employ this way to see great people will not appear worried or anxious. If they advance ahead, "there will be good fortune." "It takes the field in the south": this refers to advancing ahead.

The *Judgment* says: "Softness uses the moment to rise. There are lowliness and submission. Firmness is central and corresponds. As a result, there is great progress." The *Judgment* is remarking on the two trigram substances. The rising of softness signifies the Yield trigram traveling upward. The substance of the Low trigram is already humble and at the bottom, and the Yield trigram submits to the moment, making use of the moment to rise upward. It signifies that this is the proper moment to rise. When the soft trigram has already ascended and completed the Rise hexagram, then the Low trigram is below and the submission trigram above. A rise that uses the way of lowliness and submission may signify this moment. The second line uses the way of firmness and centrality in corresponding to the fifth, while the fifth line uses the virtues of centrality and submission in corresponding to the second, and so there can be "lowliness and submission." The rise makes use of the moment, and as a result, "there are primacy and progress." The reason the *Judgment* erroneously makes the text into "great progress" is interpreted in the Great Grasp hexagram.[1] "'**It employs the sight of great people and is without anxiety': there is delight.**" In general, the way of the Rise hexagram must have great people as its cause. If one rises into a position, kings and dukes are the cause; if one rises into the way, sages and worthies are the cause. Those who employ the way of lowliness, submission, firmness, and centrality by seeing great people will necessarily succeed in their rise. The phrase "without anxiety" refers to not being worried that one may not succeed. If it succeeds in its rise, there will be blessings and delights for it, and these blessings and delights will be extended to other things. "'**If it takes the field in the south, there will be good fortune': it acts on its tendencies.**" The south is the direction to which people turn. "It takes the field in the south": this signifies that it advances ahead. If it advances ahead, it will succeed in its rise. It will act on its tendencies, and the result will be good fortune.

The *Symbol* says: "**At the center of the earth, a tree is born: Rise. Noble people use it to submit to virtue. They accumulate what is small so as to be lofty and great.**" A tree is born at the center of the earth. It grows and rises upward, and so it symbolizes the Rise hexagram. When noble people gaze on the symbol of the Rise hexagram, they "use it to submit to" and correct their "virtue." "They accumulate" or burden themselves with what is minimal or "small," so that they may reach the point of becoming "lofty and great." If there is submission, they may advance; if there is rebellion, they will retreat. The advance of the ten thousand things always uses the way of submission to advance. If they do not accumulate what is good, it will not be sufficient to bring their fame to completion. To bring one's study and vocation to repletion and fullness, to bring one's way and virtue to veneration and loftiness—this point is always reached because one accumulates and burdens oneself with it. To accumulate what is small so as to complete what is lofty and great—this is the meaning of the Rise hexagram.

The initial "six" line: it is allowed to rise. There is great good fortune. The initial line uses softness to occupy the bottom position in the Low trigram substance. Further, it is the master of the Low trigram, it serves the firmness of the second "nine" line above it, and it refers to extreme lowliness. The second line uses the virtues of firmness and centrality, it corresponds to the ruler above it,

and it faces command over the Rise hexagram. The word "allowed" indicates
that it is believed in and attended to. The softness and lowliness of the initial
line do nothing but believe in and attend to the second line. Since it believes in
the second line and attends to it, their rise is the same and "there is great good
fortune." Concerning the virtues of the second line, one may remark that it is
firm and central; concerning its force, one may remark that it faces being put
in command. Because the initial line is *yin* and soft, and it has no corresponding or supporting line, it cannot rise by itself, but advances only by attending to
worthy people of firmness and centrality. Since this is brought about by the way
of firmness and centrality, how could its good fortune not be great? **The *Symbol***
says: "'It is allowed to rise. There is great good fortune': its tendencies are
aligned with those above." Since it agrees with those above, their "tendencies
are aligned" and their rise is the same. The phrase "those above" here refers to
the second "nine" line. Since it rises by attending to the second line, it has the
same tendencies as the second. It can believe in and attend to worthy people of
firmness and centrality, and so "there is great good fortune."

The second "nine" line: if it is trustworthy, there will be profit in employing
the lesser seasonal sacrifice. There is no blame. The second line is *yang* and
firm, but it is in a position below, while the fifth is *yin* and soft, but it occupies
a position above. As for those who use firmness to manage the affairs of softness,
or who use *yang* and attend to *yin*, they are not on the way of submissiveness,
even if there are moments for this. It may be that those who use dimness to
watch over the enlightened, or who use firmness to manage the affairs of the
weak, are goaded and exhorted to this by the propensity of the affair, but their
obedience is not sincere. When the interaction of those above and below does
not make use of sincerity, how could it continue? How could it get anything
done? Although the fifth line is *yin* and soft, it nonetheless occupies the position of respect. Although the second line is *yang* and firm, and manages the
affairs of those above, it is proper that extreme sincerity persist on the inside
and that pattern and ornament not be borrowed for the outside. If sincerity accumulates at its center, then it will not use exterior ornament when managing
its affairs. This is why the line statement says that "there will be profit in employing the lesser seasonal sacrifice," which signifies that it values sincerity and
reverence. Since antiquity, when ministers of firmness and strength have managed affairs for rulers of softness and weakness, they have never yet avoided trying to improve them with ornament. The lesser seasonal sacrifice has the most
uncomplicated disposition of any sacrifice. It says "if it is trustworthy" to signify
that, if it is already trustworthy, it is not fitting to employ pattern and ornament.

It makes unqualified use of its sincerity to affect and communicate with those above. In a case like this, "there is no blame." When ministers of firmness and strength manage affairs for rulers of softness and weakness, if they are facing the moment of the Rise hexagram, they will not be able to avoid blame unless they interact with sincere intentions. **The *Symbol* says: "The second 'nine' line is 'trustworthy': there is happiness."** If the second line can be "trustworthy" and sincere in managing the affairs of those above, it will not only enact the way of the minister without blame, as though that were all, but it should also be able to put the way of firmness and centrality into action. Its grace will extend to the world, and so "there is happiness." In general, when the *Symbol* remarks that there is delight, in such a case the blessings and delight are extended to other things. When it remarks that there is happiness, the state of affairs is already good and there should also be happiness. For instance, the Great Herd hexagram says that "it is the horn guards of the young cow. There are primacy and good fortune," and the *Symbol* says that "there is happiness."[2] In fact, it is easy to put horn guards on something young and to avoid the difficulty of controlling it with strength. In this case, there should be happiness.

The third "nine" line: it rises to an empty district. The third line uses the power of *yang* firmness while being both straightforward and lowly. Those above all submit to it, and it has a supporting or corresponding line. To rise in such a case is like entering a district with no people in it. Who will resist it? **The *Symbol* says: "'It rises to an empty district': nothing is doubtful."** As for those who enter a district with no people in it, their advance is neither doubtful nor hindered.

The fourth "six" line: the king is employed, and makes progress on Mount Qi. There are good fortune and no blame. The powers of the fourth line are softness and submissiveness. It submits to the rise of the ruler above it, and it submits to the advance of those below it. As for itself, it stops in its place. It makes use of *yin* to occupy a soft position. When *yin* is below, it has stopped in its place. In the past, King Wen occupied the bottom of Mount Qi.[3] He submitted to the son of heaven above him, and desired that the way be brought about. He submitted to the worthies of the world below him, and made them to rise and advance. As for himself, he was soft and submissive, meek and modest, and he did not go out from his position. Since his virtue was so extreme, the kingship of Zhou became his vocation, which is to be employed and make progress. If the fourth line can be like this, it "makes progress," and "there is good fortune," as well as "no blame." The powers of the fourth line are certainly good for it, but the line statement also contains the phrase "no blame." Why is this? Response: although the powers of the fourth line are good, its position is such that a warning is proper. It occupies a position near the ruler, in the moment of the Rise hexagram, but it should not itself rise. If it rises, its misfortune and blame should be recognized. This is why it says to be like King Wen, and then "there are good fortune and no blame." Nonetheless, it is placed in the position of the great minister, and so it is not that it does not manage the affairs of anyone on the rise. It is proper that it make the way of the ruler above it to rise, and the worthies of the world below it to rise. As for itself, it stops in its role. Although it is proper for it to stop in its role, it is also proper that its virtue rise, and that its way make progress. As for those who exhaust such a way—only King Wen could do it! **The *Symbol* says: "'The king is employed, and makes progress on Mount Qi': he submits to the state of affairs."** The fourth line occupies a position near the ruler, and it is the proper moment for rising. It refers to those who acquire good fortune and no blame by possessing the virtue of submissiveness. It uses softness to occupy a position in the Yield trigram, which refers to extreme submissiveness. The progress of King Wen on Mount Qi also made use of submission to the moment, and that is all. He submitted to those above him, and he submitted to those below him. As for himself, he submitted to a place in accord with his duty. This is why the *Symbol* says: "He submits to the state of affairs."

The fifth "six" line: purity brings good fortune. It rises on the ladder. The fifth line corresponds to a line of firmness and centrality below it, and this is why there is "good fortune" when it is able to occupy the position of respect. Nonetheless, its disposition or root is *yin* and soft, and it must guard its "purity" and certainty. Only then will it acquire good fortune. If it were incapable of purity and certainty, it would not devotedly believe in worthy people and, in the end, would not delegate command to them. How could there be good fortune? The word "ladder" refers to what causes people to rise. To give command to worthy people of firmness and centrality, to assist them in rising like a ladder on which they climb and advance—the line statement is remarking that the cause must be there, and then it will be easy. It is pointing to and remarking on the fifth's straightforward correspondence with the second "nine" line. In such a case, worthy people in positions below will all employ the ladder to rise. If it can employ worthy people, then people of this sort will rise. **The *Symbol* says: "'Purity brings good fortune. It rises on the ladder': it makes a great acquisition with its tendencies."** It delegates command to the powers of worthy people, and it is capable of purity and certainty. If it rises in a case like this, it should be able to bring great order to the world, and "its tendencies" should make "a great acquisition." When the way of the ruler rises, it is distressed at not receiving help from the power of worthy people. If it has their help, then it will rise as though it were on a ladder.

The top "six" line: it rises in the gloom. There is profit in purity that does not rest. This "six" line uses *yin* to occupy the limit position in the Rise hexagram, its rise is dark and gloomy, and it refers to those who know how to advance but not how to stop. It is not at all enlightened in anything it does. Nonetheless, there are moments for those whose hearts seek to rise unceasingly. If they employ "purity" and straightforwardness, and they face an affair that "does not rest," then what they do will be fitting. With their virtues of purity and straightforwardness, "noble people lead, and lead again, all day long."[4] Their strength does not rest, just like the heart of the top "six" line, which does not cease. If it is employed like this, then "there is profit." If the hearts of small people, who never cease to seek things out greedily, are converted to the virtue of advancement—could that be as good as this? **The *Symbol* says: "'It rises in the gloom' at the top: it disappears and is not wealthy."** Its rise is dark and gloomy, it is in the limit or top position, it does not know how to cease, and so it can only disappear and vanish. How could anything be attached or added to it? It is not "wealthy"—that is, nothing increases or adds to it. When the Rise hexagram has reached its limit, there is a retreat and not an advance.

47. TRAP (KUN 困)

The *Sequence of the Hexagrams* says: "If something rises ceaselessly, it will necessarily be trapped. This is why the Trap hexagram is next." Those who rise ascend from below. When something rises upward from below, it uses force to make its advance. If it rises ceaselessly, it will necessarily be trapped. This is why the Trap hexagram is next after the Rise hexagram. The Trap hexagram has the meaning of weariness and fatigue. As for the trigrams, the Joy trigram is above and the Pit trigram below. If water occupies a position above the lake, then there will be water at the center of the lake. Here it is below the lake, which symbolizes being dry, parched, and without water. These in turn have the meaning of being trapped and fatigued. Further, the Joy trigram has one *yin* line at the top, and the Pit trigram has one *yang* line occupying a position below. The top "six" line is above two *yang* lines, and the second "nine" line is snared between two *yin* lines. In both cases, lines that are *yin* and soft confine lines that are *yang* and firm, and so they constitute the Trap hexagram. When noble people are confined and concealed by small people, it is the moment of trapping and depletion.

Trap: there are progress and purity. Great people bring good fortune and no blame. There are remarks, but they are not believed. As for the powers of the trigrams, there is a trap, but also the ability to make progress and to acquire purity and straightforwardness. This is the way that great people place themselves in a trap, and is why there can be "good fortune and no blame." When great people place themselves in a trap, it is not only their way that brings them good fortune. They take pleasure in heaven and are contented with its mandate. As a result, they do not lose their good fortune. In a case where they follow the moment and place themselves well, will there be generosity?[1] "There are remarks,

376

but they are not believed": if people make remarks while facing a trap, who will believe them?

The *Judgment* says: "Trap: firmness is confined." These trigrams constitute the Trap hexagram because firmness is what softness covers and conceals. There is a snare at the bottom and a covering at the top, and so this is the Trap hexagram. What snares is also what confines. Noble people of *yang* firmness are what small people of *yin* softness cover and conceal. This is the moment when the way of noble people is trapped and obstructed. "**There are obstacles and enjoyment. There is a trap, but they have not lost what makes 'progress.' Who are they but noble people?**" The *Judgment* uses the powers of the trigrams to remark on the way of placing oneself in the Trap hexagram. The obstacle is below and enjoyment above, which refers to placing oneself in an obstacle while being capable of enjoyment. Even while at the center of a trap, depletion, hardship, and obstacle, one may still take pleasure in heaven and be contented with one's duty. This is to acquire enjoyment and pleasure for oneself. Although it is the moment of the Trap hexagram, those who place themselves without losing sight of their duty will make progress on their way: "There is a trap, but they have not lost what makes progress." As for those who can be like this, "who are they but noble people?" If it were the proper moment to be trapped, but they made progress, then they themselves might make progress, but their way would be trapped. The name "noble people" also refers to great people. "'**Purity. Great people bring good fortune': by using firmness and centrality.**" To be trapped and yet capable of purity is to be a great person, and so there will be good fortune. In fact, they use the way of "firmness and centrality." Such is the case of the fifth and second lines. If they were not firm and central, they would lose their straightforwardness when they encountered the trap. "'**There are remarks, but they are not believed': those who value their mouths will be depleted.**" Those who make remarks while facing a trap are people in whom no one believes. They want to use their mouths to avoid the trap, and so they bring about their own depletion. They use enjoyment to place themselves in the trap, and this is why the *Judgment* warns about "those who value their mouths."

The *Symbol* says: "**The lake has no water: Trap. Noble people use it to bring about the mandate and succeed in their tendencies.**" "The lake has no water," which symbolizes being trapped and fatigued. When noble people face the moment of trapping and depletion, and they have already exhausted the way of defense and apprehension, and still cannot avoid it, then it is according to the mandate. It is proper that they unfold and "bring about the mandate" so as to "succeed in their tendencies." Because they recognize that this mandate is proper, their hearts will not be moved by being depleted, choked, afflicted, and distressed. They will put their duty into action, and that is all. If they did not recognize the mandate, they would be fearful and troubled at the obstacle and difficulty. They would fall like the harvest in their depletion and peril, and what they had guarded would vanish. How could they succeed in tending to do good?

The initial "six" line: its buttocks are trapped by the tree trunks. It enters the secluded valley. For three years there is no glimpse of it. This "six" line uses *yin* softness to place itself in extreme humility. Further, it occupies the bottom position of the Pit or obstacle trigram, and it refers to those who cannot cross through the trap by themselves. They must acquire people of firmness and enlightenment in positions above to support and help them, and then they should be able to cross through the trap. The initial line corresponds straightforwardly to the fourth, but the fourth "nine" line uses *yang* to occupy a *yin* position, which is not straightforward. It has lost its firmness, it is not central, and further, it is confined by a *yin* line at the start of the trap. Having become this bad, could it make people cross through the trap? It is as though underneath a tree trunk that cannot shade or reach over it. The phrase "tree trunks" refers to trees without branches or leaves. The fourth is near the position of the ruler. In other hexagrams, it is not without help, but here it occupies a position in the Trap hexagram, and it cannot protect anything. This is why it is indicated by the "tree trunks." Buttocks are used to occupy a position. "Its buttocks are trapped by the tree trunks": this signifies that there is nothing to protect it, and so it is not contented with the position it occupies. If it occupied a position of contentment, then it would not be trapped. "It enters the secluded valley": people of *yin* softness cannot be contented with what they encounter. Since they cannot avoid the trap, they will add to their confusion with dim and faulty movement, entering the depth of the trap. The phrase "secluded valley" refers to a place that is deep and dim. Someone who adds to or enters the trap is, at the start, without the propensity to go out from it, and this is why it reaches the point that "for three years there is no glimpse of it." That is, it is trapped in the end. "There is no glimpse of it": it does not encounter anyone who is making progress. **The Symbol says: "'It enters the secluded valley': what is secluded has no light."** The word "secluded" refers to what "has no light." It signifies adding to or entering a dark and dim place, having snared oneself in the depth of the trap. If there were light, no one would reach the point of being snared.

The second "nine" line: it is trapped by food and drink. The scarlet greaves set out and arrive. There is profit in employing feasts and libations. Taking

the field brings misfortune but no blame. Food and drink are what people desire, and are used to influence other people with one's favor. The second line uses the powers of firmness and centrality to place itself in the moment of the Trap hexagram. Noble people are contented with what they encounter. Although they may be depleted and imperiled by obstacles and difficulties, there is nothing that moves their hearts, and they are not anxious about being trapped. Those who are trapped are trapped by nothing but their own desires. What noble people desire is to gratify the people of the world, and to cross with the world through the trap. The second line has not yet succeeded at what it desires or made its favor influential, and this is why "it is trapped by food and drink." Great people or noble people cherish their way, but here they are trapped in positions below. They must acquire rulers who possess the way, who will seek them out and employ them. Afterward, they will be able to have an influence with what they have collected. The second line uses the virtues of firmness and centrality, but it is trapped in a position below, while above it is the ruler of firmness and centrality referred to by the fifth "nine" line. Since their ways are the same and their virtues are aligned, they will necessarily arrive at the point of seeking each other out. This is why the line statement says: "The scarlet greaves set out and arrive." The phrase "set out and arrive" indicates that it both sets out and arrives. The scarlet greaves are pieces of clothing worn by kings that conceal their knees. Here the meaning is travel and arrival, and this is why it remarks on what conceals the knees. "There will be profit in employing feasts and libations": in feasts and libations, extreme sincerity is used to develop one's spiritual enlightenment. In the moment of the Trap hexagram, "there is profit in employing" extreme sincerity, just as in the case of "feasts and libations." When one's virtue has become sincere, one will be capable of mutual affection with those above. From the past to the present, when the worthy and wise are trapped in seclusion far away, but their virtue finally rises to be heard and their way is finally employed—it happens only because they themselves guard their extreme sincerity, and that is all. "Taking the field brings misfortune but no blame": at the start of the moment of the Trap hexagram, if it were not extremely sincere, contented with its place and awaiting the mandate, but took the field and sought it out, then it would confront the difficulty and acquire misfortune. Since it would have chosen this itself, who else could it blame? Those who take the field without measuring the moment are not contented with their place and are moved by the trap. When they lose the virtues of firmness and centrality, and choose their own misfortune and regret, who will they hate and blame? In various hexagrams, there is good fortune when the second and fifth lines use *yin* and *yang* to correspond to each other. Only in the Small Herd hexagram, together with the Trap hexagram, is *yang* imperiled by *yin*, and this is why those of the same way seek each other out. In the Small Herd hexagram, *yang* is herded by *yin*, while in the Trap hexagram, *yang* is confined by *yin*. **The Symbol says: "'It is trapped by food and drink': those with centrality will possess delight."** Although it is trapped by what it desires and cannot yet influence people with its favor, it nonetheless guards its virtues of firmness and centrality. It will necessarily be able to bring about progress, and will possess blessings and delight. Although this is not yet the moment for progress and development, it keeps guard over its virtue of centrality, which is also the way of noble people. When it makes progress, it will possess delight.

The third "six" line: it is trapped by stones. It seizes the puncture vines. It enters its palace but does not see its wife. There is misfortune. The third "six" line uses a disposition of *yin* softness without being central or straightforward, it is placed at the limit of the obstacle trigram, and it employs firmness. To occupy a *yang* position is to employ firmness, which is not good at all for someone placed in the Trap hexagram. The word "stones" refers to something that is solid and weighty, making victory difficult, and "puncture vines" are thorny things that should not be seized. If the third line uses firmness on the obstacle and advances upward, its force will not be capable of victory over the two *yang* lines above it. Since their solidity should not be confronted, it will only add to the trap: "It is trapped by stones." Since its virtue is not good and it occupies a position above the second "nine" line with its firmness and centrality, it will not be contented. It is as though its mat were made of thorns, or as though it "seizes the puncture vines." Whether it advances or retreats, it will add to the trap. It may desire contentment with its place, but it only adds to its incapacity for this. The word "palace" refers to a place one is content to occupy, and the "wife" is the master of the place of contentment. Although it recognizes that it should not advance or retreat, and it desires contentment with the place it occupies, it has lost its place of contentment. Advancing, retreating, together with staying in one place, are all impossible for it. It has nothing left but death, and that is all, and its misfortune should be recognized. The *Appended Statements* says: "If there is no trap, yet it is trapped, then its name will necessarily be disgraced. If there is nothing to seize, yet it seizes it, then its body will necessarily be imperiled. If it has already disgraced and imperiled itself, then it will soon reach the time of its death. How could it acquire the sight of its wife?"[2] That is, the two *yang* lines should not be confronted. If it confronts them, it has chosen to trap itself. This is a case where "there is no trap, yet it is trapped." Its name is disgraced because this is a bad state of affairs. The third line is above the second, which certainly indicates that it seizes it. Nonetheless, if it could descend to it with meekness and softness, there would be no harm. If it employs firmness on the obstacle so as to ride on it, it will not be contented, having chosen to trap itself, as though it had seized the puncture vines. In a case like this, "it will soon reach the time of its death." How could the master of its place of contentment be acquired or seen? **The *Symbol* says: "'It seizes the puncture vines': it rides on firmness. 'It enters its palace but does not see its wife': it is not auspicious."** "It seizes the puncture vines": this signifies that it rides on the firmness of the second "nine" line. It is not contented, as though its mat were made of thorns. When "it is not auspicious," there is no good in levying troops, and when it has lost its place of contentment, there is no good in being effective. This is why the *Symbol* says that it "'does not see its wife': it is not auspicious."

The fourth "nine" line: it arrives with hesitation, and hesitation again. It is trapped by a golden carriage. There is dismay, and it brings about its end. Force alone is not sufficient, and this is why it is trapped. Concerning the way of making progress through a trap, one will necessarily require support and help. When those above and below face the moment of the Trap hexagram, it is proper and by principle that they seek each other out. The fourth corresponds straightforwardly to the initial line, but the fourth places itself in the Trap hexagram without centrality or straightforwardness. Its power is insufficient to cross through the trap with other people. Since the initial line is close to the second, and the second has the powers of firmness and centrality, which are sufficient to rescue it from the trap, it is fitting that the initial line attend to it. The word "golden" indicates that it is firm, and "carriage" refers to something that bears loads. The second line uses firmness to bear itself in the lower trigram, and this is why it is signified by the "golden carriage." The fourth wants to attend to the initial line, but it is hindered by the second. This is why its arrival is late or doubtful, "with hesitation, and hesitation again." Such is the case of being "trapped by a golden carriage." It corresponds to something that doubts and thinks little of it, and is going toward a different line. Though it will soon attend to it, it is like a cheerful person who does not dare go forward hastily. How could it not be disappointed and dismayed? "It brings about its end": it weds itself to an affair that is straightforward. The initial line corresponds straightforwardly to the fourth, and so they will necessarily attend to each other in the end. The wife of the shivering scholar and the minister of a weak state are each content to be straightforward, and that is all. If their propensity were to select something for themselves and attend to it, their badness would be too great to be embraced by the times. The second and fourth lines both use *yang* to occupy a *yin* position.

The second also uses the powers of firmness and centrality, and so it can cross through the trap. It occupies a *yin* position, which is to value softness, but it has acquired centrality, and so it has not lost what is fitting for both firmness and softness. **The *Symbol* says: "'It arrives with hesitation, and hesitation again': it tends toward the bottom. Although its position is not proper for it, there is agreement."** The fourth corresponds to the initial line, but they are separated by the second. It tends to seek the bottom line, and this is why "it arrives with hesitation, and hesitation again." Although it occupies a position that is not proper for it—and so it is not yet good—it nonetheless corresponds straightforwardly, and the two lines agree with each other. This is why "it brings about its end."

The fifth "nine" line: it is nosed and footed. It is trapped by the red greaves. It hesitates and possesses enjoyment. There is profit in the employment of sacrifices and libations. The line statement says that "it is nosed," or that its nose is cut off, which refers to injuring the top of something. It says that it is "footed," or that its feet are removed, which refers to injuring the bottom of something. Those above and below are both confined by the *yin* lines, which is the injury or harm symbolized by nosing and footing. The fifth is the position of the ruler, but the rulers are trapped, because those above and below do not agree. The phrase "red greaves" refers to pieces of clothing worn by the lower ministers. Here the meaning of travel and arrival is chosen, and this is why it remarks on the greaves. The rulers are trapped because the world has not arrived. If all the world were to arrive, they would not be trapped. Although the fifth line is in the trap, it also possesses the virtues of firmness and centrality, and it has below it the worthy people of firmness and centrality referred to by the second "nine" line. Since their ways are the same and their virtues align, they will necessarily, after some hesitation, correspond to each other, arrive, and make a shared crossing through the trap with the world. This is the case of being trapped at the beginning, and then, after some hesitation, possessing happiness and enjoyment. "There is profit in the employment of sacrifices and libations": in an affair of sacrifice and libation, one must bring about sincerity and reverence, and afterward one will receive blessings. In the moment when the rulers are trapped, it is fitting that they also consider what is trapping the world, and seek out the worthy people of the world. If their sacrifices and libations are such that they bring about sincerity and reverence, they will also be able to bring about the worthy people of the world, who will cross with the world through the trap. If the fifth and second lines have the same virtues, why is the line statement saying that those above and below do not agree? Response: when *yin* and *yang* lines correspond to each other, their correspondence is spontaneous, as in the case of husband and wife, or meat and bone—their roles are already determined. The fifth and second are both *yang* lines, but they use the same virtues of firmness and centrality, and so they correspond to each other. They seek each other out and afterward align, as in the case of a ruler and minister, or two friends—their duties are already aligned. When they face the beginning of the Trap hexagram, how could there be agreement between those above and below? If there were agreement, there would be no trap. This is why "it hesitates" to align but, afterward, it "possesses enjoyment." The second line statement speaks of "feasts and libations," and the fifth speaks of "sacrifices and libations." The overall idea is that it is fitting to employ extreme sincerity so as to receive blessings. When one remarks on sacrifices, libations, and feasts inclusively, they should have a common object. When one remarks on each as divided from the others, sacrifices are for heavenly spirits, libations are for earthly shades, and feasts are for human ghosts. Since the fifth is the position of the ruler, its remarks concern sacrifices, and since the second is below it, its remarks concern feasts. Each makes use of what it is proper to employ. **The *Symbol* says: "'It is nosed and footed': its tendencies do not yet acquire their object. 'It hesitates and possesses enjoyment': it uses centrality and straightness. 'There is profit in the employment of sacrifices and libations': it receives blessings."** At the beginning, it is confined by the *yin* lines, and there is no agreement between those above and below. That is, it does not yet acquire the object of its tendencies when the moment of the Trap hexagram is at its starting point. "It hesitates and possesses enjoyment" by using the way of centrality and straightness. It acquires the worthy people below it and they make a shared crossing through the trap. The *Symbol* does not say "centrality and straightforwardness" concerning its alignment with the second line. It speaks only of "straightness," which is fitting. The idea of "straightness" is close to "straightforwardness," but it falls a little short. As for those who exhaust their sincere intentions—as though they were making sacrifices and libations—when they seek out the worthy people of the world, they will be able to make progress with the world through the trap. They will feast on and receive blessings and delight.

The top "six" line: it is trapped by creepers and brambles, by uproar and tumult. Its speech and movement bring regrets. It has regrets. Taking the field brings good fortune. When a thing is at its limit, it reverses itself; when a state of affairs is at its limit, it alters. Since the Trap hexagram has reached its limit, it is proper and by principle that it alter. The phrase "creepers and brambles" refers to things that act like cords and bolts, and "uproar and tumult" refers to a condition of peril and movement. This "six" line places itself at the limit of the Trap hexagram, in the cords and bolts of the trap, and it occupies the loftiest and most perilous terrain: "It is trapped by creepers and brambles" together with "uproar and tumult." "Movement brings regrets": as soon as it moves, it will have regrets, since there is no place without a trap. "It has regrets": it is blamed ahead of time for its loss. The phrase "its speech and" actually signifies "its own."[3] But if the former were possible, its speech would be just like its movement—in either case, it would acquire regret. It is proper that it alter ahead of time what it is going to do: "It has regrets." If it is capable of regret, then it will make the journey and acquire good fortune. If it takes the field at the limit of the Trap hexagram, it will go out from the trap, and this is why there is good fortune. When the third line uses *yin* at the top of the lower trigram, there is misfortune, but when the top line occupies the top of the entire hexagram, there is no misfortune. Why is this the case? Response: the third line occupies a firm position, and it is placed in the obstacle trigram. It is in the Trap hexagram, and it employs firmness on the obstacle. This is why there is misfortune. The top line uses softness to occupy a position in the enjoyment trigram, and it alone is at the limit of the Trap hexagram. Since it is at the limit of the trap, there is an alteration in the way of the trap. The top lines of the Trap and Block hexagrams are both without corresponding lines, and they occupy the end position of the hexagrams. But in the Block hexagram "it weeps blood like streams," while in the Trap hexagram "it has regrets. Taking the field brings good fortune." This is because, in the Block hexagram, the line is at the limit of the obstacle trigram, while in the Trap hexagram, it belongs to the enjoyment trigram substance. Those who advance with enjoyment and submissiveness should be able to cast off the trap. **The *Symbol* says: "'It is trapped by creepers and brambles': it is not yet proper. Its 'movement' brings 'regrets. It has regrets': its action brings good fortune."** It is in the cords of the trap and it cannot alter—that is, it has not yet acquired its way. In such a case, its place is not yet proper for it. It knows that it will acquire regrets if it moves. If it succeeds in having regrets but drives them out, it should be able to go out from the trap. In such a case, its action will bring good fortune.

48. WELL (*JING* 井)

The *Sequence of the Hexagrams* says: "When something is trapped at the top, it must revert to the bottom. This is why the Well hexagram is next." This concerns its earlier remark that "if something rises ceaselessly, it will necessarily be trapped." It signifies that if something rises ceaselessly and is trapped at the top, it will necessarily revert to the bottom. Of all the things that are below, none is like the well, and so the Well hexagram succeeds the Trap hexagram. As for the trigrams, the Pit trigram is above and the Low trigram below. The symbol of the Pit trigram is water; the symbol of the Low trigram is a tree. The meaning of the Low trigram is entry; the tree in turn is the symbol of a tool. The tree enters the water below it, and then ascends through the water, which symbolizes drawing water from a well.

Well: one may modify the district but not the well. It is not deprived of anything, and it does not acquire anything. The journey arrives at the well, and at the well again. A well is a thing that is constant and may not be modified. The district may be modified and put someplace else, but the well may not be relocated. This is why the judgment says: "One may modify the district but not the well." One draws from it and it is not drained; one gives to it and it is not filled: "It is not deprived of anything, and it does not acquire anything." Everyone who reaches it can make use of its function: "The journey arrives at the well, and at the well again." "It is not deprived of anything, and it does not acquire anything": its virtue is constant. "The journey arrives at the well, and at the well again": its function is all-encompassing. To be constant, to be all-encompassing—this is the way of the well. **To approach its extremity is not yet to pull from the well. If the bucket is crippled, there will be misfortune.** "To approach" is to be almost there, while "to pull" is to use the rope. The well has the function of sustaining things as its task. Those who are almost at its extremity have not yet made use of its function. The same holds for those who have not yet let anything down so as to pull from the well. Concerning the way of noble people, it is esteemed only when brought to completion. And so the five grains, while still unripe, are not equal to their wild cousins.[1] To dig a seventy-two foot well without reaching a spring is similar to deserting the well. To have the function of sustaining things without reaching them is similar to not having the function. Those whose "bucket is crippled" and defeated will lose it. They will be deprived of its function, and as a result, "there will be misfortune." To be crippled is to be crushed and defeated.

The *Judgment* says: "Something is lowered into the water and brings the water up: Well. The well nourishes and is not depleted. 'One may modify the district but not the well': because of its firmness and centrality." "Something is lowered" so that it enters the water below, and it "brings the water up: Well." The well's nourishment of things is never depleted, and does not cease. Though it is put to use, it is not drained, and so its virtue is constant. The district may be modified, but the well may not be relocated—this, too, indicates the constancy of its virtue. The second and fifth lines have the virtues of firmness and centrality. Since they are constant like this, the powers of the trigrams align with the meaning of the hexagram. "'To approach its extremity is not yet to pull from the well': it has not yet accomplished anything. 'The bucket is crippled': misfortune is the result." When one is almost at its extremity but has not yet made use of its function, it is the same as "not yet to pull from the well." The well has the function of sustaining things as its task. When the water goes out, it has performed its function. If the water does not yet go out, how could it have accomplished anything? When water is brought up in the bucket, it performs its function. If "the bucket is crippled" and defeated, it will not perform its function, and "misfortune is the result."

The *Symbol* says: "Above the tree, there is water: Well. Noble people use it to reassure the people and persuade them for each other's sake." The tree receives water and ascends, symbolizing a tool that draws water, which then goes out from the well. When noble people gaze on the symbol of the Well hexagram, they make the virtue of the well into their law, using it as the way of reassuring and encouraging the people, persuading and exhorting them to help each other. To reassure and encourage the people is to make the function of the well into one's law, while to persuade the people to help each other is to make the influence of the well into one's law.

The initial "six" line: the well is muddy. No one drinks from it. At the former well there is no game. The well and the tripod are both things, and it is as things that they constitute the meaning. This "six" line uses *yin* softness to occupy the bottom position, it has no corresponding or supporting line above it, and it is symbolized by the water that does not ascend. Since it cannot sustain anything, this well is one from which no one may drink. The well from which no one may drink is "muddy" and foul. The bottom of the well is here symbolized by mud. The function of a well is to nourish people with its water. If there is no water, then it will be abandoned and situated without a function. When the well water ascends, people obtain its function, but game and birds also approach and seek it out. If it is a "former" or neglected well, and people have not drunk from it because the water does not ascend, the game and birds will also not make the journey. In fact, this is because it cannot sustain anything. At its root, the well is a thing that sustains people. This "six" line uses *yin* to occupy the bottom position, and is symbolized by the water that does not ascend. This is why no one drinks from it. The well from which no one drinks is muddy, like those who face the moment for sustaining things but whose powers are weak, without support, and unable to reach them. They will be abandoned by the moment. **The *Symbol* says: "'The well is muddy. No one drinks from it': it is at the bottom. 'At the former well there is no game': the moment abandons it."** It uses *yin* to occupy the bottom of the Well hexagram, and so it is symbolized by mud. If it is "muddy" and without water, then people will not drink from it. If people do not drink from it, then the water will not ascend. It will not extend itself to "game" and birds, and the game and birds will also not reach out for it. They see that it cannot sustain anything, and so it is abandoned by the moment and situated without a function. If it could extend itself to the game and birds, then it could also have something it sustains. The word "abandons" has an ascending tone, and so it does not sound the same as when the Lead hexagram says "it is the moment for abiding."[2]

The second "nine" line: the valley well shoots the bottom dwellers. The jug is decayed and leaky. Although the second line has the power of *yang* firmness, it occupies a position below. It has no corresponding line above it, it draws close to the initial line, and it is symbolized by something below that does not ascend. The way of the well is to travel upward. The water of a "valley" brook will pour out from the side and approach the bottom. Since the second line occupies a position in the Well hexagram and approaches the bottom, it has lost the way of the well. It is a well that acts like a valley. When something goes out from the top of the well, people are nourished and things are sustained, but now it is approaching the mud and foulness at the bottom. It pours over the "bottom dwellers," and that is all. The phrase "bottom dwellers" sometimes refers to crayfish and sometimes to frogs, which are all minimal things in the mud at the center of the well. To shoot is to pour over, as when the flow of the valley descends and pours out over the bottom dwellers. "The jug is decayed and leaky"—that is, the jug is broken and leaky. The power of *yang* firmness at its root should be able to nourish people and sustain things, but if it has no corresponding or supporting line above it, it will not be able to ascend and will approach the bottom. As a result, it will not accomplish its function of sustaining things. It is like water kept in a jug. At its root it may be able to perform its function, but if it leaks because it is broken or decayed, then it will not be able to perform its function. The initial and second lines of the Well hexagram do not accomplish anything and yet the line statement does not remark on their regrets or blame. How can this be? Response: the loss of something will bring regrets, and an excess of something will bring blame. Since it has no corresponding or supporting line and cannot complete its function, there will be neither regrets nor blame. How could there be no excess when it occupies the second position and is close to the initial line? Response: there is no excess in something placed at the center. It cannot ascend because it has no support, not because it is close to the initial line. **The *Symbol* says: "'The valley well shoots the bottom dwellers': there is no agreement."** The well has making something go out at the top as its task. The second line, with its power of *yang* firmness, may at its root perform the function of sustaining things, but it is in a position below and has no corresponding or supporting line above it. As a result, it draws close to the bottom and "shoots the bottom dwellers." Were the higher line in agreement with it, it would be proper for it to be drawn upward and complete the task of the well.

The third "nine" line: the well is clean, but no one drinks from it. It makes my heart feel pity. It may be employed in the drawing of water. If the king is enlightened, he will receive its blessings. The third line uses *yang* firmness to occupy and acquire a straightforward position, and it refers to those who have the power to perform the function of sustaining things. It is at the top of the lower trigram in the Well hexagram and refers to clear and refreshing water that one may drink. The well has ascending as its function, but this line occupies a lower position and so it does not yet perform its function. The nature of *yang* is to ascend, and further, its tendency is to correspond to the top "six" line. It is placed in a firm position that exceeds the center, and it does its best to advance upward. It has the power and the function to be quite influential. If it does not yet perform its function, then it is like the clean, orderly, clear, and refreshing water that no one seems to drink, and that makes the heart feel pity and grief. The third line occupies a position during the moment of the Well hexagram and it is firm without centrality. This is why it is eager to be influential, differing from those "who act only when employed and store themselves away when abandoned."[3] Nonetheless, when the enlightened king employs people, how could he "seek only those who are perfect"?[4] This is why, "if the king is enlightened," then he will receive "blessings." The third line has sufficient power to perform the function of sustaining things. It is like the clear and refreshing water of the well: "It can be employed in the drawing of water," and one may drink from it. Were there an enlightened king above it, it would be proper for him to employ it and acquire its effectiveness. If the powers of worthy people are seen and used, they themselves will put their way into action, their rulers will feast on their accomplishments, those below will receive their grace, and those above and below will all receive their blessings. **The *Symbol* says: "'The well is clean, but no one drinks from it': action brings pity. If it seeks the enlightened king, it will receive blessings."** "The well is clean" and orderly, but no one seems to drink from it—people of power and knowledge do not seem to be employed. Not taking action makes them feel distress and pity. Since not taking action makes them feel pity, how could they avoid seeking it out? This is why "it seeks the enlightened king" and "will receive blessings"—that is, it has an ardent tendency to act.

The fourth "six" line: the well is mended. There is no blame. Although the fourth line is *yin* and soft and places itself straightforwardly, it serves the ruler referred to by the fifth "nine" line above it. Its powers are not sufficient to have a broad influence or to bring profit to things, but it is capable of guarding itself. This is why, if it can correct and order itself, it will acquire "no blame." The word "mended" refers to piling up mortar, and signifies that it is corrected and set in order. Although the powers of the fourth line are weak and it cannot accomplish any broad sustaining of things, by correcting and ordering its affairs it should not reach the point of neglect. Were it unable to correct and order itself, while also neglecting the task of nourishing other people, it would lose the way of the well and its blame would be great. It occupies a lofty position and has acquired a ruler of *yang* firmness, centrality, and straightforwardness. It is also able to place itself straightforwardly and serve the higher line without neglecting its affairs—this, too, should be considered as avoiding blame. **The *Symbol* says: "'The well is mended. There is no blame': the well is corrected."** The word "mended" refers to setting the well in order and making it correct. Although its task cannot be to sustain anything great, it can still make things correct and orderly without neglecting them. This is why "there is no blame," because it can only avoid blame, and that is all. If it were a line of *yang* firmness, it would not reach such a point. In such a case, there would be blame.

The fifth "nine" line: the well is icy. It drinks from the cold spring. The fifth line uses *yang* firmness, centrality, and straightforwardness. It occupies the position of respect, and its power and virtue exhaust the good and beautiful: "The well is icy. It drinks from the cold spring." The word "icy" here signifies that it is sweet and refreshing. It is the coldness of wells and springs that constitutes their beauty. When the cold spring is sweet and refreshing, people may drink from it. This is the best that the way of the well can do. Nonetheless, the line statement does not remark on its good fortune. The task of the well is complete only when something goes out at the top, but here it has not yet reached the top or performed its function. This is why, after it reaches the top, the line statement will remark that "there is primary good fortune." **The *Symbol* says: "'It drinks from the cold spring': there are centrality and straightforwardness."** To be able to drink from the cold spring is what is best in the way of the well. The virtues of the fifth "nine" line are centrality and straightforwardness, which means that it is extremely good.

The top "six" line: the well is brought in and is not overgrown. It is trustworthy. There is primary good fortune. The function of the well is to make something go out at its top. This line occupies the top position in the Well hexagram and completes the way of the well. The phrase "brought in" indicates that it is chosen for the drawing of water, while "overgrown" refers to being concealed or overturned. If it is chosen and not concealed, then its profit will not be depleted and the influence of the well will be broad and great. "It is trustworthy": it is constant and without alteration. To be constant and to have a liberal influence is the good fortune of great goodness. Who other than great people could give substance to the function of the well with its constancy and liberal influence? The end of other hexagrams refers to their limit and alteration. It is only the end of the Well and Tripod hexagrams that refers to the completion of their task. As a result, there is good fortune. **The *Symbol* says: "'There is primary good fortune' for the top line: this is its great completion."** The good fortune of great goodness at the top of the Well hexagram is the "great completion" of the way of the well. The top of the well is where its task is completed.

49. HIDE (*GE* 革)

The *Sequence of the Hexagrams* says: "The way of the well should not be without reform, and this is why the Hide[1] hexagram is next." When the well is
considered as a thing, the longer it persists the dirtier and more defeated it will
become. A change will make it clear and refreshing. It "should not be without
reform," and this is why the Hide hexagram is next after the Well hexagram. As
for the trigrams, the Joy trigram is above and the Cast trigram below: "At the
center of the lake, there is fire." The *ge* character of "hide" here refers to alteration. Water and fire are things that put each other to rest. Water destroys fire,
while fire parches water—they alter and reform each other. The nature of fire is
to go up, while the nature of water is to go down. Were they to draw back from
each other, they would split apart, and that is all. But in this case the fire is at
the bottom and the water is at the top, so they must approach and subdue each
other. They will destroy and put each other to rest, and so they are symbols of
the Hide hexagram. Further, "the two women occupy the same position," but
they are wedded to different men. Their tendencies are not the same—that is,
they "do not acquire each other." This is why they refer to the Hide hexagram.

**Hide: when the day is past, it is trusted. There are primacy and progress, profit
and purity. Regrets vanish.** Reformers alter what was done in the past. Since
they alter what was done in the past, people cannot believe in them right away.
This is why a day must pass, and afterward people's hearts will believe in and
attend to them. "There are primacy and progress, profit and purity. Regrets vanish": when something is decaying and declining, it may afterward be reformed.
Its development is brought about by the reform, and this is why reform should
be able to make great progress. Since the reform will bring profit to the way of
straightforwardness, it has the meaning of being able to continue and to drive

out the past. No one will regret this movement of alteration, and so "regrets vanish." If a reform that adds nothing much is likely to be regretted, what will the case be for one that does harm? And so, people of antiquity treated the production of modifications as a weighty matter.

The *Judgment* says: "Hide: water and fire put each other to rest. The two women occupy the same position. Their tendencies do not acquire each other. It is called the Hide hexagram." A lake and fire destroy and put each other to rest. Further, the tendencies of the two women "do not acquire each other." This is why it is the Hide hexagram. The *xi* character of "rest" refers to stopping, but also to being born. When things come to a stop, they are afterward born again, and this is why the character has the meaning of being born. But the putting each other to rest of the Hide hexagram signifies the rest that is a stopping. "'When the day is past, it is trusted': when there is reform, they believe in it." When affairs are altered and reformed, how could the human heart be capable of readily believing in them? The day must come to an end, and afterward they will be trusted. When those above are on the verge of making modifications, it is proper that they delineate and provide information about them, and reiterate their decrees, until they reach the point when "the day is past" and they have made people believe in them. If people's hearts do not believe in something, it may be enacted with strength, but it cannot be brought to completion. When the first kings made their government and decrees, the hearts of some people in the beginning were doubtful. Nonetheless, with their continuation, these people necessarily came to believe in them. There has never yet been a case where someone brought goodness and order to completion without being trusted in the end. **There are pattern and enlightenment, with enjoyment. There is great progress, with straightforwardness. If the reform is proper, regrets vanish.**" The *Judgment* uses the powers of the trigrams to speak about the way of reform. The Cast trigram refers to "pattern and enlightenment," and the Joy trigram refers to "enjoyment." If there are pattern and enlightenment, then principle will never be other than exhausted, and affairs will never be other than examined. If the human heart has something to enjoy, it will be harmonious and submissive. If reformers can illuminate and examine affairs and their principles, and make the human heart harmonious and submissive, they may bring about great progress, and acquire purity and straightforwardness. In a case like this, the alteration and reform will acquire what is extremely proper for them, and this is why "regrets vanish." If the affairs of the world are not reformed in this way, they will bring about the reverse: decay and harm. This is why the Hide hexagram refers to the way of having regrets. It is only when the reform is extremely proper that one's new and former regrets will both vanish. "**When heaven and earth are reformed, the four seasons are brought to completion. With Tang and Wu, there was a reform of the mandate, submission to heaven, and correspondence to people. How great is the moment of the Hide hexagram!**" The way of unfolding reform has its limit in the alteration and change of heaven and earth, in the beginning and end of the revolution of the seasons. Heaven and earth, or *yin* and *yang*, in their unfolding, relocation, modification, and change, bring the four seasons to completion. It is because of this that the ten thousand things are born, grow, then come to completion and to their end. Each of them acquires what is fitting for it. There is reform, and afterward "the four seasons are brought to completion." When the revolution of the seasons has come to its end, it will necessarily be reformed and renewed. Kings flourish when they receive a mandate from heaven, and this is why a time of change is called a "reform of the mandate." King Tang and King Wu submitted to the mandate of heaven above and corresponded to the human heart below.[2] This is "submission to heaven, and correspondence to people." When the way of heaven is altered and modified, or when the procedures of the times are relocated and changed, the reform is extremely great. This is why the *Judgment* applauds it, saying "how great is the moment of the Hide hexagram!"

The *Symbol* says: "**At the center of the lake, there is fire: Hide. Noble people use it to set the calendar in order and shed light on the seasons.**" Water and fire putting each other to rest constitute the Hide hexagram. The *ge* character of Hide refers to alteration. When noble people gaze on the symbol of alteration and reform, they unfold the relocation and change of the sun, moon, stars, and planets, and they use it to set the numbering of the calendar in order, and to shed light on the sequence of the four seasons. As for the way of alteration and change, even the greatest state of affairs, the most enlightened principle, or the most manifest of traces, is nothing like the four seasons. If they gaze on the four seasons and submit to alteration and reform, they will align themselves with the sequence of heaven and earth.

The initial "nine" line: **for confinement, it employs the hide of the yellow cow.** Alteration and reform are the greatest of affairs. One must possess the moment for them, the position for them, and the powers for them, and then, having apprehended and scrutinized them, one may move with caution. Afterward, there should be no regrets. This "nine" line makes use of the moment, but it is the initial line of the hexagram. Since it moves at the initiation of the affair, it has no intention of scrutiny or caution, and so it becomes the symbol of restless change. It makes use of its position, but it is at the bottom of the hexagram.

Since it moves at the bottom without either the moment or a supporting line, and its substance and propensity carry no weight, it will be blamed for its poaching and for other faults. It makes use of its power, but it is a *yang* line in the Cast trigram substance. The nature of the Cast trigram is to ascend, and the substance of a firm line is vigorous — both of them are rapid in their movement. Since its powers are like this, anything it does will bring extreme misfortune and blame. In fact, those whose firmness is without centrality and whose substance is restless are insufficient in their centrality and submissiveness. It is proper that they make themselves certain with centrality and submissiveness, and then they may move without fault. The word "confinement" refers to tethering and bolting down, and the "hide" is what contains or bolts it down. "Yellow" is the color of centrality and "cow" refers to something submissive. "For confinement, it employs the hide of the yellow cow": it makes itself certain using the way of centrality and submissiveness, and it moves without fault. Why does the line statement not say that there is good or bad fortune? Response: if it were to be at fault by moving, there would be misfortune and blame. Since it makes itself certain with centrality and submissiveness, there is no reform, and that is all. How could it be ready to possess either good or bad fortune? **The *Symbol* says: "'For confinement, it employs the yellow cow': it should not do anything."** The moment, position, and powers of the initial "nine" line are all of them incapable of doing anything. This is why it is proper that it make itself certain with centrality and submission.

The second "six" line: when the day has already come, there is reform. Taking the field brings good fortune and no blame. This "six" line occupies the second position, is soft and submissive, and acquires centrality and straightforwardness. Further, it is the master of pattern and enlightenment, and there is a ruler of *yang* firmness above it. They have the same virtues and correspond to each other. Since it is central and straightforward, it is not partial and does not conceal itself; since it has pattern and enlightenment, it exhausts the principle of the affair; since it corresponds to the higher line, it acquires its aptitude and propensity; since its substance is submissive, it does not draw back from or up-end it. It is in the right moment, it has acquired a position, and its powers are sufficient, which is the best that someone placed in the Hide hexagram can do. Nonetheless, it is not proper for the way of the minister to be first in reform. Further, it must wait for those above and below to believe in it, and this is why "when the day has already come, there is reform." When the power and virtue of the second line, as well as the terrain it occupies and the moment it chances on, are sufficient to reform the decay of the world and renew the order of the world, then it is proper to advance. If it assists the rulers above it and puts their way into action, then there will be "good fortune and no blame." If it does not advance, then it should lose the moment for doing something and there will be blame. The substance of the second line is soft, and so it is placed in its proper position. Since its substance is soft, its advance will be slack; since its position is proper for it, it places itself with certainty. Alteration and reform are the greatest of affairs, and this is why the line statement gives this warning. The second line acquires centrality and corresponds to a firm line, and so it has not yet reached the point of loss from its softness. Because there may be some doubt about this warning, the sage sheds light on its meaning, so that the powers of worthy people will not lose the moment when they ought to do something. **The Symbol says: "'When the day has already come, there is reform': there is excellence in its action."** "When the day has already come, there is reform. Taking the field brings good fortune and no blame": if it acts, it will possess excellence and delight. This signifies that it should be able to reform the decay of the world and renew the affairs of the world. To be placed here without acting is to have no heart for saving others from decay and crossing through the times with them. Such a one will lose the moment, and there will be blame.

The third "nine" line: taking the field brings misfortune. Purity brings danger. It remarks on the reform and approaches three times. It is trustworthy. The third "nine" line uses *yang* firmness at the top of the lower trigram. Further, it occupies the top position in the Cast trigram, it does not acquire centrality, and it refers to those who restlessly move toward reform. To be in the lower trigram and restlessly make alterations and reforms—action in such a case will bring "misfortune." Nonetheless, if it occupies the top position in the lower trigram, and it is proper that the affair be reformed, how could it not do anything? If it attempts to guard its purity and straightforwardness, and cherishes its peril and trouble, submitting and attending to public discussion, then it will be able to act without doubt. "It remarks on the reform": it is proper to discuss the reform. The word "approaches" refers either to completing it or aligning with it. It is proper to scrutinize and examine its remarks on reform up to "three times." If everyone aligns with it, then one may believe in it. If its remarks can be extremely weighty and cautious like this, then it will necessarily acquire what is extremely proper, and become "trustworthy." If what it believes in and what the crowd believes in are like this, then it should make reforms. In the moment of reform, it occupies the top position in the lower trigram, when it is proper that affairs be reformed. If it does nothing because it is trembling and troubled, then it will lose the moment and do harm. It is proper to be nothing but extremely cautious and weighty, not delegating command to its own firmness and enlightenment but scrutinizing and appraising the public discussion until it approaches three times. If it makes the reform afterward, then there will be no excess. **The *Symbol* says: "'It remarks on the reform and approaches three times': why go further?"** Since the discussion of the crowd is appraised until it "approaches three times," the affair is extremely proper. The question "why go further?" is like the customary question: "Why make another journey?"[3] If it acts in such a case, it will submit to principle and act in accord with the moment. It does not want to act on its own private intentions, and so it will necessarily acquire what is fitting.

The fourth "nine" line: regrets vanish. It is trustworthy. It modifies the mandate. There is good fortune. The fourth "nine" line refers to the abundance of reform, and its *yang* firmness refers to the power of reform. It has cast off the lower trigram substance, and its own substance advances upward, which refers to the moment of reform; it occupies the border between water and fire, which refers to the propensity of reform; it has acquired a position near the ruler, which refers to its command over reform; it is not bound to any corresponding line, which refers to its tendency of reform; since a "nine" line occupies the fourth position, firmness and softness border each other, which refers to the function of reform; since the fourth line has equipped itself like this, it may be said to be the proper moment for reform. There may be regrets over a state of affairs and afterward reform. If it is made proper by the reform, then the "regrets vanish." When the reform has made it proper, it needs only to place itself with extreme sincerity. This is why, if "it is trustworthy," then "it modifies the mandate" and "there is good fortune." The phrase "modifies the mandate" refers to modifying what it does, and signifies reform. When the state of affairs is already proper and the decay has been reformed, it has only to act with sincerity. Those above will believe in it and those below will submit to it—its "good fortune" should be recognized. Without either centrality or straightforwardness, the fourth line is extremely good. How can this be? Response: it is merely that it places itself in a soft position, and this is why its firmness is not excessive. It draws near the ruling line without pressing against it, submitting to and serving its centrality and straightforwardness, so that it becomes a person of centrality and straightforwardness. The meaning chosen by the *Book of Changes* is not constant but follows the moment, and that is all. **The *Symbol* says: "Its good fortune is that 'it modifies the mandate': they believe in its tendencies."** "It modifies the mandate" and "there is good fortune," so that those above and below believe in its tendencies. When its sincerity has become extreme, those above and below will believe in it. The way of reform has the belief of those above and below as its root. If reform is not proper and it is not trustworthy, then no one will believe in it. If reform is proper but no one believes in it, it will be as though it were unable to act. What will the case be like when reform is not proper?

The fifth "nine" line: great people are like tigers in their alteration. There is not yet divination, but it is trusted. The fifth "nine" line uses the power of *yang* firmness and the virtues of centrality and straightforwardness, it occupies the position of respect, and it refers to "great people." The way of great people is to reform the affairs of the world, so that nothing is improper and nothing disagrees with the moment. In what is exceedingly altered and transformed, the principle of affairs is luminous and manifest, like the pattern of color on tigers. This is why the line statement says they are "like tigers in their alteration." Dragons and tigers are symbols of great people. The word "alteration" refers to the alteration of affairs and things, yet it says here that the tigers are altered. How can this be? Response: what great people alter is also the alteration of great people. Those who alter and reform using the way of centrality and straightforwardness of great people will themselves become luminous, illuminated, and manifest. They do not wait for the resolutions of "divination," but know already that it is extremely proper and that the world will necessarily believe in it. When great people reform the blindness of the world, they do not wait for the resolutions of divination, but know that it is extremely proper and believe in it. **The *Symbol* says: "'Great people are like tigers in their alteration': their pattern is luminous."** When the principle of the affair is enlightened and manifest like the luminous sheen and enlightened abundance of the pattern on a tiger, how could the world not trust it?

The top "six" line: noble people are like leopards in their alteration. Small people reform their faces. Taking the field brings misfortune. Occupying a position of purity brings good fortune. The end of reform is when the way of reform is completed. The phrase "noble people" signifies good people. Those who are fine and good will attend to their own reform, and so will alter themselves. It will be manifest and apparent, like the elaborate decoration of the leopard. Although small people—whose darkness and stupidity make it difficult for them to relocate themselves—are not yet able to transform their hearts, they at least reform their faces so that they may attend to the teachings and decrees of those above. Dragons and tigers are symbols of great people, and this is why the line statement calls great people "tigers," while noble people are called "leopards." Human nature is good at its root, and everyone should be able to alter and transform. Nonetheless, there are some who are "at the bottom of stupidity," who cannot be converted even by sages.⁴ When Yao and Shun were the rulers, when sage succeeded sage for more than a hundred years, their transformation of the world could be called deep and continuous. Still there were the Miao tribe and brother Xiang, who arrived and tarried, and "gained in discipline," but in fact only reformed their faces, and that is all.⁵ When small people have been reformed on the outside, the way of reform is complete. Were someone to attend to them again, to set them in order more deeply, it would become extreme, and the extreme is not the way. This is why those who take the field when the end of reform has been reached will bring misfortune. It is proper to guard oneself with purity and certainty. If one reaches the limit of reform, but does not keep guard with purity, then what has been reformed will follow along and turn to further alteration. When the affairs of the world are at their beginning, there is distress at the difficulty of reform; when the reform has ceased, there is distress at not being able to keep guard over it. This is why, at the end of the Hide hexagram, the line statement warns that "occupying a position of purity brings good fortune." Does it warn about occupying a position of purity because this is a 'six' line? Response: it is remarking on the end of reform, when there is nothing that is not at its center. If human nature is good at its root, why are there some who may not be reformed? Response: if one is speaking about human nature, then everyone is good. If one is speaking about human powers, then some are "at the bottom of stupidity" and cannot be converted. The saying "at the bottom of stupidity" may refer either to "doing violence to oneself" or to "deserting oneself."⁶ Were people to use goodness to set themselves in order, nothing about them could not be converted. Though their darkness and stupidity might be extreme, they could all polish themselves step by step and advance. But those who do violence to themselves resist it because of their unbelief. And those who desert themselves are severed from it because they do nothing. They may occupy a position with the sages, but nothing can transform or enter into them. They are the ones said by Zhongni to be "at the bottom of stupidity."⁷ Nonetheless, not all of those in the world who desert themselves or do violence to themselves are necessarily in darkness and stupidity. Now and then, there are strong and brutal people, whose power and force exceeds that of everyone else. This was the case for Xin in the Shang dynasty.⁸ The sage refers to these people as "at the bottom of stupidity" because they sever themselves from the good. Nonetheless, one who tests what they have wedded themselves to will sincerely find them stupid. It has already been said that they are "at the bottom of stupidity," and yet the line statement says they can reform their faces. How can this be? Response: although their hearts are severed from the way of the good, if they tremble before authority and commit few crimes, they will be the same as other people. In this one respect they are the same as other people, and so it should be recognized that their crimes do not belong to their nature. **The *Symbol* says: "'Noble people are like leopards in their alteration': their pattern is decorative. 'Small people reform their faces': they submit by attending to their rulers."** Noble people attend to the good of transformation and relocation. They complete a pattern that is elaborate and decorative, whose arrangement may be seen on the outside. People in positions at the center and above are never without alteration and reform. Although small people are not converted, they still do not dare to indulge in what is bad. They reform and change on the outside, by submitting and attending to the teachings and decrees of the rulers above them. The phrase "reform their faces" refers to this. When this point is reached, the way of reform is complete. Small people may be exhorted to appear good, and this is what noble people embrace. If they make another journey to set people in order, there will be misfortune.

50. TRIPOD (*DING* 鼎)

The *Sequence of the Hexagrams* says: "To bring about the reform of things, there is nothing like the tripod. This is why the Tripod hexagram is next." When the tripod is considered according to its function, it is to bring about the reform of things. It alters the raw so that it becomes cooked; it changes the solid so that it becomes soft. Water and fire cannot be in the same place. If they can be made to align with each other in their functions and not harm each other—this is to be capable of bringing about the reform of things. And so the Tripod hexagram succeeds the Hide hexagram. As for the trigrams, the Cast trigram is above and the Low trigram below. Since they constitute a tripod, it is chosen as both the symbol and the meaning of the hexagram. As for why it is chosen as the symbol, there are two reasons: concerning the substance of the whole hexagram, one may remark that the lines planted at the bottom constitute its feet, and the full lines at the center constitute its torso, which symbolizes the reception of things at one's center. The ears extend on opposite sides toward the top, and the poles run horizontally across the top. Together they symbolize a tripod. Concerning the substances of the upper and lower trigrams, one may remark that that the center of the upper trigram is empty, and the lower trigram has feet to serve it—they, too, symbolize a tripod. As for why it is chosen as the meaning, the wood trigram attends to the fire trigram, and they are the lowliness and entry trigrams—both have the meaning of submitting and attending to something. Wood attending to fire also constitutes the symbol of the hexagram. The sole function of fire is to bake and to fry. Baking does not borrow tools, and this is why frying is chosen as the symbol, and this constitutes the Tripod hexagram. "By putting wood lower than the fire": this is the symbol of frying or braising. When the tool was constructed, was the shape of this hexagram chosen for it, or was the shape of the tool used to constitute the hexagram? Response: when the tool was constructed, the shape of this hexagram was chosen for it. The shape persists in the hexagram, but the hexagram does not necessarily precede the tool. When the sages were constructing tools, they did not wait to see the hexagrams and only afterward recognize the shapes of the tools. The crowd, on the other hand, was unable to recognize these shapes, and this is why the hexagrams were provided—to show them to the crowd. Which came first and which came afterward, the hexagram or the tool, does no harm to the meaning. Someone wonders: the shape of the tripod does not occur spontaneously, but is constituted by people. Response: certainly it is constituted by people. Nonetheless, frying or braising are capable of bringing things to completion. When a form is constructed for this, then it may have it as its function. The function is not constituted by people, but occurs spontaneously, as is also the case with the well. Although the tool precedes the hexagram, what is chosen for it is the shape of the hexagram. The hexagram, in turn, has the function of the tool as its meaning.

Tripod: there are primacy, good fortune, and progress. The judgment is remarking on the powers of the trigrams. Those who are like the powers of the trigrams should be able to bring about primacy and progress. It is proper that the judgment stop at saying "primacy and progress," but the text is distorted with the phrase "good fortune." Those who possess the powers of the trigrams should be able to bring about primacy and progress, but they are not yet ready to possess primacy and good fortune. The *Judgment*, in turn, stops at saying "primacy and progress," which sheds light on this distortion of the text.

The *Judgment* says: "The tripod is the shape." This is the Tripod hexagram because the shape of a tripod was chosen for it. A tripod is a tool, and it gives its law to the shape of the hexagram. First there is the shape, and afterward the tool. The hexagram, in turn, has the function of the tool as its meaning. A tripod is a great tool, weighty and precious, and this is why its construction is produced or formed using a mold. It gives its law to a shape that is exceptionally severe. The name of the Tripod hexagram is straightforward. The people of antiquity started with something particular—that is, they started with something real and straightforward. Concerning its form, one may remark that the ears are planted on opposite sides at the top, and the feet are divided and extended at the bottom. It is all-encompassing or spherical on both the inside and the outside. Whether it is lofty or humble, beneficial or meager, this form is never without its law, and it is extremely straightforward. Because of its extreme straightforwardness, it afterward completes a shape that is contented and weighty. This is why the tripod is a tool that gives its law to a shape, and this is the Tripod hexagram because of its shape. **"By putting wood lower than the fire, one makes progress in one's braising. Sages make progress in holding a feast for the lord on high. They make great progress so as to nourish sages and worthies."** Concerning the two trigram substances, one may remark that they refer to the function of the tripod. "By putting wood lower than fire," by making the wood attend to the fire, "one makes progress in one's braising." Considered as a tool, the tripod is something on which the lives of people are, to a great degree, dependent. The greatness of its function reaches its limit when sages "make progress in holding a feast for the lord on high. They make great progress so as to nourish sages and worthies." The sages here are the sage-kings of antiquity. The word "great" refers to their breadth. **"There is lowliness, and ears and eyes that are aware and enlightened. Softness advances and travels upward. It acquires centrality and corresponds to firmness. As a result, there are primacy and progress."** Having remarked earlier on the function of the tripod, the *Judgment* now turns its remarks to the powers of the trigrams. If people can be like the powers of the trigrams, they should be able to bring about "primacy and progress." The Low trigram substance is below and refers to lowliness and submission to principle. The Cast or enlightenment trigram with its empty center is above, and symbolizes "ears and eyes that are aware and enlightened." In general, when the Cast trigram is on top, the *Judgment* says that "softness advances and travels upward." Softness is a thing in positions below, but here it occupies the position of respect: it "advances and travels upward." It uses enlightenment to occupy the position of respect, and it "acquires" the way of "centrality and corresponds to firmness." That is, it can employ the way of *yang* firmness. The fifth line occupies the center, it makes use of softness, and it corresponds to a firm line, which is to acquire the way of centrality. Because its powers are like this, there can be "primacy and progress."

The *Symbol* says: "Above the wood, there is fire: Tripod. Noble people use it to make their positions straightforward and to crystallize the mandate." "Above the wood, there is fire," or "by putting wood lower than the fire": this is the symbol of frying or braising, and this is why these trigrams refer to the Tripod hexagram. When noble people gaze on the symbol of the tripod, they use it to "make their positions straightforward and to crystallize the mandate." A tripod is a tool that gives its law to a shape—its form is regular and straightforward, and its substance is contented and weighty. Since its regularity and straightforwardness were chosen as the symbol, they will use it to "make their positions straightforward," which signifies that they will make the positions that they occupy straightforward. That noble people must place themselves straight-forwardly even in small things is exemplified by the following: "If his mat was not straightforward, he would not sit on it," and one should neither slouch nor lean on anything.[1] Since the symbol of contentment and weight has been chosen, they will crystallize their mandate and decree, which is to make their mandate and decree contented and weighty. To "crystallize" means to gather and stop, and signifies contentment and weight. A customary expression of the present time is "to crystallize it just so," and it is used in the language of man-dates and decrees. In general, it is proper that movement always be contented and weighty.

The initial "six" line: the tripod has upset toes. There is profit in pouring out what is lacking. It acquires a concubine for the gentleman. There is no blame. This "six" line is at the bottom of the Tripod hexagram and is symbolized by the "toes." It corresponds to the fourth line above it and its toes are pointed up, which is the symbol of being "upset." When the tripod is overturned, its toes will be upset. If its toes are upset, it will overturn what fills it, which is not the way of submissiveness. Nonetheless, there are moments when it is proper to upset things. If the upset toes signify a collapse that pours out and defeats what is bad, bringing about something unpolluted and choosing something new, then it is permissible. This is why the "profit" in the upset toes lies in "pouring out what is lacking." The word "lacking" here refers to what is bad. The fourth line is near the ruler, in the position of the great minister, while the initial line is someone in a position below who corresponds to it. The higher line seeks out the lower, while the lower line attends to the higher. The higher line can employ what is good in the lower, while the lower can assist the higher in what it does, and so they should be able to bring their affairs and tasks to completion. The goodness of this way is just like the upset toes of the tripod. There are mo-ments when it is proper to upset things, and so it does not yet upend its prin-ciple. "It acquires a concubine for the gentleman. There is no blame": this "six" line is *yin* and humble, and this is why the line statement refers to it as a con-cubine. The phrase "it acquires a concubine" signifies that it acquires another person. Were it to acquire a fine concubine, she would be able to assist and help her master and there would be neither excess nor blame. The "gentleman" here refers to the master, and "for the gentleman" indicates that it brings about "no blame" for its master. This "six" line is *yin* and occupies a position below. Being humble and lowly, it attends to *yang* and is symbolized by the concubine. The upset toes reveal the meaning of a "six" line corresponding to the fourth line above it. The initial "six" line is without power or virtue at its root, but it may still be chosen. This is why it says that "it acquires a concubine." It is remarking that this will be the case if it acquires another person. **The *Symbol* says: "'The tripod has upset toes': it is not yet upended."** The tripod is overturned and has upset toes, which is the way of upending. Nonetheless, it does not necessarily constitute an upending. In fact, there are moments when a collapse will pour out what is lacking or bad. **"'There is profit in pouring out what is lacking': it attends to what is estimable."** To drive out what is old and accept what is new, or to disgorge what is bad and receive what is beautiful—this is the meaning of attending "to what is estimable." By corresponding to the fourth line, it attends to what is estimable above it.

The second "nine" line: the tripod is full. My counterpart is ill and cannot approach me. There is good fortune. The second line uses firmness and fullness to occupy the center, and is symbolized by the tripod whose center is full. If what fills the tripod is poured out at the top, then it is performing its function. The *yang* firmness of the second line has the power to perform the function of making the crossing. Since it corresponds to the fifth line and attends to the ruler—the fifth "six" line above it—it acquires straightforwardness and its way may make progress. Nonetheless, it is profoundly close to the initial line, and *yin* is what attends to *yang*. The second "nine" line occupies the center and corresponds to a central line, so that it does not reach the point of losing its straightforwardness, but the other line will necessarily seek it out, even though it guards itself. This is why the line statement warns that it can travel far away from it. If it is not made to arrive or "approach me," then "there is good fortune." The word "counterpart" refers to an opponent. *Yin* is something that opposes *yang*, and here it signifies the initial line. If they attend to each other, they will not be straightforward and duty will be harmed—this is to be "ill." It is proper that the second line guard itself with straightforwardness, making it impossible for the other line to arrive or approach it. If people can guard themselves with straightforwardness, those who are not straightforward will be unable to approach them, and so there will be good fortune. **The *Symbol* says: "'The tripod is full': it is cautious about where it goes."** What fills the tripod refers to the power and vocation of people. It is proper that they be cautious about where they rush off to. If they are not cautious about where they are journeying, they will be snared by their absence of duty. The second can avoid intimacy with the initial line while attending to its straightforward correspondence to the fifth "six" line above it—this is to be "cautious about where it goes." **"My counterpart is ill': in the end, there is no resentment."** "My counterpart is ill": it brings up only the earlier part of the text. The phrase "my counterpart" refers to its own opponent and signifies the initial line. It is not straightforward for the initial line to be close to it—this is to be "ill." Since it guards itself with straightforwardness, the other line will be unable to "approach me," and so "in the end, there is" neither excess nor "resentment."

The third "nine" line: the tripod's ears are reformed. Its action is choked off. The pheasant fat is not eaten. When the rain starts, it regrets its inadequacy. In the end, there is good fortune. The phrase "tripod's ears" refers to the fifth "six" line, which is the master of the Tripod hexagram. The third line uses *yang* to occupy the top of the Low trigram—that is, it is firm and capable of lowliness, and so its powers are sufficient to cross through this matter. Nonetheless, it is not the same as the fifth line and they do not correspond to each other. The fifth line is central without being straightforward, while the third line is straightforward without being central. They are not the same, and so it has not yet acquired its ruler. If it has not yet acquired its ruler, how could its way have an effect or be put into action? The *ge* character of "reform" refers to an alteration that does something different. The third line is different from the fifth, and they do not align. "Its action is choked off" and it cannot make progress. Since it does not align with its ruler, it does not acquire command or make its function influential. The word "fat" refers to a thing of sweetness and beauty, symbolizing a position with a wage, and "pheasant" points to the fifth line. It possesses the virtues of pattern and enlightenment, and this is why it is signified by the pheasant. The third line has the power and the function, but it has not acquired the position with a wage occupied by the fifth "six" line—that is, it has not been able to eat the pheasant fat. When noble people store up their virtue, they will necessarily display it continuously; when they keep guard over their way, they will necessarily make progress "in the end." The fifth line symbolizes awareness and enlightenment, while the third is something that advances upward in the end. When *yin* and *yang* interact smoothly, then it rains. "When the rain starts": this indicates that it is about to rain, and is remarking that the fifth and third lines are starting to, or are about to, harmonize and align. "It regrets its inadequacy. In the end, there is good fortune": this signifies that it regrets its insufficiency, and that it is proper for it to obtain good fortune in the end. The third line cherishes its power and has no partner. This is why it regrets its insufficiency. Nonetheless, it has the virtue of *yang* firmness. There are awareness and enlightenment above and lowliness and straightforwardness below. In the end, they will necessarily acquire each other, and this is why "there is good fortune." Although the third line is not at the center, it belongs to the Low trigram substance, and this is why it does not lose itself in excessive firmness.

If it were excessively firm, how could there be good fortune in the end? **The Symbol says: "'The tripod's ears are reformed': they lose sight of their duty."** In the beginning, the "tripod's ears are reformed" and made different, so that they lose sight of their duty to seek each other out. It does not correspond to the fifth line, so that it has lost the way of seeking alignment. It is not at the center, and it symbolizes those whose tendencies are not the same. As a result, its action is choked off and it does not develop. Nonetheless, there are enlightenment above and power below. They will necessarily harmonize and align in the end, and this is why there is good fortune "when the rain starts."

The fourth "nine" line: the tripod breaks its foot. It overturns the duke's pottage. His form is drenched. There is misfortune. The fourth is the position of the great minister and refers to those with command over the affairs of the world. How could one person be capable of possessing sole command over the affairs of the world? It is necessary and proper that it seek out the worthy and wise people of the world so that their forces may be allied. If it acquires these people, then it may bring about the order of the world without labor. If it does not employ these people, then it will bring defeat to the affairs of the state and endow the world with distress. The fourth corresponds to the initial line below it, but the initial line with its *yin* softness refers to small people who should not be employed. If the fourth line employs them, its command will not be victorious and it will bring defeat to its affairs, just like a tripod that "breaks its foot." If the tripod breaks its foot, it will collapse and overturn the pottage of the duke above it. The word "pottage" refers to what fills the tripod. It occupies the position of the great minister and it is proper for it to have command over the world, but it employs the wrong people and reaches the point of overturning and defeat. Its command is not victorious, and it should be extremely disappointed and humiliated. "His form is drenched": this signifies that he is flushed and sweaty, and his misfortune should be recognized. The *Appended Statements* says that "its virtue is meager, but its position is respected; its knowledge is small, but its skill is great; its force is small, but its command carries weight—it is rare that this will not extend itself further."[2] It is remarking that its command is not victorious. It conceals itself in what is private, its "virtue is meager," and its "knowledge is small." **The Symbol says: "'It overturns the duke's pottage': how could anyone believe in it?"** It is proper that great ministers have command over the world. They must be able to complete the order and contentment of the world, and then it will not be wrong for the ruler above to delegate command to them or for the people below to hope in them. Since its own personal tendency is to bring about the way of command, it will not lose sight of what it hopes to do, and others may be said to "believe in it." If this were not the case, it would lose sight of its mission and it would be wrong for those above to have faith in or delegate command to it. How could it become believable? This is why the *Symbol* says: "How could anyone believe in it?"

The fifth "six" line: the tripod has yellow ears and golden poles. There is profit in purity. The fifth line is in the upper part of the tripod and is symbolized by the "ears." The handles by which the tripod is raised are its ears, and so they are the masters of the tripod. The fifth line possesses the virtue of centrality, and this is why the line statement says that it has "yellow ears." The word "poles" refers to what attaches to the ears. The poles, as what arrive and attend to the ears, refer to the second line, which corresponds to the fifth. The second line possesses the virtues of firmness and centrality. *Yang* substances are firm, and yellow is the color of centrality. This is why it refers to the second line as "golden poles." The pattern and enlightenment of the fifth line acquire centrality and correspond to firmness, while the firmness and centrality of the second line belong to the Low trigram substance and correspond to the higher line. Their powers are not insufficient, and it is extremely good that they correspond to each other. Their profit lies in purity and certainty, and that is all. The fifth "six" line occupies the center and corresponds to a central line. It does not reach the point of losing its straightforwardness, even though its disposition is *yin* and soft at its root. This is why it gives the warning about purity and certainty at the center. **The *Symbol* says: "'The tripod has yellow ears': centrality is considered full."** The fifth "six" line considers the acquisition of centrality to be good—that is, it considers centrality to be the fullness of virtue. The sole reason why the fifth line corresponds to a firm line with awareness and enlightenment, why it is the master of the Tripod hexagram, and why it acquires the way of the tripod is that it acquires centrality.

The top "nine" line: the tripod has jade poles. There is great good fortune. Nothing is without profit. The well and the tripod both have going out at the top as their function. It is placed in the end position and completes the task of the tripod. To be at the top is symbolized by the "poles," and those who are both firm and mild are referred to as "jade." Although this "nine" line is *yang* and firm, it occupies a *yin* position and walks on a soft line. It is not at the limit of firmness, and so it is capable of mildness. Those who occupy the way that completes their task have merely placed themselves well, and that is all. When firmness and softness are suited to and fitting for each other, and movement and tranquility do not exceed each other, then "there is great good fortune" and "nothing is without profit." The word "poles" refers to being at the top.

Although it occupies a terrain without a position, it is really proper that it be employed. It is different from other hexagrams, although this is also the case for the Well hexagram. **The *Symbol* says: "The 'jade poles' are at the top: firmness and softness rein each other."** To be both firm and mild is to have a rein. The top line occupies the terrain on which the task is completed and the function is brought about.[3] Firmness and softness are centered and reined, and so "there is great good fortune" and "nothing is without profit." Since the Well and Tripod hexagrams both consider the end position to be what completes the task, why does the Tripod line statement not say that "primacy brings good fortune"? Response: the task and function of the well are both to go out at the top, and further, it has a liberal influence and the virtue of constancy. As a result, "primacy brings good fortune." The tripod has frying and braising as its task and the occupation of the top position as the completion of its virtue. It is different from the well because its "firmness and softness rein each other." This is why it acquires great good fortune.

51. SHAKE (*ZHEN* 震)

The *Sequence of the Hexagrams* says: "To be the master of tools, there is nothing like the oldest son. This is why the Shake hexagram is next." The Tripod hexagram refers to a tool, and the Shake hexagram refers to a grown man. This is why the *Sequence* chooses the master of tools as its meaning, and why it succeeds or comes after the Tripod hexagram. The oldest son will circulate through the state, and will be called to successive positions. This is why his mastery is the mastery of tools. The *Sequence of the Hexagrams* chooses the greatness of this one meaning: the meaning of succeeding each other. As for the Shake trigram, a single *yang* line is born below two *yin* lines and moves upward. This is why they constitute the Shake trigram, since the word "shake" refers to movement. It is not called the "move" trigram because shaking is a movement that means to arouse and reveal, to be shaken and disturbed. When the Lead and Yield trigrams interact, the first line is squeezed out to complete the Shake trigram. It refers to the growth of living things, and this is why it is referred to as a grown man. Its symbol is thunder, but its meaning is movement. Thunder is the symbol of what shakes and arouses, and movement has the meaning of disturbing or troubling.

Shake: there is progress. When a *yang* line is born below and advances upward, it means that "there is progress." Further, shaking refers to movement, to bringing fear and trouble, and to having the mastery. To shake is to arouse and reveal, to move and advance, to be troubled and corrected, to have the mastery and preserve one's greatness. All of these should be able to bring about progress, and this is why "there is progress" in the Shake hexagram. **When the shaking arrives, there is terror, and terror again, but then there are the chuckling and chuckling sounds of laughter.** Those who face the arrival of shaking and movement, being fearful and troubled, will not dare to make themselves serene. They will encompass and cycle through concern and apprehension, so that "there is terror, and terror again." "Terror, and terror again": its concern and apprehension do not have the appearance of contentment. The flies on a tiger are said to be in terror because they encompass it and circle around it in their concern and apprehension. They do not make themselves serene. To be placed like this in the Shake hexagram is to be able to preserve one's contentment and generosity. This is why "there are the chuckling and chuckling sounds of laughter." "Chuckling and chuckling" is the sound of laughter, which has the appearance of harmony and suitability. **When the shaking disturbs from thirty miles away, it will not be deprived of the ladle and the wine.** The judgment is remarking on the greatness of a movement that shakes, but also on the way of placing oneself there. For greatness of movement, there is nothing like thunder. The Shake trigram refers to thunder, and this is why the judgment remarks on thunder. The shaking movement of thunder can disturb people as far as thirty miles away, who are not untroubled, and who then lose themselves.[1] The sound of thunder can extend for thirty miles. Only those making sacrifices and libations in the ancestral temple, grasping the ladle and the wine, will not reach the point of deprivation and loss. For bringing about sincerity and reverence in people, there is nothing like sacrifices and libations. The ladle is used to bear what fills the tripod and raise it to the stand, and the wine is spilled on the ground to make the spirit descend. At the start, those who pour the oblation so as to seek the spirit, who offer the animal and make supplications for the feast, and who exhaust a heart of sincerity and reverence, cannot be troubled or made to lose their guard solely by the authoritative shaking of thunder. This is why, while watching over a great shaking and troubling, they can be contented and not lose themselves. They are merely sincere and reverent, and that is all, which is the way to place oneself in the Shake hexagram. The judgment does not choose to comment on the powers of the trigrams, and this is why its remarks only concern the way to place oneself in the Shake hexagram.

The *Judgment* says: "'Shake: there is progress. When the shaking arrives, there is terror, and terror again': their fear brings them blessings. 'There are the chuckling and chuckling sounds of laughter': afterward, they are regulated." The meaning of progress belongs to the Shake hexagram itself and is not effected by the powers of the trigrams. "When the shaking arrives," those who can be fearful and troubled, who make themselves correct and cautious, may bring about the reverse: blessings and good fortune. "There are the chuckling and chuckling sounds of laughter": the *Judgment* is remarking that this is how they will be. Because they can be fearful and troubled, they will afterward place themselves where there are laws and regulations. If there are regulations, then they will be contented and not troubled. This is the way to place oneself in the Shake hexagram. "'**The shaking disturbs from thirty miles away': if it disturbs those far away, it troubles those who are adjacent to it.**" The shaking of thunder extends for thirty miles. Those far away are disturbed, while those who are adjacent are troubled. The *Judgment* is remarking that it is authoritative, far away, and great. "**It goes out, and should be able to guard both the ancestral temple and the altar of land and grain as the master of sacrifices.**" The text of the *Judgment* omits the sentence: "It will not be deprived of the ladle and the wine." The hexagram judgment says that "it will not be deprived of the ladle and the wine," which refers at its root to extreme sincerity and reverence. An authority that troubles it cannot make it lose itself. The *Judgment* considers this to be fitting for the oldest son, and so, in the service of the preceding text, it employs the meaning of the oldest son to develop and interpret it. It is saying that, if his sincerity and reverence are such that he cannot "be deprived of the ladle and the wine," the ruler "goes out, and should be able to guard both the ancestral temple and the altar of land and grain as the master of sacrifices." When the oldest son is like this, he should afterward be able to guard the libations of the times, and to serve the state.

The *Symbol* says: "**There are rolls of thunder: Shake. Noble people use it to be fearful and troubled, correcting and inspecting themselves.**" The word "roll" refers to a repeated onslaught. Those above and below are both shaking, and this is why the *Symbol* refers to "rolls of thunder." When the thunder is perpetually repeated, it adds to the abundance of its authority. When noble people gaze on the symbol of rolls of thunder shaking with their authority, they use it to become fearful and troubled, to correct and dominate themselves, and to trace out and inspect themselves. If noble people tremble at the authority of heaven, they will correct themselves and become straightforward. They will reflect on and inspect their excesses, blaming and transforming them. It is proper that every case be like this—not only the shaking of thunder, but in general, when one encounters affairs that disturb and trouble.

The initial "nine" line: when the shaking arrives, there is terror, and terror again. Afterward, there are the chuckling and chuckling sounds of laughter. There is good fortune. The initial "nine" line is the master that completes the Shake trigram, and it refers to those who bring about the shaking. It is at the bottom of the hexagram, and is placed in the initial position of the Shake trigram. It recognizes that the shaking has arrived and it faces the beginning of the shaking. Were it able to be fearful and troubled, encompassing and cycling through all its concern and apprehension, there would be such "terror, and terror again" that it would not dare to stop and be serene. In the end, it would necessarily preserve its contentment and "good fortune." This is why, "afterward, there are the chuckling and chuckling sounds of laughter." **The *Symbol* says: "'When the shaking arrives, there is terror, and terror again': their fear brings them blessings. 'There are the chuckling and chuckling sounds of laughter': afterward, they are regulated."** "When the shaking arrives," if it can be fearful and troubled, and cycle through all its concern, then there will be no distress. This is to be able to bring "blessings" instead, because it is fearful and troubled. Because it is fearful and troubled, it corrects and inspects itself, and does not dare to draw back from the laws and measures. This is to be lawful and "regulated" afterward, because of the shaking, and this is why it can preserve its contentment and good fortune: "There are the chuckling and chuckling sounds of laughter."

The second "six" line: when the shaking arrives, there is danger. It is deprived of millions of shells and scales the nine hills. It does not pursue them, but after seven days it will acquire them. The second "six" line occupies the center, acquires straightforwardness, and refers to those who place themselves well in the Shake hexagram. It rides the firmness of the initial "nine" line, and the "nine" line is the master of the Shake trigram. Since it moves with firmness and shaking, and is roused to ascend, who could resist it? The word "danger" refers to its ferocity and peril. If what arrives is fierce, then it places itself in peril. The word "millions" refers to a certain measure, "shells" are its supplies, to "scale" is to rise, and the "nine hills" are the loftiest of hills. To "pursue" is to make a journey on the trail of something. Because "there is danger" when "the shaking arrives," there can be no proper measure, and it will necessarily be deprived of what it possesses. It will then evade the shaking by rising to the extremity of loftiness. The number nine is remarking on the repetition of loftiness, and the repetition of a crest of hills is the extremity of loftiness. The number nine refers to many repetitions, as in the phrases "nine heavens" and "nine earths."[2] "It does not pursue them, but after seven days it will acquire them": centrality and straightforwardness are what the second line esteems. When it encounters the arrival of shaking and trouble, although it calculates that its propensity is to be lowly and evasive, it is nonetheless proper for it to guard its centrality and straightforwardness, and then it will not lose itself. It will necessarily be deprived of millions, and this is why it evades them in a faraway place, so as to guard itself. When the moment has been exceeded, it will return to what is constant. This is a case where "it does not pursue them," but "it will acquire them." To pursue is to approach something. When it has approached something, it will lose its guard. This is why the line statement warns that "it does not pursue them." To evade them in a faraway place, so as to guard itself, is how it places itself at the great start of the Shake hexagram. As for the second line, it is proper that it place itself well in its peril and trouble. Each hexagram has six positions, so the number seven indicates a new beginning. When the affair has reached its end, the moment has already changed. If it does not lose its guard over itself, then the moment will be exceeded and the affair will cease, even though it could not resist its arrival during this one moment. It will then return to what is constant, and this is why it says that "after seven days it will acquire them." **The Symbol says: "'When the shaking arrives, there is danger': it rides firmness."** It faces the Shake hexagram and "rides firmness." As a result, it is in "danger" and imperils itself. When the shaking and firmness arrive, who could resist them?

The third "six" line: in the shaking, it revives, and revives again. If the shaking makes it travel, there will be no mistakes. It "revives, and revives again": its spirit and *qi* are in such a slackened and scattered condition that it loses itself. The third line uses *yin* to occupy a *yang* position, which is not straightforward. If it does not place itself straightforwardly and cannot be contented when the moment is peaceful, what will the case be like when it places itself in the Shake hexagram? This is why it is shaken and troubled, and "revives, and revives again." If it were able to "travel" because it is shaken and troubled, approaching a straightforward position and departing from what is not straightforward, then it could be without excess. The word "mistakes" refers to excess. If the third line travels, then it will reach the fourth position, which is straightforward for it. Movement that approaches straightforwardness is good, and this is why the second line "does not pursue them" and acquires them by itself. If the third line can travel, "there will be no mistakes." If it places itself without straightforwardness while shaken and troubled, its mistake should be recognized. **The Symbol says: "'In the shaking, it revives, and revives again': its position is not proper for it."** When it loses itself in being fearful and troubled, and "revives, and revives again," this is because it has not placed itself properly. Since it is neither central nor straightforward, how could it be contented?

The fourth "nine" line: in the shaking, it finds success in the mud. The fourth "nine" line occupies a position in the moment of shaking and movement, it is neither central nor straightforward, it is placed in a soft position, and it has lost the way of firmness and vigor. It occupies the fourth position without the virtues of centrality and straightforwardness, it is snared and drowns in the space between the repeated *yin* lines, and it refers to those who cannot shake or rouse themselves. This is why the line statement says: "It finds success in the mud." The word "mud" refers to its drowning in laziness. Since the *yang* line is not straightforward and there are repeated *yin* lines above and below it, how could it avoid the mud? The idea of the word "success" here is that it does not reverse itself. If it places itself here while shaken and troubled, it will not be able to guard itself. If it wants to shake and move, it will not be able to rouse itself. When the way of the Shake hexagram vanishes, how could it be "bright" and make progress? **The *Symbol* says: "'In the shaking, it finds success in the mud': it is not yet bright."** A *yang* line is something firm, and the meaning of the Shake hexagram is movement. If it uses firmness to place itself in movement, it will at root possess the way of being "bright" and making progress. Here it has lost its firmness and straightforwardness, and has been snared by the repeated *yin* lines. Since it brings about "success in the mud," how could it be bright? The *Symbol* says that "it is not yet bright," seeing that *yang* firmness is at root capable of shaking, but here it has lost its virtue, and this is why it is in the mud.

The fifth "six" line: in the shaking, making a journey and arriving are both dangerous. Among the millions, it is not deprived of the affair that it possesses. Although the fifth "six" line uses *yin* to occupy a *yang* position—so that its position is not proper for it and it is not straightforward—it nonetheless uses softness to occupy a firm position and acquires centrality. Here it refers to those who possess the virtue of centrality. Since it has not lost its centrality, it will not draw back from straightforwardness, and so its centrality is to be esteemed. In the various hexagrams, the centrality of the second and fifth lines is often considered beautiful even when their positions are not proper for them. Even when the positions of the third and fourth lines are proper for them, their absence of centrality is sometimes considered an excess. Ordinarily, centrality carries more weight than straightforwardness. In fact, a line with centrality will not draw back from straightforwardness, while a straightforward line will not necessarily possess centrality. There is no principle in the world that is as good as centrality. This may be seen in the case of the second "six" line and the fifth "six" line. If the movement of the fifth line makes a journey to the top, its softness will not be able to occupy the limit position of movement, but if it arrives at the bottom, it will confront a firm line: "Making a journey and arriving" are both perilous. It faces the position of the ruler and is the master of the movement hexagram, but it follows what is fitting in its correspondence and alteration, being at the center, and that is all. This is why, when it faces a measure of "millions," it "is not deprived of" or does not lose "the affair that it possesses," and that is all.

"The affair that it possesses" signifies the virtue of centrality. If it does not lose its centrality, then it will not reach the point of misfortune even though it is imperiled. The measure of millions signifies that it does not lose its centrality because it makes plans, is apprehensive, and seeks out others. The fifth line is imperiled because it is neither *yang* nor firm, and no one is helping it. If it made use of *yang* firmness and had help while remaining the master of movement, then it would be able to make progress. If making a journey and arriving are both perilous, then the moment is extremely difficult. If its only hope is not to lose its centrality, then it should be able to guard itself. Those who use softness to become the masters of movement certainly cannot bring about progress or make the crossing. **The *Symbol* says: "'In the shaking, making a journey and arriving are both dangerous': it is perilous to travel. Its 'affair' is centrality: there is greatness without deprivation."** "Making a journey and arriving are both dangerous": if it travels, it will be imperiled. When every movement imperils it, it can only be "without deprivation" in its "affair," and that is all. The phrase "its affair" signifies centrality. If it can prevent the loss of its centrality, then it should be able to guard itself. "There is greatness without deprivation": to be without deprivation is great.

The top "six" line: in the shaking, it is squeezed, and squeezed again. Its look is blurry, and blurry again. Taking the field brings misfortune. If the shaking is not in its own person but in its neighbors, there is no blame. Among the married, there are remarks. The phrase "squeezed, and squeezed again," concerning the condition of disappearing and being squeezed without persisting, signifies that its tendency and *qi* are like this. This "six" line uses *yin* softness to occupy the limit position of the Shake or movement hexagram. Extremely disturbed and troubled, its tendency and *qi* are enervated and squeezed. "Blurry, and blurry again": it does not have a contented or determinate appearance. If its tendency and *qi* are squeezed, and squeezed again, then its look or regard will be unsettled and tentative. It uses a disposition of *yin* softness without centrality or straightforwardness, and it places itself in the limit position of the Shake or movement hexagram. This is why "taking the field brings misfortune." If the shaking extends to its body, then it also extends to its "own person." If it were not in its own person, this would signify that it had not yet extended to its body. The word "neighbors" refers to those who are near its body. If it can be shaken and troubled early on, when this has not yet extended to its body, then it will not reach its limit. This is why it acquires "no blame." If it has not yet reached its limit, it will value the way of being able to transform. It is proper that there be alteration at the end of the Shake hexagram. A soft line does not keep guard with certainty, and this is why the *Symbol* says that "it is warned about the trembling in its neighbors," which means that it is capable of alteration. At the end of the Shake hexagram, the sage shows people the meaning of recognizing how to be troubled and able to transform, so as to persuade them of something deep. The word "married" refers to those who are related, and signifies those whose movement is the same. "There are remarks": there are remarks of hate and blame. This "six" line occupies the top position in the Shake hexagram. The beginning is at the head of a crowd of movements, but now "it is warned about the trembling in its neighbors," and so this line does not dare to advance. It is different from the other places in the Shake hexagram, and this is why "among the married, there are remarks." **The *Symbol* says: "'In the shaking, it is squeezed, and squeezed again': centrality is not yet acquired. Although there is misfortune, 'there is no blame': it is warned about the trembling in its neighbors."** The reason it loses itself while fearful and troubled like this is that it has not yet acquired the way of centrality, which signifies that it has exceeded the center. If it were made to acquire the center, it would not reach the point of being "squeezed, and squeezed again." If it reaches its limit and takes the field, "there is misfortune." Were it able to see the warning about its neighbors and know how to be troubled, then it would alter early on without reaching its limit and there would be "no blame." The top "six" line is at the limit of movement. Since it is at the limit of the Shake hexagram, it has the meaning of alteration.

52. CALM (*GEN* 艮)

The *Sequence of the Hexagrams* says: "To shake is to move. Things cannot be in motion to the end, but come to a stop. This is why the Calm hexagram is next. To calm is to stop." Movement and tranquility cause each other to come about. If there is movement, then there will be tranquility; if there is tranquility, then there will be movement. Things do not possess the principle of constant movement, and so the Calm hexagram succeeds the Shake hexagram. "To calm is to stop": it is not called the "stop" hexagram, even though calming has the mountain as its symbol, because its intention is to be contented, weighty, solid, and real—a meaning that cannot be exhausted by the word "stop." When the Lead and Yield trigrams interact, the third line of the Yield trigram is squeezed out to complete the Calm trigram. A single *yang* line occupies a position above two *yin* lines. *Yang* is a thing that moves and advances upward. If it has already reached the top, then it will stop. Since *yin* is a tranquil thing, what is above has stopped and what is below is tranquil. This is why these lines constitute the Calm trigram. If this is the case, how does it differ in meaning from the stopping of the Herd hexagrams? Response: the stopping that is a herding means to control the herd and bring it to a stop by force. The stopping that is a calming means to bring something to a stop with contentment, so that it stops in its place.

It calms its back, but it does not obtain its body. It travels to its court, but it does not see its people. There is no blame. When people cannot be contented where they have stopped, they are moved by desire. Since their desire guides them on ahead, they cannot acquire a place to stop, even if they seek one out. This is why, concerning the way of the Calm hexagram, it is proper that "it calms its back." What it sees is ahead of it, but its back is at its back, and this is what it does not see. If it stops in what it does not see, then its desires will not disorder its heart and it will be contented where it has stopped. "It does not obtain its body": it does not see its body, which signifies that it has forgotten itself. If it is a non-self, then it has stopped. If it cannot be a non-self, then it may not possess the way of stopping. "It travels to its court, but it does not see its people": the space of the outer court is extremely near, but if it is at its back, then it will not see it, even though it is extremely near. This signifies that it does not interact with anything. It does not respond to the things outside, and it does not sprout desires inside. If this is the case when it stops, then it will acquire the way of stopping, and in its stopping "there is no blame."

The *Judgment* says: "To calm is to stop. If the moment is for stopping, then it stops. If the moment is for acting, then it acts. Neither movement nor tranquility loses its moment. Its way is bright and enlightened." The Calm hexagram refers to stopping, and the way of stopping concerns nothing but the moment. If action and stopping, or movement and tranquility, do not make use of the moment, they will be at fault. If neither of them "loses its moment," they will submit to their principle and align with their duty. Principle refers to how a thing is, while duty refers to how a thing is placed. When movement and tranquility align with principle and duty, and neither of them loses its moment, then their way "is bright and enlightened." As for what noble people esteem in the moment, this is what made the action and stopping of Zhongni either continuous or brief.[1] The substance of the Calm trigram is devotion and fullness, which have the meaning of being "bright and enlightened." "It is calm at its stopping point. It stops in its place." "It is calm at its stopping point": this signifies that it stops when it is brought to a stop. If it can stop when it is brought to a stop, this is because "it stops in its place." If it stops without being in its place, it will be without the principle of being able to stop. Fuzi says: "When it stops, it recognizes where to stop,"[2] which signifies that there is a proper place in which to stop. "As long as there are things, there will necessarily be regulations."[3] The father stops in compassion, the child stops in filial piety, the ruler stops in humaneness, and the minister stops in reverence. Of the ten thousand things and the numberless states of affairs, there is none that does not have its place. When it is in its place it will be contented, and when it has lost its place it will be upended. And so sages can make the world submit to order, but they cannot constitute things or produce their regulations. They can only bring them to a stop, each in its place, and that is all. "Those above and below correspond as enemies. They do not agree with each other." The *Judgment* is remarking on the powers of the trigrams. The two trigram substances, "those above and below," correspond to each other "as enemies," which means that "they do not agree with each other." When *yin* and *yang* correspond to each other, their inclinations communicate and they agree with each other. In this case they are enemies, and this is why they do not agree with each other. If they do not agree with each other, then they will have their backs to each other. Each of them "calms its back," which means that they come to a stop. **"As a result, 'it does not obtain its body. It travels to its court, but it does not see its people. There is no blame.'"** They have their backs to each other, and this is why "it does not obtain its body," and "it does not see its people." As a result, they can come to a stop. Since they can come to a stop, "there is no blame."

The *Symbol* says: "There is a range of mountains: Calm. Noble people use it to reflect on not going out from their positions." Above and below there are mountains, and this is why the *Symbol* refers to "a range of mountains." When there is "this" and also "that," they refer to a range. They signify a repetition and return, and symbolize the repetition of the Calm trigram. When noble people gaze on the symbol of the Calm or stopping hexagram, they reflect on being contented where they have stopped and not going out from their positions. Their positions are the roles in which they are placed. Each of the ten thousand affairs has its place. Those that acquire their place will stop and be contented. Whether it is proper to act or stop, to be brief or continuous—those who go to excess or who do not extend far enough are both "going out from their positions." What will the case be like if they overshoot their role and do not seize it?

The initial "six" line: it calms its toes. There is no blame. There is profit in endless purity. This "six" line is at the very bottom and is symbolized by the "toes." The toes are the first to move. "It calms its toes": it stops at the initial point of the movement. When a state of affairs is stopped at its initial point, it has not yet reached the point of losing its straightforwardness, and this is why "there is no blame." As for those who use softness to place themselves below when facing the moment of stopping, if they act, they will lose their straightforwardness. This is why there is no blame if they stop. *Yin* softness is distressed because it cannot be constant and cannot be certain. This is why, when it faces the initial position of the stopping hexagram, it is warned that "there is profit" in constant or "endless purity" or certainty, so that it will not lose the way of stopping. **The *Symbol* says: "'It calms its toes': it has not yet lost its straightforwardness."** Action is not straightforward when it is proper to stop. It stops in the initial position, and this is why it does "not yet" reach the point of losing "its straightforwardness." It is easy for a state of affairs to be stopped at its beginning, when it has not yet reached the point of loss.

The second "six" line: it calms its calf. It does not rescue, but it follows. Its heart is not quickened. The second "six" line occupies the center, it acquires straightforwardness, and it refers to those who acquire the way of stopping. There is no corresponding or supporting line above it, and so it does not obtain its ruler. The third line occupies the top position in the lower trigram, it is the master of bringing the stop to completion, and it refers to those who are the masters of stopping. Since it is firm and has lost its centrality, it does not stop in a fitting place. Firmness stops at the top and cannot diminish itself to seek those below. Although the second line has the virtues of centrality and straightforwardness, the third cannot attend to it. Whether the second line acts or stops, it is bound to its master and cannot cause itself to do anything. This is why it is symbolized by the calf. When the thigh moves, the calf follows. When movement stops in the thigh, it does not persist in the calf. Since the second line has not acquired a way of centrality and straightforwardness that can "rescue" or save the third from its absence of centrality, it must be exhorted to follow it. It cannot rescue, and so it merely "follows." Although it is not blamed, how could this be what it desires? The *Symbol* remarks that it does not "listen"—that is, it does not put its way into action. This is why "its heart is not quickened"—that is, it cannot put its tendencies into action. If scholars are placed in lofty positions, they will rescue others rather than follow them. If they are in positions below, sometimes it is proper that they rescue others, sometimes it is proper that they follow others, and sometimes they will follow others after they are unable to rescue them. **The *Symbol* says: "'It does not rescue, but it follows': it does not yet retreat and listen."** The reason "it does not rescue" but merely "follows" is that those above are not yet able to attend to those below. To "retreat and listen" is to attend to those below.

The third "nine" line: it calms its perimeter. It cracks its spine, endangering and roasting its heart. The word "perimeter" refers to a division or separation, and signifies the border between those above and below. The third line uses firmness to occupy a position that is firm and without centrality, it is the master that completes the Calm trigram, and it refers to the limit of dissolution and stopping. To be already at the top of the lower trigram substance, and to be the perimeter that separates those above from those below—both have stopping as their meaning. This is why "it calms its perimeter," which refers to those who are steadfast in stopping and unable to advance or retreat. Concerning the human body, it is as though "it cracks its spine." The spine is the backbone, or the border between what is above and below. If it cracks or severs its spine, then those above and below will not attend to or heed each other. The line statement is remarking on the solidity with which it stops those below. Concerning the way of stopping, it is estimable to acquire what is fitting. If those who act or stop cannot make use of the moment but are determined to do only one thing, and if this is what constitutes their solidity and strength, then their place and time will fracture and repulse them. They will be split apart and severed from things, and their peril will be extreme. When people stop in one corner with certainty, being at no time in agreement with what is fitting, they will limp with the hardship of it. Burning with wrath, and trembling and frustrated at their center, how will they possess the principle of contentment and generosity? The phrase "endangering and roasting its heart" signifies that they roast their center and make it glow with their discontented propensities. **The *Symbol* says: "'It calms its perimeter': it is imperiling and 'roasting its heart.'"** This signifies that it has certainly stopped and cannot advance or retreat. The apprehension of its peril and trouble is constantly "roasting" its center or heart and making it glow.

The fourth "six" line: it calms its body. There is no blame. The fourth is the position of the great minister and refers to those who stop what it is proper to stop in the world. It makes use of *yin* softness and does not encounter a ruler of *yang* firmness. This is why it cannot put a stop to things, but only stops its own "body," and so there should be "no blame." There can be no blame because it stops in a straightforward position. The line statement is remarking that if it stops its body and there is no blame, then it has seen that it cannot put a stop to things. If it has an influence on the government, there will be blame. As for those in positions above, who can barely make their bodies better, it does not choose to say anything extreme to them. **The *Symbol* says: "'It calms its body': it stops itself."** It cannot stop the world, but can stop "its body," and that is all. How could this be sufficient for it to be named to the position of great minister?

The fifth "six" line: it calms its jowls. Its remarks have a sequence. Regrets vanish. The fifth is the position of the ruler, it is the master of the Calm hexagram, and it refers to those who are the masters of stopping the world. The power of *yin* softness is not sufficient to make proper use of this duty, and this is why, when the line statement remarks on stopping in a position above, it chooses the jowls as its meaning. When people stop where it is proper to be cautious, then it only remarks on their action, but the fifth line is in a position above, and this is why it remarks on the jowls. The word "jowls" refers to what cause one's remarks to go out. If "it calms its jowls," then its remarks will be in sequence and not at fault when they go out. If it reveals its remarks lightly and not in sequence, then it will have regrets. If they are stopped in the jowls, then "regrets vanish." To be in sequence is to be central and reined in by a series and sequence. The jowls, together with the cheeks and tongue, all cause one's remarks to go out, and the jowls are at their center. "It calms its jowls": this signifies that it stops at its center. **The *Symbol* says: "'It calms its jowls': its centrality makes it straightforward."** What is good for the fifth line is centrality. "It calms its jowls": this signifies that it stops at its center. The *Symbol* is remarking that the acquisition of centrality will constitute straightforwardness. It is stopped in the jowls, which keeps it from losing its centrality, and so it acquires straightforwardness.

The top "nine" line: its calm is truehearted. There is good fortune. This "nine" line uses firmness and fullness to occupy the top position, it is also the master that completes the Calm trigram, it is at the end of the Calm hexagram, and it refers to those who are extremely solid and devoted in their stopping. To be "truehearted" is to be filled with devotion. It occupies the limit position in the stopping hexagram, and this is why it is not excessive but truehearted. When people stop, it is difficult for them to continue to the end. This is why their rein is sometimes removed in the evening, their guard is sometimes lost at the end, and their affairs are sometimes neglected after long continuing. These are all the same in the distress they bring to people. The top "nine" line can be truehearted and beneficial to the end, which is the best that the way of stopping can do, and so "there is good fortune." This is the only virtue in all six of the lines that constitutes good fortune. **The *Symbol* says: "It is fortunate that 'its calm is truehearted': it is beneficial to the end."** In the affairs of the world, it is only at the end that keeping guard becomes difficult. Those who can be "truehearted" in their stopping will bring about their end. The good fortune of the top line is that it can be "beneficial to the end."

53. STEP (*JIAN* 漸)

The *Sequence of the Hexagrams* says: "To calm is to stop. Things cannot be stopped to the end, and this is why the Step hexagram is next. To step is to advance." Those that have stopped will necessarily also have their advance. This is the principle of contracting and expanding, of disappearing and coming to rest. When what has stopped is now born, this is an advance, and when what has stopped now reverses itself, this is also an advance. And so the Step hexagram succeeds the Calm hexagram. To advance in a sequence is to go step by step. Today people consider a slackened advance to be a step by step advance. What advances in a sequence does not surpass its position in the series, and so it is slackened. As for the trigrams, the Low trigram is above and the Calm trigram below. "Above the mountain, there is a tree": the tree is lofty because of the mountain, and so its loftiness has a cause. Its loftiness has a cause—that is, its advance has a sequence to it, and so these trigrams constitute the Step hexagram.

Step: when the woman is wed, there will be good fortune. There is profit in purity. The judgment is remarking at the same time on the powers of the trigrams and the meaning of the Step hexagram. The Low and Calm trigrams are alterations of the Lead and Yield trigrams. The Low trigram is put on top of the Calm trigram to constitute the Step hexagram. Concerning the substance of the Step hexagram, one may remark that the two lines at the center interact with each other. Because these two lines interact with each other, men and women will afterward each acquire their straightforward positions. Although the positions of two lines—the initial and final lines—are not proper for them, the *yang* line is above and the *yin* line below, and so they have acquired the respect and humility that are straightforward for them. Men and women will each acquire what is straightforward for them, and this, too, is to acquire a position. This hexagram and the Wed Bride hexagram are straightforwardly opposed to each other.[1] If the wedding of a woman can be straightforward like this, then "there will be good fortune." Of all the affairs of the world in which an advance must be step by step, none is like the wedding of a woman. In the advance of a minister at the palace, or in the advance of people in their affairs, it is certainly proper that there be a sequence. If they have no sequence, they will go beyond their rein and confront their duty. Misfortune and blame will follow them. Of all the cases in which duty is taken either lightly or weightily, in which the way is one of honesty or dishonesty, the greatest is when a woman attends to a man. This is why the judgment considers the wedding of a woman to be the meaning. Men and women together constitute the first of the ten thousand states of affairs. Of the various hexagrams, many say that "there is profit in purity," but its application is not always the same. Sometimes it is warning one to be doubtful about traversing anything without straightforwardness; sometimes one's state of affairs must be pure, which is to acquire what is fitting for it; sometimes it is remarking that there will be profit because there is purity. As for what was just said—"it is warning one to be doubtful about traversing anything without straightforwardness"—this refers to the second "nine" line of the Take hexagram. It is placed in a *yin* position in the enjoyment trigram, and this is why it is warned to make use of a fitting purity. "Sometimes one's state of affairs must be pure, which is to acquire what is fitting for it": this refers to the Great Herd hexagram. Its judgment remarks that, for those who are herded, "there is profit in purity." "Sometimes it is remarking that there will be profit because there is purity": this refers to the Step hexagram. Its judgment remarks that there will be good fortune because the woman is wed, and that there is profit when one's purity and straightforwardness are like this. In fact, because one is certain to possess it, no warning is provided. As for the meaning of the Step hexagram, it is fitting that one be able to make progress, and yet the judgment does not say "there is progress." In fact, progress has the meaning of attaining one's development. It does not mean a step by step advance.

The *Judgment* says: "It advances step by step. 'When the woman is wed, there will be good fortune.'" Those who advance in accordance with the meaning of the Step hexagram will have good fortune "when the woman is wed," which signifies that their advance is straightforward and step by step. The wedding of a woman is something great, but there are other such advances. **"If it advances, it will acquire a position. If it makes the journey, it will accomplish something."** In the moment of the step by step advance, the *yin* and *yang* lines each acquire their straightforward positions: "If it advances," "it will accomplish something." Because the fourth line advances upward, it acquires its straightforward position. The third line casts off the lower trigram and becomes part of the upper trigram, successfully acquiring its straightforward position. This, too, is the meaning of "if it advances, it will acquire a position." **"If it advances straightforwardly, it should be able to make the kingdom straightforward."** "If it advances" according to the straightforward way, "it should be able to make the kingdom" or state "straightforward," and also reach the world. It is generally proper for those who advance in their affairs, who advance in virtue, or who advance in position, never to be without straightforwardness. **"In this position, firmness acquires centrality."** The *Judgment* earlier said that, "if it advances, it will acquire a position. If it makes the journey, it will accomplish something." The end of this passage is remarking that the *yin* and *yang* lines have acquired their positions, and as a result, they advance and accomplish something. Now, in turn, it says that, "in this position, firmness acquires centrality." The position referred to is the fifth, because *yang* firmness, centrality, and straightforwardness have been used to acquire the position of respect. Various lines have acquired straightforwardness, and they also may be said to have acquired their positions. Nonetheless, they are not like the fifth line, which has acquired the position of respect, and this is why its remarks are specific to this line. **"There are stopping and lowliness. Its movement is not depleted."** The inner trigram refers to calming and stopping, while the outer trigram refers to lowliness and submission. Stopping symbolizes contentment and tranquility, while lowliness means harmony and submission. People who advance when moved by the desire of their hearts will be restless, and will acquire nothing step by step. This is why they are trapped and depleted. Going step by step means to have stopping and tranquility on the inside, and lowliness and submission on the outside. This is why the movement of its advance is not trapped or depleted.

The *Symbol* says: "Above the mountain, there is a tree: Step. Noble people use it to occupy positions of worth and virtue, and to make their customs good." "Above the mountain, there is a tree": its loftiness has a cause, and this is the meaning of the Step hexagram. When noble people gaze on the symbol of the Step hexagram, they use it to occupy virtues of worth and goodness, and then they transform their manners and customs, and make them beautiful. When people advance in worth and virtue, it must always be step by step. If they practice them, they can afterward be contented, but if they cannot, they will go beyond their rein, having rushed to their extremity. If this is how they act when by themselves, how will they be able step by step to enter into the teaching and transformation of other people? "The conversion of manners and the changing of customs" is not something that can be completed in a day and a night, and this is why they must go step by step when making customs good.[2]

The initial "six" line: the wild goose steps toward the shore. The small child is in danger. There are remarks but no blame. The various line statements of the Step hexagram all choose the symbol of the wild goose. Considered as a thing, the wild goose has a season for its travels and a sequence for its group. Since it does not lose its season and sequence, what it does is step by step. The word "shore" refers to the water's edge. Water birds stop at the edge of the water, when the water is extremely near, and so their advance may be called step by step. Their travels make use of the seasons, and so they also may be called step by step. Those who advance step by step without losing anything will step by step acquire what is fitting for them. This "six" line occupies the initial position, which is at the very bottom. The power of the *yin qi* is very weak and has no corresponding or supporting line above it. If it advances in such a case, it will be constantly inclined to worry. If it is a noble person, then, with its deep understanding and far-reaching illumination, it will know how to be contented with duty and principle. It will recognize what is fitting for the season and the state of affairs, and its placement will not be doubtful. Small people and young children can only see states of affairs that have already come about. They attend to the knowledge possessed by the crowd, but they cannot elucidate its principle. This is why they are imperiled and troubled, and "there are remarks." In fact, they advance because they do not know how to stay below, they are not restless because they employ softness, and they can advance step by step because there is no corresponding line. In its duty, there is "no blame." Were the initial line of the Step hexagram to advance by employing firmness in its agitation, it would lose sight of its duty to advance step by step. It would be unable to advance and there would necessarily be blame. **The *Symbol* says: "The danger of the small child: in its duty, there is 'no blame.'"** Although the "small child" is considered to be in peril and danger, there is in reality "no blame" in its duty and principle.

The second "six" line: the wild goose steps toward the boulder. It eats and drinks with satisfaction, and satisfaction again. There is good fortune. The second line occupies the center and acquires straightforwardness, it corresponds to the fifth line above it, and it refers to those who advance with contentment and generosity. On the other hand, it occupies a position in the Step hexagram, and this is why its advance is not rapid. The word "boulder" refers to a stone that is contented and level, as may be found on the banks of great rivers, and so it symbolizes a contented advance. Further, there is a step by step advance from the shore to the boulder. The second line uses the way of centrality and straightforwardness to correspond to the fifth "nine" line, or the ruler. Nothing further may be attached to the contented certainty and level ease of its advance, and this is why it "eats and drinks" with such harmony, pleasure, "satisfaction, and satisfaction again." Its "good fortune" should be recognized. **The *Symbol* says: "'It eats and drinks with satisfaction, and satisfaction again': it is not that what is simple gorges itself."** The line statement refers to its contented and level advance, and this is why it chooses to remark that it "eats and drinks" with harmony and pleasure. Fuzi fears that later generations will not get the metaphor, and so he explains it further, saying that a noble person of centrality and straightforwardness has encountered a master of centrality and straightforwardness.[3] Step by step it advances upward, and is about to put its way into action, extending it to the world. When it says that "it eats and drinks with satisfaction, and satisfaction again," this signifies that it acquires the object of its tendency with harmony and pleasure. It does not signify that what is hollow "gorges itself" with food and drink, and that is all. To be simple is to be hollow.

The third "nine" line: the wild goose steps toward the plateau. The husband takes the field and does not return. The wife becomes pregnant but does not raise the child. There is misfortune. There is profit in resisting bandits. A level and lofty place is called a "plateau"—that is, a plain. The third line is at the top of the lower trigram, and its advance reaches a plateau. *Yang* is something that advances upward. If it occupies a moment in the Step hexagram, its tendency is to advance step by step. If it has no corresponding or supporting line above it, it is proper that it guard its straightforwardness and await its moment. If it is contented with its place and the terrain is level, it will acquire the way of the Step hexagram. If it is sometimes unable to guard itself, and its desires guide it toward something, or its tendencies approach something, it will lose the way of the Step hexagram. The fourth is a *yin* line that is above it and quite close to it, which is what a *yang* line enjoys. The third is a *yang* line that is below it and related to it, which is what a *yin* line attends to. The two lines are close to each other, but they are not corresponding lines. Since they are close to each other, they will relate to each other and align with ease. Since they are not corresponding lines, it is not suitable that they seek each other. This is why the line statement gives a warning about them. A husband is a *yang* sort of thing, and so the word "husband" here signifies the third line. Were the third line not to guard its straightforwardness but to align with the fourth, it would be a case of knowing how to take the field but not knowing how to return. The phrase "take the field" refers to action, and "return" refers to reversion. To "not return" signifies that it does not revert to or concern itself with its duty and principle. The word "wife" here signifies the fourth line. Were it to align without straightforwardness, then it would not "raise the child" even if it "becomes pregnant," because it would be without its way. In a case like this, there would be "misfortune." What is profitable for the third line is "resisting bandits." The word "bandits" refers to those who reach their goals without principle.[4] If it guards its straightforward-ness and "safeguards against crookedness," it may said to resist the bandits.[5] If it cannot resist the bandits, then it will lose itself and there will be misfortune. **The *Symbol* says: "'The husband takes the field and does not return': he is uncouth and has cast off his group. 'The wife becomes pregnant but does not raise the child': she has lost her way. 'There is profit' in the employment of 'resisting bandits': they preserve each other through submissiveness."** "The husband takes the field and does not return": he has lost the straightforwardness of the Step hexagram. He attends to his desires and loses his straightforward-ness, casting off and betraying his group and kind, which one may refer to as uncouth. Of all the hexagram's various lines, none is without something good. If he does nothing but lose his straightforwardness, this is to "cast off his group" and kind. The wife "becomes pregnant," but her way is not the cause of this, and so she "does not raise the child." What is profitable is "resisting bandits," which signifies that they "preserve each other through submissiveness." When noble people are close to small people, they use straightforwardness to guard themselves, but how could noble people only keep themselves intact, and that is all? They also make small people avoid ensnaring themselves in their absence of duty. This is to preserve them using the way of submissiveness, resisting and putting a stop to what is bad in them, and this is why the line statement uses the phrase "resisting bandits."

The fourth "six" line: the wild goose steps toward the tree. Sometimes it acquires its perch. There is no blame. Facing the moment of the Step hexa-gram, the fourth line uses *yin* softness to advance and seize the *yang* firmness of the line above it. Since lines that are *yang* and firm advance upward, how could it be contented with a place below a line that is *yin* and soft? This is why the fourth line is placed on a terrain where it is not contented, like a "wild goose" that advances "toward the tree." The tree becomes lofty step by step, and symbolizes those who have no contentment. The toes of the wild goose are linked and cannot get a grip on branches. This is why it cannot roost in a tree. The word "perch" refers to a horizontal and level branch. Atop a level branch is the only place where it can be contented. This signifies that the place of the fourth line is perilous at its root. If it can "sometimes" acquire for itself a way of contentment and serenity, then "there is no blame." Like the wild goose and the tree, it is not contented at its root. If it sometimes acquires a level branch as its place, then it will be contented. When the fourth line occupies a straightforward position while being lowly and submissive, it is fitting that there be no blame. The line statement is remarking that it will necessarily acquire what it has lost. Because it acquires what it has lost, it will be enlightened as to its duty. **The *Symbol* says: "'Sometimes it acquires its perch': it is submissive and lowly."** The word "perch" refers to a level place of contentment. The way of seeking contentment is nothing but submissiveness and lowliness. If one's duty is to be submissive and straightforward and one's place is humble and lowly, how could one not be contented with this place? Such is the case for the submissiveness, straightforwardness, and lowliness of the fourth line, and so it acquires its perch.

The fifth "nine" line: the wild goose steps toward the hill. Its wife of three years has not become pregnant. In the end, nothing is victorious over it. There is good fortune. The word "hill" refers to a lofty mound. The wild goose stops in the loftiest place, which symbolizes the position of the ruler. Although it has acquired the position of respect, it is nonetheless in the moment of the Step hexagram, and it will certainly not put its way into action hastily. It corresponds straightforwardly to the second line, and their virtues of centrality and straight-forwardness are the same, but they are separated by the third and fourth lines. The third line is close to the second, and the fourth is close to the fifth, and both of these lines keep them from interacting. They have not yet been able to align, and this is why "its wife of three years has not become pregnant." None-theless, the way of centrality and straightforwardness possesses the principle of necessary progress. How could what is not straightforward be able to separate or harm them? This is why, "in the end, nothing" can be "victorious over it." Though their alignment is step by step, they will acquire "good fortune" in the end. What is not straightforward may be the enemy of centrality and straightfor-wardness, and it may do something for a moment, but can it be continuously victorious? **The *Symbol* says: "'In the end, nothing is victorious over it. There is good fortune': it acquires the object of its aspiration."** Rulers and ministers interact using centrality and straightforwardness, and it is proper that they put their way into action. Although there is a space between them, how could it be victorious in the end? They hesitate, but they must acquire "the object" of their "aspiration," which is the "good fortune" of the Step hexagram.

The top "nine" line: the wild goose steps toward the plain. Its feathers should be employed in the ceremonies. There is good fortune. Duke Hu of Anding considers the "plain" as the "high road," and the "high road" as the "cloud road," which signifies something that is empty and hollow at its center.[6] The *Erya* says that "the ninth meaning of the word 'attainment' is 'high road.'"[7] To be on the high road means to develop or attain something without hindrance or concealment. The top "nine" line is in a position of extreme loftiness, yet it adds to its advance upward and goes outside of its position. In another moment this would constitute an excess, but in the moment of the Step hexagram it occupies the limit position in the Low trigram. It will necessarily be in a sequence, like the wild geese that cast off the place where they have stopped and fly into the cloudy hollow. In the case of people, it refers to those who are transcendent and leisurely, and outside ordinary affairs. Such is the extremity of its advance, and yet it still brings about the loftiness of worth and attainment step by step. This is why it "should be employed in the ceremonies" and laws, and "there is good fortune." The word "feathers" refers to what the wild goose employs in its advance. What it employs in its advance is also the way of advancing in the case of the top "nine" line. **The *Symbol* says: "'Its feathers should be employed in the ceremonies. There is good fortune': it should not be disorderly."** The advance of noble people ascends from below. Because they are minimal, they will later become manifest—their footprints create a series, and none of them is out of sequence. Since they have not lost their sequence, there is no place in which they will not acquire good fortune. This is why the "nine" line does not lose its good fortune even though it has depleted its lofty position. What "should be employed in the ceremonies" and laws is what is in sequence. It "should not be disorderly."

54. WED BRIDE (*GUIMEI* 歸妹)

The *Sequence of the Hexagrams* says: "To step is to advance. Those who advance will necessarily wed themselves to something. This is why the Wed Bride hexagram is next." If they advance, then they will necessarily have someone that they reach. This is why the Step hexagram has the meaning of a wedding, and so the Wed Bride hexagram succeeds the Step hexagram. The Wed Bride hexagram refers to the wedding of a woman, since "bride" is a name for a young woman. As for the trigrams, the Shake trigram is above and the Joy trigram below: a young woman attends to a grown man. The man moves to her and the woman enjoys him. Further, the enjoyment and movement can mean both that the man enjoys the woman and that the woman attends to the man. There are four hexagrams that have the meaning of a man and a woman matching up and aligning: the Stir, Last, Step, and Wed Bride hexagrams. In the Stir hexagram, the man and woman affect each other. The man is below the woman, and their two kinds of *qi* affect each other and correspond. The stopping and enjoyment symbolize the inclinations of the man and woman affecting each other. The Last hexagram refers to constancy. The man is above and the woman below. She is lowly and submissive, and he is in motion. *Yin* and *yang* both correspond to each other, which is the constant way of a man and woman in the home. The husband sings the melody and the wife follows it. The Step hexagram refers to the acquisition of straightforwardness in wedding a woman. The man is below the woman, but each of them acquires a straightforward position. He has stopped himself and is tranquil, while she is lowly and submissive. Their advance is step by step, which is the way for a man and woman to match up and align. The Wed Bride hexagram refers to a woman's espousal—that is, her wedding. The man is above and the woman below, which refers to a woman

431

attending to a man, and means to have the enjoyment of youth. If it is for enjoyment that he moves, if "there are movement and enjoyment," then he will not acquire straightforwardness, and this is why none of the lines are in their proper positions. Although the initial and the top lines are in the proper positions of *yin* and *yang*, *yang* is on the bottom and *yin* is at the top. These positions, too, are not proper. The Wed Bride and Step hexagrams are straightforwardly opposed to each other.[1] The Stir and Last hexagrams refer to the way of husband and wife, while the Step and Wed Bride hexagrams have the wedding of a woman as their meaning. The Stir and Wed Bride hexagrams refer to the inclinations of men and women for each other. In the Stir hexagram there are stopping and enjoyment, while in the Wed Bride hexagram there is movement toward enjoyment, but both hexagrams refer to enjoyment. The Last and Step hexagrams have husbands and wives as their meaning. In the Last hexagram there are lowliness and movement, while in the Step hexagram there are stopping and lowliness, but both hexagrams refer to lowliness and submission. The way of men and women, and the meaning of husband and wife, are perfected in these hexagrams. As for the trigrams of the Wed Bride hexagram, "above the lake, there is thunder." The thunder shakes and the lake moves, which is the symbol of one thing attending to another. Of the things whose movement follows the movement of another, none is like water. The man moves upward and the woman attends to him, which symbolizes an espoused or wedded woman attending to a man. The Shake trigram refers to a grown man, while the Joy trigram refers to a young woman. When a young woman attends to a grown man, it is for enjoyment that they move. They move, and then they enjoy each other. What people enjoy are young women, and this is why the hexagram speaks of a bride—that is, a woman at her wedding—as the symbol. Further, the trigrams have the meaning of a grown man enjoying a young woman, and this is why they constitute the Wed Bride hexagram.

Wed Bride: taking the field brings misfortune. There is no long-term profit. It is for enjoyment that they move. They move, but it is not proper, and this is why there will be misfortune. "It is not proper" indicates that their positions are not proper for them. "Taking the field brings misfortune": if they move, then there will be misfortune. As for the meaning of the hexagram, it does not only concern the wedding of a woman. There is no journey to be made that will bring profit.

The *Judgment* says: "Wed Bride: this is the great duty of heaven and earth." A single *yin* line and a single *yang* line may be called "the way." That *yin* and *yang* affect each other, that a man and a woman match up and align—this is the constant principle of heaven and earth. In the Wed Bride hexagram, a woman is wedded to a man, which is why the *Judgment* says: "This is the great duty of heaven and earth." The man is above the woman, and *yin* attends to the movement of *yang*. This is why these trigrams symbolize the Wed Bride hexagram. **"If heaven and earth do not interact, the ten thousand things will not flourish. To wed a bride is the beginning and end of a person."** "If heaven and earth do not interact," how can the ten thousand things that attend to them be born? The wedding of a woman to a man is the way by which birth and life prolong each other. When a man and woman interact, something will afterward come to rest and live. If something comes to rest and lives, then their end will afterward not be a depletion. First there is an end, and afterward a beginning. They prolong each other without depletion, and this is "the beginning and end of a person." **"There are movement and enjoyment: what is wedded is a bride. 'Taking the field brings misfortune': its position is not proper for it."** The *Judgment* is using the two trigram substances to explain the meaning of the Wed Bride hexagram. When a man and woman affect each other, there are enjoyment and movement, which are affairs for a young woman. This is why they move for the sake of enjoyment, and "what is wedded is a bride." The reason "taking the field brings misfortune" is that none of the various lines is in its proper position. They are all placed without straightforwardness, and so how could they move without misfortune? In the great majority of cases, when people move for the sake of enjoyment, how could they not lose their straightforwardness? **"'There is no long-term profit': softness rides on firmness."** It is not only that "its position is not proper for it," but that there is an excess of riding on firmness. The third and fifth lines both ride on firm lines. Men and women have a sequence where one is respected and the other humble. Husband and wife have a ritual in which one sings the melody and the other follows it. This is a constant principle, and is like the case of the Last hexagram. Were they to discount the way of constancy and straightforwardness, and succumb to inclination, indulgence, and desire, moving only for the sake of enjoyment, then husband and wife would be disdainful and disorderly. The man would be restrained by desire and would lose his firmness, while the woman would become habituated to enjoyment and would forget to be submissive. This is like the case of riding on firmness in the Wed Bride hexagram. And so, there is misfortune and no profitable journey can be made. As for the matching up and alignment of *yin* and *yang*, or the marital interaction of a man and woman, these are constant principles. Nonetheless, if they attend to their desires and surrender to their flow, discounting duty and principle, nothing about their licentiousness and crookedness will be other than extreme. To injure one's body and defeat one's virtue—how could this be the human principle? This is the misfortune of the Wed Bride hexagram.

The *Symbol* says: "Above the lake, there is thunder: Wed Bride. Noble people use it to make their end endless and to recognize decay." The thunder shakes from above, and the lake follows its movement. The movement of *yang* is above, and *yin* enjoys and attends to it, which symbolizes a woman attending to a man. This is why these trigrams constitute the Wed Bride hexagram. When noble people gaze on the symbol of men and women matching up and aligning, of birth and coming to rest prolonging each other, they use it to make their end endless, which is to recognize that there is decay. "To make their end endless" signifies that birth and coming to rest replenish and prolong them, and that their oscillation is endless and continuous. "To recognize decay" signifies their recognition that things decay and decline, which is the way that they succeed one another. If a woman is wed, something will come to rest and live, and this is why the hexagram has the meaning of making the end endless. Further, concerning the way of husband and wife, it is proper that their constancy and endlessness have an end. They must recognize that there is a principle by which they will decay and decline, and so the *Symbol* warns and cautions them. The words "decay" and "decline" signify a casting off and breaking up. In the Wed Bride hexagram, "there are movement and enjoyment," which is different from the Last hexagram, in which "there are lowliness and movement," and the Step hexagram, in which "there are stopping and lowliness." The enjoyment belongs to a young woman, and the affection or movement belongs to the inclinations. If they move, they will lose their straightforwardness. This is not the straightforwardness of husband and wife or a way that is capable of constancy. What is continuous will necessarily decay and decline. If they recognize that it will necessarily decay, they will face it and reflect on making their end endless. The "opposed stares" of the world are all unable to make their end endless.[2] Not only in the way of husband and wife, but also in the affairs of the world, there is nothing that does not have an end and decay, but there is also nothing that does not have a way that is capable of succession, that is capable of continuity. Those who gaze on the Wed Bride hexagram will face and reflect on its warning to make their end endless.

The initial "nine" line: it weds a bride as a concubine. The lame can walk. Taking the field brings good fortune. The wedding of this woman occupies the bottom of the hexagram and is without a line that corresponds to it straightforwardly, which symbolizes the "concubine." *Yang* firmness in a wife constitutes the virtues of worth and purity. It is placed in a humble and submissive position, which is worthy and straightforward for a concubine. Placement in the enjoyment trigram occupying the bottom position has the meaning of submissiveness. Since a concubine is in a humble position below, how could she do anything, even if she is worthy? She does not exceed making her own person good so as to serve and help her ruler, and that is all. She is like the "lame" who "can walk"—the *Symbol* remarks that they cannot extend their reach very far.[3] Nonetheless, her role is good, and this is why there will be "good fortune" if she acts like this. **The *Symbol* says: "'It weds a bride as a concubine': she lasts. 'The lame can walk. There is good fortune': they serve each other."** The meaning of the Wed Bride hexagram is movement for the sake of enjoyment, which is not a way that can be constant for husbands and wives. This "nine" line is *yang* and firm, and it has the virtues of worth and purity. Although the position of a concubine is minimal, she is capable of constancy. Although she is in a position below and there is nothing she can do, just like the lame who can walk, there will nonetheless be good fortune if she takes the field, so that they can "serve" and help "each other." To be able to help her ruler is the good fortune of a concubine.

The second "nine" line: the nearsighted can look. There is profit in the purity of secluded people. The second "nine" line is *yang* and firm, it acquires centrality, and it refers to worthy and straightforward women. A higher line corresponds to it straightforwardly, but has a disposition of *yin* softness and refers to those who move for the sake of enjoyment. The woman is worthy, but she is not matched with someone fine. This is why the second line cannot successfully complete the task of helping the inner trigram, even though it is worthy. It is suitable that it should make its own person good and exercise a small influence, like the "nearsighted" who can look, and that is all. The *Symbol* remarks that they cannot extend their reach very far.[4] It is proper that the border between men and women be set by straightforwardness and ritual. Although the fifth line is not straightforward, the second guards itself with purity and straightforwardness in seclusion and tranquility, and this is where the profit lies. The second line has the virtues of firmness and straightforwardness and refers to people of seclusion and tranquility. The powers of the second line are like this, and yet the line statement remarks that there is profit in purity. Its remarks concern profit because it is fitting that someone like this be pure. It is not because of some insufficiency that the warning is given. **The *Symbol* says: "'There is profit in the purity of secluded people': they do not yet alter what is constant."** It guards its purity in seclusion and does "not yet" lose the way by which husbands and wives are "constant" and straightforward. People of the times consider lechery and carnality as what is constant, and this is why they think that purity and tranquility "alter what is constant." They do not recognize the way to be constant and continuous.

The third "six" line: the bride requires something for the wedding. Instead of being wed, she becomes a concubine. The third line occupies the top position in the lower trigram. It is not impoverished at its root, but it has lost its virtue and no other line corresponds to it straightforwardly. This is why it desires a wedding, but has not yet acquired a wedding. The word "requires" refers to waiting. It waits because it does not yet have what is suitable for it. This "six" line occupies the third position, a position that is not proper for it, and its virtue is not straightforward. To be soft and value firmness is to act without submissiveness. As the master of the enjoyment trigram, it seeks a wedding for the sake of enjoyment, which is to be moved by something other than ritual. The top line does not correspond to it—that is, it does not receive it in marriage. There is no one that is suitable, and this is why it requires something. When a young woman places herself like this, what man will choose to marry her? She should not be considered anyone's match. It is proper that, instead of being wed, she seek to become a concubine. This she may do, since she is without straightforwardness and has lost her place. **The *Symbol* says: "'The bride requires something for the wedding': it is not yet proper."** "It is not yet proper": its place, its virtue, and its way of seeking a wedding—none of them are proper. This is why no one chooses to marry it, and so it requires something.

The fourth "nine" line: she violates the period for wedding a bride. She is wedded late, when there is a moment for it. This "nine" line uses *yang* to occupy the fourth position. The fourth belongs to the upper trigram substance, which is on a lofty terrain. *Yang* firmness in a young woman refers to the virtue of straightforwardness as well as to her worthiness and enlightenment. It has no straightforwardly corresponding line—that is, it has not yet acquired a wedding. It has exceeded the moment and is not yet wed, which is why the line statement says that "she violates the period." A young woman occupies a terrain that is esteemed and lofty, she is supplied with worthiness and enlightenment, and men have the inclination and aspiration to marry her. This is why "she violates the period," but it will also be the case that "there is a moment for it." In fact, she is waiting for someone. It is not that she will not be given in marriage. She is simply waiting to acquire a decent match, and afterward she will act. This "nine" line occupies the fourth position. Although its position is not proper for it, the way of the wife is to be placed in a soft position. It has no corresponding line, and this is why it has the meaning of violating the period. The sage unfolds this principle, that a woman of worth who "violates the period" is in fact waiting for someone. **The *Symbol* says: "Her tendency is to violate the period: she waits for someone, and then acts."** She violates the period because of herself and not because of anyone else. Men aspire to marry the woman of worth, and so she violates the period. "Her tendency" or desire is to wait for someone. She is simply waiting to acquire a decent match, and afterward she will act.

The fifth "six" line: Di Yi gives the bride away at her wedding. The sleeves of the ruler are not as fine as the sleeves of the concubine. The moon is almost full. There is good fortune. The fifth "six" line occupies the position of respect and refers to an esteemed and lofty bride. It corresponds to the second line below it, which symbolizes the espousal of someone in a position below. Royal ladies sometimes espouse men in positions below them—this has been the case since antiquity. It reached the point that Di Yi and others who came after him made the ritual of marriage straightforward and shed light on the roles of men and women. Although a woman may be extremely estimable, her tendency to be estimable or arrogant will depend on whether she acquires or loses the way of softness and submissiveness. This is why, in the *Book of Changes*, when *yin* is meek and diminished in the position of respect, it says that "Di Yi gives the bride away at her wedding"—such is the case for the fifth "six" line of the Free hexagram. At the wedding of an estimable woman, if she is nothing but meek and diminished in attending to the ritual, she will possess the virtue of someone respected and lofty. This is not an affair of ornamenting one's appearance so as to be enjoyed by men. The ornamentation of one's appearance is an affair for concubines, and the sleeves on clothing are considered to be ornamentation for one's appearance. The fifth "six" line refers to a respected and esteemed woman who values ritual and does not value ornament. This is why her sleeves are "not as fine as the sleeves of the concubine." To be "fine" here is to be beautiful and preferred. "The moon is almost full": it is full of *yin*. If it is full, then it will be the enemy of *yang*. To be "almost full" is to have not yet reached the point of fullness. If the esteem and loftiness of the fifth line are constantly without reaching the limit of fullness, then it will not act proudly toward its husband: "There is good fortune." This is the way for a woman to place herself in a position of respect and esteem. **The *Symbol* says: "'Di Yi gives the bride away at her wedding,' but 'not as fine as the sleeves of the concubine': its position is at the center, so that its action may be estimable."** The *Symbol* remarks on the way in which "Di Yi gives the bride away at her wedding." Her sleeves are "not as fine as the sleeves of the concubine," since she values ritual and does not value ornament. The fifth line uses softness and centrality in the position of respect and loftiness. It is respected and esteemed, but it puts the way of centrality into action. To be soft, submissive, diminished, and contracted, valuing ritual and not valuing ornament—this is the way of centrality.

The top "six" line: the woman serves, but the basket is not filled. The scholar cuts up a sheep, but there is no blood. There is no long-term profit. The top "six" line is at the end of the wedded woman hexagram, has no corresponding line, and refers to a wedded woman who does not achieve her end. The purpose of a wife is to serve the first progenitors by presenting the sacrifices and libations. If she cannot present the sacrifices and libations, then she cannot be considered a wife. The mission of a wife is to distribute what fills the covered baskets. In antiquity, the stands for the many kinds of salted and vinegared dishes within the mansion were the mission of the prince's lady. In the sacrifices made by the various marquises, too, it was a relative who sliced up the livestock. This was also the case for the dignitaries and great officials who sliced up animals and took their blood for the sacrifice. The *Book of Rites* says that "blood is sacrificed because its *qi* is abundant."[5] It is proper that "the woman serves" and manages the affair of the covered "basket," but it "is not filled." If it is not filled, then there is nothing to sacrifice, which signifies that she cannot present the sacrifices and libations. Service in the ancestral temple is shared by husbands and wives. If the wife cannot present the sacrifices and libations, the husband will not be able to serve the sacrifices and libations. This is why he "cuts up a sheep, but there is no blood," and so it cannot be used as a sacrifice. This signifies that he cannot serve the sacrifices and libations. If the wife cannot present the sacrifices and libations, it is proper that he cast her out and sever himself from her. When husband and wife do not achieve their end because of this, how could any journey be profitable? **The *Symbol* says: "In the top 'six' line, it 'is not full': she serves an empty basket."** The basket "is not filled"—that is, the basket is hollow. How can a sacrifice be made with a hollow basket? The *Symbol* is remarking that she cannot present sacrifices and libations. If a woman cannot serve the sacrifices and libations, she is cast out and severed from her husband, and that is all. This is when a wedded woman does not achieve her end.

55. THICK (*FENG* 豐)

The *Sequence of the Hexagrams* says: "Those who acquire someone to wed will necessarily become great. This is why the Thick hexagram is next." Things that are wedded and gathered together will necessarily bring their greatness to completion. This is why the Thick hexagram is next after the Wed Bride hexagram. The word "thick" means to be abundant and great. As for the trigrams, the Shake trigram is above and the Cast trigram below. The Shake trigram refers to movement and the Cast trigram to enlightenment. If it is for enlightenment that one moves, or if one moves and can then be enlightened—both of these will bring about the way of the Thick hexagram. If the light is sufficient for illumination, and the movement is sufficient for progress, then afterward one will be able to bring about thickness and greatness.

Thick: there is progress. When the king appears, he will be without worry. It is fitting to be the sun at the center of its course. The Thick hexagram refers to abundance and greatness. Taken by itself it means progress. It is the limit of the world's brightness and greatness, but only kings can reach it. The word "appears" refers to reaching something. The respect owed to the position of heaven, the wealth of those between the four seas, the crowd of living things in their groups, the greatness in the way of the king, the way of thickness at its limit—these belong to the king alone. At the moment of the Thick hexagram, the people are complicated and numberless, and affairs and things are magnificently abundant. How could it be easy for the king to encompass them so as to set them in order? In this respect, he may be worried and apprehensive. It is fitting that he be like the abundant light and the broad illumination of "the sun at the center of its course." If there is nowhere he does not extend himself, then afterward he will not be worried.

The *Judgment* says: "To be thick is to be great. There are enlightenment and movement, and this is why it is thick." The Thick hexagram has the meaning of abundance and greatness. The Cast trigram refers to enlightenment and the Shake trigram to movement. Enlightenment and movement supply each other, and complete the thickness and greatness. "'When the king appears': he values greatness." Those who are kings possess the breadth between the four seas, the crowd of a million people, and the greatness of the world's limits. This is why only those who are kings can bring about the way of thickness and greatness. Since what they possess is already great, it is proper that their way of preserving it and setting it in order also be great. This is why what is valued by those who are kings is extreme greatness. "'He will be without worry. It is fitting to be the sun at the center of its course': it is fitting to illuminate the world." Since what he already possesses is broad, and what he has set in order is the crowd, it is proper for him to worry and be apprehensive that he may not be able to encompass or extend himself to it. It is fitting that he be like the abundant light of "the sun at the center of its course," and universally illuminate the world, so that there is no place he does not reach. Then he may be "without worry." In a case like this, he will afterward be able to preserve his thickness and greatness. The preservation and possession of thickness and greatness—how could those of small power or small knowledge be capable of it? "If the sun is at the center of its course, then it is about to set. If the moon is full, then it is about to be eaten up. If the fullness and emptiness of heaven and earth, as well as their disappearance and rest, are in agreement with the moment, what will be the case for people? What will be the case for ghosts and spirits?" Since the *Judgment* has already remarked on extreme thickness and abundance, it now turns its remarks to the difficulty of making them constant, and gives a warning. "If the sun is at the center of its course," at the limit of abundance, then it is proper for it to set and fade away. If the moon is already filled to satiety, then it will become inadequate and possess a gap. "If the fullness and emptiness of heaven and earth, as well as their disappearance and rest," value "agreement with the moment," what will be the case for people and for ghosts and spirits? "Fullness and emptiness" signify abundance and scarcity, and "disappearance and rest" signify advance and retreat. The revolution of heaven and earth also follows the moment in its advance and retreat. "Ghosts and spirits" signify the traces of creation and transformation, whose disappearance and rest may be seen in the abundance and scarcity of the ten thousand things. In the moment of thickness and abundance, it gives this warning, desiring that people guard their centrality and not reach the point of excessive abundance. To place oneself on the way of the Thick hexagram—how could it be easy?

The *Symbol* says: "Thunder and lightning are both extreme: Thick. Noble people use it to hold trials and bring about punishment." "Thunder and lightning are both extreme": the light and the shaking act together. Their two substances align with each other, and this is why the *Symbol* says that they "are both extreme." The light and the movement supply each other, and so they complete the symbol of the Thick hexagram. The Cast trigram refers to light, which symbolizes illumination and examination, and the Shake trigram refers to movement, which symbolizes authority and decisiveness. Those who "hold trials" must illuminate the inclination and reality of the case, and only enlightenment is capable of allowing this. Those who "bring about punishment" use their authority over what is vile and bad, and only their decisiveness will bring it to completion. This is why, when noble people gaze on the symbol of thunder and lightning shedding light and moving, they "hold trials and bring about punishment." Whereas the Bite Down hexagram remarked on the first kings, who gave dominion to the law, the Thick hexagram remarks on noble people, who hold trials. When the enlightenment trigram is above, and it is connected to the authority of the Shake trigram, it refers to the affairs of the king. This is why the Bite Down hexagram refers to controlling punishment and setting up the law. When the enlightenment trigram is below, and it is connected to the authority of the Shake trigram, it refers to the function of noble people. This is why the Thick hexagram refers to holding trials and bringing about punishment. In the March hexagram, the enlightenment trigram is above, and yet the *Symbol* speaks about noble people. The *Symbol* of the March hexagram chooses to speak about the cautious employment of punishment together with not delaying trials, which are always the proper actions of noble people.

The initial "nine" line: it encounters a master who is its match. Although ten days go by, there is no blame. There is value in making a journey. "Thunder and lightning are both extreme": they complete the symbol of the Thick hexagram. The light and the movement supply each other, and so they bring about the way of the Thick hexagram. Nothing can illuminate where there is no light, and nothing can act where there is no movement. They require each other like a form and its shadow, and they supply each other like surface and content. The initial "nine" line is the initial line of the enlightenment trigram, and the fourth "nine" line is the initial line of the movement trigram. It is fitting that they require each other to complete their function. This is why, "although ten days go by," they correspond to each other. They correspond to each other because of their positions, and they supply each other because of their functions. This is why the initial line statement refers to the fourth as the "master who is its match," because it is itself its match. Although "match" is a name for a mate, nonetheless here the one has almost become the other. For example, one becomes the match of heaven by becoming the match of the noble person.[1] This is why the initial line statement says that the fourth line is its match, and the fourth line statement says that the initial line is its equal. "Although ten days go by, there is no blame": the phrase "ten days" refers to things that are even with each other. When things in the world correspond to each other, they are not ordinarily even with or enemies of each other. For example, when *yin* corresponds to *yang*, softness attends to firmness, or those below depend on those above, how could they willingly attend to each other if they were enemies? It is only in the case of the initial and fourth lines of the Thick hexagram that they supply each other because of their functions and complete each other because of their correspondence. This is why, although they are even with each other—since they are both *yang* and firm—they attend to each other and there is no excess or blame. In fact, if there were no light, the movement could not go anywhere; if there were no movement, the light could not function anywhere. But here they supply each other and bring their functions to completion. Those who are in the same boat will have a single heart, even if they belong to the Hu and Yue tribes.[2] Those who share a difficulty will ally their forces even if they are hostile and hate each other. It is the propensity of the affair that brings this about. If they make the journey and attend to each other, they will be able to complete the Thick hexagram, and this is why it says that "there is value," because this may be excellent and valuable. If this were another hexagram, they would not descend to each other, but would cast each other off and break apart.

The *Symbol* says: "'Although ten days go by, there is no blame': to exceed ten days would be a disaster." Sages accord with the moment and place themselves fittingly. They follow the state of affairs and submit to principle. It is a constant principle that two even propensities will not defer to one other. Nonetheless, there are cases when, although they are enemies, they supply each other, and so they seek each other out. Such is the case for the initial and fourth lines. As a result, "although ten days go by, there is no blame." When people are the same and their forces are even, they may diminish themselves so as to seek each other, and they may ally their forces so as to attend to the state of affairs. Were they to cherish their private selves above all, and have the intention of attaching their own ascent to it, then their distress would properly be extreme. This is why the *Symbol* says that "to exceed ten days would be a disaster." When they are even, and yet each puts itself first—this is "to exceed ten days." If each seeks to be victorious alone, they cannot be the same.

The second "six" line: it curtains its thickness. The sun is at the center of its course, but it sees the north star. If it makes a journey, it will acquire doubts and illness. If it is trustworthy in what it reveals, there will be good fortune. Light and movement supply each other, and so they can complete the Thick hexagram. The second line is the master of the enlightenment trigram, it has acquired centrality and straightforwardness, and it refers to those who may be called enlightened. The fifth line is on the terrain that straightforwardly corresponds to it, but to be *yin* and soft in the fifth position is not straightforward, and so it cannot move. The second and fifth are both *yin* lines in the moment when light and movement supply each other, and they occupy terrains that correspond to each other, but the power of the fifth line is insufficient. Its power of correspondence is not sufficient to supply anything, and light alone is not capable of completing the Thick hexagram. Since it cannot complete the Thick hexagram, it will be deprived of light and movement, and this is why "it curtains its thickness." "The sun is at the center of its course": the second line has the power of extreme enlightenment, but its corresponding line does not agree with it sufficiently, and it cannot complete the Thick hexagram. It will be deprived of the accomplishment of light, and without the accomplishment of light it will be dark and dim. This is why the line statement says that "it sees the north star." The phrase "north star" refers to something seen when it is dark, and "curtain" means something that encompasses and enshrouds. It functions as a thing that shield and conceals, covering and obscuring what once was light. The north star is categorized as *yin*, and symbolizes the master of what revolves peacefully.[3] The fifth line uses *yin* softness and is in the proper position of the ruler. "The sun at the center of its course" is in the moment of abundant light, and yet "it sees the north star." Similarly, it is in the moment of thickness and greatness, and yet it encounters the master of softness and weakness. Since the north star is seen when it is dark, if the line statement remarks that "it sees the north star," this indicates that it is deprived of its light and has become dim. Although the second line has the powers of extreme enlightenment, centrality, and straightforwardness, it encounters a ruler who is soft, dim, and not straightforward. Since it is incapable of descending to seek those below itself, if it makes the journey to seek them, it will only acquire doubts and suspicions, jealousy and illness. Such is the case for the master of dimness. In such a case, what would it have to do to be capable of anything? When noble people manage the affairs of those above, but do not acquire their hearts, they will exhaust their extreme sincerity in affecting and bringing revelation to their tendencies or intentions, and that is all. If their own sincere intentions were capable of movement, they would be able to open up even the dark and blind, they would be able to assist even the soft and weak, and they would be able to make straightforward even those who are not straightforward. People of antiquity who managed the affairs of everyday rulers and ordinary masters, and who were capable of putting their way into action, made their own sincere intentions ascend and attain them. The rulers, in turn, saw that they were devoted and believable. Such were the cases of Guan Zhong and Duke Huan, and Kong Ming when he assisted his later master.[4] Those who can make themselves sincere and believable when revealing their tendencies or intentions will be able to put their way into action, and this constitutes good fortune. **The *Symbol* says: "'If it is trustworthy in what it reveals': it is believed when it reveals its tendencies."** "It is trustworthy in what it reveals": this signifies that it makes itself trustworthy and believable when affecting and bringing revelation to the hearts and tendencies of those above. If it can bring revelation, its good fortune should be recognized. Although it is soft and dim, it possesses the way of being able to bring revelation.

The third "nine" line: it bolsters its thickness. The sun is at the center of its course, but it sees the dust. It breaks its right arm. There is no blame. In the root text of antiquity, the *pei* character of "bolster" was written as the *pei* character of "banner."[5] Wang Bi considered it as referring to the streamers around a tent, which is what banners are.[6] Streamers around a tent surround and conceal what is inside. "It bolsters its thickness": the dimness here is more extreme than in the case of the curtain. The third line belongs to the enlightenment trigram, but it is dimmer than the fourth line because it corresponds to a line that is *yin* and dim. The third line occupies the top position in the enlightenment trigram substance, it is *yang* and firm, it has acquired straightforwardness, and at root it is capable of enlightenment. To complete the way of the Thick hexagram, light and movement must supply each other. The third corresponds to the top line, but the top line is *yin* and soft, has no position, and is placed at the end of the Shake trigram. Since it is at the end, it has stopped and is incapable of movement. In other trigrams, those who reach the end are at the limit, but in the Shake trigram those who reach the end have stopped. Since the third line is without the correspondence of the top line, they cannot complete the Thick hexagram. The word "dust" refers to the numerous minimal and small stars that have no names. "It sees the dust": this refers to its extreme dimness. It is in the moment of the Thick hexagram, but it encounters the top "six" line: "The sun is at the center of its course, but it sees the dust." The "right arm" is the one that people employ. When it is broken, their inability to do anything should be recognized. When the powers of the worthy and wise encounter enlightened rulers, they will be able to do things for the world. If there is no master above them on whom they can depend, they will be unable to do anything, like people who have broken their right arm. If what people do results in a loss, then it will also wed them to blame. It is saying that, because there was a specific cause, some specific other thing was brought about. Those who desire movement but have no right arm, like those who desire action but do not depend on those above, will be incapable of it, and that is all. What further remarks can be made about them? They have not wedded themselves to blame. **The *Symbol* says: "'It bolsters its thickness': there should be no great affairs. 'It breaks its right arm': in the end, it should not be employed."** The third corresponds to the top line, but the top line is *yin* and has no position. Its *yin* softness has no propensity or force, and it has already placed itself at the end. Could they make a shared crossing through some great affair? It has no one on whom to depend, as though it has broken its right arm, and so "in the end, it should not be employed."

The fourth "nine" line: it curtains its thickness. The sun is at the center of its course, but it sees the north star. It encounters a master who is its equal. There is good fortune. The fourth line is *yang* and firm, it is the master of the movement trigram, and it has acquired the position of the great minister, but it is nonetheless neither central nor straightforward. Since it encounters a master of *yin* dimness, softness, and weakness, how can it bring about thickness and greatness? This is why "it curtains its thickness." The word "curtain" refers to something that encompasses, surrounds, covers, and conceals. Since it is encompassed and surrounded, it will not be great, and since it is covered and concealed, it will have no light. "The sun is at the center of its course, but it sees the north star": it faces the moment of abundant light, but it is dark and dim. The phrase "a master who is its equal" indicates that they are equal in rank. It is because they correspond to each other that it is called a "master." The initial and fourth lines are both *yang*, and they occupy initial positions. That is, their virtue is the same, and they occupy terrains that correspond to each other. This is why there is "a master who is its equal." It occupies the position of the great minister, and has acquired worthy people below it. When those of the same virtue assist each other, how could their help be small? This is why "there is good fortune." As for those who have powers like the fourth line, and have acquired worthy people below them to give them help, will they be able to bring about thickness and greatness? Response: when those below have the agreement of people in their proper positions above them, and those above have the help

of worthy and powerful people below them, how could they not add to each
other? This is why there is good fortune. Nonetheless, when they are bringing about the thickness of the world, there must first be a ruler, and then they
will be capable of it. The fifth line is *yin* and soft, and occupies the position of
respect, but it belongs to the Shake trigram substance, and so its empty center does not symbolize lowliness and submissiveness toward the worthy people
below it. Although there are many worthy people below it, how could they do
anything? In fact, it is without *yang* firmness, centrality, and straightforwardness, so that it cannot bring about the thickness of the world. **The *Symbol* says:**
"'It curtains its thickness': its position is not proper for it." "Its position is not
proper for it": this signifies that it occupies a lofty position without centrality
or straightforwardness. As a result, it is dull and cannot bring about thickness.
"'The sun is at the center of its course, but it sees the north star': its seclusion
brings no enlightenment." The *Symbol* signifies that its seclusion and dimness
are incapable of brightness and light. This is because the ruler is *yin* and soft,
and the minister is neither central nor straightforward. **"'It encounters a mas-**
ter who is its equal': its action brings good fortune." Two lines that are *yang*
and firm have encountered each other, which is a fortunate act. It descends to
approach the initial line, and this is why the *Symbol* speaks of "its action." If it
descends to seek the initial line, this constitutes good fortune.

The fifth "six" line: the arrival of arrangement brings delight and praise.
There is good fortune. The fifth line uses the power of *yin* softness to become
the master of the Thick hexagram, and so it will certainly not be able to bring
thickness and greatness to completion. Were it able to bring about the arrival of
those below, with their powers of arrangement and beauty, and employ them,
there would be blessing and delight. In return, it would acquire beauty and
praise, which are here said to be "good fortune." The second "six' line, with its
pattern and enlightenment, centrality and straightforwardness, has the powers
of arrangement and beauty. Its sincerity can bring about a position for it from
the fifth line, which appoints it to command. It should be able to bring about
the delight of thickness and greatness, and the beauty of renown and praise.
This is why there is good fortune. The line statement remarks on the second
line as the master of the powers of arrangement and beauty. Nonetheless, the
initial, third, and fourth lines all possess the power of *yang* firmness. If the fifth
line can employ worthy people, then people of this sort will take the field. Although the second line is *yin*, it possesses the virtues of pattern and enlightenment, centrality and straightforwardness, and refers to great and worthy people
in positions below. Although the fifth and second lines do not straightforwardly

correspond as *yin* and *yang*, they are in the moment when light and movement supply each other, which means that they employ each other. Were the fifth line able to bring about "the arrival of arrangement," there would be "delight and praise," and "good fortune." Nonetheless, the fifth "six" line does not have the meaning of emptying itself and descending to worthy people. The sage has provided it with this meaning so as to teach something. **The *Symbol* says: "The good fortune of the fifth 'six' line: there is delight."** What is here called "good fortune" is to be capable of extending one's delight and blessings to the world. Although the rulers may be soft and dim, if they can employ the powers of worthy people, they should be able to bring about the blessings of the world. Their only distress is that they cannot do it themselves.

The top "six" line: it is the roof of thickness. It curtains its family and surveys its household. All is quiet, with no one around. For three years, there is no glimpse of it. There is misfortune. This "six" line uses a disposition of *yin* softness and occupies the limit position in the Thick hexagram. It is placed at the end of the movement trigram, and so its satisfaction is only apparent, and its movement is extremely restless. It is placed in the moment of thickness and greatness, and it is fitting for it to be meek and contracted, but it is in the lofty place of the limit. It brings about the accomplishment of thickness and greatness, which lies in firmness and vigor, but its substance is *yin* and soft. It faces command over thickness and greatness, which lies in making an acquisition of the moment, but its position is not proper for it. Since it is the top "six" line and its place is not at all proper for it, its misfortune should be recognized. "It is the roof of thickness": its place is great and lofty. "It curtains its family": it occupies a position without enlightenment. It uses *yin* softness to occupy a position of thickness and greatness, it is on a terrain without a position, its loftiness and pride make it dark and dim, and it has severed itself from other people—what person could agree with it? This is why it "surveys its household. All is quiet, with no one around." Since it has continued for a period of three years without knowing how to alter, it is fitting that there be misfortune. "There is no glimpse of it": this signifies that it does not value the sight of anyone—that is, it does not alter. This "six" line occupies the end position of the hexagram, which has the meaning of alteration. It is incapable of relocating itself—that is, its powers are incapable of it. **The *Symbol* says: "'It is the roof of thickness': it soars on the border of heaven. It 'surveys its household. All is quiet, with no one around': it stores itself away."** This "six" line is placed at the limit of thickness and greatness. It is in a position above, and makes itself lofty. If it flies or soars to the border of heaven, this signifies that it is extremely lofty and great. "It surveys its household" and this is "with no one around": although it occupies the limit position of thickness and greatness, in reality it is on a terrain without a position. Some people use their darkness and dimness to make themselves lofty and great, and this is why all others desert them and sever themselves from them. They store themselves away and evade others, and no one will relate to them.

56. MARCH (LÜ 旅)

The *Sequence of the Hexagrams* says: "To be thick is to be great. Those who deplete their greatness will necessarily lose the position they occupy, and this is why the March hexagram is next." When those who are thick and abundant reach the point of their limit and depletion, they will necessarily lose their place of contentment. And so the March hexagram succeeds the Thick hexagram. As for the trigrams, the Cast trigram is above and the Calm trigram below. The mountain is stopped and will not be relocated, but fire travels and does not occupy a place. Together they symbolize withdrawal and departure, and being without a place, and this is why these trigrams constitute the March hexagram. Further, the connection trigram is on the outside, which is another symbol of the March hexagram.

March: there is some small progress. The purity of the march brings good fortune. The judgment is remarking on the powers of the trigrams. Concerning the powers of the trigrams, there should be "some small progress." They have acquired the purity and straightforwardness of the March hexagram, and so there will be good fortune.

The *Judgment* says: "'March: there is some small progress': softness acquires centrality on the outside and submits to firmness. There are stopping and a connection to enlightenment. As a result, 'there is some small progress,' and 'the purity of the march brings good fortune.'" A "six" line ascends to occupy the fifth position: "Softness acquires centrality on the outside." It is connected to the firm lines above and below it, and so it "submits to firmness." The Calm trigram is below and refers to stopping, while the Cast trigram is above and refers to connection: "There are stopping and a connection to enlightenment."

A line that is soft and submissive acquires the center of the outer trigram—that is, it stops where it can connect itself to the enlightenment trigram. "As a result, 'there is some small progress'": it acquires the purity and straightforwardness of the March hexagram, and there will be good fortune. In the moment of the march or trap, there is not a line with *yang* firmness, centrality, and straightforwardness in the lower trigram to help it, and so it cannot bring about great progress. When the *Judgment* says that it "acquires centrality on the outside," it does not refer to a single sense of centrality. The March hexagram has the centrality of those on the march. If "there are stopping and a connection to enlightenment," then it will not lose what is fitting for the moment, and afterward it will acquire the way to place itself in the March hexagram. **"How great are the moment and meaning of the March hexagram!"** When managing the affairs of the world, it is proper to follow the moment, to do what is suitable and fitting in each case. But the March hexagram refers to difficulty in placing oneself, and this is why the *Judgment* salutes the greatness of its moment and meaning.

The *Symbol* says: "Above the mountain, there is fire: March. Noble people use it to become enlightened and cautious when employing punishment. They do not delay trials." When fire is lofty, its light cannot do otherwise than illuminate. When noble people gaze on the symbol of light and illumination, they "use it to become enlightened and cautious when employing punishment." They should not rely on their enlightenment, and this is why the *Symbol* warns them to be cautious in their enlightenment, and the stopping also is a symbol of caution. When they gaze on the symbol of a fire that travels without having a place, they "do not delay trials." A trial is provided when something cannot be put in the past. If one of the people commits a crime and enters into court, how could they delay in their laziness and continually put it off?

The initial "six" line: on the march, it is petty, and petty again. In such a case, what it chooses is disaster. This "six" line makes use of *yin* softness in the moment of the March hexagram, it is placed in a humble position below, and it refers to people of softness and weakness. They have placed themselves on the march or in the trap, they are humble and impoverished, and they persist at the bottom of corruption. People of humble tendencies who have placed themselves on the march or in the trap are scorned, insignificant, "petty," and paltry. There is no place they will not reach, and so they bring about regret and disgrace, and they choose "disaster" and blame for themselves. To be "petty, and petty again" is to be in an insignificant and paltry condition. Those whose power and disposition are like this, and who face the moment of the march or trap, will be unable to do anything even if they are supported by those above. The nature of the fourth line is *yang* and it belongs to the Cast trigram substance, both of which make it unable to approach those below. Further, the March hexagram is different from other hexagrams where this is the position of the great minister. **The *Symbol* says: "'On the march, it is petty, and petty again': its tendencies are depleted, and there is a disaster."** "Its tendencies" or intentions "are depleted" and suppressed. In addition, it chooses a "disaster" for itself. When the *Symbol* remarks on "a disaster and a mistake," and the two are opposed, each has its role to play.[1] When it remarks only on a disaster, it signifies the disaster of distress.

The second "six" line: on the march, it approaches its camp and cherishes its supplies. It acquires the purity of servants and children. The second line possesses the virtues of softness, submission, centrality, and straightforwardness. Since it is soft and submissive, the crowd agrees with it; since it is central and straightforward, it does not lose its proper place. This is why it can preserve what it possesses, and its servants and children will exhaust their loyalty and believability. Although it does not possess the virtues of pattern and enlightenment like the fifth line, it has the help of the lines above and below it, which is also to place oneself well in the March hexagram. The "camp" or lodging is where those on the march are contented, resources and commodities are the "supplies" of those on the march, and "servants and children" are depended on by those on the march. It acquires or "approaches" its camp or lodging, it "cherishes" or herds its supplies and resources, and it acquires servants and children who are pure and fine, which is good for someone placed in the March hexagram. The soft and weak line at the bottom is the child, while the strong and mighty line placed on the outside is the servant. The second line is soft, submissive, central, and straightforward, and this is why it acquires the hearts of those on the inside and outside. What those on the march relate and draw close to are servants and children. The line statement does not say that "there is good fortune." If those on the march are on the verge of being housed, and have avoided disaster and danger, this is already something good. **The *Symbol* says: "'It acquires the purity of servants and children': in the end, there is no resentment."** People on an expedition or march depend on "servants and children." If they have acquired the loyalty and purity of servants and children, "in the end, there is no resentment" or regret.

The third "nine" line: on the march, it burns its camp. It is deprived of the purity of servants and children. There is danger. The way to place oneself in the March hexagram is first of all to be soft, submissive, meek, and in a

position below. The third line is firm and without centrality, and further, it
occupies the top position in the lower trigram substance, and it is the top line
of the Calm trigram, which is the symbol of those who make themselves lofty.
In the March hexagram, those who are excessively firm and make themselves
lofty will bring about the way of traps and disasters. If it makes itself lofty, it
will not submit to those above. This is why the top line does not agree with it,
and it "burns its camp"—that is, it loses its place of contentment. When the
Cast trigram is on top, it symbolizes burning. If there is excessive firmness, it
will do violence to those below. This is why those below cast it off, and it is
"deprived" of the purity and belief of "servants and children," which signifies
that it has lost their hearts. Such a line is on the way of peril and danger. **The
Symbol says: "'On the march, it burns its camp': it is also injured. On the
march, it agrees with those below: it is deprived of their sense of duty."** "On
the march, it burns" or loses "its camp" or lodging, which is also to be trapped
or "injured." In the moment of the March hexagram, when the way of agreeing with those below is like this, it is proper that it be "deprived of their sense
of duty." When those on the march are excessively firm and make themselves
lofty in waiting on those below, they will necessarily be deprived of their loyalty and purity, which signifies that they have lost their hearts. When those on
the march have lost the hearts of their servants and children, they should be
imperiled.

**The fourth "nine" line: on the march, it reaches its place. It acquires its sup-
plies and a hatchet. My heart is not quickened.** The fourth line is *yang* and
firm. Although it does not occupy the center, it is placed in a soft position at
the bottom of the upper trigram substance, which symbolizes the employment
of softness and the capacity to be at the bottom. It has acquired what is fitting
in the March hexagram. Because its powers are firmness and enlightenment,
the fifth line agrees with it and the initial line corresponds to it, which is good
for someone in the March hexagram. Nonetheless, the fourth line is not in a
straightforward position, and this is why it is not like the second line approaching its camp or lodging, even though it has acquired a place to stop. Because
it possesses the powers of firmness and enlightenment, those above and below
agree with it, and so it acquires the "supplies" of commodities and resources
and the profit of tools and their functions for its march. Although this is good
for those on the march, it nonetheless has no *yang* firmness to agree with in the
line above it, but only corresponds to the *yin* softness of the bottom line. This is
why it cannot expand its powers or put its tendencies into action: its "heart is not
quickened." The line statement says "my" because it is speaking as the fourth

line. **The *Symbol* says: "'On the march, it reaches its place': it has not yet acquired a position. 'It acquires its supplies and a hatchet': its heart is not yet quickened."** The fourth line considers the position near the ruler to be proper for it, but in the March hexagram, the meaning of the ruler is not chosen for the fifth line, and this is why the fourth "has not yet acquired a position." Someone says: in such a case, to occupy the fourth position with a "nine" line, which is not straightforward, will result in blame. Response: it is fitting for firm lines to occupy soft positions in the March hexagram. This "nine" line uses the powers of firmness and enlightenment, and it desires the acquisition of the moment for putting its tendencies into action. This is why its "heart" and tendencies are "not yet quickened," even though it has acquired "supplies and a hatchet," which is good for someone in the March hexagram.

The fifth "six" line: it shoots a pheasant. One arrow vanishes. In the end, there are praise and the mandate. The fifth "six" line possesses the virtues of pattern, enlightenment, softness, and submissiveness. It is placed so as to acquire the way of centrality, and those above and below agree with it, which is what is best for someone placed in the March hexagram. People placed in the March hexagram should be called good when they can align with the way of pattern and enlightenment. If people on an expedition or march sometimes lose things when they move, then traps and disgrace will follow them. If they lose nothing when they move, they will afterward become good. The Cast trigram is indicated by the "pheasant," which is a thing of pattern and enlightenment. "It shoots a pheasant": this signifies that it chooses to be regulated by the way of pattern and enlightenment, and will necessarily align with it. In the example of shooting a pheasant, if there is one arrow and it is made to vanish, revealing that it went nowhere but the center, then "in the end" it will be able to bring about "praise and the mandate." The word "praise" refers to decrees and renown, and "mandate" refers to blessings and wages. The fifth line occupies a position of pattern and enlightenment, and it possesses the virtues of pattern and enlightenment. This is why its movement will necessarily be at the center of the way of pattern and enlightenment. The fifth is the position of the ruler, but rulers do not go on the march. If they were to go on the march, they would lose their position, and this is why the meaning of the ruler is not chosen for this line. **The *Symbol* says: "'In the end, there are praise and the mandate': the top captures it."** If it possesses the virtues of pattern, enlightenment, softness, and submissiveness, then those above and below will agree with it. The word "capture" refers to agreement. If it can submit to and serve the top line, then the top line will agree with it—that is, the top line is what captures it. The

Symbol is remarking that the top line acquires the line below it—that is, the line below is what the top line captures. In the March hexagram, those above and below agree with it, and so it brings about "praise and the mandate." The March hexagram refers to a trap, when one has not yet acquired the moment for contentment. "In the end, there are praise and the mandate": it is proper that praise and the mandate be brought about in the end. If there were already praise and the mandate, it would not be on the march. Those who are trapped, and who "have few relations," are already on the march.[2] It is not even necessary that they go outside.

The top "nine" line: the bird burns its nest. People on the march laugh at first, but afterward they call out and wail. It is deprived of a cow while at ease. There is misfortune. The word "bird" refers to what flies and soars in a lofty place. The top "nine" line is firm without centrality and it is in the loftiest place. Further, it belongs to the Cast trigram substance and its pride should be recognized. This is why the bird is chosen as its symbol. In the moment of the March hexagram, those who are meek, diminished, soft, and harmonious may preserve themselves. But it is excessively firm and makes itself lofty, losing its fitting place of contentment. The "nest" is where the bird stops and is contented. If it "burns its nest," it will lose its place of contentment and will have nowhere to stop. The top line of the Cast trigram is symbolized by burning. When *yang* firmness places itself in extreme loftiness, its intentions are quickened at the beginning, and this is why they "laugh at first." Later, it loses its contentment and nothing agrees with it, and this is why "they call out and wail." When it is light and "at ease," it is "deprived" of the virtue of submissiveness, and so "there is misfortune." The word "cow" refers to something submissive. "It is deprived of a cow while at ease": this signifies that it loses its submissiveness while oblivious and at ease. The Cast trigram refers to fire, whose nature is to ascend, and which symbolizes restlessness and ease. This statement serves the earlier one that "the bird burns its nest."[3] This is why the line statement attaches the characters for "people on the march." If it did not say "people on the march," it would be the bird that laughed and wept. **The *Symbol* says: "The top line of the March hexagram: its meaning is to burn. 'It is deprived of a cow while at ease': in the end, it hears of nothing."** Since "the top line of the March hexagram" puts itself in a lofty and respected place, how could it preserve the position that it occupies? It is proper that its meaning be the affair of burning one's nest. When it uses firmness at the limit to make itself lofty, it acquires the object of its tendencies and laughs. It does not recognize that it has deprived itself of the virtue of submissiveness in its restlessness and ease—that is, "in the end, it hears of nothing," which signifies that in the end it "hears" and recognizes nothing. If it were to make itself recollect or recognize anything, it would not reach the limit or call out and wail. When *yang* firmness without centrality is placed at the limit, it will certainly symbolize lofty pride and restless movement. In the case of the fire that flames up, it is also at its extreme.

57. LOW (XUN 巽)

The *Sequence of the Hexagrams* says: "They are on the march because no place will embrace them. This is why the Low hexagram is next. Those who are lowly will gain entry somewhere." If those on an expedition or march have few relations, and are neither lowly nor submissive, what place will choose to embrace them? If they were capable of lowliness and submissiveness, even if they were at the center of a march or trap, how could they make a journey without gaining entry somewhere? And so the Low hexagram succeeds the March hexagram. As for the trigrams, a single *yin* line is below two *yang* lines. It is lowly and submissive to *yang*, and so they constitute the Low trigram.

Low: there is some small progress. There is profit in a long journey, and profit in seeing great people. The powers of the trigrams should be able to make "some small progress," and so "there is profit in a long journey, and profit in seeing great people." The Low and Joy trigrams both possess firmness, centrality, and straightforwardness, and their meanings of lowliness and enjoyment are also one in kind. If there is joy, then there will be progress; if there is lowliness, then there will be "some small progress." Joy is the act of *yang*, while lowliness is the act of *yin*. The soft line of the Joy trigram is on the outside and refers to the function of softness. The soft line of the Low trigram is on the inside and refers to the nature of softness. And so, the progress of the Low trigram is "small."

The *Judgment* says: "The Low trigram is repeated so as to reiterate the mandate." "The Low trigram is repeated": the Low trigram is both above and below. Those above submit to the way so that the mandate will go out, while those below honor the mandate by submitting and attending to it. Those above and below are both submissive, and this is symbolized by the repetition of the

Low trigram. Further, the *chong* character of "repeated" has the meaning of "returned." Noble people give substance to the meaning of the repeated Low trigram so as to reiterate or return to their mandate and decree. To reiterate is to repeat or to return to, and signifies that they insist on it. **"Firmness is lowly in its centrality and straightforwardness, and puts its tendencies into action. Softness is always submissive to firmness. As a result, 'there is some small progress.'"** The *Judgment* is remarking on the powers of the trigrams. Lines of *yang* firmness occupy positions in the Low trigrams, and they acquire centrality and straightforwardness. This is the way to be lowly and submissive, central and straightforward. The nature of *yang* is to be above, and its tendency is to use the way of centrality and straightforwardness to travel upward. Further, the soft lines in the upper and lower trigrams are both lowly and submissive to the firm lines. When the trigram powers are like this, even if the soft line is on the inside, there should be "some small progress." **"'There is profit in a long journey, and profit in seeing great people.'"** Concerning the way of lowliness and submissiveness, there is no journey that is incapable of gaining entry somewhere. This is why "there is profit in a long journey." Although the way of lowliness and submissiveness is good, one must recognize what to attend to. To be capable of lowliness and submissiveness toward great people of *yang* firmness, centrality, and straightforwardness is profitable. This is why there is "profit in seeing great people." For example, the fifth and second lines with their *yang* firmness, centrality, and straightforwardness refer to "great people." To be lowly and submissive to those who are not great people is not necessarily without excess.

The *Symbol* says: **"'The winds follow: Low. Noble people use it to reiterate the mandate and put their affairs into action."** When two winds are set one on top of the other, "the winds follow." The word "follow" here means to succeed each other. When noble people gaze on the symbol of the repeated Low trigrams succeeding each other submissively, they use it to reiterate their mandate and decrees, and to put the affairs of government into action. When the repeated trigrams agree to follow each other, the upper and lower trigrams are both submissive. Those above submit to those below by going out to them, while those below submit to those above by attending to them. Those above and those below are both submissive—this is the meaning of the repeated Low trigrams. If their mandate, decrees, and the affairs of government are submissive to principle, they will align with the hearts of the people, and the people will submit and attend to them.

The initial "six" line: it advances and retreats. There is profit in the purity of warlike people. This "six" line uses *yin* softness to occupy a position of humility, it is lowly and without centrality, it is placed at the bottom and serves a firm line, and it refers to those who are excessively humble and lowly. When people of *yin* softness possess a great excess of humility and lowliness, their tendencies or intentions will be fearful and trembling, and they will not be contented. Sometimes they will advance and sometimes retreat, not knowing what they should attend to. What is profitable here is the "purity of warlike people." Were they able to employ the tendencies of firmness and purity possessed by warlike people, then they would do what is fitting. If they are exhorted to be firm and pure, they will not lose themselves in excessive humility, fear, and trembling. **The Symbol says: "'It advances and retreats': its tendencies are doubtful. 'There is profit in the purity of warlike people': its tendencies are orderly."** "It advances and retreats": it does not know how to be contented because "its tendencies are doubtful" and troubled. "There is profit" in employing the firmness and purity of warlike people to set up its tendencies, and then "its tendencies are orderly." The word "orderly" signifies that they are set up correctly.

The second "nine" line: lowliness is to be underneath the bed. It employs harbingers and prophets pervasively. There are good fortune and no blame. The second line occupies the moment of lowliness, it is *yang* placed in a *yin* position in the lower trigram, and it refers to those who are excessively lowly. The word "bed" refers to where people are contented. "Lowliness is to be underneath the bed": it is excessively lowly, and excessively contented. When people are excessively humble and lowly without being fearful or timid, they take up flattery and enjoyment, neither of which is straightforward. Since the second line has fullness and firmness at its center, it does not have a crooked heart, even though it belongs to the Low trigram substance, occupies a soft position, and is excessively lowly. Although an excess of modesty and lowliness is not straightforward according to ritual, it may still be far away from shame and disgrace, and it will sever itself from hatred and blame, which is also a way of good fortune. The phrase "harbingers and prophets" refers to those who communicate their sincere intentions with spiritual enlightenment, and "pervasively" indicates that there are many of them. If it is extremely sincere and contented in its meekness and lowliness, and is able to communicate many of its sincere intentions, then there will be "good fortune and no blame." This signifies that its sincerity is sufficient to move other people. If other people do not examine the sincerity of its intentions, they will consider its excessive lowliness to be flattery. **The Symbol says: "The good fortune of 'pervasively': it acquires centrality."** The second line occupies a soft position in the lower trigram and symbolizes excessive lowliness. It can, however, communicate its sincere intentions to a crowd or multitude—that is, "pervasively"—because "it acquires centrality." A *yang* line occupies the center, constituting the symbol of a center that is full. When one's center is already sincere or full, it is proper for other people to believe in it spontaneously. If one's intentions are sincere, one will not flatter or tremble before anyone, and so there will be good fortune and no blame.

The third "nine" line: it is frequently lowly. There is dismay. The third line uses *yang* to place itself in a firm position, but it does not acquire the center. Further, it is at the top of the lower trigram substance, and it occupies the moment of lowliness and submissiveness using a disposition of firmness and pride. It refers to those who cannot be lowly but exhort themselves to do something, and this is why it is routinely lost. It occupies a position in the moment of the Low hexagram, it is placed in the lower trigram, and the line above it watches over it with lowliness. Further, the fourth line relates to it with softness and lowliness, it rides a firm line, and two of the lines above it constitute a repetition of firmness. Although it does not desire lowliness, what else could it acquire? This is why it is frequently lost and "frequently lowly"—that is, it should be dismayed. **The *Symbol* says: "The dismay of being 'frequently lowly': its tendency is depleted."** The power and disposition of the third line are, at their root, incapable of lowliness. The line above it watches over it with lowliness, it serves the repetition of firmness, and its own walk has the propensity to be firm. It cannot put its tendency into action, and this is why it is frequently lost and "frequently lowly"—that is, its tendency is depleted and trapped, and it should be extremely dismayed.

The fourth "six" line: regrets vanish. It obtains three items from the field. *Yin* softness has no supporting line here. The lines it serves and rides are both firm, and so it is fitting that there be regrets. The fourth line uses *yin* to occupy a *yin* position, which is to acquire the straightforwardness of the Low hexagram. It is at the bottom of the upper trigram substance, which is to occupy a position above while capable of being below. It occupies the bottom position in the upper trigram, which is to be lowly in a position above. It uses lowliness to watch over those below, which is to be lowly toward those below. It has placed itself so well that its "regrets vanish." The reason its regrets vanish is that it is like someone who "obtains three items from the field." "It obtains three items from the field": it extends itself to those above and below. Those who hunt in the fields divide what they have obtained into three items: one that is dried and put in vessels, one that is distributed to visitors and guests, and one that is sent to "those on foot and horseback."[1] The fourth line is capable of lowliness toward the *yang* lines above and below it, like someone who obtains three items from the field. This signifies that it extends itself entirely to those above and below. The terrain of the fourth line has regrets at its root but, because it has placed itself so well, "regrets vanish" and "it accomplishes something." In the affairs of the world, even regrets can sometimes be considered an accomplishment for those who place themselves well. **The *Symbol* says: "'It obtains three items from the field': it accomplishes something."** It is lowly toward those above and below, like one who "obtains three items from the field." It extends itself entirely to those above and below, and completes the accomplishment of the Low hexagram.

The fifth "nine" line: purity brings good fortune. Regrets vanish. Nothing is without profit. It has nothing initially, but something in the end. For three days before the seventh stem, and three days after the seventh stem, there is good fortune. The fifth line occupies the position of respect, it is the master of the Low hexagram, and the mandate and decrees go out from it. It is placed so as to acquire centrality and straightforwardness, and it exhausts what is good in the Low hexagram. Nonetheless, the Low hexagram refers to the way of softness and submissiveness, and the profit here lies in purity. It is not that the fifth line is insufficient, but it is proper that there be a warning about this in the Low hexagram. Since it is already pure, there is "good fortune," "regrets vanish," and "nothing is without profit." The word "purity" refers to centrality and straightforwardness. When decrees go out from those placed in the Low hexagram, they always consider centrality and straightforwardness as good fortune. If they are soft and lowly without being pure, they will have regrets. How could it be the case that nothing is without profit? The mandate and decrees go out because there is something that needs alteration and revision. "It has nothing initially": at the beginning it is not yet good. It has "something in the end": it is made good through its revision. If it were already good, why would the mandate be employed? Why would revision be employed? "For three days before the seventh stem, and three days after the seventh stem, there is good fortune": this is the proper way for the mandate of revision and modification to go out. The first stem refers to the impetus of an affair, while the seventh stem is the beginning of its alteration and revision. Of the ten stems, the fifth and sixth constitute the center. When the center is exceeded, there is alteration, and this is why the line statement refers to it as the seventh stem. In the modification and revision of affairs, it is proper that the origin or beginning come to an opportune end, just like the meaning of "before the first stem" and "after the first stem." In such a case, there will be good fortune. This is interpreted in the Blight hexagram.[2] **The *Symbol* says: "The good fortune of the fifth 'nine' line: its position**

is straightforward and central." "The good fortune of the fifth 'nine' line" is that it places itself with straightforwardness and centrality. If it acquires the way of straightforwardness and centrality, then there will be good fortune and its regrets will vanish. The phrase "straightforward and central" signifies that it is not excessive, but there is nothing to which it does not extend itself: it has straightforwardly acquired the center. When the mandate and decrees go out from those in places of softness and lowliness, their sole good is the acquisition of centrality. Those who lose their centrality will have regrets.

The top "nine" line: lowliness is to be underneath the bed. It is deprived of its supplies and a hatchet. Purity brings misfortune. The word "bed" refers to where people are contented. To be "underneath the bed" has the meaning of exceeding the place of contentment. This "nine" line occupies the limit position in the Low hexagram and refers to those who are excessively lowly. "Supplies" are what people possess, and "hatchet" refers to something decisive. *Yang* firmness has decisiveness at its root, but this line loses its firmness and decisiveness because of its excessive lowliness. To lose what one possesses is to be deprived of "supplies and a hatchet." Because it occupies the top position and is excessively lowly, it reaches the point of losing itself. To be on the way of straightforwardness here constitutes misfortune. **The *Symbol* says: "'Lowliness is to be underneath the bed': there is depletion at the top. 'It is deprived of its supplies and a hatchet': is it straightforward? There is misfortune."** "Lowliness is to be underneath the bed": it is excessively lowly. It is placed at the top of the hexagram, and so its lowliness reaches its depletion and limit. It occupies the top position and exceeds the limit of lowliness, reaching the point of losing itself. Does it acquire straightforwardness? Then it is on the way of misfortune. The action of lowliness is good at its root, and this is why the *Symbol* speaks with such doubt: does it acquire straightforwardness? It then speaks about its decisiveness: "There is misfortune."

58. JOY (*DUI* 兌)

The *Sequence of the Hexagrams* says: "Those who are lowly will gain entry to a place. If they gain entry to it, they will afterward enjoy it. This is why the Joy hexagram is next. The word 'Joy' refers to enjoyment." When things enter each other, they enjoy each other. And when they enjoy each other, they enter each other. And so the Joy hexagram succeeds the Low hexagram.

Joy: there are progress, profit, and purity. The Joy hexagram refers to enjoyment. When there is enjoyment, it brings about the way of progress. If something can be enjoyed by things, then things will not be without their enjoyment, and will agree with it, which is sufficient to bring about progress. Nonetheless, for those on the way of enjoyment, the profit lies in purity and straightforwardness. If they seek enjoyment without the way, they will become crooked flatterers and there will be regret and blame. This is why the judgment gives the warning about "profit, and purity."

The *Judgment* says: "The word 'joy' refers to enjoyment. Firmness is at the center and softness is outside. Enjoyment makes use of 'profit and purity.' As a result, it submits to heaven and corresponds to people. If enjoyment is put before the people, the people will forget about their labor. If enjoyment is used to confront difficulties, the people will forget having to die. Surely the greatness of enjoyment is that it persuades the people!" The meaning of the Joy hexagram is enjoyment. A single *yin* line occupies a position above two *yang* lines. *Yin* is enjoyed by *yang* and refers to what *yang* enjoys. A line that is *yang* and firm occupies the center, which symbolizes a center or heart that is sincere and full. A soft line is on the outside, which symbolizes a response to things that is harmonious and soft. This is why these trigrams constitute the enjoyment hexagram, and are capable of purity. There are "profit and purity" when the way of enjoyment is fitting and straightforward. Since the trigrams have the virtue of a firm center, they can be pure. There is enjoyment, but it is capable of purity. As a result, it submits to the principle of heaven above, and corresponds to people's hearts below. And so, the way of enjoyment is extremely straightforward and extremely good. Were it to draw back from the way so as to crave the praise of the masses, it would be the way of reckless enjoyment. Were it to draw back from the way and not submit to heaven, to crave praise and not correspond to people, it would recklessly choose the enjoyment of a single moment, which is not the straightforward way of noble people. The way of noble people brings enjoyment to the people as though it were the influence of heaven and earth. When it affects their hearts, they enjoy and obey it tirelessly. This is why, if it "is put before the people," the people's hearts will enjoy and follow it, and they "will forget about their labor." If it is administered to "confront difficulties," the people's hearts will enjoy it and obey their duty, and they will not be anxious about death. The way of enjoyment is great because the people are nothing but knowledgeable and persuaded. The word "persuades" signifies that they believe in it, and exhort themselves with all their force to submit and attend to it. The way of noble people[1] has the enjoyment and obedience of the human heart as its root, and this is why the sage applauds its greatness.

The *Symbol* says: "The lakes are connected: Joy. Noble people use it to make friends in their instruction and practice." "The lakes are connected": the two lakes depend on and connect with each other. When two lakes connect with each other, their interaction will make them commingle and soak into each other, which symbolizes exchanging one's possessions, thriving, and adding to them. This is why, when noble people gaze on this symbol, they "use it to make friends in their instruction and practice." "Make friends in their instruction and practice": they exchange with and add to each other. An earlier intellectual said that, of all the enjoyable things in the world, none is like having friends in one's instruction and practice.[2] To have friends in one's instruction and practice is certainly the greatest of enjoyable things. It is proper, nonetheless, to shed light on the symbol of their adding to each other.

The initial "nine" line: the joy of harmony brings good fortune. Although the initial line is *yang*, it occupies a position at the very bottom of the enjoyment trigram substance. It is not bound to any corresponding line—this is to be capable of finding enjoyment in humility, in occupying a position below, in harmony, and in submissiveness, without being either partial or private. To consider harmony as enjoyable without being partial or private is to be straightforward in one's enjoyment. Since it is *yang* and firm, it will not be humble; since it occupies a position below, it will be capable of lowliness; since it is placed in the enjoyment trigram, it will be capable of harmony; since it has no corresponding line, it will not be partial. Such is its placement in the enjoyment hexagram, and so there is "good fortune." **The *Symbol* says: "The good fortune of the joy of harmony: its actions are not yet doubtful."** If it seeks to be in harmony with something, it will traverse crookedness and flattery. The initial line follows the moment and submits to its place. Its heart is not bound to anything, and so it has nothing to do. It is in harmony, and that is all. As a result, there is "good fortune." The *Symbol* goes further, considering its placement at the bottom of the enjoyment hexagram without centrality or straightforwardness. This is why it says that "its actions are not yet doubtful." Its actions do not yet have anything about them that should be doubted, which signifies that it does not yet seem to have lost anything. Were it to acquire centrality and straightforwardness, the *Symbol* would not make these remarks. The enjoyment hexagram has centrality and straightforwardness as its root. The line statement goes straight to declaring this meaning, while the *Symbol* unfolds and exhausts it.

The second "nine" line: the joy of being trustworthy brings good fortune. Regrets vanish. The second line serves and is close to a line of *yin* softness, but *yin* softness refers to small people. If it were to enjoy them, it would be proper that it have regrets. The second line has the virtues of firmness and centrality, it is trustworthy and believable, and its interior is replete. Although it is close to small people, it keeps guard and does not lose itself. Noble people are in harmony with them, but are not the same as they are. They do not lose their firmness and centrality to enjoyment, and this is why there is "good fortune" and "regrets vanish." If the second line were not firm and central, it would have regrets. They vanish because it guards itself. **The *Symbol* says: "The good fortune of the joy of being trustworthy: its tendency is to be believed."** What persists in the heart is one's tendency. The second line possesses firmness and fullness, and occupies the center. Trustworthiness and believability persist at its center. Since its persistent tendency is sincere and believable, how could it possess the enjoyment of small people and lose itself? As a result, there is "good fortune."

The third "six" line: the joy of arrival brings misfortune. The third "six" line refers to people of *yin* softness without centrality or straightforwardness, whose enjoyment does not make use of the way. "The joy of arrival" refers to approaching someone in search of enjoyment. It is close to the *yang* line below it, bending itself without the way. It approaches the second line in search of enjoyment, and so there is "misfortune." It goes inside to make its arrival. Those above and below are both *yang* lines, but it only goes inside one of them, because they belong to the same trigram substance, and because the nature of *yin* is to descend. It loses the way by traveling below. **The *Symbol* says: "The misfortune of the joy of arrival: its position is not proper for it.** It places itself without centrality or straightforwardness, and no line agrees with it. Its search for enjoyment is faulty, and so there is "misfortune."

The fourth "nine" line: it ponders joy but is not yet serene. If it is secure from illness, it will be happy. The fourth line ascends to serve the central and straightforward fifth line, and it descends to draw close to the soft and crooked third line. Although it is *yang* and firm, it does not place itself straightforwardly. The third line, being *yin* and soft, is what the *yang* line enjoys. This is why it cannot be resolute, but ponders and takes the measure of it. The phrase "not yet serene" signifies that it sketches out and discusses what it will attend to, but it is not yet resolute and cannot yet be determined. The space between two things is signified by the word "security," which constitutes a division or perimeter. To get the character for a "domain" of the earth, the character for "field" must be attached to it, but their meanings are the same.[3] This is why people who rein in and guard themselves are said to be secure, and those with such security will guard their straightforwardness. If illness is far away from them, together with what is crooked and bad, they "will be happy." It is straightforward to attend to the fifth line and crooked to enjoy the third line. Since the fourth is near the position of the rulers, if it can secure its firmness and guard its straightforwardness, and if illness is far from it together with what is crooked and bad, then it will make an acquisition of the rulers and put their way into action. When their blessings and delight are extended to all things, then "it will be happy." As for the fourth line, it is not yet determined whether it will acquire or lose anything—they are bound up with what it attends to. **The *Symbol* says: "The happiness of the fourth 'nine' line: there is delight."** Concerning what the line statement calls "happiness," if it guards its straightforwardness and the rulers enjoy it, then it will be able to put the way of *yang* firmness into action, and their blessings and "delight" will be extended to all things.

The fifth "nine" line: it trusts in something that wears away. There is danger. The fifth "nine" line has acquired the position of respect, it is placed with centrality and straightforwardness, and it exhausts what is good in the way of enjoyment. The sage, however, provides the warning that "there is danger." In fact, no one tastes the abundance of Yao and Shun without being given this warning. The warning given by the line statement is the warning that is proper, and that is all. Although sages and worthies are in positions above, the world has never

466 58. Joy (Dui 兑)

tasted the absence of small people, but they do not now dare to indulge what is bad in them. Sages also enjoy their ability to exhort them and "reform their faces."[4] These small people never taste any ignorance of what should be enjoyed by sages and worthies. Such was the case for the four unfortunates placed at the court of Yao, who hid their badness and submitted to the mandate.[5] The sage was not ignorant that they were bad to the end, but he made them tremble at their crimes and strengthened their humaneness. If the sincere heart of the fifth line were to believe that the apparent goodness of small people is real goodness, and were ignorant of what they contain and store away, it would be on the way of peril. As for small people, if one's preparations for them are not extreme, they will do harm to what is good. The intention of the sage's warning is deep. The phrase "wears away" refers to the disappearance of *yang*, and *yin* is what makes *yang* disappear. In fact, this phrase points to the top "six" line, and this is why, "if it trusts in something that wears away," there will be peril. The fifth line is in the moment of enjoyment, and is profoundly close to the top "six" line, which is why the warning is given. Although it may be a sage like Shun, trembling at "clever words and a commanding countenance," how could it not need a warning?[6] When enjoyment affects people, it enters easily and they should be troubled in such a case. **The *Symbol* says: "'It trusts in something that wears away': it is proper that its position be straightforward."** As for the warning that "it trusts in something that wears away," it is proper to warn the fifth line to make the position in which it places itself straightforward. It is profoundly close to *yin* softness, and possesses the way of enjoying it. This is why the *Symbol* gives a warning about believing in it.

The top "six" line: it draws out its joy. In other hexagrams, there is alteration when the limit is reached, but when the Joy hexagram reaches the limit of enjoyment, there is even more enjoyment. The top "six" line is the master of complete enjoyment, it occupies the limit position in the enjoyment hexagram, and it refers to those who do not know how to make their enjoyment cease. This is why, when its enjoyment has reached its limit, it draws it out further and makes it grow. This being the case, why does it not reach the point of regret and blame? Response: when one remarks that it does not know how to make its enjoyment cease, it cannot yet be seen whether what it enjoys is good or bad. Further, it rides the centrality and straightforwardness of the fifth "nine" line below it. It has nothing to influence with a crooked enjoyment. If it were the third "six" line, the lines it served and rode would neither of them be straightforward, and as a result, there would be misfortune. **The *Symbol* says: "'The top 'six' line: it draws out its joy': it is not yet bright."** The enjoyment hexagram has reached its limit, but it draws it out further and makes it grow. Although the heart for enjoying things has not ceased, the principle of this affair has already been exceeded, and in reality, there is nothing to enjoy. When an affair is abundant, it will possess brightness and radiance. When it has reached its limit, if strength is used to draw it out and make it grow, it will have no intention or savor at all. How could it be bright? The phrase "not yet" indicates "not necessarily," and is employed many times in the *Symbol*. It is not necessary that it be able to possess brightness and radiance, which signifies that it is unable to be bright.

59. EBB (*HUAN* 渙)

The *Sequence of the Hexagrams* says: "The word 'Joy' refers to enjoyment. If something is enjoyed, it will afterward be scattered. This is why the Ebb hexagram is next." Those who enjoy something will relax and scatter it. If the *qi* of a person is worried, then it will be knotted up and gathered together, but if that person enjoys something, then it will be relaxed and scattered. This is why enjoyment means to scatter, and so the Ebb hexagram succeeds the Joy hexagram. As for the trigrams, the Low trigram is above and the Pit trigram below. "The wind travels above the water": when water encounters wind, it ebbs and is scattered. And so, these trigrams constitute the Ebb hexagram.

Ebb: there is progress. When the king appears, he will possess a temple. There is profit in traversing a great stream. There is profit in purity. The Ebb hexagram refers to casting off and scattering. When people cast off and scatter something, the cause lies at their center. What has been cast off by the human heart is now scattered. As for bringing order to what has scattered, this also has its root at their center. If someone can bring in and align the human heart, then what has scattered may be gathered up again. This is why the meaning of both trigrams is to be master of the center. "There is profit in purity": the way of aligning what has ebbed and scattered lies in straightforwardness and certainty.

The *Judgment* says: "'Ebb: there is progress.' Firmness arrives and is not depleted. Softness acquires a position on the outside. It is the same as those above." The Ebb hexagram can make progress because the powers of the trigram are like this. The ebbing of the Ebb hexagram is completed because a "nine" line arrives to occupy the second position, and a "six" line ascends to occupy the fourth position. *Yang* "firmness arrives," and it "is not depleted" by being at the limit—that is, at the bottom. Instead, it places itself so as to acquire centrality. A soft line makes a journey, and acquires a straightforward position in the outer trigram. "It is the same as those above": it is the same as the central or fifth line. It is lowly and submits to the fifth line, which is to be "the same as those above." The fourth and fifth are the positions of the minister and ruler. They face the Ebb hexagram, and they are close to each other, so that their duties are mutual. The fourth is the same as the fifth in that it attends to centrality. Those who guard their centrality when facing the moment of the Ebb hexagram will not reach the point of being cast off or scattered, and this is why they can make progress. "'**When the king appears, he will possess a temple':** **the king is at the center.**" The meaning of the line—"when the king appears, he will possess a temple"—is delineated in the commentary on the Meet hexagram.[1] In the moment when the world is cast off and scattered, those who are kings will bring in and align people's hearts. If they reach the point of possessing temples, this is to be at the center. The phrase "at the center" signifies that they seek to acquire their center. It signifies that they are marshaling their hearts, since the center is the symbol of the heart. "Firmness arrives and is not depleted. Softness acquires a position. It is the same as those above": the meaning of the trigram powers is that mastery always lies in centrality. The way for kings to rescue people from the Ebb hexagram is to acquire centrality, and that is all. Mencius says: "There is a way to make an acquisition of the people. The way to make an acquisition of the people is to acquire their hearts."[2] The people's hearts wed themselves to the holding of feasts for the lords; they attend to setting up their temples. The way to wed the human heart is no greater than this, and this is why the *Judgment* says they reach the point of possessing a temple. The way of rescuing them from the Ebb hexagram has its limit in this. "'**There is** **profit in traversing a great stream': if it rides on the wood, it will accomplish** **something.**" Concerning the way of bringing order to the Ebb hexagram, it is proper to cross through obstacles and difficulties, and so the hexagram is symbolized by riding on wood and crossing a stream. The Low trigram is above and refers to wood; the Pit trigram is below and refers to water or to the "great stream." "There is profit in traversing" the obstacle so as to cross through the Ebb hexagram. The wood is above the water, which symbolizes riding on wood: "It rides on the wood" so as to traverse the stream. The one who traverses it "will accomplish" the crossing of the Ebb hexagram. This is the meaning of the hexagram, and this is also its symbol.

The *Symbol* says: "Wind travels above the water: Ebb. The first kings used it to hold feasts for the lords and set up temples." "Wind travels above the water," which symbolizes ebbing and scattering. When the first kings gazed on this symbol, they saved the world from ebbing and scattering. They reached the point at which they held "feasts for the lords and set up temples." When it comes to bringing in and aligning the hearts of people, nothing is like the ancestral temple. The performance of sacrifices and libations goes out from this heart. This is why the human heart weds itself to holding feasts for the lords and setting up temples. When it comes to binding the hearts of people—that is, the way of aligning what has been cast off and scattered—nothing is greater than this.

The initial "six" line: it employs the might of the horse to rescue itself. There is good fortune. This "six" line occupies the initial position, and is the beginning of the Ebb hexagram. It rescues itself at the beginning of the Ebb hexagram, and further, it acquires the "the might of the horse," and so "there is good fortune." Of the six line statements, only the initial one does not say "as it ebbs." It is fitting that the propensity to ebb and scatter be distinguished early. Those who rescue themselves from it at the start or beginning will not reach the point of ebbing—this is a teaching with depth. The word "horse" refers to what supports people. It is supported by the might of the horse, and this is why it can rescue itself from the Ebb hexagram. The "horse" signifies the second line. The second has the powers of firmness and centrality, the initial line has *yin* softness and submissiveness, and neither one has a corresponding line. Since neither has a corresponding line, they relate to and draw close to each other, and they seek each other out. The softness and submissiveness of the initial line are supported by the powers of firmness and centrality, which rescue it from the Ebb hexagram. It is like acquiring a mighty horse to travel far away. It will necessarily make the crossing, and this is why "there is good fortune." Those who possess force will easily rescue themselves at the beginning of the Ebb hexagram, because they submit to the moment. **The *Symbol* says: "The good fortune of the initial 'six' line: it is submissive."** The initial line has good fortune because it can attend submissively to the powers of firmness and centrality. To employ something and rescue oneself at the beginning of the Ebb hexagram is to be capable of submitting to the moment.

The second "nine" line: as it ebbs, it hastens to its crutch. Regrets vanish. Many of the various line statements say "as it ebbs," which signifies that this is the moment of the Ebb hexagram. It is in the moment of ebbing and being cast off, and it is placed at the center of the obstacle trigram—it should be recognized that it will have regrets. Were it able to hasten to a place of contentment, then its regrets would vanish. A "crutch" is what one stoops over and leans on so as to be contented, and to stoop over is to approach the bottom. To "hasten" is to make an agitated journey. Although the second and initial lines are not in straightforward correspondence, they face the moment of ebbing and being cast off, and neither has a line to agree with it. If *yin* and *yang* relate to and draw close to each other, and seek each other out, they will depend on each other. This is why the second sees the initial line as its crutch, while the initial line statement says that the second line is its "horse." If the second agitatedly approaches the initial line so as to be contented, it will be able to make its regrets vanish. Although the initial line belongs to the Pit trigram substance, it is not at the center of the obstacle. Someone wonders: how could the softness and minimal position of the initial line be sufficiently dependable? In fact, in the moment of the Ebb hexagram, victory is constituted by the alignment of forces. Earlier intellectuals all considered the fifth line as the crutch, which is wrong.[3] How could two *yang* lines become the same during the moment of ebbing and being cast off? Were they able to become the same, it is proper that they would be great at completing the task of crossing through the Ebb hexagram. Why would they stop at making their regrets vanish, and that is all? The word "crutch" signifies what it stoops over and approaches. **The *Symbol* says: "'As it ebbs, it hastens to its crutch': it acquires the object of its aspiration."** In the moment of ebbing and scattering, alignment constitutes contentment. Although the second line occupies the center of the obstacle, it agitatedly approaches the initial line in search of contentment. Since it depends on it like a crutch and makes its regrets vanish, it will acquire the object of its aspiration.

The third "six" line: as it ebbs, it remains itself. There are no regrets. The third line is in the moment of the Ebb hexagram, it alone has a line that corresponds to it, and it has "no regrets" from the ebbing and scattering. Nonetheless, it has a disposition of *yin* softness, its powers are neither central nor straightforward, and it occupies a terrain at the top without a position. How could it be rescued from the moment of ebbing or extend itself to other people? If it stops at "itself," then it may be without regrets, and that is all. The *huan* character of "as it ebbs" has been attached at the top. In the moment of the Ebb hexagram, it does not itself have any regrets as though it were ebbing. **The *Symbol* says: "'As it ebbs, it remains itself': it tends toward the outside."** "It tends" to correspond to the top line, which is in the "outside" trigram. It corresponds to the top line, and this is why it is able to avoid the Ebb hexagram and have "no regrets." When the line statement says that "regrets vanish," it indicates that they are there at its root but it makes them vanish. When it says that there are "no regrets," it means that there are none at its root.

The fourth "six" line: as it ebbs, it becomes a group. There is primary good fortune. As it ebbs, it reaches the summit. It does not reflect on the wasteland. In the Ebb hexagram, the meanings of two lines—the fourth and the fifth—require each other, and this is why their line statements remark on them together. This is why the *Judgment* says: "It is the same as those above." The fourth line is lowly, submissive, and straightforward, and it occupies the position of the great minister. The fifth line is firm, central, and straightforward, and it occupies the position of the ruler. When ruler and minister align their forces, firmness and softness sustain each other and rescue the world from the Ebb hexagram. In the moment of ebbing and scattering, those who employ firmness cannot make others cherish and depend on them, and those who employ softness will not be sufficient for others to rely on or wed themselves to them. The fourth line uses the straightforward way of lowliness and submissiveness, and it assists a ruler of firmness, centrality, and straightforwardness. When rulers and ministers have the same task, they will be able to cross through the Ebb hexagram. When the world has ebbed and scattered, they can make it into a "group" and gathering— this may be called the good fortune of great goodness. "As it ebbs, it reaches the summit. It does not reflect on the wasteland": this statement applauds its beauty. The word "summit" refers to the greatness of its gathering. During the ebbing and scattering it can bring about a great gathering. Its task is extremely great, its affairs are extremely difficult, and its function is extremely mysterious. The word "wasteland" refers to something level and ordinary. It cannot reflect on or extend itself to the sight of anything level or ordinary. Who but the great sages and worthies could be like this? **The *Symbol* says: "'As it ebbs, it becomes a group. There is primary good fortune': it is bright and great."** The phrase "primary good fortune" signifies that its accomplishment and virtue are bright and great. The primary good fortune, as well as the brightness and greatness, are not in the fifth but the fourth line, because the line statements remark on the meaning of the two lines together. In the fourth line they remark on their influence and function, and in the fifth they remark on the completion of their task. These are the roles of the ruler and minister.

The fifth "nine" line: as it ebbs, there is sweat, and a great call. As it ebbs, the place of the king is occupied. There is no blame. The virtues of the fifth and fourth lines, of the ruler and minister, are in alignment. Using the way of firmness, centrality, straightforwardness, lowliness, and submission, they acquire the way of bringing order to the Ebb hexagram. It has only to saturate and penetrate the hearts of other people, and they will submit and attend to it. It is proper to make the "call" and decree that will penetrate the hearts of the people, just as the "sweat" of the human body saturates its four limbs. Then they will be believed and obeyed, and people will attend to them. In a case like this, they will be able to cross through the ebbing with the world, occupying the position of the king when they are proportioned to it, and "there is no blame." The phrase "great call" refers to a great decree of the government. It signifies a great mandate to renew the people and a great government to save it from the ebb. The line statement twice says "as it ebbs." The former instance signifies that this is the moment of the Ebb hexagram, while the latter instance signifies that "there is no blame" if it places itself in the Ebb hexagram like this. The fourth line statement has already remarked on its primary good fortune, so the fifth only remarks on how it is proportioned to its position. The fourth and fifth line statements of the Ebb hexagram make their remarks together. The harm of the Ebb hexagram lies in casting off and scattering, and one is rescued from it by alignment. If rulers and ministers do not undertake the same task and align their forces, how will they be able to cross through it? The meanings of these lines require each other, which is fitting for this moment. **The *Symbol* says: "'The place of the king is occupied. There is no blame': its position is straightforward."** "The place of the king is occupied": this signifies the position of respect, which is the straightforward position of the rulers. If they can act like the fifth line, they will occupy the position of respect, since it is proportioned to them, and "there is no blame."

The top "nine" line: as it ebbs, its blood departs, recedes, and goes out. There is no blame. Many of the various lines in the Ebb hexagram are not bound to a corresponding line, which is another symbol of ebbing and being cast off. The top line alone corresponds to the third, and the third occupies the limit position in the obstacle or snare trigram. Were the top line to descend and attend to it, it would be unable to go out from the Ebb hexagram. The obstacle symbolizes injury and harm, being trembling and troubled, and this is why the line statement speaks about "blood" and care.[4] Nonetheless, this "nine" line uses *yang* firmness to place itself on the outside of the Ebb hexagram, symbolizing that it "goes out" from the ebbing. Further, it occupies the limit position in the Low trigram, indicating that it can be lowly and submit to the principle of the affair. This is why it says that, if it can make its blood depart and its care go out, then "there is no blame." The word "its" refers to what it possesses. In the moment of the Ebb hexagram, its task is to be capable of alignment. Only this "nine" line occupies the limit position in the Ebb hexagram, is bound to another line, and watches over the obstacle. This is why it is good if it can go out from the Ebb hexagram and be "far from harm." **The *Symbol* says: "'As it ebbs, its blood': it**

is far from harm." Were the line statement like the text of the *Symbol*, it would be read as "its blood ebbs," just the same as when "its richness is blocked."[5] But such is not its meaning. In fact, after the word "blood" the *Symbol* has simply omitted the word "departs." Its blood departs and its care goes out: this signifies that "there is no blame" if it can be far away from harm.

60. REIN (JIE 節)

The *Sequence of the Hexagrams* says: "To ebb is to be cast away. Things cannot be cast away to the end, and this is why the Rein hexagram is next." When one has already cast away and scattered something, it is proper to rein it in and bring it to a stop. And so the Rein hexagram succeeds the Ebb hexagram. As for the trigrams, "above the lake, there is water." There is a limit to what the lake will embrace. When water is situated above the lake, and the lake is full, it will not embrace the water—this symbolizes the possession of a rein, and is why these trigrams constitute the Rein hexagram.

Rein: there is progress. A bitter rein cannot be pure. When affairs have been reined in, they will be capable of bringing about progress and development. This is why the Rein hexagram has progress as its meaning. A rein is esteemed when it is suitable and central. If it is excessive, then it will become bitter. When a rein has reached the point of becoming bitter, how could it be constant? It cannot keep guard with certainty so as to be constant, and so it "cannot be pure."

The *Judgment* says: "'Rein: there is progress.' Firmness and softness divide, and firmness acquires centrality." The way of the Rein hexagram taken by itself has the meaning of progress. When affairs have been reined in, they can make progress. Further, in the powers of the trigrams, the firm and soft lines have divided up the places. "Firmness acquires centrality" and is not excessive— this, too, is why these lines constitute the Rein hexagram. And so, there can be progress. **"'A bitter rein cannot be pure': its way is depleted."** When the Rein hexagram reaches its limit, it becomes bitter. It cannot be solid and certain, and it cannot guard its constancy. Its way is already at its limit and depletion.

"There are enjoyment and obstacles to action. Its position is proper for it, and it uses a rein. It develops centrality and straightforwardness." The *Judgment* is remarking on the powers of the trigrams. The Joy trigram is inside and the Pit trigram outside: "There are enjoyment and obstacles to action." When people are enjoying something, they do not know how to put it in the past. But if they encounter hardships and obstacles, they will reflect on bringing it to a stop. To stop after starting with enjoyment constitutes the meaning of the Rein hexagram. "Its position is proper for it, and it uses a rein": the fifth line occupies the position of respect, which is proper for it. It is above the lake, and it has a rein. "Its position is proper for it, and it uses a rein": it is the master of the Rein hexagram, and it is placed so as to acquire centrality and straightforwardness. Since it reins itself in, it will be able to develop; since it is central and straightforward, it will develop. If it were excessive, it would become bitter. "**Heaven and earth are reined, and the four seasons are completed. The rein uses controls and measures, so that nothing injures resources or harms the people.**" The *Judgment* unfolds its remarks on the way of the Rein hexagram. Heaven and earth have a rein, and this is why they can complete the four seasons. Without a rein, they would lose their sequence. Sages set up "controls and measures" as their reins, and this is why it can be the case that "nothing injures resources or harms the people." Human desires are never depleted. If it were not the case that "the rein uses controls and measures," their extravagance and indulgence would reach the point of injuring resources and harming the people.

The *Symbol* says: "**Above the lake, there is water: Rein. Noble people use it to control their numbers and measures. They discuss virtue and action.**" There is a limit to how much water a lake will embrace. If it exceeds this limit, it will fill up and overflow. This is to possess a rein, and this is why these trigrams constitute the Rein hexagram. When noble people gaze on the symbol of the Rein hexagram, they "control" and set up "their numbers and measures." In general, whether a thing is great or small, light or weighty, lofty or below, its pattern and disposition both possess number and measure, and these are what constitute its rein. The word "numbers" refers to being few or many, and "measures" refers to laws and controls. "They discuss virtue and action": various virtues persist at their center, and are revealed on the outside as action. When the virtues and actions of people are proper and dutiful, then they are central and reined. The phrase "they discuss" signifies that they ponder the measures when seeking to be central and reined.

The initial "nine" line: it does not go out from the courtyard of the door. There is no blame. The phrase "courtyard of the door" refers to the courtyard with the outer door, just as "courtyard of the gate" refers to the courtyard with the inner gate. The initial line makes use of *yang*, it is below, it has a corresponding line above it, and it refers to those who cannot rein themselves. Further, it faces the initial position of the Rein hexagram, and this is why it is warned to guard its prudence. If it reaches the point of not going out from the courtyard of the door, there will be no blame. If it can initially guard itself with certainty, then it will sometimes adapt to this in the end, but if it is not initially prudent, what could it possess in the end? This is why there is such a severe warning in the initial line of the Rein hexagram. **The *Symbol* says: "'It does not go out from the courtyard of the door': it knows both how to develop and how to choke itself off."** The initial line statement of the Rein hexagram warns it to guard its prudence, and this is why it says that if "it does not go out from the courtyard of the door," "there is no blame." The *Symbol* fears that people will get mired in such remarks, and this is why it turns to shedding light on them. It says that, although it is proper to guard its prudence, so that "it does not go out from the courtyard of the door," it must also know whether this is the moment to develop or to choke itself off. If it develops, then it will act, but if it chokes itself off, then it will stop, meaning that if it is proper to go out, then it will go out. Wei Sheng, who did not depart when the water rose, was believable, but he did not know "both how to develop and how to choke itself off."[1] This is why noble people are pure and not indifferent. What the *Appended Statements* interprets here—in fact the only thing it remarks on—is that people have nothing to rein but words and actions. If they rein in their words, it should be recognized in their actions, but it is proper that the words come first.

The second "nine" line: it does not go out from the courtyard of the gate. There is misfortune. Although the second line has a disposition of firmness and centrality, it is placed in a *yin* position, it occupies a position in the enjoyment trigram, and it serves a soft line. It is placed in a *yin* position, indicating that it is not straightforward; it occupies a position in the enjoyment trigram, indicating that it has lost its firmness; it serves a soft line, indicating that it is near a crooked line. Concerning the way of the Rein hexagram, it is proper to make use of firmness, centrality, and straightforwardness. The second line has lost the virtues of firmness and centrality, and so it differs from the firmness, centrality, and straightforwardness of the fifth "nine" line. "It does not go out from the courtyard of the gate": it does not go outside, which signifies that it does not attend to the fifth line. The second and fifth lines do not have the straightforward correspondence of *yin* and *yang*, and this is why they do not attend to each other. If they used the way of firmness and centrality to align with each other, they could complete the task of the Rein hexagram. But it has only lost its virtue, and lost sight of the moment, and as a result, "there is misfortune." It does not align with the fifth line, and so its rein is not straightforward. To consider firmness, centrality, and straightforwardness as one's rein is to "admonish wrath and obstruct desire"—that is, to take away from the excessive and impede what has a surplus.[2] To rein oneself without straightforwardness is to be stingy in the employment of one's rein or timid in putting one's rein into action. **The Symbol says: "'It does not go out from the courtyard of the gate. There is misfortune': it loses sight of the moment and the limit."** It cannot ascend and attend to the fifth "nine" line—whose way is firm, central, and straightforward—to complete the task of the Rein hexagram. It is bound up with the privacy and intimacy of *yin* softness. In such a case, it will lose sight of the extremity or limit of the moment, and so there will be misfortune. "It loses sight of the moment": it loses sight of what is fitting.

The third "six" line: if it is not reined, there will be lamentation. There is no blame. The third "six" line is neither central nor straightforward, it rides a firm line, and it watches over the obstacle trigram. It is certainly fitting that there be blame. Nonetheless, it is soft and submissive, and harmonizes with the enjoyment trigram. If it can rein itself in and submit to its duty, then it should be able to be without excess. If such is not the case, its misfortune and blame will necessarily be extreme, and there may be injury and lamentation. This is why, "if it is not reined," then "there will be lamentation." It has itself brought this about, and so there is no one else to blame. **The Symbol says: "There is 'lamentation' when 'it is not reined': who else can it blame?"** If it is reined, it should be able to avoid excess, but if it cannot rein itself, it will bring about lamentation: "Who else can it blame?"

The fourth "six" line: it is contented and reined. There is progress. The fourth line submits to and serves the way of the fifth "nine" line with its firmness, centrality, and straightforwardness. This is to consider centrality and straightforwardness as one's rein. It uses *yin* to occupy a *yin* position, and so it is content to be straightforward. Its position is proper for it, which symbolizes the possession of a rein, and it corresponds to the initial line below it. The fourth line belongs to the Pit trigram substance, which refers to water. When water ascends and overflows, this indicates that it has no rein. It is only when it descends that it has a rein. It is similar in meaning to the fourth line, which is not reined by strength, but is contented with its rein. This is why it can bring about progress. In the Rein hexagram, contentment is to be considered something good. If it guards itself with strength and is not contented, it will be incapable of constancy. How could it make progress? **The *Symbol* says: "'There is progress' when 'it is contented and reined': it serves the way of those above."** There is no single meaning to the fourth line being contented with its rein. The *Symbol* only brings up the one that carries the most weight. It "serves the way" of the fifth "nine" line above it with its firmness, centrality, and straightforwardness—this may be considered its rein, which is sufficient for it to make progress. The rest of them, at least those that are good, do not depart from the meaning of centrality and straightforwardness.

The fifth "nine" line: it makes its rein sweet. There is good fortune, and value in making the journey. The fifth "nine" line is firm, central, and straightforward, it occupies the position of respect, and it is the master of the Rein hexagram. Its position in the Rein hexagram is proper, which signifies that it communicates its centrality and straightforwardness. It is contented to be by itself, but it also enjoys acting on the world. It attends to the sweetness and beauty of its rein, and its good fortune should be recognized. When one acts in such a case, one's accomplishment will be great. This is why, if it makes the journey, it may become excellent and valued. **The *Symbol* says: "'There is good fortune' when 'it makes its rein sweet': it occupies the central position."** It already occupies the position of respect, and it has acquired the way of centrality. As a result, there is good fortune, and it will accomplish something. In the Rein hexagram, centrality is to be esteemed. Those who acquire centrality will be straightforward, but those who are straightforward will not be able to exhaust centrality.

The top "six" line: it makes its rein bitter. Purity brings misfortune. Regrets vanish. The top "six" line occupies the limit position in the Rein hexagram and refers to the bitterness of the rein. It occupies the limit position in the obstacle trigram, which also has bitterness as its meaning. If it guards itself with certainty, there will be misfortune, but if it has regrets, the misfortune will vanish. The word "regrets" signifies that it takes away from what is excessive and attends to the center. The phrase "regrets vanish" is the same in the Rein hexagram as in the other hexagrams, but the meaning is different. **The *Symbol* says: "'It makes its rein bitter. Purity brings misfortune': its way is depleted."** When one's rein has become bitter, and one still guards it with purity and certainty, then there will be misfortune. In fact, the way of the Rein hexagram has reached the point of its limit and depletion.

61. CENTER TRUST (*ZHONGFU* 中孚)

The *Sequence of the Hexagrams* says: "Those with a rein may be believed. This is why the Center Trust hexagram is next." "Those with a rein" refers to those controlled by a rein that prevents them from exceeding or surpassing anything. If they are believed, then afterward they will be able to act. Because those above can believe in them, they will guard them; because those below can[1] believe in them, they will attend to them. "Those with a rein may be believed," and so the Center Trust hexagram succeeds the Rein hexagram. As for the trigrams, "above the lake, there is wind." The wind travels above the lake and affects the water at the center—this symbolizes the Center Trust hexagram. The *gan* character of "affect" here signifies movement. The inside and the outside are both full, but the center is empty, which symbolizes the Center Trust hexagram. Further, the second and the fifth lines are both *yang,* and so their centers are full, which is also a symbol of trust. In the two trigram substances, the center is full, while in the substance of the hexagram as a whole, the center is empty. An empty center refers to the root of being believable, while a full center refers to the disposition of being believable.

Center Trust: swine and fish bring good fortune. There is profit in traversing a great stream. There is profit in purity. Swine are restless and fish are gloomy—it is difficult to affect such things. If trust and belief can affect even swine and fish, then there is nothing they cannot reach, and so there will be good fortune. If those with loyalty and believability can tread on water and fire, what will be the case when they traverse a stream? The way to guard the belief of others lies in solidity and straightforwardness, and this is why "there is profit in purity."

The *Judgment* says: "Center Trust: softness is on the inside, and firmness acquires centrality." Two soft lines are on the inside, and their centers are empty, which symbolizes sincerity; two firm lines are at the center of the upper and lower trigram substances, and their centers are full, which symbolizes trustworthiness. And so, these trigrams constitute the Center Trust hexagram. "**There are enjoyment and lowliness. Those who are trustworthy transform the kingdom.**" The *Judgment* is remarking on the two trigram substances and on the function of the trigrams. The Low trigram is above and the enjoyment trigram below. They indicate that those above are extremely sincere, so that they can be submissive and lowly toward those below, and those below are trustworthy, so that they enjoy attending to those above. In a case like this, their trustworthiness can "transform the kingdom" and the states. If people did not enjoy attending to them, if they sometimes drew back from or brushed off their affairs and principles, how could they transform the world? "'**Swine and fish bring good fortune': belief in them extends to swine and fish.**" "Belief in them" can extend "to swine and fish." The way of belief in them is extreme, and so there is good fortune. "'**There is profit in traversing a great stream': it rides on wood in the emptiness of the boat.**" As for those who traverse obstacles and difficulties with the Center Trust hexagram, their profit is like riding on wood when crossing a stream, like using an empty boat. If the boat is empty, it will not distress them by sinking or overturning. The empty center of the hexagram is symbolized by the empty boat. "**The Center Trust hexagram uses "profit in purity": it corresponds to heaven.**" Since the Center Trust hexagram is pure, "it corresponds to heaven." The way of heaven is to be trustworthy and pure, and that is all.

The *Symbol* says: "**Above the lake, there is wind: Center Trust. Noble people use it to discuss trials and are slackened when the case concerns death.**" "Above the lake, there is wind": it affects the center of the lake. The substance of water is empty, and this is why the wind can enter it; the human heart is empty, and this is why things can affect it. When the wind moves the lake, it is like something affecting one's center, and this is why these trigrams symbolize the Center Trust hexagram. When noble people gaze on this symbol, they "use it to discuss trials and are slackened when the case involves death." When noble people discuss trials, they exhaust their loyalty, and that is all. When resolving a case that involves death, they push their pity to its limit, and that is all. This is why their sincere intention constantly seeks to be slackened. To be "slackened" is to be lenient. They never do otherwise than exhaust their loyalty in the affairs of the world, and the discussion of trials and slackness in cases involving death are the greatest of these.

The initial "nine" line: deliberation brings good fortune. If it possesses anything else, it will not be comforted. This "nine" line faces the initial position of the Center Trust hexagram, and this is why it is warned to scrutinize what it believes in. The word "deliberate" refers to measuring. It takes the measure of what it should believe in and afterward attends to it. Although it may be extreme in its belief, if it does not acquire its place, there will be regrets and blame. This is why, if it deliberates on and takes the measure of something, and only afterward believes in it, there will be good fortune. If it has already acquired what it believes in, it is proper that it be sincere and unified. Were it to possess anything else, it would not acquire comfort and contentment. "Comfort" refers to contentment and generosity. "If it possesses anything else," its tendencies will not be determinate, and if its tendencies are not determinate, it will be bewildered and not contented. The initial line corresponds straightforwardly to the fourth. The fourth belongs to the Low trigram substance and occupies a straightforward position, so that it is nothing but good. The line statement considers "skill at its beginning" as the greater meaning, and this is why it has not chosen the line correspondence as its meaning.[2] If it had employed the line correspondence, it would not speak about "deliberation." **The *Symbol* says: "In the initial 'nine' line, 'deliberation brings good fortune': its tendencies have not yet altered."** This line faces the beginning of the belief hexagram, and its tendencies do not yet attend to anything. If it deliberates on and takes the measure of what it believes, it will acquire straightforwardness, and as a result, there will be good fortune. In fact, its tendencies have not yet altered or moved. If its tendencies attend to something, this is to be altered and moved, and its deliberation will not acquire straightforwardness. The *Symbol* is remarking that the initial line seeks the way of belief.

The second "nine" line: the eloquent crane is in the *yin* region. Its child harmonizes with it. I have a preference for this goblet, but I will share it with you. The second line is firm and full at its center and refers to extreme trustworthiness. Extremely trustworthy people are capable of mutual affection. The crane is eloquent in a place of seclusion and concealment. It is not heard, but "its child" corresponds to and "harmonizes with" it. The aspirations of their centers and hearts are mutual. There is "a preference for this goblet" that "I have," and someone else is also bound to adore it—they have the same intention of enjoying or preferring the goblet. They are trustworthy at their centers, and their things are not without correspondence, because their sincerity is the same. When one's sincerity is extreme, there is no space "between those nearby and far away, between the secluded and the deep."[3] This is why the *Appended*

Statements says: "If they are good, they will correspond over more than a thousand miles. If they are not good, they will draw back for a thousand miles."[4] It is remarking on their mutual sincerity. Extreme sincerity is the principle of mutual affection. Those who recognize the way will be able to understand it. **The *Symbol* says: "'Its child harmonizes with it': this is the aspiration of its center and heart."** "This is the aspiration of its center and heart": this signifies that it aspires to have sincere intentions. This is why they communicate and correspond to each other.

The third "six" line: it acquires an enemy. Sometimes it drums, sometimes it refrains, sometimes it weeps, and sometimes it sings. The *di* character of "enemy" refers to an opposite, and signifies that it interacts with someone it trusts—that is, it straightforwardly corresponds to the top "nine" line. The third and fourth lines both use their empty centers to become the masters who complete the Trust hexagram. Nonetheless, their places are different. The fourth line has acquired a position that it occupies straightforwardly, and this is why it makes its mate vanish by attending to the higher line. The third line is not central and has lost its straightforwardness, and this is why it acquires an enemy that burdens its tendencies. It uses a disposition of softness and enjoyment, it has already bound itself to something, and it attends only to what it believes in: "Sometimes it drums" on a skin, and "sometimes it refrains" and neglects it, "sometimes it weeps" with melancholy, and "sometimes it sings" and makes music. Its movement and rest, its worry and pleasure—all these are bound to what it believes in. It binds itself only to what it believes in, and this is why it does not yet know either good or bad fortune. Nonetheless, this is not what a noble person, who has attained enlightenment, would do. **The *Symbol* says: "'Sometimes it drums, sometimes it refrains': its position is not proper for it."** It occupies a position that is not proper for it, and this is why it is the master of nothing, and attends only to what it believes in. If its placement were to acquire straightforwardness, then what it believes in would be correct.

The fourth "six" line: the moon is almost full. The horse's mate vanishes. There is no blame. The fourth line is the master of completing the Trust hexagram, it occupies a position near the ruler, it is placed straightforwardly, those above consider it extremely believable, and it refers to those whom it is proper to entrust with command. It is like the moon that is almost full, when it is extremely abundant. If it were already full, it would become an enemy. When ministers are enemies to their rulers, they will necessarily reach the point of affliction and defeat. This is why being "almost full" refers to the extremity of abundance. "The horse's mate vanishes": the fourth line corresponds straightforwardly to the initial line, which is its mate. People of antiquity employed four horses to pull their carriages. If they could not all be perfectly uniform in color, the two behind and the two in front would each be of one color. Further, the small ones and the great ones would necessarily be proportioned to each other. This is why the two horses are called "mates," which signifies that they are opposites. The word "horse" refers to a thing that travels. The initial line ascends and corresponds to the fourth, while the fourth also advances and attends to the fifth. All of them are traveling upward, and this is why they are symbolized by the horse. The way of trust lies in unity. Since the fourth is already attending to the fifth, if it were to return, descend, and bind itself to the initial line, there would be no unity, its trustworthiness would be harmed, and there would be blame. This is why, if "the horse's mate vanishes," then "there is no blame." It ascends and attends to the fifth, and does not bind itself to the initial line—this is to make its mate vanish. If it bound itself to the initial line, then it would not advance, and it would not be able to complete the task of the Trust hexagram. **The Symbol says: "'The horse's mate vanishes': it severs itself from its own kind and ascends."** "It severs itself from its own kind and ascends" to attend to the fifth line. The phrase "its own kind" signifies its corresponding line.

The fifth "nine" line: it is trustworthy, as though it were confined. There is no blame. The fifth line occupies the position of the ruler. It is proper for those on the way of rulers to use extreme sincerity concerning the mutual affection of the world. This will make the hearts of the world to believe in them. If the knots that bind them are certain, "as though" they were chained or "confined," there will be no blame. If the world's trust in its rulers cannot make it to be bound with knots that are certain like this, how could the hearts of the countless millions be preserved and not cast off? **The Symbol says: "'It is trustworthy, as though it were confined': its position is straightforward and proper."** The fifth line occupies the respected position of the ruler, which is brought about by the way of centrality and straightforwardness. It can make the world believe in it as though chained or confined with certainty, which proportions their positions. It is proper that the way of rulers be like this.

The top "nine" line: its soaring sound climbs to heaven. Purity brings misfortune. The phrase "soaring sound" refers to a sound that flies on unattended by the reality that made it. This line is placed at the end of the belief hexagram. When belief is at its end, it becomes scarce. It is deprived of loyalty and devotion on the inside, while its flowering and beauty are diffused on the outside. This is why the line statement says that "its soaring sound climbs to heaven." Its straightforwardness is also destroyed—the nature of a *yang* line is to advance upward, and the substance of the wind trigram is to fly away and diffuse. This "nine" line occupies a position in the moment of the Center Trust hexagram, it is placed at the very top, and it refers to those whose trustworthiness advances upward and does not know how to stop. At its limit, it reaches the point of sounding like wings that soar, climbing to be heard in the heavens. When its purity and certainty are like this, it will not know how to alter, and its misfortune should be recognized. Fuzi says: "As for those who prefer to believe, but do not prefer to learn, their concealment makes them treacherous."[5] This signifies that they keep guard with certainty, but do not develop. **The *Symbol* says: "'Its soaring sound climbs to heaven': how could it grow?"** In guarding its trustworthiness, if it reaches the point of its limit and depletion, and does not know how to alter, how could it grow or continue? In such a case, when it keeps guard with certainty and does not develop, there will be misfortune.

62. SMALL EXCESS (*XIAOGUO* 小過)

The *Sequence of the Hexagrams* says: "Those who believe in something will necessarily act on it. This is why the Small Excess hexagram is next." People will necessarily act on what they believe in. If they act, then there will be excess, and so the Small Excess hexagram succeeds the Center Trust hexagram. As for the trigrams, "above the mountain, there is thunder." The thunder is shaking in a lofty place, and its sound exceeds what is ordinary. This is why it refers to the Small Excess hexagram. Further, a *yin* line occupies the position of respect, while the *yang* lines have lost their positions and do not possess centrality. Their smallness exceeds what is ordinary. In fact, the hexagram refers to a smallness that is excessive, and further, to small affairs that are excessive, and also to the smallness of those who are excessive.

Small Excess: there is progress, and profit in purity. To exceed here is to exceed what is ordinary. For instance, one may improve what is bent by making it exceed the straight. Because of the excess, it has almost become straight. States of affairs have moments when they are proper, but if they wait to become excessive, they will afterward be capable of progress. This is why the Small Excess hexagram has the meaning of progress. "Profit in purity": concerning the way of excess, there is profit in purity. Those who do not lose what is fitting for the moment are said to be straightforward. **There should be a small affair; there should not be a great affair. The sound of the flying bird is distant. It is not fitting to ascend; it is fitting to descend. There is great good fortune.** Those who have become excessive now seek to approach the center. What they have exceeded is a small affair. If the affair were great, how could anyone exceed it? This discussion is elucidated in the Great Excess hexagram. "The sound of the flying bird is distant": this signifies that they have not exceeded it by far. "It is

486

not fitting to ascend; it is fitting to descend": this signifies that it is fitting to be submissive. If they are submissive, then "there is great good fortune." Those who exceed so as to approach something are, in fact, submitting to principle. Since they are excessive and yet submissive to principle, their good fortune will necessarily be great.

The *Judgment* says: "Small Excess: smallness is excessive, and so 'there is progress.'" *Yang* is great and *yin* is small. *Yin* lines have acquired positions, while "firmness loses its position and is not central." This is a case where "smallness is excessive," and this is why the hexagram refers to small affairs that are excessive, and also to the smallness of those who are excessive. There are moments when it is proper for smallness and small affairs to be excessive, and also for those who are excessive to be small—this is why these lines constitute the Small Excess hexagram. States of affairs certainly wait to become excessive, and afterward they can make progress. It is because of the excess that they can make progress. "By means of excess there is 'profit in purity.' It acts in agreement with the moment." That there is excess, but also "profit in purity," signifies that "it acts in agreement with the moment." If there is excess when it is the proper moment for excess, then it is not excess but what is fitting for the moment. Such excess may be called straightforward. "Softness acquires centrality. As a result, a small affair brings good fortune. Firmness loses its position and is not central. As a result, 'there should not be a great affair.' It is symbolized by the flying bird." Concerning the way of the Small Excess hexagram, if small affairs are excessive, there will be good fortune. The *Judgment* uses the powers of the trigrams to remark on the meaning of good fortune. "Softness acquires centrality": the second and fifth lines occupy the center. Soft *yin* lines have acquired these positions, and can bring it about that "a small affair brings good fortune." They cannot, however, cross through a great affair. "Firmness loses its position and is not central. As a result, 'there should not be a great affair'": those who manage great affairs without the power of *yang* firmness will not be able to cross through them. The third line is not at the center, and the fourth line has lost its position. As a result, "there should not be a great affair." In the moment of the Small Excess hexagram, taken by itself, "there should not be a great affair." But the powers of the trigrams are also not ready for a great affair, being aligned with the moment. "It is symbolized by the flying bird": this one sentence does not belong to the substance of the *Judgment*. In fact, it is an interpretive statement erroneously entered into the *Judgment*. The firm lines are at the center and the soft lines are outside—this is the symbol of a flying bird. The hexagram possesses this symbol, and this is why its meaning approaches that of the flying bird. "'The sound of the flying bird is distant. It is not fitting to ascend; it is fitting to descend. There is great good fortune': to ascend is to rebel, while to descend is to submit." Although the affair has its proper moment for excess, and one attends to what is fitting, how could the excess be extreme? Excess modesty, excess sorrow, and excess thrift should not be cases of great excess, and so they are cases of small excess. It is proper that what is excessive be like the distant sound of the flying bird. Although the bird flies suddenly and swiftly, and the noise goes out from a place its body has already exceeded, how could they be far from each other? The proper moment for excess in affairs is also like this. The bird's body cannot be extremely far from the noise, and the affair should not far exceed what is ordinary—this is to acquire what is fitting. "It is not fitting to ascend; it is fitting to descend": the meaning chosen here, that it is fitting to be submissive, resembles the sound of the bird even more. Concerning the way of excess, it is proper that it be like the distant sound of the flying bird. As for the noise that rebels against it and ascends, it will be in difficulties, but one that submits and descends will be at ease. This is why it is a great thing to be lofty. "Above the mountain, there is thunder," and so these trigrams constitute the excess hexagram. Concerning the way of excess, submissive action brings good fortune. As with the distant sound of the flying bird, it is fitting to be submissive, and so the excess here constitutes submission to what is fitting. Since there can be submission to what is fitting, "there is great good fortune."

The *Symbol* says: "Above the mountain, there is thunder: Small Excess. Noble people use it to be excessively modest when acting on something, excessively sorrowful when deprived of something, and excessively thrifty when employing something." The thunder is shaking above the mountain, and its sound exceeds what is ordinary. This is why these trigrams constitute the Small Excess hexagram. In the affairs of the world, there is a moment when excess is proper, but the excess should not be extreme, and this is why these trigrams constitute the Small Excess hexagram. When noble people gaze on the symbol of the Small Excess hexagram, and if excess is fitting in their affairs, they will exhort themselves to it. Such is the case when they are "excessively modest when acting on something, excessively sorrowful when deprived of something, and excessively thrifty when employing something." If excess is proper, and there is excess, then it is merely fitting. If excess were not proper, and there were excess, then it would be excessive.

The initial "six" line: because of the flying bird, there is misfortune. The initial "six" line is *yin* and soft, occupies a position below, and symbolizes small people. Further, it corresponds to the fourth line above it, and the fourth line in turn belongs to the movement trigram substance. Small people are restless and changeable, and have the help of the corresponding line above them. If they will necessarily reach the point of extreme excess even when excess is proper, what will the case be like if they are excessive when excess is not proper? Their excess is sudden and swift like the "flying bird," and so "there is misfortune." When their restlessness and swiftness are like this, their excess will be both rapid and far-reaching, and they will never reach the point at which they are saved or stopped. **The *Symbol* says: "'Because of the flying bird, there is misfortune': there is nothing to be done."** Since the swiftness of its excess is like the suddenness of the "flying bird," how could it embrace being saved or stopped? Its misfortune is fitting. "There is nothing to be done": there is no employment for its force.

The second "six" line: it exceeds its male progenitor but encounters its female ancestor. It does not extend itself to the ruler but encounters the minister. There is no blame. The higher *yang* line symbolizes the father. Respect is shown to the father because he symbolizes the "male progenitor." The fourth line is above the third, and this is why it refers to the male progenitor. The second and fifth lines occupy terrains that correspond to each other, they are the same in possessing the virtues of softness and centrality, and their tendency is not to attend to the third and fourth lines. This is why "it exceeds" the fourth and "encounters" the fifth line—that is, "it exceeds its male progenitor." The fifth line is *yin* and in the position of respect, which symbolize the female and male ancestors respectively. It has the same virtues as the second line and they correspond to each other. In other hexagrams, *yin* and *yang* seek each other out, but at the moment of the excess hexagram they will necessarily exceed what is ordinary, and this is why the case is different here. There is nothing without excess, and this is why the second line attends to the fifth and the line statement warns about its excess. "It does not extend itself to the ruler but encounters the minister": this signifies that it advances upward but it does not usurp or "extend itself to" the ruler. If the way of the minister is suitable and proper, "there is no blame." To encounter is to be proper for. If it exceeds the role of the minister, its blame should be recognized. **The *Symbol* says: "'It does not extend itself to the ruler': the minister should not exceed it."** In the moment of the excess hexagram, the state of affairs never does otherwise than exceed what is ordinary. This is why the *Symbol* warns about extending itself to the ruler when it advances upward. "The minister should not exceed" the role of the minister.

The third "nine" line: if it is not excessive in its defense, sometimes they will attend to its slaughter. There is misfortune. The Small Excess hexagram refers to the moment when *yin* lines exceed *yang* lines that have lost their positions. The third line alone occupies a straightforward position, but it is in the lower trigram and there is nothing it can do. The *yin* lines are jealous of and detest it, and this is why excess is proper for it, to be "excessive in its defense" against small people. "If it is not excessive in its defense," they will sometimes attend to it by slaying or harming it. In such a case, "there is misfortune." The third line is in the moment when *yin* is excessive, and it uses *yang* to occupy a firm position, which is to be excessive in its firmness. Since it has been warned to be excessive in its defense, it is now also warned about excessive firmness. As for the way of defense against small people, the first thing to do is to make oneself straightforward. The third line has not lost its straightforwardness, and this is why it does not necessarily have the meaning of misfortune. If it can be excessive in its defense, it will avoid it. This is always the case when those below occupy a position above, as when the third line occupies the top position in the lower trigram. **The *Symbol* says: "'Sometimes they will attend to its slaughter': what will its misfortune be like?"** In the moment when *yin* is excessive, it will necessarily do harm to *yang*. When the way of small people has become abundant, it will necessarily do harm to the noble people. It is proper that they be excessive in their defense. If their defense is not extreme, it is because of this that they will be slain. This is why the *Symbol* says: "What will its misfortune be like?" It is remarking on how extreme it will be.

The fourth "nine" line: there is no blame. It is without excess, and encounters something. It must be warned about the danger of making a journey. It does not employ endless purity. The fourth line faces the moment of the Small Excess hexagram and uses firmness to place itself in a soft position—that is, its firmness is not excessive. As a result, "there is no blame." Since it is without excess, it will align with what is fitting. This is why the line statement says that it "encounters something," which signifies that it has acquired the way. Were it to make a journey there would be peril, and so it is necessary and proper that it be warned and troubled. The phrase "making a journey" refers to departing from softness and advancing with firmness. "It does not employ endless purity": the nature of *yang* is solid and firm, and this is why it is warned to follow what is fitting and that it should not keep guard with certainty. In the moment when *yin* becomes excessive and *yang* firmness loses its position, it is proper that noble people follow the moment and submit to their placement. They should not guard their constancy with certainty. The fourth line occupies a lofty position and does not interact with those above and below. Although it is close to the fifth and corresponds to the initial line, it faces the moment when *yin* becomes excessive. How could the latter willingly attend to the *yang* line? This is why there is danger if it makes a journey. **The *Symbol* says: "'It is without excess, and encounters something': its position is not proper for it. 'It must be warned about the danger of making a journey': it cannot be lengthy in the end."** "Its position is not proper for it": this signifies that it is placed in a soft position. The fourth "nine" line faces the moment of the excess hexagram, but it is not excessively firm. On the contrary, it occupies a soft position, which is to acquire what is fitting for it. This is why the line statement says that it "encounters something": it encounters what is fitting for it. When a "nine" line occupies the fourth position, its position is not proper for it, but if it occupies a soft position, then it encounters what is fitting for it. It faces a moment when *yin* is excessive while *yang* retreats and wanes sufficiently to preserve itself. How could it become lengthy and abundant in the end? This is why it is necessary and proper to warn it that there will be peril if it makes a journey. The *chang* character of "lengthy" is pronounced with an ascending tone. Those who make it a level tone have completely lost the intention of the *Book of Changes*.[1] This may be seen in the Gaze, Solve, and Wear hexagrams together with the *Symbol* on the Solve hexagram.[2] The text is the same, but the pronunciation is different.

The fifth "six" line: dense clouds but no rain come from our western outlands. The duke picks off and chooses the one in the cave. The fifth line uses *yin* softness to occupy the position of respect. Although its desire is to do something excessive, how could it complete such a task? It is like "dense clouds" that cannot bring the rain to completion. The reason they cannot bring the rain to completion is that they come from the "western outlands." That the *yin qi* cannot bring the rain to completion has already been interpreted in the Small Herd hexagram.[3] "The duke picks off and chooses the one in the cave": to pick off is to choose something by shooting it. The meaning of the word "shoot" stops at the fact of shooting, but "pick off" also has the meaning of choosing. The word "cave" refers to a hollow at the center of a mountain. If the center is empty, then it is hollow, and so the reference to being in the cave points to the second "six" line. The fifth and the second lines do not at root correspond to each other, but one picks off and chooses the other. The position of the fifth line is proper for it, and this is why the line statement calls it the "duke," signifying that the duke is above. Even though those of the same kind choose each other, and one acquires the other, how could two *yin* lines be able to cross through great affairs? They are like dense clouds that cannot bring the rain to completion. **The *Symbol* says: "'Dense clouds but no rain': it is already at the top."** When *yang* is falling and *yin* rising, they will harmonize and bring the rain to completion if they align. If *yin* is "already at the top," how could it bring the rain to completion, even if its clouds are dense? The meaning here is that excessive *yin* cannot bring anything great to completion.

The top "six" line: it does not encounter but exceeds it. The flying bird casts it off. There is misfortune. This may be called a disaster and a mistake. This "six" line is *yin*, it belongs to the movement trigram substance, it is placed at the limit of the excess hexagram, and it does not encounter its principle. Its every movement will be excessive. It draws back from its principle and exceeds what is ordinary, just like the suddenness and swiftness of a "flying bird," and so "there is misfortune." The phrase "casts it off" refers to a far-reaching excess. "This may be called a disaster and a mistake": in this case, it is proper that there be a disaster and a mistake. The word "disaster" refers to a calamity of heaven, and "mistake" refers to something done by people.[4] Since it is at the limit of the excess hexagram, how could there merely be a human mistake? A disaster of heaven also occurs, and its misfortune should be recognized. Such is the case both for heavenly principles and human affairs. **The *Symbol* says: "'It does not encounter but exceeds it': it has already become proud."** It occupies the end of the excess hexagram. It "does not encounter" its principle "but exceeds it." In its excess, "it has already become proud," and it is fitting that there be misfortune at its limit.

63. HAS CROSSED (*JIJI* 既濟)

The *Sequence of the Hexagrams* says: "When things become excessive, they have necessarily already made the crossing. This is why the Has Crossed hexagram is next." If a thing can become excessive, it has necessarily been able to make the crossing. This is why, after the Small Excess hexagram, the Has Crossed hexagram is next. As for the trigrams, "water is above the fire." When water and fire interact with each other, they both perform their functions. Each performs its proper function, and this is why these trigrams constitute the Has Crossed hexagram. It is the moment when the world and the ten thousand things have already made the crossing.

Has Crossed: there is progress, but also the small. There is profit in purity. There is initial good fortune but disorder in the end. In the moment of the Has Crossed hexagram, the great have already made progress, while the small value the progress to be made.[1] Although it is the moment of the Has Crossed hexagram, it cannot be without small people who have not yet made any progress. The word "small" is on the right, and this is proper to the syntax. If the judgment had remarked that "there is some small progress," it would have been referring to the small degree of the progress. "There is profit in purity": when one is placed in the moment of the Has Crossed hexagram, there is profit in guarding it with purity and certainty. "There is initial good fortune": this is the moment at the start of the crossing. "But disorder in the end": when the crossing reaches its limit, it reverses itself.

The *Judgment* says: "'Has Crossed: there is progress.' The small make progress. 'There is profit in purity': firmness and softness are straightforward, and their positions are proper for them." In the moment of the Has Crossed hexagram, the great have certainly already made progress. It is only the small who are making progress.[2] Since the moment has already been crossed, it is certainly fitting that it be guarded with purity and certainty. As for the powers of the trigrams, "firmness and softness are straightforward and their positions are proper for them." Proper positions are constant positions, which means that they are straightforward and certain. There is profit in the purity that is like this. The *yin* and *yang* lines have all acquired their straightforward positions, and so these are the lines that constitute the Has Crossed hexagram. "'There is initial good fortune': softness acquires centrality." The second line makes use of softness and submissiveness, pattern and enlightenment, and it acquires centrality. This is why it can complete the task of the Has Crossed hexagram. The second line occupies a position in the lower trigram substance, which faces the initiation of the crossing. Further, it places itself well, and as a result, there is good fortune. "If it stops in the end, there is disorder. Its way is depleted." As for the affairs of the world, if they do not advance, they will retreat. There is no principle by which they could have a single determination. At the end of the crossing, they do not advance, but stop. Since they cannot constantly be stopped, they will become extremely scarce and disorderly and, in fact, their way is already at its limit and depletion. The power of the fifth "nine" line is not other than good, but at the moment of the limit "its way is depleted." Its alteration is proper, necessary, and according to principle. When sages reach this point, what can they do? Response: sages alone are capable of developing and altering when they are not yet depleted, and so they are not made to reach the point of the limit. Such was the case for Yao and Shun, and this is why, although they brought about their end, there was no disorder.

The *Symbol* says: "Water is above the fire: Has Crossed. Noble people use it to reflect on their distress and cheerfully defend against it." When water and fire have already interacted and each has acquired its function, they have made the crossing. Those who face the moment of the Has Crossed hexagram are apprehensive solely about the birth of distress and harm. This is why they "reflect" and "cheerfully defend," so that they are not made to reach the point of distress. Since antiquity, when the world has already made the crossing, it brings about affliction and disorder. In fact, it cannot reflect on its distress and cheerfully defend itself.

The initial "nine" line: it drags its wheels. Its tail glistens. There is no blame. The initial line uses *yang* to occupy the bottom position, it corresponds to the fourth line above it, it belongs to the substance of the fire trigram, and its tendency to advance is keen. Nonetheless, this is the moment of the Has Crossed hexagram, and if its advance does not cease, it will extend itself to regret and blame. This is why "it drags its wheels," and "its tail glistens," so that it will acquire "no blame." Since it travels only because of its wheels, dragging them back will keep it from advancing. When a beast traverses the water, it will necessarily expose its tail. If its tail glistens, then it will be unable to make the crossing. The initial line of the Has Crossed hexagram can stop its advance, and so it acquires no blame. If it did not know how to cease, it would reach the point of blame. **The *Symbol* says: "'It drags its wheels': it means that there is no blame."** If the initial line of the Has Crossed hexagram can stop its advance, it will not reach the limit, which means that it will not be blamed.

The second "six" line: the wife is deprived of her cloak. She should not pursue it. After seven days, she will acquire it. The second line uses the virtues of pattern, enlightenment, centrality, and straightforwardness, and it corresponds to the fifth "nine" line above it, which refers to a ruler of *yang* firmness, centrality, and straightforwardness. It is fitting for it to put its tendencies into action. Nonetheless, the fifth line has acquired the position of respect, and it is already the moment of the Has Crossed hexagram. Even if it does something without advancing, how could it intend to seek out and employ the powers of worthy people in positions below? This is why the second line does not acquire success in its action. Since antiquity, few have been able to employ people in the Has Crossed hexagram. If Taizong of the Tang dynasty employed their words but disregarded their value in the end, what will the case be like for those who came later?[3] In such a moment, firmness and centrality revert to centrality and satisfaction. It is the moment when the Pit and Cast trigrams repulse each other. People who can understand the moment and recognize its alteration should be able to make remarks on the *Book of Changes*. The second line is *yin*, and this is why the line statement remarks on "the wife." The word "cloak" refers to what wives use to conceal themselves when they go outside their gate. If she is "deprived of her cloak," then she should not travel. If the employment of the second line is not sought by the fifth, then it will not travel, just like the wife deprived of her cloak. Nonetheless, how could the way of centrality and straightforwardness be neglected? When this moment has been exceeded, then it will travel. To "pursue" something is to attend to it. If it attends to something, it will lose sight of simply keeping guard over itself. This is why it warns that "she should not pursue it." If she does not lose her guard over herself, then "after seven days" it is proper that she "acquire it." Since a hexagram has six positions, the number seven refers to alteration. "After seven days, she will acquire it": this signifies that the moment will alter. Although it is not employed by those above, there is no principle by which the way of centrality and straightforwardness may be neglected to the end. If it does not act now, it will necessarily act at a different moment. The warning of the sage is persuasive and deep. **The *Symbol* says: "'After seven days, she will acquire it': it uses the way of centrality."** Although the way of centrality and straightforwardness is not employed at this moment, there is nonetheless no principle of inaction to the end. This is why she is "deprived of her cloak," but it is proper that "after seven days" she "acquire it." This signifies that it keeps guard over its own centrality, and will necessarily act at a different moment. If it does not lose its centrality, it will be straightforward.

The third "nine" line: Gaozong attacked Guifang. It took three years to conquer it. Small people should not be employed. The third "nine" line faces the moment of the Has Crossed hexagram and it uses firmness to occupy a firm position, which is to employ extreme firmness. Such an employment of firmness in the Has Crossed hexagram is like the affair of Gaozong attacking Guifang. This Gaozong must be the Gaozong of the Shang dynasty.[4] It attacks and does violence to a faraway disorder when it has crossed through the affairs of the world. To extend one's authority to war, and to have saving the people as one's heart, are affairs of kings. Only rulers of sageliness and worth will be capable of them. To gallop toward authority in war out of wrath at the disobedient or out of greed for pieces of land is to be savage to the people and to indulge one's desires. This is why the line statement warns that "small people should not be employed." Small people do everything because of greed and wrath, which are private intentions. When they are not greedy or wrathful, they are unwilling to do anything. "It took three years to conquer it": this shows how extremely laborious and wearying it was. Because the third "nine" line employs firmness while facing the Has Crossed hexagram, the sage reveals this meaning, showing it to people as a law and a warning. How could his sight be extended only to what is shallow? **The *Symbol* says: "'It took three years to conquer it': it is weary."** The *Symbol* remarks that "it is weary" to show the extreme difficulty of this affair. If it is Gaozong that does it, he will be capable of it. Those who do not possess the heart of Gaozong will bring calamities to the people with their greed and wrath.

The fourth "six" line: it is exquisite silk, but it has raggedy clothes. At the end of the day, it is warned. The fourth line belongs to one of the crossing hexagrams and to the water trigram substance, and this is why the line statement chooses a boat as its meaning. The fourth is a position near the ruler, and so it is proper to delegate command to it. It faces the moment of the Has Crossed hexagram, and it is agitated both to defend against distress and to apprehend its alteration. It is proper that "exquisite silk" be taken as "glistening," which

signifies something waterlogged and leaky.[5] If a boat has cracks and leaks, raggedy clothes are used to choke them up. "It has raggedy clothes" to prepare
itself for the glistening leaks. Further, "at the end of the day, it is warned" to be
troubled about them and not to disregard them: it is proper to be apprehensive
about distress like this. It does not remark that there is good fortune, because
it is merely avoiding distress. In the moment of the Has Crossed hexagram it
is sufficient to avoid distress—how could one attach anything else to it? **The
Symbol says: "'At the end of the day, it is warned': there is room for doubt."**
"At the end of the day, it is warned" to be troubled, to be in constant doubt
about whether or not it will soon reach the point of distress. When placed in
the moment of the Has Crossed hexagram, it is proper to be trembling and
cautious like this.

**The fifth "nine" line: the eastern neighbor kills a cow, but it is not like the
lesser seasonal sacrifice made by the western neighbor. Because it is full, it
receives blessings.** The center of the fifth line is full and refers to being trustworthy; the center of the second line is empty and refers to sincerity. This is
why the meaning of sacrifice and libation was chosen for both. The "eastern
neighbor" is *yang* and signifies the fifth line, while the "western neighbor" is
yin and signifies the second line. The killing of a cow is an abundant sacrifice,
while the "lesser seasonal sacrifice" is a meager sacrifice. The abundant is not
like the meager—their moments are not the same. The second and fifth lines
both possess the virtues of being trustworthy, sincere, central, and straightforward, but the second line is at the bottom of the crossing hexagram and still
has somewhere to advance. This is why "it receives blessings." The fifth line
is placed at the limit of the crossing and has nowhere to advance. Because it
guards itself with extreme sincerity, centrality, and straightforwardness, it has
not yet reached the point of reversal. There is no principle of a limit or end
without a reversal. Since it has already reached the limit, although it may place
itself well, it will not be like the placement of the other line. This is why the
line statement and the *Symbol* only remark on the two moments. **The *Symbol*
says: "'The eastern neighbor kills a cow': but it is not like the moment of the
western neighbor. 'Because it is full, it receives blessings': there is the good
fortune of a great arrival."** The power and virtue of the fifth line are never other
than good, but "it is not like the moment" of the second line. The second line is
at the bottom, and is at the moment for its advance. This is why, if it is central,
straightforward, and trustworthy, "there is the good fortune of a great arrival."
This is what is signified by "it receives blessings." "There is the good fortune of
a great arrival": the moment of the Has Crossed hexagram constitutes a great

arrival. In such a moment, "there is progress, but also the small," and "there is initial good fortune."[6]

The top "six" line: its head glistens. There is danger. At the limit of the Has Crossed hexagram, there is certainly peril rather than contentment. Further, a line that is *yin* and soft is placed at the top of the obstacle trigram substance. The Pit trigram refers to water, and the crossing hexagram also chooses water as its meaning. This is why the line statement remarks that its depletion reaches the point that "its head glistens" and its peril should be recognized. When small people are placed at the end of the Has Crossed hexagram, their defeat and decline should be set up and awaited. **The *Symbol* says: "'Its head glistens. There is danger': how could it continue?"** When the Has Crossed hexagram is depleted, its peril reaches the point that "its head glistens": "How could it" grow or "continue"?

64. UNCROSSED (*WEIJI* 未濟)

The *Sequence of the Hexagrams* says: "Things are incapable of depletion, and this is why the Uncrossed hexagram is next, at the end of the book." The Has Crossed hexagram refers to the depletion of things. When things are depleted and do not alter, there is no principle by which they do not cease. The *yi* character of the *Book of Changes* refers to alteration and the avoidance of depletion. This is why the Uncrossed hexagram is next after the Has Crossed hexagram, at the end of the book. If something has not yet been crossed, then it has not yet been depleted; if it has not yet been depleted, then it has the meaning of birth and life. As for the trigrams, the Cast trigram is above and the Pit trigram below. "Fire is above the water": they do not perform their functions on each other, and this is why they refer to the Uncrossed hexagram.

Uncrossed: there is progress. The small fox approaches the crossing. Its tail glistens. There is no long-term profit. The moment of the Uncrossed hexagram possesses the principle of progress. The powers of the trigrams in turn possess the way of bringing about progress, but only if one is cautious in placing oneself. The fox can take the measure of the water, but if "its tail glistens," then it will not be able to make the crossing. Old foxes tremble at and doubt many things. This is why they listen when they walk on the ice, troubled that they might be ensnared. If the fox is small, then it is not yet capable of trembling and caution, and this is why it has the courage to make the crossing. It is proper that "approaches" be considered as "is brave at," referring to its condition of mighty courage.[1] The *Book of History* says: "That brave, brave and courageous man!"[2] The purpose of the small fox is to make the crossing, but "its tail glistens" and it cannot make the crossing. In the moment of the Uncrossed hexagram, when one seeks a way to make the crossing, it is proper to be extremely cautious, and then one will be capable of progress. Those whose purpose is like the small fox will be unable to make the crossing. Since they are unable to make the crossing, nothing will be profitable for them.

The *Judgment* says: "'Uncrossed: there is progress': softness acquires centrality." The *Judgment* is remarking on the powers of the trigrams. There can be progress because "softness acquires centrality." The fifth line uses softness to occupy the position of respect, it occupies a firm position, and it corresponds to a firm line, but it acquires the center of a soft trigram. When firmness and softness acquire centrality, they place themselves in the moment of the Uncrossed hexagram, and they should be able to make progress. "'The small fox approaches the crossing': it does not yet go out from the center." The *Judgment* is remarking on the second line. The second line uses *yang* firmness to occupy the center of the obstacle, indicating that it is about to make the crossing, and further, it corresponds to the fifth line above it. The obstacle cannot be a terrain of contentment, and there is a principle by which it is proper that the fifth line attend to the second—this is why its purpose, like that of the small fox, is to make the crossing. Its purpose is already to make the crossing, and this is why it has the distress of a glistening tail, and it cannot yet "go out from the center." "'Its tail glistens. There is no long-term profit': it is not prolonged to the end." Its advance is keen, and its retreat is rapid. Although it begins with the courage to make the crossing, it cannot be prolonged successively to the end. There is no journey to make that will bring it profit. "Although their positions are not proper for them, firmness and softness correspond." Although the *yin* and *yang* lines are not in their proper positions, it is nonetheless the case that all the firm and soft lines correspond to each other. It is proper that there be agreement about what has not yet been crossed. Were they capable of a weighty caution, they would possess the principle of being able to make the crossing. The second line approaches the crossing, and this is why "its tail glistens." As for the various lines of the hexagram, none has acquired its position, and this is why these are the lines that constitute the Uncrossed hexagram. The *Mixed Hexagrams* says: "The Uncrossed hexagram refers to the depletion of the male," which signifies that the three *yang* lines have all lost their positions. As for this meaning, I heard it from someone in Chengdu.[3]

The *Symbol* says: "Fire is above the water: Uncrossed. Noble people use it cautiously to distinguish things and make them occupy their regions." When water and fire do not interact, they do not perform the function of crossing through each other. This is why these trigrams constitute the Uncrossed hexagram. "Fire is above the water": it is not in its place. When noble people gaze on the symbol of something not in its proper place, they use it cautiously to place things and affairs. They distinguish what is proper for each, so that each occupies its own region, which signifies that they stop them in their places.

The initial "six" line: its tail glistens. There is dismay. This "six" line makes use of *yin* softness in the bottom position, it is placed in the obstacle trigram, and it corresponds to the fourth line. Since it is placed in the obstacle trigram, it is not contented with the position that it occupies, and since it has a corresponding line, its tendency is to travel upward. Nonetheless, since it is *yin* and soft in itself, and the fourth line does not have the powers of centrality and straightforwardness, it cannot support it in making the crossing. When a beast crosses the water, it will necessarily expose its tail. If its tail is glistening, then it cannot make the crossing. "Its tail glistens": this is remarking that it cannot make the crossing. If it advances without taking the measure of its power or force, it will not be able to make the crossing in the end, and it should be disappointed and dismayed. **The *Symbol* says: "'Its tail glistens': it is also at the limit of recognizing nothing."** If it advances without taking the measure of its power or force, it will reach the point at which "its tail glistens." This is the limit of "recognizing nothing."

The second "nine" line: it drags its wheels. There are purity and good fortune. In other hexagrams, a "nine" line occupying the second position is considered to be occupying a soft position and acquiring centrality. It does not have the meaning of excessive firmness. In the Uncrossed hexagram, the sage makes a deep choice of hexagram symbol as a warning, and sheds light on the way to manage the affairs of those above with modesty and submissiveness. The Uncrossed hexagram refers to the way of the ruler at a moment of hardship and difficulty. The fifth line uses softness to place itself in the position of the ruler. It is proper for it to employ the second line, which has the power of *yang* firmness and occupies a terrain that corresponds to it. Firmness has the meaning of usurping softness, and water is the symbol of victory over fire. Those who face a moment of hardship and difficulty depend on powerful ministers, for whom it is especially proper to exhaust the way of modesty and submissiveness. This is why the line statement warns that if "it drags its wheels," it will acquire straightforwardness and there will be "good fortune." To drag one's wheels backward is to kill one's propensity and slacken one's advance—it is a warning about employing excessive firmness. If its firmness is excessive, it will prefer to confront those above and its submissiveness will not be sufficient. When Guo Ziyi and Li Sheng of the Tang dynasty faced the moment of the Uncrossed hexagram with its hardship and peril, they were able to bring their modesty and submissiveness to the limit, and so they acquired straightforwardness and were able to preserve their good fortune to the end.[4] Concerning the fifth "six" line, it remarks on its purity, good fortune, brightness, and radiance, which exhaust what is good for the way of the ruler. Concerning the second "nine" line, it warns it about modesty and submissiveness, which exhaust what is straightforward for the way of the minister. Together they exhaust the way of those above and below. **The Symbol says: "The purity and good fortune of the second 'nine' line: it uses centrality to act straightforwardly."** The second "nine" line acquires straightforwardness and good fortune. It is straightforward because it "drags its wheels" and acquires the way of "centrality."

The third "six" line: it is uncrossed. Taking the field brings misfortune. There is profit in traversing a great stream. "It is uncrossed. Taking the field brings misfortune": this signifies that it occupies a position in the obstacle trigram without being employed to go out from the obstacle. If it acts, there will be misfortune. It must go out from the obstacle, and afterward it may take the field. The third line uses *yin* softness without the powers of centrality and straightforwardness. It occupies a position in the obstacle trigram without being sufficient to make the crossing. It does not yet have the way of being able to make the crossing, of being employed to go out from the obstacle, or of "taking the field," and so there is "misfortune." Nonetheless, the Uncrossed hexagram has a way of being able to make the crossing. The end of the obstacle trigram possesses the principle of going out from the obstacle, and the top line corresponds to it with *yang* firmness. If the third can traverse the obstacle and make the journey to attend to it, then it will make the crossing. This is why "there is profit in traversing a great stream." Nonetheless, how could the *yin* softness of the third line go out from the obstacle and make the journey? If this is not the moment for it, it will not be able to do it—that is, its power will not be capable of it. **The Symbol says: "'It is uncrossed. Taking the field brings misfortune': its position is not proper for it."** If there is misfortune because the third line takes the field, then "its position is not proper for it." This signifies that, when *yin* softness is neither central nor straightforward, it does not have the power to cross through the obstacle. If it could traverse the obstacle and attend to its corresponding line, then there would be profit.

The fourth "nine" line: purity brings good fortune. Regrets vanish. It employs shaking to attack Guifang. After three years it will be rewarded with a great state. The fourth "nine" line is *yang* and firm, and occupies the position of the great minister. Its master is the line above it, which has an empty center and is enlightened and submissive. Further, it has already gone out from the obstacle, and the Uncrossed hexagram has already exceeded its center. It possesses the way of being able to make the crossing. As for crossing through the hardship and difficulty of the world, those without the powers of firmness and vigor will not be capable of it. Although this "nine" line is *yang*, it occupies the fourth position, and this is why the line statement warns that there is "good fortune" and "regrets vanish" only if it is pure and certain. If it is not pure, it will not be able to make the crossing and will have regrets. The word "shaking" refers to the limit of movement. The people of antiquity employed extreme force to attack Guifang, and this is why it constitutes the meaning of the line.[5] Those who attack a faraway place with force and diligence for a period of three years will afterward "be rewarded with a great state" for their action and for completing their task. They must be people like this to be capable of making the crossing. Concerning the way of making the crossing with the world, it is proper that one be pure and certain like this. The fourth line occupies a soft position, and this is why it provides this warning. **The *Symbol* says: "'Purity brings good fortune. Regrets vanish': it puts its tendency into action."** Since the powers of the fourth line are in alignment with the moment, and it attaches purity and certainty to them, it will be able to "put its tendency into action," there will be "good fortune," and "regrets vanish." To attack Guifang is to be extremely pure.

The fifth "six" line: purity brings good fortune. It has no regrets. It is the brightness of noble people. It is trustworthy. There is good fortune. The fifth line is the master of pattern and enlightenment, it occupies a firm position and corresponds to a firm line, it is placed so as to acquire centrality, it empties its heart, and it is assisted by a *yang* line. Although it uses softness to occupy the position of respect, its placement is extremely straightforward and extremely good. There is nothing insufficient about it. It has acquired purity and straightforwardness, and this is why there is "good fortune" and "it has no regrets." Since it possesses purity and certainty, the line statement gives it no warning. When this is used to make the crossing, nothing is left uncrossed. The fifth line is the master of pattern and enlightenment, and this is why it is renowned as the "brightness of noble people." Because its virtue and radiance are abundant, it becomes renowned for the fullness of its accomplishment, which is to be "trustworthy." It says early on that it has "good fortune" because of its purity. To be soft but capable of purity is the good fortune of virtue. It says later on that it has "good fortune" because of its accomplishment. When it has become bright and trustworthy, it can cross through the moment. **The *Symbol* says: "'It is the brightness of noble people': their radiance brings good fortune."** When brightness has become abundant, it will be radiant. To be radiant is to scatter one's brightness about. Noble people accumulate and replenish their brightness, and so it becomes abundant. When it reaches the point of being radiant, this is the best it can do. This is why the line statement repeatedly says that there is "good fortune."

The top "nine" line: it is trustworthy in drinking wine. There is no blame. Its head glistens. It is trustworthy, but this is its loss. This "nine" line makes use of firmness in the top position, and so it is the limit of firmness. It occupies the top of the enlightenment trigram, and so it is the limit of enlightenment. If those at the limit of firmness can be enlightened, they will not be considered restless, but resolute. Their enlightenment can elucidate the principle and their firmness can decide on their duty. It occupies the limit position in the Uncrossed hexagram, and has not acquired a position from which to make the crossing. Since there is no principle by which it could make the crossing, it is proper for it to take pleasure in heaven and submit to the mandate, and that is all. If this were the end of the Clog hexagram, it would collapse in the alteration of the moment, but the Uncrossed hexagram does not have the principle of reaching the limit and making the crossing on its own. This is why there is a stopping at the limit of the Uncrossed hexagram. If it takes pleasure in itself, by its extreme sincerity and contentment with its duty and the mandate, then there should be "no blame." The phrase "drinking wine" refers to taking pleasure in oneself. If it does not take pleasure in its place, then it will be wrathful and restless, and fall like the harvest, entering into misfortune and blame. But if it attends to its own pleasure and gives itself to indulgence in excess of what ritual allows, it will reach the point at which "its head glistens" and it will not be able to be contented with its place. "It is trustworthy": it is believable at its center. "This is its loss": it loses what is fitting for it. In a case like this, to be trustworthy constitutes a loss. When people placed in distress and difficulty recognize that there is nothing they can do and surrender their intentions without reverting to them, how could they be contented with their duty and mandate? **The *Symbol* says: "While 'drinking wine,' 'its head glistens': it does not know how to rein itself in."** When it drinks wine to the point that "its head glistens," this is the extreme of not knowing how to rein oneself in. Because it has reached this point, it cannot be contented with its duty and mandate. If it can be contented, it will not lose what is constant.

GLOSSARY

The definitions provided in this glossary are only those used by Cheng Yi in the *Yi River Commentary on the Book of Changes*, and they are supported only with internal evidence from the text. It cannot be assumed that any term supplied here has the same definition in the broader Chinese philosophical tradition, or even in other works authored by Cheng Yi.

Center (*zhong* 中): see "centrality."

Centrality (*zhong* 中): the virtue of being in the middle or the interior of something. This is not usually the geometrical center, as those who occupy geometrical centers are not necessarily virtuous. Rather, the geometrical center serves as a metaphor for a fitting amount of something, usually a fitting amount of firmness (q.v.) in ministers and rulers. Outside the center in all directions lies excess. One can have excessively little or excessively much. Those who possess excessively little are incapable of making decisions, and so they do not know whether to act or not to act (Hexagram 57, initial line). Those who possess excessively much, on the other hand, tend to be destructive in their decisiveness. To possess centrality in this respect is to be able to delegate command (Hexagram 19, fifth line, *Symbol*). The virtue of centrality is symbolized in the *Book of Changes* by the following three geometrical centers: (1) the middle line in a trigram (Hexagram 9, *Judgment*), (2) the middle line in a group of lines that are all either *yin* or *yang* (Hexagram 24, fourth line), and (3) the point between the third and fourth lines of a hexagram (Hexagram 11, fourth line). Although centrality is usually paired with straightforwardness (q.v.), the two are not of equal worth. What is central will be straightforward, but what is straightforward will not necessarily be central (Hexagram 32, second line). For instance, a firm line in a firm position is straightforward, but it can refer to excessive firmness rather than centrality.

Constant (*chang* 常): always, ideally, or usually occurring. For instance, it is a "constant principle" that "when *yang* has fallen to the bottom, it must return to the top" (Hexagram 11, third line, *Symbol*). It is always the case that the depleted *yang qi* will begin to rise again, as when winter yields to spring. Some constant principles describe only what ideally occurs rather than what always occurs. For instance, it is a "constant principle of heaven and earth" that men and women align with each other (Hexagram 54, *Judgment*), but this does not always happen. When the *chang* character refers only to what usually occurs, it is sometimes translated as "ordinary." For instance, "it is ordinary for softness to occupy a position below" (Hexagram 15, initial line). Soft people are often in humble positions, although this is not always the case, and it is not always best for them to be there.

Correspondence (*ying* 應): a link between two things of complementary kinds, or between two or more things of the same kind. The former is the more common meaning in Cheng Yi's commentary. It first appears in a passage from the *Judgment*, which says that "the two kinds of *qi* affect and correspond to each other" (Hexagram 31, *Judgment*). That is, the *yang qi* affects and corresponds to the *yin qi*, and vice versa. In the hexagrams, such correspondence occurs when a *yang* line is either adjacent to or exactly three lines away from a *yin* line. In the latter case, the correspondence is called "straightforward" (q.v.), as the two lines occupy the same positions in their respective trigrams. For instance, a *yin* line in the initial position and a *yang* line in the fourth position have a straightforward correspondence, as they both occupy the initial positions in their respective trigrams. The second kind of correspondence—when two or more things of the same kind are linked—is described in the *Remarks on the Text*: "The same sounds correspond to each other, and the same kinds of *qi* seek each other" (Hexagram 1, *Remarks*). In this case, *yang qi* corresponds to *yang qi*, and *yin qi* corresponds to *yin qi*. Cheng Yi does not consider this the root meaning of correspondence, but it describes the bonds formed in certain adverse circumstances (Hexagram 38, initial line).

Crowd (*zhong* 眾): the group of human beings who are not capable of holding positions in government. This is by far the largest group of people in the state, often referred to by Cheng Yi as the "countless millions." The crowd tends the crops that provide the state with its material resources, and it serves as the army when military action is needed. The rulers and officials are in the awkward position of having both to respect the crowd's fundamental desire, which is for wealth (Hexagram 15, fifth line), and to correct the crowd's shortsighted pursuit of this desire. Without the crowd, the state would have no material resources and so would not exist at all, so what the crowd permits is to be regarded as proper for the state (Hexagram 35, third line). The rulers and officials are not to attempt to give the crowd a new reason for acting, but to convince it that the decisions of the rulers serve the crowd's own desires (Hexagram 9, fifth line, *Symbol*). The crowd is distinguished from the class of rulers and officials by its inability to recognize incipient problems that could later grow to overwhelm the state (Hexagram 36, initial line). Since it cannot be trusted to limit its desires when their unbridled pursuit would destroy the state, it must be kept in line with the threat of punishment (Hexagram 43, *Judgment*). The same word "crowd" is also used in a nontechnical sense to refer to any group of things, such as a "crowd of *yang* lines."

Desire (*yu* 欲): a synonym for "tendency," similar in meaning to "inclination." Desires in themselves are morally indeterminate—that is, they can tend toward either a good or a bad goal, and they can go too far in the pursuit of that goal. For this reason, Cheng Yi claims that it is a fault to move in accordance with desire (Hexagram 25, *Sequence*). If desires are not to lead to disorder through either pursuing a bad goal or pursuing it excessively, they must be made determinate (Hexagram 10, *Symbol*). Desire, then, should not be the root of human action. The root ought to be the principle of heaven (Hexagram 41, judgment), which can set a limit on desire. This is not to say that all people need to possess the root of action in themselves, so long as those in government rely on it. The crowd, for instance, may be moved by desire, while noble people govern their own actions and those of the crowd using principle. The problem arises when small people serve in government, as they are entirely devoted to their desires (Hexagram 15, judgment).

Disposition (*zhi* 質): a synonym for "tendency," with the added notion of being rooted in one's *qi*. For instance, whether one has the tendency to be firm will depend on whether one's *qi* is *yin* or *yang*. In the hexagrams, a solid line indicates a *yang* disposition, whereas a broken line indicates a *yin* disposition. A ruler with a *yang* disposition will then be symbolized by a solid line in the fifth position. Since dispositions are rooted in the *qi*, they are not easily changed, but they are not as fundamental as natures (q.v.). Dispositions may be either good or bad (Hexagram 22, second line), while natures are always good.

Duty (*yi* 義): action that serves the public good rather than private desire. For instance, Cheng Yi glosses duty as "what it is proper for them to do" (Hexagram 2, third line, *Symbol*). Duty is closely associated with principle, to the point that Cheng Yi often refers to them with one phrase, "duty and principle" (e.g., Hexagram 7, initial line). He once distinguishes the two, saying that "principle refers to how a thing is, while duty refers to how a thing is placed" (Hexagram 52, *Judgment*). One needs to know the principles of things to know how they should be employed, while the sense of duty concerns the decision to employ them. As Cheng Yi puts it, enlightenment elucidates the principle, while firmness makes one decisive in one's duty (Hexagram 64, top line). Small people cannot "place themselves in accord with their duty" but are guided by what is private (Hexagram 33, fourth line). This is not surprising, as small people are led by their desires, and attending to desire causes one to discount both duty and principle (Hexagram 54, *Judgment*). Other translators sometimes render the *yi* character as "appropriate behavior" or as "righteousness," but it has a self-denying character in Cheng Yi's commentary that makes the translation of "duty" peculiarly appropriate. Duty requires that one take away from oneself and attend to others (Hexagram 41, top line), and in fact, it requires that the self be conquered (Hexagram 43, fourth line). In short, duty serves the public rather than the private, principle rather than desire, and others rather than the self. Despite Cheng Yi's separation of duty and principle, the *yi* character does sometimes simply refer to what something is and is translated in these cases as "meaning."

Earth (*di* 地): see "terrain."

Employment (*yong* 用): see "function."

Firmness (*gang* 剛): the disposition of *yang qi*. Firmness is the virtue of being able to make a decision, and then to persist in the decision one has made. Both of these characteristics are more associated with force than with intelligence. To make a decision is to impose one's own tendency on others, while to persist is to resist any influence from others. When firmness is used by itself or taken too far, it turns into violence and becomes harmful (Hexagram 21, *Judgment*). It is a mistake, then, to regard firmness as preferable to softness (Hexagram 1, employment of the lines). To be valuable, it generally must be paired with enlightenment. Firmness makes decisions, and enlightenment makes them informed decisions (Hexagram 30, top line, *Symbol*). When enlightenment is added to firmness, it makes firmness resolute rather than restless (Hexagram 64, top line). Although firmness is generally used in relation to others, it can also be used on the self, to decide persistently against its desires and so to conquer it (Hexagram 13, *Judgment*). While it is generally applied to males as the traditional decision makers, women can also be firm. In a wife, firmness refers to "worth and purity"

(Hexagram 54, initial line); in a young woman, it refers to straightforwardness, worth, and enlightenment (Hexagram 54, fourth line).

Fullness (*shi* 實): see "reality."

Function (*yong* 用): action in accordance with one's tendency or position. Although Cheng Yi occasionally uses the term "function" to describe the potential for action (Hexagram 50, third line), he generally uses it to describe the action itself. As he puts it, "to have the function of sustaining things without reaching them is similar to not having the function" (Hexagram 48, judgment). Cheng Yi identifies the function with the position in a hexagram rather than with the line that occupies it (Hexagram 21, *Judgment*). Those in ruling positions, for instance, will exercise authority whether they have the disposition for it or not. The disposition, then, may be symbolized by the line, but the function is symbolized by the position. Because the *yong* character refers primarily to action rather than potential, it is sometimes translated as "employment."

Heaven (*tian* 天): either the visible appearance of the sky and its weather patterns or the cosmic *yang qi*. The former is referred to as the "form and substance" of heaven (Hexagram 1, judgment), but it is the latter that concerns Cheng Yi throughout most of the commentary. Both the heavenly and earthly *qi* work together to bring about the ten thousand things (Hexagram 31, *Judgment*). Cheng Yi refers to the heavenly *qi* as their beginning, while it is the earthly *qi* that gives them life (Hexagram 42, *Judgment*). Heaven provides the impetus, and the earth brings it to fruition. Heaven is identified with principle (Hexagram 11, fourth line, *Symbol*), as it not only provides an impetus, but also the structure of relationships through which that impetus is brought to completion. Human kings are simply the agents of heaven, requiring a mandate from heaven (Hexagram 49, *Judgment*), and giving substance to the way of heaven (Hexagram 1, *Judgment*). For this reason, the term "heaven" sometimes serves merely as a symbol for the human king (Hexagram 7, second line, *Symbol*).

Hexagram (*gua* 卦): a figure composed of two trigrams stacked one on top of the other. A trigram, in turn, is a figure composed of three lines stacked one on top of the other, each line being either solid or broken at its center. Solid lines symbolize the *yang qi*, and broken lines symbolize the *yin qi*.

Idea (*yi* 意): see "intention."

Inclination (*qing* 情): a synonym for tendency (Hexagram 11, *Judgment*), but with the added notion of "moving only for the sake of enjoyment" (Hexagram 54, *Judgment*). Such a tendency is present in human beings of every age but is most identified with youth (Hexagram 32, *Sequence*). Human beings possess a general inclination from their childhood to pursue pleasure and avoid pain, but they also share an inclination for and against certain specific objects. For instance, "it is human inclination to be made ill by and to detest those who are full and satiated" (Hexagram 15, *Judgment*). Other shared human inclinations include "taking pleasure in loftiness" and "being made happy by victories" (Hexagram 15, third line). Inclinations share several characteristics with other kinds of tendency. Like dispositions, they are separate from ornament (Hexagram 22, *Symbol*), and like desires, they must be controlled by laws (Hexagram 37, initial line).

Intellectual (*ru* 儒): a pejorative term for scholars of the classics. When it occurs elsewhere in Cheng Yi's works, this character may be translated as "Confucian" or "Ruist" without any pejorative connotation, but in his commentary on the *Book of Changes* he uses it to refer to any scholar who has expressed an inaccurate or incomplete view of a classical text.

Intention (*yi* 意): a synonym for "tendency" (Hexagram 16, initial line), but referring only to those tendencies that occur in thought. As a result, it can only describe the tendencies of human beings, not of other animals or inanimate things. Cheng Yi is primarily concerned that intentions be sincere—that is, that they be unitary (Hexagram 4, judgment). Unity of intention does not appear to mean tending in one direction, as even a bad intention may tend in only one direction. Instead, an intention becomes unitary when it preserves the unity of one's essence (Hexagram 20, judgment). An essence is not a private thing but connects the individual with the world as a whole. A private intention, by contrast, redefines the world according to what one desires (Hexagram 13, judgment). The same *yi* character can also simply mean "idea," or what is expressed in words (Hexagram 16, *Judgment*).

Marquis (*hou* 侯): a governor of a state in classical China. The "various marquises" ruled the states of classical China ostensibly in the name of the son of heaven (q.v.). The third position in a hexagram is the position of the various marquises (Hexagram 14, third line).

Meaning (*yi* 義): see "duty."

Minister (*chen* 臣): a person who serves the authority of the ruler on the one hand, and governs the people on the other. Although ministers govern the people, their function is *yin* rather than *yang* (Hexagram 2, fifth line), since they are not in positions of absolute authority. Rulers decree what must be done, and ministers carry it out (Hexagram 2, judgment). Rulers may also delegate author-ity to their ministers, but in either case the ministers labor over affairs for which they do not have absolute responsibility. The "great minister" (*dachen* 大臣) is symbolized by the fourth line (Hexagram 16, fourth line) and occupies a posi-tion closer to that of the ruler than other ministers.

Moment (*shi* 時): a hexagram or a position within a hexagram understood as enabling certain specific actions to occur, and changing in a predictable man-ner. Cheng Yi frequently refers to "the moment of" a particular hexagram — "the moment of the Blind hexagram" for instance (Hexagram 4, fourth line, *Symbol*). At other times he says that hexagrams refer to states of affairs, while the lines within the hexagrams refer to "the moments of these states of affairs" (Hexagram 3, top line, *Symbol*). Less often, Cheng Yi uses the term broadly to refer to any configuration of things that enables specific actions to occur, such as the "moment of washing" during the ancestral sacrifices (Hexagram 20, judgment).

Nature (*xing* 性): whatever a thing does not acquire on its own, but receives from heaven (Hexagram 1, *Judgment*). In the commentary, the term refers al-most exclusively to the tendency to rise or fall. "The nature of fire is to go up, while the nature of water is to go down" (Hexagram 49, *Sequence*), while the nature of *yang* is to go up (Hexagram 61, top line), and the nature of *yin* is to go down (Hexagram 58, third line). A nature in itself is always good, but it may not be able to express this goodness. For instance, the powers by which the nature is expressed may corrupt it, resulting in bad actions (Hexagram 49, top line). In the symbolic structure of the *Book of Changes*, this may be expressed by a *yang* line in a *yin* position, which loses the ability to act straightforwardly as *yang* (Hexagram 43, fourth line, *Symbol*).

Noble people (*junzi* 君子): the group of human beings who are motivated by a sense of duty to serve as ministers in government. Among their defining char-acteristics are an attention to principle (Hexagram 13, *Judgment*) and the ability to see the incipient (Hexagram 16, second line). Although these are good char-acteristics, it is not necessary that everyone in the state possess them (Hexagram 7, top line). It is also not the case that one must be entirely noble to be worthy of the name. That is, one may be noble in one respect and not in another (Hexagram 34, third line). Noble people are different from kings, since kings establish the law while noble people merely uphold it (Hexagram 55, *Symbol*). Noble people are also better able to survive the destruction of the state than their rulers, since rulers cease to be rulers when they leave their posts, while noble people can retreat into private life (Hexagram 18, top line). There is no easy way to tell whether a hexagram line refers to noble people. A *yin* line may refer to noble people, since the way of noble people requires submissiveness (Hexagram 2, *Judgment*), but Cheng Yi also describes the way of noble people as *yang* (Hexagram 24, initial line), presumably because *yin* is incapable of conquering its own desires and doing its duty (Hexagram 34, top line). Any line, then, may refer either to noble people or to small people.

Ordinary (*chang* 常): see "constant."

Pattern (*wen* 文): the manner in which an action is performed. This manner may be simple or complicated. For instance, the action of making a sacrifice may be performed in a simple or complicated manner, depending on the number of parts into which it is broken. Feasts and libations have an "extremely complicated" pattern (Hexagram 41, judgment). The more complicated a pattern becomes, the more it can be considered as separate from the action that it enables. It may be identified as ornament (Hexagram 8, initial line), and distinguished from reality (Hexagram 22, *Judgment*) as well as from inclination (Hexagram 22, *Symbol*). Although Cheng Yi criticizes pattern on this score, he nonetheless regards it as necessary. No action can be performed without being performed in a certain manner, and so what has no pattern cannot act (Hexagram 22, judgment). When the well-governed state makes principles (q.v.) manifest by clarifying the relation between the various virtues and the actions that result from them, it makes these principles like patterns. In the well-governed state, principle becomes "luminous and manifest, like the pattern of color on tigers" (Hexagram 49, fifth line). At least part of this manifestation takes the form of action. If there is a pattern, then "principle will never be other than exhausted" (Hexagram 49, *Judgment*). As what makes something manifest, and as having a complicated character of its own, the *wen* character can refer to a written composition, and so it is sometimes translated as "text."

People, the (*min* 民): see "crowd." Note that there is a difference between "people" (*ren* 人) and "the people." The former refers to human beings generally, while the latter refers specifically to those who are not capable of holding a position in government.

Position (*wei* 位): either an office in government, or one of the six terrains (q.v.) occupied by lines in a hexagram. These two meanings are not entirely independent of one another, since the second, third, fourth, and fifth terrains of each hexagram are symbols for offices in government. Nonetheless, Cheng Yi is careful to keep the two meanings separate (Hexagram 21, initial line).

Power (*cai* 才): a synonym for "virtue," but often referring to a virtue symbolized by a trigram or by a particular hexagram line. For instance, the powers of the trigrams in the Small Herd hexagram are "vigor" and "lowliness" (Hexagram 9, *Judgment*), and the second line of the Great Grasp hexagram has the power of "firmness" and "vigor" (Hexagram 14, second line). Cheng Yi occasionally refers to the "three powers" mentioned in the *Explanation of the Trigrams*: heaven, earth, and human beings (Hexagram 12, judgment).

Principle (*li* 理): a relation between an action and the virtue or position that makes it possible. For instance, there is a principle by which those who possess the virtue of sincerity will acquire help from other people (Hexagram 16, fourth line). Sometimes Cheng Yi refers to the virtue or position itself as the principle of the action, as when he says that the virtue of sincerity is the principle of mutual affection (Hexagram 61, second line). The *Book of Changes* may be understood as an attempt to describe "the crowd of principles" (Hexagram 3, top line, *Symbol*), with each hexagram describing the actions that are possible for a person of a given virtue and position at a given moment. All the different kinds of action may be understood as gathering and dispersing things, and so all principle may be understood as the principle of gathering and dispersing (Hexagram 45, *Judgment*). Cheng Yi famously says that "the tendencies of the world have ten thousand peculiarities, but their principle is one" (Hexagram 13, *Judgment*). While the character for "principle" is similar in meaning to "pattern" and "coherence," and has in fact been rendered with these words by other translators, principle is "extremely minimal" ("Preface") and "has no form" (Hexagram 1, initial line). Pattern and coherence, however, make principle manifest (Hexagram 22, *Judgment*). Pattern and coherence also do not have a normative character, whereas principle is elucidated with the laws of the state (Hexagram 21, *Symbol*).

Propensity (*shi* 勢): the ability or inability to put one's tendency into action. To be able to put one's tendency into action is to have a weighty or strong propensity. Cheng Yi often identifies blocks of lines as possessing this strong propensity. When the *yang qi* is ascending from the center of the earth, symbolized by a block of *yang* lines ascending from the bottom of a hexagram, its propensity is strong (Hexagram 9, second line, *Symbol*). On the other hand, a single *yin* line that attends to a *yang* line when no other lines are doing so has a weak propensity (Hexagram 23, third line). A line's propensity may also depend on other configurations of lines in the hexagram (Hexagram 26, second line) or on the position of one other line in the hexagram (Hexagram 31, initial line). As for human beings, their propensity belongs to the overall configuration of the environment that surrounds them, while their tendency and desire are within them.

Qi (氣): the expanding and contracting material of life. When a thing first comes about, its *qi* is extremely minimal (Hexagram 24, judgment). People nourish their *qi* by eating and drinking (Hexagram 5, *Symbol*), and particularly by making themselves tranquil (Hexagram 24, *Symbol*). The contraction of their *qi* causes them to feel worried, while the expansion of their *qi* causes them to feel emotions like well-being (Hexagram 58, *Sequence*). The cosmos as a whole also experiences the expansion and contraction of the *qi* that constitutes it. In the spring, the balance of the cosmic *qi* tilts in favor of *yang*, which expands, whereas in the autumn, the balance of the cosmic *qi* tilts in favor of *yin*, which contracts. The activities of the *yang* and *yin qi* are described in the first two hexagrams respectively (Hexagram 2, *Judgment*). Human beings may experience one or other tilt of the *qi* in them, and so it is possible to speak of the *qi* of rulers and ministers (Hexagram 19, fifth line, *Symbol*).

Reality (*shi* 實): sometimes a synonym for "disposition" (Hexagram 29, fourth line), and sometimes the ability to act on one's disposition. As a synonym for "disposition," it can refer to either the *yin* or *yang* character of a line (Hexagram 18, fifth line). Since *yin* lines have a tendency to descend, a *yin* line stuck in a high position has lost the ability to act on its tendencies, and so may be said to have lost its reality (Hexagram 11, fourth line). A *yin* line, though, is able to act on its tendencies to the extent that it occupies a *yin* position, and so a *yin* line in a *yin* position may be said to acquire reality (Hexagram 39, fourth line, *Symbol*). The *shi* character is also sometimes translated as "fullness," especially when it refers to a line that has a solid center (Hexagram 5, judgment).

Ride (*cheng* 乘): the relationship of a line in a hexagram to the line immediately below it. For example, the third line of a hexagram rides the second. See "serve" for a line's relationship to the line immediately above it.

Ruler (*jun* 君): the person charged with authority over a group. The best rulers are sages (q.v.), and in this sense, the rulers serve as the model of the five constant virtues. Rulers are expected to be humane (Hexagram 52, *Judgment*), and to make themselves straightforward so that everyone else will be straightforward as well (Hexagram 1, *Remarks*). However, the distinctive virtues of rulers are not those of sages. Without someone to enforce them, laws go into decline (Hexagram 37, *Judgment*). The virtue of the ruler, then, is to occupy the position of respect with *yang* firmness (Hexagram 8, *Judgment*). Firmness is required because it prevents one from depending on others for one's position

(Hexagram 16, fifth line). The self-sufficiency imparted by firmness includes being able to make decisions for others (Hexagram 40, second line). This virtue may also be identified with the virtue of primacy, which means "mastery" in the case of rulers (Hexagram 45, fifth line). The state does not necessarily go into decline when a ruler fails to possess this virtue. Rulers may delegate command, in which case the force of the decision remains with them while the reasoning behind it may lie with their ministers. The result is no different than if the whole process had occurred within the ruler (Hexagram 4, fifth line). It is, then, more important for enlightenment to lie in the ministers than in the rulers (Hexagram 39, fifth line). The best rulers are those who combine authority, so that laws do not go into decline, and submissiveness, so that they are able to delegate command to enlightened ministers (Hexagram 15, fifth line). Unlike noble people, who can retreat into hiding when the state declines, rulers are always in public. They are unable to flee from the declining state (Hexagram 33, fifth line), and they cannot leave their post to go on the march (Hexagram 56, fifth line). While remaining in public, they simply become unable to influence the world around them (Hexagram 3, fifth line) and should try not to stand out (Hexagram 36, fifth line). Although they have great power to destroy the state, they are also exposed to the consequences of their bad decisions.

Sage (*sheng* 聖): a person whose teaching effectively reveals the principle of things. There were sages in antiquity who held the position of rulers, but ministers can also be sages (Hexagram 39, fifth line). It is not their position in government that makes people sages, but their possession of great virtue (Hexagram 30, *Symbol*). The greatness of their virtue does not make them superhuman, as they remain one in kind with other people (Hexagram 1, *Remarks*), and they are not all-powerful. They cannot put their way into action whenever they choose but must wait for the appropriate moment to act (Hexagram 25, second line). What they put into action is not their own creation—they simply put things in a position to follow their own innate laws (Hexagram 52, *Judgment*). Sages do not act alone but choose to be assisted by others (Hexagram 28, third line). There will be some moments when they cannot act at all. When the disorder of the world becomes great, for instance, even sages will not be able to stop it (Hexagram 26, fourth line). Like noble people (q.v.), sages will not openly oppose such disorder but will cultivate their virtue on the inside while submitting to the course of affairs on the outside (Hexagram 36, *Judgment*). Sages appear to differ from noble people only in that sages are often rulers, whereas noble people never are. The *Book of Changes* is itself a teaching of the sages. When Cheng

Yi refers to "the sage" in the singular, he is always referring to the author of the *Book of Changes* or one of its ancient commentaries.

Serve (*cheng* 承): the relationship of a line in a hexagram to the line immediately above it. For example, the second line of a hexagram serves the third. See "ride" for a line's relationship to the line immediately below it.

Small people (*xiaoren* 小人): the group of human beings who are motivated by private desire to serve as ministers in government. The more small people there are in government, the fewer noble people there will be (Hexagram 11, Judgment), and vice versa (Hexagram 12, Judgment). The defining characteristic of small people is to act only on "their private intentions" (Hexagram 13, judgment). These private intentions are greed and wrath (Hexagram 63, third line). Small people are incapable of suppressing their desires. When they want something, "they must struggle to achieve it" (Hexagram 15, judgment). Unlike noble people, who are able to see the incipient, small people can only see states of affairs when they are fully manifest and have already come about (Hexagram 53, initial line). Despite the threat that they pose to the state, no one should try to get rid of small people completely, as they can never entirely vanish (Hexagram 58, fifth line). When the text of the *Book of Changes* uses the phrase "small people," it is synonymous with "the people" (Hexagram 20, initial line).

Softness (*rou* 柔): the disposition of *yin qi*. Softness is the ability to receive the influence of others, and to turn that influence into something profitable. Each of these abilities becomes destructive when taken by itself. Those who value softness without qualification become lethargic and haughty (Hexagram 14, fifth line). Excessive receptivity leads to lethargy, as one is sapped of all initiative; excessive concern for profit leads to haughtiness, as one is continually enlarging one's own possessions. The best that soft people can do is to "trace out what is ordinary and keep guard over themselves" (Hexagram 18, fourth line). Since they cannot initiate new action, they "cannot struggle with the moment" (Hexagram 5, fourth line, *Symbol*). If they have the help of firm people, then they can maintain themselves (Hexagram 27, fifth line). In other words, softness avoids becoming excessive by maintaining a relationship with something firm, not by becoming firm itself. The very lack of initiative in softness can be a virtue, as it prevents people from becoming restless (Hexagram 53, initial line) and arrogant (Hexagram 54, fifth line).

Son of heaven (*tianzi* 天子): the ruler of the world. While each of the various marquises governs a single state, "the son of heaven nourishes the world" (Hexagram 27, second line). The world in question here is composed of the states or kingdoms occupying the central plain of classical China. The term is much less common in the *Book of Changes* than the synonymous term "king."

Spontaneous (*ziran* 自然): occurring without reflection or intention, but not by chance. When people act spontaneously, their action is not based on their previous knowledge or evaluation of the situation (Hexagram 20, *Symbol*); when they cause something outside of them to happen spontaneously, it does not come about because of their intention or desire (Hexagram 25, second line); when things occur spontaneously by themselves, it is not by chance, but by the pattern of action contained in their disposition (Hexagram 22, *Judgment*). Although the word *ziran* is composed of one character that means "self" and another that means "thus," and so literally means "self-thus" or "what has come to be so by itself," spontaneity nevertheless requires the help of others. That is, spontaneous activity comes about because of a particular configuration of things, rather than because of one person's reflection or intention, or because of one thing's internal structure. For instance, when people assist receptive officials spontaneously (Hexagram 42, second line), the officials must make themselves receptive, but there must also be other people to come and assist them. The spontaneous principle links the action of the people with the virtue of the officials.

Straight (*zhi* 直): see "straightforwardness."

Straightforwardness (*zheng* 正): the virtue of regularity or extending in a straight line. Cheng Yi occasionally means geometrical straightness (Hexagram 50, *Symbol*), but straightness is usually a metaphor for a relation between things with an obvious similarity. Such things are better able to perform their distinctive function by teaming up. When a *yang* line is in a *yang* position, it is said to be in its straightforward position, better able to carry out the distinctive function of *yang*. The same goes for *yin* lines—straightforwardness is a virtue that belongs equally to *yin* and *yang* (Hexagram 59, fourth line). The receptivity of *yin*, however, makes it liable to change when it receives different commands, and so it is incapable of "great straightforwardness" (Hexagram 40, third line). Lines in the same relative positions in the lower and upper trigrams have the ability to correspond straightforwardly, so long as one of them is *yang* and one is *yin*. Straightforward correspondence may occur no matter which line is on top, but in general, it is straightforward for *yang* to be above *yin* (Hexagram 53, judgment). The position above is a *yang* position, and *yang* lines are straightforward when in *yang* positions. Straightforwardness is more or less synonymous with the rarer term "straightness" (*zhi* 直), although Cheng Yi says that "straightness" is of slightly less significance (Hexagram 47, fifth line, *Symbol*).

Substance (*ti* 體): either a thing's *qi* or its form. On rare occasion, it describes the form of an entire hexagram (Hexagram 25, *Judgment*). More often, it refers to the form of a trigram (Hexagram 30, third line). Three *yang* lines, for instance, constitute the Lead trigram substance. No line has its own substance; each line is part of the substance of the trigram by its relation to two nearby lines. As describing the visible form of a thing, the *ti* character is often used as a verb. It refers to drawing close to something and making it effective (Hexagram 1, *Remarks*), as when "the king gives substance to the way of heaven" (Hexagram 1, *Judgment*). The way of something, or the function of something, cannot accomplish anything until there is someone to give it substance.

Tendency (*zhi* 志): a potential for action, usually a line's potential for movement up or down within a hexagram. This potential will actualize itself unless an outside force prevents it. *Yang* lines have a tendency to move upward. *Yin* lines have a tendency to move downward. Various kinds of tendency may be referred to as "desire," "disposition," "inclination," and "intention" (q.v.).

Terrain (*di* 地): a synonym for "position," but referring properly to all possible positions and not only those in government. Cheng Yi frequently uses the phrase "terrain without a position" when discussing people who do not have a position in government, but who do have a function to perform (Hexagram 19, top line). Possibly thinking of the term's use in military strategy, he often refers either to a perilous terrain or a terrain of peace and ease (Hexagram 39, judgment). In these cases, the meaning of the term comes close to the meaning of "propensity" (q.v.). The *di* character may also refer to the earth itself, in which case it is translated as "earth." The earth is what brings things to birth and completion (Hexagram 2, judgment). It also possesses the ability to yield (Hexagram 2, *Symbol*), in both senses of the English word. It yields to the activity of heaven, and it yields life on its own surface.

Text (*wen* 文): see "pattern."

Trigram (*gua* 卦): see "hexagram."

Virtue (*de* 德): a synonym for "tendency." The two basic virtues of Cheng Yi's commentary are *yang* firmness, which is the virtue of the ruler (Hexagram 8, *Judgment*), and *yin* softness, which is the way of the minister (Hexagram 2, judgment). There are two other sets of virtues that appear throughout the commentary. The first set is "primacy, progress, profit, and purity" (Hexagram 1, judgment). Primacy is one of these virtues, but it also contains the rest (Hexagram 1, *Judgment*). It is the virtue of the ruler, and so is associated with *yang* firmness (Hexagram 8, *Judgment*). The second set of virtues consists of centrality (q.v.) and straightforwardness (q.v.). Noble people cultivate virtue before they try to influence other people (Hexagram 5, *Symbol*). In fact, one of the distinctive features of noble people is the ability to possess virtue without occupying a position in government (Hexagram 15, judgment). Such virtue is not complete. Virtue is completed when it leads to action (Hexagram 1, *Remarks*), and only someone with political power can bring this action about. Those who have it should "visit the king's court" to make the force of their wisdom effective (Hexagram 20, fourth line). By the same token, those who have already reached a state of abundance no longer need virtue, as there is nothing left to be done (Hexagram 35, *Sequence*). Virtue is not entirely useless without political power. People can still model themselves on the virtue of noble people who have no position in government (Hexagram 20, top line, *Symbol*). Since virtue is simply the tendency to do something, it can be bad (Hexagram 47, third line), as in the case of the virtue of rebellion (Hexagram 30, fourth line).

Way (*dao* 道): the link between the virtue that allows one to occupy a position and the position that one occupies. It is more familiar to Western readers when Romanized as "Tao," as in Taoism and the *Tao Te Ching*. Because the way constitutes a link rather than the virtue and position that it links together, it can be described as the way of either the virtue or the position. For instance, ministers are said to be on the way of submissiveness, but submissiveness is also the way of ministers (Hexagram 64, second line). Cheng Yi treats "way" as synonymous with "law" (Hexagram 1, *Remarks*), perhaps because he thinks of laws not primarily as decrees but as necessary connections between things. Since connections by themselves are not things, the way is of no value in itself but must be given substance (Hexagram 25, *Symbol*) or put into action (Hexagram 40, second line). Some ways are good and some are bad. There are ways of misfortune (Hexagram 3, fifth line), of peril (Hexagram 9, top line), and of confusion (Hexagram 24, top line). When used without qualification, the term "way" refers to the way of heaven and earth, which is the way of *yin* and *yang* (Hexagram 15, *Judgment*). This is why noble people can control their desires with the way (Hexagram 33, fourth line), because the way of heaven and earth is impersonal.

Yang (陽): possessing the tendency to rise and lead. This tendency can arise either from one's position or from one's substance or *qi*. Rising and leading cannot occur in isolation. There must something displaced by one's ascent, just as there must be something that one leads, and so *yang* cannot act without its *yin* counterpart. In the cosmos, the *yang qi* appears at the center of the earth on the winter solstice (Hexagram 24, *Sequence*), and it slowly grows and rises over the next six months, bringing heat and dryness. When it begins to interact with the *yin qi* above it, they produce clouds and thunder (Hexagram 3, *Sequence*). When their interaction is complete, rain falls (Hexagram 9, judgment), which is ultimately responsible for the birth and growth of everything on the surface of the earth. In human beings, *yang* takes the form of decisiveness (Hexagram 57, top line) and enjoyment (Hexagram 57, judgment). To lead effectively one must be able to make decisions, and the ordinary goal of the decisions is to satisfy oneself. Since *yin* carries out the decisions *yang* has made, it provides enjoyment to *yang*, and is itself often identified as what *yang* enjoys (Hexagram 33, third line).

Yin (陰): possessing the tendency to descend and yield. This tendency can arise either from one's position or from one's substance or *qi*. Descending and yielding cannot occur in isolation. There must be something displaced by one's descent, as there must be something to which one yields, and so *yin* cannot act without its *yang* counterpart. In the cosmos, the *yin qi* appears at the center of the earth on the summer solstice (Hexagram 23, *Judgment*), and it slowly grows and rises over the next six months, bringing cold and dampness. In human beings, *yin* takes the form of beauty (Hexagram 44, second line) and lowliness (Hexagram 57, judgment). The beauty of *yin* is what draws the attention of *yang*, but it must also conceal this beauty (Hexagram 2, third line) so as not to usurp its *yang* counterpart and lose the quality of lowliness.

NOTES

TRANSLATOR'S NOTE

1. Richard Wilhelm and Cary F. Baynes, trans., *The I-Ching or Book of Changes* (1950; Princeton, NJ: Princeton University Press, 1967), 163.
2. Richard John Lynn, trans., *The Classic of Changes: A New Translation of the I Ching as Interpreted by Wang Bi* (New York: Columbia University Press, 1994), 129; John Minford, *I-Ching* (New York: Penguin Books, 2015), 9.

INTRODUCTION

1. Richard J. Smith, *Fathoming the Cosmos and Ordering the World* (Charlottesville: University of Virginia Press, 2008), 1.
2. Kidder Smith Jr. et al., *Sung Dynasty Uses of the I-Ching* (Princeton, NJ: Princeton University Press, 1990), ix. See also G. E. Kidder Smith Jr., "Cheng Yi's (1033–1107) Commentary on the *Yijing*" (PhD diss., University of California, Berkeley, 1979), iv–v.
3. Tze-ki Hon 韓子奇, *The Yijing and Chinese Politics* (Albany: State University of New York Press, 2005), 1–2.
4. Lynn, *Classic of Changes*, 7–8.
5. Hon, *Yijing and Chinese Politics*, 4.
6. Lynn, *Classic of Changes*, 9.
7. For the various titles and formats taken by the commentary, see Bent Nielsen, *A Companion to Yi Jing Numerology and Cosmology* (London: RoutledgeCurzon, 2003), 32–33. There are no extended biographical resources on Cheng Yi in English. In Chinese, see Yao Mingda 姚名達, *Cheng Yichuan nianpu* 程伊川年譜 (Shanghai 上海: Shangwu yinshuguan 商務印書館, 1937). There are two English-language monographs on the philosophy of Cheng Yi and his brother Cheng Hao: A. C. Graham, *Two Chinese Philosophers: The Metaphysics of the Brothers Ch'êng* (1958; La Salle, IL: Open Court, 1992); Yong Huang, *Why Be Moral? Learning from the Neo-Confucian Cheng Brothers* (Albany: State University of New York Press, 2014).

8. See Cheng Yi's "Preface to the Commentary on the *Book of Changes*."

9. Lynn, *Classic of Changes*, 6 claims that previous English translations "for the most part are principally derived directly or indirectly from some combination of the commentaries of the Neo-Confucians Cheng Yi (1033–1107) and Zhu Xi (1130–1200)," and that most modern Chinese editions "also closely follow the commentaries of Cheng Yi and Zhu Xi." See also Smith, "Cheng Yi's (1033–1107) Commentary on the *Yijing*," iv.

10. James Legge, *The Yî King* (Oxford, UK: Clarendon Press, 1882); Richard Wilhelm, *I-Ging: das Buch der Wandlungen* (Jena, Germany: E. Diederichs, 1924).

11. These two features of Cheng Yi's commentary were both noticed by Zhu Xi, although Zhu Xi considered them defects. On the thoroughness of the *Yi River Commentary*, see *Zhuzi yulei* 朱子語類, "Xuewu" 學五, 116: "Even when something has already been discussed, he discusses it further. This is why, when people today contemplate the *Book of Changes*, they no longer read the original classic, but only study his commentary." On the philosophy of the *Yi River Commentary*, see *Zhuzi yulei*, "Yisan" 易三, "Chengzi Yizhuan" 程子易傳, 12: "Yi River simply used the *Book of Changes* to produce metaphorical interpretations." For more on Zhu Xi's criticisms, see Smith et al., *Sung Dynasty Uses of the I-Ching*, 179–88.

12. This set of figures is divided into two unequal parts, one with the first thirty and the other with the remaining thirty-two. On possible reasons for this division, see Edward A. Hacker and Steve Moore, "A Brief Note on the Two-Part Division of the Received Order of the Hexagrams in the *Zhouyi*," *Journal of Chinese Philosophy* 30, no. 2 (June 2003): 219–21.

13. Smith, "Cheng Yi's (1033–1107) Commentary on the *Yijing*," 90. Smith says that Hu's "concerns are similar to Cheng Yi's, but their expression is rudimentary. Hu lacks the subtle inquisitiveness of Cheng's investigation of the principles of the world. Nor does he possess Cheng's willingness to consider the range of negative and positive possibilities." For a detailed study of Hu's commentary, see Tze-ki Hon, "Eremitism, Sagehood, and Public Service: the *Zhouyi Kouyi* of Hu Yuan," *Monumenta Serica* 48 (2000): 67–92; Hon, *Yijing and Chinese Politics*, 49–68.

14. There has been some discussion in recent years about whether the Chinese character *li* is better translated as "coherence" than "principle." Willard Peterson, in "Another Look at Li," *Bulletin of Sung and Yüan Studies* 18 (1986): 13–31, argues for translating it as "coherence." In *Ironies of Oneness and Difference: Coherence in Early Chinese Thought* (Albany: State University of New York Press, 2012), 9, Brook Ziporyn explains why he refers to *li* as "coherence" while also acknowledging that it may sometimes be better translated as "principle" or some other word. Philip J. Ivanhoe, in his review of Peter K. Bol, *Neo-Confucianism in History*, in *Dao: A Journal of Comparative Philosophy* 9 (2010): 471–75, argues for continuing to translate *li* as "principle."

15. Hexagram 64, *Sequence*. Cheng Yi's remarks on the *Sequence* occur in the first paragraph of his commentary on each hexagram. For other meanings of the *yi* character, see Hon, *Yijing and Chinese Politics*, 31.

16. Hexagram 43, second line, *Symbol*.

17. See Smith, *Fathoming the Cosmos*, 229–31.

18. See Smith et al., *Sung Dynasty Uses of the I-Ching*, 212–14.

19. For the claim that Cheng Yi never recommends divination, see Smith et al., *Sung Dynasty Uses of the I-Ching*, 164, 212. On whether the *Book of Changes* is a divination text, according to Cheng Yi, see Smith et al., *Sung Dynasty Uses of the I-Ching*, 182–84; Wing-tsit Chan 陳榮捷, *Reflections on Things at Hand* (New York: Columbia University Press, 1967), xxxiv–xxxv.

20. Hexagram 41, fifth line. See also Hexagram 42, second line. For other interpretations of this passage, see Lynn, *Classic of Changes*, 395n18.

21. Hexagram 49, fifth line.

22. Hexagram 8, judgment.

23. On the actions symbolized by the eight trigrams, see Hexagram 29, *Sequence*.

24. Hexagram 3, top line, *Symbol*.

25. Graham, *Two Chinese Philosophers*, 159; Don J. Wyatt, *The Recluse of Loyang: Shao Yung and the Moral Evolution of Early Sung Thought* (Honolulu: University of Hawai'i Press, 1996), 86–88.

26. Cheng Yi says that principle is without form at *Er Cheng ji* 二程集 (Beijing: Zhonghua Shuju, 1981), 271; see also Hexagram 1, initial line. On the concept of principle in Cheng Yi, see Graham, *Two Chinese Philosophers*, 8–22; Huang, *Why Be Moral*, 200–208; Michael Harrington, "Principle and Place: Complementary Concepts in Confucian *Yijing* Commentary," *Philosophy East and West* 66, no. 3 (2016): 861–82.

27. For women as *yin*, see Hexagram 2, fifth line; for women as *yang*, see Hexagram 54, fourth line.

28. For noble people as *yang*, see Hexagram 11, judgment; for noble people as *yin*, see Hexagram 2, judgment: "The actions of noble people are soft and submissive."

29. Hexagram 32, *Judgment*.

30. See Hexagram 12, *Judgment*.

31. Compare the claim made in the *Huainanzi* 淮南子, "Yuandaoxun" 原道訓, 4–5, that employing *yin* and *yang* is like riding a horse or steering a chariot. For an English translation, see Liu An 劉安, *The Huainanzi: A Guide to the Theory and Practice of Government in Early Han China*, trans. John S. Major et al. (New York: Columbia University Press, 2010), 52.

32. Cheng Yi explains this model of hexagram construction at Hexagram 22, *Judgment*.

33. On using *yin* and *yang* in evaluating the balance and imbalance of functions in the human body, see Robin R. Wang, *Yinyang: The Way of Heaven and Earth in Chinese Thought and Culture* (Cambridge: Cambridge University Press, 2012), 163–81.

34. See Smith, *Fathoming the Cosmos*, 67.

35. See Chan, *Reflections on Things at Hand*, 12.

36. See *Er Cheng ji*, 148/4, 165/9. Cheng Yi is not saying that *qi* itself is produced or destroyed, but that the always-existing "primary *qi*" (*zhenyuan zhi qi* 真元之氣) produces new *yin* or *yang qi* rather than relocating previously existing *yin* or *yang qi*. Graham, *Two Chinese Philosophers*, 41–42, claims that this account represents "strong personal opinions" of Cheng Yi himself rather than "current views" concerning *qi*.

37. On categorization as a method for acquiring knowledge in classical China, see Derk Bodde, "Types of Chinese Categorical Thinking," in *Essays on Chinese Civilization*,

ed. Charles Le Blanc and Dorothy Borei (Princeton, NJ: Princeton University Press, 1981), 141–60. For the specific discussion of *lei*, see Yuan Jinmei, "'Kinds, Lei 類' in Ancient Chinese Logic: A Comparison to 'Categories' in Aristotelian Logic," *History of Philosophy Quarterly* 22, no. 3 (2005): 181–200; Wang, *Yinyang*, 85–96.

38. See Hexagram 13, *Symbol*.

39. Hon, *Yijing and Chinese Politics*, 113: "The commentary was not merely another reading of the *Yijing*, but also a testimony of late Northern Song politics and an attempt to redefine the role of the educated elite in an age of factionalism." See also 134: "in emphasizing the need for civil bureaucrats to form their own factions in government and to transform society through moral education, he gave the educated elite a new identity."

40. For Shun, see Hexagram 45, fifth line; for King Cheng, see Hexagram 16, fifth line; for the Duke of Zhou, see Hexagram 18, second line.

41. See Hexagram 14, third line.

42. See Hexagram 10, *Symbol*.

43. See Lynn, *Classic of Changes*, 33.

44. See Hexagram 21, initial line.

45. On the straightforwardness of a *yin* line in the initial position and a *yang* line in the sixth position, see Hexagram 53, judgment.

46. *Er Cheng ji*, 164/5. For more on this subject, see Smith et al., *Sung Dynasty Uses of the I-Ching*, 156.

47. See "Preface to the Commentary on the *Book of Changes*."

48. Cheng Yi describes the *Book of Changes* as "altering and moving without constancy" in Hexagram 12, initial line. See also Hexagram 36, fifth line, and Hexagram 45, third line.

PREFACE TO THE COMMENTARY ON THE *BOOK OF CHANGES*

1. *Appended Statements* (Xici 繫辭) 2.10; *Explanation of the Trigrams* (Shuogua 說卦), 2; *Appended Statements* 1.11. Where no printed edition is mentioned, references to Chinese texts include their paragraph number at the Chinese Text Project (http://www.ctext.org), edited by Donald Sturgeon. The project is an open-access digital library of Chinese texts. All translations are mine.

2. *Appended Statements* 1.10.

3. Hexagram 1, *Remarks on the Text* (Wenyan 文言).

4. *Appended Statements* 1.2.

5. *Appended Statements* 1.8.

6. This is the year 1099. The Yuanfu 元符 era of emperor Huizong 徽宗 began in 1098.

1. LEAD (QIAN 乾)

1. All text in boldface belongs to the *Zhouyi zhengyi* 周易正義 edition of the *Book of Changes* and its ancient commentaries. The rest is Cheng Yi's commentary. All numbered endnotes are my own.

2. The three powers are heaven, earth, and human beings. See the *Explanation of the Trigrams*, 2. The sage who invented the trigrams is traditionally understood to be Fu Xi 伏羲, but Cheng Yi 程頤 never identifies him explicitly.

3. See Hexagram 1, *Remarks on the Text*.

4. The claim that these four virtues appear only in Hexagrams 1 and 2 cannot be taken at face value, as they can be found together in many other hexagram judgments. More likely, Cheng Yi means that only Hexagrams 1 and 2 give them the specific meanings he has just described. As he goes on to say, their meanings are different when they are found in other hexagrams.

5. Cheng Yi is explaining why the *Book of Changes* (*Yijing* 易經) refers to a *yang* 陽 line as a "nine" line. The "*yang* numbers" are the odd numbers, and the number nine is the "most abundant" of these because there is no higher odd number in the number series. On the identification of *yang* lines as "nine" and *yin* 陰 lines as "six," see Richard J. Smith, *Fathoming the Cosmos and Ordering the World* (Charlottesville: University of Virginia Press, 2008), 26.

6. In his commentary on the *Judgment* (*Tuan* 彖) of Hexagram 49, Cheng Yi notes that the *xi* 息 character of "comes to rest" can mean either "stops" or "is born." Here it means "is born."

7. The respect shown to Shun by his neighbors when he plowed and fished is described in Sima Qian 司馬遷, *The Grand Scribe's Records* 史記, "Wudi benji" 五帝本紀, 21. For an English translation, see Ssu-ma Ch'ien, *The Grand Scribe's Records—Volume I: The Basic Annals of Pre-Han China*, ed. William H. Nienhauser Jr. (Bloomington: Indiana University Press, 1995), 11.

8. That is, the lines of Hexagram 1 are uniformly *yang*, and the lines of Hexagram 2 are uniformly *yin*.

9. The third and fourth positions are traditionally regarded as belonging to humanity. The initial and second positions belong to earth, while the fifth and top positions belong to heaven.

10. *Book of History* (*Shujing* 書經), "Shundian" 舜典, 1. See James Legge, trans., *The Chinese Classics*, vol. 3, *The Shoo King* (1865; Hong Kong: Hong Kong University Press, 1960), 29. The sage-king Yao 堯 heard of the "mysterious virtue" of Shun 舜 when the latter was simply an unmarried man without an official position.

11. *Book of History*, "Yaodian" 堯典, 3 (Legge, 26). The sage-king Yao sent his two daughters to be the wives of Shun, intending to see whether Shun was capable of bringing harmony to his family. This was his "test."

12. Only Hexagrams 1 and 2 have a seventh line statement, referred to as the "employment of the lines." Commentators disagree on the meaning of this line, and Cheng Yi offers no interpretation of his own.

13. The *Judgment* consists of the first and second of the classical commentaries on the *Book of Changes* known as the Ten Wings (*Shiyi* 十翼). Its comments on the first thirty hexagram judgments constitute the first Wing, and the second Wing contains comments on the remaining hexagram judgments. Cheng Yi's text puts the portion of the *Judgment* that is relevant to a particular hexagram immediately after the judgment of that hexagram.

14. Fuzi 夫子 simply means "the master" and is a respectful way of referring to Confucius (*Kongzi* 孔子). Cheng Yi, like many of his contemporaries and predecessors, considers Confucius the author of the Ten Wings.

15. The five constant virtues are humaneness, duty, ritual, wisdom, and believability.

16. The *Symbol* (*Xiang* 象) consists of the third and fourth of the classical commentaries on the *Book of Changes* known as the Ten Wings. The third Wing—sometimes called the *Great Symbol* (*Daxiang* 大象)—identifies the symbolic content of the two trigrams composing each hexagram, and the use to which this content may be put. In Cheng Yi's text, it has been divided up into sixty-four sections, with the relevant section for each hexagram located after the portion of the *Judgment* that comments on that hexagram. The fourth Wing—sometimes called the *Small Symbol* (*Xiaoxiang* 小象)—makes brief comments on each of the line statements, and these comments have also been divided up and located after the lines on which they comment.

17. The *Remarks on the Text* is the seventh of the classical commentaries known as the Ten Wings. Its comments are restricted to Hexagrams 1 and 2.

18. Reading "ritual" (*li* 禮) with the *Er Cheng quanshu* 二程全書 (n.p.: 1865), rather than "substance" (*ti* 體) with Wang Xiaoyu 王孝魚, ed., *Er Cheng ji* 二程集 (Beijing 北京: Zhonghua shuju 中華書局, 1981).

19. The *Er Cheng ji* notes that one text has "straightforward" rather than "pure" here.

20. *Book of History,* "Yaodian," 4 (Legge, 26). When the sage-king Yao was looking for his successor, he asked one of his ministers to find for him either someone among the enlightened or someone "ensconced among the rustics." The minister proposed Yao's eventual successor Shun as an example of the latter.

21. *Mencius* 5B1. See James Legge, trans., *The Chinese Classics,* vol. 2, *The Works of Mencius* (Oxford: Clarendon Press, 1895), 372. The quoted passage describes the character of Kongzi using a metaphor from music. When many instruments play together, there must be a "sorting according to principle" so that they harmonize. Some should play first, and others should play afterward. Kongzi likewise is capable of displaying each component of his character at the appropriate time.

22. The saying that "people are things" (*ren wu ye* 人物也) occurs several times in the work of Wang Chong 王充, who uses the phrase to argue that human beings do not differ radically from other creatures. A similar view appears in the work of Cheng Yi's contemporary and rival Shao Yong 邵雍. See Don J. Wyatt, *The Recluse of Loyang: Shao Yung and the Moral Evolution of Early Sung Thought* (Honolulu: University of Hawai'i Press, 1996), 183.

23. Hexagram 6, initial line, *Symbol.*

24. See Hexagram 48, initial line, *Symbol,* for Cheng Yi's claim that the *she* 舍 character should not be translated as "abandonment" here.

25. The *Er Cheng ji* notes that one text says that the world "sees its pattern and enlightenment and is transformed."

26. Yu 禹 was the successor to the sage-king Shun. Neither Yu nor Shun inherited the throne by being the son of the previous king but were chosen by the previous king because of their worthiness.

27. Yi Yin 伊尹 worked in the fields before becoming minister to the Shang 商 dynasty king Cheng Tang 成湯, as noted at *Mencius* 5A7 (Legge, 360). Fu Yue 傅說 was a

builder before becoming minister to the Shang dynasty king Wu Ding 武丁, as noted at *Mencius* 6B15 (Legge, 446).

2. YIELD (*KUN* 坤)

1. The configuration of the trigrams known as "later heaven" locates the Yield trigram in the southwestern corner. See the depiction of this configuration in Smith, *Fathoming the Cosmos*, 47.

2. Reading "in the number eight" (*ba* 八) with the *Er Cheng quanshu*, rather than "in its entrance" (*ru* 入) with the *Er Cheng ji*. At *Er Cheng ji*, 250, Cheng Yi claims that people mistakenly refer to "six" as old *yin* and "eight" as lesser *yin*. He says there that it is the Yellow River Chart (*Hetu* 河圖) that clarifies why, if the number six is exceeded, *yang* has already appeared and there is no longer uniform *yin*. For the Yellow River Chart, see Bent Nielsen, *A Companion to Yi Jing Numerology and Cosmology* (New York: RoutledgeCurzon, 2003), 103–5.

3. *Mencius* 2A2 (Legge, 190). The full statement reads: "It is extremely great and extremely firm, because it is nourished by straightness." Mencius is saying that people whose actions are "straight" will thereby nourish their *qi* 氣, which will then become "extremely great and extremely firm."

4. On Fuzi, see Hexagram 1, *Judgment* and note.

5. Hou Yi 后羿 was an archer who seized the throne from King Taikang 太康 of the Xia 夏 dynasty. See Herbert A. Giles, *A Chinese Biographical Dictionary* (1898; Taipei: Literature House, 1962), 268–69. Wang Mang 王莽 was an official during the Han 漢 dynasty who first served as regent to several young emperors, then declared himself emperor and established the short-lived Xin 新 dynasty. See Denis Twitchett and Michael Loewe, eds., *The Cambridge History of China* (Cambridge: Cambridge University Press, 1986), 1:224–31.

6. Nu Wa 女媧 is a mythical figure sometimes regarded as one of the first rulers of China. See Giles, *A Chinese Biographical Dictionary*, 601. Wu Zetian 武則天 was the only woman in Chinese history to claim the title "emperor" (*huangdi* 皇帝). See Denis Crispin Twitchett, ed., *The Cambridge History of China—Vol. 3: Sui and T'ang China, 589–906, Pt. 1* (Cambridge: Cambridge University Press, 1979), 306.

7. For the affairs of Tang 湯 and Wu 武, see Hexagram 49, *Judgment*.

8. For the phrase "endless end," see Hexagram 54, *Symbol*.

9. See the hexagram judgment: "At first, there is confusion, but later acquisition and the mastery of profit."

3. BLOCK (*ZHUN* 屯)

1. Beginning with Hexagram 3, Cheng Yi quotes and discusses a relevant portion of the eighth of the Ten Wings—the *Sequence of the Hexagrams* (*Xugua* 序卦)—before turning to the judgment of each hexagram.

2. In classical China, the "marquises" (*hou* 侯) or "various marquises" (*zhuhou* 諸侯) ruled the various states in the name of the emperor.

3. That is, there is no difference in meaning between "it is someone blocked" and "it is like someone blocked."

4. Duke Zhao 昭公, the nominal ruler of the state of Lu 魯, tried to assert his authority over the powerful Ji 季 family but failed and was forced into exile: *The Grand Scribe's Records*, "Lu Zhougong shijia" 魯周公世家, 62. For an English translation, see Ssuma Ch'ien, *The Grand Scribe's Records—Volume V.1: The Hereditary Houses of Pre-Han China, Part I*, ed. William H. Nienhauser Jr. (Bloomington: Indiana University Press, 2006), 155–56. The Duke of Gaogui Village 高貴鄉公 was a title given to Cao Mao 曹髦, who became emperor of Wei 魏 and was killed while trying to take power from his regents. See Victor Cunrui Xiong, *A Historical Dictionary of Medieval China* (Lanham, MD: Scarecrow Press, 2009), 73.

5. Pan Geng 盤庚 and King Xuan 宣王 both reestablished the power of their respective royal houses over the various marquises. Before Pan Geng took the throne of the Shang dynasty, the various marquises had not come to the imperial court for several years. Pan Geng's virtue is said to have moved them to attend on him at court. See *The Grand Scribe's Records*, "Yin benji" 殷本紀, 21 (Nienhauser, 1:47). During his lengthy reign, King Xuan sought to restore the power of the Zhou 周 royal house over the various marquises. See Michael Loewe and Edward L. Shaughnessy, eds., *The Cambridge History of Ancient China: From the Origins of Civilization to 221 B.C.* (Cambridge: Cambridge University Press, 1999), 345–48.

6. See Hexagram 2, initial line, *Symbol* for the line "it steadily brings about its way."

7. The Tang 唐 dynasty collapsed during the reigns of emperors Xizong 僖宗 and his younger brother Zhaozong 昭宗. Xizong was in the control of his chief eunuch and has sometimes been regarded as abandoning affairs of government for study and amusement. See Twitchett, *Cambridge History of China—vol. 3, pt. 1*, 714–15. Zhaozong was powerless to save the dynasty from the conflict created by eunuchs at court. See Twitchett, *Cambridge History of China—vol. 3, pt. 1*, 773–81.

4. BLIND (MENG 蒙)

1. *Mencius* 2B2 (Legge, 214).

2. *Book of Rites* (*Liji* 禮記), "Xueji" 學記, 8. See James Legge, trans., *The Sacred Books of China: The Texts of Confucianism, Parts III-IV—The Lî Kî* (Oxford: Clarendon Press, 1885), 2:86. Cheng Yi quotes the same passage in Hexagram 26, fourth line.

3. *Book of Rites*, "Yueji" 樂記, 26 (Legge, 2:107).

4. A reference to *Analects* (*Lunyu* 論語) 2.3. See James Legge, trans., *The Chinese Classics*, vol. 1, *Confucian Analects, The Great Learning, and the Doctrine of the Mean* (Oxford: Clarendon Press, 1893), 146.

5. The Warring States period Confucian Xunzi 荀子 uses this phrase to criticize the improper application of punishment at "Fuguo" 富國, 14. See Eric L. Hutton, trans., *Xunzi: The Complete Text* (Princeton, NJ: Princeton University Press, 2014), 92.

6. "Immensity" refers to tolerance and generosity in Cheng Yi's commentary on Hexagram 2, *Judgment*.

7. *Book of History*, "Lüxing" 呂刑, 3 (Legge, 593). In this chapter, an unidentified sage-king (presumably Shun) asks questions of the people and hears widows make

statements against the Miao 苗 tribe (presumably because the tribe killed their husbands).

8. See the *Book of History*, "Dayumo" 大禹謨, 19 (Legge, 64–65).

9. The "three deputies" are Guan 管, Cai 蔡, and Huo 霍, all brothers of the Duke of Zhou. They served as marquises when the Duke of Zhou was regent, but when they rebelled against him, he put Guan to death, imprisoned Cai, and stripped Huo of his title. See the *Book of History*, "Caizhongzhiming" 蔡仲之命, 1 (Legge, 487).

10. Huang 皇, who reunified China and founded the Qin 秦 dynasty, also engaged in a campaign of territorial expansion. See Twitchett and Loewe, *Cambridge History of China—vol. 1*, 64–66. Wu 武, the seventh emperor of the Han dynasty, waged massive military campaigns to expand the territory of China. See Twitchett and Loewe, *Cambridge History of China—vol. 1*, 163–70.

5. NEED (*XU* 需)

1. On Fuzi, see Hexagram 1, *Judgment* and note.

2. *Book of Rites*, "Zhongyong" 中庸, 14 (Legge, 2:306–7).

6. FIGHT (*SONG* 訟)

1. *Book of History*, "Yaodian," 3 (Legge, 25).

2. *Mencius* 1B4 (Legge, 160).

7. TROOP (*SHI* 師)

1. *The Grand Scribe's Records*, "Sima Rangju liezhuan" 司馬穰苴, 1. For an English translation, see Ssu-ma Ch'ien, *The Grand Scribe's Records—Volume VII: The Memoirs of Pre-Han China*, ed. William H. Nienhauser Jr. (Bloomington: Indiana University Press, 1995), 33–34. Zhuang Jia 莊賈 was appointed to watch over the army of Duke Jing 景 of Qi 齊 until his general Sima Rangju 司馬穰苴 had earned the respect of the troops, but Zhuang Jia showed his own form of disrespect by showing up late for a meeting. By putting Zhuang Jia to death, Sima gained the respect of the troops.

2. *The Grand Scribe's Records*, "Huaiyinhou liezhuan" 淮陰侯列傳. For an English translation, see Burton Watson, trans., *Records of the Grand Historian—Han Dynasty I* (1961; New York: Columbia University Press, 1993), 163–84.

3. The phrase "soldier of duty" is common in classical Chinese sources. At *Wuzi* 吳子, "Tuguo" 圖國, 5, it is employed as the name for one of five kinds of soldier, the kind that "prohibits violence and saves others from disorder." See Ralph D. Sawyer, trans., *The Seven Military Classics of Ancient China* (Boulder, CO: Westview Press, 1993), 208.

4. *Book of History*, "Zhonghuizhigao" 仲虺之誥, 2 (Legge, 180). When the founder of the Shang dynasty restored order to the east with his troops, those in the west wished he would do the same for them.

5. The story of how the Duke of Zhou came to receive the honors of a king is told in *The Grand Scribe's Records*, "Lu Zhougong shijia," 12 (Nienhauser, 5.1: 139–40).

6. *Mencius* 4A19 (Legge, 310).

7. Cheng Yi here follows his teacher at the imperial academy in Kaifeng 開封, Hu Yuan 胡瑗. The *Zhouyi kouyi* 周易口義, a record of Hu's lectures on the *Book of Changes*, reads the phrase *yushi* 輿尸 as meaning a "crowd of masters." See the *Yingyin Wenyuange Siku quanshu* 影印文淵閣四庫全書 (Taibei 台北: Shangwu 商務, 1983–1986), 8–224. For the more customary reading of it as "carriages to transport corpses," see Richard John Lynn, trans., *The Classic of Changes: A New Translation of the I Ching as Interpreted by Wang Bi* (New York: Columbia University Press, 1994), 179.

8. *Book of History*, "Shundian," 12 (Legge, 44).

9. Cheng Yi names emperors infamous for their use of brutal military force. The founder of the Qin dynasty used military force to reunify China, while the seventh emperor of the Han dynasty used it to expand the territory of China. See also Hexagram 4, top line.

10. The general Xun Linfu 荀林父 advocated making peace with the armies of Chu 楚, but others in his army forced a confrontation. Their defeat at Bi 邲 is graphically described in the *Zuozhuan* 左傳, "Xuangong shiernian" 宣公十二年, 2. See James Legge, trans., *The Chinese Classics*, vol. 5, *The Ch'un Ts'ew* [*Chunqiu* 春秋], *with the Tso Chuen* (1872; Hong Kong: Hong Kong University Press, 1960), 316–21. Guo Ziyi 郭子儀 was one of two generals charged with leading the imperial army against the Anshi 安史 rebellion. When retreating from the rebel stronghold at Xiangzhou 相州, each general retreated toward his own base, bringing about defeat. See David Graff, *Medieval Chinese Warfare, 300–900* (London: Routledge, 2002), 222.

11. Ying Bu 英布 and Peng Yue 彭越 fought for the king of Han during the early years of the Han dynasty. The king rewarded Ying by making him king of Huainan 淮南, but Ying later led a rebellion against him. Likewise, the king rewarded Peng by making him king of Liang 梁, only to find evidence that Peng, too, was planning a revolt. See *The Grand Scribe's Records*, "Weibao Pengyue liezhuan" 魏豹彭越列傳 and "Qingbu liezhuan" 黥布列傳 (Watson, 148–62).

8. CLOSE (*BI* 比)

1. *Mixed Hexagrams* (*Zagua* 雜卦), 2.

2. *Zuozhuan*, "Zhaogong Yuannian" 昭公元年, 2 (Legge, 578). Zixi 子晳 and Zinan 子南 competed for a woman's hand in marriage. She observed that Zixi was beautiful, but Zinan was grand.

3. *Zuozhuan*, "Xuangong Shiernian" 宣公十二年, 2 (Legge, 824). Shusun Wushu 叔孫武叔 says this when Ranyou 冉有, a student of Confucius, refuses to discuss military affairs with him.

4. The *Er Cheng ji* notes that one text has "depend on" rather than "assist."

5. In historical works, the phrase "constrain each other" is sometimes used of states that are in competition without either of them gaining the upper hand. See, for instance, *The Grand Scribe's Records*, "Xiangyu Benji" 項羽本紀, 34 (Nienhauser, 1:202).

6. That is, it is without a beginning, as Cheng Yi makes clear in his commentary on the top line.

7. *Analects* 18.8 (Legge, 336).

8. Both Yi Yin and the Marquis of War 武侯 had to be visited several times by their rulers before they would agree to become ministers. Yi Yin wanted to serve the Shang dynasty king Cheng Tang, but Tang's representatives had to visit him five times before he would agree to go with them. See *The Grand Scribe's Records*, "Yin benji," 5 (Nienhauser, 1:43). "Marquis of War" is a title given to Zhuge Liang 諸葛亮. Liu Bei 劉備, ruler of the state of Shu 蜀 during the Three Kingdoms period, had to visit him several times before he would consent to become a minister. See Rafe de Crespigny, *A Biographical Dictionary of Later Han to the Three Kingdoms (AD 23–220)* (Leiden: Brill, 2007), 1172–73. For a classical use of the phrase "waiting for ritual," see *Zuozhuan*, "Zhaogong shisannian," 昭公十三年, 2 (Legge, 653).

9. *Qianfu lun* 潛夫論, "Bianyi" 邊議, 3.

10. *Mencius* 1A7 (Legge, 146).

11. *Book of Rites*, "Wangzhi" 王制, 21 (Legge, 1:220).

12. See *The Grand Scribe's Records*, "Yin benji," 6 (Nienhauser, 1:43). King Tang saw someone who had put nets on all four sides of a field to trap its game. Tang removed the nets on three sides of the field and prayed that the animals would leave the field if they wished.

13. King Tang prayed that his net would catch only those animals who did not employ his mandate and leave the field through its three open sides. See *The Grand Scribe's Records*, "Yin benji," 6 (Nienhauser, 1:43).

14. *Analects* 1.3 (Legge, 139). Cheng Yi cites the same passage at Hexagram 58, fifth line.

15. See Hexagram 17, fifth line, *Symbol*.

16. See Hexagrams 5 and 6, fifth line, *Symbol*.

9. SMALL HERD (*XIAOXU* 小畜)

1. For the claim that *yang qi* arises in the northeast and *yin qi* in the southwest, see the *Huainanzi* 淮南子, "Quanyanxun" 詮言訓, 20. For an English translation, see Liu An 劉安, *The Huainanzi: A Guide to the Theory and Practice of Government in Early Han China*, trans. John S. Major, Sarah A. Queen, Andrew Seth Meyer, and Harold D. Roth (New York: Columbia University Press, 2010), 569.

2. Cheng Yi appears to overlook the fact that the phrase "it is called" also occurs in the *Judgment* of Hexagrams 13, 14, and 21. His point still holds, that the phrase may be supplied by the reader when it is absent in the text.

3. *Appended Statements* 1.3.

4. Reading "entwine themselves around" (*luan* 孌) rather than following the *Er Cheng ji* and *Er Cheng quanshu*, which have "climb up" (*pan* 攀).

5. *Book of Poetry* (*Shijing* 詩經), "Shengmin" 生民, 1.3. See James Legge, trans., *The Chinese Classics*, vol. 4, *The She King* (1871; Hong Kong: Hong Kong University Press, 1960), 468.

10. WALK (*LÜ* 履)

1. See Hexagram 54, *Judgment*.
2. The single character *lü* 履 can refer both to walking and to being walked on. Cheng Yi here assumes that it refers to the latter.
3. The *Er Cheng ji* provides the note from the Yuan 元 edition that "one text has 'does not agree.'"
4. A reference to the *Book of Poetry*, "Shengmin," 10.3 (Legge, 501).
5. See Hexagram 10, *Judgment*.
6. Cheng Yi is referring to his discussion of the various negative outcomes brought about by purity in the commentary on Hexagram 11, top line.

11. FREE (*TAI* 泰)

1. See Hexagram 2, *Judgment*.
2. The *Er Cheng ji* provides the note from the Yuan edition that "one text has 'immensity.'"
3. The *Er Cheng ji* notes that one text has "ensconced among the rustics" rather than "crass and rustic."
4. This is the interpretation of Wang Bi 王弼. See Lynn, *Classic of Changes*, 207 and 210n6.
5. *The Grand Scribe's Records*, "Yin benji," 2 (Nienhauser, 1:42), says that "after Zhu Gui 主癸 died, his son Tian Yi 天乙—the one who is called Cheng Tang—was enthroned."
6. *Book of History*, "Duoshi" 多士, 2 (Legge, 456–57).

12. CLOG (*PI* 否)

1. The three powers are heaven, earth, and human beings. See *Explanation of the Trigrams*, 2.
2. While the *feiren* 匪人 characters must elsewhere be translated as "outlaws," Cheng Yi here follows his main sources—Kong Yingda 孔穎達 and Hu Yuan—in regarding them as equivalent to "no one" (*fei* 非人).
3. The *Er Cheng ji* notes that the Yuan edition has "use the virtues of thrift and taking away" rather than "be thrifty or take away from their virtue."
4. The *Er Cheng ji* provides the note from the Yuan edition that "one text has 'in the Clog hexagram.'"
5. The *Er Cheng ji* notes that the Yuan edition has "exhausting" rather than "taking it as the symbol of."
6. Wang Yun 王允 planned the assassination of a warlord who had seized power toward the end of the Han dynasty, but he himself was put to death when a pardon was not issued for the warlord's troops. See de Crespigny, *Biographical Dictionary*, 841–43. Li Deyu 李德裕 was a court official during the reign of several Tang dynasty emperors. He amassed great power but made many enemies with his unyielding behavior and was forced into exile. See Twitchett, *Cambridge History of China—Vol. 3, Pt. 1*, 671–72.

7. *Appended Statements* 2.5.
8. *Appended Statements* 2.1.

13. SAME MEN (*TONGREN* 同人)

1. *Appended Statements* 1.8.
2. *Appended Statements* 1.8.

14. GREAT GRASP (*DAYOU* 大有)

1. See Lynn, *Classic of Changes*, 223.
2. The phrase "great progress" occurs in the *Judgments* of Hexagrams 3, 17, 19, 25, 46, 49, and 50. Cheng Yi claims that, when the hexagram judgment mentions all four of the virtues (primacy, progress, profit, and purity), then the *Judgment* will use the phrase "great progress," although he acknowledges that this is not the case in Hexagrams 1 and 2.
3. See Hexagram 1, *Judgment*.
4. This may be a reference to *Analects* 3.17 (Legge, 161).
5. *Book of Poetry*, "Qifeng" 齊風, 10.3 (Legge, 160).
6. *Book of Poetry*, "Wenwang" 文王, 2.8 (Legge, 436).
7. *Appended Statements* 1.12.

15. MEEK (*QIAN* 謙)

1. The characters for "sustains" (*ji* 濟) and "borders" (*ji* 際) sound the same. Cheng Yi is claiming that one has been substituted for the other here.
2. *Book of Poetry*, "Beifeng" 邶風, 17.3 (Legge, 69).
3. For the phrase "to the pasture," see the initial line, *Symbol*.
4. *Appended Statements* 1.8.
5. The *Er Cheng ji* notes that one text has "it is saying that titles and fame are the results of their goodness" rather than "it would be saying that titles and fame are the reasons why they become good."

16. CHEER (*YU* 豫)

1. *Book of History*, "Kangwangzhigao" 康王之誥, 3 (Legge, 567).
2. See Hexagram 1, *Remarks on the Text*.
3. *Book of Rites*, "Sangdaji" 喪大記, 56 (Legge, 2:194).
4. The *Er Cheng ji* notes that the Yuan edition has "they are not aligned with the moment" rather than "their powers are aligned with the moment."
5. The *Book of Rites*, "Ruxing" 儒行, 7 (Legge, 2:404) describes intellectuals as not regretting what has passed and as not being cheerful about what is to come. This is their "special setup"—that is, this is what distinguishes them from other people.
6. *Appended Statements* 2.5.

7. On Fuzi, see Hexagram 1, *Judgment* and note.

8. For the "early distinctions," see Hexagram 2, *Remarks on the Text*.

9. Cheng Yi is thinking of periods in Chinese history when the rulers were forced to submit to their subordinates. The final emperor of the Han dynasty, Liu Xie 劉協, was famously under the control of one of his ministers, the eunuch Cao Cao 曹操. See Twitchett and Loewe, *Cambridge History of China*—vol. 1, 350–56. The young final rulers of the Wei dynasty, Cao Mao and Cao Huan 曹奐, never successfully escaped the control of their regents. See *Historical Dictionary of Medieval China*, 73. Cheng Yi elsewhere mentions Cao Mao, the penultimate ruler, who was killed when he tried to take power from his regents. See Hexagram 3, fifth line and note.

10. Tai Jia 太甲 and King Cheng are Cheng Yi's favorite examples of rulers who delegated great power to their ministers. See Hexagram 17, fourth line and note.

17. FOLLOW (SUI 隨)

1. *Book of Rites*, "Tangong shang" 檀弓上, 42 (Legge, 1:136).

2. These three ministers all spent some time as rulers. Yi Yin exiled the Shang dynasty king Tai Jia for several years and ruled in his stead. See *The Grand Scribe's Records*, "Yin benji," 12–13 (Nienhauser, 1:45). The Duke of Zhou served as regent to the Zhou dynasty king Cheng. See *The Grand Scribe's Records*, "Lu Zhougong shijia," 3 (Nienhauser, 5.1:134). The name Kong Ming 孔明 refers to Zhuge Liang, who served as regent to Liu Shan 劉禪, ruler of the state of Shu 蜀 during the Three Kingdoms Period. For more on Zhuge Liang, see Hexagram 8, second line, *Symbol* and note.

3. Guo Ziyi was a Tang dynasty general and military governor. Unlike Cheng Yi's other examples in this passage, he never occupied a position of absolute authority. Cheng Yi later takes him as an example of a strong minister serving a weak ruler. See Hexagram 39, fifth line.

4. *Mencius* 1B15 (Legge, 176).

18. BLIGHT (GU 蠱)

1. The character for "blight" (*gu* 蠱) is composed of the characters for "insect" (*chong* 蟲) and "vase" (*min* 皿).

2. *Zuozhuan*, "Zhaogong Yuannian" 昭公元年, 2 (Legge, 581).

3. This statement may be found between the passages from the *Sequence* quoted by Cheng Yi at the beginning of Hexagrams 18 and 19.

4. Reading "already occurred" (*ji* 既) with the *Er Cheng quanshu*, rather than "approached its occurrence" (*ji* 即) with the *Er Cheng ji*.

5. The ten heavenly stems, combined with the twelve earthly branches, constitute a calendar of sixty days used since at least the Shang dynasty. See David N. Keightley, *The Ancestral Landscape: Time, Space, and Community in Late Shang China (ca. 1200–1045 B.C.)* (Berkeley, CA: Institute of East Asian Studies, 2000), 31. On the origins of the system, see 37n1.

6. Cheng Yi explains the meaning of the "seventh stem" in his commentary on the fifth line of Hexagram 57.

7. Instead of "he," the *Er Cheng ji* provides the note from the Yuan edition that "one text has 'his mother.'"

8. Fu Xi and Huang Di 黃帝 are legendary figures traditionally thought to have ruled China before the historical dynasties. Both of them are credited with the invention of basic technologies used by the ancient Chinese. See Giles, *Chinese Biographical Dictionary*, 233–34 and 338. Yao and Shun are sage-kings associated more with virtue than with invention. Cheng Yi frequently refers to them in delineating the characteristics of the sage, as at Hexagram 4, second line.

9. The Shang dynasty king Tai Jia allowed his virtuous minister Yi Yin to serve as ruler for three years. While the Zhou dynasty king Cheng was young, the virtuous Duke of Zhou served as his regent. See Hexagram 17, fourth line and note.

10. The Shang dynasty king Cheng Tang sought out Yi Yin while he was working in the fields. See Hexagram 8, second line, *Symbol*. The Zhou dynasty king Wen 文 sought out Taigong Wang 太公望 while he was fishing on the river Wei 渭. See *The Grand Scribe's Records*, "Qitaigong shijia" 齊太公世家, 2 (Nienhauser, 5.1:35–38). *Mencius* 4B31 (Legge, 338–40) tells the story of Zengzi 曾子, who left his city when it was threatened, and Zisi 子思, who remained in office. The disciples of Zengzi questioned whether it was proper for him to leave his post in the face of a threat.

19. WATCH (*LIN* 臨)

1. Han Kangbo 韓康伯 wrote commentaries on the *Appended Statements*, the *Sequence of the Hexagrams*, the *Mixed Hexagrams*, and the *Explanation of the Trigrams*. Their inclusion in the *Zhouyi zhengyi* made them the "official" commentaries on these texts. Cheng Yi is here quoting from Han's commentary on the *Sequence of the Hexagrams* for Hexagram 19.

2. Cheng Yi's point is that the *Judgment* of Hexagram 43 connects the concepts of enjoyment and harmony.

3. Cheng Yi is literally referring to the eleventh lunar month (which overlaps with the solar month of December) and the sixth lunar month (which overlaps with the solar month of July).

4. Hexagram 31, *Judgment*.

5. The *Er Cheng ji* notes that one text has "moment" rather than "state of affairs."

6. *Mencius* 2B8 (Legge, 223).

7. *Mencius* 3B10 (Legge, 285).

8. *The Grand Scribe's Records*, "Fansui Caize liezhuan" 范睢蔡澤列傳, 24 (Nienhauser, 7:244–45).

20. GAZE (*GUAN* 觀)

1. The *Er Cheng ji* provides this note from the Yuan edition: "pronounced with a level tone." When the *guan* 觀 character is pronounced with a modern first tone, it means "to look."

2. The *Er Cheng ji* provides this note from the Yuan edition: "pronounced with a departing tone." When the *guan* character is pronounced with a modern fourth tone, it means "watchtower" or "platform."

3. Hu Yizhi 胡翼之 is the courtesy name of Hu Yuan, Cheng Yi's teacher at the imperial academy. This statement does not appear word for word in Hu's *Zhouyi kouyi*, but it may be understood as a rough paraphrase of his commentary on Hexagram 53, top line. See the *Siku quanshu*, 8–403.

4. The *Er Cheng ji* notes that one text has "they are constantly solemn" rather than "it is proper that they be solemn."

5. *Mencius* 7A21 (Legge, 459).

6. See Lynn, *Classic of Changes*, 263.

7. Cheng Yi is paraphrasing the top line of Hexagram 53.

21. BITE DOWN (*SHIHE* 噬嗑)

1. Cheng Yi is wondering whether the text should read "lightning and thunder" rather than "thunder and lightning," so as to match what it goes on to say about the first kings. They first act as lightning by shedding light on the penalties, and then as thunder by enforcing their laws.

2. *Appended Statements* 2.5.

3. For Wang Bi's position, see Lynn, *Classic of Changes*, 33–34. In what follows, Cheng Yi agrees with Wang that the initial and top positions primarily refer to the beginning and end of the activity indicated by the hexagram, but he denies that these positions are without the character of *yin* or *yang*.

4. Cheng Yi is saying that the word "position" can mean two things: an official position in government or any place that has a *yin* or *yang* character. The initial and top positions are positions only in the latter sense.

5. Reading "constrain" (*chi* 持) rather than following the *Er Cheng ji* and *Er Cheng quanshu*, which have "wait for" (*dai* 待).

6. *Appended Statements* 2.5.

22. DRESS (*BI* 賁)

1. *Book of Rites*, "Liqi" 禮器, 2 (Legge, 1:395).

2. The *Zhouyi zhengyi* text used by Cheng Yi omits a portion of this line. Where the official text reads "there is a pattern of heaven," the full text should read "the intersection of firmness and softness is the pattern of heaven."

3. Hexagram 32, *Judgment*.

4. Hexagram 42, *Judgment*.

5. Hexagrams 6 and 25 have the Lead trigram in the upper position. Because it is entirely composed of *yang* lines, none of them could have left it to form part of the lower trigram.

6. The *Er Cheng ji* provides the note from the Yuan edition that "one text has 'the dress of.'"

7. It is then the second line rather than the top line that is the master of the hexagram.

8. *Book of Poetry*, "Wenwang," 8.2 (Legge, 457).

23. WEAR (BO 剝)

1. Cheng Yi is literally referring to the ninth lunar month, which overlaps with the solar month of October.
2. *Book of History*, "Wuzizhige" 五子之歌, 2 (Legge, 158).
3. Lü Qiang 呂強 was a eunuch during the time of emperor Ling 靈. Other eunuchs had persuaded the emperor to persecute the Confucians, who, as a result, were likely to join the Yellow Turban Rebellion. Lu persuaded the emperor to pardon the Confucians so as to ensure their loyalty. Other eunuchs resented Lu and accused him of treachery. He committed suicide. See de Crespigny, *Biographical Dictionary*, 629–30.
4. The *Er Cheng ji* notes that the Yuan dynasty edition has "there is a principle by which it will be reborn" rather than "will soon see its way to the principle of rebirth."
5. See Wing-tsit Chan 陳榮捷, *Reflections on Things at Hand* (New York: Columbia University Press, 1967), 12.
6. *Book of Poetry*, "Guifeng" 檜風, 4 (Legge, 218); "Caofeng" 曹風, 4 (Legge, 224). Each occupies the end of a section.

24. TURN (FU 復)

1. The Turn hexagram is associated with the eleventh lunar month, which must always overlap with the winter solstice.
2. Cheng Yi is literally referring to the eleventh, twelfth, and first lunar months, which overlap with the solar months of December, January, and February.
3. The *Er Cheng ji* notes that the Yuan edition omits "and earth."
4. See, for instance, Wang Bi's interpretation in Lynn, *Classic of Changes*, 286.
5. The character in the text is "extol" (*zhi* 祇). Cheng Yi says it should be pronounced like the character for "foundation" (*di* 柢) and have the meaning of the character for "achieve" (*di* 抵).
6. The *Jade Chapters* (*Yupian* 玉篇) is a dictionary originating in the southern Liang dynasty but repeatedly revised before the time of Cheng Yi. See Edwin G. Pulleyblank, *Middle Chinese: A Study in Historical Phonology* (Vancouver: University of British Columbia Press, 1984), 144.
7. Hexagram 29, fifth line.
8. See *Appended Statements* 2.5. On Fuzi, see Hexagram 1, *Judgment* and note.
9. Lu Deming 陸德明 was a Tang dynasty scholar and author of a glossary called *Explaining the Text of the Classics* (*Jingdian shiwen* 經典釋文). See Yong Heming and Peng Jing, *Chinese Lexicography: A History From 1046 BC to AD 1911* (Oxford: Oxford University Press, 2008), 214–15. The *Characters of the Five Classics* (*Wujing wenzi* 五經文字) is a Tang dynasty dictionary compiled by Zhang Shen 張參. See *Chinese Lexicography*, 195. *Discerning the Pronunciation of the Various Classics* (*Qunjing yin bian* 羣經音辨) is a Song 宋 dynasty dictionary compiled by Jia Changchao 賈昌朝. See *Chinese Lexicography*, 200.
10. On this distinction, see also Hexagram 62, top line.

25. NO FAULT (WUWANG 無妄)

1. Hexagram 1, *Judgment*.
2. Hexagram 1, *Remarks on the Text*.
3. Hexagram 1, *Judgment*.
4. Reading "on the waters" (*shui* 水) rather than following the *Er Cheng ji* and *Er Cheng quanshu*, which have "endlessly" (*yong* 永). This is a reference to the sage-king Yu's moving of the waters. See *Mencius* 4B26 (Legge, 331).
5. The *Er Cheng ji* notes that one text has "do" instead of "want to do."
6. The *Er Cheng ji* notes that one text here inserts: "If the case is like this, then there will be no faults. If there are no faults, then a journey will bring profit and not harm."
7. Hexagram 19, second line, *Symbol*.
8. That is, they use herbal medicine and acupuncture needles. "Crookedness" and "straightforwardness" here refer to crooked and straightforward *qi*. For more on them, see the *Huangdi neijing* 黃帝內經, "Lihe zhenxie" 離合真邪.
9. For the Miao tribe, as well as Guan and Cai, see Hexagram 4, top line. Shusun Wushu criticizes Confucius in *Analects* 19.23 and 19.24 (Legge, 347–48).

26. GREAT HERD (DAXU 大畜)

1. *Book of Rites*, "Xueji," 8 (Legge, 2:86). Cheng Yi quotes the same passage in Hexagram 4, *Judgment*.
2. *Analects* 12.18 (Legge, 258). Confucius speaks these lines to the leader of the Jisun 季孫 clan, meaning that the people will not steal if their rulers are not themselves filled with desire.
3. "Teacher Hu" is Hu Yuan, Cheng Yi's teacher at the imperial academy. His assertion that "what is" was added by a copyist appears in the *Zhouyi kouyi*. See the *Siku quanshu*, 8–300.

27. FEED (YI 頤)

1. On Fuzi, see Hexagram 1, *Judgment* and note.
2. The phrase "pastoral agents" (*simu* 司牧) comes from the *Book of History*, "Lizheng" 立政, 6 (Legge, 516).
3. Hexagram 3, initial line, *Symbol*. The word "causes" appears in Hexagram 27, top line.
4. *Book of History*, "Jinteng" 金縢, 2 (Legge, 359).

28. GREAT EXCESS (DAGUO 大過)

1. Hexagram 62, *Symbol*.
2. For the abdications of Yao and Shun, see the *Grand Scribe's Records*, "Wudi benji," 26 (Nienhauser, 1:16). For the attacks of Tang and Wu, see Hexagram 49, *Judgment* and note.

3. *Appended Statements* 1.8.

4. This is one in a series of petitions written by Liu Kun 劉琨, a Jin 晉 dynasty official. On Liu Kun, see Stephen Owen, ed., *The Cambridge History of Chinese Literature — Volume I: To 1375* (Cambridge: Cambridge University Press, 2010), 195–98.

5. The two characters, though written differently, have the same pronunciation. On Zheng Xuan 鄭玄, see Nielsen, *A Companion to Yi Jing Numerology and Cosmology*, 333–34.

6. The *Er Cheng ji* provides the note from the Yuan edition that "one text has 'willing.'"

7. The *Zhouyi zhengyi* refers to the ridgepole as "ample and raised up."

29. DOUBLE PIT (*XIKAN* 習坎)

1. Both of these are commonly used phrases.

2. In the *Liezi* 列子, "Huangdi" 黃帝, 12, these lines are spoken by Zixia 子夏, a disciple of Confucius. Zixia attributes to Confucius the claim that someone with harmony is capable of passing "through metal and stone, and treading both fire and water." He is prompted to make this claim in response to the report of a person who has literally walked through a rock wall and across a burning field. See A. C. Graham, trans., *The Book of Lieh-tzŭ: A Classic of Tao* (1960; New York: Columbia University Press, 1990), 46.

3. Reading "attend to it" (*cong* 從) with the *Er Cheng quanshu*, rather than "come afterward" (*hou* 後) with the *Er Cheng ji*.

4. This phrase occurs in several classical Chinese texts and means simply to repeat a command several times. See, for example, *The Grand Scribe's Records*, "Sunzi Wuqi liezhuan" 孫子吳起列傳, 1 (Nienhauser, 7:38).

5. The Yan 燕 feast is mentioned in the *Book of Rites*, "Wangzhi," 54 (Legge, 1:240).

6. *Book of Poetry*, "Shengmin," 10.6 (Legge, 502).

7. See the *Maoshi zhengyi* 毛詩正義 on "Shengmin," 10.6.

8. The emperor Gaozu 高祖 planned to remove the title of crown prince from the son of his first wife and give it to the son of Qi Ji 戚姬, one of his concubines. His ministers Zhang Liang 張良, Shusun Tong 叔孫通, and Zhou Chang 周昌 argued against this, one of them on the basis of historical examples, another by becoming angry and blustering, but the emperor refused to listen to them. The four old men changed his mind by praising the character of his first wife's son. See *The Grand Scribe's Records*, "Liuhou shijia" 留侯世家, 24–25; "Zhangchengxiang liezhuan" 張丞相列傳, 5 (Watson, 111–12, 209).

9. "Turning over one's hand" is a metaphor for easy action. See *Mencius* 2A1 (Legge, 181).

10. During the Warring States period, the state of Zhao 趙 sought an alliance with the state of Qi. Qi agreed to the alliance on condition that the prince of Chang'an 長安 be sent to Qi as a hostage. The dowager queen was initially unwilling to agree to this, but Chu Long 觸龍 convinced her by pointing out that this was an opportunity for her son to make a name for himself. See the *Zhanguo ce* 戰國策, "Zhaosi" 趙四, 18.

11. *Mencius* 7A40 (Legge, 473).

12. Hexagram 24, initial line. There, too, Cheng Yi explains the proper pronunciation and meaning of the character.

13. See, respectively, Hexagram 13, third line, and Hexagram 3, second line.

30. CAST (LI 離)

1. See Hexagram 51, *Symbol*; Hexagram 57, *Symbol*.
2. Cheng Yi has already referred several times to the story of Yao handing the throne to Shun. Boyi 伯夷 handed the throne over to Qi 啟, who became ruler of the Xia dynasty. Yao and Boyi both demonstrated the spirit of "lowliness and abdication" by abdicating the throne to a worthy successor.
3. *Book of History*, "Yinzheng" 胤征, 1 (Legge, 168–69). The marquis of Yin 胤 speaks the quoted lines after being commissioned to put several unworthy ministers to death.

31. STIR (XIAN 咸)

1. By "aligned trigram substances," Cheng Yi means that each of the *yang* lines in one trigram is in a position occupied by a *yin* line in the other trigram, and vice versa.
2. Hexagram 32, *Judgment*.
3. A trigram with only one *yin* line, at the top, refers to a young woman. A trigram with only one *yang* line, at the top, refers to a young man.
4. The Buddhist term "non-self" (*wuwo* 無我) also occurs in Hexagram 31, fourth line and Hexagram 52, *Judgment*.
5. The *Symbol* was originally an independent commentary on the *Book of Changes*. It was not divided up into pieces and collated with the relevant sections of the *Book of Changes*, as it is in the official edition used by Cheng Yi.
6. *Appended Statements* 2.5.
7. On Fuzi, see Hexagram 1, *Judgment* and note.
8. I follow Cheng Yi in giving the meaning of "expand" (*shen* 伸) to the *xin* 信 character as it occurs in this passage from the *Appended Statements*, although the *xin* character is everywhere else translated as "be believable."

32. LAST (HENG 恆)

1. A trigram with one *yang* line, at the bottom, refers to an old man. A trigram with one *yin* line, at the bottom, refers to an old woman.
2. Xunzi, "Youzuo" 宥坐, 1 (Hutton, 318) quotes Confucius as saying that something will be straightforward so long as it is central. Cheng Yi repeats his analysis of the relation between straightforwardness and centrality in Hexagram 41, second line, *Symbol*; Hexagram 51, fifth line; and Hexagram 60, fifth line, *Symbol*.

33. FLEE (DUN 遯)

1. All the people mentioned supported rulers against external and internal threats to their authority during periods of decline. Confucius is said to have held office briefly in the state of Lu and to have supported Duke Ding 定公 against the three powerful families

who threatened his authority. He withdrew from office during a particularly licentious period in the duke's own administration, described laconically at *Analects* 18.4 (Legge, 332). Mencius served several rulers during the Warring States period. He held office in the state of Qi and was involved in the decision to invade the state of Yan 燕, purportedly to bring order to it. On his holding office in Qi, see *Mencius* 2B8–9 (Legge, 222–25); on his resignation, see 2B10–14 (Legge, 226–33). Wang Yun successfully plotted the assassination of the warlord Dong Zhuo 董卓 during the rule of the Han dynasty's emperor Xian 獻. See Hexagram 12, fifth line. Xie An 謝安 curbed the power of the warlord Huan Wen 桓溫. See the *Historical Dictionary of Medieval China*, 577–78.

2. The phrase "small people and women" refers to *Analects* 17.25 (Legge, 330). The "small people" here are not participants in government but family members. This is why Cheng Yi goes on to say that "the case of noble people waiting on small people is not like this." It is not that noble people do not have private bonds, as becomes clear in his commentary on the next line, but that this line does not concern the political relationship between noble people and small people.

3. The Han dynasty ruler Liu Bei was known as the "first master of Shu" (*Shuxianzhu* 蜀先主). See de Crespigny, *Biographical Dictionary*, 479–84.

4. *Analects* 12.1 (Legge, 250).

34. GREAT MIGHT (DAZHUANG 大壯)

1. The *Er Cheng ji* notes that one text has "growth" rather than "coming to rest."
2. *Analects* 12.1 (Legge, 250).
3. *Daodejing* 道德經, 33.
4. *Book of Rites*, "Zhongyong," 10 (Legge, 2:303). The first of the exclamations is also from "Zhongyong," 10, but the other two are not found there.
5. *Analects* 17.23 (Legge, 329).
6. That is, the crossbar is not the axle but the spokes of the wheel.

35. LIFT (JIN 晉)

1. *Zuozhuan*, "Huangong ernian" 桓公二年, 2 (Legge, 40).
2. These words are spoken by Tan Zouyi 譚奏議 to the emperor in the *Hanshu* 漢書, "Jiaosi zhixia" 郊祀志下, 29.

36. WASTE LIGHT (MINGYI 明夷)

1. Zhou 紂 is a derogatory name for Di Xin 帝辛, the last king of the Shang dynasty. On Wen managing the affairs of Zhou, see *The Grand Scribe's Records*, "Zhou benji" 周本紀, 7–9 (Nienhauser, 1:57–58).
2. Jizi 箕子 assisted Di Xin, the last king of the Shang dynasty. As Cheng Yi explains in his commentary on the fifth line, Jizi pretended to go mad to avoid being killed by Di Xin, and was imprisoned instead. See *The Grand Scribe's Records*, "Yin benji," 33 (Nienhauser, 1:51).

3. See Hexagram 2, *Judgment*.

4. According to the *Hanshu*, "Wanggong lianggongbao zhuan" 王貢兩龔鮑傳, 72, Xue Fang 薛方 was a county official. When Wang Mang 王莽, who had usurped the Han dynasty throne and founded the short-lived Xin dynasty, invited him to court, he declined in such a way that Wang Mang accepted his refusal. See Michael Loewe, *A Biographical Dictionary of the Qin, Former Han and Xin Periods, 221 BC–AD 24* (Leiden: Brill, 2000), 626. Yang Xiong 楊雄, in contrast, held a position at Wang Mang's court. See Loewe, *Biographical Dictionary*, 637–39. On Wang Mang himself, see Hexagram 2, fifth line.

5. *Hanshu*, "Chu Yuanwang zhuan" 楚元王傳, 7. Mu Sheng 穆生 withdrew from the court of Chu after the king served him a drink he considered disrespectful. Mu Sheng's fellow ministers Bai Sheng 白生 and Shen Gong 申公 were unable to prevent his departure. See Loewe, *Biographical Dictionary*, 3.

6. Cheng Yi is paraphrasing the *Hou Hanshu* 后漢書, "Deng Zhang Xu Zhang Hu liezhuan" 鄧張徐張胡列傳, 22. During the Han dynasty, Yuan Hong 袁閎 saw that there was about to be civil strife, and so he sealed himself up in an earthen room, avoiding the suppression of the "faction" of Confucian officials and their student supporters. See de Crespigny, *Biographical Dictionary*, 1006.

7. Cheng Yi is referring to a crossbow supported by the feet and drawn with both hands.

8. For Tang and Wu, see Hexagram 49, *Judgment*.

9. *Book of History*, "Jiugao" 酒誥, 10 (Legge, 412).

10. *Book of History*, "Biming" 畢命, 3 (Legge, 574).

11. This claim appears to contradict Cheng Yi's later references to the top line as "the master of injury to the enlightened."

12. On Yang Xiong, see Hexagram 36, initial line, and note.

37. FAMILY (*JIAREN* 家人)

1. Wen Zhongzi 文中子 is a posthumous name given to Wang Tong 王通, the Sui 隋 dynasty intellectual thought to have compiled the text known as the *Zhongshuo* 中說.

2. *Explanation of the Trigrams*, 5.

3. Cheng Yi does not think that the characters for "is chided, and chided again" (*hehe* 嗃 嗃) express the meaning of the line. Instead, he invites the reader to consider an alternative: "wails, and wails again" (*aoao* 嗷嗷), based on the fact that it sounds similar to the other characters, and that its meaning better fits with the rest of the line statement.

4. The name of King Wen's consort is Tai Si 太姒. See *The Grand Scribe's Records*, "Guan Cai shijia" 管蔡世家, 1 (Nienhauser, 5.1:191).

5. On Fuzi, see Hexagram 1, *Judgment* and note.

6. *Mencius* 7B9 (Legge, 482).

38. SPLIT (*KUI* 睽)

1. A trigram with one *yin* line, at the top, refers to a young woman. A trigram with one *yin* line, in the middle, refers to a middle-aged woman.

2. This account of *yang* falling and *yin* rising also appears in Cheng Yi's commentary on Hexagram 11, third line, *Symbol*, and Hexagram 62, fifth line, *Symbol*.

3. See Hexagram 2, *Judgment*.

4. See Hexagram 12, second line.

5. On Fuzi, see Hexagram 1, *Judgment* and note.

6. This phrase occurs frequently in classical Chinese texts, but see especially *Mencius* 5B8 (Legge, 391–92).

7. On Fuzi, see Hexagram 1, *Judgment* and note.

8. When the Zhou dynasty king Cheng was young, the Duke of Zhou served as his regent. See Hexagram 17, fourth line and note.

9. Duke Ji 姬 refers to Ji Li 姬歷, who undertook military campaigns on behalf of the Shang dynasty king Wen Ding 文丁. He was also the father of the Zhou dynasty king Wen. See Loewe and Shaughnessy, *Cambridge History of Ancient China*, 301–2. Kong Ming is the courtesy name of Zhuge Liang, who served as regent to Liu Shan. See Hexagram 17, fourth line and note.

10. See Hexagram 34, top line, *Symbol*.

11. For the other appearances of this statement in the *Book of Changes*, see Hexagram 3, second line, and Hexagram 22, fourth line.

39. LIMP (*JIAN* 蹇)

1. The "later heaven" configuration of the trigrams locates the Yield trigram in the southwest corner. See Hexagram 2, judgment.

2. The "later heaven" configuration of the trigrams locates the Calm trigram in the northeast corner. See Hexagram 2, judgment.

3. On Fuzi, see Hexagram 1, *Judgment* and note.

4. *Mencius* 4A4 (Legge, 295).

5. See, for instance, the *Spring and Autumn Annals*, "Yingong yuannian" 隱公元年, 2 (Legge, 1). The *Annals*, here as elsewhere, pairs the characters for "arrive" and "wed" in a single phrase.

6. On Tang and Wu, see Hexagram 49, *Judgment*. Yi Yin served as minister to Cheng Tang, and Lü Shang 呂尚, also known as Taigong Wang, served as minister to kings Wen and Wu 武.

7. All the ministers mentioned served their rulers at some point as generals. Kong Ming is the courtesy name of Zhuge Liang, who undertook military campaigns on behalf of Liu Bei and Liu Shan, rulers of Shu during the Three Kingdoms period. See Hexagram 17, fourth line. Guo Ziyi served as general to the Tang dynasty emperor Suzong 肅宗; Li Sheng 李晟 served as general to the Tang dynasty emperor Dezong 德宗. Guo Ziyi and Li Sheng also appear together in Hexagram 64, second line.

8. Li Gu 李固 served as minister to several Han emperors. He called for the dismissal of many officials, made many enemies, and was put to death when they gained power. See de Crespigny, *Biographical Dictionary*, 412–14. On Wang Yun, see Hexagram 12, fifth line. Zhou Yi 周顗 interceded with the Jin dynasty emperor Yuan 元 on behalf of Wang Dao 王導 but chose to let Wang Dao think that he opposed him. When Wang

was restored to favor, he did not support Zhou Yi, who was soon put to death. Wang was filled with remorse when he learned what Zhou Yi had done for him. See the *Jinshu* 晉書, "Liezhuan disanshijiu" 列傳第三十九, 49.

40. LOOSE (JIE 解)

1. On Tang and Wu, see Hexagram 49, *Judgment*.
2. That is, the judgment is not referring to any "it" here, but is simply saying that "an arrival and return will bring good fortune."
3. Hexagram 30, *Symbol*. Cheng Yi is claiming that the hexagram title is the direct object of the verb "produce" in Hexagram 30, but not in Hexagram 40.
4. Huan Yanfan 桓彥範 and Jing Hui 敬暉 participated in the coup that overthrew the empress Wu Zetian, who was mentioned earlier by Cheng Yi in his commentary on Hexagram 2, fifth line. They did not take action against her nephew, Wu Sansi 武三思, who became an adviser to the emperor Zhongzong 中宗 and who quickly acquired enough power to have them banished. See Twitchett, *Cambridge History of China—vol. 3, pt. 1*, 321–23.
5. *Appended Statements* 1.8.
6. *Appended Statements* 2.5. On Fuzi, see Hexagram 1, *Judgment* and note.

41. TAKE (SUN 損)

1. The *Er Cheng ji* provides the notes from the Yuan edition that "one text has 'they are constant'" and "one text has 'improper.'"
2. On Fuzi, see Hexagram 1, *Judgment* and note.
3. *Book of Rites*, "Liqi," 2 (Legge, 1:395).
4. These two sentences also appear in Hexagram 32, second line.
5. *Appended Statements* 2.5.
6. For the origin of this quotation, see Hexagram 35, third line and note.

42. ADD (YI 益)

1. See *Analects* 10.16 (Legge, 236).
2. *Mencius* 6B13 (Legge, 444).
3. *Book of Rites*, "Jiaotesheng" 郊特牲, 9 (Legge, 1:420–21).
4. *Analects* 4.12 (Legge, 169). On Fuzi, see Hexagram 1, *Judgment* and note.
5. *Mencius* 1A1 (Legge, 126–27).
6. *Appended Statements* 2.5.

43. SOLVE (GUAI 夬)

1. See Hexagram 45, *Symbol*.
2. *Book of History*, "Dayumo," 21 (Legge, 66). Shun sent Yu to fight against the Miao tribe. After thirty years, the Miao were still in a state of rebellion, so Yu withdrew his

troops, and Shun chose instead to "promulgate pattern and virtue." Within seventy days, the Miao leader submitted to Shun.

3. See Lynn, *Classic of Changes*, 405, with the explanation at 409n4.

4. "Duke of Anding" is a posthumous name given to Hu Yuan, Cheng Yi's teacher at the imperial academy. His reordering of the line appears in the *Zhouyi kouyi*. See the *Siku quanshu*, 8–361.

5. As Cheng Yi explains below, he does not think that the two phrases—"it encounters rain" and "it seems to glisten"—belong together. The first phrase refers to the correspondence of the third and top line, while the second phrase refers to their lack of correspondence, as would occur if the third line referred to noble people. Cheng Yi claims that the original line statement must have interposed "noble people solve, and solve again," to indicate that the second phrase applies only to noble people.

6. Cheng Yi is claiming that, since rain glistens, someone thought these two phrases had the same subject and rewrote the line statement to reflect this.

7. On Fuzi, see Hexagram 1, *Judgment* and note.

8. When "call" (*hao* 號) is pronounced with a "departing tone" or with a modern fourth tone, it means to command. When it is pronounced with a "level tone" or with a modern second tone, it means to shout out. As Cheng Yi goes on to explain, the earlier instances of "call" in this hexagram mean to command or employ, but here it means to shout out.

44. PAIR (GOU 姤)

1. See *Analects* 17.25 (Legge, 330).

2. Hexagram 20, *Symbol*.

3. Hexagram 24, *Symbol*.

4. Gaozong 高宗 here refers to the Shang dynasty king Wu Ding, who dreamed that the High Lord had sent him a minister. He had images made of the minister's face, and sent them out with messengers to find the original, which turned out to be the builder Fu Yue. On King Wen's discovery of the fisherman Taigong Wang, see Hexagram 18, top line and note.

45. MEET (CUI 萃)

1. *Mencius* 6A8 (Legge, 409).

2. *Book of Poetry*, "Dangzhishi" 蕩之什, 2.7 (Legge, 515). This line is quoted in the *Book of Rites*, "Zhongyong," 16 (Legge, 2:308).

3. The sacrifices of jackals and otters appear in the *Book of Rites*, "Wangzhi," 22 (Legge, 1:221).

4. "Lesser seasonal sacrifice" translates the *yue* 禴 character. The *Shuoyuan* 說苑, "Xiuwen" 脩文, 26 says this character refers to the summer sacrifice. Wang Bi says that it refers to the spring sacrifice: see Lynn, *Classic of Changes*, 419–20. Cheng Yi says only that it is meager. Hence it is translated here as "lesser seasonal sacrifice."

5. *Appended Statements* 1.3.

6. Chen Heng 陳恆 became ruler of Qi by assassinating Duke Jing. In the *Zuozhuan*, "Aigong shisinian" 哀公十四年, 2 (Legge, 840), Confucius says Chen has lost the support of half the people of Qi, and so he may easily be attacked by the state of Lu. Cheng Yi is here more interested in the implication that half the people of Qi support Chen even though he is an assassin. The Jisun clan was one of three powerful families in the state of Lu during Confucius's time there. Numerous examples of its power and amorality may be found in the *Analects*, starting with 3.1 (Legge, 154).

7. See Hexagram 43, judgment.

8. The phrase "not yet ready" (*weibian* 未便) occurs here and there in Song dynasty texts. Cheng Yi uses it himself at Hexagram 33, *Judgment*; Hexagram 50, judgment.

46. RISE (SHENG 升)

1. See Hexagram 14, *Judgment*.

2. Hexagram 26, fourth line.

3. King Wen's grandfather moved his family to the base of Mount Qi 岐山, an event mentioned by Cheng Yi in his commentary on the top line of Hexagram 17. Lynn, *Classic of Changes*, 428n7 thinks Cheng Yi is here referring to an act of King Wen himself.

4. Hexagram 1, third line.

47. TRAP (KUN 困)

1. The *Er Cheng ji* notes that the Yuan edition has "blame" rather than "generosity." The modern editor, Wang Xiaoyu, suggests a further change to make the clause read "how could there be blame" instead of "will there be generosity?"

2. *Appended Statements* 2.5.

3. That is, the character that means "its speech" (*yue* 曰) should in fact read "its own" (*zi* 自).

48. WELL (JING 井)

1. A reference to *Mencius* 6A19 (Legge, 421).

2. Hexagram 1, *Remarks on the Text* contains the same written phrase, *shishe* (時舍), that is here translated as "the moment abandons it." Cheng Yi is claiming that the *she* character is pronounced with an "ascending tone," or with a modern third tone, and so means "abandonment." In Hexagram 1, it is presumably to be pronounced with a modern fourth tone, and so means "abiding" or "residing."

3. *Analects* 7.10 (Legge, 197). This passage says specifically that Confucius and Yan Hui are only capable of acting when they are in office.

4. *Analects* 13.25 (Legge, 274), 18.10 (Legge, 338). Both passages say that noble people do not seek perfection from everyone.

49. HIDE (GE 革)

1. The *ge* 革 character means both "reform" and "the hide of an animal." In this text it is translated as "hide" and "reform" according to context.
2. Both Tang and Wu founded new dynasties after defeating the last ruler of the previous dynasty. Cheng Tang overthrew the Xia dynasty king Jie 桀 and founded the Shang dynasty. Wu overthrew the Shang dynasty king Di Xin and founded the Zhou dynasty. See Loewe and Shaughnessy, *Cambridge History of Ancient China*, 309–10.
3. Cheng Yi himself refers to making another journey in his commentary on the top line, *Symbol*.
4. See *Analects* 17.3 (Legge, 318).
5. On the Miao tribe, see Hexagram 43, judgment and note. Xiang 象 was the supercilious brother of the sage-king Shun. It is said that, by living with Shun, he "gained in discipline." See the *Book of History*, "Yaodian," 4 (Legge, 26).
6. See *Mencius* 4A10 (Legge, 301).
7. Zhongni 仲尼 is the courtesy name of Confucius.
8. Di Xin is the last king of the Shang dynasty, more often referred to by Cheng Yi as King Zhou. See Hexagram 36, *Judgment*.

50. TRIPOD (DING 鼎)

1. See *Analects* 10.9 (Legge, 233). On the prohibition against slouching and leaning on things, see the *Book of Rites*, "Neize" 內則, 12 (Legge, 1:453).
2. *Appended Statements* 2.5.
3. The *Er Cheng ji* notes that one text has "nothing is employed" rather than "the function is brought about."

51. SHAKE (ZHEN 震)

1. The reference is to one hundred *li*, each of which is about one-third of an English mile.
2. For a nontechnical use of both phrases, see the *Art of War* (*Sunzi bingfa* 孫子兵法), "Junxing" 軍形, 2, although they occur in many classical texts. An English translation may be found in Sun Tzu, *The Art of War*, trans. Samuel B. Griffith (Oxford: Oxford University Press, 1963), 85.

52. CALM (GEN 艮)

1. Zhongni is the courtesy name of Confucius.
2. *Book of Rites*, "Daxue" 大學, 7 (Legge, 2:415–16). On Fuzi, see Hexagram 1, *Judgment* and note.
3. *Book of Poetry*, "Dangzhishi," 6.1 (Legge, 541).

53. STEP (*JIAN* 漸)

1. If each line of the Stir hexagram is turned from *yin* to *yang* and vice versa, it becomes the Wed Bride hexagram. Cheng Yi refers to hexagrams that have this relationship as "straightforwardly opposed" (*zhengxiangdui* 正相對), although their more common name is "inverted hexagrams" (*hugua* 互卦).
2. *Book of Rites*, "Yueji," 26 (Legge, 2:107).
3. On Fuzi, see Hexagram 1, *Judgment* and note.
4. The *Er Cheng ji* notes that one text has "ritual" rather than "principle."
5. See Hexagram 1, second line, *Remarks on the Text*.
6. See the edition of the *Zhouyi kouyi* in the *Siku quanshu*, 8–403.
7. The *Erya* 爾雅 is the oldest extant dictionary of the Chinese language. *Erya*, "Shigong" 釋宮, 30, lists nine definitions of the word "attainment" (*da* 達), the last of which is "high road" (*kui* 逵).

54. WED BRIDE (*GUIMEI* 歸妹)

1. For the meaning of straightforward opposition, see the note on Hexagram 53, judgment.
2. See Hexagram 9, third line.
3. The *Symbol* commentary on the third line of the Walk hexagram, where the statement "the lame can walk" appears, says "not enough for action."
4. The *Symbol* commentary on the third line of the Walk hexagram says "not enough for enlightenment."
5. *Book of Rites*, "Jiaotesheng," 39 (Legge, 1:445).

55. THICK (*FENG* 豐)

1. The phrase "match of heaven" occurs relatively frequently in classical Chinese texts. In the *Book of Rites*, "Zhongyong," 32 (Legge, 2:327), the sage becomes the match of heaven by possessing a number of characteristics, such as liberality, that resemble those of heaven.
2. Classical Chinese texts often refer to the Hu 胡 and Yue 越 as two tribes with dramatically different practices. The *Huainanzi*, "Zhushuxun" 主術訓, 8 (Major, 304) observes that certain things, like weights and measures, do not vary even between tribes with different customs like the Hu and the Yue.
3. The *Er Cheng ji* notes that the Yuan, Lü 呂, and Xu 徐 editions all have "master of revolution" rather than "master of what revolves peacefully."
4. Guan Zhong 管仲 served Duke Huan 桓公 of Qi during the Spring and Autumn Period. See *Analects* 14.16–18 (Legge, 281–83). Kong Ming is the courtesy name of Zhuge Liang. See Hexagram 17, fourth line and note. Liu Shan is referred to as his later master because he had earlier served Liu Bei.
5. That is, the character for "bolster" (*pei* 沛) was originally the character for "banner" (*pei* 旆).
6. See Lynn, *Classic of Changes*, 490.

56. MARCH (*LÜ* 旅)

1. See Hexagram 62, top line.
2. See the *Mixed Hexagrams*, 39.
3. That is, the "it" in the statement that "it is deprived of a cow" refers to the bird, not to the people on the march.

57. LOW (*XUN* 巽)

1. The phrase occurs several times in the *Book of Poetry*. See, for instance, "Tonggong-zhishi" 彤弓之什, 5.7 (Legge, 290), where it occurs in the context of hunting, as it does here. The first two of the three items are found in Lynn, *The Classic of Changes*, 504. Wang Bi in turn relies on the *Book of Rites*, "Wangzhi," 21 (Legge, 1:220).
2. See Hexagram 18, judgment.

58. JOY (*DUI* 兌)

1. The *Er Cheng ji* notes that one text has "people who rule" rather than "noble people."
2. Cheng Yi is referring to Kong Yingda's comment on the *Symbol* here. For a transla-tion of Kong's comment, see Lynn, *Classic of Changes*, 510n3.
3. That is, to get the character for "domain" (*jie* 界), the character for "field" (*tian* 田) must be added to the character for "security" (*jie* 介).
4. See Hexagram 49, top line.
5. The four unfortunates are mentioned by Sima Qian in *The Grand Scribe's Records*, "Wudi benji," 23 (Nienhauser, 1:13). They were either clans or individual men who were banished, rather than put to death, by Shun, while he served as minister to the sage-king Yao. The four unfortunates were sent to the border regions to take charge of "goblins and demons."
6. *Analects* 1.3 (Legge, 139). Cheng Yi cites the same passage at Hexagram 8, fifth line.

59. EBB (*HUAN* 渙)

1. See Hexagram 45, judgment and *Judgment*.
2. *Mencius* 4A9 (Legge, 300).
3. These intellectuals do not include Wang Bi, Kong Yingda, or Hu Yuan, who agree with Cheng Yi in regarding the initial line as the crutch.
4. This line statement does not, in fact, speak about "care" explicitly, but Cheng Yi sees it as making the same point as Hexagram 9, fourth line—"its blood departs and its care goes out"—which he later quotes.
5. Cheng Yi is saying that the name of the hexagram could be used as a verb, as in Hexa-gram 3, fifth line: "Its richness is blocked."

60. REIN (*JIE* 節)

1. Wei Sheng 尾生 is a legendary figure who arranged to meet his wife under a bridge. While he was waiting, the river began to rise. He refused to break the arrangement he

had made with his wife by leaving his position, and so he drowned. At *Er Cheng ji*, 320, Cheng Yi says that Wei Sheng possessed the virtue of being believable, but in his case it was not to be esteemed.

2. See Hexagram 41, *Symbol*.

61. CENTER TRUST (*ZHONGFU* 中孚)

1. Reading "can" (*neng* 能), rather than following the *Er Cheng ji* and *Er Cheng quanshu*, which have "then" (*ze* 則).
2. For "skill at its beginning," see Hexagram 6, *Symbol*.
3. *Appended Statements* 1.10.
4. *Appended Statements* 1.8.
5. *Analects* 17.8 (Legge, 322). On Fuzi, see Hexagram 1, *Judgment* and note.

62. SMALL EXCESS (*XIAOGUO* 小過)

1. The *chang* 長 character means "lengthy" when pronounced with an "ascending tone" or a modern second tone. It means "grow" when pronounced with a "level tone" or a modern third tone.
2. The Gaze hexagram does not use the word "lengthy" (*chang* 長), but the word "gaze" also has different meanings depending on the pronunciation. See Hexagram 20, *Sequence* and note. Cheng Yi's other references are to the word "grow" (*zhang* 長), which looks the same as "lengthy" but has a different pronunciation. See Hexagram 23, *Judgment*; Hexagram 43, *Judgment*; Hexagram 43, top line, *Symbol*.
3. See Hexagram 9, judgment.
4. On this distinction, see also Hexagram 24, top line.

63. HAS CROSSED (*JIJI* 既濟)

1. The *Er Cheng ji* provides the note from the Yuan edition that "one text has 'have not yet made progress.'"
2. The *Er Cheng ji* provides the note from the Yuan edition that "one text has 'have not yet made progress.'"
3. Emperor Taizong 太宗 was served by highly capable ministers, some of whom were nonetheless eventually exiled or put to death by him.
4. The Shang dynasty king Gaozong ruled under the name of Wu Ding. Gaozong's attack on Guifang 鬼方 is discussed in Herrlee Glessner Creel, *The Origins of Statecraft in China* (Chicago: University of Chicago Press, 1970), 232. See also Loewe and Shaughnessy, *Cambridge History of Ancient China*, 919. Guifang, which literally means "the region of ghosts," is a pejorative term for the region occupied by certain barbarian peoples and for the peoples themselves.
5. The character for "exquisite silk" (*xu* 繻) differs only in its radical from the character for "glistening" (*ru* 濡).
6. See Hexagram 63, judgment.

64. UNCROSSED (*WEIJI* 未濟)

1. Cheng Yi is advising that the character for "approaches" (*qi* 汔) should really be understood as the similar character for "brave" (*yi* 仡).
2. *Book of History*, "Qinshi" 秦誓, 2 (Legge, 628).
3. Cheng Yi is saying that the meaning of the Uncrossed hexagram is not determined by every line being out of its position, but only by the *yang* lines being out of position. Paul-Louis-Félix Philastre, *Le Yi king* (1885–1893; Paris: Zulma, 1992), 776, takes *chengdu* 成都 not to be the name of a city but to mean "on pénètre tout," so he reads "I heard it from someone in Chengdu" as "si on l'entend, on pénètre tout ce qui y est caché."
4. On Guo Ziyi and Li Sheng, see Hexagram 39, fifth line and note.
5. On Guifang, see Hexagram 63, third line and note.

INDEX

553

Index